48

44
48
63
___
107
48
___
155

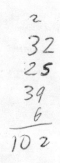

2
32
25
39
6
___
10 2

D0573795

Building
The United States

Building The United States

Jerome R. Reich   Arvarh E. Strickland   Edward L. Biller

 Harcourt Brace Jovanovich, Inc.
New York   Chicago   San Francisco   Atlanta   Dallas

About the Authors

Jerome R. Reich has taught history and the social studies in elementary and secondary classrooms in the Chicago public school system for nearly twenty years. Most of his teaching and administrative career has been concerned with inner city schools. Dr. Reich was principal in several Chicago schools, including Murray, Abbott, and Shakespeare Elementary Schools, from 1955 to 1965.

Dr. Reich is Professor of History at Chicago State College, South. His professional experience also includes teaching education courses and supervising practice teachers in history and the social sciences.

Dr. Reich received his Ph.D. in History from the University of Chicago in 1949. He has written a study of Leisler's Rebellion, and he has contributed articles to *Social Education,* the *Illinois Schools Journal* and the *Journal of Negro History.* He also is co-author of the American history textbook *Building the American Nation,* and co-author of the world history textbook *Building the Modern World.*

Arvarh E. Strickland has taught history and the social sciences in secondary school in Mississippi and at Tuskegee Institute in Alabama. He was principal of a high school in Madison County, Mississippi. And from 1957 to 1959, he was the Supervisor of Schools in Madison County.

Dr. Strickland is Professor of History at the University of Missouri at Columbia. His professional experience also includes teaching history at Chicago State College and teaching history during a summer-school session at the University of Illinois. During his career, Dr. Strickland has taught courses in both Afro-American history and American history. In 1968, he was one of the nationally known historians invited to a symposium on "Civil Rights and the Truman Administration" held at the Truman Library.

Dr. Strickland received his Ph.D. in History from the University of Illinois in 1962. He has written a *History of the Chicago Urban League* and has contributed articles and book reviews to the *Journal of the Illinois State Historical Society, Mid-continent American Studies Journal,* and the *Illinois Schools Journal.*

Edward L. Biller has been a social studies teacher and supervisor in the Baltimore city school system for many years. He is now Supervisor of Social Studies in the Baltimore city public schools, where he also served as Curriculum Coordinator, Specialist in Social Studies, and Supervisor of Geography. In these positions, Mr. Biller has been active in curriculum development and teacher training programs in the social studies.

Mr. Biller has taught history, geography, and civics in junior high classrooms, and he was principal of the Roland Park Elementary-Junior High School in Baltimore. He was also a member of the working committee, and later adviser, of the High School Geography Project.

Mr. Biller is co-author of a geography textbook, *The World Around Us.* He also is co-author with Dr. Reich of *Building the American Nation* and *Building the Modern World.* And he is an educational consultant on the new junior high American history textbook *America, Its People and Values.*

Copyright © 1971 by Harcourt Brace Jovanovich, Inc.

All rights reserved. No part of this publication may be reproduced or transmitted in any form or by any means, electronic or mechanical, including photocopy, recording, or any information storage and retrieval system, without permission in writing from the publisher.

Printed in the United States of America

ISBN 0-15-371420-4

Contents

Introduction 1

Part I. **The Colonial Years** 16

UNIT 1. **Europe Settles the New World** 17

CHAPTER 1.	The First Discovery of America	18
CHAPTER 2.	Europe Discovers a New World	24
CHAPTER 3.	The First Americans	30
CHAPTER 4.	Spain in the New World	36
CHAPTER 5.	European Empires in the New World	42

UNIT 2. **The English Start Colonies in America** 47

CHAPTER 6.	England Decides to Settle Colonies	48
CHAPTER 7.	The First English Colonies	54
CHAPTER 8.	Pilgrims and Puritans Settle Colonies	60
CHAPTER 9.	The Start of New England	66
CHAPTER 10.	The Other English Colonies	72

UNIT 3. **How the Colonists Made Their Living** 77

CHAPTER 11.	Colonial Farming	78
CHAPTER 12.	Colonial Trade	84
CHAPTER 13.	Colonial Industry and Towns	90

UNIT 4. **The People Who Settled the Colonies** 95

CHAPTER 14.	Newcomers to America	96
CHAPTER 15.	Slavery in the Colonies	102
CHAPTER 16.	Slave Life	108

UNIT 5. **Life in the Colonies** 113

CHAPTER 17.	Daily Life in the Colonies	114
CHAPTER 18.	Colonial Thought	120
CHAPTER 19.	The Frontier	126

UNIT 6. **The Colonies Win Their Independence** 131

CHAPTER 20.	Colonial Government	132
CHAPTER 21.	The French and Indian War	138
CHAPTER 22.	British Plans for the Colonies	144
CHAPTER 23.	The Start of the Revolutionary War	150

CHAPTER 24.   The Colonies Declare Their Independence   156
CHAPTER 25.   Winning the Revolutionary War   162

Part II.   Building the American Nation   168

UNIT 7.   **Building A Strong New Government**   169

CHAPTER 26.   The Confederation Government   170
CHAPTER 27.   The Constitution of the United States   176
CHAPTER 28.   The Nation's New Government   182
CHAPTER 29.   President Washington's Second Term   188
CHAPTER 30.   President Adams and President Jefferson   194

UNIT 8.   **America Deals with Other Nations**   199

CHAPTER 31.   The War of 1812   200
CHAPTER 32.   Fighting the War of 1812   206
CHAPTER 33.   The United States and the World, 1815–1860   212

UNIT 9.   **The Sections of the Nation**   217

CHAPTER 34.   The Northeast   218
CHAPTER 35.   The South   224
CHAPTER 36.   The West   230

UNIT 10.   **Americans Enjoy More Freedom**   235

CHAPTER 37.   The Era of Good Feelings   236
CHAPTER 38.   The Sections and the Government   242
CHAPTER 39.   Jackson as President   248
CHAPTER 40.   Changes in the Nation after Jackson   254

UNIT 11.   **American Life From 1800 to 1860**   259

CHAPTER 41.   Everyday American Life, 1800–1860   260
CHAPTER 42.   Changes in American Thought   266
CHAPTER 43.   Americans Work for a Better Nation   272
CHAPTER 44.   Black Americans in the North   278
CHAPTER 45.   Black Americans in the South   284

UNIT 12.   **America Spreads from Coast to Coast**   289

CHAPTER 46.   Westward to the Pacific Coast   290
CHAPTER 47.   Winning the Mexican War   296
CHAPTER 48.   The United States in the 1850's   302

Unit 13.   **Americans Fight a Terrible War**   307

    Chapter 49.   A Nation Divided by Slavery   308
    Chapter 50.   Moving Toward War   314
    Chapter 51.   The War Between the North and the South   320
    Chapter 52.   Fighting the War   326

Part III.   **The Nation Becomes a World Leader**   332

Unit 14.   **Americans Rebuild the Nation**   333

    Chapter 53.   Reconstruction of the Nation   334
    Chapter 54.   The End of Reconstruction   340
    Chapter 55.   The New South   346

Unit 15.   **America Becomes an Industrial Nation**   351

    Chapter 56.   Settling the Last Frontier   352
    Chapter 57.   Farmers on the Last Frontier   358
    Chapter 58.   The Growth of Railroads   364
    Chapter 59.   The Growth of American Industries   370
    Chapter 60.   Problems of Industrial America   376

Unit 16.   **Changes in American Life After 1865**   381

    Chapter 61.   Problems of American Workers   382
    Chapter 62.   The Growth of American Cities   388
    Chapter 63.   Changes in American Life   394
    Chapter 64.   American Thought, 1865–1900   400

Unit 17.   **Americans Try to Improve Their Life**   405

    Chapter 65.   American Government, 1865–1900   406
    Chapter 66.   American Workers Organize   412
    Chapter 67.   American Farmers Protest   418
    Chapter 68.   Progressives Work for a Better Nation   424
    Chapter 69.   Progressives Work for Better Government   430

Unit 18.   **The Progressives Reform the Nation**   435

    Chapter 70.   President Roosevelt and the Square Deal   436
    Chapter 71.   The Nation Under President Taft   442
    Chapter 72.   President Wilson and the New Freedom   448

Unit 19.   **The United States and the World**   453

    Chapter 73.   The United States and the World, 1865–1900   454
    Chapter 74.   The Spanish-American War   460

CHAPTER 75.   The United States and the World, 1900–1917   466
CHAPTER 76.   The United States Enters World War One   472
CHAPTER 77.   Fighting World War One   478
CHAPTER 78.   Peace-Making After World War One   484

Part IV.   **Problems at Home and in the World**   490

UNIT 20.   **The American Nation in the 1920's**   491

CHAPTER 79.   American Government in the 1920's   492
CHAPTER 80.   American Problems in the 1920's   498
CHAPTER 81.   American Life in the 1920's   504
CHAPTER 82.   American Thought in the 1920's   510

UNIT 21.   **Changes in America in the 1920's**   515

CHAPTER 83.   Changes in America in the 1920's   516
CHAPTER 84.   Expansion of American Businesses   522
CHAPTER 85.   The Great Depression   528

UNIT 22.   **The American Nation in the 1930's**   533

CHAPTER 86.   Franklin D. Roosevelt and the New Deal   534
CHAPTER 87.   New Laws Under the New Deal   540
CHAPTER 88.   The Last Years of the New Deal   546
CHAPTER 89.   American Life in the 1930's   552
CHAPTER 90.   American Thought in the 1930's   558

UNIT 23.   **America Deals with Other Nations**   563

CHAPTER 91.   The United States and the World, 1920–1930   564
CHAPTER 92.   The United States and the World, 1930–1940   570
CHAPTER 93.   Moving Toward World War Two   576
CHAPTER 94.   World War Two Begins   582

UNIT 24.   **America Fights in World War Two**   587

CHAPTER 95.   The United States in World War Two   588
CHAPTER 96.   The Home Front in World War Two   594
CHAPTER 97.   The Battle Fronts in World War Two   600
CHAPTER 98.   Planning for Peace After the War   606

Part V.   **The Nation in the Modern Age**   612

UNIT 25.   **The American Nation After the War**   613

CHAPTER 99.   The United States After the War   614
CHAPTER 100.   President Truman's Fair Deal   620
CHAPTER 101.   The Nation Under President Eisenhower   626

The North Atlantic Treaty Organization 635
President Truman and General MacArthur 641
The Development of Television 652
James Meredith and the University of Mississippi 670
Warren Burger—Fifteenth Chief Justice 689
The Peace Corps 696
The Post Office Department 714
Dr. King's "Dream" 719

Maps

The United States Today 15
Routes of the Crusaders 21
Trade Routes Between Europe and Asia 26
The Search for New Routes to Asia 27
Important Indians of the New World 32
Spain in the New World 38
France in the New World 44
The Tobacco-Growing Colonies 57
The Massachusetts Colonies 63
The Beginning of New England 68
Other English Colonies 74
The Thirteen English Colonies 80
Colonial Trade Routes 87
The Frontier of the Colonies 128
The French and Indian War 141
The Beginning of the Revolutionary War 154
The Main Battles of the Revolutionary War 164
The Northwest Territory 173
The Louisiana Purchase 197
The War of 1812 208
The Northeast as a Section 220
The South as a Section 226
The West as a Section 232
The Missouri Compromise 238
Roads and Canals, 1800 to 1860 244
The United States in 1846 292
Victory in the Mexican War 298
The Growing United States 299
The United States After the Compromise of 1850 304

New Territories Open to Slavery 311
The Union and the Confederacy 322
The Union War Plans 328
The West, 1865 to the 1890's 354
Railroads by the Early 1900's 366
American Cities by the Early 1900's 390
New Overseas Territories of the United States 456
The Spanish-American War in Cuba 462
The United States and the Panama Canal 469
Europe in the Year 1914 476
The Fighting in World War One 481
Europe After World War One 486
The Tennessee Valley Authority 542
The Axis Powers by 1939 584
The Attack on Pearl Harbor 590
World War Two—Victory in Europe 602
World War Two—Victory in Asia 603
A Divided Germany 608
The Cold War in Europe 634
The Cold War in Asia 640

Charts

The First Thirteen States 184
The Northeast 222
The South 228
The West 233
The Growing Nation, 1791–1821 239
The Growing Nation, 1836–1859 294
The Growing Nation, 1861–1896 361
The Growing Nation, 1907–1959 628

Introduction
to Building
The United States

▲ A modern American city.

Introduction

Life in America today often seems confusing. So many changes are taking place at such a rapid rate that it is difficult to keep up with them. These changes are taking place in many parts of American life. For example, changes are taking place in the way our government works, and in the way our nation deals with other nations. Changes are taking place in the way Americans earn their living, and in the way they enjoy themselves. Changes are also taking place in the way Americans work to make all citizens equal members of the nation. These and many other parts of American life are changing. Almost every day, American life seems to be just a little different from the way it was yesterday.

Today, Americans are concerned about our nation's present and its future. They want to understand the changes taking place in America today, and they want to shape a strong and good future for America. But in order for Americans to understand their nation today and to shape the future of America, they must know about America's past. For this reason, it is very important for all Americans to study their nation's history.

History is the past record of a nation and its people. In this book you will study the history of the United States. Of course, no textbook can include everything that has happened in our nation's past. Instead, it must choose the most important events and ideas. The book you are now reading will give special attention to these six basic themes in American history:

1. How the American people developed a free government.
2. How the American people worked to improve life in the United States.
3. How all groups of Americans helped to build the United States.
4. How Americans earned their living and developed America's economy.
5. How Americans developed their own way of life and thought.
6. How the United States dealt with other nations.

In order to show that all six of these topics are still important today, this book begins with a picture introduction of American life in the late 1960's and in the 1970's. This picture introduction shows you how these six topics are important in American life today. After this introduction, you will begin your study of America's history to discover how the American nation developed over the years.

America's Government

▶ The Supreme Court building. *(right)*

▼ The Capitol building. *(below)*

The White House. ▲ *(above, right)*

▶ President Nixon giving the State of the Union speech to Congress. *(right)*

◀ Supporters of Hubert Humphrey at the Democratic Party's 1968 Convention. *(left)*

▲ Supporters of Richard Nixon at the Republican Party's 1968 Convention. *(above, left)*

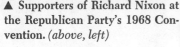

▶ Eugene McCarthy and supporters during the Presidential election campaign of 1968. *(right)*

▶ Richard Nixon in a parade during the Presidential election campaign of 1968. *(right)*

▲ Robert Kennedy giving a speech during the Presidential election campaign of 1968. *(above)*

Life in America's Cities

▶ A modern American city.
(right)

▲ Air pollution is a problem many American cities face. *(above)*

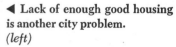

▲ Lack of playgrounds is a problem in American cities. *(above)*

◀ Lack of enough good housing is another city problem. *(left)*

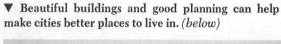
◄ Building new housing, transportation systems, and playgrounds will help solve some city problems. *(left)*

▼ Beautiful buildings and good planning can help make cities better places to live in. *(below)*

▲ Monorails and other improved transportation systems may improve city living. *(above)*

► Overcrowding also is a major city problem. *(right)*

Working for Equality in America

▶ Important civil rights leaders.
Charles Evers *(above, left)*
Carl Stokes *(above, right)*
Martin Luther King, Jr. *(below, left)*
Cesar Chavez *(below, right)*

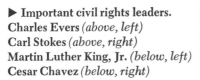

▲ The March on Washington. *(above, left)*

Mexican-Americans march in ▲ California. *(above, right)*

▶ Resurrection City in Washington, D.C. *(right)*

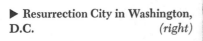

▶ Black students in a college class. *(right)*

▼ Indians smoking a peace pipe on Alcatraz Island. *(below)*

▲ The Wall of Dignity painted by black Americans. *(above, right)*

◀ A sign on the island of Alcatraz, which was taken over by a group of Indians. *(left)*

America's Modern Economy

▶ A new American test plane. *(right)*

▲ A helicopter spraying crops. *(above)*

An automated factory making butter. ▲
(center, right)

▶ A modern ice cream machine. *(right)*

◀ A modern hospital's intensive care unit. *(left)*

▼ The first American walks on the moon. *(below)*

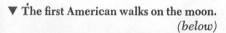

◀ An automated plant that turns salt water into fresh water. *(above, left)*

◀ A laser beam. Laser beams have many uses in industry. *(left)*

▲ An automated steel mill.

Enjoying Life in America

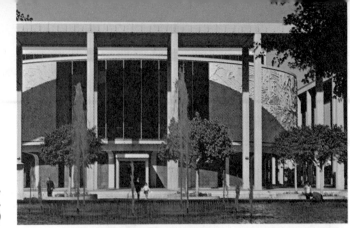

▶ The Los Angeles civic center. Plays, concerts, and other events are held here. *(right)*

▲ Americans looking at paintings in a museum. *(above, left)*

An artist working on a painting in his studio. *(above, right)* ▲

▶ Sports are very popular in the United States. At *(right)* scenes from a football game and a baseball game.

▶ A group of young musicians play at an outdoor art show. *(right)*

▲ Boys ducking for apples at a county fair. *(above, left)*

A traveling theater group performs a play ▲ for city children. *(above, right)*

▶ An outdoor rock concert. *(right)*

▶ Americans rowing boats in a city park. *(right)*

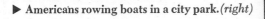

America's Dealings
With Other Nations

▶ Delegates of the United States, North Viet Nam, and South Viet Nam at a meeting of the Paris peace talks. *(right)*

▲ President Nixon meets with President de Gaulle in Paris.
(above, left)

The United Nations. ▲
(above, right)

▶ President Nixon during his visit to Rumania. *(right)*

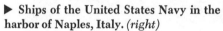
◀ United States troops being withdrawn from South Viet Nam boarding ships to return home. *(left)*

▶ Ships of the United States Navy in the harbor of Naples, Italy. *(right)*

◀ The United States building at Expo 70, the 1970 World's Fair in Japan. *(left)*

CAN

To Alaska

Everett
Tacoma Seattle Columbia R.
Olympia Spokane
WASHINGTON
Astoria Yakima Walla Walla
Vancouver
Portland Pendleton
Salem
Corvallis
Eugene OREGON
Medford
Klamath Falls

Kalispell
Coeur d'Alene Havre
Great Falls
Missoula MONTANA Missouri R.
Butte Helena Miles City
Anaconda
Bozeman Billings

Lewiston
IDAHO
Boise

Idaho Falls
Twin Falls Snake R. Pocatello

Cody Sheridan

WYOMING Casper

Rock Springs

Laramie
Cheyenne
Fort Collins
Greeley
Boulder
Denver Aurora
COLORADO
Colorado Springs
Pueblo Arkansas R.

Minot
Grand Forks
NORTH DAKOTA
Bismarck Fargo

Aberdeen
Watertown
SOUTH DAKOTA
Pierre
Rapid City Sioux Falls
Sioux

Norfolk
NEBRASKA
Scottsbluff
North Platte Grand Island
McCook Lincoln

Concordia
KANSAS Salina
Dodge City Hutchinson
Wichita

PACIFIC

Eureka
Redding
Marysville
Berkeley Sacramento
San Francisco Oakland
Carson City
San Jose CALIFORNIA
Monterey Salinas Fresno

Winnemucca Elko
Reno
NEVADA
Ely

Logan
Ogden
Orem Salt Lake City
Provo
Price
UTAH

Cedar City
Monticello

Grand Junction

Durango
Trinidad

To Hawaii

OCEAN

Las Vegas
Colorado R.

Santa Barbara
Bakersfield
Los Angeles Glendale
Torrance Pasadena
Long Beach San Bernardino
Anaheim Santa Ana
San Diego

Yuma

Prescott
ARIZONA

Flagstaff
Winslow
Phoenix Tempe
Mesa

Silver City

Gallup
Santa Fe
Albuquerque
NEW MEXICO Clovis

Roswell

Tucson

Nogales Douglas

El Paso

Las Cruces
Carlsbad
Hobbs

Amarillo
Oklahoma City
OKLAHOMA
Norm

Lawton
Wichita Falls
Lubbock

Abilene
Odessa
San Angelo TEXAS

Enid

Fort Worth

Wac

Aust

MEXICO

Rio Grande

San Antonio

Corpus Christi

Brownsville

ARCTIC OCEAN
SIBERIA (U.S.S.R.)
Arctic Circle
Fort Yukon
Nome
Yukon R.
Fairbanks CANADA
ALASKA
Anchorage Valdez
Cordova
Seward Skagway
Juneau
Sitka Petersburg
Ketchikan
BERING SEA
PACIFIC OCEAN
Dutch Harbor
0   500
Scale of miles

160°
NIIHAU KAUAI
OAHU
Honolulu MOLOKAI
LANAI MAUI
PACIFIC OCEAN
20°
Hilo
HAWAII HAWAII
0   200
Scale of miles

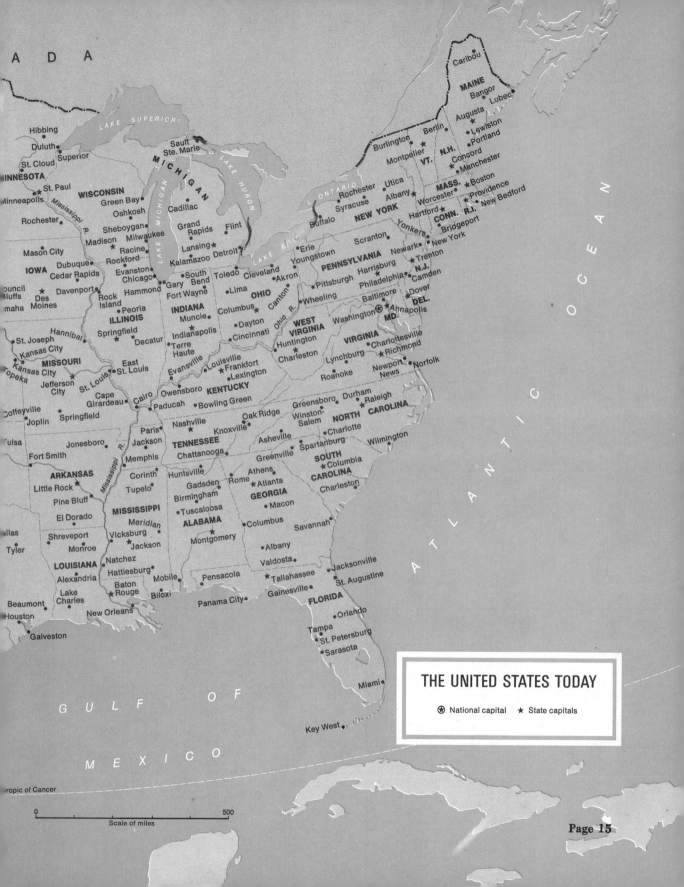

THE UNITED STATES TODAY

⊕ National capital   ★ State capitals

PART I

The
Colonial
Years

1000 to 1783

THE UNITS IN PART I ARE

Unit 1   Europe Settles the New World
Unit 2   The English Start Colonies in America
Unit 3   How the Colonists Made Their Living
Unit 4   The People Who Settled the Colonies
Unit 5   Life in the Colonies
Unit 6   The Colonies Win Their Independence

Europe Settles the New World

Columbus discovers a New World.

THE CHAPTERS IN UNIT 1 ARE

CHAPTER 1   The First Discovery of America
CHAPTER 2   Europe Discovers a New World
CHAPTER 3   The First Americans
CHAPTER 4   Spain in the New World
CHAPTER 5   European Empires in the New World

THE YEARS OF THIS UNIT ARE 1000 TO 1700

1000   1700   1975

The First Discovery of America

Norsemen discover America.

BEFORE YOU BEGIN THE CHAPTER

Know What to Look For

1. On a hot August day in 1898, a Minnesota farmer named Olaf Ohman found a strange stone as he was clearing away trees on his farm. On the stone was the ancient writing of Norsemen. This writing told about an unsuccessful journey by Norsemen. But what was this stone, and why was it found at Kensington, Minnesota?

Some experts said that the stone was put there as a joke. Other experts believed that it was real and proved that Norsemen may have settled briefly in parts of North America. And later on, other evidence of such early Norse settlements was found. In this chapter, you will read about the first discovery of North America by Norsemen. You will learn why most Europeans in the year 1000 were not ready to explore a New World beyond their own homeland.

2. Read the title of the chapter. Then look through the chapters and read each heading. Why did Europeans know little about the world outside their own neighborhood? How did this change?

3. Look at the pictures in the chapter and read the captions, or the words that describe each picture. What occupations are shown in the pictures? Examine the map on text page 21. To what location do all the routes from Europe lead? Note also the time line at the beginning of the chapter. Compare the chapter time line to the unit time line on page 17.

4. Read the last part of the chapter called Summing Up. What changes resulted from the Crusades? What will you find out about in the next chapter?

Know These Important Terms

Norsemen	Crusades
barter	raw materials

Know the Main Idea

Here is the MAIN IDEA of this chapter.

America was first discovered by Norsemen in the year 1000, but most Europeans did not become interested in other lands until after the Crusades.

Keep this MAIN IDEA in mind as you study the chapter. Ask yourself the following questions as you read. They will help you remember the MAIN IDEA.

1. What name did the Norsemen give to the part of North America they discovered?

2. What did Europeans hope to accomplish by the Crusades?

3. What events began to happen as trade between Europe and Asia increased?

THE YEARS OF THIS CHAPTER ARE 1000 TO 1300

1000   1300   1700

THE CHAPTER LESSON BEGINS HERE

The Norsemen Discovered America

The **Norsemen** were brave sailors from northern Europe who were the first people to discover America. Led by Leif Ericson (LEEF ER-ick-son), the Norsemen sailed far out into the Atlantic Ocean and landed on the northeastern coast of North America in the year 1000. Leif Ericson named this new land Vinland, or Vineland, because many grape vines grew there. The Norsemen tried to settle Vinland, but after several tries they gave up and returned to Europe. Their discovery of America was soon forgotten, because in the year 1000, the people of Europe were not ready to explore and to settle other parts of the world.

Europe Was Divided into Many Warring States

In the year 1000, kings in Europe did not have very much power. Europe was divided into a great many small states ruled by noblemen, or powerful lords. These noblemen usually did what they pleased because the king was not able to control them. They spent most of their time fighting each other. These rulers were not interested in discovering or exploring new lands.

Most Europeans Were Farmers

Most of the people of Europe were farmers, called serfs. These serfs had little freedom.

Most of the people of Europe were farmers. They had little freedom, and many never left the farm where they were born.

They were not even free to leave the farm where they were born. In some years, they grew enough food to feed themselves. But in other years, many of them grew very little food, and they starved. These serfs were too busy farming the land to think about new lands.

Europe Had Little Trade and Few Cities

Hardly any trade was carried on in Europe in the year 1000. If a farmer grew a little extra wheat, he might **barter**, or exchange it, for another kind of food or for some tool. This kind of trade took place right in the village where the farmer lived. Europe had only a few cities, and towns were few and far between.

News Traveled Slowly in Europe

Very few people in Europe knew how to read or write in the year 1000. The people of Europe had no printed books, no newspapers, and very few schools. When Leif Ericson and his men discovered America, they had no way of spreading the news of their discovery of a new land.

The Crusades Opened the Way to Asia

However, life in Europe did not remain like this. Many changes took place in Europe after the year 1000. Some of these changes were caused by the **Crusades** (kroo-SADES). The Crusades were religious wars that began in 1096. In these wars, armies from several countries in Europe set out to try to capture the Holy Land—the birthplace of the Christian religion—from the Moslems. The Holy Land, called Palestine, was located in Asia, on the eastern shore of the Mediterranean Sea.

Although the Crusades lasted almost 200 years, the Crusaders failed to win the Holy Land from the people of the Moslem religion. But they learned a great deal about the lands of Asia. When the Crusaders returned to Europe, they told amazing stories about the great cities and the wealth of Asia. They brought back richly colored carpets, fine silk cloth, and sharp steel weapons. The Crusaders also brought back pepper and other spices. In those days, spices were necessary to keep food from spoiling as well as to make it taste good.

ROUTES OF THE CRUSADERS

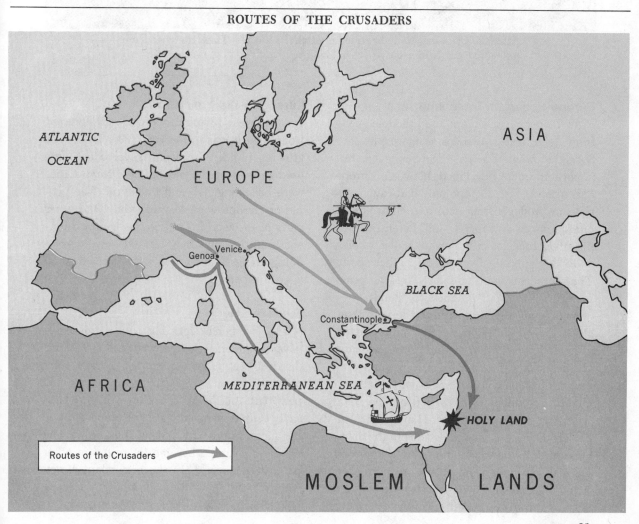

ATLANTIC OCEAN

ASIA

EUROPE

Genoa

Venice

BLACK SEA

Constantinople

AFRICA

MEDITERRANEAN SEA

HOLY LAND

Routes of the Crusaders

MOSLEM LANDS

After the Crusades, trade became important in Europe. These merchants are unloading goods in a busy port in Europe.

Europe Began to Trade with Asia

As the people of Europe used the fine goods from Asia, their lives became more pleasant. Soon they wanted more of the new goods. An important trade developed between Europe and Asia. At first, Europe only had **raw materials,** or products from nature, such as animal hides, lumber, and furs, to sell. Later, the people of Europe learned how to make woolen and silk cloth, metalwares, and leather goods. These products were traded by the Europeans in return for Asian products, or goods.

As a result of the growing trade with Asia, cities grew rapidly and new trading towns grew up in many parts of Europe. Seaports developed along the coast of Europe, and they became busy and important places. The merchants, or traders, who carried on the trade with Asia lived in the cities. Many poor farmers left their farms, and they came to the towns and cities. In the towns and cities, the farmers learned new jobs. They began to earn their living by making goods such as woolen and silken cloth to be traded with Asia.

Europe in the Year 1300

By the year 1300, Europe was very different from what it was in the year 1000. Trade was growing rapidly. Gold and silver coins were used instead of the old barter system. Cities were becoming rich and important. The people of Europe were learning about the other parts of the world. Traders traveled to different countries, and they learned new ways of doing things. New ideas were spreading all over Europe.

Summing Up

The Norsemen from northern Europe discovered America in the year 1000. But this discovery was soon forgotten because the rulers of Europe were not ready to explore new parts of the world. However, the Crusades caused many changes in Europe. Europe began to trade with Asia. Cities grew. The people of Europe became interested in other parts of the world. In the next chapter, you will find out how these changes in Europe helped lead to the discovery of America.

AFTER YOU READ THE CHAPTER

Do You Know These Important Terms?

For each sentence below, choose the term that best completes the sentence.

1. (Norsemen/Serfs) were brave sailors from Northern Europe who first discovered America.
2. A type of trade made by exchanging one item for another is called (buying/barter).
3. The (Moslems/Crusades) were religious wars that lasted almost 200 years.
4. Products obtained directly from nature are called (raw materials/trade goods).

Do You Remember This Person?

Tell something about Leif Ericson and why he is important. Visit your school library to find out more about Leif Ericson.

Can You Locate These Places?

Use the map on page 21 to answer the following questions.

1. Where did the Crusades begin? In which land were the Crusades fought?
2. What cities were important to the Crusaders, whether they took an overland route or went by sea?

Do You Know When It Happened?

In what year did each of the following events happen?

1. The Norsemen landed in North America.
2. The Crusades began in Europe.

Discovering More About the Main Idea

America was first discovered by Norsemen in the year 1000, but most Europeans did not become interested in other lands until after the Crusades.

Tell how each of the following developments is related to the MAIN IDEA:

Europeans in the year 1000 were not ready to explore or settle other parts of the world.

Little trade was carried on in the year 1000.

As a result of the Crusades, Europeans began to trade with Asia.

By the year 1300, European trading centers were busy places, and new ideas were spreading over Europe.

Can You Discuss the Chapter?

Use the information you learned in this chapter to answer the following questions.

1. Why was the discovery of America by the Norsemen unknown or soon forgotten in Europe?
2. Explain the statement, "The Crusades were both a failure and a success."
3. How was the growing trade between Europe and Asia related to the growth of cities and towns?
4. Why was Europe in the year 1300 different from Europe in the year 1000?
5. If you had lived during the time of the Crusades, which Asian products might you have wanted most? Why?

Can You Connect the Past and the Present?

1. Raw materials are still very important in trade today. What raw materials are produced near your city or town?
2. Knowledge and communication are closely related. Explain why one is not very important without the other. Compare the story of the Norsemen with the American astronauts' first walk on the moon.

CHAPTER 2

Europe Discovers a New World

Magellan's voyage around the world.

BEFORE YOU BEGIN THE CHAPTER

Know What to Look For

1. When sail boats need to sail into the wind, they move ahead along a slow zig-zag course. This way of sailing is called "tacking." In the days of the early European explorers, sailing ships had no motors, and they were powered by the wind. The brave seamen of Europe were guided on their ocean voyages by the wind and the stars.

In this chapter, you will read about the famous voyages of one of these seamen—Christopher Columbus. You will learn that Columbus' crew became worried after they sailed steadily westward with the wind for several weeks. They were worried because they knew their ships might be forced to tack slowly against the wind in order to return to Europe. And they might not have enough supplies to make this long journey back home to Spain.

2. Read the title of the chapter. Then look through the chapter and read each heading. To what part of the world did the nations of Europe want to establish new trade routes?

3. Look at the pictures in the chapter and read each picture caption. Examine the map on page 26. What three trade routes are shown on the map? Which route to Asia was the shortest route? Now look at the map on page 27. What trade routes are shown on this map? What years are included in this chapter? Compare this chapter time line to the unit time line on page 17.

4. Read the last part of the chapter called Summing Up. What nation first discovered a new route to Asia?

Know These Important Terms

trade routes   Indians

astrolabe   New World

continent

Know the Main Idea

Here is the MAIN IDEA of this chapter.

Europeans discovered a New World while searching for new trade routes to Asia.

Keep this MAIN IDEA in mind as you study the chapter. Ask yourself the following questions as you read. They will help you remember the MAIN IDEA.

1. What nations were ruled by powerful kings in the years of the 1400's?

2. What new inventions helped sailors sail their ships more easily?

3. Which European explorer reached Asia by sailing around Africa?

THE YEARS OF THIS CHAPTER ARE 1300 TO 1522

1000	1300	1522	1700

THE CHAPTER LESSON BEGINS HERE

Traders Helped Build Strong Nations

The growth of trade after the Crusades helped lead to the rise of united nations ruled by powerful kings in Europe. European merchants, or traders, found it difficult to trade in Europe. Every time they crossed a nobleman's land or used a bridge, the merchants had to pay a tax.

Most merchants wanted their country to become a nation united under the rule of a powerful king. In a nation, the merchants did not have to pay so many different taxes. Therefore, the merchants backed the king, and they paid taxes to him. With this tax money, the king hired an army and bought guns and cannons. Because of his strong army, the king was now able to take control of his nation. He was able to make the noblemen obey him and rule the entire nation. By the years of the 1400's, powerful kings ruled the strong united nations of Portugal, Spain, England, and France.

Italian Cities Controlled
the Trade with Asia

After Portugal, Spain, England, and France grew into strong nations ruled by powerful kings, each wanted a larger share of the trade with Asia. However, during the 1400's, the trade with Asia was controlled by the Italian cities of Venice (VEN-us) and Genoa (JEN-uh-wuh). Venice and Genoa controlled the

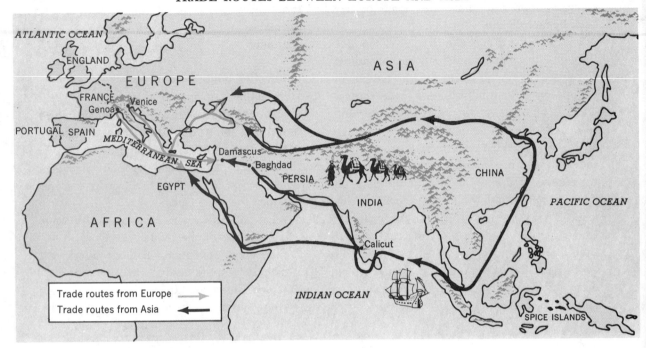

trade routes, or trade paths, between Europe and Asia. Goods came by land from China to India to the Mediterranean Sea. From the Mediterranean Sea, Italian ships carried the goods to Europe.

European Nations Wanted to Find New Trade Routes to Asia

Traders from other European nations had to buy the Asian goods from Venice or from Genoa. Because the goods came such a long way, their price was very high. The kings of the European nations wanted to send their own ships to buy the goods from Asia more cheaply. Since Venice and Genoa controlled the trade routes, the European nations wanted to find new trade routes to Asia.

New Inventions and Ideas Helped the European Explorers

In the years between 1000 and the 1400's, new discoveries helped make it possible to find new trade routes. Larger ships which carried more supplies were built. The compass showed in what direction a ship was sailing. The **astrolabe** (As-truh-lab), which measures a ship's position at sea, helped ship captains find their way across the open seas. Better maps of Europe, Asia, and Africa also helped sailors find their way more easily.

The printing press—invented in the 1450's—also helped Europeans find new trade routes. Since many books were now printed, the European people began to learn about the world. Travel books like the one written by Marco Polo, an Italian trader who traveled to China, stirred up European interest in Asia.

The Portuguese Sailed Around Africa to India

In the early years of the 1400's, Prince Henry of Portugal started looking for a new sea route to Asia. He sent Portuguese explorers southward along the west coast of Africa. In 1488, Bartholomeu Dias (bahr-THOL-uh-myoo DEE-uhs) sailed all the way down the coast of Africa and rounded the Cape of Good Hope, the southern tip of Africa. Ten years later, a Portuguese sea captain, Vasco da Gama (VASS-koh duh GAH-muh), sailed around Africa and reached India.

Portugal was the first European nation to find this new sea route to Asia. Portuguese traders now were able to buy goods from Asia at fairly low prices. Then they sold these goods for very high prices in Europe. Portugal soon became a strong and rich nation because of its growing trade with Asia.

Columbus Sailed Westward in Search of Asia

Portugal's neighbor, Spain, also wanted to share in the riches of the trade with Asia. Christopher Columbus, an Italian sea captain from Genoa, told the Spanish rulers, King Ferdinand and Queen Isabella, that the best way to reach Asia was by sailing westward across the Atlantic Ocean. They decided to let him try this daring voyage. In 1492, Columbus sailed across the Atlantic with three ships.

Columbus had the right idea. It was possible to reach Asia by sailing westward from Spain. But Columbus did not know how long a voyage this was. He thought the world was much smaller than it is. He also did not know that another **continent,** or huge body of land, blocked the path to Asia.

Columbus Discovered a New World

On October 12, in 1492, after ten weeks at sea, Columbus and his men reached the island of San Salvador (SAN SAL-vuh-door) in the

THE SEARCH FOR NEW ROUTES TO ASIA

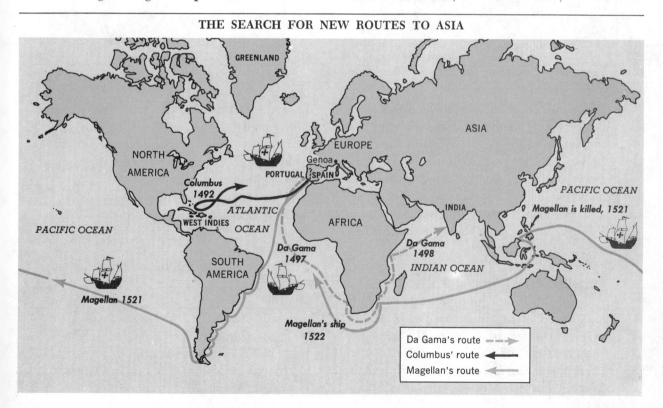

Columbus says good-bye to the king and queen of Spain. His men are boarding the ships for the voyage.

West Indies. Columbus thought that he had landed on an island near India. For this reason, he called the people living on the island **Indians.** In later years, Columbus made three more trips across the Atlantic, but he never knew that he had discovered a new continent and opened up a **New World** to the nations of Europe. This New World later came to be called America.

Magellan Sailed Around the World

In the year 1519, Ferdinand Magellan (muh-JELL-un), a sea captain, tried to reach Asia by sailing westward from Spain. He left Spain with five ships and sailed around South America to the Pacific Ocean and then on to Asia. The trip was long and dangerous, and Magel-

lan was killed on the way. Only one of his ships completed the trip. In 1522, this ship returned to Spain after sailing around the world. Magellan's voyage showed that two large continents, North America and South America, stood between Europe and Asia. It also proved that the world was round.

Summing Up

After the nations of Europe became united and strong, they looked for new sea routes to Asia. Portugal was the first nation to find a new trade route to Asia. Columbus tried to discover a sea route to Asia from Spain, but he discovered America instead. In the next chapter, you will read about the people Columbus found in America.

AFTER YOU READ THE CHAPTER

Do You Know These Important Terms?

For each sentence below, select the term that best completes the sentence.

1. (**Trade routes/Markets**) were trade paths between Europe and Asia.
2. An instrument which helped measure a ship's position at sea was the (**compass/astrolabe**).
3. A (**continent/country**) is a huge body of land.
4. Columbus called the people of the New World (**Asians/Indians**).
5. Columbus never knew that he had opened up a (**New World/New Asia**) to the nations of Europe.

Do You Remember These People?

Tell something about each of the following persons.

Marco Polo
Prince Henry of Portugal
Bartholomeu Dias
Vasco da Gama
King Ferdinand
Queen Isabella
Christopher Columbus
Ferdinand Magellan

Can You Locate These Places?

Use the maps in this chapter to do the following map work.

1. Locate each of these places:

Spain
Portugal
France
England
Venice
The West Indies
The Cape of Good Hope
The Spice Islands
Genoa

Do You Know When It Happened?

In what year did each of the following events happen?

1. Vasco da Gama reached India.
2. Dias sailed around the Cape of Good Hope.
3. Magellan's ship sailed around the world.
4. Columbus landed in the West Indies.

Discovering More About the Main Idea
Europeans discovered a New World while searching for new trade routes to Asia.

Tell how each of the following developments is related to the MAIN IDEA.

European nations were jealous of the Italian cities' control of the trade with Asia.

Portuguese seamen explored southward along the coast of Africa.

Columbus believed that he would reach Asia by sailing westward.

Can You Discuss the Chapter?

Use the information you learned in this chapter to answer the following questions.

1. Why did European merchants want their nation to be united under a powerful king?
2. Columbus' idea about sailing westward to reach Asia was a good one, but what two important facts did he not know?
3. Why were European nations searching for new trade routes to Asia?
4. Why did none of the explorers try to reach Asia by sailing across the Mediterranean Sea?

Can You Connect the Past and the Present?

1. The discovery of America might be called an accident. Can you name some other important discovery that happened accidentally?
2. The meeting of the Spanish and Indians, the Portuguese and Africans, and the Europeans and Asians caused serious conflicts between different cultures. Can you guess what some of these conflicts were about?

CHAPTER 3

The First Americans

A group of Iroquois Indians.

BEFORE YOU BEGIN THE CHAPTER

Know What to Look For

1. Carbon-14 dating is a new method which scientists use to find out the age of objects. Most experts have long agreed that Indians were the first settlers in North America. However, for many years these experts believed that the Indians arrived here only several thousand years before the Europeans. Then in 1925, a black cowboy found the bones of an animal killed by a spear tip. The age of

the spear tip was estimated to be 10 thousand years old.

In recent years, using Carbon-14 dating, scientists have learned that the Indians lived here 25 thousand years ago. In this chapter, you will read about these early American people and the kind of cultures they had developed when the first Europeans arrived.

2. Read the title of the chapter. Then look

through the chapter and read each heading. From the chapter headings, do you think the same Indian people lived in all parts of the Americas?

3. Look at the pictures in the chapter and read each caption. What do the pictures tell you about the ways Indians lived? Look at the map on page 32. What information does the map show? Compare this information to the chapter headings. Use the time line here to determine the years in this chapter. Compare this chapter time line with the unit time line on page 17.

4. Read the last part of the chapter called Summing Up. What does it tell you about the Indians of North America?

Know These Important Terms

Maya Indians
Aztec Indians
Inca Indians

Plains Indians
Southwestern
Indians

Eastern Woodland
Indians
Iroquois Indians

Pueblo Indians
Northwestern
Indians

Know the Main Idea

Here is the MAIN IDEA of this chapter.

Many different Indian peoples lived in the Americas. These Indian peoples taught the European settlers many things that helped Europeans live in the New World.

Keep this MAIN IDEA in mind as you study the chapter. Ask yourself the following questions as you read. They will help you remember the MAIN IDEA.

1. What three great Indian nations developed in America?

2. How were the North American Indians different from the Indian nations of Central America, Mexico, and South America?

3. What important ways of living did European settlers learn from the Indians?

THE YEARS OF THIS CHAPTER ARE 1000 TO 1650

1000

1650 1700

THE CHAPTER LESSON BEGINS HERE

The Indians Settled in the Americas

The Indians were the first people to arrive in America. They came from Asia by crossing the Bering Strait, which now separates Asia from North America. The Indians arrived about 25 thousand years before any European landed on the shores of America. They slowly moved southward, settling in both North America and South America. This Indian move across the Americas lasted for thousands of years.

At first, the Indians hunted, fished, or gathered fruits and berries. Later, they settled down and became farmers who grew corn, beans, and squash. The Indians made most of

their own tools and weapons of stone, but they never learned to use the wheel. Even so, three great Indian nations developed in America.

The Maya Indians Developed a Great Culture

Over a thousand years before Columbus came to America, the **Maya** (MY-yuh) **Indians** settled in Central America, where they developed a great culture, or way of life. This Maya culture lasted for more than a thousand years. The Mayas built huge pyramids which still stand today in Mexico and Central America.

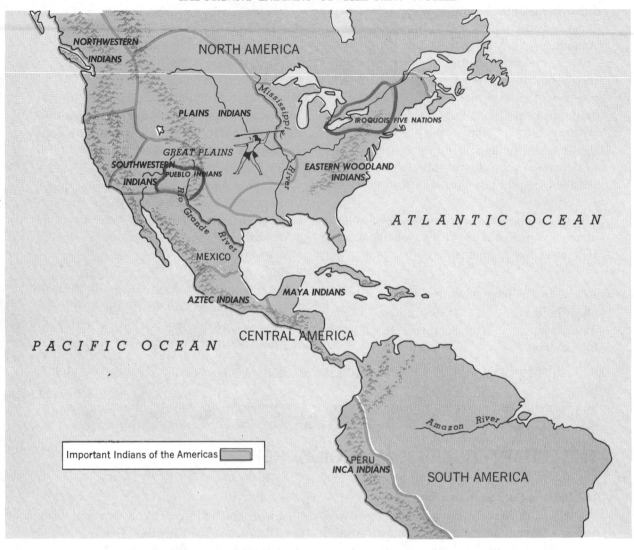

They developed a number system and made a calendar in which the year was 365¼ days long. This Maya calendar was better than the one the Europeans used at that time.

The Aztec Indians Were Fighters and Traders

By the early 1400's, the **Aztec** (az-teck) **Indians** took over the Mayas' land and much of the Maya culture. They used the Maya calen-dar, and they built pyramids like the Maya pyramids. The Aztec Indians built their beautiful capital city in what is the present-day Mexico City.

The Aztec Indians were great fighters. They conquered many other Indian groups and forced them to pay taxes in gold, cotton, and other valuable products. The Aztec traders then sold these goods to the people of Central America.

The Inca Indians Built a Large and Rich Empire

The third great nation, the **Inca** (INK-uh) **Indians,** developed an empire stretching across the present-day nations of Peru (puh-ROO), Bolivia (boh-LIV-ee-uh), and Ecuador (EK-wuh-dor).

Good roads and bridges tied the Inca empire together. Swift runners carried messages to all parts of the empire over these roads. Like the Maya Indians, the Inca Indians built many large buildings, and they were outstanding craftsmen. Their pottery, woven cloth, and metal work were very beautiful.

The Indians of North America

In 1492, about 850 thousand Indians lived within what is now the United States. These Indians who lived in North America were not as advanced as those living in Mexico, Central America, and South America. The North American Indians did not build great empires or own gold or silver mines. They had little skill in mathematics or science. However, the North American Indians lived in ways suited to their needs.

The Eastern Woodland Indians

The **Eastern Woodland Indians** lived in the forests along the eastern coast of North America. These Indians lived by farming, hunting, and fishing. They built their houses of wooden poles and wood bark.

The **Iroquois** (EER-uh-kwoy) **Indians** were the most powerful Eastern Woodland Indians. They were divided into five groups, called nations. The Iroquois were strong because they always fought together against any enemy.

The Plains Indians

The **Plains Indians** roamed the Great Plains of North America, which stretch from the Mississippi River to the Rocky Mountains. They

The Aztec Indians of Mexico built this temple and city.

lived by hunting buffalo. The buffalo supplied the Plains Indians with food, clothing, and the coverings for their tents.

The Southwestern Indians

The **Southwestern Indians** lived on the lands of the southwestern part of North America. Some of these Southwestern Indians were hunters. Some of the Southwestern Indians, called **Pueblo** (PWEB-low) **Indians,** were farmers. The Pueblo Indians lived in villages. ("Pueblo" means village in Spanish.) They built mud brick houses four to six stories high. The Pueblo Indians were skilled weavers and pottery makers.

The Pyramid of the Sun.

AMERICAN PYRAMIDS

Many people have heard of the Aztec Indians of Mexico. But few people know about the Toltecs. The Toltecs were a group of Indians who lived in central and southern Mexico in the years between 900 and 1100. The Aztecs borrowed much of their civilization from the Toltecs.

Today, the ruins of a beautiful Toltec city are found about twenty-five miles outside Mexico City. A road about one mile long runs down the center of this ancient city. The ruins of almost 300 pyramids are located along the road. The two largest pyramids are called the Pyramid of the Sun and the Pyramid of the Moon. The Pyramid of the Sun is over 200 feet tall, and it is almost as large as the Great Pyramid of Egypt.

The Toltecs built their pyramids either of solid stone or of large mounds of earth covered with stone. Their pyramids were flat and usually had a temple on top. One pyramid is covered with the carvings of snakes. It is thought that this pyramid was built in honor of the Plumed Serpent, one of the chief gods of the Toltecs. Today, many tourists visit this ancient city.

The Northwestern Indians

The **Northwestern Indians**, who lived along the Pacific coast of North America, were fishermen. Some of them were so skilled at fishing that they were able to catch huge whales. The Northwestern Indians were also skilled wood carvers. They made fancy canoes, and they carved totem poles.

The Indians Helped Make Possible European Settlement

The North American Indians are important in the history of the United States. The skill and knowledge of the Indians made it possible for the Europeans to settle in America. The Indians taught the Europeans how to plant corn, potatoes, and many other vegetables. The Indian canoe and snow shoes helped the settlers to travel across the new continent. And the Indians taught the Europeans how to grow tobacco, which became the most important crop grown in the Southern colonies.

Although the Indians helped the settlers, they often fought the settlers to protect or to win back their land. Because the Indian tribes usually did not fight together, and because they lacked guns, they were never strong enough to defeat the settlers. Sometimes, the Indians slowed up the European settlement, but they never stopped it completely.

Summing Up

Many groups of Indians lived in the Americas when Columbus landed. Three Indian groups developed great cultures in Mexico, Central America, and South America. The North American Indians were not as advanced. They lived in ways that best suited their needs. Although the North American Indians often fought the settlers, they also helped make the European settlement of America possible. In the next chapter, you will read more about the arrival of the European settlers.

AFTER YOU READ THE CHAPTER

Do You Know These Important Terms?

Read this list of Indian peoples. Then choose the numbered description below that tells about each of these Indian peoples.

Maya Indians   Plains Indians

Aztec Indians   Southwestern

Inca Indians   Indians

Eastern Woodland   Pueblo Indians

   Indians   Northwestern

Iroquois Indians   Indians

1. Built houses of poles and bark.
2. Built villages of mud brick houses.
3. Invented a calendar.
4. Were skilled fishermen.
5. Had good roads and bridges.
6. Were divided into five nations.
7. Depended on the buffalo.
8. Built an empire in Mexico.
9. Some were hunters.

Can You Locate These Places?

Use the map on page 32 to answer the following questions.

1. Which Indian people lived in South America?
2. Which North American Indians lived closest to your town or city?
3. The five nations of the Iroquois were part of what larger Indian group?

Do You Know When It Happened?

Place the following events in the order in which they occurred.

The Aztec Indians built a great nation in Mexico.

Early Indians came to North America across the Bering Strait.

The Indians taught the Europeans how to plant corn and other vegetables.

The Maya Indians developed an accurate calendar.

Discovering More About the Main Idea

Many different Indian peoples lived in the Americas. These Indian peoples taught the European settlers many things that helped Europeans live in the New World.

Tell how each of the following developments is related to the MAIN IDEA.

* Indian movements across the Americas lasted for thousands of years.

Great Indian nations developed in Mexico, Central America, and South America.

Most Indians lived in ways best suited to their needs and surroundings.

Can You Discuss the Chapter?

Use the information you learned in this chapter to answer the following questions.

1. Why do you think the Indians never invented the wheel?
2. Explain the statement, "The North American Indians lived in ways suited to their needs."
3. Why were the Iroquois the most powerful group of Eastern Woodland Indians?
4. Why do you think the Indians were never powerful enough to stop the Europeans from settling and taking over the Americas?

Can You Connect the Past and the Present?

1. Whenever two groups of people with different cultures live side by side, each culture learns something from the other. Give some examples of this from the chapter. Give some examples from your own city or town.
2. What might happen today if one group of people tried to settle on land that was already occupied by another people? Why did this not happen when Europeans began to settle in the Americas?

CHAPTER 4

Spain in the New World

Cortés meets the Aztec ruler.

BEFORE YOU BEGIN THE CHAPTER

Know What to Look For

1. The search for riches and adventure has always had a magic attraction. Stories of gold and silver treasure played an important part in bringing Spanish explorers and soldiers to the New World. These adventurous Spaniards were called conquistadors—the Spanish word for conquerers. One of the most famous and most daring conquistadors was Hernando Cortés.

Dressed in shiny metal armor and riding magnificent war horses, Cortés and his men terrified the Aztec Indians. The Aztec Indians, who had never seen horses, thought that the Spanish soldier, his armor, and his horse were all one strange and terrible creature. In this chapter, you will read how Spanish conquistadors like Cortés, with only a small army, conquered powerful Indian nations and built a rich and great Spanish empire in the New World.

2. Read the title of the chapter. Then look through the chapter and read each heading. What can you tell about the Spanish empire in the New World by reading these headings?

3. Look at the pictures in the chapter and read each picture caption. What difference can you see between the Indians and the Spaniards? Look at the map on page 38. Name some Spanish explorers whose routes are shown on the map. Which lands did they explore? Notice also the time line at the beginning of the chapter. What years are included in this chapter? Compare the chapter time line to the unit time line on page 17.

4. Read the last part of the chapter called Summing Up. What nation first established successful colonies in the New World?

Know These Important Terms
colonists   missions

Know the Main Idea
Here is the MAIN IDEA of this chapter.
In the 1500's, Spain built a rich and powerful empire in the New World. Spanish colonists established ways of living that were used by later settlers.

Keep this MAIN IDEA in mind as you study the chapter. Ask yourself the following questions as you read. They will help you remember the MAIN IDEA.

1. Which two Spanish explorers captured great riches from the New World?

2. How did the Spanish colonists find the workers they needed?

3. What things did Spaniards bring to America? What things did they borrow?

THE YEARS OF THIS CHAPTER ARE 1500 TO 1600

| 1000 | | 1500 | 1600 | 1700 |

THE CHAPTER LESSON BEGINS HERE

Spaniards Searched for Gold

Although Columbus found only a small amount of gold in America, many other Spaniards—people from Spain—soon arrived in America. These daring men came to America in search of gold, silver, and jewels. One of the first of these adventurers was Vasco de Balboa (duh bal-BOH-uh). In 1513, Balboa explored Central America in search of gold and pearls. Balboa found neither gold nor pearls, but he did discover the Pacific Ocean.

In the same year, 1513, Ponce de León (PON-suh DAY lee-OHN), the Spanish governor of Puerto Rico, sailed northward from Puerto Rico looking for gold and "the Fountain of Youth." Ponce de León, an old man, believed the Indians' stories of a fountain with waters which made men young forever. On his voyage Ponce de León found neither gold nor the fountain, but he discovered Florida.

Some Spaniards Found Gold

Some Spaniards did find gold in America. In 1519, Hernando Cortés (er-NAN-doh kor-TEZ) led a small Spanish army into Mexico, the land of the Aztec Indians. Cortés and his army defeated the Aztecs and captured the Aztecs' rich treasure. After Cortés conquered Mexico, the gold and the silver he captured soon helped to make Spain the richest nation in Europe.

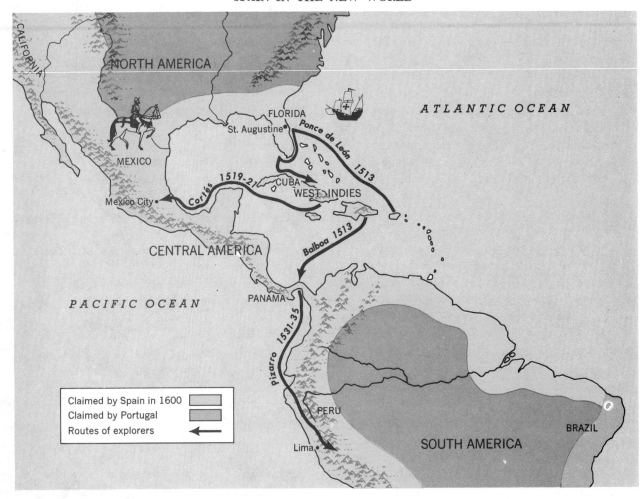

During the early 1530's, another Spaniard, Francisco Pizarro (pih-ZAHR-roh), defeated the Inca Indians of Peru. He captured an even richer treasure of gold and silver than Cortés had. Later, many other Spanish explorers also searched for riches. However, none of them were as successful as Cortés and Pizarro.

Spaniards Settled Colonies in the New World

By the year 1580, Spain's search for gold ended, and Spaniards began to come to the New World to settle. Spanish colonies were established in South America, Central America, Mexico, the West Indies, Florida, California, and the southwestern part of what is now the United States.

The Spaniards Brought African Slaves to America

Most Spanish **colonists,** or settlers, were farmers. Others ran mines or ranches. All of the Spanish settlers needed many workers. At first, the Spaniards forced the Indians to work for them as slaves. But the Indians often were poor workers, and many died or ran away.

Pizarro arrives in the capital of the Inca empire with the Inca ruler. He conquered this rich empire for Spain.

By the middle years of the 1500's, the Spanish started using black people from Africa as slaves. The Africans were good workers, and thousands were brought to the Spanish colonies. Later, the English colonists in North America borrowed the system of slavery from the Spanish colonies.

Spain Ruled Its Colonies
in the New World

The Spanish colonists had little part in their government. Instead, Spain ruled the colonies. The king of Spain decided how the colonies were governed. All the colonies' laws came from Spain, and Spain also controlled the colonies' trade.

Spain split its empire in the New World into two main parts. These two parts were then divided up into separate states. A governor sent by Spain ruled in each of these Spanish states, with the help of a small group of men. The governor ruled in the king's name, but he had to obey all the king's orders.

Learning and Religion Were Important
in the Spanish Empire

The Spaniards in America were interested in education, art, and learning. Two fine universities were opened in the 1500's. One was located in Lima, Peru, and the other was in Mexico City. Books, plays, and music were written and enjoyed in the Spanish colonies.

Religion was also an important part of the Spanish colonists' life. Almost all the Spanish colonists belonged to the Catholic Church. It built most of the churches, schools, and hospitals in the colonies. The Catholic Church tried to make the colonists treat the Indians fairly.

The Catholic Church wanted the Indians to become Christians. Brave Spanish priests journeyed into jungles and deserts to bring the Christian religion to the Indians. These priests set up many **missions,** or religious centers, for the Indians. The Indians lived in the missions, farmed the fields around the missions, and were taught the Christian religion by the Spanish priests.

A mission built by the Spanish in the 1600's. It is located in the state of New Mexico.

The Spanish Established a New Way of Life in America

The Spanish settlers brought many products from Europe with them. They planted the first wheat, rice, oranges, cherries, olives, and figs in America. The Spanish brought the first horses and sheep to America. And, in turn, the Spanish took many American products, such as corn, potatoes, tomatoes, and cocoa, back to Europe. Spanish settlers learned how to do many things which were later copied by colonists from other nations who settled in the New World. The Spanish settlers learned how to grow sugar, tobacco, and rice on large farms, and how to raise sheep and cattle on large ranches.

The Spanish Empire Left Its Mark on the United States

The Spanish held their colonies in America for about 300 years. During this long period (from the 1500's to the 1800's), over half the land in what is now the United States belonged to Spain. Reminders of these years of Spanish rule are all around us today. The names of many places like Florida or Santa Fé (SAN-tuh FAY) are Spanish. St. Augustine, the oldest city in the United States, was built by the Spaniards. Buildings in the southwestern part of the United States are still often built in the Spanish style. And today, many Americans still speak the Spanish language and follow Spanish customs.

Summing Up

Spain built the first rich and powerful colonies in the New World. The Spanish colonists developed a new way of life in America. Many of the achievements of the Spanish colonists later were copied by settlers from other European nations. You will read about these other settlers in the next chapter.

AFTER YOU READ THE CHAPTER

Do You Know These Important Terms?

For each sentence below, choose the term that best completes the sentence.

1. Spanish settlers who came to live in the New World were called (**migrants/colonists**).
2. Religious centers that the Spaniards set up for the Indians were called (**missions/compounds**).

Do You Remember These People?

Tell something about each of the following persons.

Vasco de Balboa   **Francisco Pizarro**
Ponce de León   **Hernando Cortés**

Can You Locate These Places?

Use the map on page 38 to do the following map work.

1. Locate each of the following places, and tell how it is connected with events in this chapter.

   Pacific Ocean   **Mexico City**
   Peru   **St. Augustine**
2. Which lands that are now part of the United States once belonged to Spain?

Do You Know When It Happened?

What are the years of this chapter? Place the following events in the order in which they occurred.

Africans were imported as slaves.

The Spanish empire reached its largest extent.

Cortés conquered the Aztec Indians.

Balboa discovered the Pacific Ocean.

Discovering More About the Main Idea

In the 1500's, Spain built a rich and powerful empire in the New World. Spanish colonists established ways of living that were used by later settlers.

Tell how each of the following developments is related to the MAIN IDEA.

Spanish colonies were established in South America, Central America, Mexico, the West Indies, Florida, California, and the southwestern United States.

Africans were brought to the Spanish empire to work as slaves.

The king of Spain governed all the Spanish colonies and controlled the colonies' trade.

A new way of life developed in the colonies which was a mixture of Spanish and Indian ways.

Can You Discuss the Chapter?

Use the information you learned in this chapter to answer the following questions.

1. Why were Africans brought to the Spanish empire to work as slaves?
2. How were the Spanish colonies governed?
3. In what ways was religion an important part of life in all the Spanish colonies?
4. How did the Spanish settlers establish a new way of life in America?
5. How did Spain benefit as the first European nation to establish colonies in the New World?
6. What do you think was good about the Spanish empire? What do you think was bad?

Can You Connect the Past and the Present?

1. How was the way the Spanish colonies were governed different from Americans' ideas about government today?
2. Can you give some evidence that the Spanish empire had a lasting result on ways of living in America?

CHAPTER 5

European Empires in the New World

Cartier arrives in the New World.

BEFORE YOU BEGIN THE CHAPTER

Know What to Look For

1. Every spring as soon as the ice on the rivers melted, adventurous Frenchmen left the city of Montreal. These Frenchmen, called voyageurs, paddled bark-covered canoes loaded with blankets, cloth, knives, and other European-made goods. Crowds of people gathered along the river banks to watch them leave. The voyageurs were the traders of New France.

For many months each year, voyageurs traveled deep into the unsettled forest land. They explored the interior of North America. They traded their goods with the Indians, who gave them furs of muskrats, beavers, foxes, otters, and other animals. The voyageurs often lived more like Indians than Frenchmen. Then finally, the voyageurs returned to Montreal, with their canoes filled with furs.

In this chapter, you will read how France and other nations established colonies in the New World.

2. Read the title of the chapter. Then look through the chapter and read each heading. What nations besides Spain established colonies in the New World?

3. Look at the first chapter picture in the chapter and read the picture caption. Study the map on page 44. What does the map show? Note also the time line at the beginning of the chapter. What years are included in this chapter? Compare the chapter time line to the unit time line on page 17.

4. Read the last part of the chapter called Summing Up. Which nations' colonies are discussed in this chapter?

New France   **trading company**

Here is the MAIN IDEA of this chapter.

Portugal, France, Sweden, and the Netherlands all started colonies in the New World.

Keep this MAIN IDEA in mind as you study the chapter. Ask yourself the following questions as you read. They will help you remember the MAIN IDEA.

1. Why did Brazil belong to Portugal rather than to Spain?

2. What trade was most important to the French settlers in North America?

3. Where were the Swedish settlements in North America located?

THE YEARS OF THIS CHAPTER ARE 1500 TO 1682

| 1000 | 1500 | 1682 | 1700 |

THE CHAPTER LESSON BEGINS HERE

Portugal Started a Colony in the New World

After Columbus' discovery of America, both Spain and Portugal claimed lands in the New World. Each country wanted a share of the New World. To prevent Spain and Portugal from becoming enemies over lands in the New World, the Pope drew a line running north to south about 1100 miles west of the Azores (AY-zorz). All the land to the west of this line belonged to Spain. All the land east of the line belonged to Portugal.

In the year 1500, a Portuguese sea captain, Pedro Cabral (kuh-VRALL), was sailing along the coast of Africa when strong winds blew his ship off course and forced him westward across the Atlantic Ocean. He reached the coast of what is now Brazil (bruh-ZIL) and

claimed Brazil for Portugal. Because Brazil is located farther east than any other part of South America, it was on the Portuguese side of the line drawn by the Pope. Soon Portugal sent settlers to Brazil, which remained a Portuguese colony for over 300 years. These settlers set up many sugar plantations in Brazil.

The French Settled in Canada

France also showed interest in the New World. In the early 1500's, the king of France sent Giovanni Verrazano (VAIR-uh-ZAHN-oh) and Jacques Cartier (KAR-te-ay) to North America. They sailed along the northeastern coast of North America looking for a water route to Asia. Although neither Cartier nor

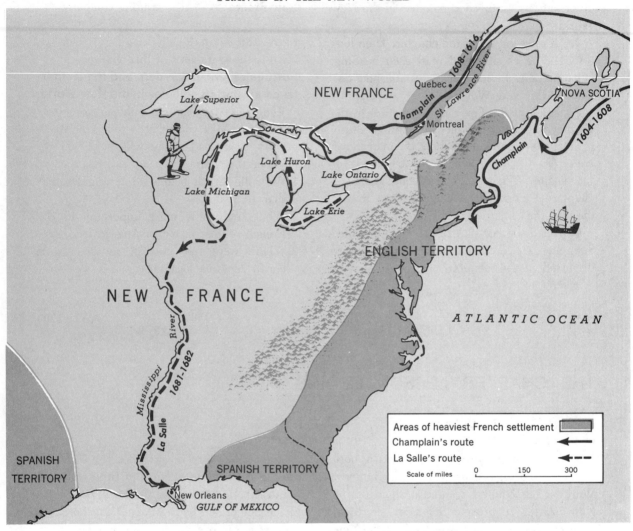

Verrazano found a water route to Asia, they gave France a claim to North America.

The first French settlers in the New World did not arrive in Canada until the early years of the 1600's. Their settlements, in Nova Scotia (NOH-vuh SKOH-shuh) and along the St. Lawrence River, were called **New France.** Samuel de Champlain (duh sham-PLAYN) led the exploration and settlement of New France. He started Quebec (kuih-BECK), which was the most important settlement in New France.

Explorers Added More Lands to New France

The explorations of Jean Nicolet (nee-ko-LE), Father Jacques Marquette (mar-KET), and Louis Joliet (JOL-ee-et), in the years of the 1600's, gave France a claim to the lands around the Great Lakes. And because of Robert La Salle's (luh SAL) trip down the Mississippi (MISS-uh-SIP-ee) River in 1682, France claimed all the land along the Mississippi River. Soon, small French settlements were established in different parts of New France. However, few Frenchmen wanted to settle in the New World, and the French population of New France remained small.

The Fur Trade Was Important in New France

Most Frenchmen who came to America were fur traders. They bought furs cheaply from the Indians in New France and sold them for high prices in Europe. Because the French were interested in the Indians' furs rather than the Indians' lands, the French and the Indians lived together in friendship. Some French fur traders lived with the Indians. These men dressed like Indians, married Indian women, and even led the Indians in war.

The towns of Quebec and Montreal (mon-tree-ALL) were the centers of the French fur trade. Each spring, hundreds of fur traders and Indians came to trade their furs at trading fairs held in Quebec and Montreal. At the fairs, the Indians traded their furs for knives, guns, blankets, foods, jewelry, and whisky. When the fairs were over, the French traders shipped the furs to Europe and prepared for the next season's trapping.

How the French Empire Was Governed

The government of New France was very much like the government of the Spanish empire in America. French settlers had little part in their own government. The French king sent two men to run New France for him. Only Catholics were allowed to settle in New France. And the Catholic Church worked hard to bring the Christian religion to the Indians.

The Swedish Started Settlements in North America

In the 1600's, Sweden also started colonies in North America. These colonies were located along the Delaware River in what are now the states of Delaware and Pennsylvania (PENN-sul-VANE-yuh). The Swedish colonists farmed and traded with the Indians. They lived in log cabins, which later became the kind of homes built by most other American settlers. Within a short time, however, the Swedish settlements were taken over by the Dutch colony of New Netherland.

New Netherland Was Taken Over by England

A Dutch **trading company,** or group of businessmen, formed the colony of New Netherland in the 1620's. Most of the settlers were farmers or fur traders. Very few Dutch people ever came to New Netherland. Instead, many of the settlers in New Netherland came from other nations in Europe. However, the Dutch trading company allowed the settlers from other European nations to follow their own customs and religion. The colonists who came to New Netherland started the cities of New York and Albany (ALL-buh-nee). And the New Netherland colony began to grow.

The colony of New Netherland did not last, because the Dutch trading company was more interested in trade than in settlement. Just a few years after the Dutch took over the Swedish settlements, an English fleet sailed into the harbor of New Amsterdam (New York). Since the Dutch were too weak to fight, New Netherland became an English colony and was renamed New York.

Summing Up

Portugal, France, Sweden, and the Netherlands (Holland) all formed colonies in the New World. None of these colonies were as successful as the colonies of Spain. England also started colonies in the New World. In the next chapters, which are in Unit 2, you will find out about the start of the English colonies in the New World.

AFTER YOU READ THE CHAPTER

Do You Know These Important Terms?

For each sentence below, choose the term that best completes the sentence.

1. The French settlements in North America were called (**Nova Scotia/New France**).
2. A group of businessmen who joined together to trade and to start colonies was called a (**trade expedition/trading company**).

Do You Remember These People?

Tell something about each of the following persons.

Pedro Cabral   **Giovanni Verrazano**
Jacques Cartier   **Jacques Marquette**
Jean Nicolet   **Samuel de Champlain**
Louis Joliet   **Robert La Salle**

Can You Locate These Places?

Use the map on page 44 to do the following map work.

1. What kind of transportation routes were most important in New France?
2. Along which river was the area of heaviest French settlement?
3. What French city was located near the mouth of the Mississippi River?
4. Name the two most important settlements in New France.

Do You Know When It Happened?

What are the years of this chapter? When did the first French settlers arrive in the New World?

Discovering More About the Main Idea

Portugal, France, Sweden, and the Netherlands all started colonies in the New World.

Tell how each of the following developments is related to the MAIN IDEA.

The Pope drew a line and divided the lands of the New World between Spain and Portugal.

The French population of New France remained small.

Frenchmen explored the rivers and lakes in the interior of North America.

The Swedish settlements in North America were taken over by the Dutch colony of New Netherland.

Can You Discuss the Chapter?

Use the information you learned in this chapter to answer the following questions.

1. Why did the Pope draw a line to divide the New World between the countries of Spain and Portugal?
2. Why did the French get along with the Indians better than the settlers in the other colonies did?
3. Compare the government of New France with the government of the Spanish colonies.
4. How was New Netherland different from most other colonies in North America?
5. Which colony do you think was the best to settle in? Why?

Can You Connect the Past and the Present?

1. Which part of present-day Canada do you think contains the largest number of people whose ancestors were Frenchmen?
2. What language do you think is spoken today in Brazil? Why do you think this language is spoken there?

The English Start Colonies in America

Courtesy Plimoth Plantation.

The "Mayflower"

THE CHAPTERS IN UNIT 2 ARE

CHAPTER 6   England Decides to Settle Colonies
CHAPTER 7   The First English Colonies
CHAPTER 8   Pilgrims and Puritans Settle Colonies
CHAPTER 9   The Start of New England
CHAPTER 10   The Other English Colonies

THE YEARS OF THIS UNIT ARE 1500 TO 1752

| 1500 | 1752 | 1975 |

CHAPTER 6

England Decides to Settle Colonies

The defeat of the Spanish Armada.

BEFORE YOU BEGIN THE CHAPTER

Know What to Look For

1. You probably know a certain football team that seems unbeatable. It may even seem foolish to try to beat them. To many people in England in 1588, a great fleet of Spanish ships sent to conquer England seemed unbeatable. This same fleet controlled the Atlantic Ocean, and it guarded the Spanish treasure ships that sailed between the New World and Spain.

However, the small English navy watched and waited. Then the English struck with daring and speed! Their well-planned attack surprised the Spanish, and the mighty Spanish fleet was forced to leave England's coast. Soon after, Spain's fleet was destroyed by a severe storm at sea. Now the Atlantic Ocean was open to other nations to sail to the New

World. In this chapter, you will read why England wanted to start colonies in the New World.

2. Read the title of the chapter. Then look through the chapter and read each heading. From these headings, list some reasons why England might want to start colonies in the New World.

3. Look at the pictures in the chapter and read the picture captions. What do the pictures show you about life in England? Also note the time line at the beginning of the chapter. What years are included in this chapter? Compare this time line to the unit time line on page 47.

4. Read the last part of the chapter called Summing Up. What were three important reasons for England's wanting colonies in the New World?

Know These Important Terms

Spanish Armada   market
Church of England

Know the Main Idea

Here is the MAIN IDEA of this chapter.
England became interested in starting colonies in the New World in the late 1500's.

Keep this MAIN IDEA in mind as you study the chapter. Ask yourself the following questions as you read. They will help you remember the MAIN IDEA.

1. Whose voyages gave England a claim to lands in the New World?

2. What change in using land in England made fewer farm workers necessary in the years of the 1500's?

3. What things might a colony supply to the mother country?

THE YEARS OF THIS CHAPTER ARE 1500 TO 1588

1500   1588   1752

THE CHAPTER LESSON BEGINS HERE

England Also Claimed North America

In 1497, England sent John Cabot to search for a water route to Asia. Cabot sailed westward from England until he reached North America. He sailed along the northern part of the east coast of North America, but he found no route to Asia. Cabot's journey, however, gave England a claim to North America.

England Ended Spain's Control of the Atlantic Ocean

During the first half of the 1500's, England did not try to settle colonies in North America. England left North America to Spain because the Spanish navy controlled the Atlantic Ocean. Also, England had many troubles at home and was not ready to settle colonies. After 1560, however, the English navy grew stronger. English sea captains, such as John Hawkins and Francis Drake, attacked and captured many Spanish treasure ships.

In 1588, the Spanish king decided to stop these English attacks. He sent a large fleet of ships, called the **Spanish Armada** (ar-MAH-duh), to conquer England. In a great sea battle off the coast of England, the English fleet defeated the Spanish Armada. England's victory against the Spanish Armada ended Spain's control of the Atlantic Ocean. Now that Spain's sea power was broken, England was free to set up colonies in North America.

These English workers are making wool cloth at home. England's growing
wool industry made many farm workers jobless.

Colonies Provided a Chance for Jobs

Both the English people and the English
government had reasons for wanting to set up
colonies in North America. One reason for
England's interest in colonies was the large
number of Englishmen who had no jobs. In
the 1500's, English land owners found they
made more money by raising sheep and selling
wool than by farming. Therefore, many English land owners changed from farming to
sheep raising. Sheep raising required fewer
workers than farming. As a result, many English farm workers lost their jobs.

Some of these English workers found new

jobs, but most of them did not. Many of these
jobless men became beggars. The English government did not know what to do with them.
Sending these jobless men to colonies in North
America might give them a chance for a better
life.

Land Owners Sought Better Land
in North America

Many English land owners also faced hard
times. In the years of the 1500's, prices in England were very high. Many land owners found
it cost them more money to live than they
earned from their lands. Therefore, some land

These Englishmen are breaking objects in a Catholic church. All English people had to attend the Church of England.

owners sold their lands. With the money from the sale of their land, these English land owners hoped to buy land in America.

Religious Differences Helped Settlement

Religious differences also made many Englishmen think of settling in America. Until the 1530's, the English people were all members of the Roman Catholic Church. However, in 1534, King Henry the Eighth split with the Catholic Church. He formed a new church, the **Church of England,** and had a law passed which said that every Englishman had to attend this new church.

Many English people were unhappy with the Church of England. Some people wanted to remain in the Catholic Church. Others felt that the Church of England was too much like the Catholic Church. They wanted to change the Church of England. Still others wanted to start new churches.

King Henry the Eighth, and the rulers who followed him, made life difficult for the people who refused to join the Church of England. Some people were fined. Some were jailed. Some were even killed. Therefore, many of these people decided to settle in the New World. The English government was willing

This picture shows a dock in London. Trade was very important to England.

to let them go to the New World, where they were free to practice their religion and to attend the church of their choice.

Colonies Supplied Products

The English government had other reasons for wanting to start colonies in the New World. England needed many goods that it did not make or grow. In England, the weather was too cold to grow sugar cane. England did not have enough trees to supply the wood needed to build ships. Because Englishmen needed such goods as sugar and wood, England spent large amounts of money to buy them from other countries.

England did not want to spend its money in other countries. As a result, England decided to set up colonies that supplied the raw materials, or products from nature, it needed. The New World was an ideal place for such colonies.

Colonies Gave England Many Advantages

England gained much by settling colonies in the New World. The people who settled in the colonies needed many goods and supplies. England sent them these goods, and the colonies became a new **market** for English goods. A market is a place to sell products. Because of this new colonial market, more jobs opened up for Englishmen. English merchants who shipped the goods between England and the colonies needed sailors for their ships. English shops needed workers to make the tools, cloth, and other goods needed by the settlers in colonies.

Many Englishmen grew rich from this trade between England and the colonies. The English government also grew rich by taxing the people who shipped the goods to the colonies. The colonies also strengthened England's claim to North America.

Summing Up

England was interested in colonies for three main reasons: (1) Colonies gave many English people a chance for a new start in life, and a place where they could attend the church of their choice. (2) Colonies provided raw materials for England, and opened a new market for English goods. (3) Colonies brought the English government wealth from taxes, and gave it a strong claim to North America. In the next chapter, you will read about the first English colonies in the New World.

AFTER YOU READ THE CHAPTER

Do You Know These Important Terms?

For each sentence below, choose the term that best completes the sentence.

1. The large fleet of ships sent to conquer England was called the (**Spanish Rovers/ Spanish Armada**).
2. The official church formed by King Henry the Eighth was the (**Church of England/ Roman Catholic Church**).
3. A (**market/claim**) is a place to sell products.

Do You Remember These People?

Tell something about each of the following persons.

John Cabot   **King Henry the Eighth**
John Hawkins   **Francis Drake**

Can You Locate These Places?

Use the map in your classroom to do the following map work.

1. From the account in the first paragraph on page 49, trace the route of John Cabot's voyage in 1497.
2. Locate England. Locate the land that is now the United States. Which place is closest to the North Pole? What might this indicate about the climate of the two places?

Do You Know When It Happened?

In what year did each of the following events happen?

1. English sea captains began to raid Spanish treasure ships.
2. The Church of England split with the Roman Catholic Church.
3. The Spanish Armada was defeated.
4. John Cabot's voyage gave England a claim to land in North America.

Discovering More About the Main Idea

England became interested in starting colonies in the New World in the late 1500's.

Tell how each of the following developments is related to the MAIN IDEA.

The Spanish Armada was destroyed.

Unemployment and religious differences were causing unrest in England.

Colonies might supply raw materials and a market for English products.

Can You Discuss the Chapter?

Use the information you learned in this chapter to answer the following questions.

1. Why was the defeat of the Spanish Armada such an important victory for England and other European nations?
2. Why was unemployment in England such a serious problem during the 1500's?
3. Why were many people unhappy when Henry the Eighth formed the official Church of England?
4. How might colonies help to increase overseas trade?
5. What arguments might you have used to get a friend to go with you to the New World if you had lived in England in the late 1500's or early 1600's?

Can You Connect the Past and the Present?

1. How have Americans tried to solve the problem of unemployment caused by great changes in ways of doing things?
2. Since few countries today have colonies with which to trade, how do they trade and sell their goods?

CHAPTER 7

The First English Colonies

The first day at Jamestown.

BEFORE YOU BEGIN THE CHAPTER

Know What to Look For

1. In every person's life, one or two years will be outstanding ones. These will be years remembered because something special happened—probably something exciting or unusual. For the new settlers at Jamestown, 1619 was such a year.

Three memorable events occurred at James-town in 1619. The first colonial law-making group was elected. The first black men and women arrived in the colony. And finally, sixty English women were brought to the colony to become the wives of some of the colonists. In this chapter, you will read about the beginning of the Virginia Colony and its struggle to survive. You will also learn about the founding of Maryland, a colony near Virginia.

2. Read the title of the chapter. Then look through the chapter and read each heading. What new crop helped the two neighboring colonies to prosper?

3. Look at the pictures in the chapter and read each caption. Which of the men in the picture on page 54 might be the leader? What makes you think so? Examine the map on page 57. In what part of the Virginia Colony was Jamestown located? Note also the time line at the beginning of the chapter. What are the years of this chapter? Compare this chapter time line to the unit time line on page 47.

4. Read the last part of the chapter called Summing Up. What colonies are mentioned in this section? What will the next chapter be about?

Know These Important Terms

legislature   proprietor

House of Burgesses   Toleration Act

plantations

Know the Main Idea

Here is the MAIN IDEA of this chapter.

The first successful English colony in America was founded at Jamestown, Virginia, in 1607. Soon, Maryland, another English colony, was started north of Virginia.

Keep this MAIN IDEA in mind as you study the chapter. Ask yourself the following questions as you read. They will help you remember the MAIN IDEA.

1. What two unsuccessful attempts were made to settle English colonies?

2. What was John Smith's one important rule that he forced the colonists to obey?

3. What kinds of governments did Virginia and Maryland have?

THE YEARS OF THIS CHAPTER ARE 1583 TO 1650

| 1500 | 1583 | 1650 | 1752 |

THE CHAPTER LESSON BEGINS HERE

The First English Colonies Failed

The first try at starting an English colony in North America was made by Sir Humphrey Gilbert in 1583. But Gilbert was lost at sea and the colony was never started. Two years later, in 1585, Gilbert's half brother, Sir Walter Raleigh, tried to start a colony on Roanoke (ROH-uh-nohk) Island, off the coast of what is now the state of North Carolina. After one year, the colonists sent by Raleigh left Roanoke and sailed back to England. Raleigh then sent another group of colonists to Roanoke. But in 1590, when an English ship visited the colony, the colonists were gone. To this day, no one knows what happened to the "Lost Colony" of Roanoke.

Jamestown Was Founded in 1607

These tries at starting colonies taught Englishmen an important lesson. They learned that one man was not able to start a colony alone. Instead, a group of men, a large amount of money, and careful planning were needed. As a result, in the 1600's, King James the First of England gave a group of men who formed the London Company the right to start a colony in North America.

The first ship load of women arrive to settle in the Virginia Colony. They came in the year 1619.

In the spring of 1607, over 100 men sent by the London Company arrived in what is now Virginia. There they formed a settlement and named it Jamestown, in honor of King James. However, Jamestown nearly became a "lost colony." At first, the settlers spent their time looking for gold or searching for a water route to Asia. Few of them planted crops or hunted for food. Lack of food, sickness, and Indian attacks killed many of the settlers and almost wiped out the colony.

Jamestown Became a Success

The leadership of one man, Captain John Smith, saved the colony of Jamestown during its first winter. Smith, a rough soldier, made the colonists obey one important rule: Work or starve! Under Smith's leadership, the colonists planted crops and built homes and forts.

It was John Rolfe who made Jamestown a success. He learned how to grow and cure tobacco from the Indians. Since smoking was very popular in Europe, tobacco was sold there for high prices. Tobacco growing soon brought money and better times to Jamestown. Other English settlements were started in other parts of Virginia, and more colonists came to settle and grow tobacco.

The Virginia Colonists Helped Make Their Laws

At first, a governor and his officials ran the Virginia Colony. However, the London Company wanted more people to settle in Virginia. For this reason, the Company gave the Virginia colonists the right to help make the laws of the colony. The colonists were able to elect a **legislature,** or law-making group.

The Virginia legislature, called the **House of Burgesses,** met for the first time in 1619. This Virginia legislature set an important example for all the English colonies. From 1619 on, English colonists demanded the right to help make their own laws. Even when King

James the First decided to rule Virginia himself, the House of Burgesses still kept meeting.

The Virginia Colonists Were Given Their Own Land

When Jamestown was first settled, the London Company owned all the land in the Virginia Colony. The settlers worked for the Company. In a few years, however, the Company divided the land among the colonists. Those settlers who brought other people with them from England were given a larger amount of land. In this way, some colonists in Virginia became the owners of large farms, or **plantations.**

Maryland, Another Tobacco-growing Colony, Was Formed

When Virginia succeeded as a tobacco-growing colony, the English government wanted to start other tobacco-growing colonies. In the 1630's, the king of England gave the land just north of Virginia to his friend Lord Baltimore. Lord Baltimore was the **proprietor** (pruh-PRY-uh-tur), or owner, of this new colony called Maryland. Because of help

THE TOBACCO-GROWING COLONIES

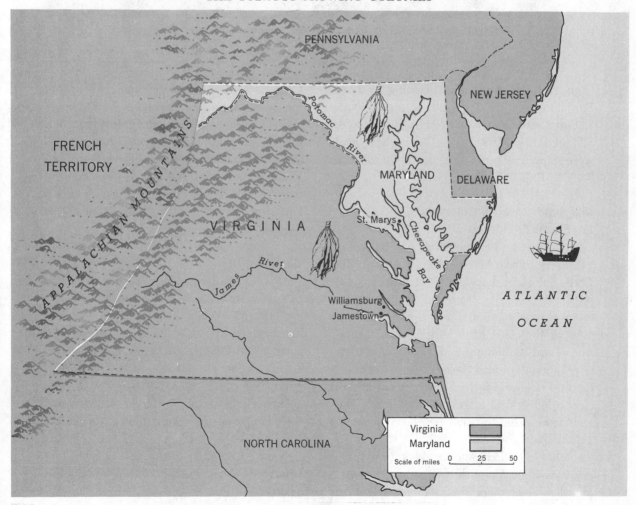

These colonists are growing tobacco. It was the most important crop grown in the Virginia Colony.

from Virginia, and careful planning by Lord Baltimore, Maryland got off to a good start. The first settlers arrived in Maryland in 1634. Within a few years, the settlers in Maryland were shipping thousands of pounds of tobacco back to England.

Maryland Gave Its Colonists Important Freedoms

The king of England gave Lord Baltimore the power to rule Maryland as he wished. But Lord Baltimore knew that in order to get settlers to come to Maryland, he must offer them as much land and as much self-government as the colonists of Virginia had. Therefore, Lord Baltimore sold the new settlers large amounts of land cheaply. He also allowed them to take part in their government and to elect a legislature, or law-making group. This legislature made the laws for the colony.

Lord Baltimore was a Catholic. He wanted Catholics to settle in Maryland and to worship as they wished. From the beginning, however, Maryland had more Protestant settlers than Catholic settlers. Lord Baltimore knew that the colony's success depended on Catholics and Protestants getting along together. For this reason, Maryland passed a law in 1649 called the **Toleration** (TAHL-uh-RAY-shun) **Act.** This law allowed all Christians to worship as they wished. The Toleration Act was an important step toward freedom of religion in the English colonies.

Summing Up

After two failures, England started its first successful American colony at Jamestown, Virginia, in 1607. When the settlers started growing tobacco, Virginia became a successful colony. The Virginia settlers owned their own land, and they elected a legislature. Like Virginia, Maryland was started as a tobacco colony. The colonists in Maryland also owned their land, and they were allowed to elect a legislature. Maryland also gave the colonists freedom of religion. In the next chapter, you will read about another group of English colonies.

AFTER YOU READ THE CHAPTER

Do You Know These Important Terms?

For each sentence below, choose the term that best completes the sentence.

1. A law-making group is called a (republic/legislature).
2. The law-making group in Virginia was called (Parliament/House of Burgesses).
3. Large Virginia farms were sometimes called (plantations/stations).
4. A (proprietor/Burgess) was the owner of a colony.
5. The Maryland law which allowed all Christians to worship as they wished was called the (Toleration Act/Freedom Code).

Do You Remember These People?

Tell something about each of the following persons.

Sir Humphrey Gilbert　　Sir Walter Raleigh
James the First　　　　　Captain John Smith
John Rolfe　　　　　　　Lord Baltimore

Can You Locate These Places?

Use the map on page 57 to do the following map work.

1. Locate the settlement at Jamestown. Locate the colony of Virginia. Locate Maryland. What large, protected body of water borders these two colonies? Why might this location help the colonies?
2. What mountains marked the western limit of Virginia?

Do You Know When It Happened?

What are the years of this chapter? Tell why all of the following are important dates in American history.

1607　　　　　　1619　　　　　　1634

Discovering More About the Main Idea

The first successful English colony in America was founded at Jamestown, Virginia, in 1607. Soon, Maryland, another English colony, was started north of Virginia.

Tell how each of the following developments is related to the MAIN IDEA.

Tobacco growing soon brought money and better times to Jamestown.

Colonists of Virginia and Maryland were given their own land and took part in their own government.

The Toleration Act was an important step toward religious freedom in America.

Can You Discuss the Chapter?

Use the information you learned in this chapter to answer the following questions.

1. What important lesson was learned through the failure of the first English colonies?
2. Why was the House of Burgesses such an important example for all the English colonies?
3. Why did the colony of Maryland get off to a much better start than did the first settlement in Virginia?
4. How was the settlement of Maryland different from the settlement of Virginia? How was it similar?

Can You Connect the Past and the Present?

1. Elected law-making groups are still very important to American democracy today. How can members of your community take part in their own local government?
2. The Toleration Act was an important step toward religious freedom. Yet this law allowed only one religion. How does this differ from our ideas of religious freedom today?

CHAPTER 8

Pilgrims and Puritans Settle Colonies

The Pilgrims land at Plymouth.

BEFORE YOU BEGIN THE CHAPTER

Know What to Look For

1. Squanto was an Indian who proved to be a valuable friend to the first colonists settling in Massachusetts. He taught these settlers how to plant crops, how to gather foods, and how to hunt and fish. He lived with the Pilgrims for many years, and he was responsible, perhaps more than anyone else, for the success of the colony. However, Squanto himself had

led an adventurous life before the Pilgrims arrived. Years earlier, he was captured by a trader, and sold as a slave in Spain. Then he escaped to England, and made several voyages across the Atlantic.

In this chapter, you will read about the beginning of the Plymouth Colony, where many settlers came to find religious freedom.

You also will read about another group of religious settlers who arrived later and established a much larger colony nearby.

2. Read the title of the chapter. Then look through the chapter and read each heading. What two different groups of people are discussed in this chapter? Use the headings only to find your answer.

3. Look at the pictures in the chapter and read each caption. What does the picture on page 60 show the Pilgrims doing? Also examine the map on page 63. Which colonies are shown on this map? Find Plymouth Colony. Finally, look at the chapter time line on this page. What years are included in this chapter? Compare the chapter time line to the unit time line on page 47.

4. Read the last part of the chapter called Summing Up. What two important ideas can you learn about the Puritans?

Know These Important Terms

Pilgrims	Puritans
Mayflower Compact	town meetings

Know the Main Idea

Here is the MAIN IDEA of this chapter.

The Pilgrims and Puritans came to America to find religious freedom. Later, they joined together and formed a large and successful colony.

Keep this MAIN IDEA in mind as you study the chapter. Ask yourself the following questions as you read. They will help you remember the MAIN IDEA.

1. Where did the Pilgrims first move to find religious freedom?

2. How did the Pilgrims draw up their first plan of government for their new colony?

3. Who was allowed to vote at a Massachusetts town meeting?

THE YEARS OF THIS CHAPTER ARE 1620 TO 1691

1500	1620	1691	1752

THE CHAPTER LESSON BEGINS HERE

The Pilgrims Left England and Went to Holland

You may remember that some English people did not want to join the Church of England. They wanted to attend their own churches. One such group of people was the **Pilgrims.** The English government fined and jailed the Pilgrims for not going to the Church of England. As a result, some of the Pilgrims left England and went to Holland.

The Pilgrims attended their own church in Holland, but they still were not happy. They had trouble finding jobs, and their children were forgetting English customs. The Pilgrims, therefore, decided to go to America, where they hoped to be able to set up their own church and to live as Englishmen.

The Pilgrims Settled in America

The Pilgrims had very little money. In return for supplies and a ship to take them to America, the Pilgrims promised to work without pay for an English company for seven years. About 100 English people made the trip to America. Only thirty-five of them were Pilgrims. These Englishmen planned to settle in the northern part of Virginia. But after a stormy trip across the Atlantic Ocean in the

The Pilgrims sign the Mayflower Compact. In this agreement the colonists formed their own government.

ship "Mayflower," they landed on the shores of what is now the state of Massachusetts (MASS-uh-CHOO-suts).

The Pilgrims Set Up a Government in a New Colony

Even before they landed, the Pilgrims knew that they needed a plan for governing themselves. For this reason, the men on the ship drew up an agreement called the **Mayflower Compact**. In this agreement, the settlers agreed to make fair laws and to obey them. The Mayflower Compact was very important. For the first time, settlers in the English colonies formed their own government.

The Pilgrims started their new colony, called Plymouth, in December, 1620. It was too cold to plant crops, and many of the settlers died during the first winter. Under the leadership of their governor, William Bradford, and with the help of the Indians, some of the Pilgrims were able to live through the winter. Then during the summer, they grew good crops and had enough food for winter. From then on, Plymouth Colony grew and did well. Plymouth Colony proved that people were able to set up successful colonies in the northern part of America.

The Puritans Settled Massachusetts Bay Colony

The **Puritans** were another group of English people who were unhappy with the Church of England. The Puritans tried to change the Church of England. When the Church of England refused to accept their changes and began to make their lives hard, the Puritans, too, decided to settle in Massachusetts. Unlike the Pilgrims, the Puritans were rich enough to start their own company, the Massachusetts

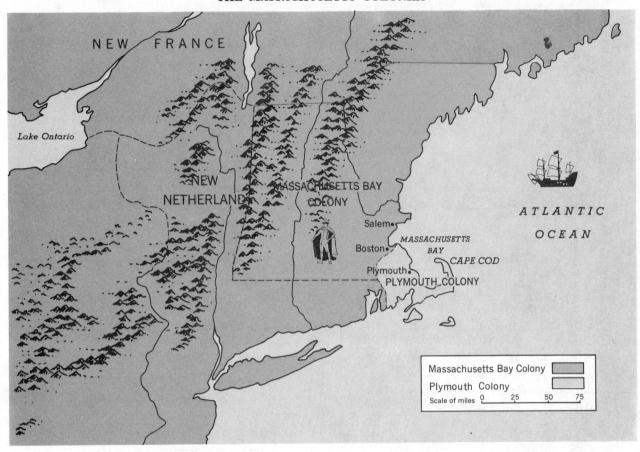

Bay Company. This company ran the colony.

In the year 1630, the Massachusetts Bay Company sent about 1 thousand colonists to America. The Puritans settled north of Plymouth Colony. They called their colony Massachusetts Bay. By 1640, about 20 thousand more Puritans joined them. Later, in 1691, Plymouth Colony and Massachusetts Bay Colony joined together into one colony, called Massachusetts Bay.

The Puritans Won the Right to Govern Themselves

At first, the settlers in Massachusetts Bay had a very small part in the government of the colony. Only members of the Massachusetts Bay Company had the right to govern the colony. John Winthrop, the governor, and a few other men were the only members of the Massachusetts Bay Company. These few men governed the colony. Finally, some of the other settlers asked to take part in the government. Governor Winthrop gave these men the right to vote. They then elected a council, or a group, of eighteen men, to help the governor run the colony.

Soon, however, the other Puritan men all demanded the right to vote. In time, they won this right. These Puritan men then elected a legislature, which was made up of two or three

JOHN WINTHROP—
PURITAN GOVERNOR

The Massachusetts Bay Company chose John Winthrop to be the first governor of the Massachusetts Bay Colony. Winthrop was a Puritan land owner who decided to leave England and settle in the New World. He was an outstanding leader, and because of his leadership the Massachusetts Bay Colony became a success. Within a few months after Massachusetts was settled, homes were built and farms were set up.

Because of his position as governor of the colony, Winthrop was able to rule Massachusetts Bay almost by himself. However, he decided to let other members of the colony take part in its government. And he soon gave the right to vote to all the men who were members of the Puritan church. These men elected the colony's legislature and governor. Winthrop was elected as governor twelve times.

Winthrop was a respected member of the colony and a popular governor. At one time, he had money problems. The legislature voted his wife 3 thousand acres of land and the people of the colony raised money to help him.

men from each town. This legislature made all the important laws for the colony.

The Puritans Settled in Towns

Unlike the settlers of Virginia and Maryland, the Puritans settled close together in towns. The Puritans built their houses and their church in the center of the town. Fields, pastures, and woodland made up the rest of the town.

The people governed the towns. They elected town officers and met together in **town meetings.** Many different questions were decided at these meetings. All the citizens of the town were allowed to attend the town meetings and to take part in them. However, only the Puritans were allowed to vote at the town meetings.

The Puritans Did Not Allow Religious Freedom in the Colony

The Puritans came to America to find freedom of religion. Yet the Puritans did not give freedom of religion to the other people in the colony. Only the Puritan church was allowed in the colony. Everyone had to attend the Puritan church and to pay taxes to support it. All the settlers had to obey laws passed by the Puritan legislature. However, some of these laws took freedom away from the people. For example, laws were passed against wearing fancy clothes or smoking in public.

Summing Up

The Pilgrims and Puritans came to America to find freedom of religion. They settled in Massachusetts. In the Pilgrim and Puritan colonies, the settlers learned how to govern themselves. However, the Puritans made everyone in the colony attend the Puritan church. The next chapter tells about settlers who left Massachusetts because the Puritans did not allow them freedom of religion.

AFTER YOU READ THE CHAPTER

Do You Know These Important Terms?

For each sentence below, choose the term that best completes the sentence.

1. Some (**Pilgrims/Puritans**) left England for Holland to attend their own church.
2. The plan of government for the Plymouth Colony was called the (**Mayflower Compact/Magna Carta**).
3. (**Pilgrims/Puritans**) were the group who wanted to change religious practices in the Church of England.
4. At (**town burgesses/town meetings**), Puritan townspeople met to elect their own officers and to decide local questions.

Do You Remember These People?

Tell something about each of the following persons.

William Bradford   **John Winthrop**

Can You Locate These Places?

Use the map on page 63 to do the following map work.

1. Locate Cape Cod. What colony was located there? What settlement was first built in this colony?
2. Locate the Massachusetts Bay Colony. Name some settlements in that colony.

Do You Know When It Happened?

What are the years of this chapter? Tell how each of the following dates is related to the events in this chapter.

1620   1630   1691

Discovering More About the Main Idea

The Pilgrims and Puritans came to America to find religious freedom. Later, they joined together and formed a large and successful colony.

Tell how each of the following developments is related to the MAIN IDEA.

The Mayflower Compact was a plan of government agreed upon by the Pilgrims' leaders.

Thousands of Puritans came to the Massachusetts Bay Colony. They established a legislature for the colony and held town meetings to settle problems of local government.

The Puritans did not give freedom of religion to the other people in their colony. Only the Puritan church was allowed.

Can You Discuss the Chapter?

Use the information you learned in this chapter to answer the following questions.

1. Why were the Pilgrims unhappy with their life in Holland? How were they able to make the trip to America?
2. Why did the Puritans find it easier to make the trip to America than did the Pilgrims?
3. How did the people of Massachusetts Bay Colony win the right of self-government?
4. What was the Puritans' idea about freedom of religion for the other people in their colony?
5. What might have happened if settlers had landed at Plymouth before they had agreed on a plan of government?

Can You Connect the Past and the Present?

1. What ideas about democratic government were included in the Mayflower Compact that are still important today?
2. What do you think about the town meeting type of government? Would it work in your city or town? Why or why not?

CHAPTER 9

The Start of New England

Puritans going to settle in Connecticut.

BEFORE YOU BEGIN THE CHAPTER

Know What to Look For

1. The Puritans were very strict about religion. To the Puritans, Sunday was a day of rest and prayer. The entire family went to church together. Everyone had to go to church, and church services often lasted four or five hours. Puritan ministers, or church leaders, preached long sermons to the people. They told the people how they should behave and what they should believe.

In this chapter, you will learn that some people who did not like strict Puritan rules left or were forced to leave the Massachusetts Bay Colony. Soon new colonies were formed, and the frontier settlements of the older colonies began to move westward.

2. Read the title of the chapter. Then look through the chapter and read each heading. What new colonies were started in New

England by people from the Massachusetts Bay Colony?

3. Look at the pictures in the chapter and read the captions. Which picture shows colonists leaving the Puritan colony? Look at the map on page 68. What is the title of the map? What symbol shows early New England colonies? Note also the time line at the beginning of the chapter. What years are included in the chapter? Compare this chapter time line to the unit time line on page 47.

4. Read the last part of the chapter called Summing Up. What does this section say about those who left the Massachusetts Bay Colony?

Know These Important Terms
Parliament
constitution
frontier
New England colonies
New England Confederation

Know the Main Idea
Here is the MAIN IDEA of this chapter.
Some colonists left the Massachusetts Bay Colony to start other English colonies nearby. The New England colonies were formed in this way.

Keep this MAIN IDEA in mind as you study the chapter. Ask yourself the following questions as you read. They will help you remember the MAIN IDEA.

1. What settlement that later became part of Rhode Island was started by Roger Williams?
2. What two new ideas of freedom became laws in the Rhode Island Colony?
3. For what purpose was the New England Confederation formed?

THE YEARS OF THIS CHAPTER ARE 1636 TO 1675

1500	1636	1675	1752

THE CHAPTER LESSON BEGINS HERE

Roger Williams Started the Rhode Island Colony

Roger Williams, a Puritan leader, spoke out against the harsh Puritan rule in Massachusetts. Williams said that the Puritan government did not have the right to force people to attend the Puritan church. He believed that all people had the right to worship as they wished. Williams also said that the land of Massachusetts belonged to the Indians, not to the Massachusetts Bay Company. The Puritans thought that Williams was a troublemaker, and they decided to send him back to England. However, in 1636, Williams fled from Massachusetts Bay.

Shortly after he left Massachusetts, Williams and some friends settled the town of Providence (PRAHV-uh-dunts). Within a few years, three more towns were settled near Providence by other people who were forced to leave Massachusetts. These four towns asked **Parliament,** the English law-making group, to allow them to become a colony. Parliament agreed, and in 1644 the four towns were joined together into the colony of Rhode Island.

Rhode Island Gained Important Freedoms

Roger Williams became the first governor of

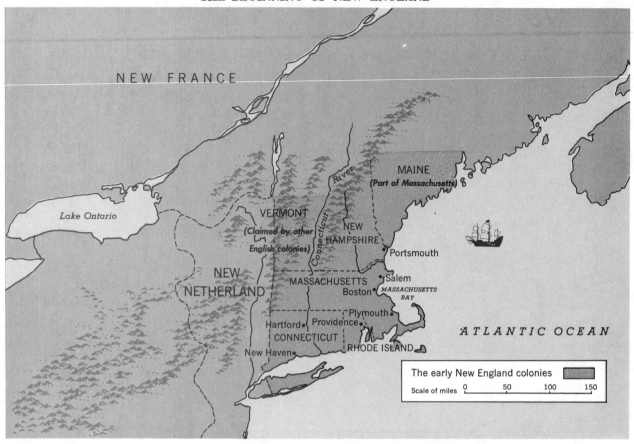

The early New England colonies
Scale of miles 0 50 100 150

Rhode Island. As governor, he passed many laws that gave the colonists important freedoms. One law gave everyone in Rhode Island freedom of religion. Another law said that churches and the government had to be kept separate. This means that the government cannot force people to attend a certain church. Also, churches can have no part in the government. Rhode Island began this important American idea that churches and the government had to remain apart.

Rhode Island colonists also had more control over their government than the colonists in any other English colony had. Many people who were unhappy in other New England colonies

settled in Rhode Island. Most Rhode Island colonists were farmers. Others raised horses and cattle. Most people who lived in the town of Newport, Rhode Island, made their living from trade.

Colonists from Massachusetts Settled Connecticut

Other settlers who were not happy in Massachusetts left and settled in the Connecticut (kuh-NET-ik-KUT) River Valley. In 1636, a church leader named Thomas Hooker led his entire church group to Connecticut, where they settled the town of Hartford. Hooker and his followers left Massachusetts because

Roger Williams was forced to leave Massachusetts Bay. He stayed with friendly Indians before settling Rhode Island.

they wanted more freedom. They also were looking for good farm land.

Soon, several other towns were started along the Connecticut River. These towns joined with Hartford, and they formed a new colony, called Connecticut. In 1639, the people of the Connecticut colony drew up the first written **constitution,** or plan of government, in America. This Connecticut constitution even allowed people who did not attend any church to vote. But the people of Connecticut did not have as much control over their government as the people of Rhode Island did.

Connecticut Was an Early Example of the Westward Movement

The settlement of Connecticut was an early example of the movement of people to the **frontier,** or the unsettled land, in the colonies. Most of the people who went to the frontier moved westward in search of land and free-

dom. This movement westward to the frontier helped to settle much of the land that later became the United States.

However, the westward movement also had a tragic result. As they moved west, the settlers drove the Indians off their lands. To protect their lands, the Indians fought back. For example, when settlers moved into Connecticut, a war between the settlers and the Indians broke out. As in most of these wars, the Indians in Connecticut lost, and many of them were killed.

People from Massachusetts Settled Maine and New Hampshire

Some settlers from Massachusetts also moved to New Hampshire. John Wheelwright, a church leader who also disagreed with the Puritans in Massachusetts, led his followers to New Hampshire in 1638. Wheelwright and his followers settled in New Hampshire and set up

page 69

The Puritans had strict rules that had to be obeyed. Colonists who did not obey were sometimes put in stocks.

their own church there. At first, New Hampshire was ruled by Massachusetts, but later it became a colony controlled by the English king.

Other settlers from Massachusetts moved into Maine. Unlike New Hampshire, Maine remained part of Massachusetts. Not many people moved into Maine or New Hampshire. Both colonies had poor soil and cold weather. And they were often attacked by the French and the Indians from nearby New France.

The Colonists Set Up the New England Confederation

The New England colonies—Massachusetts, Rhode Island, Connecticut, and New Hampshire—shared many problems. Their most important problem was the danger of attack by the Indians, the French, or the Dutch. England was far away and was not able to protect the New England colonies. Therefore, in 1643, Massachusetts, Plymouth, and Connecticut joined together and formed the **New England**

Confederation (kun-FED-uh-RAY-shun) to defend themselves. Two men from each colony represented their colony in the Confederation. These men met once a year to try to solve the colonies' problems. They worked to settle boundary disputes and to meet the danger of Indian attacks. The Confederation helped to protect the New England colonies, and it also brought them closer together.

Summing Up

Some people who settled in Massachusetts Bay Colony were not happy there. They wanted freedoms that the Puritans did not allow in the colony. These settlers left Massachusetts Bay Colony, and they started the other New England colonies of Rhode Island, Connecticut, and New Hampshire. The people in most of these colonies had an important part in their government. In some of these colonies, the people also had freedom of religion. The next chapter tells about another group of English colonies.

AFTER YOU READ THE CHAPTER

Do You Know These Important Terms?

For each sentence below, choose the term that best completes the sentence.

1. The law-making group in England is called the (Assembly/Parliament).
2. A (compact/constitution) is a plan of government.
3. Unsettled land in the colonies was called the (frontier/wilderness).
4. Massachusetts, Rhode Island, Connecticut, and New Hampshire were called the (New England/North England) colonies.
5. In the (New England Confederation/Assembly), several colonies worked together to solve common problems.

Do You Remember These People?

Tell something about each of the following persons.

Roger Williams   **Thomas Hooker**
John Wheelwright

Can You Locate These Places?

Use the map on page 68 to do the following map work.

1. Locate these places: Massachusetts, Rhode Island, Connecticut, and New Hampshire. Which colony was claimed by several other colonies?
2. Find the colony in which each of the following settlements was located.

   Boston   **Portsmouth**
   New Haven   **Plymouth**
   Providence   **Hartford**

Do You Know When It Happened?

In what year did each of the following events happen?

1. Roger Williams fled from Massachusetts.
2. Rhode Island became a colony.
3. Thomas Hooker left Massachusetts.

Discovering More About the Main Idea

Some colonists left the Massachusetts Bay Colony to start other English colonies nearby. The New England colonies were formed in this way.

Tell how each of the following developments is related to the MAIN IDEA.

Rhode Island, Connecticut, and New Hampshire were settled by colonists from Massachusetts Bay Colony.

The westward movement of colonists into unsettled land was the beginning of the frontier movement.

The New England colonies began to work together in order to settle problems faced by all the colonies.

Can You Discuss the Chapter?

Use the information you learned in this chapter to answer the following questions.

1. Why did Rhode Island's law provide for the separation of the church and the government?
2. Why has Massachusetts sometimes been called the "mother of New England"?
3. Why did the colonial frontier keep advancing farther west?
4. Why did the settlements in New Hampshire and Maine not grow as quickly as those in Connecticut and Rhode Island?

Can You Connect the Past and the Present?

1. Give some examples in your own community to illustrate that the church is separate from the government.
2. Have any groups of people you know about used a plan like the New England Confederation to try to solve their common problems? Explain.

CHAPTER 10

The Other English Colonies

William Penn signs a treaty with the Indians.

BEFORE YOU BEGIN THE CHAPTER

Know What to Look For

1. Have you ever owed money to anyone? It may not be pleasant, especially if you are not able to repay it. In England during the 1600's, people were put into prison if they were not able to pay money they owed—even when the debts they owed were small. A prisoner in a debtors' prison was only released when the debt was paid.

But how was a person in prison able to earn money to pay his debt? Often, a debtor spent many years in prison. Some people felt that this was unjust. These people were able to get some of the prisoners freed, and to send them to America as colonists, where the prisoners might start a new life. Many of these prisoners went to Georgia. In this chapter, you will read about Georgia and the other English colonies along the Atlantic coast.

2. Read the title of the chapter. Then look through the chapter and read each heading. From the headings alone, how many colonies can you name?

3. Look at the first chapter picture and read the caption. What does the picture show? Examine the map on page 74. How many new colonies are shown on it? Look at the time line at the beginning of the chapter. What years are included in the chapter? Compare this chapter time line to the unit time line on page 47.

4. Read the section called Summing Up at the end of the chapter. How many English colonies were there on the Atlantic coast?

Know These Important Terms

royal colonies   Quaker

indigo

Know the Main Idea

Here is the MAIN IDEA of this chapter.

By 1732, England had founded thirteen American colonies along the Atlantic coast from Canada to Florida.

Keep this MAIN IDEA in mind as you study the chapter. Ask yourself the following questions as you read. They will help you remember the MAIN IDEA.

1. How did England obtain the colonies of New York and New Jersey? What former Dutch colony were the colonies of New York and New Jersey formed from?

2. What man helped to found the colony of Georgia? Why did he want to start the colony of Georgia?

3. Why did William Penn get along well with the Indians when he settled the colony of Pennsylvania?

THE YEARS OF THIS CHAPTER ARE 1644 TO 1752

1500	1644	1752

THE CHAPTER LESSON BEGINS HERE

England Took New Netherland from the Dutch

You may remember that New Netherland was the Dutch colony located along the Hudson and Delaware rivers. New Netherland soon became a threat to the English colonies. The Dutch settlement separated the New England colonies from Virginia and Maryland. Dutch warships off the coast of New Netherland often attacked English ships. And the Dutch merchants in New Netherland took much of the fur trade away from the English colonies. In the year 1664, England sent a fleet of warships to New Netherland, and the English took the colony of New Netherland from the Dutch.

England Formed New York and New Jersey

England divided New Netherland into the colonies of New York and New Jersey. The king of England gave both New York and New Jersey to his brother, the Duke of York. The Duke of York then gave New Jersey to two of his friends, Lord Berkeley and Sir George Carteret. They became the proprietors, or owners, of New Jersey. New York was ruled by the Duke of York. He allowed the New York colonists freedom of religion, but he refused to let them have their own legislature. Later, both New York and New Jersey became **royal colonies,** or colonies that were ruled directly by the English king.

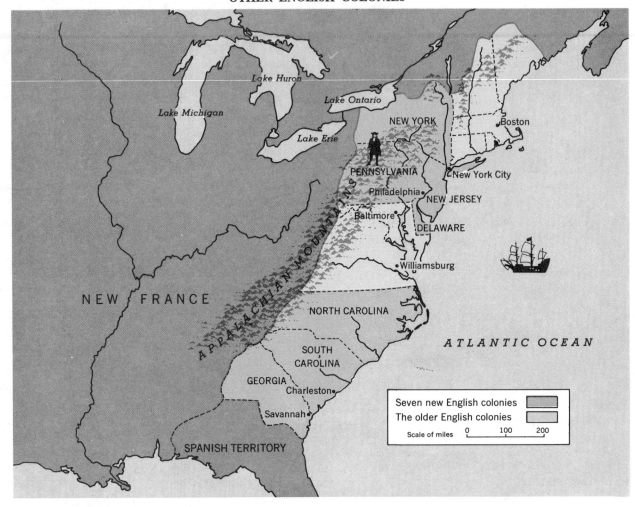

The Carolina Colonies Were Started

In 1663, the king of England gave the lands which are now the states of North Carolina and South Carolina to eight of his friends. The northern part of the Carolina Colony was settled mainly by small tobacco farmers from Virginia. The eight proprietors allowed these settlers to elect their own legislature.

Other settlements were formed farther south in Carolina. This southern part of Carolina had good soil, a warm climate, and a fine seaport which grew into the town of Charleston. The colonists in the south planted large crops of rice and **indigo,** a plant which produced a useful blue dye. These colonists were not allowed as much part in their government as the colonists who lived in the northern part of Carolina. The two parts of the Carolina settlement were different in other ways, too. In 1729, they were split into the colonies of North Carolina and South Carolina, and both became royal colonies ruled by the English king.

Georgia Was Started to Protect South Carolina

South Carolina was always in danger of an attack by Spain. Spain claimed that South Carolina was part of Spain's colony of Florida. The English government wanted to protect its valuable colony of South Carolina. Therefore, in the year 1732, England agreed to set up the colony of Georgia between South Carolina and Florida.

The leader of the Georgia Colony was General James Oglethorpe (OH-gul-thawrp). Oglethorpe wanted Georgia to be a place where Englishmen who were in prison because they owed debts might start a new life. He also wanted Georgia to supply England with valuable products that England needed but was not able to grow at home.

The founders of Georgia set up strict rules for the colony. They did not allow slavery or the sale of liquor. To prevent a few men from taking all the land, all farms had to be less than 500 acres in size. However, in 1752, when the king of England took control of the colony, these rules ended. Georgia then became much like its neighbor, South Carolina.

William Penn Started a Quaker Colony in Pennsylvania

One of the most successful of the English colonies was Pennsylvania. Pennsylvania was started by William Penn, who was the proprietor, or owner, of the colony. Pennsylvania was given to Penn by the English king to repay a debt the king owed to Penn's father.

William Penn was a **Quaker.** The Quakers were another group of Englishmen who disagreed with the religious beliefs of the Church of England and wanted freedom of religion. They felt that each man had to live in the way he believed was good and right for him.

Quakers refused to take off their hats or bow to anyone, because they believed that all men

were equal. The Quakers believed that all men must learn to live together in peace. Since Quakers believed that fighting was wrong, they refused to serve in the army. Their beliefs set them apart from many other Englishmen, who thought that they were strange. In fact, the English government thought that the Quakers were dangerous, and put many of them in jail. Penn wanted to start a colony for the Quakers in America. He hoped to make Pennsylvania a place where the Quakers were free to live as they wished.

Pennsylvania Became a Successful Colony

William Penn arrived in his colony in 1682. Penn had great plans for his colony. One of the first things he did was to make friends with the Indians. Penn paid the Indians for their land and always tried to treat them fairly. In return, the Indians allowed the settlers of Pennsylvania to live in peace.

Penn also treated his colonists very well. He allowed them to worship as they wished and to help make their own laws. He also sold them land at very low prices. Not only Quakers, but thousands of other people from England and other European nations settled in Pennsylvania. Later, the southeastern part of the colony became a separate colony known as Delaware. Penn's colony grew very quickly. In fact, by the early 1700's, Pennsylvania was the largest of the English colonies.

Summing Up

The settlement of the colonies of New York, New Jersey, Pennsylvania, Delaware, North Carolina, South Carolina, and Georgia completed the English settlement of North America. England had thirteen colonies located along the Atlantic coast of North America. In the next chapters, which are in Unit 3, you will read about life in the thirteen English colonies in North America.

AFTER YOU READ THE CHAPTER

Do You Know These Important Terms?

For each sentence below, select the term that best completes the sentence.

1. Colonies ruled directly by the English king were called (**royal/official**) colonies.
2. Settlers in the Southern colonies grew (**rice/indigo**), a plant which produced a blue dye.
3. A religious group which did not believe in war and which the English government thought was dangerous was the (**Catholics/Quakers**).

Do You Remember These People?

Tell something about the following persons.

Duke of York   **Lord Berkeley**
George Carteret   **James Oglethorpe**
William Penn

Can You Locate These Places?

Use the map on page 74 to do the following map work.

1. Name the English colonies located between New England and Maryland and Virginia.
2. Which colony was located farthest south? What foreign nations owned land bordering this colony?
3. How can you tell the difference between the names of colonies and the names of settlements within the colonies?

Do You Know When It Happened?

What are the years of this chapter? Place the following events in the order in which they occurred.

North Carolina and South Carolina became two separate colonies.

William Penn founded the colony of Pennsylvania.

England took over the colony of New Netherland.

Discovering More About the Main Idea

By 1732, England had founded thirteen American colonies along the Atlantic coast from Canada to Florida.

Tell how each of the following developments is related to the MAIN IDEA.

New Jersey and New York were formed from the Dutch colony of New Netherland.

The Carolina Colony began as a proprietary colony, but it later split into two colonies ruled by the king.

William Penn founded the colony of Pennsylvania as a safe place for Quakers.

Georgia was founded more than a hundred years after the first English colony was started.

Can You Discuss the Chapter?

Use the information you learned in this chapter to answer the following questions.

1. What freedom did the people of New York enjoy after the English took over? What freedoms did they lack?
2. Why was South Carolina well suited for agriculture? What crops were grown in North Carolina?
3. Why was Georgia an important colony to the English?
4. Why was William Penn so successful in dealing with the Indians? in attracting settlers to his colony?

Can You Connect the Past and the Present?

1. What happens to people today when they are not able to pay their debts?
2. What rights and freedoms were the colonists seeking in America? Are Americans still concerned about these same rights today? Explain.

UNIT 3

How the Colonists Made Their Living

The port of Philadelphia.

THE CHAPTERS IN UNIT 3 ARE

CHAPTER 11   Colonial Farming
CHAPTER 12   Colonial Trade
CHAPTER 13   Colonial Industry and Towns

THE YEARS OF THIS UNIT ARE 1607 TO 1750

1600   1607   1750   1975

CHAPTER 11

Colonial Farming

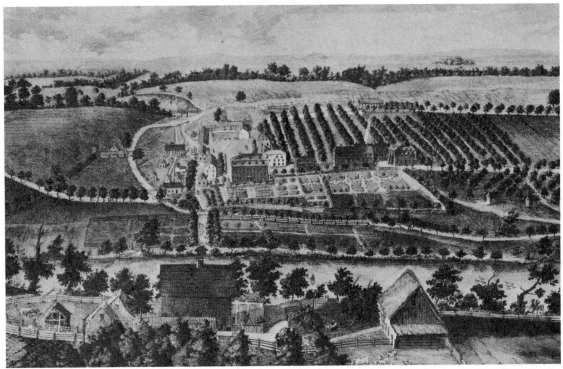

Farms in the Middle colonies.

BEFORE YOU BEGIN THE CHAPTER

Know What to Look For

1. Have you ever heard of "cloud seeding"? Cloud seeding is a new method scientists use to make it rain in an area where it has not rained in a long time. An airplane drops dry ice or other chemicals into the clouds and this sometimes causes it to rain. Today, scientists are just beginning to learn how to control certain things that happen on earth.

During colonial days, most Americans were farmers. However, at this time, Americans did not know how to control their surroundings. Farmers did not have fertilizers or insect killers, and they did not know about scientific farming methods. They had no control over the land or the weather. In this chapter, you will read about farming in the American colonies. You will find out how farming differed in the colonies because the soil, weather, and amount of good farming land differed in the colonies.

2. Read the title of the chapter. Then look through the chapter and read each heading. Name the three sections, or groups, of colonies in America.

3. Look at the pictures in the chapter and read each caption. What do the pictures tell you about farming in the American colonies? Study the map on page 80. What kind of information does the map show you? Note also the time line at the beginning of the chapter. What are the years of this chapter? Compare the chapter time line to the unit time line on page 77.

4. Read the last part of the chapter called Summing Up. What was the most important way of making a living in all three sections of colonial America?

Know These Important Terms
girdling   indentured servants

coastal plain   breadbasket colonies
subsistence farming   commercial farming

Know the Main Idea
Here is the MAIN IDEA of this chapter.
Farming was an important way of making a living in all three sections of colonial America. Because the soil, weather, and amount of good farm land was different in each section, farming differed in each section.

Keep this MAIN IDEA in mind as you study the chapter. Ask yourself the following questions as you read. They will help you remember the MAIN IDEA.

1. Name the colonies that made up the section known as the Middle colonies in colonial America.
2. What was the most important crop grown in the Middle colonies?
3. What kind of workers did farmers in the Middle colonies use to help on their large farms? in the Southern colonies?

THE YEARS OF THIS CHAPTER ARE 1607 TO 1750

1600   1607   1750

THE CHAPTER LESSON BEGINS HERE

The Indians Helped the First English Settlers to Farm

When the English settlers arrived in America, they tried to farm just as they had back home in England. They soon learned that their old farming ways often did not work. For example, wheat, the most important English crop, did not grow well in some parts of America. The English settlers had to learn how to grow crops which were suited to the lands in America. They also had to learn new ways of farming the land.

The Indians showed the early colonists how to grow corn and other crops which grew well in America. The colonists copied the Indian method of **girdling**, or tearing the bark off the trees. Girdling killed the trees, and after a while they died and fell down by themselves.

Three Groups of Colonies

The thirteen English colonies were divided into three sections, or groups, of colonies.

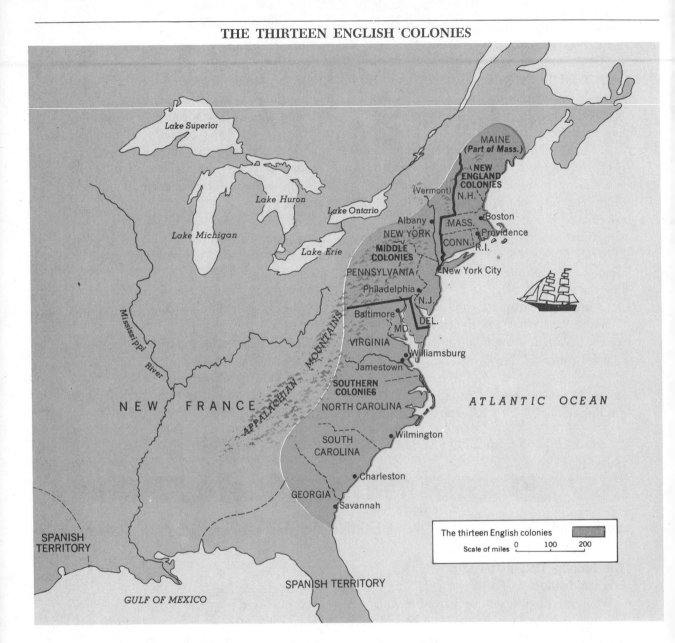

Lake Superior

Lake Huron

Lake Ontario

Lake Michigan

Lake Erie

MAINE
(Part of Mass.)

NEW ENGLAND COLONIES

(Vermont) N.H.

Albany

MASS.

Boston

NEW YORK

Providence

MIDDLE COLONIES

CONN.

R.I.

PENNSYLVANIA

New York City

Philadelphia

N.J.

Baltimore

DEL.

MD.

VIRGINIA

Williamsburg

Jamestown

SOUTHERN COLONIES

NORTH CAROLINA

Wilmington

SOUTH CAROLINA

Charleston

GEORGIA

Savannah

NEW FRANCE

Mississippi River

APPALACHIAN MOUNTAINS

ATLANTIC OCEAN

SPANISH TERRITORY

SPANISH TERRITORY

GULF OF MEXICO

The thirteen English colonies

Scale of miles 0 100 200

These three sections were the New England colonies (New Hampshire, Massachusetts, Connecticut, and Rhode Island), the Middle colonies (New York, New Jersey, Pennsylvania, and Delaware), and the Southern colonies (Maryland, Virginia, North Carolina, South Carolina, and Georgia). The weather,

the soil, and the amount of good farm land were different in each of these three sections of the colonies.

Farming Was Difficult in New England

The New England colonies were not well suited for farming. Most of the soil in New

A farm in the New England colonies. Most New England farms were small, and they were run by the farmer and his family.

England was poor and rocky. Short, cool summers made the growing season short. And much of New England was hilly. Only the **coastal plain,** or level land along the Atlantic coast, was not hilly. Therefore, New England farms were usually small family farms which were worked by the farmer and his family.

Corn was the most important New England grain, but oats, barley, and rye were also grown. Most New England farmers grew fruits and vegetables, and also raised animals such as oxen, horses, sheep, cattle, and hogs. Most New England farmers grew just enough to feed themselves and their families. They did not grow enough crops to sell for money. This kind of farming is called **subsistence** (sub-SIS-tens) **farming.**

The Middle Colonies Grew Large Crops of Food

The Middle colonies were better suited to farming than New England. They had rich soil and a mild climate. Farms in the Middle colonies were larger than those in New England, and workers were needed to help on

these large farms. Many of these workers were **indentured** (in-DEN-churd) **servants.** Indentured servants were people who agreed to work for a master for a certain number of years in order to pay for their journey to the colonies. When their time was up, indentured servants were given their freedom, and they were able to set up their own farms.

The main food crops grown in the Middle colonies were wheat, rye, barley, corn, vegetables, and fruit. The settlers also raised many cattle, sheep, and hogs for their meat and skins. Much of the wheat and cattle raised in the Middle colonies was sold in the other colonies or to other nations. In fact, the Middle colonies grew and sold so much wheat that they became known as the **breadbasket colonies.**

Tobacco Was the Most Important Southern Crop

The Southern colonies were best suited for farming because the Southern soil was rich, the growing season was long, and the weather was warm. The Southern colonies had much flat land because the coastal plain was wider

A large plantation in the Southern colonies. Rice, tobacco, and indigo were the chief crops grown on plantations.

in the South than in New England or the Middle colonies. At first, the settlers in the Southern colonies started small farms. But when tobacco, rice, and indigo—a plant used to make blue dye—became important crops, the Southern farms increased in size. Some colonists came to own thousands of acres of land, and these huge farms were called plantations.

Tobacco was the main crop grown in Virginia, Maryland, and North Carolina. Because tobacco required a great deal of care, Southern tobacco plantations needed many workers. However, workers were hard to get in the colonies. At first, Southern planters used indentured servants. Later, as you will read, the Southern colonies used black slaves as workers.

Rice and Indigo Were Important Southern Crops

In South Carolina and Georgia, the most important crops were rice and indigo. Settlers in South Carolina began to grow rice in the 1690's. Within a few years, South Carolina was growing the best rice in the world. In the 1740's, the people of South Carolina started to grow indigo, which soon became South Caro-

lina's second most important crop. Like tobacco, rice and indigo needed much care while they were growing. Almost all of the work on the rice and indigo farms was done by slaves.

Southern Crops Were Grown to Be Sold

Although the Southern colonies also raised wheat, corn, fruits, vegetables, cattle, and hogs, these crops were used by the farmer's family. Southern farmers used most of their land to raise "cash" crops, or crops grown to be sold. In Virginia the cash crop was tobacco. In South Carolina it was rice or indigo. This type of farming is called commercial (kuh-MUR-shul) farming.

Summing Up

The thirteen colonies were divided into three sections—the New England colonies, the Middle colonies, and the Southern colonies. In all three sections, farming was an important way of making a living. Because the soil, the weather, and the amount of good farm land differed in each section, farming differed in each section. In the next chapter, you will read about colonial trade.

AFTER YOU READ THE CHAPTER

Do You Know These Important Terms?

For each sentence below, choose the term that best completes the sentence.

1. Colonial farmers learned to clear their land by copying the Indian method of (**pruning/ girdling**), or killing the trees by removing the bark.
2. The level land along the Atlantic coast was called the (**shoreline/coastal**) plain.
3. The type of farming in which farmers produce just enough food to feed themselves and their families is called (**subsistence/ plantation**) farming.
4. (**Indentured/Immigrant**) servants were workers who agreed to work for a master for a number of years in order to pay for the cost of their journey to America.
5. The Middle colonies produced so much wheat they were sometimes called the (**gristmill/breadbasket**) colonies.
6. The kind of farming in which farmers produce a "cash" crop is called (**commercial/ intensive**) farming.

Can You Locate These Places?

Use the map on page 80 to do the following map work.

1. Locate the New England colonies, the Middle colonies, and the Southern colonies.
2. Name some of the crops grown in each of the three sections.
3. Why might you expect the soil, weather, and amount of good farm land in the Southern colonies to be greatly different from those in the New England colonies?

Do You Know When It Happened?

What are the years of this chapter? The farming methods used by farmers in the three sections of the American colonies took a number of years to develop. What might make you think that farming methods sometimes change over the years?

Discovering More About the Main Idea

Farming was an important way of making a living in all three sections of colonial America. Because the soil, weather, and amount of good farm land was different in each section, farming differed in each section.

Tell how each of the following developments is related to the MAIN IDEA.

Most farmers in the New England colonies were subsistence farmers.

Farmers in the Middle colonies grew many different crops which they were able to sell to other colonies or to other nations.

In the Southern colonies farmers used most of their land to grow "cash" crops.

Can You Discuss the Chapter?

Use the information you learned in this chapter to answer the following questions.

1. How did the soil, weather, and amount of good farm land in each section make farming different in each section?
2. How was commercial farming different in the Middle colonies and the Southern colonies?
3. Name some of the important "cash" crops raised in the Southern colonies.
4. Do you think that the soil, weather, and amount of good farm land in each section had anything to do with the size of the farms in each section?

Can You Connect the Past and the Present?

List some of the ways man has discovered to control or change his surroundings on earth.

CHAPTER 12

Colonial Trade

New York harbor in the early 1700's.

BEFORE YOU BEGIN THE CHAPTER

Know What to Look For

1. Colonial traders often became very rich and important men. One colonial trader, William Phipps, started out as a poor carpenter. He married a well-to-do woman and soon built his own trading ships.

On one of his voyages in 1687, he discovered a sunken Spanish trading ship in the West Indies. For two months, his men dove into the sea and brought up a fortune in gold, silver, and jewels. By law, part of his treasure went to the king of England. However, in return the king knighted Phipps, and he became Sir William Phipps. A few years later, the king appointed him governor of Massachusetts. In this chapter, you will learn about trade in the American colonies.

2. Read the title of the chapter. Then look through the chapter and read each heading. Which of the three sections of colonial America was the first one to become a trading section?

3. Look at the pictures in the chapter and read each caption. What do the pictures tell you about trade in the colonies? Look at the map on page 87. What is the title of the map? Examine the time line at the beginning of the chapter. What years are included in the chapter? Compare the chapter time line to the unit time line.

4. Read the last part of the chapter called Summing Up. What laws did England pass to control the colonies' trade?

Know These Important Terms

Navigation Acts   triangular trade
smuggling

Know the Main Idea

Here is the MAIN IDEA of this chapter.

Trade was very important to all the colonies. Although England tried to control the colonies' trade, the colonists paid no attention to the English trade laws and traded with nations all over the world.

Keep this MAIN IDEA in mind as you study the chapter. Ask yourself the following questions as you read. They will help you remember the MAIN IDEA.

1. Why did the English government pass the Navigation Acts? What were the three main rules that made up these trade laws known as the Navigation Acts?

2. Name some of the products the New England colonists traded. From which section of the colonies did these products come?

3. What were the three main seaports in the colonies?

THE YEARS OF THIS CHAPTER ARE 1607 TO 1750

1600 1607   1750

THE CHAPTER LESSON BEGINS HERE

England Passed Laws to Control the Colonies' Trade

The English colonies in America were not free to trade with all nations. To control the colonies' trade, the English government passed laws known as the **Navigation** (NAV-uh-GAY-shun) **Acts.** The Navigation Acts were trade laws made up of the following rules.

1. All goods shipped to or from the English colonies were to be carried in English ships or in colonial ships manned by English or colonial sailors.

2. Certain colonial products were to be sold only to England or to the other English colonies. These products included tobacco, rice,

indigo, furs, cotton, tar, pitch, and turpentine.

3. All goods from foreign nations had to be brought to England before they were shipped to the colonies. In England, a duty, or tax, was placed on the foreign goods.

The Colonists Disliked the Navigation Acts

In some ways the Navigation Acts helped the colonists. Many ships were needed for the trade between England and the colonies. This need led to the development of the shipbuilding industry in the colonies. The Navigation Acts also gave the colonists a place to sell some

Whaling was an important way of making a living in some of the colonies.

of their goods. However, the Navigation Acts also hurt the colonies in some ways. Because foreign goods had to be brought to England first and then shipped to America in English or colonial ships, the colonists paid higher prices for the foreign goods.

Most colonists disliked the Navigation Acts. The colonists knew that these trade laws were passed to help English businessmen, not to help the colonists. Most colonial merchants and sea captains paid no attention to the Navigation Acts. **Smuggling,** or unlawful trade, became common. And the colonists usually got away with this unlawful trade.

New England Produced Valuable Products

The lack of good farm land caused many New Englanders to turn to other ways of making a living. The colonists in New England wanted such goods as fancy cloth and weapons, which were made in Europe. In order to get these goods, they needed products to trade for them. Therefore, New England colonists began making products which they were able to sell in many parts of the world.

Some New Englanders set up lumber mills and cut down the tall trees which grew in all parts of New England. Much of the wood, or lumber, was used to make ships in New England. But much lumber was still left over to trade with other nations.

Because New England was located near some of the best fishing places in the world, many New England colonists turned to the sea for a living. New England fishermen caught tons of fish. Much of the catch was dried, salted, and sold in Europe and the West Indies.

Another important New England product was rum. Rum was a popular drink in every English colony and in many nations of the world.

New England Carried on a Busy Trade

Lumber, fish, and rum from New England, wheat and cattle from the Middle colonies, and tobacco, rice, and indigo from the Southern colonies were the products the colonists traded. New England ships traded goods from the colonies in many parts of the world. However, the most important colonial trade followed a trade route shaped like a triangle. For this reason, it was called the **triangular trade.** Rum from New England was sent to Africa,

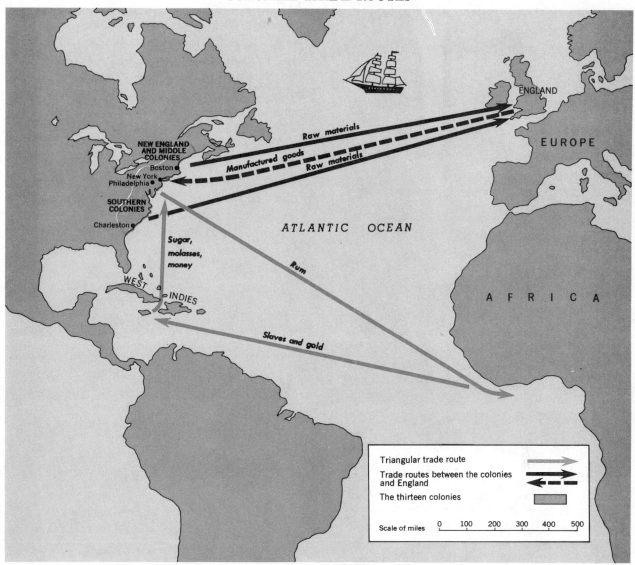

where it was traded for slaves and gold. The slaves then were taken to the West Indies and traded for sugar, molasses, and money. With the money they earned from the West Indies trade, the New England colonists bought the goods they needed from England.

Another important trade route was between New England, the West Indies, and England.

Lumber, fish, wheat, and cattle were carried to the West Indies, where they were traded for sugar and molasses. The New England colonists used these goods to make rum, which was sold in England. The New England colonies used the money from this trade to buy goods made in England. They needed all kinds of English goods.

page 87

Blackbeard the Pirate

PIRATES IN COLONIAL AMERICA

Pirates were welcome guests at most ports in the British colonies in America. The main reason for this welcome was that pirates had large amounts of gold and silver which they spent freely in the colonies. Governors and other high officials often invited them to their homes and entertained them. And most colonial merchants were eager to trade with the pirates because they bought goods with gold and silver.

But pirates were not always to be trusted. Often, they captured the ships belonging to the merchants who traded with them. At one time, the famous pirate Blackbeard (Edward Teach) blocked the port of Charlestown. He stopped all ships trying to get in or out of Charlestown. Then, he sailed away to North Carolina with his captured treasure.

The governors of the Carolinas were not able to stop Blackbeard. But the governor of Virginia sent two ships to capture him. After Blackbeard refused to surrender to the two Virginia ships, a battle broke out. Both sides suffered heavy losses. Blackbeard was killed in the battle after receiving twenty-five wounds. After this, pirates stayed away from the Carolinas.

Foreign Trade Was Very Important to the Colonies

During the 1660's, most colonial trade passed through Boston, the main seaport in New England. But in the 1700's, Philadelphia and New York, the two main seaports in the Middle colonies, became the most important ports in the colonies.

The colonies had to trade with other nations of the world besides England. Since the colonies bought more from England than they sold to England, they always owed money to English merchants. The trade with the West Indies and the other nations of Europe made it possible for colonial merchants to pay the money they owed to England and still make money for themselves.

Money Was a Problem in the Colonies

Even with their foreign trade, the colonies were always short of money—especially gold and silver coins. Indian wampum beads, tobacco, corn, sheep, cattle, rice, rum, and many other things were used as money at one time or another in the colonies. But these articles were difficult to carry around, and their value kept changing.

Massachusetts tried to coin silver money, but the English government stopped this. During the 1700's, most of the colonies printed paper money. However, businessmen both in England and the colonies refused to accept the paper money.

Summing Up

Trade was very important to the colonies. To control the colonies' trade, England passed trade laws called the Navigation Acts. However, the colonists paid no attention to these laws and traded with nations all over the world. In the next chapter, you will learn about the other ways the colonists made a living.

AFTER YOU READ THE CHAPTER

Do You Know These Important Terms?

For each sentence below, choose the term that best completes the sentence.

1. Laws passed by the English government to control the colonies' trade were called the (**Mercantile/Navigation**) Acts.
2. Illegal, or unlawful, trade is called (**pirating/smuggling**).
3. The (**triple/triangular**) trade was the name given to the trade route from New England, to Africa, to the West Indies, and back to New England.

Can You Locate These Places?

Use the map on page 87 to do the following map work.

1. Trace the trade routes that show the trade between England and the colonies. What products were traded between England and the colonies?
2. Trace the trade route from New England to Africa, to the West Indies, and back to New England. What goods were involved in this trade?

Do You Know When It Happened?

What are the years of this chapter? Place the following events in the order in which they occurred.

Philadelphia and New York became the most important seaports in the colonies.

The Navigation Acts were passed.

Boston was the main seaport in the colonies.

Discovering More About the Main Idea

Trade was very important to all the colonies. Although England tried to control the colonies' trade, the colonists paid no attention to the English trade laws and traded with nations all over the world.

Tell how each of the following developments is related to the MAIN IDEA.

The Navigation Acts helped the colonies to build up trade. But most colonists disliked these laws, and they often paid no attention to them.

The colonies, especially the New England colonies, built up important trade routes which involved trade with many parts of the world.

Colonial traders usually owed money to English merchants. The trade with other nations made it possible for them to pay the money they owed to England and still make money for themselves.

Can You Discuss the Chapter?

Use the information you learned in this chapter to answer the following questions.

1. What were the three main rules that made up the Navigation Acts?
2. Why did many New Englanders turn to trade as a way of making a living?
3. Explain how the triangular trade route worked.
4. Why were the colonies always short of money? Why was paper money not very successful?
5. Do you think that colonial traders had the right to break the Navigation Acts because they did not like these laws? Why or why not?

Can You Connect the Past and the Present?

1. What happens to a nation when it buys more products from other nations than it sells to them? Can you think of any nations that this is true of today?
2. How does the American government control trade today? How is this different from the Navigation Acts?

CHAPTER 13

Colonial Industry and Towns

From the Collections of the Maryland Historical Society.

The town of Baltimore in 1752.

BEFORE YOU BEGIN THE CHAPTER

Know What to Look For

1. "Thar she blows" was the shout of the lookout on a whaling ship when he saw a whale coming up for air. The colonial sailors then lowered a small boat into the water, and the crew rowed hard to catch up with the whale. Standing in the bow, or front end of the boat, the harpooner threw his spear into the whale. The long rope connected to the harpoon kept the whale attached to the boat.

Whaling was very dangerous. The whale might wreck the small boat with its tail, or pull it under the water as it tried to escape. But if the small boat held onto the whale until it died, and the whaling ship brought it back to shore, much money was to be made. Valuable products were manufactured from the whale. The colonists used the whale oil as fuel for lamps. Whalebones were used in women's clothing. In this chapter, you will read about other types of manufacturing in the colonies.

2. Read the title of the chapter. Then look through the chapter and read each heading. Name some of the types of industry carried on by the colonists by reading the headings in the chapter.

3. Look at the pictures in the chapter and read each caption. What important colonial towns are shown in the pictures? Note also the time line at the beginning of the chapter. What years are included in this chapter? Compare the chapter time line to the unit time line on page 77.

4. Read the last part of the chapter called Summing Up. Where were most of the goods that were made to be sold manufactured in the colonies?

Know These Important Terms

manufacturing   commercial industry
domestic industry   naval stores

Know the Main Idea

Here is the MAIN IDEA of this chapter.

Manufacturing was important in all the colonies. Most manufacturing was carried on in the towns, which were the centers of business, trade, and social life.

Keep this MAIN IDEA in mind as you study the chapter. Ask yourself the following questions as you read. They will help you remember the MAIN IDEA.

1. What types of goods did the colonists manufacture in their homes?

2. What type of mining was important?

3. Name some of the problems faced by the colonists who lived in the large towns.

THE YEARS OF THIS CHAPTER ARE 1607 TO 1750

1600 1607   1750

THE CHAPTER LESSON BEGINS HERE

England Tried to Stop Manufacturing in the Colonies

The English government wanted the colonists in America to buy their manufactured (MAN-yuh-FAK-churd) goods from England. For this reason, the English government passed several laws to stop the colonies from **manufacturing** certain goods. Manufacturing means to make products such as cloth, guns, weapons, and tools. The three following laws were the most important.

1. The **Wool Act** of 1699 allowed woolen goods to be sold only in the colony in which they were made.

2. The **Hat Act** of 1732 did not allow the sale of beaver hats outside the colony in which they were made.

3. The **Iron Act** of 1750 allowed only certain types of iron products to be made in the colonies.

These laws were unpopular in America.

Most Colonists Made the Goods That They Needed

These English laws to stop manufacturing in the colonies were not very successful. Most of the colonists needed manufactured goods, and they had very little money to buy them from England. Therefore, they decided to manufacture some of the goods they needed themselves. The colonists paid no attention to the English laws against manufacturing.

Most colonial products were manufactured in the home. The colonial family usually produced its own food, drink, clothing, furniture, candles, soap, and tools. These products were for the family's use and were not sold. This type of manufacturing is called household industry, or **domestic industry.**

Forest Industries Brought Much Money to the Colonies

The colonists also manufactured goods which were meant to be sold. This type of manufacturing is called **commercial** (kuh-MUR-shul) **industry.** Lumbering was one of the main commercial industries in the colonies. The wood from the trees was made into furniture, barrels, houses, and ships. Some of these products were sold in the nations of Europe, as well as in the colonies.

American forests also provided other products that were needed in the colonies and in England. **Naval stores** were products such as tar, resin, pitch, and turpentine, which were necessary in the shipbuilding industry. All thirteen colonies produced naval stores. They also made potash, a wood product needed in the colonies and in the English woolen industry.

Mining Was an Important Colonial Industry

Mining was another important commercial industry in America. Although the thirteen English colonies had no gold or silver, almost all of them had iron ore. The Southern colonies mined iron ore. New England and the Middle colonies turned the iron ore into finished iron products.

Iron was used in the manufacture of nails, pots and pans, tools, and weapons. Even a family which made most of its own goods had to buy these iron products. Much iron was used to manufacture goods in the colonies, but there was still plenty of iron left to send to England.

The Fur Trade Became an Important Industry

The fur trade was also an important industry. In the New England colonies and the Middle colonies, the colonists trapped beavers. In the Southern colonies, they caught deer. The skins of both these animals were sold for high prices in Europe.

Colonists in the Middle colonies used beaver skins to make hats. This colonial hat-making industry did so well that England passed the Hat Act to end the manufacture of hats in the colonies. But this law failed to stop the colonists from making hats.

Many Other Industries Began in Colonial America

Many other industries were carried on in colonial America. Glassmaking, brickmaking, papermaking, shoemaking, and flour milling were all important colonial industries. However, American manufacturing was only in an early stage during the colonial period.

The Colonies Did Not Have Enough Workers

Manufacturing required many skilled workers. However, very few such skilled workers as carpenters, bricklayers, blacksmiths, millers, shoemakers, barrelmakers, weavers, tailors, brewers, and bakers lived in the colonies. The only way to get them to come to America was to pay them high wages. Although some colonies passed laws to keep wages low, both skilled and unskilled workers made more

This is the town of Boston in colonial days. Along with New York and Philadelphia, it was one of the largest towns in the colonies.

money in America than they did in England. Even so, in the colonies many skilled workers often saved their money, gave up their jobs, and bought farms.

Towns Became Important in Colonial America

Most skilled workers settled in towns, where they were able to get plenty of work. The largest towns of the colonial period were located near good harbors. The goods going to and from Europe passed through these large towns.

By the 1750's, Philadelphia, New York, Boston, Newport, and Charleston were the largest towns in the English colonies in America. They shared many of the same problems faced by American cities today. Fire was always a danger because most houses were built of wood. Crime was hard to control since there were not enough police. The streets were dark and narrow, and often they were unpaved and filled with garbage.

In spite of these problems, towns were the busiest places in the colonies. They were the centers of business and trade. Towns were also the centers of social life, government, and education in the colonies.

Summing Up

Manufacturing soon became important in the colonies. Although England passed laws to stop the colonies from manufacturing certain goods, the colonists continued to make these goods. The colonists made many goods they needed in their own homes. They also made goods which were meant to be sold. These goods were made in the towns, which were the centers of business, trade, and social life in the colonies. In the next chapter, which begins Unit 4, you will read about the many people from Europe who came to America.

AFTER YOU READ THE CHAPTER

Do You Know These Important Terms?

For each sentence below, select the term that best completes the sentence.

1. The making of products such as cloth, tools, and weapons is called (**trade/manufacturing**).
2. The type of manufacturing in which products are produced in the home for the family's use and are not sold is called (**local/domestic**) industry.
3. The type of manufacturing in which products are made to be sold is called (**commercial/national**) industry.
4. (**Ships/Naval**) stores were forest products which were necessary in the shipbuilding industry.

Can You Locate These Places?

Use the map on page 80 to do the following map work.

1. Locate the following towns and tell in which colony each is located.

   Philadelphia   Boston
   New York   Providence
   Charleston

2. All of these towns are located near the Atlantic Ocean. Why do you think this helped them to become important colonial towns?

Do You Know When It Happened?

What are the years of this chapter? How do the years of this chapter compare with the years of Chapter 12, which told about the growth of trade in the colonies?

Discovering More About the Main Idea

Manufacturing was important in all the colonies. Most manufacturing was carried on in the towns, which were the centers of business, trade, and social life.

Tell how each of the following developments is related to the MAIN IDEA.

The English government tried to stop the colonies from manufacturing certain goods, but the colonists paid little attention to these laws.

Although manufacturing was only in an early stage during colonial days, many skilled workers were needed in the colonies. Workers usually made more money in America than they did in England.

In spite of many problems, the towns were the busiest places in the colonies.

Can You Discuss the Chapter?

Use the information you learned in this chapter to answer the following questions.

1. Why did England pass laws like the Wool Act, the Hat Act, and the Iron Act to stop the colonies from manufacturing certain goods?
2. Name some raw materials which the colonists were able to manufacture into useful products.
3. Why did skilled and unskilled workers from England often come to work in the colonies?
4. Why do you think skilled workers sometimes gave up their jobs and bought farm land?

Can You Connect the Past and the Present?

1. Which type of manufacturing, domestic or commercial, is hardly carried on in the United States today? Why?
2. Compare the problems of colonial towns in the 1700's with the problems in your town or city. How are they similar? How are they different? What is your city trying to do about these problems today?

The People Who Settled the Colonies

Pioneers setting up a home on the frontier.

THE CHAPTERS IN UNIT 4 ARE

CHAPTER 14   Newcomers to America
CHAPTER 15   Slavery in the Colonies
CHAPTER 16   Slave Life

THE YEARS OF THIS UNIT ARE 1619 TO 1775

1600   1619   1775   1975

Newcomers to America

Pilgrims leaving England.

BEFORE YOU BEGIN THE CHAPTER

Know What· to Look For

1. It was not easy for a person to come to the English colonies in America. After finally deciding to make the journey, he had to have the money to pay for his voyage. If he was not able to pay for the voyage, he agreed to become an indentured servant for a period of about seven years. The voyage to America was dangerous and often took as long as two months.

Once the newcomer arrived he faced many dangers and hardships in this new land. The soils, climates, and plants were different from the ones he was used to. Most newcomers were farmers, and it took them a while to learn how to farm this new land over 3 thousand miles away from their homeland. Still, settlers came in great numbers from many nations in Europe. And these newcomers carved thriving farms and towns out of the American wilderness. In this chapter, you will read about the many newcomers who came and helped to build the colonies in America.

2. Read the title of the chapter. Then look through the chapter and read each heading. Use the chapter headings to tell what countries many of the colonists came from.

3. Look at the pictures in the chapter and read each caption. What group of people does the picture on page 96 show leaving England? Study the time line at the beginning of the chapter. What years are included in the chapter? Compare the chapter time line to the unit time line on page 95.

4. Read the last part of the chapter called Summing Up. Why were the newcomers who came to the colonies important to life in the colonies?

Know These Important Terms
immigrants   Huguenots
Scotch-Irish

Know the Main Idea
Here is the MAIN IDEA of this chapter.
Immigrants came to America from many nations, and they came for many different reasons. They brought new ideas and ways of doing things.

Keep this MAIN IDEA in mind as you study the chapter. Ask yourself the following questions as you read. They will help you remember the MAIN IDEA.
1. Most settlers who arrived in the colonies during the 1600's came from what country?
2. What occupation did most of the settlers from Germany follow?
3. In what colony did many Scots settle?

THE YEARS OF THIS CHAPTER ARE 1640 TO 1775

1619   1640   1775

THE CHAPTER LESSON BEGINS HERE

The First Colonial Settlers Were English

During the years of the 1600's, almost all of the settlers who came to the English colonies in America came from England. Most of the settlers who were not English lived in colonies that were taken over by England. Such people were the Dutch, who lived in New York, and the Swedes, who lived along the Delaware River. But toward the end of the 1600's, many settlers from other nations in Europe began to come to the English colonies. All the settlers who came to America from Europe were called **immigrants** (IM-uh-grunts).

Many Germans Came to America

In the late 1600's, large numbers of German settlers came to America. During the 1600's, Germany suffered from many wars. These wars destroyed many farms and also destroyed trade and industry in Germany. The nation of Germany was not united under a powerful king. Instead, Germany was divided into hundreds of small states, each ruled by a prince. Each German ruler taxed his people heavily, and he often forced them to attend the church he belonged to.

For these reasons, and because the colonies offered them a chance for a better life, many Germans wanted to settle in America. However, many Germans did not have the money to pay for their journey to America. Therefore, they agreed to let ship captains take them to America and then sell them as indentured servants. Although these Germans had to work for a master from four to seven years, after this period of time they were free to start a new life in America.

The Germans Became Farmers in America

Most German immigrants settled in Pennsylvania, where they were able to buy land cheaply and to worship as they wished. Others went to the unsettled lands located in the western parts of the Middle colonies and the Southern colonies. The Germans lived close together. They kept their German customs and spoke the German language. Most of the German immigrants became farmers. They took special care with their farms, and they were probably the best farmers in the colonies.

The Scotch-Irish Were Unhappy in Ireland

Another important group of immigrants who came to the English colonies in America were the **Scotch-Irish.** The Scotch-Irish were Scotsmen who settled in northern Ireland during the early years of the 1600's. In Ireland they became farmers, cattle and sheep raisers, and woolen manufacturers.

Most frontier farmers built houses called log cabins. Here, frontier farmers are having a bee, or a party.

The Scotch-Irish had many troubles in Ireland. The English government refused to let the Scotch-Irish sell their goods in England. The Scotch-Irish were members of the Presbyterian (PREZ-buh-TIR-ee-un) Church, and not members of the Church of England. For this reason, they were not able to serve in the English government or the English army. In addition, they were forced to pay taxes to support the Church of England.

The Scotch-Irish Settled on the Frontier

During the 1700's, many Scotch-Irish came to America because of their troubles in Ireland. Like the Germans, many Scotch-Irish came to America as indentured servants. They also settled first in Pennsylvania, and then some of them moved to the colonies in the South. Because most Scotch-Irish settlers had no money to buy land, they usually moved to the unsettled land on the frontier.

Many Scots Settled in America

Another group of Scots, from the northern highlands of Scotland, also came to America. These Scots came to America because they did not like the English government.

In 1707, the government of England and the government of Scotland were joined together into a kingdom called Great Britain. Some Scots were against the joining of England and Scotland. They refused to accept the king of England as their king and they rebelled, or fought against, England twice.

After the rebellion in 1745, the Scottish clans, or tribes, were broken up, and their lands were taken away from them. Many Scots then came to America. Some Scots came on their own. Others were forced to leave Scotland by the English government. The largest number of them settled in North Carolina. Most of these Scots were farmers, but others were merchants or skilled workers.

COLONIAL COWBOYS

Cattle raising makes us think of Texas and the West during the 1800's, when cowboys herded cattle on the open range. But cattle raising was important even during the colonial period. Colonists keep cattle, horses, sheep, and hogs pastured on the open range just west of the earliest settlements.

The colonial cattle raiser had many of the same problems as the later Western cattle raiser. Many cattle escaped and roamed free. Cattle rustlers were a constant danger. Some owners tried to solve these problems by fencing in their livestock. But most cattle still roamed free. Colonial legislatures tried to prevent cattle stealing by making the punishments for rustling very harsh. Cattle thieves were whipped, branded, or had their ears cut off. Some were even hanged. Still another danger for the cattle raiser was Indian raids.

Cattle raising in the colonies was very much like cattle raising in the 1800's. As early as the 1660's, roundups and cattle branding began to take place. During the colonial period, corrals were used but they were called cow pens. And even in colonial days, the men in charge of the cattle were called cowboys. These cowboys drove large herds of cattle to market in the towns along the Atlantic coast.

Children of a Huguenot family who settled in America in the 1600's.

French Protestants Came to America

A small but important group of European immigrants who came to the English colonies in America were the **Huguenots** (HYOO-guh-NOTZ). The Huguenots were French Protestants who were not allowed to worship as they wished in France. Nor were they allowed to settle in the French colonies. Some Huguenots left France and settled in the larger towns of the English colonies along the Atlantic coast. Many Huguenots became rich and important in the colonies.

Many Other Peoples Settled in America

People from many other nations in Europe also settled in the English colonies. As early as 1654, Jews arrived in America. Many people from Ireland, Wales, and Switzerland also came to America in order to make a better living or to worship as they wished.

Immigration Was Important to the Colonies

The European immigrants who came to America in the 1700's—like later immigrants—were very important to the growth of America. European immigrants moved west and settled the frontier in America. Immigrants brought new and better ways of farming, trading, and manufacturing with them. They helped develop the American idea that people from all European nations were free and equal in America.

Summing Up

European immigrants came to America from many nations. They came for many different reasons. Immigrants brought new ideas and ways of doing things to America. In the next chapter, you will read about another group of people who also helped build America. But these people came to America against their will.

AFTER YOU READ THE CHAPTER

Do You Know These Important Terms?

For each sentence below, choose the term that best completes the sentence.

1. (Immigrants/Emigrants) were settlers who came to America from Europe.
2. Scotsmen who settled in northern Ireland during the early years of the 1600's were called (Presbyterians/Scotch-Irish).
3. (Huguenots/Presbyterians) were French Protestants, some of whom settled in the colonies.

Can You Locate These Places?

Use a wall map of Europe to do the following map work.

1. Locate each of the following places on the map. Tell why settlers from this area came to the colonies.

German states   Scotland

Northern Ireland   France

2. Now use the map on page 128. Locate the frontier, or the unsettled land, in the western part of the colonies in 1775. Why did many newcomers to the colonies go to the frontier? Compare the frontier in 1775 with the frontier in 1700.

Do You Know When It Happened?

What are the years of this chapter? How do they compare with the years of the last three chapters you read? Tell what event in this chapter each of the following dates is related to.

1654   1707   1745

Discovering More About the Main Idea

Immigrants came to America from many nations, and they came for many different reasons. They brought new ideas and ways of doing things.

Tell how each of the following developments is related to the MAIN IDEA.

Most immigrants who came to America during the 1600's came from England.

During the 1700's, immigrants came to America from many European nations. The immigrants usually came to America because of troubles in their homeland.

Immigrants brought new and better ways of farming, trading, and manufacturing. They helped develop the American idea that people from all European nations were free and equal in America.

Can You Discuss the Chapter?

Use the information you learned in this chapter to answer the following questions.

1. How did the indentured servant system work for immigrants who were unable to pay their passage to America?
2. Why did many newcomers move to the frontier after their time as indentured servants was over?
3. Why did events in 1707 and 1745 cause many Scotsmen to leave their homeland?
4. Name some of the important groups of immigrants that settled in America.
5. Why were the immigrants important to the colonies?

Can You Connect the Past and the Present?

1. During the early years of American history, immigration was encouraged and was not controlled. Why do you think immigration is controlled in America today?
2. How can a mixture of many different peoples living together help to develop a feeling of freedom and equality? Do you think it might also lead people not to trust people who seem strange or different?

CHAPTER 15

Slavery in the Colonies

A slave being sold in New Netherland.

BEFORE YOU BEGIN THE CHAPTER

Know What to Look For

1. Sailors said you were able to smell a "slaver" before you saw it because the smell of death hung around it. Slavers were the ships that carried the African slaves to the New World. This trip across the ocean from Africa was terrible. The slaves were packed together on the ship. Many died from sickness, lack of food, and beatings. Some killed themselves during the voyage. Those who

died during the voyage were thrown overboard. As a result, a school of man-eating sharks usually followed the slavers on their trip across the ocean.

What led men to treat other men so cruelly? In this chapter, you will read how the Africans in the colonies were changed from free men into slaves. You will also read how the slave trade brought thousands of Africans to the colonies to meet the need for workers.

2. Read the title of the chapter. Then look through the chapter and read each heading. How do the headings help tell you what the chapter is about?

3. Look at the pictures in the chapter and read each caption. What do the pictures show you about the way slaves were treated? Note also the time line at the beginning of the chapter. What years are included in this chapter? Compare this chapter time line to the unit time line on page 95.

4. Read the last part of the chapter called Summing Up. Why did slavery begin in the English colonies? What will the next chapter be about?

Know These Important Terms
middle passage   seasoned

Know the Main Idea

Here is the MAIN IDEA of this chapter.

Slavery began in the English colonies because of the need for workers. Thousands of Africans were captured and brought to the colonies and used as slaves.

Keep this MAIN IDEA in mind as you study the chapter. Ask yourself the following questions as you read. They will help you remember the MAIN IDEA.

1. Which two colonies first passed laws that made black people slaves?

2. In what ways did most Africans make their living before they were captured and sold as slaves?

3. How did the slave trade become different after slaves were brought to the New World?

THE YEARS OF THIS CHAPTER ARE 1619 TO 1750

1619   1750   1775

THE CHAPTER LESSON BEGINS HERE

The First Africans in America Became Indentured Servants

In 1619, a Dutch ship arrived at Jamestown with twenty Africans. All twenty were sold to colonists as indentured servants. At first, the black Africans who came to America were treated much the same as the white indentured servants in the colonies. After a few years as indentured servants, they were given their freedom.

Southern planters soon found that indentured servants were not the answer to their need for workers. When an indentured servant's period of service was ended, he was free to leave, and his master had to give him clothes, tools, and sometimes even land. Often, indentured servants ran away.

Laws Made Black Indentured Servants Slaves

Because indentured servants failed to meet their need for workers, Southern planters began to look for other ways to get workers. They knew that Africans worked as slaves in the Spanish colonies. Why, some planters asked, were they not able to use black men as slaves in the English colonies? Some planters thought that black slaves were the answer to their need for workers.

In time, laws were passed which forced black indentured servants to work for longer periods of time than white indentured servants. Before long, black indentured servants became servants for life. Their children also were made servants for life. By the 1660's,

Virginia and Maryland had passed laws that made black people slaves, rather than indentured servants. And soon, all the other English colonies also passed laws that allowed slavery. Even so, many free black men were still found in the English colonies.

Slavery Grew Rapidly in the Southern Colonies

During the 1600's, not many slaves were brought to America. By the year 1700, about 25 thousand black slaves lived in the English colonies. White indentured servants were still the largest group of workers in the colonies. But after 1700, thousands of slaves were brought to the Southern colonies. By 1760, the number of slaves living in the English colonies increased to almost 400 thousand, or to about one sixth of all the people in the colonies. And most of these slaves lived in the Southern colonies and worked on the large tobacco, rice, and indigo plantations.

Here, a slave holds the horse of a rich Southern planter. Slaves were found in all the colonies in America.

Strong Black Nations in Africa

The Africans who came to America came against their will. Many of them came from important black nations located in the western part of Africa. Although the greatest periods in the history of Ghana (GAH-nuh), Mali (MAH-lee), and Songhai (SOWNG-hy) were ended by the 1600's, many strong black nations still ruled in Africa.

Most Africans were farmers. That is one reason why they were so much in demand as slaves in the Spanish colonies. However, the people of Africa also made their living in many other ways. Many of them hunted, fished, or raised cattle. Many Africans were skilled workers. They were especially skilled as metalworkers, weavers, jewelers, artists, and woodcarvers.

A New Type of Slavery Was Started in the New World

Slavery was not a completely new idea to the people of Africa. For centuries, Arab slave traders had captured and sold African slaves. Some African nations made slaves of other black people that they captured in wars. But it was not until slaves were brought to the English colonies in America that the slave trade became so large—or so cruel.

Captured slaves were often forced to march hundreds of miles to the coast of Africa. Many Africans died or were killed during this long march. Once they reached the coast, the slaves who lived through this terrible trip were branded and sold to a merchant or a sea captain. They were then taken to the New World.

Many Slaves Died on the Trip to America

The trip across the ocean was known as the **middle passage**. Everything about slavery was terrible, but the middle passage was perhaps the worst part. The slaves were chained together below the ship's decks. Each slave was

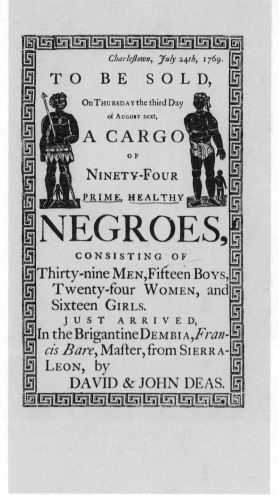

This is a poster telling of the sale of slaves in the town of Charlestown.

crammed into a space about five feet long, sixteen inches wide, and three feet high. A shipload of slaves might live crowded together, with no room to stand or stretch, for two months or longer.

Many slaves did not live through the trip. Some slaves died from rotten food. Others died from sickness that spread through the ship. And still others killed themselves by jumping overboard or choking themselves with their chains. Sometimes, the slaves tried

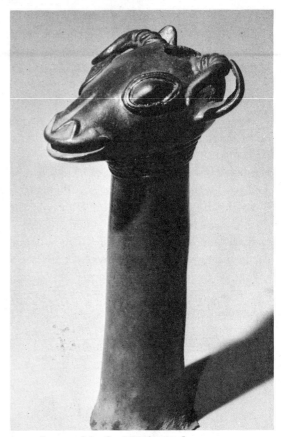

The African art work at the left is an ivory mask carved in the 1500's. At the right is a bronze ram's head made in the 1750's.

to revolt, or to take over the ship, but they seldom succeeded.

Slaves Were Trained in the West Indies

During the colonial period, most slaves were landed in the West Indies. There they were **seasoned**, or broken in, by older slaves. Slaves from the same tribe were split up. They were forced to speak English and to give up their African habits and customs.

The seasoning time was also a period when the new slave was taught his duties. He also learned that he was no longer treated as a human being, but was considered as property, without rights or freedom. The seasoning time

lasted from one to three years. Only about half of the slaves lived through the seasoning time.

Summing Up

Slavery began in the New World because of the need for workers. The English colonies in America copied the idea of using black slaves from the Spanish colonies. In the 1700's, large numbers of black Africans were brought to the English colonies as slaves. The trip from Africa to America was a terrible one, and many slaves died. In the next chapter, you will read about the life of these slaves in the English colonies in America.

AFTER YOU READ THE CHAPTER

For each sentence below, choose the term that best completes the sentence.

1. The trip of the African slaves across the ocean was called the (**middle/dark**) passage.
2. In the West Indies, new slaves were (**seasoned/drilled**), or broken in by older slaves.

Can You Locate These Places?

Use a wall map of Africa and a globe to do the following map work.

1. Locate the western part of Africa where most slaves were captured. Locate the West Indies. What part did these islands play in the life of a slave?
2. Trace the middle passage. Across what bodies of water did slave ships sail?

Do You Know When It Happened?

What are the years of this chapter? In what year did each of the following events happen?

1. The number of slaves living in the colonies was about one sixth of all the people in the colonies.
2. The first Africans were sold to colonists in Jamestown as indentured servants.
3. Virginia and Maryland passed laws that made black people slaves.

Discovering More About the Main Idea

Slavery began in the English colonies because of the need for workers. Thousands of Africans were captured and brought to the colonies and used as slaves.

Tell how each of the following developments is related to the MAIN IDEA.

Although the first Africans were indentured servants like many white settlers, in time, laws were passed that made black people slaves.

The slaves came from the west coast of Africa, where they had been farmers, herders, or craftsmen. Most slaves were used on the large plantations in the Southern colonies.

The slave trade was very cruel, especially the middle passage and the years of seasoning in the West Indies.

Only about half the Africans lived through the middle passage and the seasoning time.

Can You Discuss the Chapter?

Use the information you learned in this chapter to answer the following questions.

1. How were the Africans in the colonies changed from indentured servants into slaves?
2. Which part of Africa did most slaves come from? How did the Africans make their living before they were captured and sold as slaves?
3. Why was slavery not a new idea to the African people?
4. What happened to a slave during the seasoning time?
5. If you had lived during the early 1700's, what do you think you might have thought about slavery? Why?

Can You Connect the Past and the Present?

1. Some present-day nations in Africa took their names from the great African nations of the past. Can you name some of these nations?
2. Do you think it is important for a black American today to learn about the history of Africa? Why?

CHAPTER 16

Slave Life

Slave houses on a Southern plantation.

BEFORE YOU BEGIN THE CHAPTER

Know What to Look For

1. Slaves who worked in the fields of a large Southern plantation led a very hard life. They were awakened each day before dawn and, after a small breakfast, marched off to the fields. The slaves were divided into groups, and each group was given a special job to do. They usually worked in the fields until dark. After they returned home, they cooked their own dinner and then went to sleep on a pile of straw on the dirt floor of their huts. All slaves did not live alike. Although slaves had no rights or freedom, some were reasonably well treated. However, some slaves were treated cruelly. In this chapter, you will read more about the life of a slave in the English colonies in America.

2. Read the title of the chapter. Then look through the chapter and read each heading. Using only the headings, what can you learn about the life of a slave?

3. Look at the pictures in the chapter and read each caption. What do the pictures tell you about the life of a slave? Note also the time line at the beginning of the chapter. What years are included in this chapter? Compare this chapter time line to the unit time line on page 95.

4. Read the last part of the chapter called Summing Up. What does the summary tell you about slave life?

slave codes   field hands
house servants   slave revolt

Know the Main Idea

Here is the MAIN IDEA of this chapter.

Although all slaves were not treated alike, they were considered to be the property of their master. Slaves were unhappy and wanted to win their freedom.

Keep this MAIN IDEA in mind as you study the chapter. Ask yourself the following questions as you read. They will help you remember the MAIN IDEA.

1. What were some of the laws that were used to control the lives of slaves?

2. Which group of slaves worked the hardest and were cared for the least?

3. What makes you think that slaves wanted to win their freedom?

THE YEARS OF THIS CHAPTER ARE 1619 TO 1750

1619   1750   1775

THE CHAPTER LESSON BEGINS HERE

Slaves Had No Rights or Freedoms

By law a slave was considered property, and he was not allowed to own any property himself. Because a slave belonged to his master, the master was able to sell or rent out his slave at any time. Even a slave's family was owned by the master. When a master sold slaves, often he separated husbands from wives, or children from their parents.

All the English colonies in America passed **slave codes,** or laws to control the lives of slaves. These codes made it a crime for a slave to leave the plantation without his master's permission. Punishments for running away or breaking any of the slave codes included whipping and branding. Slaves were not allowed to meet together, to have weapons, or to learn to read or write. They were not able to speak in a court against a white settler. If a slave broke a law, he was often punished more harshly than a white settler.

Not All Slaves Were Treated Alike

Not all slaves were treated alike. How they were treated depended greatly on their job on the plantation. **House servants,** the slaves who worked as cooks, maids, and coachmen in the master's house, were generally dressed and fed better than other groups of slaves. They also were treated better than other slaves by the master and his family. House servants sometimes even were regarded as part of the master's family.

Another group of slaves were the skilled workers. Because very few free workers settled in the South, certain slaves were taught such trades as tailoring, bricklaying, and also

page 109

carpentry. A slave who knew a trade was important to a plantation. Therefore, he was usually treated fairly well.

Most slaves were **field hands,** or the slaves who did the farm work on the plantation. Field hands were the worst treated of all slaves. They were worked the hardest, were cared for the least, and were punished the most cruelly.

The Kind of Lives that Slaves Lived

Although all slaves were not treated alike, their lives usually were difficult and filled with hardships. House servants sometimes ate the food that was left over from the master's table. Other slaves ate corn meal, salt pork, and bacon—the cheapest foods. A few masters let their slaves have small gardens to raise their own fruits and vegetables. Most slave families cooked their own food after their day's work was finished.

House servants sometimes wore the old clothes of the master and his wife. Other slaves wore clothes that they made out of the cheapest and longest wearing cloth. Most Southern slaves wore shoes and jackets only during the winter.

The houses the slaves lived in were poorly made. Usually they were small huts with dirt floors, no windows, and little furniture. Many did not even have beds in them. Often many slaves were crowded together in these huts. Too many people crowded together in these dirty small huts often caused much sickness and death among the slaves.

Slaves Wanted to Win Their Freedom

Many slaves who came to America tried to get their freedom. Some slaves ran away from their masters. Some tried to slow down the work on the plantation by breaking their tools or starting fires. Some slaves killed themselves rather than spend their lives in slavery. And some slaves killed their masters.

But what the Southern planters feared most was a **slave revolt,** or slave uprising. As early as 1663, slaves in Virginia planned a revolt. This was the first of many slave revolts in the

Some slaves worked as house servants on Southern plantations. Here, two slaves are shown working as coachmen.

The slaves shown in this picture are field hands. They did the farm work on the Southern plantations.

colonies in America. During the colonial period, slave revolts broke out in New England and in New York as well as in the Southern colonies. Usually, many slaves who were fighting for their freedom were killed when these revolts were put down.

Freedom Was Hard to Win

As you read, the English colonies in America copied the idea of slavery from the Spanish colonies in America. But in some ways, slavery in the English colonies was worse than in the Spanish colonies. The main difference was that a slave in the Spanish colonies had a better chance to win his freedom.

In the Spanish colonies, a master often gave his slaves some free time to earn money. Each slave had the right to keep the money that he earned. Once a slave saved enough money, he was able to buy his freedom. In the Spanish colonies, a slave owner often celebrated very happy family events, such as births and

marriages, by freeing one or more of his slaves.

In the English colonies, it was much more difficult for a slave to get his freedom. If a slave was hired out as a worker on another plantation, his master took the money he earned. Sometimes, a master allowed the slave to keep a little of the money. In this way, a few slaves were able to save enough money to buy their freedom. But most slaves had no chance to buy their freedom.

Summing Up

Slaves had no freedom and were forced to do what their masters wanted. Harsh laws controlled the lives of slaves. Although not all slaves were treated alike, their lives were full of hardships. Many slaves fought against this life and tried to gain their freedom. A few slaves were able to buy their freedom. In the next chapter, which begins Unit 5, you will read about the life of other Americans during the colonial period.

AFTER YOU READ THE CHAPTER

Do You Know These Important Terms?

For each of the statements below, select the term that best completes the sentence.

1. Laws to control the lives of slaves were called slave (**deeds/codes**).
2. (**Personal/House**) servants were the slaves who worked as cooks, maids, or coachmen in the planter's home.
3. (**Field hands/Labor crews**) were the slaves who did the farm work on the plantations in the South.
4. A slave uprising, or a slave (**revolt/revolution**), was a fear of most Southern planters.

Can You Locate These Places?

Use the map on page 80 to do the following map work.

1. Locate each of the following sections of the colonies:

   New England colonies
   Southern colonies
   Middle colonies

2. In which of these sections might you expect slavery to be most like the way it is described in this chapter? In which section might you expect it to be least like the description in this chapter?

Do You Know When It Happened?

What are the years of this chapter? Compare the date of an early slave revolt in Virginia (page 110) with the date when Virginia first passed laws making black people slaves (page 103). What connection do you see between these two dates?

Discovering More About the Main Idea

Although all slaves were not treated alike, they were considered to be the property of their master. Slaves were unhappy and wanted to win their freedom.

Tell how each of the following developments is related to the MAIN IDEA.

The lives of slaves were strictly controlled by laws which were set up to control large numbers of slaves and to prevent slave revolts.

All slaves were not treated alike. Usually, however, the field hands were the worst treated of all slaves.

It was more difficult for a slave in the English colonies in America to win his freedom than for one in the Spanish colonies. American slaves showed they wanted to win their freedom in many ways.

Can You Discuss the Chapter?

Use the information you learned in this chapter to answer the following questions.

1. A slave was considered to be property rather than a human being. How did this affect the rights or freedoms of a slave?
2. Describe the kind of life that slaves lived.
3. How do you know that many slaves wanted to win their freedom?
4. How was a slave able to get his freedom in the Spanish colonies? in the English colonies?
5. Everyone's life is regulated by a number of rules. How were the slave codes different from the rules in your school?

Can You Connect the Past and the Present?

1. Do you think that slavery helped to cause any of the problems between black Americans and white Americans today?
2. How were the slave revolts different from the demonstrations that are sometimes held by groups of Americans who are unhappy with life in America today?

UNIT 5

Life in the Colonies

Pilgrims going to church.

THE CHAPTERS IN UNIT 5 ARE

CHAPTER 17   Daily Life in the Colonies
CHAPTER 18   Colonial Thought
CHAPTER 19   The Frontier

THE YEARS OF THIS UNIT ARE 1640 TO 1775

| 1600 | 1640 | 1775 | 1975 |

Daily Life in the Colonies

A colonial wedding.

BEFORE YOU BEGIN THE CHAPTER

Know What to Look For

1. The ice cubes we take so easily from our refrigerators do not seem very important. Most of us are used to iced cold drinks and frozen foods. But in colonial times, ice was a real luxury. Each winter, in places where ponds and lakes froze, the colonists sawed off huge blocks of ice and stored them deep in the ground with straw or some other material. They were able to keep the ice in these "ice houses" for fairly long periods of time. Sometimes, on a hot summer day, the colonists still had a bit of ice left in the ice house from the winter before.

Since ice was such a luxury it had to be used with care. Some ice was even shipped on boats to places where water did not freeze in the winter and sold for a good profit. The cutting of ice in the winter was only one small part of the way of life in colonial America. In this chapter, you will read about other ways of daily life among the colonists.

2. Read the title of the chapter. Then look through the chapter and read each heading. From reading the headings, what parts of daily life in the colonies do you expect to be included in the chapter?

3. Look at the pictures in the chapter and read each caption. What do the pictures show you about the way the colonists dressed and traveled? Note the time line at the beginning of the chapter. What years are included in this chapter? Compare the chapter time line to the unit time line on page 113.

4. Read the last part of the chapter called Summing Up. What group of people did not share the colonial ways of living described in this chapter? What topic will you read about in the next chapter?

Know This Important Term
social classes

Know the Main Idea
Here is the MAIN IDEA of this chapter.
Colonists were divided into social classes, but it was fairly easy to change one's social class. For the most part, colonists had good homes, plenty of food, and enough time to enjoy themselves.

Keep this MAIN IDEA in mind as you study the chapter. Ask yourself the following questions as you read. They will help you remember the MAIN IDEA.

1. What groups of people made up the middle class of the three social classes?

2. What methods did the colonists use to keep food from spoiling?

3. What sports were popular during colonial times?

THE YEARS OF THIS CHAPTER ARE 1640 TO 1750

1640   1750   1775

THE CHAPTER LESSON BEGINS HERE

Americans Were Divided into Groups

In the English colonies in America, people were divided into groups, or **social classes.** You have already read about one group of Americans, the unfree class of people made up of indentured servants and slaves. The other colonists in America were divided into three social classes—the upper class, the middle class, and the lower class. The upper class was made up of large land owners, rich merchants, leading church men, lawyers, and doctors. Farmers, small businessmen, and skilled workers made up the middle class. And the lower class was formed of unskilled city workers and farm laborers.

Although the social classes in America were copied from the social classes in England, they were different in one important way. In America, it was fairly easy for a man from a lower social class to climb to a higher social class. Even people who came to the colonies as indentured servants were able to become members of the upper class. This easy movement from a lower class to a higher class helped make America a land of opportunity for people from Europe. Slaves were the only people who were not able to improve their lives. And most free black men were outside the social class system.

A Puritan in the stocks.

COLONIAL PUNISHMENTS

Colonial law was quite different from English law. Some crimes, for example, stealing a horse, were punished more harshly in the colonies than in England. Other crimes, which might be punished by death in England, were treated much more lightly in the colonies.

Very few jails were found in the colonies. Instead, most punishments were public. The idea of public punishment was to shame the lawbreaker into giving up his evil ways. Every colonial town had a whipping post and a pillory, or stocks, to punish colonists who broke the law. A colonist who was put into the stocks was usually made fun of by the other people in town. Sometimes they threw eggs or even stones at him. Women who gossiped were punished by being placed on a ducking stool and dipped into the cold water of a pond or lake.

Still another way to punish a colonist who broke the law was to sew on his clothes the letter which stood for the crime he committed. For example, the letter T stood for thief. In cases where the colonist committed the same crime again, he might have the letter which stood for his crime branded on his forehead. And for serious crimes, the criminal might be sold as an indentured servant or even hanged.

The Colonial Family Worked Together

Family life was very important in the colonies. Most colonists married young. Men usually married by the age of twenty, while women married as early as fourteen. Large families with ten to fifteen children were common, but children often died young.

Colonists married young and had large families, because large families were needed to get the work done on a farm. The colonists had to grow their own food, make their own clothes, and provide almost all of the other things that they needed. This work kept every member of the family busy. A large family was necessary for a farmer to do well.

Marriage in the Colonies

Marriage in colonial days was different from what it is today. Rich families decided whom their sons or daughters were to marry. They did this because marriage was a way to join together two large farms or two large fortunes. In all colonial families, children had to receive their parents' permission to marry. Once a couple was married, it was almost impossible for them to get a divorce.

The Colonists Ate Well

Colonial Americans had plenty of corn, wheat, fish, meat, fruits, and vegetables to eat. Most colonists ate a lot and drank a lot. Beer, apple cider, and rum were the favorite drinks of most colonists. Rich colonists often drank wine and brandy from Europe.

Keeping food from spoiling was an important problem, because people in colonial days did not have ice or refrigerators. Vegetables such as potatoes and turnips were stored in cool cellars. Some foods, such as pork, were salted. Others were dried or pickled to keep them from spoiling. Meat and fish were kept from spoiling by smoking them over large fires. Smoking also gave foods a good flavor.

The Clothes the Colonists Wore

The clothes people wore in colonial days were very different from the clothes worn today. Women of the upper class wore long, fancy dresses made of silk or satin. Rich men dressed in bright-colored coats, tight knee-length pants, silk stockings, and shoes with buckles. Upper-class men and women often wore powdered wigs. Most settlers, however, wore simple, homemade clothes made of strong materials. The men who lived on the frontier usually wore leather clothing and fur caps. Children wore clothes which usually were handed down from child to child until the clothes were completely worn out. And most colonists had few clothes.

Building Styles in the Colonies

The first houses built in the colonies were very much like huts. In time, however, the colonists started to build wooden houses which were one or one and a half stories high. Because these houses were heated by fireplaces, the ceilings were low and the windows were small to keep in the heat.

In the 1700's, colonists in the upper class started to build Georgian style homes, which were copied from a style of building popular in England. These Georgian homes often were built of brick, and they were large and airy. Most people, however, lived in small, one-story, wooden houses. And settlers on the frontier built log cabins.

In colonial days, travel was difficult and took a long time. Colonists traveled in stage coaches or on horseback.

This painting shows a fox hunt. Fox hunting and other types of hunting were enjoyed by many colonists.

How the Colonists Enjoyed Themselves

The people in the colonies liked to have a good time. Colonists liked to get together at plowing parties, quilting bees, house-raisings, and cornhuskings. Colonial men liked to hunt and fish. They also enjoyed such sports as wrestling, foot racing, swimming, and shooting. Horse racing, outdoor bowling, and billiards were games that men of the upper class enjoyed.

Music, dancing, and parties were popular with most colonists. Colonial men liked to meet at inns or taverns to play cards, to drink, and to talk about news or business. Shows that traveled from city to city and to country fairs brought music and fun to many colonists.

Summing Up

The colonists were divided into social classes. Most colonists had good homes, enough clothes, and plenty of food. Colonial families worked together to supply their own needs. Even though they worked hard, most colonists found time to enjoy themselves. Slaves, however, did not share these freedoms or ways of living. In the next chapter, you will read more about life during the colonial period.

AFTER YOU READ THE CHAPTER

Do You Know This Important Term?

For the sentence below, choose the term which best completes the sentence.

People were divided into groups or (**social classes/separated classes**) in the English colonies in America.

Can You Locate These Places?

Use the map on page 80 to do the following map work.

1. Locate and name the thirteen English colonies in America.
2. Locate and name the five largest towns in the English colonies in America. Are all of these towns seaports?

Do You Know When It Happened?

What are the years of this chapter? Use the time lines on pages 115 and 95 to compare the years of this chapter with the years of the last unit. Which of the following statements best describes this comparison?

The events in this chapter happened before the events in the last unit.

The events in this chapter happened at about the same time as events in the last unit.

The events in this chapter happened after the events in the last unit.

Discovering More About the Main Idea

Colonists were divided into social classes, but it was fairly easy to change one's social class. For the most part, colonists had good homes, plenty of food, and enough time to enjoy themselves.

Tell how each of the following developments is related to the MAIN IDEA.

Most colonists married young and had very large families.

Most colonists had plenty to eat. One of the main problems was to keep food from spoiling.

Rich men and women in the colonies wore fancy clothes, while most settlers wore simple, homemade clothes of strong materials.

Although the settlers worked hard, no matter what social class they were in they found time to enjoy themselves.

Can You Discuss the Chapter?

Use the information you learned in this chapter to answer the following questions.

1. How were the social classes in America different from the social classes in England during colonial days?
2. Why was it necessary for a farm family to be large in colonial times?
3. Describe the clothes and homes of rich colonists and those of most other settlers.
4. In what ways did the colonists enjoy themselves?
5. Do you think it is important to be a member of the highest social class? Why or why not?

Can You Connect the Past and the Present?

1. Compare the social classes of colonial America with the social classes in America today. How are they alike? How are they different? Is it as easy to change one's social class today as it was in colonial times?
2. The marriage customs of settlers in colonial days were different from the ones today. In what ways were they different?

CHAPTER 18

Colonial Thought

A colonial printing press.

BEFORE YOU BEGIN THE CHAPTER

Know What to Look For

1. A teacher must keep order in his class so that students can learn. This was as true in colonial times as it is today. The colonial teacher, however, used some ways to control students which we do not use today. Sometimes, unruly students were made to hold heavy books at arm's length in front of themselves or to hold an imaginary nail in the floor without bending their knees. Students were often hit with a stick or a paddle when they were bad. Another method of punishing a student was to make him sit on a stool in front of the class and wear a tall, pointed cap with the word "DUNCE" written on it in large letters. In this chapter, you will read more about schools and education in the colonies.

2. Read the title of the chapter. Then

look through the chapter and read each heading. By reading the chapter heads, name some of the topics beside schools which are included in this chapter.

3. Look at the pictures in the chapter and read each caption. What does the picture on page 122 show you about schools in the colonies? Look at the time line at the beginning of the chapter. What years are included in this chapter? Compare this chapter time line to the unit time line on page 113.

4. Read the last part of the chapter called Summing Up. What event led colonists to take a greater interest in religion, education, and government?

Know These Important Terms

tutors   almanacs

academies   Great Awakening

Know the Main Idea

Here is the MAIN IDEA of this chapter.

Most Americans were educated, and they were interested in books, newspapers, and education for all Americans. Religion was also important in the colonies.

Keep this MAIN IDEA in mind as you study the chapter. Ask yourself the following questions as you read. They will help you remember the MAIN IDEA.

1. What subjects were taught in the high schools called academies?

2. Which colony was the first to require that schools be set up in towns and supported by taxes? Why did this colony require schools to be set up?

3. What were the results of the Great Awakening? When did the Great Awakening take place?

THE YEARS OF THIS CHAPTER ARE 1640 TO 1750

1640   1750   1775

THE CHAPTER LESSON BEGINS HERE

Education in the Colonies

In England, only children of the upper class went to school. They attended private schools or church schools. For a time, this same idea was followed in the English colonies in America. Only upper-class children went to school. Many of them also went to private schools or church schools. Others had **tutors,** or private teachers, who taught them at home. These upper-class children often went to a college in England to finish their education.

Most workers' children in America did not go to school. But sometimes they were taught to read and write at the same time they were taught a trade. Girls seldom went to school. Instead, they stayed home and were taught to cook, sew, and to care for children by their mothers.

Most boys who were able to go to school went only to elementary school. The few who did attend high school studied Latin and Greek, which were required to get into college. Later, high schools called **academies** (ah-KAD-uh-meez) were started, and they began to teach more useful subjects, such as mathematics, science, geography, and bookkeeping.

All Children Attended School in New England

An important change in education took

Some schoolrooms in the colonies looked like this. Massachusetts was the first colony to set up public schools.

place in the New England colonies. They started the idea that all children were to go to school. The Puritans believed that everyone had to learn to read the Bible. They also believed that people who had an education made better citizens and better workers. For these reasons, the Massachusetts legislature passed a law in the year 1642 requiring that all parents make sure that their children learned to read.

Five years later, in 1647, Massachusetts passed a law which required all small towns to set up an elementary school, and all large towns to set up an elementary school and a high school. All the children in the town had to attend these schools. Although these schools were supported by taxes, parents still had to pay a small amount of money for their children to attend.

Colleges Were Started in the Colonies

Colleges were also started in the colonies. Harvard, in Massachusetts, was the first. Next came William and Mary, in Virginia, and Yale, in Connecticut. Later, six other colleges were started in the colonies. These new colleges began to offer courses in science, mathematics, and history. The colleges in the colonies were attended by many young men who later became leaders in the colonies.

Books and Newspapers in the Colonies

Many colonists were able to read. The most widely read book in the colonies was the Bible. **Almanacs** (ALL-muh-naks) were the most popular books in the colonies. Almanacs were books that contained stories, jokes, calendars, and helpful ideas for farmers. They were somewhat like the magazines of today.

The first successful American newspaper, the *Boston News Letter,* began in 1704. Many other newspapers soon appeared. Most of these colonial newspapers were printed once a week. They contained colonial news, European news, and advertisements.

Some Americans Wrote Books

Some colonists owned large numbers of books. However, most colonists had very few books. Therefore, many towns opened public libraries where colonists were able to borrow books at little or no cost. Although most books came from England, some books were written in America. American colonial writers wrote about religion, the history of the colonies, their travels, and their adventures with the Indians.

Religion in the Colonies

Religion was an important part of colonial life. All the New England colonies except Rhode Island, and all the Southern colonies, had an official church, or a church everyone was supposed to attend. Sunday was a very special day. Everyone was expected to attend church services and to spend the whole day reading the Bible and thinking about it. Most colonies passed laws which forbade dancing, drinking, playing sports or games, and many other amusements on Sunday. By the early 1700's, however, many colonists were becoming less interested in religion.

But in the 1730's, a new interest in religion began, called the **Great Awakening.** As a result of the Great Awakening, thousands of colonists began to go to church again. Many new religious groups were formed, and this led to greater freedom of religion. The Great Awakening also helped education. New colleges were set up to train ministers and teachers. The Great Awakening also caused many colonists to become interested in government.

Harvard College in 1770.

STUDENT LIFE AT HARVARD COLLEGE

Harvard, America's first college, was founded in 1636. In order to attend Harvard, students had to know Latin and Greek. They also had to pay to attend. Although the payment was small, few students were able to pay in cash. As a result, the college accepted grain, meat, fruit, and almost any other type of food in payment. These products were used to feed students. Some students were not able to pay at all. Some of them received scholarships. Others were able to work their way through college.

The student's day at Harvard began at dawn. Morning prayers were said at 5 or 6 o'clock depending on the season. After prayers, the students ate a light breakfast. From 8 o'clock to 11 o'clock students attended classes. Dinner was served at 11. Students then returned to classes from 2 o'clock to 5 o'clock. The day ended with a light snack, evening prayers, and supper at 7:30. Lights-out came at 11 o'clock.

At first, Harvard's school year lasted twelve months. Later, a six-week summer vacation became common. Students were supposed to stay on school grounds at all times. However, this rule was often broken. Punishment for breaking this or other Harvard rules included warnings, whippings, or even being expelled.

The ducking stool was used to punish women who talked or gossiped too much. They were dipped into the cool waters of a pond or lake.

Because the colonists now had a great part in church matters, they also wanted a larger part in government.

The Colonies Produced Many Educated Men

Many colonists who went to college became ministers, but others became doctors or lawyers. A few Americans became good scientists. The most famous of them was Benjamin Franklin. Franklin developed a stove, reading glasses, and the famous lightning rod. The American colonies also had some famous painters. Painters usually learned their art from another artist. Most early American artists painted portraits for a living. The most

famous colonial artists were John Singleton Copley and Benjamin West.

Summing Up

Americans were better educated than most Europeans of their day. Many schools and colleges were started in the colonies. Many colonists were able to read, and they took a great interest in books, newspapers, and education. Some Americans even wrote books. Religion was very important in the colonies. In the 1730's, the Great Awakening started, and it led the colonists to take a greater interest in religion, education, and government. In the next chapter, you will learn how the colonists on the frontier lived.

AFTER YOU READ THE CHAPTER

Do You Know These Important Terms?

For each sentence below, choose the term that best completes the sentence.

1. Private teachers who teach children in their homes are called (**tutors/coaches**).
2. Colonial high schools which taught useful subjects in addition to Latin and Greek were called (**academies/grammar schools**).
3. (**Yearbooks/Almanacs**) were the most popular books because they contained stories, jokes, calendars, and helpful hints.
4. A new interest in religion in the 1730's was called the (**Grand Revival/Great Awakening**).

Do You Remember These People?

Tell something about each of the following people.

Benjamin Franklin

John Singleton Copley

Benjamin West

Can You Locate These Places?

Use the map on page 80 to do the following map work.

1. Locate the colony of Massachusetts. How is this colony connected with the events in this chapter?
2. Locate the colony in which each of the following colleges was located.

   Harvard College   **Yale College**

   William and Mary College

Do You Know When It Happened?

What are the years of this chapter? Tell why each of the following dates was important.

1647   1704   1730's

Discovering More About the Main Idea

Most Americans were educated, and they were interested in books, newspapers, and education for all Americans. Religion was also important in the colonies.

Tell how each of the following developments is related to the MAIN IDEA.

All children were required to attend school in the New England colonies.

Books and newspapers became popular in the colonies, and some Americans began to write books.

Religion was a very important part of colonial life. The Great Awakening not only started a new interest in religion but it also helped the colonists to become interested in education and government.

Can You Discuss the Chapter?

Use the information you learned in this chapter to answer the following questions.

1. Why did the Puritans in the New England colonies think that education was so important?
2. What is the connection between colonial colleges and colonial leaders? What is the connection between education and the popularity of books and newspapers?
3. What did American colonial writers write books about?
4. How did the Great Awakening help education and government in the colonies?

Can You Connect the Past and the Present?

1. Sunday is still thought of as a religious day. What are some laws or customs in your community that show this is true?
2. A college education was less important to people in colonial days than it is today. Why is education more important today?

CHAPTER 19

The Frontier

Moving to the frontier.

BEFORE YOU BEGIN THE CHAPTER

Know What to Look For

1. Today it takes weeks or even months to build a house. But on the American frontier the settlers built a house or a barn in one day. When a couple was married and needed a home, neighbors came from miles around to help with the "house raising." The men sawed the wood and nailed the timbers of the house, while the women prepared food and talked. A house raising was not only the time to build a house, it was also an important social event. Frontier life, however, was not always as pleasant as a house raising. In this chapter, you will find out more about life and problems on the frontier.

2. Read the title of the chapter. Then look through the chapter and read each heading. What group of colonists did the frontier farmer usually not get along with?

3. Look at the first chapter picture and read the caption. What does the picture tell you about going to the frontier? Look at the map on page 128. To what mountains did the frontier reach by 1775? Study the time line at the beginning of the chapter. What years are included in the chapter? Compare the chapter time line to the unit time line on page 113.

4. Read the section called Summing Up at the end of the chapter. What group of people usually settled on the frontier?

Know These Important Terms

Appalachian Mountains
pioneer farmers
Bacon's Rebellion

Paxton Boys
Regulators

Know the Main Idea

Here is the MAIN IDEA of this chapter.

The American frontier was settled by pioneer farmers who developed new ideas of freedom and equality. They often disagreed with the colonists in the more settled parts of the colonies, located along the Atlantic coast.

Keep this MAIN IDEA in mind as you study the chapter. Ask yourself the following questions as you read. They will help you remember the MAIN IDEA.

1. Who were the first people who usually arrived on the frontier? Did they settle the frontier?

2. Why did the Western settlers want the colonies to build better roads to the Western frontier lands?

3. Who helped to settle the trouble between the Western settlers and the Eastern colonists in Pennsylvania? Why did they agree to go back home?

THE YEARS OF THIS CHAPTER ARE 1640 TO 1775

1640   1775

THE CHAPTER LESSON BEGINS HERE

The Frontier Became Settled

In the 1600's, most of the Atlantic coast of what is now the United States was covered with forests. At that time, the Atlantic coast was the frontier, or unsettled land, in the colonies. By the early 1700's, the frontier was only about 100 miles inland from the Atlantic coast. But by 1775, the frontier was as far west as the **Appalachian** (AP-uh-LAY-chun) **Mountains.** By this time, about 250 thousand people lived on the frontier lands of the English colonies in America.

The first people to move into the frontier lands usually were hunters and fur traders. But these men did not settle the frontier. The colonists who settled the frontier lands were **pioneer farmers.**

The Farmers on the Frontier

Most pioneer farmers were European immigrants who settled in the western parts of the Middle colonies and the Southern colonies. They cut clearings in the forest and set up farms there. At first, they raised just enough food for themselves and their families. In time, however, many pioneer farmers were able to grow larger crops, and they sold some of their crops in the eastern part of the colonies.

THE FRONTIER OF THE COLONIES

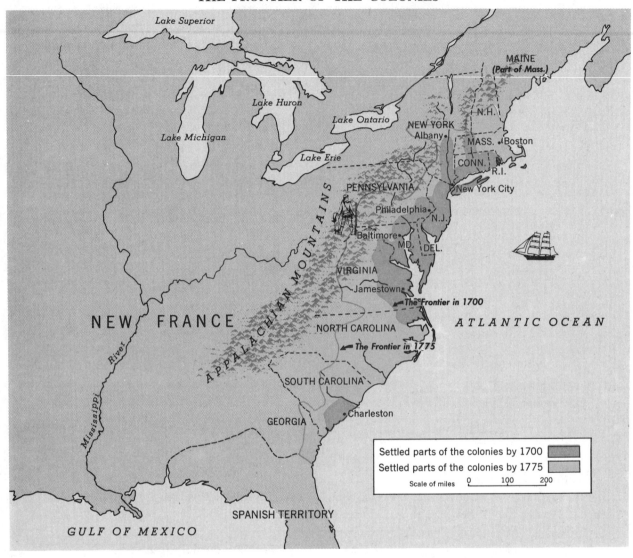

Settled parts of the colonies by 1700
Settled parts of the colonies by 1775
Scale of miles 0 100 200

The Frontier Helped Shape the American People

Most settlers on the frontier lived a different kind of life from the life of the colonists in the older settlements in the eastern part of the colonies. Frontier homes were smaller. Frontier settlers wore plainer clothes and ate simpler foods. Life was hard on the frontier, and this forced the settlers to make their own rules for getting along from day to day. Scotch-Irish, Germans, and Scots worked together, and they began to feel free and equal. These frontier settlers forgot their pasts and began to think of themselves as Americans.

Western Settlers and Eastern Colonists

Settlers on the Western frontier lands often disliked the colonists who lived in the older settlements in the East. Western settlers felt that they were not allowed to elect enough members of the legislatures. They believed that the Eastern colonists controlled the government in each colony. The Western settlers felt that the Eastern colonists were not interested in helping them.

The Western settlers also felt that the Eastern colonists did not do enough to help protect them from Indian attacks. And Western settlers were also angry because the legislatures refused to build roads to the Western frontier lands. Without roads, the Western farmers were not able to send their crops to the East, or to buy the goods they needed.

The Western settlers who lived in the Southern colonies did not like to pay taxes to support the official church in the eastern part of the colonies. Many of them did not belong to this church. For these reasons, hard feelings grew up between the Western settlers and the Eastern colonists.

Western Settlers Fought the Eastern Colonists in Virginia

In some colonies, actual fighting broke out between the Eastern colonists and the Western settlers. As early as 1676, **Bacon's Rebellion** took place in Virginia. This rebellion, or uprising, was caused by the Western settlers' unhappiness with the Virginia government. They were angry because the Eastern colonists refused to send soldiers to protect them from Indian attacks. The Western settlers also felt they did not have enough members in the Virginia legislature. And they were unhappy with the high taxes and the low prices for tobacco.

Nathaniel Bacon, a young Virginia settler, led the rebellion. First, he defeated the Indians. Then he led his army to Jamestown and took control of the colony. However, Bacon died, and his rebellion ended with his death.

Although the rebellion failed, the colonists got what they wanted. The Indians were defeated, and Western settlers were allowed to elect members to the legislature.

Western Settlers in Pennsylvania and North Carolina Also Had Troubles

Trouble between Eastern colonists and Western settlers took place in other colonies. In Pennsylvania, the Western settlers felt they did not have enough members in the legislature. The Western settlers also were not being protected against Indian attacks. As a result, a group of Western farmers, called **Paxton Boys** (from a town in Western Pennsylvania), marched on Philadelphia to force the legislature to treat them more fairly. Benjamin Franklin met them and was able to talk them into going back home. In return, they were promised more members in the legislature.

In North Carolina, the trouble between the Western settlers and the Eastern colonists was not settled as easily. Western farmers in North Carolina were unhappy about the same things —Indian attacks, too few members in the legislature, and high taxes. These farmers formed a group called the **Regulators.** The governor of North Carolina raised an army which fought and defeated the Regulators. Many of the Regulators later left Carolina.

Summing Up

The unsettled land in the colonies was called the frontier. Many European immigrants settled on the frontier lands. Life on the frontier was different from life in the eastern part of the colonies. Often, the Western settlers and the Eastern colonists did not get along well. Sometimes, they even fought. In the next chapters, which are in Unit 6, you will learn how the colonists were governed, and why they fought against England.

AFTER YOU READ THE CHAPTER

Do You Know These Important Terms?

For each sentence below, choose the term that best completes the sentence.

1. By 1775, the frontier was as far west as the (**Rocky Mountains/Appalachian Mountains**).
2. The frontier was usually settled by (**pioneer farmers/hunters and trappers**).
3. (**Bacon's/Henry's**) Rebellion was an uprising in 1676 caused by the Western settlers' unhappiness with the Virginia government.
4. Farmers from western Pennsylvania who marched to Philadelphia to protest the unfair treatment were named (**Pine tree/Paxton**) Boys.
5. (**Regulators/Volunteers**) were Western farmers in North Carolina who were defeated in a rebellion and later moved to Tennessee.

Do You Remember These People?

Tell something about each of the following people.

Nathaniel Bacon   **Benjamin Franklin**

Can You Locate These Places?

Use the map on page 128 to do the following map work.

1. Locate the frontier in 1700 and in 1775.
2. Locate the frontier in Virginia, Pennsylvania, and North Carolina. What events that you read about in this chapter happened in these places?

Do You Know When It Happened?

What are the years of this chapter? Which of the following events happened first?

The frontier reached the Appalachian Mountains.

Bacon's Rebellion took place in Virginia.

Paxton Boys marched to Philadelphia.

Discovering More About the Main Idea

The American frontier was settled by pioneer farmers who developed new ideas of freedom and equality. They often disagreed with the colonists in the more settled parts of the colonies, located along the Atlantic Coast.

Tell how each of the following developments is related to the MAIN IDEA.

The pioneer farmers were usually European immigrants. They believed that no one was any better off than his neighbor.

Western settlers felt that the colonists in the eastern parts of the colonies were not interested in their problems.

Sometimes the differences between the Western settlers and the Eastern colonists caused them to fight.

Can You Discuss the Chapter?

Use the information you learned in this chapter to answer the following questions.

1. What happened to the pioneer farmers who did not do well on their frontier lands?
2. How did frontier living help develop new feelings of freedom and equality?
3. Why did the Western settlers often dislike the colonists in the older settlements in the eastern parts of the colonies?
4. Name three incidents in which differences between Western settlers and Eastern colonists led to fighting. What were the results of each of these uprisings?

Can You Connect the Past and the Present?

For many years during America's history, the frontier presented a challenge for the American people. What new challenges have Americans found to take the place of the frontier?

UNIT 6
The Colonies Win Their Independence

Celebrating the Declaration of Independence.

THE CHAPTERS IN UNIT 6 ARE

CHAPTER 20   Colonial Government
CHAPTER 21   The French and Indian War
CHAPTER 22   British Plans for the Colonies
CHAPTER 23   The Start of the Revolutionary War
CHAPTER 24   The Colonies Declare Their Independence
CHAPTER 25   Winning the Revolutionary War

THE YEARS OF THIS UNIT ARE 1619 TO 1783

1600	1619	1783	1975

Colonial Government

A colonist speaks in the Virginia legislature.

BEFORE YOU BEGIN THE CHAPTER

Know What to Look For

1. The colonists often talked about the rights of Englishmen. What were these rights and how did the people win them? The first big victory came when King John signed the Magna Carta in the year 1215. This ended the absolute rule of the king in England.

During the 1600's, while colonists were struggling to settle North America, two other great documents were signed in England. Both

of these gave Englishmen many important rights. In 1628, the Petition of Rights guaranteed all Englishmen a jury trial. It also gave Parliament the right to set taxes. Then, in 1688 the English Bill of Rights was written. This made the Parliament more powerful than the king and gave Englishmen even more rights. In the colonies, settlers were also interested in the rights of Englishmen. In this chapter, you will see how colonial governments were based on these rights.

2. Read the title of the chapter. Then look through the chapter and read each heading. What parts of the colonial governments can you name just by reading the headings?

3. Look at the pictures in the chapter and read each caption. What do the pictures show you about how government was carried out in the thirteen colonies? Note also the time line at the beginning of the chapter. What years are included in the chapter? Compare the chapter time line to the unit time line on page 131.

4. Read the last part of the chapter called Summing Up. How was England able to watch over the colonies?

Know These Important Terms

self-governing colonies   veto

proprietary colonies   council
royal colonies   assembly

Know the Main Idea

Here is the MAIN IDEA of this chapter.

The colonists in all the English colonies were able to win the right to take an important part in their government.

Keep this MAIN IDEA in mind as you study the chapter. Ask yourself the following questions as you read. They will help you remember the MAIN IDEA.

1. What are the names of the three kinds of colonies?

2. What group of men usually made up the council, or upper house of the colonial legislature?

3. How did the English king still control the American colonies? What special group helped him deal with the colonies?

THE YEARS OF THIS CHAPTER ARE 1619 TO 1750

1619   1750   1783

THE CHAPTER LESSON BEGINS HERE

Three Kinds of English Colonies

The thirteen English colonies in America were divided into three kinds of colonies: royal colonies, proprietary (pruh-PRY-uh-TERR-ee) colonies, and self-governing colonies. The two **self-governing colonies** were Rhode Island and Connecticut. They governed themselves and were almost free from English control. Maryland, Pennsylvania, and Delaware were **proprietary colonies.** In these three colonies, the proprietors, or owners, had the power to rule the colony as they wished. The other eight English colonies were **royal colonies,** or colonies under the control of the king. But in all three kinds of colonies, the

colonial governments were set up and operated in nearly the same way.

The Colonial Governor Was Very Powerful

Each colony had a governor. In a royal colony, the governor was appointed, or given his job, by the king. In a proprietary colony, the governor was appointed by the proprietor. In a self-governing colony, the governor was elected by the voters. But in all thirteen English colonies, the duties and powers of the governor were about the same.

The governor commanded the armed forces in his colony. But most important of all, he governed the colony. The governor called for meetings of the legislature, and he had the right to approve all laws before they were passed. If he disagreed with a law, he had the right to **veto,** or turn down, that law. The governor appointed judges and other colonial officials. And he had great control over the trade of the colony and over Indian matters in the colony.

The Legislature Was Made Up of Two Parts

A small group of men who made up the governor's **council** helped the governor to rule the colony. The members of the council usually were the richest and most important men in the colony. The governor's council often served as the highest court in the colony.

It was also one of the two houses, or parts, which made up the colony's legislature. The council was the upper house in the legislature.

As the upper house in the colonial legislature, the council had to approve all laws before they were passed. But the more powerful part of the colonial legislature was the lower house, or the **assembly.** In all the English colonies, the members of the assembly were elected by the voters.

The Assemblies Won Great Power

Colonial assemblies had many of the same rights as the House of Commons, the lower house in the English legislature, Parliament. The assemblies won the right to make laws for the colony and to discuss freely all matters of importance to the colony. Colonial

This picture shows a group of colonists going to a town meeting. Town meetings were held in some New England colonies.

assemblies also had the right to help the governor set up courts and to decide how they wanted to carry on business in the assembly. And, most important of all, only the colonial assemblies had the right to raise money by passing tax laws.

The assembly's control over money and taxes in the colony gave the assembly much power. If the assembly did not like the things the governor did, they refused to raise the taxes to pay his salary. As a result, most governors tried to get along with the assembly in the colony.

Not All Colonists Were Able to Vote and Hold Office

Not all colonists had the right to vote for members of the assembly. By the 1700's, colonists had to own a certain amount of land or have a certain income in order to vote. Many colonies refused to give the right to vote to Catholics, Quakers, and Jews. All the colonies refused to give the right to vote to Indians, slaves, and free black men. And, although a few tried, women were not allowed to vote during colonial days.

In the colonies, the voting age was anywhere from sixteen to twenty-four, but twenty-one was the common voting age. The colonists did not go into a voting booth and vote in secret, as people do today. Instead, they voted out loud at meetings held for voting. In some colonies, the colonists marked their votes on ballots and then dropped the ballots into ballot boxes. Not every voter in the colonies was able to hold office. To hold

A group of men voting in colonial days. Men voted out loud or used ballots which were placed in ballot boxes.

This picture shows Margaret Brent, a Maryland colonist, asking for the right to vote in the Maryland Assembly.

From the Collections of the Maryland Historical Society.

an office, colonists had to own an even greater amount of land than they did to vote.

The English Government Tried to Control the Colonies

The English king appointed a group of men to help him deal with colonial matters. During the 1700's, this group was known as the Board of Trade. The Board of Trade studied all colonial matters, but it especially looked into business and government in the colonies. It checked over all colonial laws. If the Board did not like a colonial law, it suggested that the king disallow, or turn down, the law. The king did not disallow many colonial laws. Usually a colonial law was disallowed only if it disagreed with an English law or if it hurt English business interests. But the colonists became very angry whenever the king turned down a colonial law.

Summing Up

In all thirteen English colonies, the colonial governments had a great deal of freedom. Each colony had a powerful governor and a legislature. The assembly in the legislature had much power. However, England still had the Board of Trade to watch over the colonies. In the next chapter, you will read about how the English colonies got into a war against the French settlements in North America.

AFTER YOU READ THE CHAPTER

Do You Know These Important Terms?

For each sentence below, select the term that best completes the sentence.

1. Colonies that governed themselves and were almost completely free of English control were called (**proprietory/self-governing**) colonies.
2. Colonies in which the owners of the colony had the power to rule the colony as they wished were (**royal/proprietary**) colonies.
3. Colonies under the control of the king were (**self-governing/royal**) colonies.
4. The governor of the colony had the right to (**veto/disallow**), or turn down a law.
5. The (**assembly/council**) was a small group of men who helped the governor.
6. The most powerful part of the colonial legislature was the (**council/assembly**).

Can You Locate These Places?

Use the map on page 80 to do the following map work.

1. Locate the royal colonies.
2. Locate the proprietory colonies.
3. Locate the self-governing colonies.

Do You Know When It Happened?

What are the years of this chapter? Place the following events in the order in which they occurred.

Connecticut became a self-governing colony.

The House of Burgesses first met.

The English king appointed a Board of Trade.

Discovering More About the Main Idea

The colonists in all the English colonies were able to win the right to take an important part in their government.

Tell how each of the following developments is related to the MAIN IDEA.

The powers and duties of the colonial governor were about the same in all thirteen English colonies.

The colonial legislatures were made of two houses, or parts, the most important of which was the assembly.

Not all the colonists were able to vote or hold an office in the government.

The king of England still kept control over the American colonies.

Can You Discuss the Chapter?

Use the information you learned in this chapter to answer the following questions.

1. Why was the governor such an important part of the colonial governments?
2. Why was the assembly the most important house in the colonial legislatures?
3. Why were some colonists not able to vote during colonial times?
4. Why did the king of England usually disallow a colonial law?
5. What do you think of the fact that everyone in the colonies was not able to vote? Which of the reasons that prevented colonists from voting was most unjust?

Can You Connect the Past and the Present?

1. During colonial times, the assembly was able to control the governor because it controlled money and taxes in the colony. This is called the "power of the purse." How is this method of control used in your community? your family?
2. Compare the laws for allowing people to vote in colonial times with the laws for allowing people to vote in your community today. How are they different?

CHAPTER 21

The French and Indian War

A battle of the French and Indian War.

BEFORE YOU BEGIN THE CHAPTER

Know What to Look For

1. On a still winter morning in February 1704, the citizens of Deerfield, a small town in Massachusetts, were fast asleep. Suddenly, the sound of Indian war cries broke the stillness in the snow-covered town. Settlers leaped out of bed and grabbed their guns. But it was too late to stop the attack and the town was burned. Forty-nine settlers were killed and about 100 more were captured and taken to Canada.

Not all the men attacking Deerfield that morning were Indians. Fifty French soldiers also took part in the raid. Why was one group of Europeans attacking another European settlement? The attack at Deerfield took place while Great Britain and France were at war.

Both nations were struggling to become the most powerful nation in Europe and to control the American continent. In this chapter, you will read more about the fight between Great Britain and France to control North America, and the results this struggle had upon the British colonies in America.

2. Read the title of the chapter. Then look through the chapter and read each heading. Using only the headings, what do you think the outcome of the French and Indian War was?

3. Look at the pictures in the chapter and read each caption. What do the pictures tell you about how the French and Indian War was fought? Look at the map on page 141. What is the title of the map? How are British victories shown? How does the map show British territory and French territory? Study the time line at the beginning of the chapter. What years are included in this chapter? Compare the chapter time line to the unit time line on page 131.

4. Read the last part of the chapter called Summing Up. Why were the colonists unhappy with Great Britain after the French and Indian War? What will the next chapter be about?

Know These Important Terms

French and Indian War   Albany Plan
Albany Congress   peace treaty
Proclamation of 1763

Know the Main Idea

Here is the MAIN IDEA of this chapter.

Great Britain gained a large part of North America as a result of the French and Indian War. The colonists were unhappy because Great Britain refused to allow them to settle in the Ohio Valley.

Keep this MAIN IDEA in mind as you study the chapter. Ask yourself the following questions as you read. They will help you remember the MAIN IDEA.

1. Who was sent to order the French to leave the Ohio Valley?

2. What were the results of the peace treaty that Great Britain made with France and Spain at the end of the war?

3. What Indian chief led an attack on the British forts after the French and Indian War?

THE YEARS OF THIS CHAPTER ARE 1750 TO 1763

1619   1750   1763   1783

THE CHAPTER LESSON BEGINS HERE

Great Britain and France Were Rivals

In the early 1700's, England joined with Scotland, and the two nations then became known as Great Britain. Great Britain's greatest rival was France. Great Britain did not want France to control Europe. And Great Britain and France were rivals for some of the same land in America. This rivalry in Europe and America led to many wars between the two nations during the 1700's.

The first wars between Great Britain and France were fought mainly in Europe. The fighting in America was not too important. In the 1750's, war again broke out between these two nations. This time, however, many of the battles of the war were fought in America. The colonists fought to protect their lands.

General Wolfe climbing up to Quebec.

MONTCALM AND WOLFE

For more than two months during the summer of 1759, the British and French armies faced each other near Quebec. The leader of the French army was General Montcalm. The leader of the British army was General James Wolfe. Both generals knew that this battle might decide who won the French and Indian War. General Wolfe had tried several times, but he was not able to capture Quebec because of its location on a high, well-guarded cliff.

But on the evening of September 12, the British found a path leading up the cliff to the city. The British were able to overpower the French guards. Then, during the night, over 4 thousand British soldiers climbed up the path. The next morning the British soldiers were in Quebec. General Montcalm ordered the French to attack. After fierce fighting, the British won a great victory.

During the battle, both Montcalm and Wolfe were wounded. Wolfe died on the battlefield. Montcalm died in Quebec the next day. By September 17, the British controlled Quebec. In less than a year, they captured Montreal. And in 1763, all of Canada became British territory.

The French and Indian War

Both Great Britain and France wanted to own Nova Scotia because of the rich fishing waters located along its coast. Both nations also wanted the Ohio Valley, located west of the Appalachian Mountains. France needed the Ohio Valley to tie together the French settlements in Canada and Louisiana. France also wanted the Ohio Valley because of its valuable fur trade there. However, Great Britain also wanted to control the fur trade in the Ohio Valley. In addition, some British colonists wanted to settle there.

The French government sent soldiers into the Ohio Valley and these soldiers built several forts there. The governor of Virginia sent a young Virginia colonist named George Washington to order the French soldiers to leave the Ohio Valley. The French refused to leave, and in 1754, Washington and his soldiers fought several small battles with the French. These battles were the beginning of the **French and Indian War.**

The Colonies Failed to Join Together

After the war began, the British government called for a meeting of the colonies at Albany, New York. The British called for this meeting, known as the **Albany Congress,** for two reasons. They wanted to win the support of the Iroquois Indians in the war, and they wanted to organize the colonies to help fight the war. At the meeting, the Iroquois promised to help Great Britain. Also, Benjamin Franklin presented the **Albany Plan,** a plan to join the colonies together to fight the war. However, Franklin's plan to unite the colonies was turned down.

Great Britain Defeated France

The French and Indian War began badly for Great Britain. General Edward Braddock (BRAD-uk), the British commander-in-chief,

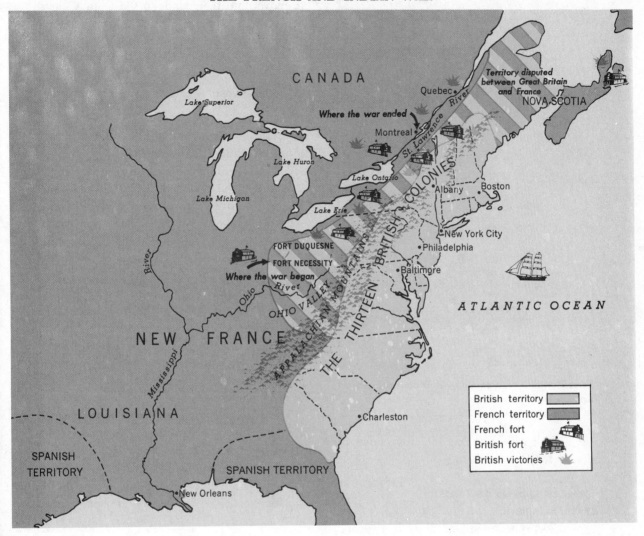

fought the French in the Ohio Valley. Braddock lost the battle and was killed. Other British generals did almost as poorly.

In the year 1756, however, William Pitt became the leader of the British government. Pitt picked younger generals who fought in ways better suited to the American forests. Pitt also sent more men and supplies to America, and he won more help from the colonists.

Pitt's methods, or ways, worked, and soon Great Britain won battle after battle. The most important battle of the war was fought near Quebec. The British army, led by General James Wolfe, surprised and defeated the French army led by General Montcalm (mahnt-KAHM). Both generals were killed, but the British army captured Quebec. A year later, Montreal was captured by the British army. Spain entered the war in 1762 to help France, but it was too late. In 1763,

Chief Pontiac led a number of Indian attacks on forts on the frontier.

the French gave up, and the war ended in victory for Great Britain.

Great Britain Gained Most of North America

In 1763, Great Britain signed a **peace treaty,** or an agreement ending the war, with France and Spain. This peace treaty gave Great Britain all the land in North America between the Appalachian Mountains and the Mississippi River, except for the city of New Orleans. Canada, a French colony, and Florida, a Spanish colony, now became British colonies. The English colonists no longer had to worry about attacks from the French in Canada. And they were now free to move into the Ohio Valley.

The Indians knew that the colonists planned to move onto their lands in the Ohio Valley. In 1763, the Indians, led by a great Indian chief named Pontiac (PAHNT-ee-ak), attacked on the frontier. They captured all the British forts on the frontier except Detroit. Finally, after three years, Pontiac was forced to make peace.

The British Government Closed the Ohio Valley to Settlement

After the French and Indian War, Great Britain decided to keep settlers out of the Ohio Valley. The British government had three reasons for not wanting American colonists to settle in the Ohio Valley. The Indian war with Pontiac frightened the British. They wanted to stop Indian attacks on the frontier. Also, the British government wanted the British fur traders to keep control of the fur trade in the Ohio Valley. Finally, the British government wanted to keep the colonists near the Atlantic coast to trade with Britain and to see that they obeyed the Navigation Acts and the laws against manufacturing.

The British government, therefore, passed a law called the **Proclamation** (prahk-luh-MAY-shun) **of 1763.** This proclamation made it unlawful for any colonists to settle on land west of the Appalachian Mountains. The Proclamation of 1763 was a very unpopular law in America.

Summing Up

The French and Indian War ended French power in North America. The peace treaty gave Great Britain almost all the land in North America between the Appalachian Mountains and the Mississippi River. But the American colonists found that Great Britain was not going to let them settle the land won in the French and Indian War. In the next chapter, you will read about some other changes Great Britain made in the colonies.

AFTER YOU READ THE CHAPTER

Do You Know These Important Terms?

For each sentence below, choose the term that best completes the statement.

1. The North American part of the war between Great Britain and France in the 1750's was called the (**French and Indian War/War of the Roses**).
2. A meeting held by the British to win the support of the Iroquois Indians and to unite the colonies was called the (**Albany Congress/New York Review**).
3. The (**Navigation Acts/Proclamation of 1763**) made it unlawful for colonists to settle west of the Appalachian Mountains.
4. The (**Colonial/Albany**) Plan was presented by Benjamin Franklin to join the colonies together to fight the war.
5. An agreement ending a war is called a (**surrender/peace treaty**).

Do You Remember These People?

Tell something about each of the following persons.

George Washington   **Benjamin Franklin**
Edward Braddock   **William Pitt**
James Wolfe   **General Montcalm**
Pontiac

Can You Locate These Places?

Use the map on page 141 to do the following map work.

Locate the following places.

Ohio Valley   **Albany**
Nova Scotia   **Montreal**
Appalachian Mountains   **Quebec**
Mississippi River

Do You Know When It Happened?

Place the following events in the order in which they occurred.

The British captured Montreal.

The British government issued the Proclamation of 1763.

Great Britain gained control of Canada, Florida, and all lands east of the Mississippi River.

Discovering More About the Main Idea

Great Britain gained a large part of North America as a result of the French and Indian War. The colonists were unhappy because Great Britain refused to allow them to settle in the Ohio Valley.

Tell how each of the following developments is related to the MAIN IDEA.

The French and Indian War was part of a much larger struggle for power between Great Britain and France.

At first, the war went badly for the British, but new leadership in the government and new methods helped Great Britain to win.

Can You Discuss the Chapter?

Use the information you learned in this chapter to answer the following questions.

1. Why was the struggle for power between Britain and France in the 1750's different from the wars fought between these two nations earlier?
2. What new lands in North America did Great Britain gain as a result of the peace treaty in 1763?
3. Why didn't the British government want colonists to settle in the Ohio Valley after 1763?

Can You Connect the Past and the Present?

How were the French able to keep such a strong alliance with the Indians? Can this same idea be used in our friendships with other people today? Explain.

CHAPTER 22

British Plans for the Colonies

Colonists pull down a statue of the British king.

BEFORE YOU BEGIN THE CHAPTER

Know What to Look For

1. The colonists were often unfriendly to British officials they did not like. They especially disliked the British stamp masters sent to collect the new stamp tax. Because the colonists threatened to harm the stamp masters who collected the tax, many stamp masters resigned, or give up their office, before they sold a single stamp. When Zachariah Hood,

the stamp master for Maryland, refused to resign, a mob of colonists tore his store down to the ground. Hood was almost killed but he managed to escape. He was followed by the angry crowd as far as New York, where he finally resigned as stamp master.

Such incidents took place in the other colonies, and many tax collectors were beaten and chased out of town. In this chapter, you will discover why the colonists disliked the stamp masters so much. You will also find out how the colonies felt about Great Britain's changes in governing the colonies and its new taxes for the colonies.

2. Read the title of the chapter. Then look through the chapter and read each heading. Name some of the new British taxes that Parliament passed.

3. Look at the pictures in the chapter and read each caption. What do the pictures show you about the colonists' feelings about the new British plans and taxes? Examine the time line at the beginning of the chapter. What years are included in this chapter? Compare this chapter time line to the unit time line on page 131.

4. Read the last part of the chapter called Summing Up. How did the colonists feel about the new British changes and taxes for the colonies?

Know These Important Terms

writs of assistance   Sons of Liberty
Sugar Act   Stamp Act Congress
Stamp Act   repeal

Know the Main Idea

Here is the MAIN IDEA of this chapter.

Great Britain made changes in governing the American colonies and passed new taxes for the colonies. The colonists were against the new tax laws.

Keep this MAIN IDEA in mind as you study the chapter. Ask yourself the following questions as you read. They will help you remember the MAIN IDEA.

1. Why did Great Britain decide to make changes in governing the American colonies?

2. What older laws did Great Britain try to make the colonists obey?

3. What tax did the colonists force Great Britain to end?

THE YEARS OF THIS CHAPTER ARE 1763 TO 1766

1619   1763   1766   1783

THE CHAPTER LESSON BEGINS HERE

Great Britain Made Changes in Governing the Colonies

After the French and Indian War, Great Britain gained new colonies in Asia and Africa, as well as in North America. Governing all these colonies and paying off the large debt from the war were great problems for Great Britain. To solve these problems, Great Britain decided to make changes in the governing of the American colonies.

Important Changes in the Colonies

At the same time, important changes were also taking place in the colonies. During the French and Indian War, the British government bought supplies manufactured in the colonies. As a result, in 1763, colonial business was richer and stronger than ever before. During the war, colonial governors needed men and supplies. In order to get supplies and men for the army from the colonies, the governors had to give new rights to the assembly. These rights gave the colonists a greater part in their government.

page 145

Many Colonists Began to Consider Themselves as Americans

Also, over the years, many settlers in the colonies came to think of themselves as Americans, and not as Englishmen. Most Englishmen came to America because they were not able to earn a living or worship as they wished in Great Britain. These colonists no longer had strong ties to Great Britain. Many settlers came from other European nations and never thought of themselves as Englishmen. All these settlers came to think of themselves as one group of people—Americans.

Great Britain Tightened Up the Navigation Acts

The British government did not understand that the colonists no longer thought of themselves as Englishmen. Great Britain expected the colonists to help pay the British debt.

Therefore, Great Britain went ahead with its new plans for the colonies.

Part of the British plan was to make the colonists obey the Navigation Acts. Great Britain wanted to get the money it was losing because the colonists were not paying taxes on the goods they smuggled. Large rewards were given for news about smuggled goods. People accused of breaking the trade laws were now tried in British courts without juries, not in colonial courts.

The British government also began to make more use of **writs of assistance** (RITZ of uh-SIS-tunts). Writs of assistance were court orders which gave British officials the right to enter a person's house, ship, or warehouse to search for smuggled goods. The colonists disliked these writs of assistance because they believed that the writs were a danger to their rights as free citizens.

England's Parliament, shown below, passed many new trade and tax laws for the colonies. The colonists did not like these new laws.

This is the Place to affix the STAMP.

The stamp at left was the British tax stamp. The stamp at right was printed by colonists who disliked the stamp tax.

Parliament Put a Tax on Sugar

After the French and Indian War, a British army was kept in America to protect the frontier. The British government needed money to pay for this army. Because people in England were already paying high taxes, the British government decided that the American colonists had to help support this army. Therefore, in 1764, the British Parliament passed a tax law called the **Sugar Act.** This law put a tax on sugar, molasses, and other products brought into the colonies from other countries. Businessmen in New England and the Middle colonies were hit hard by this tax. Many colonists talked of refusing to pay the tax.

Parliament Passed the Stamp Act

The Sugar Act did not raise enough money to support the British army in America. Therefore, in 1765, Parliament passed another tax law called the **Stamp Act.** The Stamp Act put a tax on newspapers, books, business and law papers, calendars, and playing cards sold in the colonies. All these things were to be stamped to show that the tax was paid.

The British Parliament had taxed colonial trade before. The Sugar Act was an example of a tax placed on colonial trade. But the British Parliament had never before taxed the colonists directly. Only colonial legislatures—not Parliament—had taxed the American colonists.

The Stamp Act Set Off Trouble

At first, the stamp tax was paid by almost all the colonists. But lawyers, newspapermen, businessmen, and ministers were especially hit by the stamp tax. These men were among the most important men in the colony, and they helped stir up many colonists. Before long, no one in the colonies was willing to pay the stamp tax. Some colonists formed an organization called the **Sons of Liberty** to

This picture shows angry colonists burning British tax stamps. Many colonists refused to pay the stamp tax.

make sure no one paid the tax. The Sons of Liberty even used force to make sure that no tax stamps were sold.

In October of 1765, a group of leaders from nine colonies met in New York City. This meeting was called the **Stamp Act Congress.** The Stamp Act Congress asked the British Parliament to **repeal,** or end, the Stamp Act. The Stamp Act Congress said that Parliament had no right to tax the colonies because the colonists did not elect members to Parliament. Only the colonial legislatures had the right to tax the American colonies.

The Stamp Act Was Ended

The Stamp Act Congress asked the colonists not to buy any British goods as long as the Stamp Act was in force. Soon British merchants, manufacturers, and ship owners lost a great deal of their colonial trade and money. They asked Parliament to repeal the tax, and in 1766, Parliament ended the Stamp Act.

Summing Up

After the French and Indian War, Great Britain decided to make changes in governing the American colonies. Great Britain tried to make the colonists obey the Navigation Acts, and they passed new tax laws to raise money. But the colonists fought against these taxes. The British government was forced to end one tax law, the Stamp Act. In the next chapter, you will read about actions of the British government which led the colonists to fight for their freedom.

AFTER YOU READ THE CHAPTER

Do You Know These Important Terms?

For each sentence below, choose the term that best completes the sentence.

1. Court orders which gave British officials the right to search for smuggled goods were called (**search warrants/writs of assistance**).
2. The (**Sugar/Military**) Act was passed to raise taxes to help support a British army in the colonies.
3. The (**Stamp/Paper**) Act placed a tax on newspapers, books, business papers, and many other things sold in the colonies.
4. The (**Paxton Boys/Sons of Liberty**) was an organization formed by some colonists to see that no one paid the stamp tax.
5. A group of leaders from nine colonies held the (**Stamp Act/Albany**) Congress to decide what to do about the Stamp Act.
6. The British Parliament was asked to (**enact/repeal**) the Stamp Act.

Can You Locate These Places?

Use the maps in your classroom to do the following map work.

1. Locate the continents of Asia and Africa. How are they related to the events of this chapter?
2. Locate Great Britain, the American colonies, and Canada.

Do You Know When It Happened?

What are the years of this chapter? In what year did each of the following events happen?

The Stamp Act was passed.

The Navigation Acts were more strictly enforced.

The Sugar Act was passed.

The Stamp Act was repealed.

The Stamp Act Congress was held in New York City.

Discovering More About the Main Idea

Great Britain made changes in governing the American colonies and passed new taxes for the colonies. The colonists were against the new tax laws.

Tell how each of the following developments is related to the MAIN IDEA.

Great Britain considered the American colonies as part of its growing empire and passed laws to make the colonies help pay for the British debt.

The colonists felt that Parliament did not have the right to tax the colonies because the colonists did not elect members to Parliament.

Can You Discuss the Chapter?

Use the information you learned in this chapter to answer the following questions.

1. Why did many colonists think of themselves as Americans rather than as Englishmen?
2. Why did the colonists dislike the writs of assistance so much?
3. Why did colonists object more to the Stamp Act than they did to the Sugar Act even though both taxes were to be used to support a British army in the colonies?
4. How were the colonists able to make Parliament repeal the Stamp Act?

Can You Connect the Past and the Present?

1. Americans pay many taxes today without complaining too much. What is the great difference between tax laws today and the tax laws Britain passed for the colonies?
2. The colonists were able to get Britain to repeal the Stamp Act by refusing to buy British goods. Explain how this withholding of trade is still an effective weapon today. Give some examples.

CHAPTER 23

The Start of the Revolutionary War

The Boston Tea Party.

BEFORE YOU BEGIN THE CHAPTER

Know What to Look For

1. No one knows for sure who fired the first shot that started the Revolutionary War at Lexington, or just how many men were involved in the battle at Lexington. The accounts of those who saw the battle and all the official reports disagree. The number of Minutemen in the battle ranges from forty to 300 depending upon what report is read. Some reports say the British fired first. Others state that the Minutemen fired first. Also, there is no agreement on how many men were killed or wounded. Experts will probably continue to argue and disagree for many years about who fired the first shot. But the fact remains that shots were fired and that fighting between the colonists and British began. In this chapter, you will read how fighting between the colonies and Great Britain began.

2. Read the title of the chapter. Then look through the chapter and read each heading. Using only the headings, outline briefly the steps leading to the Revolutionary War.

3. Look at the pictures in the chapter and read each caption. In the picture of the Boston Tea Party how are some of the colonists dressed? What are they doing? Examine the map on page 154. In which of the colonies did the fighting actually begin? Note also the time line at the beginning of the chapter. What years are included in this chapter? Compare this chapter time line to the unit time line on page 131.

4. Read the last part of the chapter called Summing Up. When were the first battles of the Revolutionary war fought?

Know These Important Terms
Declaratory Act
Townshend Acts
Tea Act
First Continental Congress
Minutemen
Revolutionary War

Know the Main Idea
Here is the MAIN IDEA of this chapter.
When the American colonies were unable to settle their differences peacefully with Great Britain, events led quickly to war.

Keep this MAIN IDEA in mind as you study the chapter. Ask yourself the following questions as you read. They will help you remember the MAIN IDEA.

1. What act stated that Parliament had the right to pass any laws it wished to make for the colonies?

2. How did some colonists react to the Tea Act?

3. Why did the British army move to the town of Concord?

THE YEARS OF THIS CHAPTER ARE 1766 TO 1775

1619   1766   1775   1783

THE CHAPTER LESSON BEGINS HERE

Parliament Tried New Tax Laws

The same day the Stamp Act was repealed, Parliament passed the **Declaratory** (di-KLAR-uh-tor-ee) **Act.** The Declaratory Act said that Parliament had the right to pass any law it wished to make for the colonies. The colonists were so happy about the end of the Stamp Act that they hardly noticed this new British law.

In 1767, however, Parliament passed new tax laws called the **Townshend** (TOUN-zend) **Acts.** The Townshend Acts put taxes on all glass, lead, paper, paint, and tea brought into the colonies. Part of this money was to be used to support the British army in the American colonies. The rest was to be used to pay the salaries of the colonial governors.

The Colonists Forced the Repeal of the New Tax Laws

The colonists wanted to keep control of their governors' salaries. They also felt that they were able to protect themselves without the help of a British army. Therefore, the colonists fought the Townshend Acts. Colonial merchants promised not to buy any British goods until the Townshend Acts were

THE BOSTON MASSACRE

One of the most famous black heroes of colonial times died in a fight that many people consider the first battle of the American Revolution. His name was Crispus Attucks, and he died in a fight which is known as the Boston Massacre.

Not too much is known about Crispus Attucks. A Boston newspaper of October 2, 1750 mentions a runaway slave named "Crispas." It is believed that this runaway slave was Crispus Attucks. Crispus Attucks was never recaptured. For twenty years, he worked as a seaman and on the docks of Boston.

Most people are not even sure what happened at the Boston Massacre. On the night of March 5, 1770, a crowd of men and boys gathered at the Boston customs house. A group of British soldiers tried to break up the crowd. Attucks and the others refused to move. Someone gave an order to fire, and the British shot at the crowd. Crispus Attucks and two other men were killed on the spot. Two more men died later. As John Adams later wrote, "On that night (of the Boston Massacre) the foundation of American independence was laid."

repealed. The Sons of Liberty saw to it that the colonists kept this promise. Once again the British Parliament gave in, and in 1770, all the Townshend Acts were repealed except the tax on tea. This tax on tea was kept to show the American colonists that Parliament still had the right to tax them if it wished.

Some Colonists Feared More Trouble

In the years from 1770 to 1773, many colonists disagreed over how to settle the colonies' troubles with Great Britain. Colonial merchants, businessmen, and land owners believed that Great Britain was not going to bother them any more. But many other colonists, especially workers, shop keepers, and small farmers, feared more trouble with Great Britain. Many of these colonists joined the Sons of Liberty.

Samuel Adams was the leader of these colonists. By the early 1770's, Samuel Adams was already thinking about the colonies being completely independent, or free, from Great Britain. In 1772, he helped to form Committees of Correspondence in Massachusetts, and soon the idea spread to other colonies. The Committees were groups of colonists who exchanged letters telling what was happening in the other colonies and in Great Britain.

A New Tea Act Led to Tea Parties

In 1773, Parliament passed a law called the **Tea Act.** The Tea Act allowed the British East India Company to sell its tea directly to the colonies without paying a duty, or tax, to the British government. In this way, the East India Company was able to sell its tea at a low price in the colonies.

Most American colonists disliked the Tea Act. Colonial merchants were angry because they were not able to sell their tea as cheaply as the East India Company. Many colonists were angry because they still had to pay the tax on tea. Therefore, some colonists boarded the East India Company's ships at Boston and other seaports, and they had "tea parties" by dumping the tea into the harbor. The most famous was the Boston Tea Party.

The British Government Punished Boston

The British government was very angry, and it decided to punish the colonists in Boston. The port of Boston was to be closed until the colonists agreed to pay for the tea they destroyed. The powers of the Massachusetts legislature and the town meetings were cut down. General Thomas Gage, the leader of the British army, was made governor of Massachusetts and was given great powers.

The First Continental Congress Met

In September of 1774, leaders of the American colonies met at Philadelphia to talk about the colonies' problems with Great Britain. This meeting was called the **First Continental** (KAHN-tuh-NEN-tul) **Congress.** Most of the

men at the First Continental Congress wanted to settle the colonies' problems with Great Britain peacefully. But they felt that Parliament must first stop punishing Massachusetts and must stop taxing the colonies. To back up these demands, the Congress asked all colonies to stop trading with Great Britain.

Some British leaders wanted to give in to the colonists. But King George the Third and most members of Parliament refused. Parliament finally promised not to tax the colonies if the colonies agreed to tax themselves. But the colonies refused to tax themselves.

The Revolutionary War Began at Lexington and Concord

By 1775, some Americans were planning for war with Great Britain. Samuel Adams and John Hancock were gathering guns and training colonists to fight. General Gage, the British commander, learned that many of these guns were stored in the town of Concord. In April of 1775, General Gage sent British soldiers from Boston to capture these

In this picture, British soldiers are leaving the town of Concord after fighting a battle with the Minutemen.

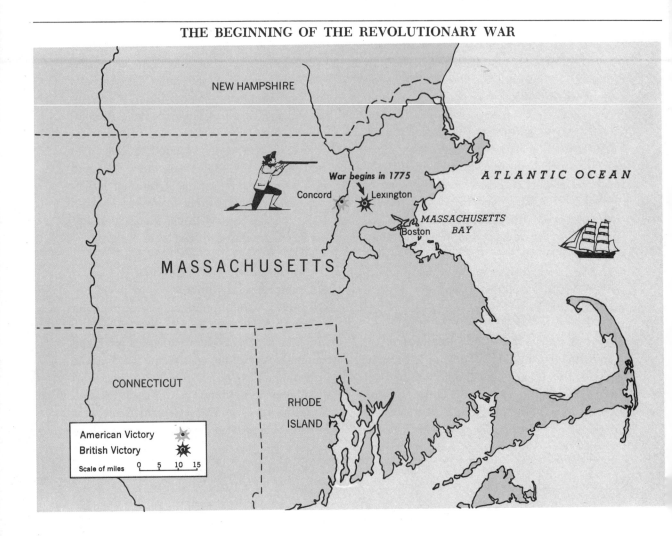

NEW HAMPSHIRE

War begins in 1775

Concord   Lexington

ATLANTIC OCEAN

MASSACHUSETTS BAY

Boston

MASSACHUSETTS

CONNECTICUT

RHODE ISLAND

American Victory
British Victory
Scale of miles   0   5   10   15

guns and to arrest Adams and Hancock. But the colonists found out about Gage's plan. Paul Revere (ruh-VEER) and William Dawes (DAWZ) warned the colonists, and Adams and Hancock escaped.

When the British soldiers reached the town of Lexington, they were met by a group of armed **Minutemen.** The Minutemen were colonists trained to be ready to fight at a minute's notice. Shots were fired, and some of the Minutemen were killed or wounded. Soon after, another battle took place at Concord. These battles fought at Lexington and Concord on April 19, 1775, were the beginning of the **Revolutionary War.**

Summing Up

From 1765 to 1775, Americans tried unsuccessfully to settle their problems with Great Britain peacefully. Finally the troubles between Great Britain and the colonies turned into a war. The first battles of the Revolutionary War were fought on April 19, 1775, at Lexington and Concord in Massachusetts. In the next chapter, you will find out why the colonies decided to fight for independence.

AFTER YOU READ THE CHAPTER

Do You Know These Important Terms?

For each sentence below, choose the term that best completes the sentence.

1. The act that said Parliament had the right to pass laws for the American colonies was the (**Declaratory/Colonial**) Act.
2. The (**Townshend/Williams**) Acts put a tax on glass, lead, paper, paint, and tea.
3. The act that gave the British East India Company a trade advantage in the colonies was the (**India/Tea**) Act.
4. The (**First/Second**) Continental Congress met in Philadelphia to talk about settling the colonies' problems with Great Britain peacefully.
5. Colonists ready to fight on short notice were called (**Continentals/Minutemen**).
6. The war between the colonies and Great Britain was called the (**Revolutionary/ Colonial**) War.

Do You Remember These People?

Tell something about each of the following persons.

Samuel Adams	Thomas Gage
King George the Third	John Hancock
Paul Revere	William Dawes

Can You Locate These Places?

Use the map on page 154 to do the following map work.

1. Locate the places where the battles of Lexington and Concord were fought.
2. These battles took place near what large city located on the Atlantic coast?

Do You Know When It Happened?

What are the years of this chapter? Place the following events in the order in which they occurred.

The Boston Tea Party was held.

The Townshend Acts were repealed.
The First Continental Congress met.

Discovering More About the Main Idea

When the American colonies were unable to settle their differences peacefully with Great Britain, events led quickly to war.

Tell how each of the following developments is related to the MAIN IDEA.

The colonists were successful in getting some tax laws repealed.

When some colonists in Boston destroyed a tea shipment, Great Britain decided to punish Boston by closing its port and cutting down the power of the Massachusetts legislature.

Fighting broke out when the British army tried to capture guns stored by the colonists and to arrest two colonial leaders.

Can You Discuss the Chapter?

Use the information you learned in this chapter to answer the following questions.

1. How were the colonists able to force Parliament to repeal some of the new tax laws?
2. How did the Tea Act lead to the punishment of Boston by Great Britain?
3. Why was the First Continental Congress not able to settle the colonies' problems with Great Britain?
4. How did the actual fighting of the Revolutionary War begin?
5. If you had lived in Britain in 1775, how do you think you might have felt about the fighting at Lexington and Concord?

Can You Connect the Past and the Present?

Why is it so important today to maintain communication between nations and to settle problems between nations peacefully?

CHAPTER 24

The Colonies Declare Their Independence

Thomas Jefferson presents the Declaration of Independence.

BEFORE YOU BEGIN THE CHAPTER

Know What to Look For

1. Treason, or the betrayal of one's country, is a serious crime. In 1776, the brave men who signed the Declaration of Independence, which declared that the colonies were free of Great Britain, became traitors. They were guilty of treason against Great Britain, and they all knew the punishment if they were captured or if their cause failed. By law, traitors to the British government were hung by

the neck and "drawn and quartered." That is, the prisoner's stomach was cut so that his insides slowly spilled forth . . . a slow and painful death! In this chapter, you will find out why these men took such a big step even though Great Britain's army and navy seemed to be much stronger than the American army and navy.

2. Read the title of the chapter. Then look

through the chapter and read each heading. If you did not already know the outcome of the war, how might you tell who won the war by reading only the headings?

3. Look at the pictures in the chapter and read each caption. Which men in the pictures are American soldiers? members of Congress? helpers from a foreign nation? Note also the time line at the beginning of the chapter. What years are included in this chapter? Compare this chapter time line to the unit time line on page 131.

4. Read the last part of the chapter called Summing Up. When did the colonies declare their independence from Great Britain? What is the topic of the next chapter?

Know These Important Terms

Second Continental Congress
Common Sense
Declaration of Independence
Loyalists

Know the Main Idea

Here is the MAIN IDEA of this chapter.

The American colonists declared their independence and fought the Revolutionary War against Great Britain to win their freedom.

Keep this MAIN IDEA in mind as you study the chapter. Ask yourself the following questions as you read. They will help you remember the MAIN IDEA.

1. What actions were taken by the Second Continental Congress in 1775 to prepare for war?

2. What helped Americans make up their minds to declare their independence?

3. What advantages did the Americans have in the war?

THE YEARS OF THIS CHAPTER ARE 1775 TO 1776

1619   1775   1776   1783

THE CHAPTER LESSON BEGINS HERE

The American Colonists Prepared for War

In May of 1775, the leaders of the colonies met again at Philadelphia to attend the **Second Continental Congress.** Most of the men at this Congress still hoped to settle the colonies' problems with Great Britain peacefully. They wrote King George the Third that the American colonies were willing to remain in the British empire if Parliament agreed not to tax them.

If you remember, however, fighting between the American colonists and British soldiers took place at Lexington and Concord in April of 1775. The leaders of the Second Continental Congress also felt that they had

to be ready for a war with Great Britain. Therefore, they voted to raise money and men for an army and a navy. George Washington was made the head of the American army.

An Attack on Canada Failed

In May of 1775, a small group of American soldiers took over Fort Ticonderoga (TY-kon-duh-ROH-guh) in upper New York State. This victory was important because the Americans captured much-needed cannons and guns. It also opened the way for an attack on Canada. During the fall of 1775, the American army attacked Canada, and an American army captured Montreal. However, Quebec held out against the American attack, and the French population remained loyal to Great Britain.

The Battle of Bunker Hill

In June of 1775, an important battle was fought near Boston. By mistake, this battle was called the Battle of Bunker Hill. The Battle of Bunker Hill was actually fought at Breed's Hill. The British army attacked Breed's Hill three times. After the first two attacks, they were forced to pull back because of heavy losses. Finally, the British took the hill on their third try when the Americans ran out of ammunition.

When King George the Third heard about the Battle of Bunker Hill, he declared that the American colonies were fighting against Great Britain and that the colonists were rebels. Great Britain began to capture American ships and the ships of any nations that tried to trade with America. Also, the British government hired German troops to fight against the American colonists and to force them to obey the British government.

Americans Began to Think of Independence

After the Battle of Bunker Hill, George Washington took command of the American army in Boston. In March of 1776, the American army surrounded Boston. The British were no longer able to hold Boston, and the British army left Boston and went by ship to Canada.

British soldiers who fought in the Battle of Bunker Hill are landing in Boston. This British ship is shelling the city.

By 1776, many American colonists believed that they must fight for their independence from Great Britain. Great Britain's actions after the Battle of Bunker Hill angered the Americans. Also, Thomas Paine wrote a short book called **Common Sense,** which helped many Americans to make up their minds in favor of independence. Paine showed that Americans had everything to gain by becoming independent.

The Colonies Declared
Their Independence

The men at the Second Continental Congress also began to favor American independence. In June of 1776, Richard Henry Lee of Virginia demanded that the colonies declare their independence. The Congress appointed a committee including Thomas Jefferson, John Adams, and Benjamin Franklin to write a Declaration of Independence to explain why the American colonies were forming a new nation.

On July 2, 1776, the Second Continental Congress voted to declare the colonies independent of Great Britain. And on July 4, 1776, the Congress approved the **Declaration of Independence.** The Americans had formed a new, independent nation—the United States of America.

Great Britain Was Not as Strong
as It Seemed

Although the American colonies had declared their independence, they had to fight a long war before they won their independence. Great Britain had a strong army and navy. And the British army expected help from the Indians and the **Loyalists,** or Americans who were against independence.

But the British army was not as strong as it seemed. The British army had to depend on hired German soldiers who did not want to

Here, a family of Loyalists is leaving the colonies to go to Canada.

fight and die for Great Britain. Nor did the British navy do as well as expected. The British navy was never able to cut off trade between Europe and America. And the British did not get very much help from the Indians or the Loyalists.

Some Europeans helped the Americans fight for their freedom. Here, Baron von Steuben drills soldiers at Valley Forge.

America Had Many Strengths

America had certain advantages in the war. America was very large, and it was far away from Great Britain. This made it hard for Great Britain to supply its army. Also, American generals knew their own land, and therefore they were often able to trap and defeat the British. Because of America's great size, Great Britain was never able to capture the Southern, Middle, and New England states (called colonies before) all at the same time. And when one section was captured, the other two kept fighting. Great Britain found it was too difficult to win a war 3 thousand miles away from home.

France, Spain, and other European nations helped the Americans win the war by giving them men, money, and war supplies. Baron von Steuben (STOO-ban) of Prussia and General Kosciusko (kahs-ee-OOS-koh) and General Pulaski (puh-LASS-kee) of Poland helped train the American army. And two French officers, the Marquis de Lafayette (mahr-KEE duh lahf-ee-ET) and Baron de Kalb (KALP), helped lead the American army. The outstanding leadership of George Washington also helped win the war.

Summing Up

As the war went on, most Americans came to favor independence from Great Britain. On July 4, 1776, the colonies declared their independence. Although Britain had a strong army and navy, the Americans had many advantages. In the next chapter, you will learn how the Americans won their independence.

AFTER YOU READ THE CHAPTER

Do You Know These Important Terms?

For each sentence below, choose the term that best completes the sentence.

1. The leaders of the (**First/Second**) Continental Congress prepared for war.
2. (**Freedom for All/Common Sense**) was the title of a book that helped many Americans make up their minds in favor of independence.
3. The reasons why Americans felt they had a right to form a new nation were written in the (**Committees of Correspondence/Declaration of Independence**).
4. (**Loyalists/Colonists**) were Americans who were against independence.

Do You Remember These People?

Tell something about each of the following persons.

Thomas Jefferson   Richard Henry Lee
John Adams   Benjamin Franklin
Thomas Paine   Baron von Steuben
General Kosciusko   General Pulaski
Marquis de Lafayette   Baron de Kalb
George Washington

Can You Locate These Places?

Use the map on page 164 to do the following map work.

Locate Fort Ticonderoga. Why did the capture of this fort open the way to Canada? Locate Montreal and Quebec. How are these cities related to the Revolution?

Do You Know When It Happened?

What are the years of this chapter? Place the following events in the order in which they occurred.

Independence was declared.

American forces invaded Canada.

The Battle of Bunker Hill was fought.

Discovering More About the Main Idea

The American colonists declared their independence and fought the Revolutionary War against Great Britain to win their freedom.

Tell how each of the following developments is related to the MAIN IDEA.

Great Britain declared the American colonies were fighting against Great Britain and sent soldiers to force them to obey the British government.

Great Britain had a strong army and navy and expected to win the war quickly.

Size, distance, knowledge of the land, and help from other European nations were advantages for the Americans.

Can You Discuss the Chapter?

Use the information you learned in this chapter to answer the following questions.

1. Why were the British no longer able to hold Boston after March of 1776?
2. Why was the Declaration of Independence such an important step for the colonies?
3. Why did many people feel that Great Britain would quickly win the war? Explain why this did not happen.

Can You Connect the Past and the Present?

1. Since 1946, many former colonies have become independent nations. Name some of these new nations. Which nations had to fight a revolution before they became independent?
2. The Declaration of Independence stressed equality and freedom. The present-day civil rights movement also stresses equality and freedom. In what ways is the civil rights movement like the American Revolution? How is it different?

CHAPTER 25

Winning the Revolutionary War

The Battle of Yorktown.

BEFORE YOU BEGIN THE CHAPTER

Know What to Look For

1. During a war, there are always some men who are especially brave. Because of their brave actions, these men are thought of as heroes. The American Revolution produced many great heroes. Among them were many black men. One black hero was Salem Poor. He was cited, or spoken of in a report, by his commanding officer for his outstanding bravery during the Battle of Bunker Hill.

Wars are not won by heroes alone. A nation must have many other things to win. It must have good leaders who plan their strategy, or moves in the war, well. A nation must also have a strong army and navy, and its forces must work together as a team. In this chapter, you will read about the events of the Revolutionary War and the peace treaty which ended the war.

page 162

2. Read the title of the chapter. Then look through the chapter and read each heading. In what section of the colonies was the Revolutionary War finally won?

3. Look at the pictures in the chapter and read each caption. What are the Americans doing in the picture on page 162? Examine the map on page 164. What is the title of the map? What symbol is used to show American victory? British advance? Notice also the time line at the beginning of the chapter. What years are included in this chapter? Compare this chapter time line to the unit time line on page 131.

4. Read the last part of the chapter called Summing Up. In what year was the peace treaty signed with Great Brittain? What is the topic of the next chapter?

THE YEARS OF THIS CHAPTER ARE 1775 TO 1783

1619   1775 1783

Know This Important Term

Treaty of Paris

Know the Main Idea

Here is the MAIN IDEA of this chapter.

After many years of hard fighting, the new American nation won its independence from Great Britain.

Keep this MAIN IDEA in mind as you study the chapter. Ask yourself the following questions as you read. They will help you remember the MAIN IDEA.

1. Where did the British army attack after it was forced to leave Boston?

2. What battle is considered the turning point of the Revolutionary War?

3. What battle marked the end of the fighting in the Revolutionary War?

THE CHAPTER LESSON BEGINS HERE

Black Americans Fought in the War

When the Revolutionary War broke out, no group was more eager to serve in the American army than black Americans. They fought bravely at the battles of Lexington, Concord, and Bunker Hill. However, when the American army was formed by the Continental Congress in 1775, no new black soldiers were allowed to join it. Later, when more soldiers were needed, black men were able to join the American army.

Before the Revolutionary War was over, about 5 thousand black soldiers—both free and slave—fought side by side with white troops. Many black men also served in the American navy. And some slaves won their freedom by fighting on the British side.

The British Captured New York and Philadelphia

After the British army was forced to leave Boston in 1776, the British decided to attack New York City. Although General Washington fought hard, he was not able to stop the British from taking New York. The following year, a British army also took over the city of Philadelphia. However, the British did not follow up these victories.

The American Victory at Saratoga Brought Help from France

Meanwhile, another British army, led by General John Burgoyne (bur-GOYN), marched south from Canada to attack New England. Burgoyne planned to cut New England off

THE MAIN BATTLES OF THE REVOLUTIONARY WAR

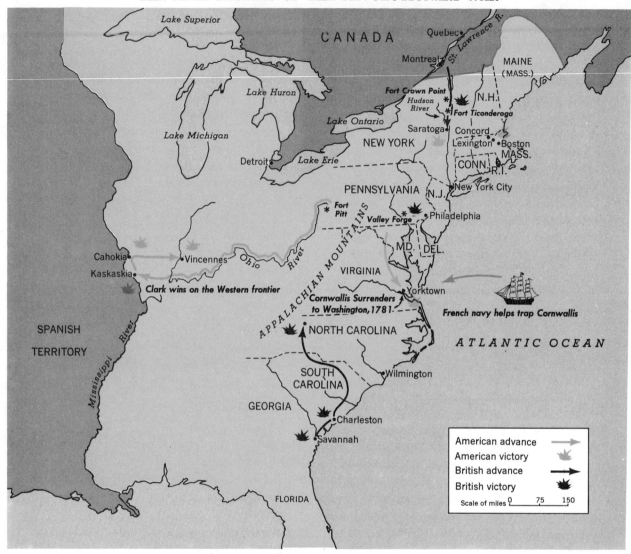

CANADA

Lake Superior

Quebec

Montreal

MAINE
(MASS.)

Fort Crown Point

N.H.

Hudson River

Fort Ticonderoga

Saratoga

Concord

Lexington

Boston

MASS.

NEW YORK

CONN.

R.I.

Lake Huron

Lake Ontario

Lake Michigan

Detroit

Lake Erie

PENNSYLVANIA

N.J.

New York City

Fort Pitt

Valley Forge

Philadelphia

Cahokia

Vincennes

Ohio River

MD.

DEL.

Kaskaskia

VIRGINIA

Yorktown

Clark wins on the Western frontier

APPALACHIAN MOUNTAINS

Cornwallis Surrenders
to Washington, 1781

French navy helps trap Cornwallis

SPANISH

TERRITORY

NORTH CAROLINA

ATLANTIC OCEAN

Mississippi River

SOUTH
CAROLINA

Wilmington

GEORGIA

Charleston

Savannah

American advance
American victory
British advance
British victory

Scale of miles 0   75   150

FLORIDA

from the other American states. However, an American army surrounded Burgoyne's army, and he was trapped at Saratoga in New York State. Burgoyne had to surrender his whole army to the Americans.

The Battle of Saratoga, fought in October, 1777, was the turning point of the Revolutionary War. It was the greatest victory won by either side up to that time. After the

Battle of Saratoga, the French government decided to help the United States.

The British Tried to Make Peace

Almost from the beginning of the Revolutionary War, the British government hoped to make peace with the Americans as soon as possible. This is one reason why General Howe did not follow up his victories at New

Some battles of the Revolutionary War were fought at sea. Here, the American ship "Bon Homme Richard" is in battle with a British ship.

York and Philadelphia. When the British government heard that France was going to help the United States, it decided to act quickly.

In 1778, the British government offered the United States freedom from taxation, the repeal of all the British laws passed since 1763, and pardons for all the leaders of the Revolution. However, the British offer came too late. With France backing them, the Americans demanded complete independence from Great Britain. But the British government refused to agree to this.

The Americans Won
Important Victories in the West

Most of the important fighting in the year 1778 took place along the Western frontier. During the war, the British encouraged the Indians to attack American frontier settlements north of the Ohio River. The state of Virginia sent George Rogers Clark, a frontier leader, to end these attacks. Clark captured several British forts in what are today Indiana and Illinois. Clark's victories stopped the Indian attacks and gave the United States a strong claim to this Western frontier land after the war ended.

The Americans Fought at Sea

During the war, the United States built up a navy. Although the American navy was very small, it fought bravely. The great American naval leader and hero of the Revolutionary War was John Paul Jones. He did a great deal of damage to British shipping. But it was the French navy that helped the Americans win the greatest victory of the war.

The Americans Won the War in the South

In 1778, the British decided that their best chance to win the war was to take over the Southern states. By the end of 1778, Georgia was captured. In 1780, South Carolina was captured. And in 1781, the British army, led

General Cornwallis surrenders his army to General Washington at Yorktown. This American victory ended the war.

by General Charles Cornwallis (korn-WALL-us), marched into North Carolina and Virginia. General Cornwallis settled at Yorktown, Virginia, and he set up a base there.

George Washington moved his army from New York to Yorktown, and the American army surrounded the British army at Yorktown. General Cornwallis and his army tried to escape by sea. However, a French fleet defeated a British fleet off the Virginia coast, and this prevented Cornwallis from escaping by sea. Cornwallis was trapped, and in October, 1781, he surrendered his army to General Washington.

A Peace Treaty Was Signed

After the American victory at Yorktown, Great Britain knew it was not possible to win the war. By 1782, the British government and the British people decided that they must end the war and make peace with the United States. Great Britain still hoped that America might remain part of the British empire, but

it was willing to agree to America's independence.

Benjamin Franklin, John Adams, and John Jay went to Great Britain to work on a peace treaty to end the war. In 1783, the **Treaty of Paris,** which ended the war, was signed. The treaty included the following four points:

1. The United States became an independent nation.

2. The Mississippi River became the western boundary of the United States.

3. American fishermen were allowed to fish off the coast of Newfoundland.

4. Great Britain gave Florida back to Spain.

Summing Up

After years of hard fighting, the new American nation won its independence. The peace treaty with Great Britain was signed in 1783. In the next chapter, which begins Unit 7, you will find out about important changes in America after the Revolutionary War.

AFTER YOU READ THE CHAPTER

Do You Know This Important Term?

For the sentence below, choose the term that best completes it.

The Treaty of (**Paris**/**London**) in 1783 ended the Revolutionary War.

Do You Remember These People?

Tell something about each of the following persons.

William Howe   John Burgoyne
George Rogers Clark   John Paul Jones
Charles Cornwallis   George Washington
Benjamin Franklin   John Adams
John Jay

Can You Locate These Places?

Use the map on page 164 to do the following map work.

1. Locate the place where the battle of Saratoga was fought. In which state was it fought? Who was victorious?
2. Name and locate the battles that were important to the Americans in the West.
3. Follow the British advance through the South. What port cities were captured? Locate the place where the battle of Yorktown was fought.

Do You Know When It Happened?

What are the years of this chapter? Place the following events in the order in which they occurred.

George Rogers Clark captured British forts in the West.

The British attacked New York City.

The victory at Saratoga made France an ally of the Americans.

The peace treaty ending the Revolutionary War was signed.

Cornwallis surrendered to the American forces at Yorktown.

Discovering More About the Main Idea

After many years of hard fighting, the new American nation won its independence from Great Britain.

Tell how each of the following developments is related to the MAIN IDEA.

Many black men served in the armed forces of both sides.

After the battle of Saratoga, France decided to enter the war on the side of the Americans, and Britain tried to end the war.

Great Britain was unable to capture and hold all three sections of the American states at the same time. In the later years of the war, Great Britain decided its best chance to win the war was to take over the Southern states.

After the army surrendered at Yorktown, the British made peace and recognized the independence of the new nation.

Can You Discuss the Chapter?

Use the information you learned in this chapter to answer the following questions.

1. Why did some black men fight on the side of the British during the Revolution?
2. How did Britain try to make peace with the United States in 1778?
3. Why were American victories in the West important?
4. What four agreements were included in the Treaty of Paris of 1783?

Can You Connect the Past and the Present?

1. When dealing with other nations, a country will often not "show its hand" until it feels it has an advantage. How did France follow this idea during the American Revolution?
2. What might have happened to the United States if the British were successful in stopping the Revolution?

PART II

Building The American Nation

1783 to 1865

THE UNITS IN PART II ARE

Unit 7 Building A Strong New Government

Unit 8 America Deals with Other Nations

Unit 9 The Sections of the Nation

Unit 10 Americans Enjoy More Freedom

Unit 11 American Life From 1800 to 1860

Unit 12 America Spreads from Coast to Coast

Unit 13 Americans Fight a Terrible War

Building A Strong New Government

The Founding Fathers sign the Constitution.

THE CHAPTERS IN UNIT 7 ARE

CHAPTER 26   The Confederation Government
CHAPTER 27   The Constitution of the United States
CHAPTER 28   The Nation's New Government
CHAPTER 29   President Washington's Second Term
CHAPTER 30   President Adams and President Jefferson

THE YEARS OF THIS UNIT ARE 1776 TO 1804

| 1700 | 1776 | 1804 | 1975 |

CHAPTER 26

The Confederation Government

General Washington is cheered in New York City.

BEFORE YOU BEGIN THE CHAPTER

Know What to Look For

1. Airline passengers flying over the Midwestern part of the United States for the first time are often interested in the checkerboard pattern made by the roads, fields of grain, and the fences separating one farm from another. This checkerboard pattern did not develop by accident. It was the result of the Land Ordinance passed by the new government of the United States in 1787. Under this law, the land was measured and divided up into one-mile squares and, therefore, from the air the land looks like a giant checkerboard.

This same land law also set up a plan of government for new lands added to the United States. It was the most important law passed by the new government set up by the Articles of Confederation. All American states were settled under the plan set up by this law. As you read this chapter you will see that the new government set up by the Articles of Confederation was too weak.

2. Read the title of the chapter. Then look through the chapter and read each heading. Name three topics that will be discussed in more detail in the chapter.

3. Look at the pictures in the chapter and read each caption. What is happening in the picture on page 170? Study the map on page 173. Locate the Northwest Territory. Note also the time line at the beginning of the chapter. What years are included in this chapter? Compare the chapter time line to the unit time line on page 169.

4. Read the last part of the chapter called Summing Up. What was the main problem of the nation's first government?

bill of rights
Articles of Confederation

Northwest Ordinance
territory
Shays' Rebellion

Here is the MAIN IDEA of this chapter.
Many important changes took place in American life after the Revolution. The first national government proved to be too weak for the nation.

Keep this MAIN IDEA in mind as you study the chapter. Ask yourself the following questions as you read. They will help you remember the MAIN IDEA.

1. In which groups of states did slavery come to an end after the Revolution?

2. How many states had to agree before the national government might pass a law?

3. What event finally made many people realize the new government was too weak and that the nation needed a stronger government?

THE YEARS OF THIS CHAPTER ARE 1776 TO 1787

1776   1787   1804

THE CHAPTER LESSON BEGINS HERE

The Revolution Improved American Life

The American Revolution brought about many important changes in America. After the war, many states raised money to open new elementary schools, high schools, and even colleges. Laws were changed so that prisoners were treated more fairly. And most states no longer had official churches.

The Revolution Helped End Slavery in some States

Many Americans believed that slavery had no place in the new nation and that all Americans must have freedom. A large number of slaves won their freedom by fighting in the Revolutionary War. Within twenty years after the end of the war, many New England and Middle states passed laws to abolish, or to end, slavery.

For a while, it looked as if the Southern states might also do away with slavery. Some of the Southern states passed laws which stopped people from bringing in new slaves and which made it easier to free the slaves already there. But the growers of rice and

page 171

Thomas Cushing

Q. WALKER—FREE MAN

Was his name Quork, Quock, Quaco, or Quarko? No one is sure. But it is certain that his last name was Walker. And he was a man who was not afraid to stand up for his rights.

Walker was a slave belonging to Dr. Nathaniel Jennison. Dr. Jennison's wife, before she died, promised to free Walker when he was twenty years old. But Walker was now twenty-eight years old, and he was still a slave. Therefore, he ran away. Dr. Jennison and some of his friends caught Walker and beat him.

In 1781, Walker took Dr. Jennison to court for beating him. Dr. Jennison was found guilty of beating Walker. Dr. Jennison appealed the case to the Supreme Court of Massachusetts. In the Supreme Court trial, Dr. Jennison claimed he had the right to beat Walker because Walker was his slave. But Chief Justice Thomas Cushing pointed out that the Massachusetts constitution of 1780 said that "all men are born free and equal." He declared that this meant Walker was a free man. This decision was an important one. It not only gave Walker his freedom, but it also outlawed slavery in Massachusetts.

indigo still believed that they needed slaves. And the invention of the cotton gin by Eli Whitney in 1793 greatly increased the demand for slaves in the South.

The States Wrote New Constitutions

During the Revolutionary War, all the states except Connecticut and Rhode Island drew up new constitutions, or plans of government. Almost all of these constitutions contained a **bill of rights,** or a list of freedoms, that all the people of the state were to have. These freedoms usually included the right to worship as they wished, the right to meet together, the right to speak and to write as they wished, and the right to a fair trial.

The new state constitutions were very much alike. All the state constitutions except one set up a two-house legislature. All of them gave the governors less power. And most states allowed only property owners to vote or hold office. However, this was not very unfair because many more Americans owned land after the American Revolution. Some men were given land for fighting in the Revolutionary War. Many other men were able to buy land which belonged to Loyalists, who left the United States during or after the war. All these men were now able to vote.

Articles of Confederation

As early as 1776, the Continental Congress began to work on a plan for a national government, or a government for the whole nation. In 1781, this plan, called the **Articles of Confederation** (kun-FED-uh-RAY-shun), was finally approved by all the states.

The Articles of Confederation set up the first national government for the new nation. Since the states did not want to give up their powers, the Confederation government was a weak government. It had no single leader such as a President to head the government.

Instead, the nation was governed by a one-house legislature. Each state had one vote in this Congress. Nine of the thirteen states had to agree before Congress passed any important laws. But the most important weakness of the Confederation government was that the Congress did not have the power to make laws about trade or to raise taxes.

Congress Passed an Important Land Law for the Nation

Although the Congress of the Confedera-tion was weak, it did pass an important land law in 1787. This law, called the **Northwest Ordinance** (OR-duh-nuns), set up a plan for settling and governing the Northwest Terri-tory, or the land north of the Ohio River. This law forbade slavery in the Northwest Ter-ritory.

The Northwest Ordinance also set up a plan for organizing new states. When 5 thou-sand people lived in any part of the North-west Territory, this part was organized as a **territory.** A territory was an area owned by

THE NORTHWEST TERRITORY

Boundary not certain

BRITISH TERRITORY
(CANADA)

Claimed by the United States and Great Britain

Lake Superior

Lake Huron

Lake Michigan

Lake Ontario

Lake Erie

MAINE
(Mass.)

N.H.

NEW YORK

MASS.

CONN. R.I.

NORTHWEST TERRITORY

PENNSYLVANIA

N.J.

DEL.

Ohio River

MARYLAND

Mississippi River

VIRGINIA

ATLANTIC OCEAN

SPANISH TERRITORY

NORTH CAROLINA

SOUTH CAROLINA

Claimed by the United States and Spain

GEORGIA

The United States in 1787

Boundary of the Northwest Territory

British fur-trading posts

GULF OF MEXICO

SPANISH TERRITORY
(FLORIDA)

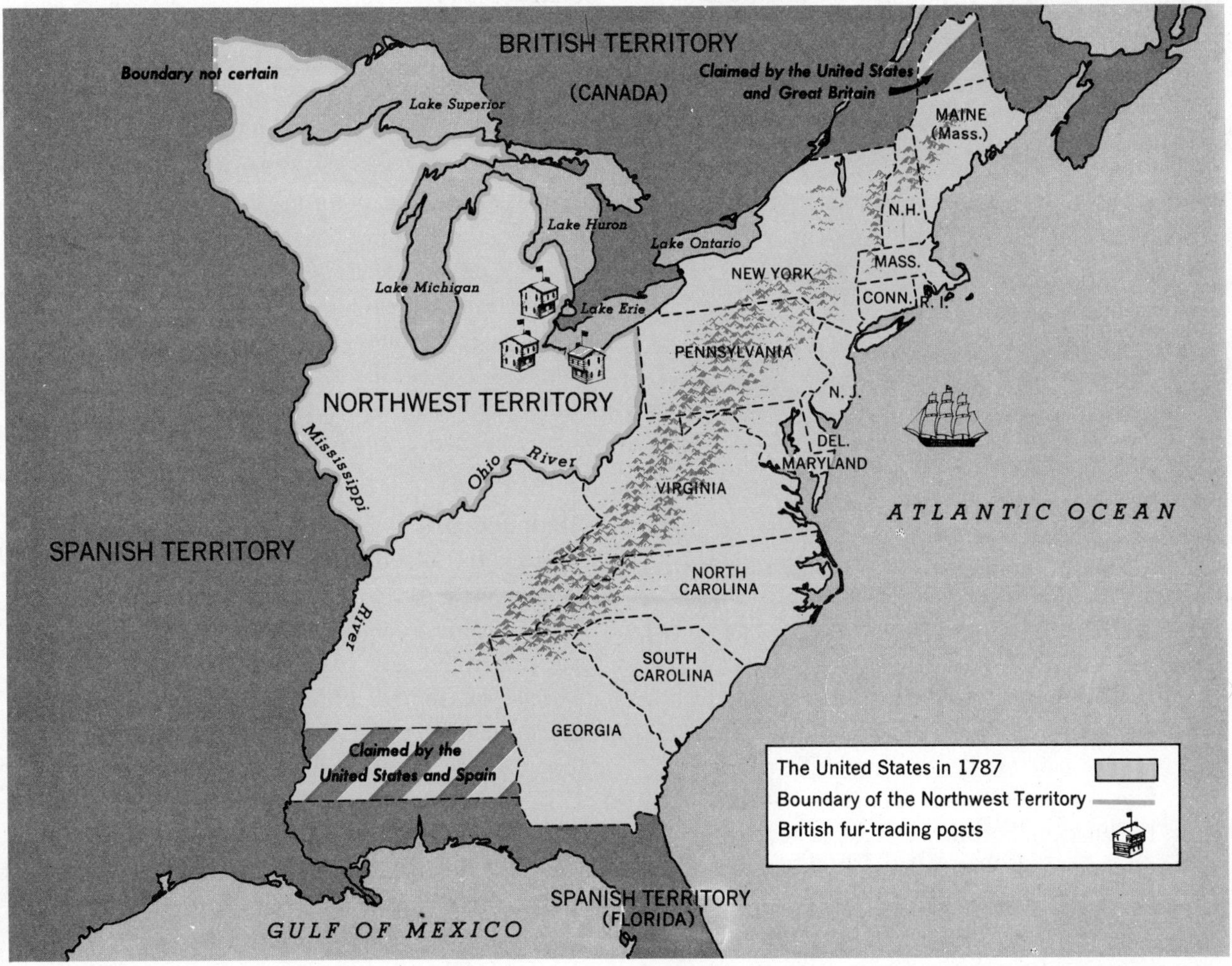

A scene in Shays' Rebellion. This uprising showed that the American government was too weak.

the United States which was later able to become a state. When 60 thousand settlers lived in any part of the Northwest Territory, they had the right to ask Congress to allow this territory to become a state. The Northwest Ordinance declared that new states were to be fully equal to the thirteen original states. This plan helped the nation to grow.

The Confederation Government Was Too Weak

The Congress under the Confederation passed a good land law, but Congress was weak and lacked the powers to settle the nation's problems. Congress never had enough money. Therefore, Congress had very little power over the states, and it was not able to make the states obey the laws it passed. And since the Confederation government had no army, it was not able to stop Britain or Spain from stirring up the Indians on the Western frontier.

By 1785, hard times came to the United States. Many farmers lost their land because they had no money to pay their debts or their taxes. In the winter of 1786–1787, the farmers of western Massachusetts banded together to force the state government to help them. The leader of this rebellion, or uprising, was Daniel Shays, a captain in the Revolutionary War.

The Congress of the Confederation had no troops to put down **Shays' Rebellion.** Finally, Shays and his followers were defeated by an army raised by the state of Massachusetts. Many Americans now realized that the United States needed a much stronger national government.

Summing Up

After the Revolutionary War, many important changes took place in American life. Slavery came to an end in many states. Most states wrote new constitutions. And the Articles of Confederation set up the first national government for the new nation. Although this government was too weak, in 1787 it passed an important land law, the Northwest Ordinance. In the next chapter, you will learn how the Constitution was written. It set up a new plan of government for the nation.

AFTER YOU READ THE CHAPTER

Do You Know These Important Terms?

For each sentence below, select the term that best completes the sentence.

1. A list of freedoms that all people were to have was written in the (**preamble/bill of rights**) of the new state constitutions.
2. The plan of national government approved by all the states was called the (**Confederation of States/Articles of Confederation**).
3. The (**Northwest Ordinance/Ohio Land Act**) set up a plan for settling and governing the land north of the Ohio River.
4. A (**protectorate/territory**) was an area owned by the United States which was later able to become a state.
5. (**Shays'/Paxton's**) Rebellion proved the new government was too weak and lacked the power to settle the nation's problems.

Can You Locate These Places?

Use the map on page 173 to do the following map work.

1. Name the large lakes that border or touch the Northwest Territory. What river marks its western boundary? What river marks its southern boundary?
2. Locate areas where two nations claim the same land. What nations are involved in these disputes?

Do You Know When It Happened?

What are the years of this chapter? Find the following dates in the chapter and tell why each is important.

1781   1787   1786

Discovering More About the Main Idea

Many important changes took place in American life after the Revolution. The first national government proved to be too weak for the nation.

Tell how each of the following developments is related to the MAIN IDEA.

After the war, new laws made changes in education, the treatment of prisoners, official churches, slavery, individual freedoms, and voting qualifications.

The government under the Articles of Confederation did not have the power to make laws about trade or to raise taxes.

The new government passed a land law which set up a plan for settling and organizing new lands.

Can You Discuss the Chapter?

Use the information you learned in this chapter to answer the following questions.

1. Why was slavery not ended in the South at the same time it was ended in many of the New England and Middle states?
2. Why was the fact that most states only allowed property owners to vote really not too unfair after the American Revolution?
3. Describe how the first national government was set up under the Articles of Confederation.
4. How did the plan for organizing new states under the Northwest Ordinance work?
5. Do you think a strong or a weak national government is better? Why?

Can You Connect the Past and the Present?

1. Earlier you found out that the colonial assemblies were powerful because they controlled money and taxes in the colony. Explain how the new government set up by the Articles of Confederation did not have this important power. Who controls this governmental power in your community?
2. What are our two newest states? When did they become states?

CHAPTER 27

The Constitution of the United States

Independence Hall in Philadelphia.

BEFORE YOU BEGIN THE CHAPTER

Know What to Look For

1. Benjamin Franklin was a remarkable man. During his long and busy life, he won fame as a publisher, writer, scientist, inventor, and American leader. A list of his inventions and the groups he started would cover pages.

Whenever he saw a need, Franklin tried to find a way to meet it. He invented America's first practical stove, eye glasses, the lightning rod, street lamps, and many other useful things. He set up Philadelphia's first fire department and first public library.

When he was eighty-one, he and other American leaders faced the most important job of their careers. They had to improve the nation's government. In the last chapter, you read how the government set up by the Articles of Confederation was too weak to solve the nation's problems. In this chapter, you will find out how a new and stronger national government was formed.

2. Read the title of the chapter. Then look through the chapter and read each heading. Using only the information in the headings tell what American leaders did about the weaknesses in the government.

3. Look at the pictures in the chapter and read each caption. Can you name any of the men in the picture who are signing the Constitution? Note also the time line at the beginning of the chapter. What years are included in this chapter? Compare the chapter time line to the unit time line on page 169.

4. Read the last part of the chapter called Summing Up. How were the powers of government divided under the Constitution?

Know These Important Terms

Constitutional   executive branch
  Convention   legislative branch

Great Compromise   judicial branch
federal government   separation of powers

Know the Main Idea

Here is the MAIN IDEA of this chapter.

American leaders met to strengthen the nation's government. They succeeded in establishing a stronger plan for governing the nation under a new constitution.

Keep this MAIN IDEA in mind as you study the chapter. Ask yourself the following questions as you read. They will help you remember the MAIN IDEA.

1. How many American leaders met in Philadelphia in May, 1787? Who were some of these leaders?

2. What were the powers given to the President?

3. In a federal government, how are the powers of government divided?

4. Name the three branches, or parts, of the federal government.

THE YEARS OF THIS CHAPTER ARE 1787 TO 1788

1776   1787   1788   1804

THE CHAPTER LESSON BEGINS HERE

American Leaders Decided a New Constitution Was Necessary

If you remember, many Americans realized that the Articles of Confederation were too weak. They felt that the national government had to be made stronger. In May of 1787, an outstanding group of Americans met in Philadelphia, Pennsylvania, to work out a plan to make the national government stronger. George Washington, James Madison, Alexander Hamilton, and Benjamin Franklin were among the fifty-five men who attended these meetings, which were held in Independence

Hall. Most of these men served before in state governments or in the Continental Congress.

At first, these leaders planned only to improve the Articles of Confederation. Soon, however, they decided that they must write a new constitution which gave more power to the national government. The men who met in Philadelphia became the Founding Fathers of this new government, and the meeting became known as the **Constitutional Convention.**

The Founding Fathers Wrote the Constitution

In writing the Constitution of the United States, the Founding Fathers had many problems to overcome. They had to decide if Congress—the law-making group—was to have one or two houses. They had to decide how to elect members to Congress. They also had to decide what powers to give to Congress, and to the President, and whether to set up national courts. And they had to decide what to do about slavery.

The Founding Fathers worked on the Constitution from May until September of 1787. They had to please both the large states and the small states. They also had to please both Northerners and Southerners. And they had to write a constitution which set up a national government strong enough to govern the country well, but not so strong that it took freedom away from the people.

A Two-House Congress Was Formed

While they wrote the Constitution, the Founding Fathers settled their problems by making compromises, or agreements in which both sides got only part of what they wanted. For example, the small states wanted all the states to have the same number of members, or representatives (REP-rih-ZENT-uh-tivz), in Congress. The large states wanted to have more representatives in Congress than the small states.

The Constitutional Convention finally decided that Congress was to be made up of two houses—the Senate and the House of Representatives. Each state was to elect two members to the Senate. Each state was to elect members to the House of Representatives according to the number of people in the state. This plan was called the **Great Compromise,** and it pleased both the large states and the small states.

This picture shows an artist's idea of the Founding Fathers signing the Constitution of the United States.

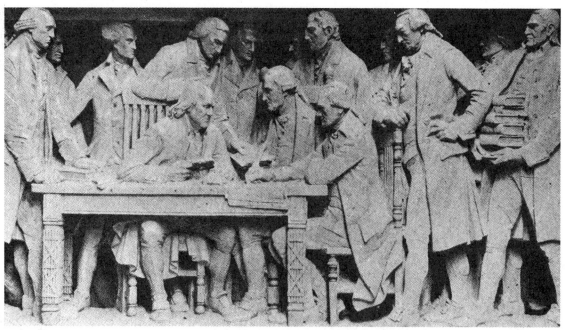

Samuel F. B. Morse, *The Old House of Representatives.* In the Collection of the Corcoran Gallery of Art.

The Constitution set up a Congress made up of two houses. Here, one house, the House of Representatives, is shown.

Congress Was Given Important Powers

If you remember, under the Articles of Confederation, the national government was not able to make laws to control trade between the states or with other nations. Nor was it able to raise taxes. The Founding Fathers gave both these important powers to the new Congress. They also gave the new Congress many other powers.

A President Headed the Government

Another weakness of the Articles of Confederation was that the nation had no leader to see that the laws passed by Congress were carried out. Therefore, the new Constitution provided for a President. The President was to be the highest official in the nation's government. And he was given the powers to

lead the nation and to make sure that the laws passed by Congress were carried out.

A Supreme Court Was Formed

Under the Articles of Confederation, the national government had no courts of its own. The new Constitution provided for a Supreme Court and for other national courts to be formed under it.

The Constitution and Slavery

Although some of the Founding Fathers were against slavery, they did not try to settle the slavery problem at the Constitutional Convention. The Founding Fathers were determined to set up a new and stronger government. But Southerners were sure to leave the Constitutional Convention if North-

page 179

The Constitution is read so Americans can think about the new plan of government.

The Constitution Formed a New Type of Government

In the Constitution, the Founding Fathers drew up a plan for a **federal government.** In a federal government, the powers of government are divided between the national government and the state governments. For example, the national government has the power to declare war and to coin money. The state governments have the power to make laws about such matters as marriage and divorce.

The powers of the federal government were divided between three separate branches, or parts, of the government. The **executive branch** was headed by the President. The **legislative branch** was made up of the Congress. And the **judicial branch** was made up of the federal courts. This **separation of powers,** or division of powers, among the three branches of government allowed each branch to serve as a check on the other branches.

Most Americans liked this separation of powers between the national and state governments, and between the three branches of the federal government. They believed that the new Constitution formed a government that was strong enough to rule the country well. Yet the separation of powers in the government protected the freedoms Americans won during the American Revolution.

Summing Up

The Founding Fathers wrote a Constitution that gave the nation a strong national government. The Constitution set up a federal government in which the powers of the government were divided between the national government and the state governments. In the next chapter, you will find out how the new government set up under the Constitution worked out its problems.

erners talked about ending slavery. Therefore, the problem of slavery was not dealt with. Many Americans believed that slavery was going to end by itself in a short time anyway. The Constitution, however, did not allow any more slaves to be brought into the United States after the year 1808.

AFTER YOU READ THE CHAPTER

Do You Know These Important Terms?

For each sentence below, choose the term that best completes the sentence.

1. The meeting where the new plan of government was drawn up was called the (**Independence/Constitutional**) Convention.
2. The plan which set up a two-house Congress and which pleased both the large and small states was the (**Great Compromise/Three-fifth Compromise**).
3. A (**federal/republican**) government is one in which the powers of government are divided between the national government and the state governments.
4. The (**executive/legislative**) branch was headed by the President.
5. The (**executive/legislative**) branch was made up of the Congress.
6. The federal courts are under the (**monetary/judicial**) branch of government.
7. Each branch of government serves as a check on the other two branches. This is called (**division of labor/separation of powers**).

Do You Remember These People?

Tell something about each of the following persons.

George Washington   James Madison
Alexander Hamilton   Benjamin Franklin

Do You Know When It Happened?

What are the years of this chapter? Tell why each of the following dates is important.

1787   1808

Discovering More About the Main Idea

American leaders met to strengthen the nation's government. They succeeded in establishing a stronger plan for governing the nation under a new constitution.

Tell how each of the following developments is related to the MAIN IDEA.

The Constitution established a Congress made up of two houses which pleased both the large states and the small states.

The Constitutional Convention drew up a plan for a federal government in which the powers of government were divided between the national government and the state governments.

The Constitution established a national government with three separate branches.

Can You Discuss the Chapter?

Use the information you learned in this chapter to answer the following questions.

1. How did the Great Compromise solve the problem of how many representatives each state was to have?
2. Why was the slavery problem not settled at the Constitutional Convention? What did the Constitution say about allowing new slaves into the United States?
3. What are the three branches of the national government? What does each branch do?
4. Why did most Americans like the new form of government set up by the Constitutional Convention?

Can You Connect the Past and the Present?

1. The Founding Fathers made it possible to change the Constitution to fit changing needs. Are any changes in the Constitution being considered at the present time?
2. How do the people in your local community feel about the powers of the national government and the state governments? Should the state governments have more power? the national government?

CHAPTER 28

The Nation's New Government

George Washington is inaugurated as President.

BEFORE YOU BEGIN THE CHAPTER

Know What to Look For

1. On December 23, 1783, General George Washington appeared at a meeting of the Continental Congress in Annapolis, Maryland. Here he resigned, or gave up his job, as commander in chief of the Continental army. At this time, Washington was the most powerful man in America. Some Americans urged him to take over the government. But Washington had just fought a long, hard war

because he believed the American nation should be ruled by the people, not by a king or an army. When George Washington walked down the aisle and left the meeting, he was just another American citizen on his way home for Christmas.

Washington did not realize that in six years, he was to be called to serve his nation again. Only this time he was to become the first President of the United States. In this chapter, you will read how the new government set up by the Constitution was started.

2. Read the title of the chapter. Then look through the chapter and read each heading. From the headings, can you tell what problem the new government faced?

3. Look at the pictures in the chapter and read each caption. What is happening in the picture on page 182? Note also the time line at the beginning of the chapter. What years are included in this chapter? Compare this chapter time line to the unit time line on page 169.

4. Read the last part of the chapter called Summing Up. What information does this paragraph contain about the chapter? What is the topic of the next chapter?

Know These Important Terms

Anti-Federalists Secretary of War
Federalists   Attorney General

Cabinet   amendments
Secretary of State Bill of Rights
Secretary of the unconstitutional
 Treasury

Know the Main Idea

Here is the MAIN IDEA of this chapter.

The Constitution was approved, and under George Washington's leadership as President the new government got off to a good start.

Keep this MAIN IDEA in mind as you study the chapter. Ask yourself the following questions as you read. They will help you remember the MAIN IDEA.

1. Why did some people not favor the Constitution?

2. What name was given to the group of men President Washington asked to help him lead the government?

3. What problem did President Washington face in the Northwest Territory?

THE YEARS OF THIS CHAPTER ARE 1788 TO 1796

1776	1788	1796	1804

THE CHAPTER LESSON BEGINS HERE

The Constitution Was Approved

After the Constitution was finished, it had to be approved by nine states before it went into operation. The men who supported the Constitution had a hard time getting the American people to approve the Constitution. Some Americans felt that the Constitution gave the President too much power. Others did not want to approve the Constitution because it did not have a bill of rights.

People who did not favor the Constitution were called **Anti-Federalists** (AN-ti-FED-uh-ruhl-ists). The people who supported the Constitution were called **Federalists** (FED-uh-ruhl-ists). The Federalists were well organized, and they worked very hard in order to get the Constitution approved. They promised to add a bill of rights to the Constitution. By the summer of 1788, most of the states had approved the Constitution, and it became the new plan of government of the United States.

Washington Became President of the New Government

George Washington became the leader of

THE FIRST THIRTEEN STATES

No.	State	Year It Approved the Constitution
1.	Delaware	December 7, 1787
2.	Pennsylvania	December 12, 1787
3.	New Jersey	December 18, 1787
4.	Georgia	January 2, 1788
5.	Connecticut	January 9, 1788
6.	Massachusetts	February 6, 1788
7.	Maryland	April 28, 1788
8.	South Carolina	May 23, 1788
9.	New Hampshire	June 21, 1788
10.	Virginia	June 26, 1788
11.	New York	July 26, 1788
12.	North Carolina	November 21, 1789
13.	Rhode Island	May 29, 1790

the new government when he was elected the first President of the United States in 1789. The American people trusted Washington, and he was one of the most popular men in the country. Washington was sworn in as President in New York City.

President Washington asked several outstanding men to help him lead the new American government. This group of men became known as the President's **Cabinet.** Thomas Jefferson was **Secretary of State** in the Cabinet, and he advised Washington on how to deal with foreign nations. Alexander Hamilton became **Secretary of the Treasury,** and he advised Washington on money problems. The two other cabinet officers were Henry Knox, the **Secretary of War,** and Edmund Randolph, the **Attorney** (uh-TUR-nee) **General.**

The Bill of Rights Was Added to the Constitution

One of the first and most important laws Congress passed was the Judiciary (joo-DISH-e-er-ee) Act. This act set up the system of federal courts. Congress also suggested ten amendments (uh-MEND-munts), or changes, to be added to the Constitution. These first ten amendments were called the **Bill of Rights.** The Bill of Rights promised all American citizens many important rights, or freedoms. These freedoms included the right to worship as they wished, the right to speak and to write as they wished, the right to meet together, and the right to a fair trial.

Hamilton Developed a Plan to Pay Government Debts

One of the big problems facing the new American government was money. The government owed money it had borrowed from its own citizens and from foreign nations during the Revolutionary War. Some states also owed money they had borrowed to fight the war. Alexander Hamilton, who was the Secretary of the Treasury, developed a plan to pay both these debts. Hamilton wanted the federal government, or national government, to pay back in full the money owed by the states and by the federal government.

Hamilton's Plan Was Approved

All the states agreed that the federal government's debt should be paid. However, the Southern states were against the federal government paying the state debts. Most of the Southern states had already paid their debts, and they did not want to be taxed to help pay the debts of the other states.

However, with the help of Thomas Jefferson, Hamilton was able to get his plan through Congress. Congress voted to pay the federal debt in full. And the Southern states

President George Washington meets with his Cabinet. The men in the Cabinet helped the President run the government.

agreed to the federal government paying the state debts. In return, the capital of the United States was to be located in the South, the present-day Washington, D.C.

Hamilton Planned a National Bank

Hamilton next asked Congress to approve the setting up of a national bank. This national bank was to be owned both by the government and private citizens. The bank was to hold the federal government's tax collections and to print paper money for the nation. Many people disapproved of a national bank. Some Americans thought that the bank favored only the rich merchants and businessmen of the North.

Thomas Jefferson was against a national bank because he thought it was **unconstitutional.** That is, he did not believe that Congress had the power to open a bank because the Constitution did not give Congress this power. Hamilton argued that the Constitution gave Congress the power to do whatever was necessary to carry on the government's work. Congress and President Washington agreed with Hamilton. Congress approved the bank, and the Bank of the United States opened in 1791.

Anthony Wayne makes a peace treaty with the Indians. This treaty made the Northwest Territory safe for American settlement.

Courtesy Chicago Historical Society.

The West Settled Down

While the new government was working out its problems, thousands of Americans were moving westward to the frontier lands gained in the Revolutionary War. During the 1790's, Kentucky, Tennessee, and Vermont became new states. Most of the settlers in these states were farmers. After Spain gave American citizens the right to ship their farm products down the Mississippi River in 1796, the farmers south of the Ohio River began to enjoy good times.

However, the Indians north of the Ohio River in the Northwest Territory continued to attack American frontier settlements. They defeated several armies that President Washington sent against them. In 1794, Anthony Wayne, a famous Revolutionary War general, defeated the Indians at the battle of Fallen Timbers in Ohio. Wayne's victory made the Northwest Territory safe for American settlers for many years afterward.

Summing Up

The Constitution was approved, and it became the new plan of government for the United States. Washington's first term as President was successful. A Cabinet was formed to help the President lead the nation. The Bill of Rights was added to the Constitution. And Alexander Hamilton developed plans which helped settle the nation's money problems. In the next chapter, you will read about Washington's second term as President.

AFTER YOU READ THE CHAPTER

Do You Know These Important Terms?

For each sentence below, choose the term that best completes the sentence.

1. People who did not favor the Constitution were called (**Federalists/Anti-Federalists**).
2. People who favored the Constitution were called (**Federalists/Anti-Federalists**).
3. The group who helps lead the American government is the (**Cabinet/Council**).
4. The (**Secretary of State/Attorney General**) advises the President on how to deal with foreign nations.
5. The (**Cabinet/Secretary of the Treasury**) advises the President on money problems.
6. The man who helped President Washington solve problems of defense was the (**Secretary of War/Chief of Staff**).
7. The (**Attorney General/Congress**) advises the President on the law.
8. Changes in the Constitution are called (**applications/amendments**).
9. The first ten amendments to the Constitution are the (**Bill of Rights/Judiciary Act**).
10. A law that goes against the rules set up in the Constitution is said to be (**illegal/unconstitutional**).

Do You Remember These People?

Tell something about each of the following persons.

George Washington	Thomas Jefferson
Alexander Hamilton	Henry Knox
Edmund Randolph	Anthony Wayne

Can You Locate These Places?

Use the map on page 208 to do the following map work.

1. Locate the new states of Kentucky, Tennessee, and Vermont.
2. Locate the Ohio River and the Northwest Territory.

Do You Know When It Happened?

What are the years of this chapter? Tell why each of the following dates is important.

1789   1794   1796

Discovering More About the Main Idea

The Constitution was approved, and under George Washington's leadership as President the new government got off to a good start.

Tell how each of the following developments is related to the MAIN IDEA.

The first actions of Congress were to pass the Judiciary Act and to add the Bill of Rights to the Constitution.

The money problems of the new nation were solved by the Secretary of the Treasury, Alexander Hamilton.

The Mississippi River was opened to Western farmers in 1796, but the Northwest Territory was largely unsettled at the time.

Can You Discuss the Chapter?

Use the information you learned in this chapter to answer the following questions.

1. What were some of the rights, or freedoms, the Bill of Rights promised?
2. Why were the Southern states against the federal government paying the state debts?
3. Why was Thomas Jefferson against Hamilton's idea of a national bank?
4. Why did farmers south of the Ohio River enjoy good times after they were able to use the Mississippi River?

Can You Connect the Past and the Present?

The Bill of Rights promises certain rights to all American citizens. What recent events in your community have been related to the Bill of Rights?

CHAPTER 29

President Washington's Second Term

Copyright by White House Historical Association.
Photograph by National Geographic Society.

The White House in 1800.

BEFORE YOU BEGIN THE CHAPTER

Know What to Look For

1. In the 1790's, many frontier farmers were not able to haul their crops of grain, such as corn, over the long, rugged forest trails to the markets in the East. To solve this problem, the frontier farmers turned their corn into whisky. They were able to bring the kegs of whisky to the markets in the East easily and cheaply by putting them on pack animals. And the whisky brought good prices in the East.

But under Alexander Hamilton's money plans, the new government placed a tax on whisky. In 1794, farmers in western Pennsylvania refused to pay the new tax. President Washington sent 15 thousand troops to Pennsylvania, and this Whisky Rebellion, as it was called, was ended. The Whisky Rebellion was just one of the problems faced by the new government during President Washington's second term.

2. Read the title of the chapter. Then look through the chapter and read each heading. How many political parties developed in the United States?

3. Look at the pictures in the chapter and read each caption. What differences do you see between the White House in the early 1800's and the White House today? Note also the time line at the beginning of the chapter. What years are included in this chapter? Compare the chapter time line to the unit time line on page 169.

4. Read the last part of the chapter called Summing Up. Who was elected President in 1796?

Know These Important Terms
neutral   **Republican Party**

political parties   **Farewell Address**
Federalist Party

Know the Main Idea
Here is the MAIN IDEA of this chapter.
During Washington's second term, the United States was able to stay out of a war. Two political parties developed, and John Adams was elected as the second President.

Keep this MAIN IDEA in mind as you study the chapter. Ask yourself the following questions as you read. They will help you remember the MAIN IDEA.

1. A war between what two nations caused problems for the United States during President Washington's second term?

2. Name the first two political parties to develop in the United States.

3. Who was elected President in 1796? To which political party did he belong? Who became the Vice-President?

THE YEARS OF THIS CHAPTER ARE 1792 TO 1796

1776		1792	1796		1804

THE CHAPTER LESSON BEGINS HERE

Washington Was Elected for a Second Term

When George Washington became President, the bad times of the 1780's were ending and good times for the nation were beginning. Farmers, businessmen, ship owners, and shop keepers earned a good living. Many Americans believed that the new Constitution and the new government had helped to bring about these good times for the country.

At the end of his first term, George Washington did not wish to run for a second term. But most Americans wanted him to become President for a second term. Washington finally agreed to run for a second term, and he was reelected President in 1792.

The United States Tried to Stay Out of War

At the beginning of Washington's second term in 1793, war broke out between Great Britain and France. This war was a result of the French Revolution, which started in 1789. Great Britain and other European nations

This picture shows election day in Philadelphia. As political parties were formed, elections became exciting events.

went to war with France to crush the Revolution. France expected help from the United States in return for the help it gave the Americans during the Revolutionary War.

Many Americans took sides in the war. Thomas Jefferson favored France in the war. Alexander Hamilton was for Great Britain. But President Washington wanted the United States to stay out of this European war and remain at peace. Therefore, he announced that the United States was **neutral** (NOO-trul), or not taking any side, in the war.

The United States Signed a Treaty with Great Britain

The United States soon found that it was not easy to remain neutral. Ships of the British navy captured American ships that traded with France. Also, Great Britain refused to give up its forts in the Northwest Territory even though these forts were on

American territory. By 1793, it looked as if the United States and Great Britain were heading for war. To prevent war, Washington sent John Jay to Great Britain to try to settle the troubles between the two nations.

Most Americans were not happy with the treaty Jay worked out with Great Britain. In Jay's Treaty, the British promised to give up the forts in the Northwest Territory. But Great Britain refused to stop capturing American ships that traded with France. The Senate barely approved the Jay Treaty. President Washington was not too pleased with Jay's Treaty, but he finally signed it.

Two Political Parties Developed

By the 1790's, Americans were beginning to take sides over what was happening in the United States and in the world. Americans sometimes disagreed about what their new government was to do. They disagreed about setting up the national bank, paying the state governments' debts, and at first, about approving the Constitution. As Americans developed their ideas, they organized **political parties.** Political parties are made up of groups of people who share certain ideas about government and what it must do.

George Washington did not want political parties to develop in the United States. He was afraid that they might divide the nation. But during Washington's second term as President, two political parties developed. One party was the **Federalist Party.** The other party was called the **Republican Party.**

The Federalists and Republicans Had Different Ideas

The leader of the Federalist Party was Alexander Hamilton. Most of the members of the Federalist Party were large land owners, merchants, and bankers. The Federalists favored a strong President and a strong federal government controlled by rich and important people. They did not think that the ordinary man was able to take part in government. In foreign affairs, the Federalists favored Great Britain over France. The Federalist Party was strong in the New England states.

The leaders of the Republican Party were Thomas Jefferson and James Madison. The members of the Republican Party were planters, small farmers, and city workers. Republicans were afraid of a strong federal government. They felt the ordinary man was able to take part in the government. In foreign affairs, the Republicans favored France over Great Britain. The Republican Party was strong in the Southern states, Pennsylvania, and New York.

John Adams Was Elected President in 1796

At the end of his second term, Washington

Tarring and feathering a tax collector.

THE WHISKY REBELLION

In the 1790's, only rugged mountain roads connected western Pennsylvania with the cities along the Atlantic coast. Farmers in western Pennsylvania were not able to carry their grain to the market towns over these rugged roads. As a result, the farmers used their grain to make whisky because it was easier to transport.

In 1791, the federal government placed a tax on whisky. The farmers in western Pennsylvania became very angry and refused to pay the tax. Collectors of the whisky tax were often attacked. One tax collector was tarred and feathered, and some others were run out of the area. The local sheriffs were not able to stop the attacks. And the federal government was not able to collect the tax.

President Washington felt strong action must be taken. In 1794, he sent 15 thousand soldiers to put down the Whisky Rebellion, as it was called. As soon as the troops arrived, the farmers gave in. A few farmers were arrested and given trials. Two men were found guilty of treason, but Washington pardoned them. The Whisky Rebellion was important, for it showed that the federal government was able to enforce the nation's laws.

Detail from Portrait of John Adams (after J. S. Copley). Courtesy Museum of Fine Arts, Boston. Seth K. Sweetser Residuary Fund.

John Adams was elected as the second President of the United States in 1796. Thomas Jefferson became Vice-President.

refused to run for a third term as President. Both the Federalists and the Republicans wanted the man they favored to win the election of 1796. The Federalist candidate (KAN-duh-dayt), or choice, for President was John Adams. Adams was the Vice-President under Washington.

The Republicans chose Thomas Jefferson as their candidate. The election was close, but Adams won and became President. Jefferson, who had the next highest number of votes, became Vice-President. The nation now had a Federalist President and a Republican Vice-President.

Washington Tried to Advise the Nation

When George Washington refused a third term, he set an example that was followed by other American Presidents for almost 150

years. Before he left office, Washington gave Americans some advice in his **Farewell Address,** or speech. In this address, Washington warned Americans against forming political parties. He also advised them to remain friendly with other nations but to keep out of these nations' affairs.

Summing Up

During Washington's second term the United States was able to stay out of the war between Britain and France. At this time, Americans formed two political parties—the Federalists and the Republicans. In the election of 1796, John Adams, a Federalist, was elected President. In the next chapter, you will read about what Adams did as President. You will also read about what Thomas Jefferson did when he became President.

AFTER YOU READ THE CHAPTER

Do You Know These Important Terms?

For each sentence below, choose the term that best completes the sentence.

1. The United States tried to remain (**peaceful/neutral**), or not to take sides, in the war.
2. (**Political/Electoral**) parties are made up of groups of people who share certain ideas about government and what it must do.
3. The party that favored a strong President and a strong federal government was the (**Democratic/Federalist**) Party.
4. The party that felt the ordinary man was able to take part in the government was the (**Democratic/Republican**) Party.
5. Washington's last great speech before he left the Presidency is called his (**Farewell/Mount Vernon**) Address.

Do You Remember These People?

Tell something about each of the following persons.

George Washington	Alexander Hamilton
Thomas Jefferson	John Jay
James Madison	John Adams

Can You Locate These Places?

Use maps in your classroom to locate the following places. Tell how each location is connected to the events in this chapter.

Great Britain	France
Northwest Territory	

Do You Know When It Happened?

What are the years of this chapter? Place the following events in the order in which they occurred.

Senate approved the Jay Treaty.
John Adams became President.
French Revolution began.
Washington gave his Farewell Address.

Discovering More About the Main Idea

During Washington's second term, the United States was able to stay out of a war. Two political parties developed, and John Adams was elected as the second President.

Tell how each of the following developments is related to the MAIN IDEA.

The United States barely avoided war with Great Britain. The problems between the two nations were settled by the unpopular Jay Treaty.

Political parties developed because groups of people had different ideas about foreign affairs and the operation of the government.

Can You Discuss the Chapter?

Use the information you learned in this chapter to answer the following questions.

1. Why was it difficult for the United States to remain neutral in the war between Britain and France?
2. Why were most Americans not pleased with the Jay Treaty?
3. What were the views of the Federalist Party? Who were their leaders?
4. If you had lived in the 1790's, would you have been a Republican or a Federalist? Why?

**Can You Connect the Past
and the Present?**

1. Political parties are still very important in America today. Which political party is most popular in your community? How can you tell?
2. The United States tried to remain neutral, or stay out of conflicts between other nations, when it was a new nation. Examine some of the new nations in Africa and Asia. Which ones are trying to remain neutral?

CHAPTER 30

President Adams and President Jefferson

President Jefferson meets with his Cabinet.

BEFORE YOU BEGIN THE CHAPTER

Know What to Look For

1. In the spring of 1805, a woman of the Shoshone Indian tribe called Sacajawea and her French husband agreed to lead a party of thirty Americans to the source of the Missouri River. Some years before, Sacajawea had been kidnapped from her own Indian tribe. She now lived with the Mandan Indians because her husband, a French fur trader, lived among them. This trip gave

Sacajawea a chance to look for her own tribe.

Sacajawea proved to be an excellent guide. Along the way, she found her own tribe of Shoshones. Her brother, who was now the Chief of the tribe, agreed to help the Americans reach the Pacific coast. In 1806, the party returned to St. Louis. This group of Americans had been sent to explore the lands added to the United States by the Louisiana

Purchase. In this chapter, you will read about President Adams. You will also read about President Jefferson and the purchase of Louisiana.

2. Read the title of the chapter. Then look through the chapter and read each heading. What was the name of the territory that was purchased by the United States? From what country was it purchased?

3. Look at the first chapter picture and read the caption. Examine the map on page 197. What is its title? How did the Louisiana Purchase compare in size to the United States east of the Mississippi River? Note also the time line at the beginning of the chapter. What years are included in this chapter? Compare this chapter time line to the unit time line on page 169.

4. Read Summing Up at the end of the chapter. List some topics you expect to read about in this chapter. What topic will you find out about in the next chapter?

Know These Important Terms

aliens	Sedition Act
Alien Acts	Louisiana Purchase

Know the Main Idea

Here is the MAIN IDEA of this chapter.

President John Adams prevented a war with France. Under President Thomas Jefferson, the United States purchased Louisiana and doubled the size of the nation.

Keep this MAIN IDEA in mind as you study the chapter. Ask yourself the following questions as you read. They will help you remember the MAIN IDEA.

1. What incident angered many Americans and caused them to prepare for war with France?
2. What law was used to silence Republican newspapers that disagreed with the Federalists' policies?
3. What doubts did President Jefferson have about the purchase of Louisiana?

THE YEARS OF THIS CHAPTER ARE 1796 TO 1804

1776   1796   1804

THE CHAPTER LESSON BEGINS HERE

President Adams Prevented a War with France

As soon as Adams became President, trouble broke out between the United States and France. This trouble was caused by the French navy, which began to capture American ships that traded with Great Britain. President Adams decided to send three American officials to France to settle this trouble.

Three Frenchmen met the Americans. The Frenchmen demanded that the Americans pay France a large sum of money before the French government agreed to any talks with

them. When the American people learned about this, they became angry and started to prepare for war. In 1798, many ships were added to the American navy, and the navy chased French ships away from the Atlantic coast.

Alexander Hamilton, the head of the Federalist Party, wanted the United States to fight against France and its ally, or friend, Spain. In this way, Hamilton hoped to take both Florida and Louisiana away from Spain.

But President Adams refused to agree to this plan. And by 1801, France and the United States were on friendly terms again.

The Federalists Passed Unpopular Laws

In 1798, while the nation was preparing for war, the Federalists passed several laws which were very unpopular. Three of these laws dealt with **aliens** (AY-lee-unz), or people who came to settle in the United States from foreign nations. These **Alien Acts** were aimed mainly at the French aliens in the United States, whom the Federalists believed were stirring up trouble. One of the acts increased the time it took for an alien to become a citizen of the United States from five years to fourteen years. Another act gave the President the power to force aliens to leave the United States if he thought they were dangerous.

But the law that caused the most trouble was the **Sedition** (seh-DISH-un) **Act.** This act made it a crime to write or say anything against the government or the President of the United States. The Federalists used the Sedition Act to silence Republican newspapers that disagreed with them. Led by Madison and Jefferson, the states of Virginia and Kentucky insisted that the Alien and Sedition Acts were unconstitutional. Most Americans agreed with them.

Jefferson Won the Election of 1800

In the election for President in 1800, Jefferson and Adams again ran against each other. This time Jefferson, the Republican candidate, won. The Republicans also won control of both houses of Congress.

Jefferson had ideas about government that were different from Adams' and the Federalists' ideas. He believed that ordinary men were able to rule themselves. They did not need a strong government or rich men to rule them.

That is why Jefferson felt that a strong government was not necessary.

As President, Jefferson repealed many Federalist laws. The first Federalist laws to be repealed were the Alien and Sedition Acts. Jefferson also lowered taxes. However, Jefferson did keep some Federalist ideas. He continued the Bank of the United States, and he cut down the amount of money the government spent to pay off the national debt.

Louisiana Was Important Both to France and the United States

During Jefferson's first term as President, thousands of farmers moved to the lands located between the Appalachian Mountains and the Mississippi River. Because of poor roads, Western farmers were not able to send their crops by land to the Eastern cities on the Atlantic coast. Instead, they floated their crops on rafts down the Mississippi River to New Orleans. At New Orleans, the farm products were loaded on ships and taken to the port cities along the Atlantic coast.

In 1801, President Jefferson learned that Spain was going to give Louisiana back to France. Louisiana was an extremely large territory stretching from the Mississippi River westward to the Rocky Mountains and from the Gulf of Mexico northward to Canada. Napoleon (nuh-POHL-yun), the ruler of France, planned to make Louisiana into a large French empire.

Napoleon Decided to Sell Louisiana

In 1802, Americans learned that the French were not going to let them use the port of New Orleans. Jefferson quickly sent James Monroe to France to try to buy New Orleans or, at least, to have the port reopened.

Meanwhile, Napoleon changed his plan about building a French empire in America. Napoleon had sent a French army to put

THE LOUISIANA PURCHASE

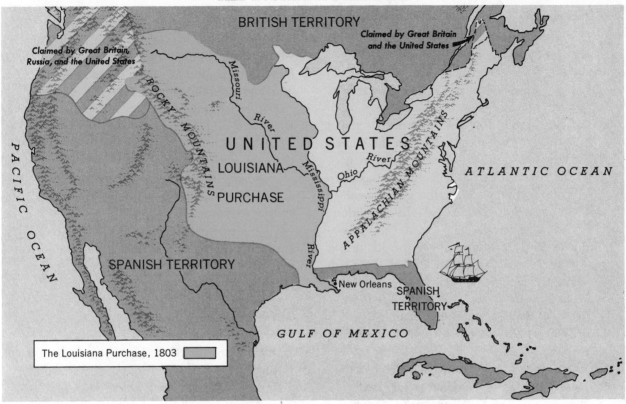

The Louisiana Purchase, 1803

down a revolt in the French West Indies. But his army was defeated by the black forces led by General Toussaint L'Ouverture (too-SAN loo-ver-TYUR). Also at this time, Napoleon had plans to conquer Europe. This meant a war with Great Britain. Therefore, Napoleon had no troops left to send to Louisiana. He needed his armies at home.

Louisiana Was Purchased by the United States in 1803

Before James Monroe arrived in France, Napoleon decided he wanted to sell all of Louisiana to the United States for 15 million dollars. Jefferson was not sure if the Constitution gave him the right to buy new territory from a foreign country. However, Jeffer-

son felt that Louisiana was too good a deal to turn down, and he decided to buy it anyway. This **Louisiana Purchase** doubled the size of the United States.

Summing Up

John Adams prevented a war with France. However, during his term as President, the Federalists passed some unpopular laws—the Alien and Sedition Acts. Thomas Jefferson won the election of 1800 and became President. During his first term, Jefferson bought the Louisiana territory from France. It doubled the size of the United States. In the next chapter, which begins Unit 8, you will find out about American troubles with Great Britain and France.

AFTER YOU READ THE CHAPTER

Do You Know These Important Terms?

For each sentence below, choose the term that best completes the sentence.

1. People from foreign nations who settle in the United States are called (**emigrants/ aliens**) before they become citizens.
2. Laws passed by the Federalists aimed mainly at the French settlers in the United States were called (**French/Alien**) Acts.
3. The law which made it a crime to say or to write anything against the government or the President was called the (**Sedition/ Censoring**) Act.
4. The large territory bought for 15 million dollars from France was called the (**Louisiana/New Orleans**) Purchase.

Do You Remember These People?

Tell something about each of the following persons.

John Adams	**Alexander Hamilton**
James Madison	**Thomas Jefferson**
Napoleon	**Toussaint L'Ouverture**

Can You Locate These Places?

Use the map on page 197 to do the following map activity.

1. Locate the Mississippi River. Name two rivers that flow into the Mississippi.
2. Locate the Louisiana Purchase. What nation claimed North American territory beyond the Louisiana Purchase?

Do You Know When It Happened?

What are the years of this chapter? Place the following events in the order in which they occurred.

The United States and France were on friendly terms again.

Jefferson was elected President.

Louisiana Territory was purchased.

Discovering More About the Main Idea

President John Adams prevented a war with France. Under President Thomas Jefferson, the United States purchased Louisiana and doubled the size of the nation.

Tell how each of the following developments is related to the MAIN IDEA.

The Federalists passed the Alien and Sedition Acts which were unpopular laws.

President Thomas Jefferson repealed some Federalist laws, but he also kept some Federalist ideas.

The port of New Orleans in the Louisiana Territory was very important to western farmers because it controlled the trade of the Mississippi River.

Can You Discuss the Chapter?

Use the information you learned in this chapter to answer the following questions.

1. Why did Alexander Hamilton want the United States to fight against France?
2. Why were the Alien and Sedition Acts such unpopular laws?
3. Why was President Jefferson interested in buying New Orleans?
4. Why was the United States able to buy all of Louisiana instead of the city of New Orleans?

Can You Connect the Past and the Present?

1. The Sedition Act made it a crime to write anything against the government or the President. Can newspapers write things disagreeing with the government today? Do newspapers have any effect on how the government acts?
2. The purchase of new lands is one way a nation can increase its size. What are some other methods that nations sometimes use?

America Deals with Other Nations

The Battle of New Orleans.

THE CHAPTERS IN UNIT 8 ARE

CHAPTER 31   The War of 1812
CHAPTER 32   Fighting the War of 1812
CHAPTER 33   The United States and the World, 1815–1860

THE YEARS OF THIS UNIT ARE 1804 TO 1860

| 1800 | 1804 | 1860 | 1975 |

CHAPTER 31

The War of 1812

The British ship "Leopard" fires on the "Chesapeake."

BEFORE YOU BEGIN THE CHAPTER

Know What to Look For

1. British sailors often did not want to stay in the British navy. Life aboard a British man-of-war in the early 1800's was hard and dangerous. Sailors sometimes jumped ship and got jobs aboard other ships. During the early years of the 1800's, British ships began stopping and searching American merchant ships for British sailors who deserted, or left the British navy. They checked the crews on

American ships and arrested any man who had been a British sailor. They sometimes found former British sailors. But they also captured many American sailors and forced these helpless men to serve in the British navy. In this chapter, you will read more about America's trouble with foreign nations who refused to leave American ships alone. These troubles led to the War of 1812.

2. Read the title of the chapter. Then look through the chapter and read each heading. How did most Americans feel about a war?

3. Look at the pictures in the chapter and read each caption. What is happening in the picture on page 202? Note the time line at the beginning of the chapter. What years are included in this chapter? Compare this chapter time line to the unit time line on page 199.

4. Read the last part of the chapter called Summing Up. When did the United States go to war with Great Britain?

Know These Important Terms

impressed	Macon's Bill Number 2
Embargo Act	War Hawks

Know the Main Idea

Here is the MAIN IDEA of this chapter.

Both President Jefferson and President Madison had trouble with France and Great Britain. In 1812, the United States declared war against Great Britain.

Keep this MAIN IDEA in mind as you study the chapter. Ask yourself the following questions as you read. They will help you remember the MAIN IDEA.

1. How did President Jefferson try to solve American problems with Great Britain and France instead of going to war?

2. What political party did not like the Embargo Act?

3. What Indian leader fought to keep the Americans from taking Indian lands? At what battle were the Indians defeated?

THE YEARS OF THIS CHAPTER ARE 1804 TO 1812

1804   1812   1860

THE CHAPTER LESSON BEGINS HERE

The United States Had Trouble with France and Great Britain

In 1804, Thomas Jefferson was elected President again. During his second term, Jefferson had problems with foreign nations. Jefferson's problems grew out of a war between Great Britain and France. Great Britain and France tried to cut off each other's trade with foreign nations. This meant that Great Britain captured American ships it found trading with France. And France captured American ships it found trading with Great Britain.

Great Britain not only captured American ships, but it also **impressed** American sailors, or forced them to serve on British ships. In 1807, the British warship "Leopard" attacked the American warship "Chesapeake" in American waters. The British then impressed four of the Chesapeake's men into the British navy.

The United States Cut Off All Trade with Europe

Many Americans wanted the United States to go to war against Great Britain. But President Jefferson thought he had a better plan. Jefferson believed that the United States must cut off trade with Great Britain. This was the way to force Great Britain to stop capturing American ships and impressing American sailors.

Congress agreed with Jefferson's plan, and

This picture shows the British capturing sailors from the American ship "Chesapeake." The sailors were forced to serve on British ships.

in 1807, Congress passed an **Embargo Act.** The Embargo Act forbade American ships to sail to any foreign port. It also forbade foreign ships to carry goods away from the United States or bring goods to the United States.

The Embargo Act Failed

However, the Embargo Act hurt the United States more than it hurt Great Britain. Great Britain was still able to trade with Canada and South America. But American trade was completely cut off. American sailors and ship

builders lost their jobs, and American business-men lost much money. American farmers were also hurt because they were not able to sell their crops to other nations.

The Embargo Act led to a great deal of smuggling, or unlawful trading, with Canada. Many Americans, especially those in New England, showed their dislike of the Embargo Act by electing Federalists to Congress. Finally, Jefferson agreed that the Embargo Act had failed. In 1809, he signed a law that repealed the Embargo Act.

James Madison Was Elected President in 1808

By 1808, the Federalist Party had grown strong again because many Americans, especially those in New England, did not like the Embargo Act. But the Republican Party was able to elect James Madison as President of the United States in 1808. Madison had been Secretary of State under Jefferson for eight years, and as President he tried to continue Jefferson's ideas.

The United States Stopped Trading with Great Britain

Under Madison, the United States refused to trade with Great Britain or France. Then in 1810, Congress passed a new law, **Macon's Bill Number 2.** This law opened up trade with both Great Britain and France. But it also said that if either Great Britain or France stopped capturing American ships, the United States promised to cut off all trade with the other nation.

Napoleon, the ruler of France, quickly promised to leave American ships alone. Napoleon did not plan to keep his promise, but the American government did not know that. When the British government refused to make the same promise to the American government, President Madison cut off all American trade with Great Britain.

The United States Moved Closer to War With Great Britain

Trade with Great Britain was cut off in February of 1811. In June 1812, Great Britain finally decided to stop capturing American ships. But before the United States learned about this British action, Congress declared war on Great Britain. What caused the United States to declare war on Great Britain? To find out, it is necessary to look at events on the Western frontier during this period.

Bowdoin College Museum of Art, Brunswick, Maine.

James Madison was elected President in 1808. He was the nation's fourth President.

Indian Troubles in the West

By 1812, Americans were pushing westward in larger numbers than ever before. The Americans wanted more land because most of the Western frontier lands were settled. Therefore, Westerners planned to take over the Indian lands farther west, and they also began to think of taking over Canada and Florida.

The Indians did not want the Americans to take their lands. Led by Tecumseh (tuh-KUM-suh) and his brother the Prophet (PRAHF-ut), the Indian tribes joined together to protect their lands. In November of 1811, General

This picture shows the Battle of the Thames in which Tecumseh, the famous Indian leader, was killed.

William Henry Harrison, governor of the Indiana Territory, fought and defeated the Indians at the Battle of Tippecanoe. This battle led to an Indian war in the Northwest. Many Westerners believed that the British leaders in Canada were helping the Indians. These Westerners wanted the United States to go to war with Great Britain and conquer Canada.

Most Americans Wanted War

By 1811, many members of Congress wanted to go to war. Many of these Congressmen, or members of Congress, came from the West. Because of their demands for a war with Great Britain, they were given the name **War Hawks.**

The War of 1812 Began

President Madison finally asked Congress to declare war in 1812. He said that the United States must fight Great Britain because Great Britain refused to stop capturing American ships.

In the election of 1812, Madison ran for a second term as President. A vote for Madison was a vote in favor of the war. Madison won the election, and the War of 1812 continued.

Summing Up

President Jefferson had problems with France and Great Britain in his second term. He tried to solve these problems with the Embargo Act, but failed. When James Madison became President in 1808, he also had to deal with Great Britain and France. In 1812, the United States went to war with Great Britain. In the next chapter, you will learn how the War of 1812 was fought.

AFTER YOU READ THE CHAPTER

Do You Know These Important Terms?

For each sentence below, choose the term that best completes the sentence.

1. The British navy (enlisted/impressed) American sailors, or forced them to serve on British ships.
2. An act which forbade any trade with Britain or France was called the (Embargo/Boycott) Act.
3. The law passed in 1810 which opened trade with Britain and France was called (Macon's Bill Number 2/Trade Repeal Bill).
4. Congressmen, especially those from the West, who wanted to go to war with Britain were called (War Doves/War Hawks).

Do You Remember These People?

Tell something about each of the following persons.

Thomas Jefferson   James Madison
Tecumseh   The Prophet
William Henry Harrison

Can You Locate These Places?

Use the map on page 208 to locate the Indiana Territory. How was this part of the Northwest Territory connected to the start of the War of 1812?

Do You Know When It Happened?

What are the years of this chapter? Place the following events in the order in which they occurred.

Congress passed Macon's Bill Number 2.
James Madison was elected President.
War was declared against Great Britain.
Congress passed the Embargo Act.
Tecumseh was defeated.
The Embargo Act was repealed.

Discovering More About the Main Idea

Both President Jefferson and President Madison had trouble with France and Great Britain. In 1812, the United States declared war against Great Britain.

Tell how each of the following developments is related to the MAIN IDEA.

The Embargo Act failed because it hurt the businesses of the United States more than it hurt those of France and Great Britain.

Many Congressmen, especially from the West, wanted to take over Canada and to take over certain Indian lands.

The United States cut off trade with Britain in 1811 and declared war in 1812.

Can You Discuss the Chapter?

Use the information you learned in this chapter to answer the following questions.

1. Why was the Embargo Act unsuccessful?
2. Why did the United States cut off trade with Great Britain in 1811?
3. Why were the War Hawks so interested in Canada, Florida, and Indian lands?
4. How do we know that many Americans favored war with Great Britain in 1812?
5. How do you feel about American settlers taking over the Indian lands in the Northwest Territory? Explain your answer.

Can You Connect the Past and the Present?

1. The idea of an embargo, or cutting off trade with another nation, is still used today. Against what nation does the United States now have an embargo? Do you know why?
2. The term "hawk" usually refers to war and the term "dove" to peace. How are these terms used to describe the views of certain Congressmen today?

CHAPTER 32

Fighting the War of 1812

Perry accepts surrender of British ships on Lake Erie.

BEFORE YOU BEGIN THE CHAPTER

Know What to Look For

1. During the War of 1812, Francis Scott Key went aboard a British ship to arrange for an exchange of prisoners. Just as he came aboard the ship, the British attack on the city of Baltimore began. The fighting went on all night. By morning the British attack had failed. Key watched the fight from the British ship. When he saw the American flag still flying above Fort McHenry in the morning

light, he knew the Americans won the battle.

Key was so moved by this sight that he wrote the famous poem which begins: "Oh, say can you see, by the dawn's early light." This poem was later put to music and became the American national anthem, or song. In this chapter, you will read more about the events of the War of 1812.

2. Read the title of the chapter. Then

look through the chapter and read each heading. By using only the headings, can you tell how the war turned out?

3. Look at the pictures in the chapter and read each caption. What do the pictures show you about the War of 1812? What is the title of the map on page 208? What symbol is used to show American victories? British victories? Note also the time line at the beginning of the chapter. What years are included in the chapter? Compare the chapter time line to the unit time line on page 199.

4. Read the last part of the chapter called Summing Up. What was unusual about the peace treaty ending the War of 1812?

Know These Important Terms

privateers   Treaty of Ghent

Know the Main Idea
Here is the MAIN IDEA of this chapter.
The United States fought the War of 1812, but the war settled very little. In 1818, the United States and Great Britain settled most of their differences.

Keep this MAIN IDEA in mind as you read the chapter. Ask yourself the following questions as you read. They will help you remember the MAIN IDEA.

1. Instead of capturing Canada in 1812, what happened to the United States?
2. What American officer defeated the British fleet and forced the British to call off their attack from Canada?
3. What battle of the war was fought after the peace treaty had already been signed? Why was it fought?

THE YEARS OF THIS CHAPTER ARE 1812 TO 1818

1804   1812   1818   1860

THE CHAPTER LESSON BEGINS HERE

The War Got Off to a Slow Start
The United States was not prepared to fight the War of 1812. It lacked money, supplies, and men. At first, Congress refused to vote the taxes needed to build an army and navy and to fight the war. And the United States had trouble getting men to join the army.

The American armies that were sent to attack Canada in 1812 failed badly. Instead of conquering Canada, the United States lost Detroit, Fort Dearborn (the present city of Chicago), and much of the land around the Great Lakes to the British. However, this lost territory was regained from the British the next year. Captain Oliver Hazard Perry, an American naval officer, defeated a British fleet on Lake Erie, and General Harrison won the Battle of the Thames.

The United States Did Well at Sea
The Americans did much better in the war at sea. Although the British navy had many more ships than the American navy, the American ships were able to capture and destroy many British ships. The most famous American ship, the "Constitution," won the name "Old Ironsides" for its victories against British warships.

Near the end of the war, the British navy blocked up most of the American warships in their home ports. However, privately owned ships called **privateers** (pry-vuh-TEERS) still sailed the seas and captured British ships.

THE WAR OF 1812

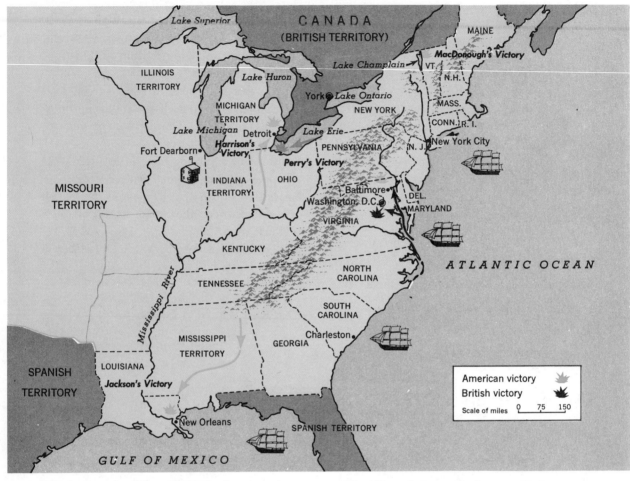

All during the War of 1812, the American people were very proud of their brave sailors. Many of these brave sailors were black men.

A British Attack from Canada Failed

In 1814, the British finally defeated Napoleon, and the war in Europe came to an end. Great Britain was now able to send thousands of trained soldiers to America. The British planned to attack New England and New York from Canada, then to raid important cities along the Atlantic coast, and finally to attack New Orleans by sea. They planned to end the war with these attacks.

The United States had a small fleet commanded by Captain Thomas Macdonough (muk-DAHN-uh) on Lake Champlain. The British had to defeat this fleet in order to move their men and supplies southward from Canada. But the American fleet led by Macdonough defeated the British fleet, and the British attack on the United States from Canada had to be called off.

The British Attacked Washington and Baltimore

The British next landed soldiers near Washington, D.C., and attacked the capital in

page 208

August, 1814. An American army tried to defend Washington against the British attack but failed. The British army captured Washington, D.C., and they burned many government buildings. A few days later, the British army attacked Baltimore. However, the British army was unable to capture Baltimore and the troops returned to their ships.

The Final Battle at New Orleans

The final British attack took place at New Orleans early in 1815. There the British army found an American army waiting for them. The American army was led by General Andrew Jackson and was made up of frontiersmen, free black men, and army men. The British general felt he had an easy fight. But when the Battle of New Orleans was over, 2 thousand British soldiers were dead or wounded. The Americans had less than 100 men who were dead or wounded.

The Battle of New Orleans was a great American victory. But the **Treaty of Ghent,** the peace treaty which ended the war, was signed two weeks before the battle was fought. News of the treaty did not reach the United States in time to stop the battle. Many people thought that the War of 1812 had been fought for nothing. The Treaty of Ghent ended the fighting, but it did not solve any of the problems that caused the war.

The United States and Great Britain Settled Their Differences

However, after the war in Europe ended, Great Britain no longer tried to stop American ships. In 1818, Great Britain and the United States settled many of their differences. Both nations agreed to keep their warships off the Great Lakes, and they fixed most of the boundary line between the United States and Canada.

The Battle of New Orleans.

"OLD HICKORY" AND THE BATTLE OF NEW ORLEANS

Andrew Jackson won the nickname "Old Hickory" because of his ability as a military leader. This ability was shown at the Battle of New Orleans. To prepare for the battle, Jackson put the city of New Orleans under strict military law. Then he asked the free black citizens of New Orleans and the French pirates, led by Jean Lafitte, to join his army of frontiersmen.

The Battle of New Orleans took place on January 8, 1815. The British attack was well planned. But the British soldiers were met by Jackson's army made up of Tennessee frontiersmen, black citizens of New Orleans, and French pirates. During the fierce battle, the British general, Sir Edward Pakenham, was wounded in the arm. Bravely, he returned to the battle but he was soon killed. By noon the battle was over.

Over 2 thousand British soldiers died in the battle. Thirteen Americans were killed. The people of New Orleans honored Jackson with a huge parade. Congress gave him a gold medal. President James Madison congratulated him on his "glorious victory." Old Hickory was now a great American hero. In 1828, he was to become President of the United States.

J. Queen and P. Duval (after T. Birch): *Capture of H.M. Ships Cyane and Levant, by the U.S. Frigate Constitution.* Yale University Art Gallery, Mabel Brady Garvan Collection.

The American ship "Constitution" forces two British ships to surrender. This ship was nicknamed "Old Ironsides."

The War Brought About Changes

The New England states were against the War of 1812 more than any other part of the United States. But, as it turned out, they gained most from the war. During the war, the United States had to manufacture its own goods because British goods were not sent to the United States. New England was a good place for manufacturing, and by the end of the war, New England became the leading manufacturing section of the United States.

The West was also helped by the War of 1812. The Indians around the Great Lakes and south of the Ohio River were defeated by American armies during the war. The Western frontier was now safe for American settlement. Because plenty of good land was open for settlement, Canada was no longer important to the United States.

The War of 1812 made most Americans feel proud of their country. Americans soon forgot their defeats in the War of 1812 and only remembered their victories. Generals such as William Henry Harrison and Andrew Jackson became great American heroes. After the war, Americans felt their country was strong and important.

Summing Up

From 1812 to 1815, the United States and Great Britain fought the War of 1812 on land and at sea. The peace treaty that ended the war did not really settle anything. But in 1818, Great Britain and the United States settled most of their differences. In the next chapter, you will find out that the United States also settled many of its problems with other nations in the world.

AFTER YOU READ THE CHAPTER

Do You Know These Important Terms?

For each sentence below, choose the term that best completes the sentence.

1. Privately owned ships that captured British ships were called (**clipper ships/privateers**).
2. The Treaty of (**Paris/Ghent**) ended the War of 1812.

Do You Remember These People?

Tell something about each of the following persons.

Oliver Hazard Perry   General Harrison
Thomas Macdonough   Andrew Jackson

Can You Locate These Places?

Use the map on page 208 to do the following map work.

1. Locate the Great Lakes. What two important forts on the Great Lakes were lost to the British?
2. Locate Lake Champlain. Why was this battle important to the Americans?
3. Locate Washington, D.C., and Baltimore. Locate also the city of New Orleans. Why do you think the British wanted to capture that city?

Do You Know When It Happened?

What are the years of this chapter? Place the following events in the order in which they occurred.

The city of Washington, D.C., was captured by the British.

Captain Perry defeated a British fleet on Lake Erie.

Americans invaded Canada.

Americans were victorious at the Battle of New Orleans.

A British attack from Canada was stopped at Lake Champlain.

Discovering More About the Main Idea

The United States fought the War of 1812, but the war settled very little. In 1818, the United States and Great Britain settled most of their differences.

Tell how each of the following developments is related to the MAIN IDEA.

The War of 1812 started off badly for the United States. The United States was able to recapture the territories it lost.

The United States and Great Britain agreed to keep warships off the Great Lakes, and they fixed most of the boundary line between the United States and Canada.

The War of 1812 made Americans feel proud of their country. As a result of the war, manufacturing improved, and new lands were opened to settlement.

Can You Discuss the Chapter?

Use the information you learned in this chapter to answer the following questions.

1. Why did the War of 1812 get off to such a bad start for the United States?
2. Why did many people feel that the War of 1812 was fought for nothing?
3. What three big changes did the war bring about in the United States? Explain each change.
4. How might faster news travel have helped the course of events in the War of 1812?

Can You Connect the Past and the Present?

1. Heroes are a very important part of American history. Who are some present-day people who are American heroes?
2. Few nations have been able to live side by side without trouble as have the United States and Canada. Why do you think this is true?

CHAPTER 33

The United States and the World, 1815-1860

The Cabinet talks over the Monroe Doctrine.

BEFORE YOU BEGIN THE CHAPTER

Know What to Look For

1. When Commodore Perry sailed his ships into Tokyo harbor, he gave the Japanese emperor gifts from the American President. Most of the gifts he gave to the emperor were strange and new products for the Japanese. The gift that especially captured the interest of the Japanese was a small steam locomotive that pulled several small cars around an oval track. The Japanese were

fascinated as they watched the train ride around the tracks.

Commodore Perry's arrival in Japan was one of the important American dealings with foreign nations in the early 1800's. In this chapter, you will read more about American dealings with other nations during the 1800's.

2. Read the title of the chapter. Then look through the chapter and read each heading. By reading the headings, can you tell whether the United States had successful or unsuccessful dealings with other nations during the early 1800's?

3. Look at the pictures in the chapter and read each caption. What are the American leaders talking over in the picture on page 212? How did Americans dress at this time? What two leaders are shown on page 214? Notice also the time line at the beginning of the chapter. What years are included in this chapter? Compare this chapter time line to the unit time line on page 199.

4. Read the last part of the chapter called Summing Up. What does this summary tell you about American dealings with other nations during the early 1800's? What is the topic of the chapters in Unit 9?

Know These Important Terms
Adams-Onís Treaty   Webster-Ashburton
Monroe Doctrine   Treaty

Know the Main Idea
Here is the MAIN IDEA of this chapter.
In the years from 1815 to 1860, the United States was generally successful in its dealings with other nations.

Keep this MAIN IDEA in mind as you study the chapter. Ask yourself the following questions as you read. They will help you remember the MAIN IDEA.

1. How much money did the United States pay for Florida?
2. How was trade with the West Indies reopened?
3. What nation paid its debt to America?

THE YEARS OF THIS CHAPTER ARE 1815 TO 1860

1804   1815   1860

THE CHAPTER LESSON BEGINS HERE

The United States Bought Florida

After the War of 1812, the United States still had to settle some problems with foreign nations. One problem was Spain's control of Florida. Spain was too weak to control its colony of Florida. Therefore, Indians from Florida raided American settlements. Also, runaway slaves escaped to the safety of Florida. Many Americans wanted Florida to be made part of the United States.

In 1818, Andrew Jackson chased a group of raiding Indians back into Florida and took over part of it. Soon after, Spain decided to sell Florida to the United States. In 1819, the United States and Spain signed the **Adams-Onís** (oh-NEES) **Treaty.** In this treaty, the United States bought Florida from Spain for

5 million dollars. However, American settlers were slow to move into Florida. It did not become a state until 1845.

Spain Lost Its American Colonies

Spain was willing to sell Florida because it lost all of its American empire except Cuba and Puerto Rico. Under the leadership of such men as José de San Martín (hoh-ZAY day SAN mar-TEEN) and Simón Bolívar (see-MOHN boh-LEE-var), the nations of Central and South America revolted against Spain's rule and won their independence. The people of the United States were happy that their Spanish neighbors had followed their example and were now free.

At left is Simón Bolívar, a leader of the South American revolutions. At right is José de San Martín, another great revolutionary leader.

However, in the early 1820's, it looked as if some of the nations of Europe were going to help Spain reconquer its American colonies. The government of the United States did not want Spain to conquer South America again. The British government also wanted South America to remain free because Great Britain traded a lot with South America, and it did not want this trade to end.

The Monroe Doctrine Warned Europe

The British government asked the government of the United States to join it in warning Spain and the other European nations to leave the new nations of South America alone. But John Quincy Adams, President Monroe's Secretary of State, wanted the United States to give its own warning to the European nations. He wanted the United States, not Great Britain, to protect South America. Monroe agreed with Adams' idea.

Late in 1823, Monroe gave a speech to Congress which became known as the **Monroe Doctrine.** In this Monroe Doctrine, President Monroe told the nations of Europe to stay out of the affairs of North America and South America. In return, the United States promised to stay out of European affairs.

At this time, the United States was not strong enough to protect South America by itself. But the United States knew that Great Britain was willing to help protect South America. However, the danger of a European attack on South America had passed by the time Monroe made his speech. But the Monroe Doctrine was important because it declared that all American nations must be free of European control. It also made the United States the protector of freedom in North America and South America.

The West Indian Trade Was Reopened

Before the Revolutionary War, the American colonies carried on an important trade with the British West Indies. However, for many years after the Revolutionary War, Great Britain refused to allow American ships to trade freely with the West Indies.

After Andrew Jackson became President in 1829, he succeeded in getting Great Britain to allow the United States to trade with the West Indies. Jackson offered to allow British ships freedom of trade with the United States in return for the freedom of American ships to trade with the West Indies. The West Indies needed American farm products and lumber. Therefore, Great Britain decided to accept Jackson's offer and reopened the West Indies to American trade.

The United States Collected Its Debt from France

President Jackson was also successful in dealing with France. Since the early years of the 1800's, France owed money to the United States. In 1831, the French government promised to pay this debt. But in 1833 when the payment was due, the French refused to pay. President Jackson was very angry, and he threatened to take over all French property in the United States.

For a few years, it looked as if the United States and France might go to war. Finally, France paid the money, and the two nations once again were on friendly terms.

The United States and Great Britain Settled the Maine Boundary

In 1818, the United States and Great Britain fixed the boundary between the United States and Canada except for the area of the Oregon Territory. But in the 1830's, a question over the boundary between the state of Maine and Canada came up. However, the United States and Great Britain settled the boundary between Maine and Canada peacefully in the **Webster-Ashburton Treaty** of 1842.

The United States Started to Trade with Japan

During the 1800's, a small but important trade grew up between the United States and China. Because of this trade, the United States also wanted to trade with Japan, China's neighbor. But Japan refused to allow any foreign ships to visit its ports. In 1852, the United States sent a fleet commanded by Commodore Matthew C. Perry to Japan. Perry was to talk the Japanese into opening up their seaports to trade with the United States.

Perry arrived at just the right time. Many Japanese knew that their old ways must change. Therefore, in 1854, the Japanese government signed a treaty with the United States, which opened two Japanese ports to American trade.

Summing Up

In the years from 1815 to 1860, the United States was generally successful in its dealings with other nations. In the next chapters, which are in Unit 9, you will read about changes in the United States itself after 1815.

AFTER YOU READ THE CHAPTER

Do You Know These Important Terms?

For each sentence below, choose the term that best completes the sentence.

1. In the (Adams-Onís/Spanish Cession) Treaty, the United States bought Florida from Spain.
2. A speech which told the nations of Europe to stay out of the affairs of North America and South America was called the (Jackson/Monroe) Doctrine.
3. The (Adams-Webster/Webster-Ashburton) Treaty established the boundary between Maine and Canada.

Do You Remember These People?

Tell something about each of the following persons.

Andrew Jackson   José de San Martín
Simón Bolívar   John Quincy Adams
James Monroe   Matthew C. Perry

Can You Locate These Places?

Use maps in your classroom to do the following map work.

1. Locate the nations of South and Central America. What two nations in this area remained Spanish colonies?
2. Locate Florida, France, the West Indies, and Japan. Explain how each was connected to the events in this chapter.

Do You Know When It Happened?

What are the years of this chapter? Place the following events in the order in which they occurred.

France paid its debt to the United States.

The boundary was established between Maine and Canada.

The United States bought Florida.

President Monroe issued his Doctrine.

Commodore Perry visited Japan.

Discovering More About the Main Idea

In the years from 1815 to 1860, the United States was generally successful in its dealings with other nations.

Tell how each of the following developments is related to the MAIN IDEA.

Spain lost most of its colonies in the New World and sold Florida to the United States.

The Monroe Doctrine declared that all American nations must be free of European control and made the United States the protector of freedom in North and South America.

The United States started to trade with China and Japan.

Can You Discuss the Chapter?

Use the information you learned in this chapter to answer the following questions.

1. Why did many Americans want Florida to be made part of the United States?
2. Why did President Monroe give the speech that became known as the Monroe Doctrine in 1823? What were its effects?
3. Why was the United States unable to trade with the West Indies after the Revolution?
4. Why was Commodore Perry's visit to Japan important?
5. What do you think might have happened if Spain had not sold Florida or Japan had not wanted to trade? Explain your answer.

Can You Connect the Past and the Present?

1. At one time the Monroe Doctrine protected North America and South America. What organization, or group, now protects North and South America?
2. China and Japan both started to trade with America and met Americans at about the same time. Which of these nations has accepted or used many American ways?

UNIT 9
The Sections of the Nation

Shipping goods by canalboat.

THE CHAPTERS IN UNIT 9 ARE

CHAPTER 34 The Northeast
CHAPTER 35 The South
CHAPTER 36 The West

THE YEARS OF THIS UNIT ARE 1800 TO 1850

1800	1850	1975

The Northeast

New York City in 1836.

BEFORE YOU BEGIN THE CHAPTER

Know What to Look For

1. Two ideas of modern manufacturing were first used in the early 1800's. Eli Whitney, an inventor, signed an agreement with the American government to make muskets, or guns, for the army. Up to this time, muskets were made by skilled workmen one at a time. When the worker finished one gun he started another. These guns always were slightly different from one another and there-

fore, the parts of one gun could not be used in another gun.

Eli Whitney had a new plan. Instead of workers making a complete gun, each worker was to make parts of guns. Each part was made exactly alike so that a part from one musket would fit any other musket. After the gun parts were finished, they were put together to make complete guns. These two ideas are now called "the division of labor" and "the use of interchangeable parts." In this chapter, you will read about how the Northeast became a manufacturing center by using these and other ideas.

2. Read the title of the chapter. Look through the chapter and read each heading. What can you tell about the Northeast just by reading the headings?

3. Study the pictures in the chapter and read each caption. What do the pictures show about manufacturing in the Northeast? Look at the map on page 220. What is the title of the map? Name the states in the Northeast. Note the time line at the beginning of the chapter. What years are included in this chapter? Compare the chapter time line to the unit time line on page 217.

4. Read the section called Summing Up at the end of the chapter. What information does it tell you about the Northeast section of the nation?

Know This Important Term
Northeast

Know the Main Idea
Here is the MAIN IDEA of this chapter.

In the 1800's, the Northeast became the leading manufacturing, trading, and banking section of the nation.

Keep this MAIN IDEA in mind as you study the chapter. Ask yourself the following questions as you read. They will help you remember the MAIN IDEA.

1. What two older sections made up the Northeast?
2. Why were factories started in New England?
3. Name some of the problems caused by the quick growth of cities.

THE YEARS OF THIS CHAPTER ARE 1800 TO 1850

1800   1850

THE CHAPTER LESSON BEGINS HERE

Trade in the Northeast

As the American nation grew, three main sections, or parts, of the nation were developing in different ways. One section, the **Northeast,** was made up of two older sections, the New England states and the Middle states. During the early 1800's, the most important men in the Northeast were merchants and traders. Most of these businessmen lived in Philadelphia, New York, and Boston, which were the leading seaports of the Northeast.

Traders from the Northeast sailed their ships all the way around South America to China. They stopped in Oregon to buy furs and in Hawaii (huh-WAH-ee) to pick up valuable wood. Furs and wood were needed in China, and they were traded there for tea, dishes, and silk. These products were then brought back to the United States and sold at very high prices. Businessmen from the Northeast also traded with Europe and South America.

Factories Developed in the Northeast

The War of 1812 greatly encouraged manufacturing in the United States. New England soon proved to be a good place for manufacturing, because it had many skilled workers and plenty of swift streams to supply water

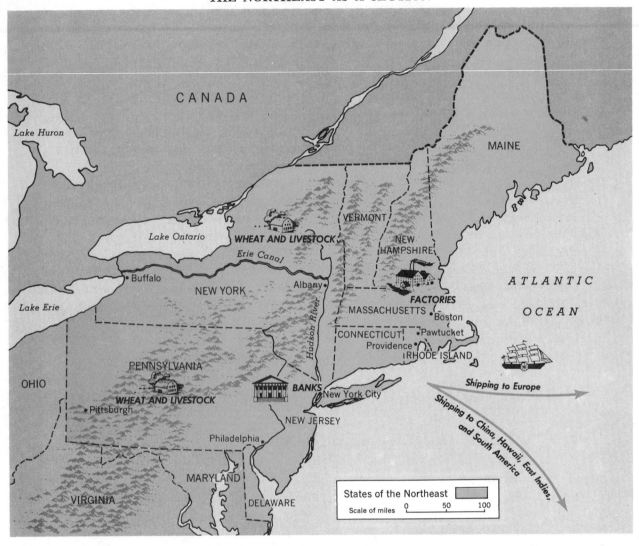

power to run machines. New England also had many rich businessmen who had the money to build and open factories.

The first American factories made cotton goods. Later, other factories made woolen goods, shoes, clothing, leather goods, machinery, and all types of metal products. The factories in the Northeast sold their manufactured goods in the Northeast and also in the South and the West.

Large Factories Cost Money

Before long, many factories also opened up in the Middle states, especially in Pennsylvania and in New York. Most of these factories were small and had only a few workers. But others were quite large. These large factories made large amounts of money, but few men had the money necessary to build and open them.

Some businessmen solved their problem by

An iron foundry located in the Northeast. In this factory the workers are making iron parts for ships.

forming a corporation. In a corporation, many people put their money into a business, and these people own the business together. Instead of one man owning a business, many people own it. However, before 1850, there were very few corporations. Most corporations were not formed until after the 1850's.

The Start of Labor Unions

Most of the workers in the early factories were women and children. Many of them came from farms, and they were happy to earn a little extra money. But as factories became larger, factory owners became harder on their workers. They paid their workers very low wages—often as low as $1.25 a week. They made them work long hours, sometimes as much as sixteen hours a day. And the early factories were often terrible places to work in. They were dirty, dangerous, and poorly lit.

THE NORTHEAST

New England States

Maine

New Hampshire

Vermont

Rhode Island

Massachusetts

Connecticut

Middle States

New York

Pennsylvania

New Jersey

Delaware

In time, the workers tried to help themselves by joining together and starting unions. Sometimes these unions went on strike, or stopped work, to try to get the factory owners to do what the unions wanted. These early unions were weak, and their strikes were usually unsuccessful. However, in time, working conditions for skilled workers improved. But unskilled workers continued to work long hours for low pay.

The Problems of Growing Cities

As industry became more important in the Northeast, the cities in the Northeast also began to change. One change was the quick growth of cities. In 1820, 43 thousand people lived in Boston, 112 thousand people lived in Philadelphia, and 123 thousand people lived in New York City. By 1850, four times as many people lived in New York City, while three times as many people lived in Boston and Philadelphia. This quick growth of cities caused many problems. Cities were not able to provide all the people living there with good housing, enough police, enough fire protection, and clean water and streets. The rich people were able to live in fine houses. Some

other people bought homes at the edge of the city. But some poor people were forced to live in dirty, unhealthy slums.

The Northeast Was a Banking Center

The Northeast was the leading manufacturing and trading section of the nation. It had the largest cities and the largest factories in the nation. The Northeast also had the largest banks in the nation. Many banks were opened in Philadelphia and New York because factory owners often had to borrow money to carry on their businesses. These banks helped factory owners and merchants to get the money that they needed. The Bank of the United States, the federal government's own bank, also had its main office in Philadelphia.

The Northeast Was Still an Important Farming Section

Even though manufacturing was important in the Northeast, most people living there were still farmers. Farmers in the Northeastern states grew large crops of wheat. They also raised many sheep and cattle. Although factory owners and bankers became the most important people in the Northeast, these farmers still had an important part in government. Many Congressmen were elected from the Northeast. Farmers made up a large group of voters, and therefore, they had a lot of power among these Congressmen.

Summing Up

The Northeast was made up of New England and the Middle states. In the 1800's, the Northeast became the leading manufacturing, trading, and banking section of the nation. But it also was an important farming section. In the next chapter, you will read about the South, which was developing in a different way.

AFTER YOU READ THE CHAPTER

Do You Know This Important Term?

For the sentence below, choose the term that best completes the sentence.

The (**Urban East/Northeast**) was made up of the older sections called New England and the Middle states.

Can You Locate These Places?

Use the map on page 220 to do the following map work.

1. Locate the states that make up the Northeast. Name some of the important cities of the Northeast. In which state is each city located?
2. Find the symbols that show the routes of trade. Where does one of these routes go? Where does the other one go?

Do You Know When It Happened?

What are the years of this chapter? How many years does the chapter cover? In what century did these events take place?

Discovering More About the Main Idea

In the 1800's, the Northeast became the leading manufacturing, trading, and banking section of the nation.

Tell how each of the following developments is related to the MAIN IDEA.

Northeast traders visited almost every part of the world.

The first American factories developed in New England, and later many factories also opened up in the Middle states. Corporations and labor unions began in the factories of the Northeast.

Manufacturing and trade drew people to the cities. The quick growth of cities caused new and different problems. Some cities became banking centers.

Although factory owners and bankers became the most important people in the Northeast, most people in the Northeast were still farmers in the early 1800's.

Can You Discuss the Chapter?

Use the information you learned in this chapter to answer the following questions.

1. Why did the Northeast develop into the leading manufacturing section of the nation?
2. Why did workers start labor unions? What did these early unions do? Were they successful?
3. What was the connection between the growth of manufacturing and the problems of the cities? the growth of manufacturing and the opening of banks?
4. Why did farmers still have an important part in government in the Northeast?
5. If you had a choice of a section of the nation in which to live in the early 1800's, would you select the Northeast? Why or why not?
6. Why did businessmen begin to form corporations? Were there many corporations in the United States before the 1850's?

Can You Connect the Past and the Present?

1. In the early 1800's, the Northeast became the leading manufacturing, trading, and banking section of the nation. What section in the United States is the leading manufacturing, trading, and banking section today?
2. Compare the problems of the rapidly growing cities of the early 1800's with the problems in your city today. How are they alike? different?

CHAPTER 35

The South

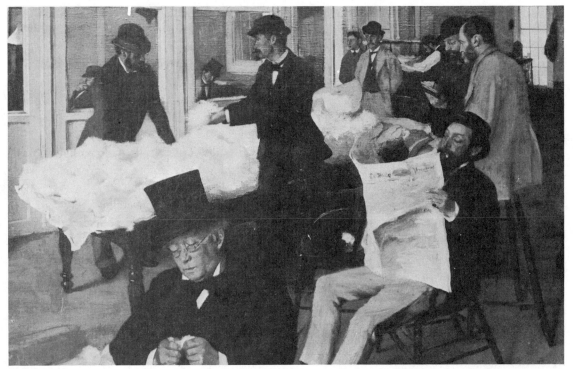

Buying and selling cotton at a cotton exchange.

BEFORE YOU BEGIN THE CHAPTER

Know What to Look For

1. Benjamin Banneker was a free black man who lived in the South. He attended school for a short time and then continued to educate himself. Banneker was especially good in mathematics, and he also became an expert in astronomy, or the study of the stars and planets. He published an almanac which gave the times of sunrise and sunset, and the position of heavenly bodies.

Banneker is most known for his work in

helping to plan and build the city of Washington, D.C. When Pierre L'Enfant, the chief planner of Washington, angrily returned to France with all the plans for the city, Banneker redrew them from memory. Although some free black men lived in the South, most black men in the South were slaves. In this chapter, you will read about the section of the nation called the South.

2. Read the title of the chapter. Then

look through the chapter and read each heading. What crop was grown in the South?

3. Look at the pictures in the chapter and read each caption. What do the pictures show you about life in the South? Examine the map on page 226. What is the title of the map? Name the states in the South. Note the time line at the beginning of the chapter. What years are included in this chapter? Compare the chapter time line to the unit time line on page 217.

4. Read the last part of the chapter called Summing Up. What was the connection between slavery and cotton growing?

Know These Important Terms

cotton gin   **Old Southwest**
Old South

Know the Main Idea

Here is the MAIN IDEA of this chapter.

In the 1800's, cotton became the main crop of the South. As cotton growing grew in importance, the number of slaves increased in the South.

Keep this MAIN IDEA in mind as you study the chapter. Ask yourself the following questions as you read. They will help you remember the MAIN IDEA.

1. What invention helped to make cotton the most important crop in the South? Who was the inventor?

2. Where did the South sell most of the cotton it grew?

3. What percentage of the white families in the South did not own any slaves? How many free black men lived in the South?

THE YEARS OF THIS CHAPTER ARE 1800 TO 1850

1800   1850

THE CHAPTER LESSON BEGINS HERE

The South Changed from Tobacco Growing to Cotton Growing

Most of the people in the South were farmers. Before the Revolutionary War, farmers in the Southern states grew tobacco, rice, and indigo. However, after the Revolutionary War, the price of tobacco went down. Many Southern farmers then started to grow wheat and other products.

In the early years of the United States, cotton was grown in the South. But at first, cotton growing cost the planter too much money because a worker had to work a whole day to remove the seeds from one pound of cotton. In 1793, however, Eli Whitney, a young New Englander, invented the **cotton gin.** The cotton gin was a machine that re-

moved seeds from picked cotton fifty times faster than a worker was able to remove them by hand. Cotton was needed for the cotton mills in Great Britain and the United States. Cotton soon became the most important crop in the South.

Southerners Moved West

In the early years of the United States, the South was made up of the states of Maryland, Virginia, North Carolina, South Carolina, and Georgia. However, as the United States grew, the section known as the South also grew.

Between the years 1815 and 1850, the South spread westward to include a huge area of

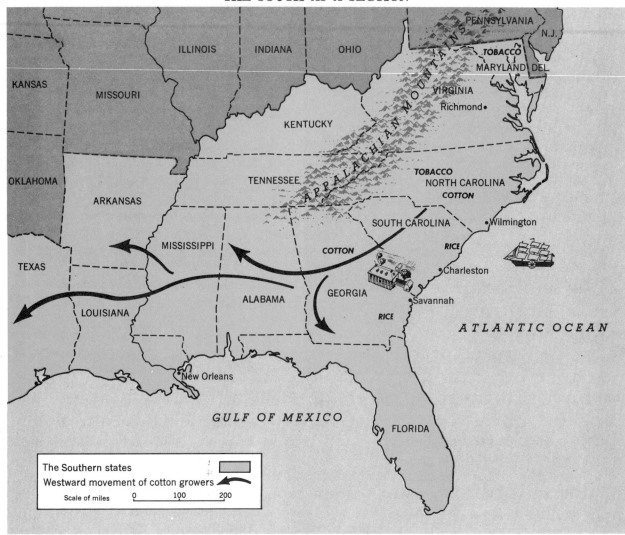

land. The South was made up of three parts: (1) the **Old South,** the Southern states located along the Atlantic coast, (2) the **Old Southwest,** the lands south of the Ohio River, and (3) certain lands west of the Mississippi River—Louisiana, Arkansas, and Texas.

During the 1800's, the factories in Great Britain and the United States needed more and more cotton. The states in the Old South were not able to grow enough cotton to meet

this need. Therefore, after 1815, farmers moved westward, and they started growing cotton in Alabama and Mississippi in the Old Southwest. Later, they moved even farther westward. Soon all these western lands became part of the Cotton Kingdom.

Cotton Growing Required Slavery

At the same time that tobacco growing was ending in the South, it looked as if slavery might also end. After the Revolutionary War, many Southerners thought that slavery was wrong. Since growing wheat did not require as many workers as growing tobacco, many Southerners were willing to end slavery. But as soon as planters began to make money from cotton growing, they changed their minds. Southern planters came to believe that slaves were needed for growing cotton because cotton growing required many workers. Many Southerners were even sorry that they had agreed in the Constitution not to allow any more slaves to come into the United States after the year 1808.

Slaves Were Traded Within the United States

The number of slaves in the United States grew from 1 million in 1800 to over 4 million in 1860. Prices for slaves also went way up during this period. In 1800, a good field worker sold for about 300 dollars in Virginia. By 1860, a good field worker sold for over 1 thousand dollars in Virginia and almost 2 thousand dollars in New Orleans, Louisiana. Slaves sold for more money in the western lands of the South.

The demand for slaves in the western lands led to a growing slave trade within the United States. Slave traders bought most of their slaves in Virginia, Maryland, Tennessee, and Kentucky. They then shipped the slaves to New Orleans. From New Orleans, the slaves were sold to the planters in the Old Southwest and the other Southern states.

Almost All Southerners Backed Slavery

The South, however, was not a land of large plantations. Even in 1860, only about 10 thousand families in the South owned more than fifty slaves. Some families owned a few slaves. And three fourths of the white families in the South owned no slaves at all.

Mill girls going to work.

THE LOWELL GIRLS

By the 1820's, many cotton manufacturing factories were located in Lowell, Massachusetts. But almost all of these factories were short of skilled workers. To solve this problem, one of the factory owners, Francis Cabot Lowell, encouraged young women between the ages of sixteen and twenty to work in his factory. Other factory owners began hiring girls also. These young working women became known as the Lowell girls.

Many young women from New England farm families worked in the factories. They were attracted by the high (for that day) wages paid by the factory owners. Their wages were about 2 dollars a week plus room and board. For this the young women worked twelve hours a day, six days a week. Many of them were even able to save money out of their salaries.

The young women lived in boarding houses owned by the factories. Many of them read books and attended lectures in their free time. The Lowell girls even put out a magazine of their own stories and poems. But by the 1840's working conditions in the factories became harder. Soon New England girls stopped coming to work in Lowell. Immigrant girls replaced them, and the day of the "Lowell girls" ended.

THE SOUTH

Old South	Old Southwest
Maryland	**Kentucky**
Virginia	**Tennessee**
North Carolina	**Mississippi**
South Carolina	**Alabama**
Georgia	

Lands West of Mississippi River

Louisiana

Arkansas

Texas

An artist's idea of how a cotton plantation in the South looked.

Why then did almost all Southerners believe slavery was necessary to the South? The planters believed that slaves were needed for cotton growing and that slavery was profitable. A planter got a lot more out of his slaves than they cost him. The more slaves he owned, the more money he made, and the more important he was.

The man with one or two slaves supported slavery because he planned to buy more slaves some day and become rich and important. Even the man without any slaves did not want the slaves to be freed. He, too, had hopes of becoming a slave owner.

Free Black People in the South

However, not all the black men in the South were slaves. About 250 thousand were free men. Some black men were given their freedom, and others bought their freedom. A few, especially in Louisiana, became very rich. But most free black men were small farmers or city workers. Slave owners felt that these free men were a danger to slavery.

For this reason, many laws were passed in the South to control free black people. Free black men had to carry papers with them at all times to prove they were free. They were not able to vote, hold office, or, in most states, to testify in court against a white man. Other laws kept them from moving from place to place, from holding certain types of jobs, and from owning guns.

Summing Up

In the early 1800's, cotton became the most important crop grown in the South. The change from tobacco growing to cotton growing helped many people in the South. But it also made slavery an important part of Southern life. In the next chapter, you will read about life in another section, the West. This was the largest of the sections.

AFTER YOU READ THE CHAPTER

Do You Know These Important Terms?

For each sentence below, choose the term that best completes the sentence.

1. A (cotton gin/cotton seeder) was a machine that removed the seeds from cotton fifty times faster than a worker was able to remove them by hand.
2. The states of the South located along the Atlantic coast were called the (Cotton Kingdom/Old South).
3. The lands south of the Ohio River were known as the (Natchez Trace/Old Southwest).

Do You Know This Person?

Tell how this person from the Northeast influenced life in the South.

Eli Whitney

Can You Locate These Places?

Use the map on page 226 to do the following map work.

1. Name the states of the South. Which states make up the Old South? the Old Southwest? Which Southern states are west of the Mississippi River?
2. Follow the symbols that show the westward movement of the cotton growers. From what ports do you think the cotton planters shipped their crops?

Do You Know When It Happened?

What are the years of this chapter? Why is the year 1793 important?

Discovering More About the Main Idea

In the 1800's, cotton became the main crop of the South. As cotton growing grew in importance, the number of slaves increased in the South.

Tell how each of the following developments is related to the MAIN IDEA.

The invention of the cotton gin made cotton the chief crop of the South.

Southerners believed that slaves were needed to grow cotton. The price and number of slaves as well as the slave trade increased as the cotton crop increased.

Although only a small number of Southerners owned slaves, almost all white Southerners supported the idea of slavery.

Can You Discuss the Chapter?

Use the information you learned in this chapter to answer the following questions.

1. Why did cotton farmers move westward in the South?
2. Why did Southerners change their minds about slavery when they changed from tobacco and wheat growing to cotton growing?
3. How can you show that slavery was connected to the growing of cotton?
4. Why did Southerners want to control the activities of free black men in the South?
5. Why did almost all Southerners support the idea of slavery?

Can You Connect the Past and the Present?

1. The economy of the South was based on one crop—cotton. The economy of some countries today is also based on one crop, mineral, or product. What are the dangers of such an economy?
2. The cotton gin had a revolutionary effect on the South in the early 1800's. What new inventions can you name that have had a revolutionary effect on Americans in the 1900's?

CHAPTER 36

The West

A Mountain Man in the West.

BEFORE YOU BEGIN THE CHAPTER

Know What to Look For

1. Fanny Kemble, an English actress, visited the United States in the early 1800's. At this time, traveling across the United States was still difficult. Most people used stagecoaches to travel. Miss Kemble described her trip on a stagecoach like this: "Away galloped the four horses ... and away we went after them, bumping, thumping, jumping, jolting, shaking, tossing, and tumbling over the wickedest road...."

Miss Kemble liked traveling by canals better. Her only complaint about canal boats was that passengers often had to flatten themselves on the deck so that they were not brushed overboard by the many low bridges which crossed the canal. Stagecoaches and canal boats helped connect the West with other parts of the nation. In this chapter, you will read about the section of the nation called the West.

2. Read the title of the chapter. Then

look through the chapter and read each heading. What information can you find about the West by reading only these headings?

3. Look at the picture in the chapter and read the caption. What does the picture show you about the section known as the West? Look at the map of the West on page 232. What symbol is used on this map to show the lands of the West? Note the time line at the beginning of the chapter. What years are included in this chapter? Compare this chapter time line to the unit time line on page 217.

4. Read the last part of the chapter called Summing Up. What helped the West to grow and become rich?

Know These Important Terms

West	**canals**
Old Northwest	**Erie Canal**
squatters	**Mountain Men**
turnpikes	**Mormons**

Know the Main Idea

Here is the MAIN IDEA of this chapter.

By the 1800's, the West was the largest and fastest growing section of the nation.

Keep this MAIN IDEA in mind as you study the chapter. Ask yourself the following questions as you read. They will help you remember the MAIN IDEA.

1. What three parts of the nation made up the section known as the West in the years between 1820 and 1846?

2. What improvements in travel helped the West to grow? In what ways did they help the West to grow?

3. What group of people settled around the Great Salt Lake in what is now Utah?

THE YEARS OF THIS CHAPTER ARE 1800 TO 1846

1800   1846   1850

THE CHAPTER LESSON BEGINS HERE

The West Was a Large and Growing Section

As the United States grew in size and population, the West grew, too. The word **West** itself was used to include different lands in different years of America's history. During the colonial years, the West was the unsettled land inland from the Atlantic coast. Then colonists moved westward and settled this land. By the time of the Revolutionary War, the West included the lands between the Appalachian Mountains and the Mississippi River.

Between the years 1820 and 1846, the West included all the lands west of the Appalachian Mountains to the Rocky Mountains and cer-

tain lands beyond the Rocky Mountains. This area was made up of three parts: (1) the **Old Northwest,** located north of the Ohio River, (2) the lands west of the Mississippi River to the Rocky Mountains, and (3) the Oregon Country. In these same years, certain western lands which were made up of the Old Southwest, Arkansas, Louisiana, and Texas became part of the South.

By the 1800's, the West was the largest section of the nation. The West was also the fastest growing section of the nation. In 1820, one fourth of all the people in the United States lived in the West, and by 1840 one

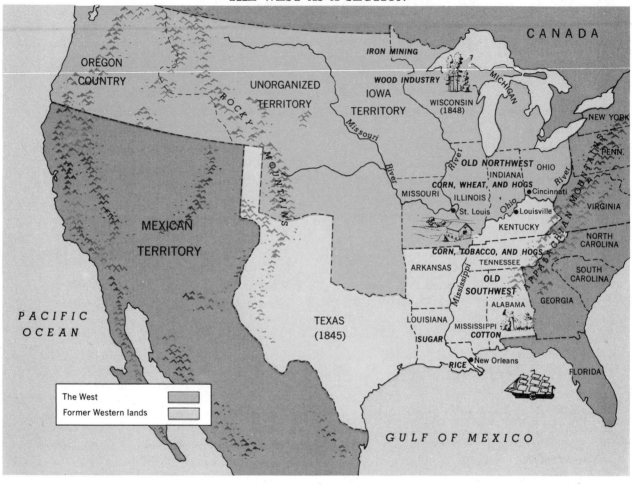

The West As A Section map showing Oregon Country, Unorganized Territory, Iowa Territory, Wisconsin (1848), Michigan, Mexican Territory, Texas (1845), Old Northwest, Old Southwest, and surrounding states.

Legend:
- The West
- Former Western lands

third of the people in the United States lived there.

Land Brought People West

Americans usually moved to the West to find good land. In 1820, Congress passed a law which made it possible for a settler to buy eighty acres of land for 100 dollars. However, settlers without money often just settled the land without paying for it. These settlers were called **squatters.** In 1841, Congress passed a law which gave squatters the chance to buy the land they had settled before it was

put up for sale by the government.

Roads, Canals, and Steamboats Brought People West

At first, the roads which took settlers to the West were poor, but in time better roads, called **turnpikes,** were built. In the 1820's and 1830's, many people also traveled west on **canals,** or man-made waterways. The most famous canal was the **Erie Canal.** The Erie Canal ran over 350 miles across New York State and connected the Great Lakes with the Hudson River. Soon other states rushed to build canals, and by 1837, over 3 thousand miles of canals had been built.

The steamboat also played an important part in the westward movement. Robert Fulton's steamboat, the "Clermont," traveled up the Hudson River in 1807. By the 1830's, hundreds of steamboats were traveling up and down the Mississippi and other western rivers. Roads, canals, and steamboats not only brought people to the West, they also carried the crops of the Western settlers eastward, and they carried manufactured goods from the East westward.

The Old Northwest Was a Farming Area

One of the parts which made up the West was the Old Northwest, located north of the Ohio River. The Old Northwest was settled by several groups of people. Michigan, Wisconsin, and the northern parts of Ohio, Indiana, and Illinois were settled by people from the Northeast. The southern parts of Ohio, Indiana, and Illinois were settled by farmers from the South. And in the 1840's, many newcomers from Europe also settled in the Old Northwest.

The Old Northwest was a rich farming section. Farmers raised wheat, corn, hogs, and cattle. The wheat was sold in the East. Farmers used the corn to feed and fatten hogs and cattle, which they then sold in the East. In the northern part of the Old Northwest, iron mining and lumbering were also important.

Towns Grew Up in the West

As more people moved westward, towns began to develop in the West. These towns grew up along rivers or lakes or where roads or canals joined together. These towns soon became centers of trade and industry in the West. In the Old Northwest, the leading towns were Cincinnati and St. Louis, and, in later years, Chicago.

THE WEST

Old Northwest

Ohio
Indiana
Illinois
Wisconsin
Michigan

*Lands West of the Mississippi River
to the Rocky Mountains*
The Oregon Country

The Lands West of the Mississippi

In the early years of the 1800's, Meriwether Lewis, William Clark, and Zebulon Pike explored the lands west of the Mississippi River. During the 1820's, American traders started an important trade with the Mexican settlers in Santa Fé, New Mexico. About the same time, American fur trappers called **Mountain Men** explored the Rocky Mountain area.

Some Americans began to settle in Texas and Oregon. But one of the largest groups to settle in the West was the **Mormons** (MORE-muns). The Mormons were a religious group founded in the 1820's. The Mormon religion allowed men to have several wives. One of the early Mormon settlements was in Illinois. When they were forced to leave Illinois in 1846, the Mormons moved farther west and settled around the Great Salt Lake in Utah.

Summing Up

By the 1800's, the West was the largest and fastest growing section of the nation. Cheap land and good travel routes helped all parts of the West to grow and become rich. In the next chapters, which are in Unit 10, you will read about the part the three sections played in American government.

AFTER YOU READ THE CHAPTER

Do You Know These Important Terms?

For each sentence below, choose the term that best completes the sentence.

1. During colonial times, the unsettled land inland from the Atlantic coast was called the (**West/tidewater**).
2. The lands north of the Ohio River were called the (**Ohio Territory/Old Northwest**).
3. (**Bountymen/Squatters**) were people who just settled on land without paying for it.
4. (**Avenues/Turnpikes**) were improved roads built during the early 1800's.
5. Man-made waterways are called (**canals/channels**).
6. The (**Mohawk/Erie**) Canal connected the Great Lakes with the Hudson River.
7. Fur trappers who first explored the Rocky Mountain area were called (**explorers/Mountain Men**).
8. The (**Quakers/Mormons**) were a religious group founded in the 1820's.

Do You Remember These People?

Tell something about each of the following persons.

Robert Fulton   **Zebulon Pike**
Meriwether Lewis   **William Clark**

Can You Locate These Places?

Use the map on page 232 to do the following map work.

1. Locate each part of the West.
2. Locate Cincinnati, St. Louis, the Old Northwest, and the Rocky Mountains.

Do You Know When It Happened?

What are the years of this chapter? Tell how each of the following dates was important to the settlement of the West.

1807   1820   1841   1846

Discovering More About the Main Idea

By the 1800's, the West was the largest and fastest growing section of the nation.

Tell how each of the following developments is related to the MAIN IDEA.

The section of the nation called the West included different lands in different years of America's history.

The improved roads, canals, and the steamboat helped settlers to reach the West.

The Old Northwest developed into a rich farming section.

In the 1800's, settlers were moving to the Rocky Mountains and beyond. One of the first of these groups was the Mormons.

Can You Discuss the Chapter?

Use the information you learned in this chapter to answer the following questions.

1. Explain why the West was such an important section from 1800 to 1846.
2. What land laws passed by Congress helped in the settlement of the West?
3. Why was the Old Northwest described as a rich farming section?
4. Where did the Mormons settle after they were forced to leave Illinois?
5. If you had to choose a section of the nation in which to live during the early 1800's, might you select the West? Why?

Can You Connect the Past and the Present?

1. What part of the nation do we think of as the West today? How does this differ from the West between 1820 and 1846?
2. Because of religious differences many Americans did not trust Mormons and they often treated them unfairly. Are people ever treated unfairly because of religious differences in your community?

Americans Enjoy More Freedom

A candidate speaks to voters.

THE CHAPTERS IN UNIT 10 ARE

CHAPTER 37   The Era of Good Feelings
CHAPTER 38   The Sections and the Government
CHAPTER 39   Jackson as President
CHAPTER 40   Changes in the Nation after Jackson

THE YEARS OF THIS UNIT ARE 1816 TO 1844

1800   1816   1844   1975

CHAPTER 37

The Era of Good Feelings

Moving west on the National Road.

BEFORE YOU BEGIN THE CHAPTER

Know What to Look For

1. In the early 1800's, America was growing and on the move. An Englishman named Morris Birkbeck traveled westward in 1817 on the new National Road, which connected the West with the East. Birkbeck was amazed at the number of people traveling across America. He discovered that 12 thousand wagons had passed between Baltimore and Philadelphia during that year. Besides these, many stages completely filled with passengers, and large numbers of travelers on horseback, on foot, or in light wagons had also traveled between Baltimore and Philadelphia. The stages were so full that it was often difficult to get a seat on one. In fact, on one part of his trip, Birkbeck had to walk because he was not able to get a stagecoach. Birkbeck felt that America was moving westward because he saw so many families traveling to settle in the West. In this chapter, you will find out some of the ways in which the American nation was growing.

2. Read the title of the chapter. Look through the chapter and read each heading. From reading the headings, tell what problem faced the United States.

3. Look at the pictures in the chapter and read each caption. What does the first chapter picture show you about settlers who moved West? Look at the map on page 238. How many slave states and how many free states were in the United States in 1820? Note also the time line at the beginning of the chapter. What years are included in this chapter? Compare this chapter time line to the unit time line on page 235.

4. Read the last part of the chapter called Summing Up. What was the period between 1816 and 1824 called?

Know These Important Terms
Tariff Act of 1816
National Road
American System
Marbury against Madison
judicial review
McCulloch against Maryland
Missouri Compromise

Know the Main Idea

Here is the MAIN IDEA of this chapter.

The period between 1816 and 1824 was a time when the American nation and government became stronger. Americans settled the problem of slavery for awhile.

Keep this MAIN IDEA in mind as you study the chapter. Ask yourself the following questions as you read. They will help you remember the MAIN IDEA.

1. Who was President during the "Era of Good Feelings"?
2. What name did the Republicans give to their plan to help the United States grow during the 1800's?
3. What was a free state? How many free states were there in 1819? How many slave states were there?

THE YEARS OF THIS CHAPTER ARE 1816 TO 1844

1816   1824   1844

THE CHAPTER LESSON BEGINS HERE

The Federalist Party Ended, but Federalist Ideas Lived On

During the War of 1812, many members of the Federalist Party, especially those from New England, refused to support the war. Because of this, the Federalist Party became weak, and it ended soon after the war. Although the Federalist Party ended, some Federalist ideas were taken over by the Republican Party.

In the years between 1816 and 1824, the Republican Party was the only important political party in the United States. For this reason, the period between 1816 and 1824 is called the "Era of Good Feelings." James Monroe was President during the "Era of Good Feelings." He was elected President in 1816 and again in 1820.

The United States Tried to Protect Its Factories

Before Monroe became President, Congress passed the **Tariff Act of 1816.** A tariff is a tax collected on goods coming into one country from another nation. The tariff of 1816 was not the first tariff law passed in the United States. But the purpose of the earlier tariffs was to raise money for the federal government. The purpose of the tariff of 1816 was to keep foreign manufactured goods out of the United States. Congress wanted this tariff to protect American factories and to give them a chance to grow.

The United States Built Roads

Western farmers wanted better roads in order to send their crops to Eastern markets. As factories developed in the 1800's, factory owners also wanted good roads in order to send their manufactured products to the West. To meet the need for roads from the East to the West, the federal government built the **National Road.** When the National Road was finished, it ran from Cumberland, Maryland, to southern Illinois. Many states also built roads which ran from the East to the West.

A New National Bank Was Opened

The Republicans in Congress let the first Bank of the United States come to an end in 1811. They soon saw that they had made a mistake. Without the bank, the government had no way to handle the money affairs of

THE MISSOURI COMPROMISE

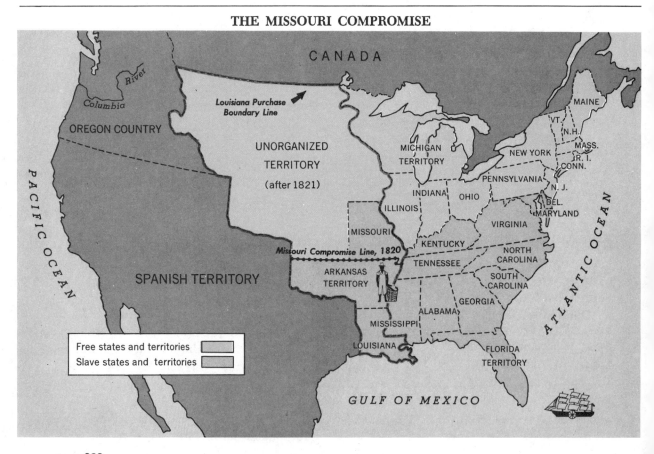

the nation. Therefore, in 1816, Congress approved the opening of the second Bank of the United States. This bank, like the first Bank of the United States, held the government's tax collections and printed paper money.

The Republican Plan Was Called the American System

The tariff, better roads, and the National Bank were the parts of a plan Republicans in Congress worked out to help the United States grow. Republicans called this plan the **American System.** Henry Clay, a great Congressman from Kentucky, gave the plan its name.

The Supreme Court Became Important

The Supreme Court was also helping to build a stronger American nation. The Chief Justice of the Supreme Court was John Marshall, a Federalist who was appointed to the Court by John Adams in 1801. As Chief Justice, Marshall built up the power of the Supreme Court.

One of the most important cases ever to come to the Supreme Court was the case of **Marbury against Madison.** In this case, John Marshall stated that the Supreme Court had the power to declare a law of Congress unconstitutional. The Court has used this power, called **judicial** (joo-DISH-uhl) **review,** ever since.

The Supreme Court Strengthened the Federal Government

The Supreme Court helped to strengthen the federal government. John Marshall stated that the Supreme Court was able to declare a state law unconstitutional. The Court usually declared a state law unconstitutional when that law took away some power from Congress. The best example of this was his deci-

THE GROWING NATION 1791 to 1821

No.	State	Date Admitted
14.	Vermont	March 4, 1791
15.	Kentucky	June 1, 1792
16.	Tennessee	June 1, 1796
17.	Ohio	March 1, 1803
18.	Louisiana	April 30, 1812
19.	Indiana	December 11, 1816
20.	Mississippi	December 10, 1817
21.	Illinois	December 3, 1818
22.	Alabama	December 14, 1819
23.	Maine	March 15, 1820
24.	Missouri	August 10, 1821

sion in the case of **McCulloch against Maryland** in 1819.

In this case, Marshall told the state of Maryland that it did not have the right to tax the Bank of the United States. Marshall then declared that Congress has the right to do whatever is "necessary and proper" to carry out any of its powers. Marshall's decision helped make the American System a success because it made the bank and other parts of the American System constitutional.

The Problem of Slavery Caused Trouble

Certain problems developed in the "Era of Good Feelings" that proved that the nation's feelings were not always all "good." One important problem developed in 1819, when the people of Missouri asked to become a slave state. At that time, the United States had eleven slave states and eleven free states, or states where slavery was not allowed. The free states did not want Missouri to become a slave state because they did not want the slave states to have more votes in the Senate.

The first Bank of the United States was located in Philadelphia. The bank handled the money affairs of the nation.

A Congressman from New York suggested that over a period of years slavery be ended in Missouri. The slave states refused to accept this suggestion. The question of Missouri was finally settled by the **Missouri Compromise** of 1820. This agreement allowed Missouri to come in as a slave state and Maine to come in as a free state. Congress also drew a line on the map across the Louisiana Purchase territory. No slavery was allowed north of this line, but slavery was allowed south of the line. The Missouri Compromise settled the question of slavery for awhile.

Summing Up

The years from 1816 to 1824 were called the "Era of Good Feelings." The Republicans carried out some Federalist ideas, and they helped the nation grow with their American System. The Supreme Court's rulings strengthened the federal government. Slavery began to be a serious problem, but the Missouri Compromise settled this problem for awhile. In the next chapter, you will read about the three sections of the United States and the elections of 1824 and 1828. Each section wanted the federal government to favor its interests.

AFTER YOU READ THE CHAPTER

Do You Know These Important Terms?

For each sentence below, choose the term that best completes the sentence.

1. The first tariff passed to protect American factories was the Tariff Act of (**1816/Abominations**).
2. The (**National Road/Eastern Turnpike**) was built by the federal government to join the East to the West.
3. The plan that Republicans in Congress worked out to help the nation grow was named the (**Plan of Union/American System**).
4. The case of (**Flagg against Clay/Marbury against Madison**) started the idea that the Supreme Court has the power to declare an act of Congress unconstitutional. This power is called (**judicial review/checks and balances**).
5. One case that strengthened the power of the federal government over the states was (**Marshall against West Virginia/McCulloch against Maryland**).
6. The (**Missouri/Louisiana**) Compromise settled the question of slavery for awhile.

Do You Remember These People?

Tell something about each of the following persons.

James Monroe   **Henry Clay**
John Marshall

Can You Locate These Places?

Use the map on page 238 to do the following map work.

1. Locate the states of Illinois and Maryland. How were these two states important in the early growth of the nation?
2. Locate the state of Missouri. What slave states are south of the Missouri Compromise line?

Do You Know When It Happened?

What are the years of this chapter? Tell why each of the following years is important in American history.

1816   **1819**   **1820**

Discovering More About the Main Idea

The period between 1816 and 1824 was a time when the American nation and government became stronger. Americans settled the problem of slavery for awhile.

Tell how each of the following developments is related to the MAIN IDEA.

The "Era of Good Feelings" was a time when there was only one political party.

The government helped industries to grow and built better roads. This plan was called the American System.

The Supreme Court at this time helped to build a stronger American nation.

Can You Discuss the Chapter?

Use the information you learned in this chapter to answer the following questions.

1. How did the Tariff Act of 1816 help give American industries a chance to grow?
2. Why was a second Bank of the United States necessary?
3. What was John Marshall's decision in the case of McCulloch against Maryland?
4. Why did the entry of Missouri as a new state cause problems in 1819?

Can You Connect the Past and the Present?

1. How has the Supreme Court recently shown that it has the power to declare state laws unconstitutional?
2. Protective tariffs are still used today. Do you think protective tariffs are necessary in today's world?

CHAPTER 38

The Sections and the Government

Canals helped join the sections together.

BEFORE YOU BEGIN THE CHAPTER

Know What to Look For

1. On March 4, 1829, the nation's capital was jammed with Americans wishing to see Andrew Jackson inaugurated as President. The high point of the day was the party held at the White House. This party was usually only for high officials. But, the new President ordered that no one was to be turned away.

A large crowd arrived at the party at the White House. This huge mob poured into

the White House. They overturned furniture, knocked down waiters, broke glasses and china, and spilled food and drinks on the rugs. For awhile, it looked as if the whole house was going to be ruined. Only when someone announced that punch was to be served on the lawn was the crowd cleared from the White House. Jackson was truly a new kind of President. He was so different from other

Presidents that his election as President has been called the "Revolution of 1828." You will read about Jackson's election in this chapter.

2. Read the title of the chapter. Then look through the chapter and read each heading. Who was elected President in the election of 1824? in the election of 1828?

3. Look at the pictures in the chapter and read each caption. What does the first picture show you? Look at the map on page 244. Examine the time line at the beginning of the chapter. What years are included in this chapter? Compare this chapter time line to the unit time line on page 235.

4. Read the last part of the chapter called Summing Up. What did the sections of the nation have to do to elect a President?

Know These Important Terms

internal improvements   spoils system
  Democratic Party   Tariff of 1828

Know the Main Idea

Here is the MAIN IDEA of this chapter.

The three sections each had different interests and wanted different things from the federal government. When Andrew Jackson was elected as President, he started new ideas about the government.

Keep this MAIN IDEA in mind as you study the chapter. Ask yourself the following questions as you read. They will help you remember the MAIN IDEA.

1. What three things did the Northeast want from the federal government? Did the other sections also want things?

2. Who received the largest number of votes in the election of 1824? Who became President?

3. What kind of leader did Andrew Jackson believe the President must be? How were Jackson's ideas as President different from those of earlier Presidents?

THE YEARS OF THIS CHAPTER ARE 1824 TO 1828

1816	1824	1828	1844

THE CHAPTER LESSON BEGINS HERE

The Northeast Tried to Protect Manufacturing

The Northeast, the South, and the West each had its own interests and wanted to be favored by the federal government. The Northeast was mainly concerned about manufacturing. It wanted three things from the federal government.

1. The Northeast wanted a high tariff in order to keep out European goods and to protect its own factories.

2. The Northeast wanted **internal improvements,** or roads and canals, to be built by the federal government in order to send its manufactured goods to the West.

3. The Northeast wanted high prices for Western lands so that workers could not leave their jobs and buy land in the West.

The South Tried to Protect Cotton and Slavery

The South was mainly concerned about cotton and slavery. The South also wanted the federal government to help it in certain ways.

1. The South wanted a low tariff because it bought many manufactured goods from

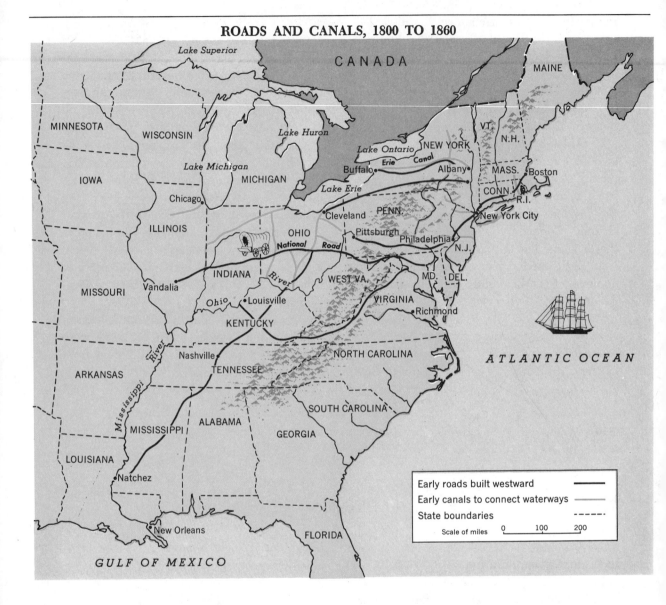

Europe, and a high tariff made the prices of these goods higher.

2. The South did not want the federal government to build roads and canals. It felt that only the states had the right to build roads and canals.

3. The South wanted high prices for Western lands. High land prices cut down the amount of cotton grown in the West, and

Southern planters were able to charge higher prices for their cotton.

The West Tried to Protect Farming

The West was mainly concerned with farming, and it wanted the federal government to help Western farmers.

1. The West wanted a high tariff to keep farm products from Europe out of the United

States. In this way, American farmers were able to sell more farm products.

2. The West wanted the federal government to build roads and canals so that Western farmers were able to send their farm products to the East and receive manufactured products from the East.

3. The West favored low prices for Western lands to attract more settlers.

John Quincy Adams Won the Election of 1824

In the election of 1824, each section tried to elect its candidate for President. The Northeast backed John Quincy Adams of Massachusetts. The South backed William H. Crawford of Georgia. The West backed two candidates. One candidate was Henry Clay of Kentucky, the Republican leader in the House of Representatives. The other candidate was Andrew Jackson, Senator from Tennessee and a hero of the War of 1812.

Andrew Jackson received the largest number of the people's votes as well as the largest number of electoral votes. But Jackson did not have the majority of the electoral votes which the Constitution says a candidate must have to be elected. In such a case, the President is elected by the House of Representatives. In the election in the House of Representatives, Clay supported Adams because both men favored a high tariff and internal improvements. Because of Clay's support, Adams won the election. In the election of 1824, the Northeast and the West joined together and elected a President.

Jackson Won the Election of 1828

During the next four years, Jackson's friends in Congress fought against all the laws President Adams wanted. The only important law passed during President Adams' term was the **Tariff of 1828.** This was the highest tariff ever

John Quincy Adams was elected President in 1824. He was President John Adams' son.

passed by Congress. Meanwhile, Jackson and his followers formed the **Democratic Party** and planned for the election of 1828.

Jackson won the election of 1828 by gaining the support of the people of the West and

Jackson Forever!
The Hero of Two Wars and of Or'eans!
The Man of the People!
HE WHO COULD NOT BARTER NOR BARGAIN FOR THE
PRESIDENCY!

Who, although " *A Military Chieftain*," valued the purity of Elections and of the Electors, **MORE** than the Office of **PRESIDENT** itself! Although the greatest in the gift of his countrymen, and the highest in point of dignity of any in the world,

BECAUSE
It should be derived from the
PEOPLE!

No Gag Laws! No Black Cockades! No Reign of Terror! No Standing Army or Navy Officers, when under the pay of Government, to browbeat, or
KNOCK DOWN

Old Revolutionary Characters, or our Representatives while in the discharge of their duty. To the Polls then, and vote for those who will support
OLD HICKORY
AND THE ELECTORAL LAW.

A campaign poster for Andrew Jackson in the Presidential election of 1828.

the South. They felt that President Adams was only interested in helping the businessmen of the Northeast. Also by 1828, many more people were able to vote. During the 1820's, most states gave all white male citizens the right to vote. These new voters were the people who elected Jackson as President in 1828. For this reason, Jackson was called the "people's President."

Jackson's Ideas as President

Jackson's ideas of the Presidency were different from those of earlier Presidents. He believed that the President must be a strong leader and that he must serve all the people of the United States. Jackson felt that the

President had just as much right as Congress or the Supreme Court to decide what laws were good for the nation.

Jackson was the first President to veto, or turn down, a law because he did not like it. Earlier Presidents vetoed laws only if they believed that these laws were unconstitutional. Only nine laws were vetoed by earlier Presidents. But Jackson vetoed twelve laws during his eight years as President.

Jackson Was the Leader of His Political Party

Andrew Jackson also believed that the President must be the leader of his political party. He thought that political party members deserved rewards for their service and that this system of rewards helped build a strong party. As President, Jackson had the power to appoint and remove federal job holders. He removed about 900 job holders, and he replaced them with loyal Democrats.

Jackson was not the first President to appoint his friends to government jobs. But he gave more jobs to his friends than any other President before him. This rewarding of party members with government jobs was called the **spoils system.** Jackson believed in the spoils system because it gave more men a chance to hold government jobs. He believed that all men, not just rich and important men, were able to serve in government.

Summing Up

The three sections of the country each had different interests and wanted to be favored by the federal government. In the election of 1824, the Northeast and the West worked together and elected John Quincy Adams President. In 1828, the South and the West elected Andrew Jackson President. Jackson had new ideas about the Presidency. In the next chapter, you will read about Jackson as President.

AFTER YOU READ THE CHAPTER

Do You Know These Important Terms?

For each sentence below, choose the term that best completes the sentence.

1. Roads and canals that are built by the federal government are called (**federal projects/internal improvements**).
2. The followers of Andrew Jackson formed the (**Democratic/Whig**) Party.
3. The rewarding of party members with government jobs was called the (**spoils/paternal**) system.
4. The Tariff of (**1816/1828**) was the highest tariff ever passed by Congress.

Do You Remember These People?

Tell something about each of the following persons.

John Quincy Adams   William H. Crawford
Henry Clay   Andrew Jackson

Can You Locate These Places?

Use the map on page 244 to do the following map work.

1. Locate the three sections of the nation. Why do you think the people of the West favored internal improvements?
2. Locate the state of Tennessee. Which man that you read about in this chapter came from this state?

Do You Know When It Happened?

What are the years of this chapter? Place the following events in the order in which they occurred.

The highest tariff was passed by Congress.
Andrew Jackson was elected as President.
John Quincy Adams was elected as the nation's President.
Andrew Jackson started the spoils system.
The Democratic Party was formed by Jackson and his followers.

Discovering More About the Main Idea

The three sections each had different interests and wanted different things from the federal government. When Andrew Jackson was elected as President, he started new ideas about the government.

Tell how each of the following developments is related to the MAIN IDEA.

It was necessary for at least two of the sections to get together to elect a President.

Andrew Jackson was a favorite of the people, especially those who had just received the right to vote.

Jackson believed the President must serve all the people and that he must be the leader of his party.

Can You Discuss the Chapter?

Use the information you learned in this chapter to answer the following questions.

1. Compare the feelings of each of the three sections about internal improvements, the tariff, and the price of western land.
2. Explain why Jackson, who received the largest number of votes in the election of 1824, did not become President.
3. Why was Andrew Jackson called the "people's President"?
4. What new ideas did Jackson have about the Presidency?

Can You Connect the Past and the Present?

1. What system is used in your community today to fill government jobs? Do you agree with this system?
2. How does your community feel about internal improvements? Who do you think should pay for these improvements—the local, state, or federal government? Why?

CHAPTER 39

Jackson as President

President Jackson on his way to Washington, D.C.

BEFORE YOU BEGIN THE CHAPTER

Know What to Look For

1. The Cherokee Indians were among the group of Indians that Americans spoke of as the "civilized tribes." These Indians successfully took many new ideas from the white man. In fact, they lived almost like the white settlers. In the early 1800's, one member of the Cherokees, named Sequoya, developed an alphabet. The Cherokees now had a written language. Up to that time, no group of Indians had a written language. With their new written language the Cherokees were able to record their history and save it for future generations.

The Cherokees were shocked when President Jackson forced them to give up their land and moved them to lands west of the Mississippi. The removal of all Indians to lands west of the Mississippi was one action taken by President Jackson.

2. Read the title of the chapter. Then look through the chapter and read each heading. Using the information in the headings, list the things Jackson did during his years as President.

3. Look at the pictures in the chapter and read each caption. What is happening in the first chapter picture? Note also the time line at the beginning of the chapter. What years are included in this chapter? Compare this chapter time line to the unit time line on page 235.

4. Read Summing Up in the last part of the chapter. What things did Jackson do as President?

Compare this chapter time line to the unit time line on page 235.

Know These Important Terms
nullify   state banks
secede

Keep this MAIN IDEA in mind as you study

Know the Main Idea
Here is the MAIN IDEA of this chapter.

President Jackson did much to please the West and the South. He proved to be a strong President, and he showed that all states were expected to obey the laws of the United States.

Keep this MAIN IDEA in mind as you study the chapter. Ask yourself the following questions as you read. They will help you remember the MAIN IDEA.

1. What two Indian wars resulted from President Jackson's decision to move all Indian tribes to lands west of the Mississippi River?
2. What action on western lands displeased people in the Northeast section?
3. What action did President Jackson take toward the Bank of the United States?

THE YEARS OF THIS CHAPTER ARE 1828 TO 1836

1816   1828   1836   1844

THE CHAPTER LESSON BEGINS HERE

Jackson Moved the Indians West
One of Jackson's first acts as President was to ask all Indians to move west of the Mississippi River. Many Indian tribes signed treaties, or agreements, giving up their lands east of the Mississippi. Almost 100 tribes moved west of the Mississippi during the years Jackson was President.

However, some tribes fought for their lands. Two Indian wars broke out because some Indians did not want to leave their lands. The Black Hawk War in Illinois only lasted a short time. But the Seminole (SEM-uh-nohl) Indians of Florida, supported by runaway slaves, fought for years before their lands were taken away. The Cherokee (CHER-uh-kee) Indians

of Georgia went to court to protect their lands. Although the Supreme Court backed the Cherokee Indians, the state of Georgia still took their lands.

Jackson Slowed Down Internal Improvements
President Jackson pleased the people of both the South and the West by moving the Indians. However, the South and the West disagreed over internal improvements. The West wanted the federal government to build roads and canals into Western lands. But the South believed that only the states had this power.

President Jackson was called the "people's President." He was popular with Americans.

President Jackson tried to please both sections. He agreed to the building of roads when he felt they served the needs of the whole nation. But when the road only served a part of the nation, he refused to build it. Some Westerners did not like Jackson's plans, which slowed down road building and canal building by the federal government.

Jackson and the Sale of Western Lands

But President Jackson soon won back Western support by favoring lower prices for Western land. Southerners also backed the West in favoring low prices for Western land because the South wanted the West's support for a low tariff. The Northeast, however, was against cheap land. In fact, the Northeast wanted the sale of Western land to be stopped completely.

The land question caused a big fight in Congress. President Jackson backed the Westerners and the Southerners. As a result, the sale of Western land continued. But the price of Western land remained the same, $1.25 an acre. The Northeast was not pleased by this settlement.

The South Wished to Disobey the Tariff Law

An even bigger fight broke out over the tariff which Congress passed in 1828. This Tariff of 1828 was the highest ever passed in the United States. The people of the South were strongly against the new tariff. Southerners were not against a tariff that raised money for the government. But they felt that a tariff, such as the Tariff of 1828, to protect factories in the Northeast was unfair and unconstitutional.

Vice-President John C. Calhoun of South Carolina spoke for the South. Calhoun developed the states' rights argument. He declared that a state had the right to **nullify**

(NUL-uh-fy), or refuse to obey, a law which the state thought was unfair and unconstitutional. Some Southerners went even further than Calhoun. They believed that a state had the right to **secede** (suh-SEED), or leave the United States, if the state felt a federal law was unfair.

Jackson Forced South Carolina to Accept the Tariff Law

In 1832, Congress passed a lower tariff, but South Carolina also refused to accept this tariff. South Carolina nullified the Tariff of 1832 and threatened to secede from the United States if the federal government tried to force it to obey the tariff. Calhoun even gave up his job as Vice-President in order to lead the fight against the tariff in Congress.

President Jackson did not favor the tariff, but he soon showed that he expected every state to obey the laws of the United States. To make sure South Carolina obeyed the tariff, Jackson sent warships to Charleston, South Carolina. He also threatened to lead an army to South Carolina himself. South Carolina and President Jackson decided to settle the problem peacefully. Congress worked out an agreement which lowered the tariff, and South Carolina accepted this lower tariff.

Jackson Ends the Bank of the United States

You may remember that the second Bank of the United States was opened in 1816. Unless Congress passed a new law, the Bank was to go out of business in 1836. Many Congressmen thought the Bank was doing a good job and wanted to allow it to remain open for another twenty years.

But President Jackson was against the Bank, and he wanted the Bank to end. Jackson felt that the Bank had too much power because it held the government's tax collections. Jackson

Indians moving to the West.

INDIANS GO WEST

As early as 1803, Thomas Jefferson suggested sending all the Indians west of the Mississippi River. They were to be resettled in part of the territory included in the Louisiana Purchase. Small numbers of Indians did move West during the years between 1810 and 1820. But during this time, the Indians themselves were able to decide whether or not they wanted to move.

By the middle of the 1820's, the government began to encourage the Indians to move further West. The Indians were offered a territory of their own. No white men were to be able to settle in this territory. Then, Andrew Jackson became President. He believed that the Indians must move West whether they wished to or not. If they remained in the East, they were to lose the right to govern themselves by their own laws.

The Land Removal Act of 1830 put this policy into force. The Supreme Court tried to protect the Indians but failed. By 1840, most Indians left the area east of the Mississippi River. Some left peacefully. Others, such as the Seminoles, fought bravely but unsuccessfully against moving. Only a few Indian tribes remained east of the Mississippi.

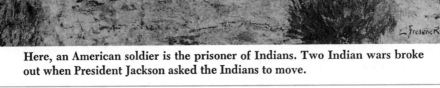

Thomas Gilcrease Institute, Tulsa, Oklahoma.

Here, an American soldier is the prisoner of Indians. Two Indian wars broke out when President Jackson asked the Indians to move.

and his supporters in the South and West also believed that the Bank was used mostly to help the businessmen of the Northeast, and not to help the whole nation.

In 1832, Congress passed a law allowing the Bank to remain open. Jackson quickly vetoed this law. After he won the election of 1832, Jackson decided to end the Bank. He took the federal government's money out of the Bank of the United States and put it into **state banks.** This weakened the Bank, and it went out of business in 1836.

Summing Up

Jackson proved to be a strong President. He moved many Indian tribes west of the Mississippi River. Jackson had the federal government build some roads, and he supported the sale of Western lands. He upheld the power of the federal government when he forced South Carolina to accept the Tariff of 1832. And Jackson ended the Bank of the United States. In the next chapter, you will read about changes Jackson made in American life.

AFTER YOU READ THE CHAPTER

Do You Know These Important Terms?

For each sentence below, choose the term that best completes the sentence.

1. To (avoid/nullify) means to refuse to obey a law which a state thinks is unfair and unconstitutional.
2. The right of a state to leave the United States was called the right to (succumb/secede).
3. President Jackson took the federal government's money out of the Bank of the United States and put it into (state/farmers') banks.

Do You Remember These People?

Tell something about each of the following persons.

Andrew Jackson   John C. Calhoun

Can You Locate These Places?

Use maps in your classroom to do the following map work.

1. Locate Florida. Locate the Mississippi River. How are these locations related to the events in this chapter?
2. Locate the port city of Charleston. In which state is it located? Why was it necessary to send warships to this harbor?

Do You Know When It Happened?

What are the years of this chapter? Tell what event each of the following dates is related to.

1828   1832   1836

Discovering More About the Main Idea

President Jackson did much to please the West and the South. He proved to be a strong President, and he showed that all states were expected to obey the laws of the United States.

Tell how each of the following developments is related to the MAIN IDEA.

President Jackson moved the Indians to lands west of the Mississippi River. He favored low prices for western lands, and he slowed down internal improvements.

The tariff caused problems for President Jackson. He showed that all states must obey the tariff law of the United States.

President Jackson took the government's money out of the Bank of the United States and placed it in state banks.

Can You Discuss the Chapter?

Use the information you learned in this chapter to answer the following questions.

1. President Jackson asked the Indians to move west of the Mississippi River. What were the results of this act?
2. How was President Jackson able to please the people in both the South and the West?
3. Which sections were in favor of the high protective tariff? Why did Jackson force South Carolina to obey the tariff?
4. Why was President Jackson against the Bank of the United States?
5. Do you think President Jackson was right to move the Indians west of the Mississippi River? Why or why not?

Can You Connect the Past and the Present?

1. Jackson tried to stay popular by pleasing people in the South and the West even when these people had different interests on such things as internal improvements and the tariff. How do political leaders in your community deal with groups who have different interests?
2. What can an individual or state do today if he or it disagrees with a federal law?

CHAPTER 40

Changes in the Nation After Jackson

Detail from George C. Bingham (after) *The County Election, 1854.* Courtesy Museum of Fine Arts, Boston. M .& M. Karolik Collection.

Americans voting in the 1800's.

BEFORE YOU BEGIN THE CHAPTER

Know What to Look For

1. "Tippecanoe and Tyler, too" was a famous slogan, or saying, in the Presidential election of 1840. Tippecanoe was General William Henry Harrison, who defeated the Indians in the Northwest Territory at the Battle of Tippecanoe. Tyler was his running mate for Vice-President.

Today, election slogans are often colorful and clever but they do not win many votes.

In 1840, however, there were no television sets, and candidates were not able to campaign by speaking to millions of people. Instead, candidates used brass bands, colorful parades, and election banners to win votes. Slogans were an easy way to help Americans remember candidates for President. In this chapter, you will read more about the election of 1840 and why it was important.

2. Read the title of the chapter. Then look through the chapter and read each heading. By reading just the headings, tell why you think the election of 1840 was important.

3. Look at the pictures in the chapter and read each caption. What do the pictures show you about American elections in 1840? Examine the time line at the beginning of the chapter. What years are included in this chapter? Compare this chapter time line to the unit time line on page 235.

4. Read the last part of the chapter called Summing Up. In what years did the United States suffer from hard times? What is the topic of the next chapter?

Know These Important Terms

Jacksonian Democracy	depression
Whigs	treasuries

Know the Main Idea

Here is the MAIN IDEA of this chapter.

Jacksonian Democracy gave the people a larger part in their government, but in the years between 1837 and 1844, the nation suffered from hard times.

Keep this MAIN IDEA in mind as you study the chapter. Ask yourself the following questions as you read. They will help you remember the MAIN IDEA.

1. How did the Democratic Party feel about free public schools?

2. Which one of Jackson's ideas helped to cause the hard times that began in 1837? When did good times begin to come back to the United States?

3. What did the Whigs plan to do if they won the election of 1840? Were they able to carry out these plans?

THE YEARS OF THIS CHAPTER ARE 1836 TO 1844

1816   1836   1844

THE CHAPTER LESSON BEGINS HERE

Jackson's Ideas Helped City Workers

The ideas of Jackson and his followers are often called **Jacksonian Democracy.** These ideas made important changes in American life. Many of Jackson's strongest followers were the workers who lived in the large cities in the Northeast. City workers had hard lives. They worked long hours for very low pay.

You may remember that some city workers formed unions to help improve their working conditions, but these early unions were not too successful. Many workers then joined Jackson's new Democratic Party because it promised to help the workers. The Democratic Party was able to get some states to pass laws that cut down the workday and made factories safer. The Democratic Party also worked to get laws passed starting free public schools.

Changes in State Government

Jacksonian Democracy helped to make changes in the state governments. The men who wrote the state constitutions just after the Revolutionary War did not believe that the common man was able to take part in government. Therefore, only property owners were allowed to vote or to hold office. And the members of the state legislature, not the voters, appointed the governor and other state officials.

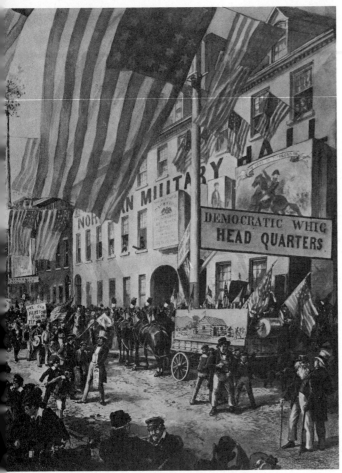

A rally for William Henry Harrison, the Whig candidate, in the election of 1840.

Jacksonian Democracy changed all this. New state constitutions were written. These constitutions gave most white male citizens the right to vote, and also allowed them to hold office. Under the new constitutions, the governors were elected by the people, and the powers of the governors were increased. The voters also elected judges and other state officials. Under Jackson, workers began to have an important part in government.

Van Buren Was Elected President in 1836

In 1835, President Jackson decided not to run for a third term. As a result, the Democratic Party chose Vice-President Martin Van Buren as their candidate in the election of 1836. The people who disliked Jackson and his ideas formed a new political party called the **Whigs.** The Whigs supported three men for President—each of them was from a different section of the nation. But Van Buren was elected President.

Hard Times Began in 1837

Almost as soon as Van Buren became President, a **depression,** or hard times, hit the United States. This depression was largely the result of one of Jackson's ideas.

If you remember, in 1833 President Jackson took the federal government's money out of the Bank of the United States and put it into certain state banks. Some of these state banks printed too much paper money, and they were not able to back up this money with gold and silver to give it value. The banks loaned this paper money to people who wanted to buy Western lands.

In 1836, President Jackson ordered that Western land had to be paid for with gold or silver. But few Americans had gold or silver. Most Americans had the cheap paper money printed by state banks. When they demanded that the banks give them gold or silver for their paper money, the banks were not able to do so. Soon many banks had to close.

The Depression Continued

Without banks to borrow money from, many factories and businesses had to close down. Thousands of workers lost their jobs. Farmers were hard hit too because many people did not have the money to buy farm products. Also, the value of their land went down.

Van Buren, and most other Americans at this time, did not know how to end a depression. The government did nothing to help city

In this picture, William Henry Harrison is being inaugurated as President. He died after serving only one month in office.

workers, farmers, or businessmen. President Van Buren took the federal government's money out of the state banks. He had Congress pass an act which set up **treasuries,** or places to store the government's money. The government treasuries kept the money safe, but they did not help bring back good times to the nation.

Harrison Was Elected President in 1840

The depression hurt the Democratic Party because many Americans blamed the depression on the Democratic party. For this reason, the Whigs were sure that they had a good chance to elect a President in 1840. To win Western votes, the Whigs chose William Henry Harrison, the hero of the Battle of Tippecanoe, as their candidate. To win Southern votes, the Whigs chose John Tyler of Virginia to run as Vice-President.

The Whigs told voters that Van Buren ate off gold dishes and wasted the people's money. They said Harrison was a poor farmer who lived in a log cabin and drank hard cider. However, Harrison really was a rich man from an old Virginia family. But the Whig plan worked. William Henry Harrison defeated Van Buren in the election of 1840.

Good Times Returned to the United States

The Whigs planned to open a new Bank of the United States, to pass a higher tariff, and to give the money raised from the sale of Western lands to the states. But Harrison died early in 1841, and John Tyler became President. Tyler did not have the same ideas. He agreed with the Democrats rather than with the Whigs. Although the tariff was raised a little while Tyler was President, he vetoed the other parts of the Whig plan. He was against a new bank and a higher tariff.

By 1844, good times began to come back to the United States. Farmers began to make more money. And business got back to normal. Once again most workers were able to find jobs.

Summing Up

Jacksonian Democracy gave the American people a larger part in their government. However, one of Jackson's ideas failed, and in the years from 1837 to 1844, the United States suffered hard times. By 1844, business began to improve again. In the next chapters, which are in Unit 11, you will learn about important changes in American life in the years between 1800 and 1860.

AFTER YOU READ THE CHAPTER

For each sentence below, choose the term that best completes the sentence.

1. The ideas of Jackson and his followers are often called Jacksonian (**Politics/Democracy**).
2. People who disliked Jackson and his ideas formed a new political party called the (**Whigs/Federalists**).
3. A (**depression/recession**), or hard times, hit the United States in 1837.
4. Places to store the government's money were called (**vaults/treasuries**).

Do You Remember These People?

Tell something about each of the following persons.

Martin Van Buren
William Henry Harrison
John Tyler

Can You Locate These Places?

Use maps of the United States on pages 220, 226, and 232 to review the location of these three sections.

Northeast   South   West

Be sure that you know the states that are included in each section.

Do You Know When It Happened?

What are the years of this chapter? Place the following events in the order in which they occurred.

President Harrison died.
Martin Van Buren became President.
John Tyler became President.
Hard times hit the nation.
The Whig Party was formed.

Discovering More About the Main Idea

Jacksonian Democracy gave the people a larger part in their government, but in the years between 1837 and 1844, the nation suffered from hard times.

Tell how each of the following developments is related to the MAIN IDEA.

The followers of Jackson made important changes in state government which gave more people the right to vote and gave more power to the voters.

The depression of 1837 was largely the result of state banks printing too much paper money and not being able to back this money with gold and silver.

Can You Discuss the Chapter?

Use the information you learned in this chapter to answer the following questions.

1. Why were city workers usually members of the Democratic Party?
2. Describe some of the changes Jacksonian Democracy made in American life.
3. Why did a depression hit the United States between 1837 and 1844?
4. What was the plan used by the Whigs to win the election of 1840?
5. If you had lived in the 1830's and 1840's, would you have favored the Democrats or the Whigs? Why?

Can You Connect the Past and the Present?

1. City workers were once strong supporters of the Democratic Party. Which party do most workers in your city favor today?
2. In 1837, the government did very little about the depression because it did not know what to do. Can you name some ways in which the government controls the nation's money system today?

American Life From 1800 to 1860

Winter in Brooklyn, New York, in the 1800's.

THE CHAPTERS IN UNIT 11 ARE

CHAPTER 41 Everyday American Life, 1800–1860
CHAPTER 42 Changes in American Thought
CHAPTER 43 Americans Work for a Better Nation
CHAPTER 44 Black Americans in the North
CHAPTER 45 Black Americans in the South

THE YEARS OF THIS UNIT ARE 1800 TO 1860

1800   1860   1975

Everyday American Life, 1800-1860

The McCormick reaper.

BEFORE YOU BEGIN THE CHAPTER

Know What to Look For

1. At one time, the coming of the circus was one of the big events of the year for families all over America. Every spring, the circus started its yearly tour to hundreds of American towns. A few weeks before the show came to town, posters were put up telling when the circus was coming. For weeks, people saved their money to go to the circus. They looked forward to seeing the strange and exciting world of the circus. Here they saw elephants, trained bears, roaring lions, giants, bearded ladies, clowns, and jugglers. When the circus left town, many young boys and girls dreamed of leaving home and joining the circus. Some did. But most stayed home and waited for next year's show. In this chapter, you will read more about everyday life in America.

2. Read the title of the chapter. Then look through the chapter and read each heading. From reading the headings, what are some topics that you might expect to read about in this chapter?

3. Look at the pictures in the chapter and read each caption. What do the pictures show you about American life? Note also the time line at the beginning of the chapter. What years are included in this chapter? Compare this chapter time line to the unit time line on page 259. How do the years of this chapter compare with the years of the unit?

4. Read the last part of the chapter called Summing Up. In what ways did life in the United States change in the years from 1800 to 1860? What will the next chapter be about?

Know These Important Terms

reaper   revival meetings

Know the Main Idea

Here is the MAIN IDEA of this chapter.

In the years from 1800 to 1860, life changed in the United States. City families and farm families were developing different ways of life.

Keep this MAIN IDEA in mind as you study the chapter. Ask yourself the following questions as you read. They will help you remember the MAIN IDEA.

1. Name one machine which helped change the life of the farmer.

2. Name some new types of amusements that appeared during the early 1800's.

3. Who led the fight for free public schools?

THE YEARS OF THIS CHAPTER ARE 1800 TO 1860

1800   1860

THE CHAPTER LESSON BEGINS HERE

Farm Life Became Easier

In the years between 1800 and 1850, most farm families lived very much like farm families of the colonial period. They still made most of the things they needed. However, during the 1850's, life began to change for American farmers. For the first time, they began to buy large amounts of manufactured goods.

During the 1850's, life became easier for farmers. New farm machines such as the steel plow made it possible for farmers to grow larger crops in less time. One of the most important of these new machines was the **reaper** invented by Cyrus McCormick. The McCormick reaper helped the farmer to speed up the cutting and gathering of his crops.

People Developed New Ways of Living in the Cities

During the years between 1800 and 1860, people in the cities began developing ways of living that were different from the ways people lived on farms. City people were able to buy many of the things they needed. They did not grow their own food, make their own clothes, or make products they needed for the house.

In the 1820's, Americans learned how to pack food in cans. Packing food in cans stopped it from spoiling. Canned foods were important in helping American cities grow because they made it possible to feed the large numbers of people who were now living in cities.

Detail from *Skating in Central Park*. City Art Museum of St. Louis.

Americans who lived in the city and the country enjoyed winter sports.
Here, city families are skating in Central Park in New York City.

New Clothing Styles Were Worn

Clothing styles also changed during the 1800's. The changes in clothing styles were greater in the cities than on the farms. The new clothing styles were much simpler than the fancy clothes and large wigs that American colonists wore before the Revolutionary War.

Men wore long pants rather than the knee breech pants of colonial times. American women began to copy their clothing styles from Paris instead of from London. Dresses were long and graceful with wide hooped skirts.

Americans Enjoyed a Good Time

Many of the amusements that were popular with Americans during colonial times were still popular during the 1800's. Hunting, fishing, and horse racing were amusements still favored by many Americans. Music, dancing, traveling shows, and winter sports were enjoyed by Americans who lived in the cities and in the country.

City people also became interested in indoor amusements. Cities had theaters and music halls which offered plays and concerts all year round. Plays from foreign countries and American plays were both very popular. Many famous British actors came to America to perform in theater plays.

Americans Developed New Types of Amusements

Some amusements were started by Americans. One of these amusements was the minstrel show. The first minstrels were black men who played and sang the plantation songs of the South. Later, white men painted their faces black and took the parts in the minstrel shows. Stephen Foster wrote many of his most famous songs for these minstrel shows.

Phineas T. Barnum's American Museum in New York City was another kind of amusement which started in America. In his museum, Barnum put on concerts and Wild West Shows. He also showed such people as the world's fattest lady and tallest man, gave lectures and speeches, and held beauty contests for babies. Many years later, Barnum and J. A. Bailey opened the famous Barnum and Bailey Circus.

Religion in American Life

In the 1800's, religion still played an important part in American life. Many American churches gained new members. In New England, a new church called the Unitarian Church was started.

You may remember reading about the Great Awakening of American religion in the 1700's. About the year 1800, another awakening of religion took place along the frontier. Groups of people came together to attend **revival meetings.** These revival meetings were religious meetings, and they were often held outdoors. Sometimes, they lasted several days. The ministers or preachers who spoke at these meetings urged people to lead better lives by following the teachings of their religion. They also encouraged people to help each other. This helped make frontier life better.

Americans attending a revival meeting. These religious meetings became popular on the frontier in the 1800's.

Many American women read the popular fashion magazine, "Godey's Lady's Book," to find out what the latest fashions were.

Free Public Schools Were Started

Americans wanted a good education for their children. After the Revolutionary War, Americans stopped using British textbooks in their schools. They started using American books such as Noah Webster's famous *Spelling Book*. Webster also wrote a dictionary of American words. Webster's dictionary of the American language and other American textbooks helped Americans to be proud of their nation.

Until about 1830, the United States had few public schools. Rich people sent their children to private schools. Most workers' children did not go to school. However, some of them were able to attend church schools. American workers realized that their children needed an education to get ahead. But many Americans did not want to pay taxes to send other people's children to school.

Horace Mann of Massachusetts led the movement for free public schools. He told

Americans it was necessary for all children to receive a good education because education made better citizens and better workers. In time, more and more Americans agreed with Mann. By the 1850's, the states of the Northeast and the states of the Old Northwest had free public elementary schools which were supported by taxes. Most high schools, however, were still private.

Summing Up

Life changed in the United States in the years from 1800 to 1860. City families and farm families were developing different ways of life. Clothing styles changed, and Americans found many new amusements. Americans remained interested in religion, and many people attended revival meetings. Free public schools were set up in many states. In the next chapter, you will find out what Americans were reading and writing from 1800 to 1860.

AFTER YOU READ THE CHAPTER

Do You Know These Important Terms?

For each sentence below, choose the term that best completes the sentence.

1. The (scythe/reaper) was a machine that helped the farmer speed up the cutting and gathering of crops.
2. (Gospel/Revival) meetings were religious meetings often held outdoors.

Do You Remember These People?

Tell something about each of the following persons.

Cyrus McCormick   Stephen Foster

Phineas T. Barnum   J. A. Bailey

Noah Webster   Horace Mann

Can You Locate These Places?

Use the maps in your classroom to do the following map work.

1. Locate some cities of the early 1800's.
2. Locate the Northeast and the Old Northwest. What relationship did these areas have to free public education?

Do You Know When It Happened?

What are the years of this chapter? Place the following events in the order in which they occurred.

Horace Mann led the fight for free public schools.

Revival meetings were held on the frontier.

The Northeast and Old Northwest had free elementary schools.

A new American industry began—canned food packing.

Discovering More About the Main Idea

In the years from 1800 to 1860, life changed in the United States. City families and farm families were developing different ways of life.

Tell how each of the following developments is related to the MAIN IDEA.

The life of the farmer became easier as new farm machines were used to raise larger crops and to speed up the cutting and gathering of crops at harvest time.

New clothing styles and new types of amusements appeared.

Many Americans remained interested in religion and in leading better lives.

Free public elementary schools were set up in the states of the Northeast and Old Northwest.

Can You Discuss the Chapter?

Use the information you learned in this chapter to answer the following questions.

1. How did the life of the farmer change between 1800 and 1860? the city dweller?
2. Compare the amusements that were popular with Americans in the early 1800's with those of colonial days. Which were alike? Which were different and new?
3. Why were some persons against free public schools? How did Horace Mann show Americans that education was important?
4. How did the textbooks used in schools during the early 1800's change?
5. If you lived between 1800 and 1860, what might have been your favorite type of amusement?

Can You Connect the Past and the Present?

1. The idea of free public elementary schools was new in the early 1800's. How many years of free public education is it possible to get in your community today?
2. Sometimes older people are concerned about the clothing styles that younger people wear. Explain how this is not new.

CHAPTER 42

Changes in American Thought

The University of Michigan in 1856.

BEFORE YOU BEGIN THE CHAPTER

Know What to Look For

1. When the last morning bell rang in the one-room schools of the 1800's, students quickly took their seats. The school day began when the teacher, or one of the older students, read from the Bible. After this, the students sang a hymn and said a prayer. Then, a student often recited a poem he had memorized. This poem might be about America or everyday life. But almost always, the poem recited

in class was written by an American writer.

By the 1830's and 1840's, Americans were writing great books and poetry. They were also producing low priced magazines and newspapers. These books, magazines, and newspapers were popular with many Americans because so many Americans enjoyed reading. In this chapter, you will read more about American culture in the 1800's.

2. Read the title of the chapter. Then look through the chapter and read each heading. What part of the United States produced great writers and poets?

3. Look at the pictures in the chapter and read each caption. What do the chapter pictures show you about American culture in the 1800's? Note the time line at the beginning of the chapter. What years are included in this chapter? Compare the chapter time line to the unit time line on page 259.

4. Read the last part of the chapter called Summing Up. What did Americans become interested in? What is the topic of the next chapter?

Compare the chapter time line to the unit time line on page 259.

Know These Important Terms

lyceum lectures   penny newspapers

Know the Main Idea

Here is the MAIN IDEA of this chapter.

In the 1800's, America produced great writers and poets. The American people became interested in learning, in reading, and in listening to speakers.

Keep this MAIN IDEA in mind as you study the chapter. Ask yourself the following questions as you read. They will help you remember the MAIN IDEA.

1. Who were the first two American writers to become famous all over the United States?
2. Name the most famous Southern writer and poet. What kind of stories is he famous for writing?
3. How can you prove that Americans of the early 1800's enjoyed art?

THE YEARS OF THIS CHAPTER ARE 1800 TO 1860

1800   1860

THE CHAPTER LESSON BEGINS HERE

American Writers Stopped Using European Styles

In the year 1837, Ralph Waldo Emerson (EM-ur-sun), a great American writer and thinker, made a speech in which he urged Americans to free themselves from European ideas and tastes. But long before Emerson made his speech, American writers stopped copying European styles. They no longer depended on Europe for their ideas. Instead, American writers began to write about American life and history. The first American writers to become famous all over the United States were James Fenimore Cooper and Washington Irving.

Cooper wrote adventure stories about the sea and the frontier. His most famous book is

The Last of the Mohicans. Washington Irving wrote humorous stories of life in New York when it was called New Netherland and was ruled by the Dutch. His stories "Rip Van Winkle" and "The Legend of Sleepy Hollow" are still popular today.

Two Americans Developed New Styles of Writing

Later, American writers moved even farther away from European styles. Herman Melville (MELL-vill) wrote sea stories. In his books, Herman Melville tried to show that red men, yellow men, brown men, and black men all have ways of life that are worthy of respect.

page 267

George Eastman House.

At left is Walt Whitman, who developed a new form of poetry. At right is Ralph Waldo Emerson, another great American writer.

Melville's most famous book was *Moby Dick,* the strange story of the captain of a whaling ship and his hunt for a white whale called Moby Dick.

Walt Whitman was a poet who developed his own style of writing. Whitman broke away from the old forms of poetry and wrote in what is now called free verse. Whitman was the poet of the common man because he believed in the American nation and the abilities of all its people. His most famous work, *Leaves of Grass,* is full of hope for the growing American nation and its people. Both Whitman and Melville were ahead of their time. They are read much more now than they were in their own day.

New England Produced Many Great Writers and Poets

Cooper, Irving, Melville, and Whitman were all from New York. But the most famous writers of the period between 1830 and 1860 came from New England. Nathaniel Hawthorne (HAW-thorn) wrote *The Scarlet Letter* and other books about the early Puritans. Ralph Waldo Emerson and Henry David Thoreau (THOR-oh) wrote books which tried to teach men to lead better lives.

The most famous poet from New England was Henry Wadsworth Longfellow. He wrote about America's early history in such poems as "Paul Revere's Ride" and *The Song of Hiawatha.* James Russell Lowell and John Greenleaf Whittier wrote poems against slavery. Two other famous New England poets whose works are still enjoyed today were William Cullen Bryant and Oliver Wendell Holmes.

The South Also Produced Famous Writers

The South produced many writers, but most of them spent their time writing books to defend slavery. However, William G. Simms of South Carolina and John P. Kennedy of Maryland wrote good books about the South and the Old Southwest. But the most famous Southern writer and poet was Edgar Allan Poe. Poe's moving poems and his stories of mystery and terror made him one of the greatest writers of his time.

Americans Learned by Listening to Speakers

In the years from 1800 to 1860, many Americans wanted to become better educated. Americans wanted to learn about the world. Hundreds of thousands of people all over America learned by attending **lyceum** (ly-SEE-um) **lectures,** or talks. Many writers, scientists, and government leaders spoke at these lectures. The lyceum gave Americans a chance to learn about the important things going on in the world.

Magazines Became Very Popular

Another way that Americans learned what was going on in the world was by reading magazines. By the 1840's, hundreds of magazines were put out in the United States. Some of these magazines contained stories and poems, and they gave Americans the chance to read the writings of the best American and European writers. The most popular of this type of magazine was *Harper's Monthly Magazine,* which still comes out today. The most popular ladies' magazine was *Godey's Lady's Book,* which showed the latest fashions.

Noah Webster

EARLY AMERICAN SCHOOL BOOKS

Almost as soon as the United States won its independence, Americans wanted their own school books. The first American speller was written by Noah Webster in 1783. This speller became very popular, and it was used in almost every elementary school in America. It was still being printed over one hundred years after it was written, and nearly 100 million copies were sold over the years.

Webster also wrote the first American school reader. This book, which came out in 1785, was popular, but it did not sell as well as the speller. Its main competition came from readers written by Caleb Bingham. Bingham's books contained writings of Jefferson, Franklin, and other American leaders. Its purpose was to teach children to lead good lives.

The first American geography book, *Geography Made Easy,* was written by Reverend Jedediah Morse in 1784. At first, the book had 214 pages. Over the years, the book grew to over 400 pages. Morse described each American state separately. He described the state's geography and also its plants, animal life, government, and history. Morse also wrote about other nations.

In one-room country schools, such as the one above, students read poems and books written by American writers.

Detail from *The Country School* by Winslow Homer. City Art Museum of Saint Louis.

Americans Read the New Penny Newspapers

Americans also learned by reading the popular **penny newspapers**, or newspapers that sold for one cent. The *New York Sun,* the first successful penny newspaper, came out in 1833. Later, it was followed by the *New York Herald* and *New York Tribune.* Then penny papers began to appear in other cities.

Each of these newspapers was somewhat different. The *New York Sun* and the *New York Herald* carried stories of crime and scandal. The *New York Tribune,* Horace Greeley's paper, supported causes such as the end of slavery and more rights for women. All these penny newspapers were easy to read, and by the 1840's, they also began to have pictures.

Americans Enjoyed Art

Few of the American artists of the early 1800's are well known today. Their work does not appeal to modern Americans. But the people of the 1800's liked their work, and usually even the poorest families had copies of their favorite paintings in their homes.

Summing Up

In the years between 1800 and 1860, America produced great writers and poets. These writers stopped using European styles. Americans became interested in learning, and they began to read and enjoy books, newspapers, and magazines. Lectures were also a popular way of learning about the world. In the next chapter, you will learn about how some Americans tried to improve life in America.

AFTER YOU READ THE CHAPTER

Do You Know These Important Terms?

For each sentence below, choose the term that best completes the sentence.

1. Hundreds of thousands of people all over America learned by attending talks called (**night classes/lyceum lectures**).
2. Newspapers that sold for only one cent during the early 1800's were called (**daily papers/penny newspapers**).

Do You Remember These People?

Tell something about some of the following persons.

Ralph Waldo Emerson
James Fenimore Cooper
Walt Whitman
Henry David Thoreau
James Russell Lowell
William Cullen Bryant
William G. Simms
Edgar Allan Poe
Washington Irving
Herman Melville
Nathaniel Hawthorne
Henry Wadsworth Longfellow
John Greenleaf Whittier
Oliver Wendell Holmes
John P. Kennedy
Horace Greeley

Can You Locate These Places?

Use the maps in your classroom to locate the following places. Tell how each place is related to the chapter.

New York State   **New England**
The South   **New York City**

Do You Know When It Happened?

What are the years of this chapter? When did the first penny newspaper appear? When did the newspapers start to have pictures?

Discovering More About the Main Idea

In the 1800's, America produced great writers and poets. The American people became interested in learning, in reading, and in listening to speakers.

Tell how each of the following developments is related to the MAIN IDEA.

American writers began to write about American life and history rather than copying European styles.

Americans learned by reading books, magazines, and newspapers and by listening to lectures by writers, scientists, and government leaders.

Although the American artists of the early 1800's are not popular today, the people of the 1800's liked their work.

Can You Discuss the Chapter?

Use the information you learned in this chapter to answer the following questions.

1. Which two Americans tried new styles of writing?
2. Why didn't the South produce many writers that are still remembered today?
3. Why do you think so many people attended the lyceum lectures?
4. How did magazines and newspapers help the writers and poets?
5. If you had lived in New York City in the 1840's, which of the penny newspapers might you have bought? Why?

Can You Connect the Past and the Present?

1. Today, there are many famous American writers and poets. Can you name a famous present-day writer or poet?
2. Many Americans think that people today spend too much time watching television and do not read enough. Do you agree?

CHAPTER 43

Americans Work For a Better Nation

Presenting a temperance petition to a state legislature.

BEFORE YOU BEGIN THE CHAPTER

Know What to Look For

1. As the cold, gray dawn of a January morning began to light up the sky, William Lloyd Garrison finished the first issue of a new newspaper. The name of this newspaper was *The Liberator*. Its aim was to liberate, or set free, the slaves in the United States.

The first issue of *The Liberator* appeared on New Year's Day in 1831. By then the United States had made great advances, but many problems still had to be solved. The worst of these problems was slavery. With his new newspaper, Garrison hoped to strike a blow against his life-long enemy—slavery. Many Americans at this time were interested in improving life for their fellow citizens. You will read about some of these people and how they were trying to make America a better place in this chapter.

2. Read the title of the chapter. Then look through the chapter and read each heading. Make a list of things some Americans were trying to improve during the early 1800's by reading the headings.

3. Look at the pictures in the chapter and read each caption. What do the pictures show you about the work of reformers? Note also the time line at the beginning of the chapter. What years are included in this chapter? Compare this chapter time line to the unit time line on page 259.

4. Read the last part of the chapter called Summing Up. Which movement became the most important reform movement?

Know These Important Terms
abolition movement   reform

immediate abolition   gradual abolition
temperance movement

Know the Main Idea
Here is the MAIN IDEA of this chapter.

In the years between 1820 and 1860, many reform movements developed in the United States to improve life. The abolition movement, or the effort to end slavery, became the most important.

Keep this MAIN IDEA in mind as you study the chapter. Ask yourself the following questions as you read. They will help you remember the MAIN IDEA.

1. What did prison reformers want to do?
2. What religious group was one of the first to speak out against slavery?
3. What did all abolitionists agree about?

THE YEARS OF THIS CHAPTER ARE 1820 TO 1860

1800   1820   1860

THE CHAPTER LESSON BEGINS HERE

Many Americans Wanted to Improve Life

In the years between 1820 and 1860, many Americans wanted to make the world a better place to live in. They wanted to **reform,** or to make things better for the people of the United States. These Americans were called reformers.

Reformers Helped Prisoners and Sick People

One reform movement tried to improve the treatment of prisoners and insane, or mentally ill, people. In the 1800's, prisons were horrible, cold, and dirty places. The young prisoners learned new methods of crime from the older prisoners. Prison reformers tried to improve conditions in prisons. They wanted to turn prisons into places to prepare prisoners to lead a better life.

One of the women active in prison reform was Dorothea L. Dix. She discovered that many insane people were locked up in prisons. As a result, Dorothea Dix worked to set up hospitals where mentally ill people were given proper treatment and where they might be cured.

Reformers Tried to End Alcoholic Drinks

Some reformers felt that Americans drank too much. They believed that heavy drinking

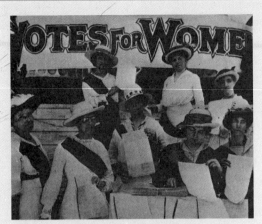

Women asking for the vote.

WOMEN'S RIGHTS

The struggle for women's rights in America has a long history. As early as colonial times, women asked for equal rights. In the 1830's and 1840's, women joined reform movements to work for the end of slavery and for temperance laws. But most men did not welcome women in these movements. As a result, women decided to work to improve their own position.

In 1848, a Women's Rights Convention met in Seneca Falls, New York. Mrs. Elizabeth Cady Stanton wrote a "declaration of independence" for women at this convention. This declaration made twelve demands. One of these demands was that women be allowed to vote. Frederick Douglass, the black leader, strongly supported this demand.

Susan B. Anthony was another important leader in the struggle for women's rights. Just before the Civil War, Miss Anthony was able to get several states to give married women the right to own property and to manage their own affairs. In 1869, the state of Wyoming gave the right to vote to women. But by 1916, only ten other states followed Wyoming's example. Finally in 1920, with the Nineteenth Amendment to the Constitution, all American women gained the right to vote.

caused people to lose their jobs and to turn to crime. This movement against the use of alcoholic drinks was called the **temperance movement.**

Some reformers in the temperance movement just wanted people to cut down on their drinking. But others wanted to end drinking altogether. In time, the temperance movement became strong enough to force some states to pass laws against using alcoholic drinks. Maine was the first state to pass such a law, in 1846.

Women Worked for Equal Rights

Women reformers began to work for equal rights with men. In the 1800's, women were not able to own property, to go to college, or to hold most jobs. And women were not allowed to vote or to hold office. To fight for equal rights, a group of American women held a Women's Rights Convention in 1848. At this meeting, the women wrote a "declaration of independence" for women.

Women such as Emma Willard, Lucy Stone, Elizabeth Cady Stanton, and Lucretia Mott led the reform movement for women's rights. It took many years before women won the right to own property, to go to college, and to become schoolteachers.

Reformers Brought About
Other Changes

American reformers tried to improve life in many other ways. Some reformers worked for peace and talked about a "Congress of Nations" to settle world problems. Others worked for better conditions for factory workers. Still other reformers opened schools for deaf people or blind people.

Reformers Worked Against Slavery

In time, the most important reform groups were those groups that were formed to end slavery. The Quakers were among the first Americans to speak out against slavery. In the early 1800's, other religious groups in the North also began to teach that slavery was wrong. Soon, many Americans who were members of other reform groups joined the effort to end slavery. This effort became known as the **abolition movement**. Members of this movement were called abolitionists.

Before 1830, leaders of the abolition movement like Benjamin Lundy believed that slavery must be ended slowly and that planters must be paid for their slaves. This was called **gradual abolition.** Even some Southerners agreed with this program. Many Americans favored gradual abolition as a way to settle the slavery problem.

Reformers Were Agreed that Slavery Must Be Ended

On January 1, 1831, however, a Northern abolitionist named William Lloyd Garrison started putting out a newspaper called *The Liberator.* In this paper, Garrison demanded that all slave owners begin freeing their slaves immediately without receiving any payment. Soon after, Garrison helped form the New England Anti-Slavery Society, which supported his program of **immediate abolition.**

Other leading Northern abolitionists— Wendell Phillips, Gerrit Smith, and Theodore D. Weld—did not always agree with Garrison's ideas. All abolitionists agreed, however, that slavery was evil and must be ended. But some abolitionists felt that the slaves needed a period of training before they were finally freed. Abolitionists also disagreed on the way to gain an end to slavery. Some felt they needed to form their own political party. Others wanted to work through the older political parties. And still others wanted to work on their own to end slavery apart from political parties.

This slave is a field hand. In the 1800's reformers worked to end slavery.

An angry mob attacks Elijah Lovejoy, the famous abolitionist, and sets fire to the warehouse where he printed his newspaper.

Many Northerners Disagreed with the Abolitionists

At first, many Northerners disagreed with the abolitionists. Slaves were considered to be property, and Northern property owners did not like the idea of taking a man's property away from him without paying him in return. Northern businessmen were afraid that the abolition movement might hurt their trade with the South. Northern workers were afraid of losing their jobs, or of being paid less money, if the slaves were freed and these freed slaves came to the North looking for jobs.

For a while, some Northerners tried to stop the abolitionists. They used force to break up abolitionists' meetings. Mobs smashed the abo-

litionists' printing presses. One time, Garrison had to be put in prison in order to protect him from a mob. And Elijah Lovejoy, a famous Illinois abolitionist, was killed by a mob. But the abolitionists were not stopped.

Summing Up

Many reform movements developed in the United States between the years 1820 and 1860. Reformers worked to have prisoners and mentally ill people treated better, to gain equal rights for women, and to end drinking. But the abolition movement, or the effort to end slavery, became the most important reform movement in America. In the next chapter, you will find out how black Americans tried to win their freedom.

AFTER YOU READ THE CHAPTER

Do You Know These Important Terms?

For each sentence below, choose the term that best completes the sentence.

1. The fight to end slavery became known as the (**freedom/abolition**) movement.
2. The demand that all slave owners begin freeing their slaves immediately without any payment was called (**instant freedom/ immediate abolition**).
3. The movement against the use of alcoholic drinks was called the (**temperance/abstinence**) movement.
4. Between 1820 and 1860, many Americans wanted to (**correct/reform**), or make things better for the people of the United States.
5. The idea that slavery must end slowly and that planters must be paid for their slaves was called (**gradual abolition/progressive freedom**).

Do You Remember These People?

Tell something about some of these people.

Dorothea L. Dix
Lucy Stone
Lucretia Mott
Gerrit Smith
Elijah Lovejoy
William Lloyd
  Garrison

Emma Willard
Benjamin Lundy
Wendell Phillips
Theodore D. Weld
Elizabeth Cady
  Stanton

Can You Locate These Places?

Use the map on page 292 to locate the following places. Tell how each location is related to the chapter events.

    Maine   Illinois

Do You Know When It Happened?

What are the years of this chapter? Why are the following dates important?

        1831   1848

Discovering More About the Main Idea

In the years between 1820 and 1860, many reform movements developed in the United States to improve life. The abolition movement, or the effort to end slavery, became the most important.

Tell how each of the following developments is related to the MAIN IDEA.

Prison improvements, the temperance movement, and the fight for equal rights for women began during the early 1800's.

Reformers began to demand an end to slavery. All abolitionists agreed that slavery must be ended.

Many Northerners as well as Southerners were against the idea of immediate abolition.

Can You Discuss the Chapter?

Use the information you learned in this chapter to answer the following questions.

1. What were the aims of prison reformers during the early 1800's?
2. What were some of the important reform movements in the early 1800's?
3. Why do you think the abolitionists were not as successful as they might have been?
4. Why were many Northerners against the abolition movement?
5. If you lived during the early 1800's, would you have favored gradual or immediate abolition? Why?

Can You Connect the Past and the Present?

1. What reform groups are active today? Describe some of their activities in your community.
2. Women claim they are sometimes treated unfairly in certain jobs because they are women. Can you give an example of how women are treated unfairly in jobs today?

CHAPTER 44

Black Americans in the North

Abolition meeting held by black Americans.

BEFORE YOU BEGIN THE CHAPTER

Know What to Look For

1. Ira Aldridge, a black man, became one of the most famous actors in the world during the early 1800's. He learned to act at the African Free School in New York. He also attended the University of Glasgow in Scotland. Aldridge began his acting career in London, where he won great success performing for the kings and queens of Europe. He was especially famous for his role in Shake-speare's play *Othello* and in plays about slavery. In many of his parts, Aldridge had to wear white makeup in order to play the role of a white man.

At this time, many black people in the North led difficult lives. In this chapter, you will read about the black people in the North and how they worked to help themselves and the black people who were still in slavery.

2. Read the title of the chapter. Then look through the chapter and read each heading. From reading the headings, what topics do you expect to read about in this chapter?

3. Look at the pictures in the chapter and read each caption. What do the pictures show you about the fight against slavery in the North? Note also the time line at the beginning of the chapter. What years are included in this chapter? Compare this chapter time line to the unit time line on page 259.

4. Read the last part of the chapter called Summing Up. For what two things were free black people in the North fighting? What will be the topic of the next chapter?

Know These Important Terms
segregated   benefit societies

poll tax   black conventions
boycotted

Know the Main Idea
Here is the MAIN IDEA of this chapter.

Free black people in the North had many problems. They struggled to gain equal rights and to end slavery.

Keep this MAIN IDEA in mind as you study the chapter. Ask yourself the following questions as you read. They will also help you remember the MAIN IDEA.

1. What type jobs did most free black people in the North hold during the early 1800's?
2. Who were the most important black abolitionist speakers?
3. What actions did free black people in the North take to help themselves?

THE YEARS OF THIS CHAPTER ARE 1800 TO 1860

1800   1860

THE CHAPTER LESSON BEGINS HERE

Black Americans Had Problems in the North

You may remember reading about the problems of free black Americans in the South. In the North, their life was not much better. In most states, black men were not allowed to vote or to serve on juries. They were **segregated,** or separated, from whites in schools, churches, hospitals, hotels, restaurants, streetcars, and railroads.

In the early years of the 1800's, black Americans in the North lived in mixed neighborhoods. As time went on, however, they were forced to live in their own neighborhoods. Making a living also became more difficult for black men. Most black men were not able to find jobs as skilled workers because skilled white workers refused to work with them. Even black men who learned a trade were forced to work at unskilled jobs. When large numbers of immigrants arrived in the United States between 1830 and 1860, they took away many of these unskilled jobs from black workers.

In spite of all these problems, many black men did well—especially in the service trades. They became tailors, restaurant owners, and hotel keepers. James Forten of Philadelphia made a fortune as a manufacturer of ship sails. Other black men owned grocery stores, barber shops, and stables. A few became lawyers, doctors, ministers, and teachers.

Black Americans Struggled for Their Rights

Black Americans in the North struggled to win their rights. They asked state legislatures to end unfair laws. Some refused to pay the state **poll tax,** or voting tax, unless they were actually allowed to vote. Black people often **boycotted,** or refused to ride, the segregated streetcars, or they sat in the seats set aside for whites. One woman in New York City even sued the streetcar company. She won her case, but this did not end segregated streetcars.

Black people stood in the aisles of churches rather than sit on segregated benches. Some black people refused to pay school taxes as long as schools were segregated. One man sued the Boston school board for forcing him to send his daughter to a segregated school. He lost his case in court, but in 1855, a state law was passed which ended segregation in all Massachusetts schools.

A Few Black Americans Wanted to Return to Africa

In most cases, black Americans lost their struggle for equal rights. A few decided to return to Africa. Paul Cuffe, a wealthy black ship owner from Massachusetts, sent thirty-eight people to Africa. Some Southerners also sent their slaves to Liberia after freeing them.

Some slaves who gained their freedom went to settle in Liberia in Africa. The capital city of Liberia, Monrovia, is shown below.

A few other free black Americans settled in Liberia with the help of the American Colonization Society. But most free black people wanted to remain in the United States. They wanted to work for equal rights for themselves and freedom for those who were still in slavery.

Black Americans Formed Groups to Fight for Freedom

To fight for equal rights and freedom, black Americans found it necessary to join together and form groups. Even before 1800, free black people of the Northeast formed **benefit societies,** or self-help groups. Black men also started their own churches. In the 1800's, Richard Allen, a former slave, helped form the African Methodist Episcopal Church. Black Baptists also formed their own churches. The benefit societies and the black churches tried to help their members to get an education, to hold jobs, and to win equal rights.

Black abolitionist groups were formed long before any white abolitionist groups were started. These black abolitionist groups worked hard against slavery, but they were not very successful. However, black abolitionists had a strong influence on William Lloyd Garrison, a famous white abolitionist, who put out the newspaper *The Liberator.*

Black Speakers Helped the Abolition Movement

Black men and women also joined abolitionist groups as speakers. They told many terrible stories about their own lives as slaves. These stories helped many Northerners to learn how horrible slavery was and made many people decide that slavery was wrong. The most famous black speakers were Harriet Tubman, Sojourner Truth, and Frederick Douglass.

SOJOURNER TRUTH

As a slave in New York, she was called Isabella. When she became free in 1827, Isabella changed her name to Sojourner Truth. She called herself Sojourner Truth because she was to sojourn, or travel around, and tell people the truth about slavery. Sojourner Truth was six feet tall and very thin. Although she was not able to read or write, she had a brilliant mind. Sojourner Truth became the first black woman to speak for the abolition movement. She traveled all over the nation telling Americans about life as a slave. Her moving speeches completely captured her listeners' attention.

In the 1840's, Sojourner Truth also became interested in the women's rights movement. In 1852, she attended the second National Women's Suffrage Convention. At this meeting, the women tried to stop Sojourner Truth from speaking because she was black. But during the meeting she suddenly got up and gave her speech. It was one of the best speeches of the meeting.

During the Civil War, Sojourner Truth worked as a nurse. She also worked to end segregation on the streetcars of Washington, D.C. And until her death in 1883, she worked to improve life for her people.

This picture shows Frederick Douglass, an escaped slave, who became an important leader in the abolition movement.

Frederick Douglass was an escaped slave. He showed great courage by making these public speeches. He was always in danger of being captured. Douglass spoke and wrote against slavery all over the North. Because of his great abilities, Douglass became one of the most important abolitionists. Douglass showed that black men wanted their freedom.

Black Americans Worked to Help Themselves

Even after white abolitionist groups were formed, black Americans kept trying to help themselves. In the early 1830's and the 1840's, several **black conventions,** or meetings, were held. These conventions backed such political actions as appeals to Congressmen to abolish slavery and to win equal rights for free black people. Conventions were an important joint action by black men, and they called attention to the conditions black Americans lived under.

Some black leaders were not satisfied with this program. In the North, these leaders urged black men to do business only with other black men. And they hoped to open a museum and library to build up pride in black people and their past. A few even wanted to stir up slave revolts and to fight against the practice of returning runaway slaves to their masters in the South.

Summing Up

Free black Americans in the North had many problems. But they fought against unfair treatment and worked to gain equal rights. Free black Americans in the North also fought to end slavery. In the next chapter, you will learn what slaves were doing to help themselves.

AFTER YOU READ THE CHAPTER

Do You Know These Important Terms?

For each sentence below, choose the term that best completes the sentence.

1. Black people were (**discriminated/segregated**), or separated, from whites in schools, churches, hospitals, hotels, restaurants, streetcars, and railroads.
2. A voting tax is called a (**ballot/poll**) tax.
3. Black people often (**stimulated/boycotted**), or refused to ride, segregated streetcars.
4. Some groups of black people formed (**benefit societies/church circles**), or self-help groups, to fight for equal rights.
5. Large meetings held by black Americans in the 1830's and 1840's were called black (**convocations/conventions**).

Do You Remember These People?

Tell something about these people.

James Forten	William Lloyd Garrison
Richard Allen	Sojourner Truth
Harriet Tubman	Frederick Douglass
Paul Cuffe	

Can You Locate These Places?

Use maps of the United States and Africa to locate the following places. Tell how each place is connected with the events in this chapter.

New York City   Massachusetts   Liberia

Do You Know When It Happened?

What are the years of this chapter? Place the following events in the order in which they occurred.

Segregation ended in the Massachusetts schools.

Black conventions appealed for action.

Black people lived in mixed neighborhoods.

Black people formed benefit societies.

Discovering More About the Main Idea

Free black people in the North had many problems. They struggled to gain equal rights and to end slavery.

Tell how each of the following developments is related to the MAIN IDEA.

Free black people in the North were segregated from whites. In many states they were not able to vote or to serve on juries.

Black people in the North struggled to win their rights and to end segregation. They were not very successful in their efforts.

Black people formed their own abolition groups and also worked with white abolitionists.

Can You Discuss the Chapter?

Use the information you learned in this chapter to answer the following questions.

1. Why did making a living become more difficult for black men during the 1800's?
2. How did some black people try to gain their equal rights?
3. Why did most free black people want to remain in America instead of returning to Africa?
4. Why was Frederick Douglass such an important leader in the abolition movement?
5. How do you think black people in the North might have tried to win their rights during the early 1800's?

Can You Connect the Past and the Present?

1. Are some citizens in your community segregated or prevented from enjoying their equal rights? How is this done?
2. What similarities can you see between the black American's struggle for rights in the 1800's and the civil rights movement of today?

CHAPTER 45

Black Americans in the South

Slaves on a Southern plantation in 1862.

BEFORE YOU BEGIN THE CHAPTER

Know What to Look For

1. Harriet Tubman was born a slave, but when she was in her early twenties she escaped from the South and fled to the North. Once free, she wanted to help free other slaves. She made about nineteen trips to the South over a period of ten years and helped more than 300 slaves reach freedom. Each time Harriet Tubman returned to the South, she risked her own freedom and even her

life. At one time, Southern plantation owners offered 40 thousand dollars for the capture of Harriet Tubman, dead or alive. Again and again she escaped capture.

Later, she became a spy for the North during the Civil War. Harriet Tubman was one of the many black people who tried to win freedom for those in slavery. In this chapter, you will read how slavery conditions became worse as cotton growing spread westward, and how slaves worked to win their own freedom.

2. Read the title of the chapter. Then look through the chapter and read each heading. How did slaves show they were unhappy as slaves? Use only the headings for your information.

3. Look at the pictures in the chapter and read each caption. What do the pictures show about the lives of slaves in the South? Note also the time line at the beginning of the chapter. What years are included in this chapter? Compare this chapter time line to the unit time line on page 259.

4. Read the last part of the chapter called Summing Up. How did slaves try to win their freedom? What is the topic of the next chapter?

Know These Important Terms

overseers   Underground Railroad

petitions

Know the Main Idea

Here is the MAIN IDEA of this chapter.

Black people never accepted slavery. They tried to gain their freedom in many different ways.

Keep this MAIN IDEA in mind as you study the chapter. Ask yourself the following questions as you read. They will help you remember the MAIN IDEA.

1. What was the relationship between the westward spread of cotton growing and slave conditions?

2. Which slave revolt was most successful?

3. What was the Underground Railroad? How did it operate?

THE YEARS OF THIS CHAPTER ARE 1800 TO 1860

1800   1860

THE CHAPTER LESSON BEGINS HERE

Slavery Became Worse

As you read earlier, cotton growing spread from the Old South to the Old Southwest and to lands even farther west. As cotton growing spread, slavery conditions became worse. Slave codes, or the rules controlling the slaves, became more strict. Cotton growing turned into a big business, and planters became more interested in making money. At the same time, they became less interested in slave conditions. Some Southerners did not live on their plantations. And some Southerners owned more than one plantation. These Southern plantation owners usually hired **overseers,** or managers, to run their plantations for them.

Overseers were paid more money if they grew more cotton. Therefore, overseers often worked the slaves hard, and some overseers whipped slaves to get them to work harder. The plantation owner usually did not like to see his slaves treated this way, but he was not around often enough to stop it. And besides, he too made more money if the overseers produced a larger crop.

Some Slaves Tried to Revolt

Slave revolts were as old as slavery itself. But during the 1800's, slave revolts in the South became more serious. In the year 1800, a slave blacksmith named Gabriel Prosser

Nat Turner led a slave revolt in Virginia in 1831. Here, he is shown planning the revolt with other slaves.

planned a revolt of the slaves around Richmond, Virginia. Over a thousand slaves marched on the city, but someone told the city leaders about the revolt and the soldiers were ready. The revolt failed, and Gabriel Prosser and about thirty of his followers were hanged.

In 1822, Denmark Vesey (VEE-zee), a free black man, tried to carry out a revolt of the slaves around Charleston, South Carolina. Once again someone told the city leaders about the planned revolt. No one is sure just how many slaves were in with Vesey. But many were arrested, and Vesey and many others were hanged.

The most famous slave revolt took place in Virginia in 1831. This revolt was led by Nat Turner, a preacher, who believed that it was his duty to lead the slaves to freedom. Nat Turner and a small band of men started out by killing Nat's owner and his owner's family. Then as Nat traveled through the countryside, he gathered other slaves around him. Within a few days, nearly sixty white Southerners were killed. Armed troops put down Nat Turner's revolt. Nat Turner was later

captured, and he and many of his followers were hanged.

Slave Revolts Upset the South

These slave revolts made Southerners very angry. They were angry at Northern abolitionists. They blamed Nat Turner's revolt on a free Northern black man, David Walker. In 1829, Walker put out *Appeal,* a short book which urged all slaves to fight for their freedom. After Nat Turner's revolt, Southern postmasters refused to deliver abolitionist writings. And for many years, Southern leaders refused to allow Congress to even talk about any **petitions,** or requests, to end slavery.

White Southerners were also frightened by slave revolts. They tightened up the slave codes, or rules regulating the slaves. Slaves were not allowed to meet together anywhere unless a white man was present. And slaves were not allowed to meet with free black men at all. Special patrols, or groups of guards, were organized to make sure that these rules were carried out. These patrols dealt harshly with any slave who left his plantation without a pass.

This picture shows a house in Ohio that was used as a station on the Underground Railroad. How did the Underground Railroad work?

Many Slaves Ran Away

Not all slaves started slave revolts. Some broke their tools. Some killed their masters. Some killed themselves. And thousands of slaves tried to escape from slavery by running away to the North. During the years between 1830 and 1860, over 60 thousand slaves succeeded in reaching the North. Slaves used all kinds of ways to reach freedom. Some slaves used false passes. One slave, Henry Brown, gained his freedom by hiding in a box that was shipped to the North.

It took a great deal of courage for a slave to try to escape. He often had to travel hundreds of miles without food or other supplies. Slave patrols and law officers in each town were hunting for him. If a runaway slave was caught, he often was cruelly whipped. But slaves were willing to take this chance to win their freedom. Many slaves also ran away to try to join their families.

Slaves Were Helped to Escape

Runaway slaves were helped by the famous **Underground Railroad.** This Underground Railroad was a group of people who helped slaves to escape. The Underground Railroad had "conductors," or persons who led slaves out of the South. Every ten or twenty miles, slaves were able to eat and rest at "stations," which were houses or farms. Other people in the North helped runaway slaves to get a new start in life in the North or to move to Canada.

Although many white persons helped, most conductors on the Underground Railroad were black people. Harriet Tubman and Josiah Henson were famous conductors who helped hundreds of slaves to escape. Frederick Douglass used his home and office in Rochester as "stations." And many other free black people gave their time and money to make the Underground Railroad a success.

Summing Up

Slaves never accepted slavery, and they tried to gain their freedom in many ways. Some slaves revolted. Nat Turner's revolt was the most famous slave revolt. Many slaves ran away. The Underground Railroad helped many slaves to escape to freedom. In the next chapter, which begins Unit 12, you will read about how the growth of the United States only made the slavery problem more serious.

AFTER YOU READ THE CHAPTER

Do You Know These Important Terms?

For each sentence below, choose the term that best completes the sentence.

1. Managers hired by plantation owners were called (**slave drivers/overseers**).
2. Requests made by various groups to Congress are called (**petitions/favors**).
3. The (**Underground Railroad/Freedom Train**) was a group of people who helped slaves to escape.

Do You Remember These People?

Tell something about each of the following persons.

Gabriel Prosser	Denmark Vesey
Nat Turner	David Walker
Harriet Tubman	Josiah Henson

Can You Locate These Places?

The routes of the Underground Railroad were located mainly in the North. The Northern cities that were located near the slave states or port cities in the North were important centers of the Underground Railroad. Examine the map of the United States. Which cities do you think might have been important centers of the Underground Railroad?

Do You Know When It Happened?

What are the years of this chapter? Place the following events in the order in which they occurred.

David Walker wrote *Appeal*.
Gabriel Prosser planned a revolt of slaves.
Nat Turner led a revolt in Virginia.
Denmark Vesey tried to carry out a revolt.

Discovering More About the Main Idea

Black people never accepted slavery. They tried to gain their freedom in many different ways.

Tell how each of the following developments is related to the MAIN IDEA.

Slavery conditions grew worse as cotton growing spread westward, and the demand for cotton increased.

Some slaves tried to revolt. Many others escaped or tried to escape. Strict rules were set up to regulate the lives of slaves, and slave patrols were organized to make sure these rules were carried out.

The Underground Railroad helped runaway slaves to escape to Canada or to a city in the North.

Can You Discuss the Chapter?

Use the information you learned in this chapter to answer the following questions.

1. Why did slavery conditions grow worse as cotton growing spread westward?
2. How did the people of the South react to the slave revolt led by Nat Turner? Why did they react this way?
3. Why was it difficult for a slave to escape?
4. How did the Underground Railroad operate?
5. How might you feel about the Underground Railroad, if you were a slave owner? a slave? an abolitionist? a free black person? a Northern bounty-hunter?

Can You Connect the Past and the Present?

1. Whether a person is a hero or not sometimes depends upon your own beliefs. Harriet Tubman and Nat Turner were not heroes to slave owners, but they were heroes to many slaves. Show how a person today might be a hero for one group but not for another.
2. How do you think a state government might handle a revolt today?

America Spreads from Coast to Coast

Moving West by train and wagon.

THE CHAPTERS IN UNIT 12 ARE

CHAPTER 46   Westward to the Pacific Coast
CHAPTER 47   Winning the Mexican War
CHAPTER 48   The United States in the 1850's

THE YEARS OF THIS UNIT ARE 1820 TO 1860

1800   1820   1860   1975

CHAPTER 46

Westward to the Pacific Coast

Settlers moving West on the Oregon Trail.

BEFORE YOU BEGIN THE CHAPTER

Know What to Look For

1. The Alamo is an old mission in San Antonio, Texas. In this tiny mission in 1836, less than 200 Americans had been under attack by a Mexican army for two weeks. On March 6, 1836, 3 thousand Mexican troops made their final attack. The Americans in the Alamo fought until the last man was dead. Among those lying dead, were the famous Jim Bowie and Davy Crockett. "Re-

member the Alamo" became the battle cry of Americans fighting in Mexico. In this chapter, you will read about the growth of the United States during the early 1800's. Americans wanted the United States to reach all the way to the Pacific Ocean.

2. Read the title of the chaper. Then look through the chapter and read each heading. Using information from only the headings, in what three land areas were the Americans especially interested?

3. Look at the pictures in the chapter and read each caption. What do the pictures show you about the westward movement in the United States? Look at the map on page 292. What information does this map show? Note also the time line at the beginning of the chapter. What years are included in this chapter? Compare this chapter time line to the unit time line on page 289.

4. Read the last part of the chapter called Summing Up. What did the rapid, westward movement of the United States lead to?

Know These Important Terms

Manifest Destiny   **Oregon Trail**
Lone Star Republic

Know the Main Idea

Here is the MAIN IDEA of this chapter.

Most Americans wanted the United States to reach all the way to the Pacific coast. Americans settled in Texas, Oregon, and California.

Keep this MAIN IDEA in mind as you study the chapter. Ask yourself the following questions as you read. They will help you remember the MAIN IDEA.

1. What section of the United States did most of the settlers who went to Texas come from?

2. What other nation besides the United States was interested in Oregon?

3. What nation did California belong to in the early 1840's? When did California become part of this nation?

THE YEARS OF THIS CHAPTER ARE 1820 TO 1859

1820   1859   1860

THE CHAPTER LESSON BEGINS HERE

Americans Wanted Their Nation to Grow

During most of America's history, Americans have moved westward. In the 1840's, the term **Manifest Destiny** (MAN-uh-fest DES-tuh-nee) was used to describe this westward movement. Manifest Destiny meant that the American people wanted the United States to take over all the land between the Atlantic Ocean and the Pacific Ocean. Americans wanted this land for several reasons.

Americans wanted more farm land, and they were interested in the cheap land that the West offered. Also, Americans were interested in developing American trade with China and Japan. Traders wanted to use the good harbors located along the Pacific coast

to trade with China and Japan. And finally, Americans were afraid that Great Britain might take over Oregon and Texas if the United States did not take them first.

Texas Won Its Independence

During the 1820's, many Americans became interested in Texas. But Texas was then a part of Mexico. Mexico had just won its independence from Spain in 1821. At first, the Mexican government allowed about 20 thousand Americans—almost all Southerners—to settle in eastern Texas. But in 1830, the Mexican government passed a law which stopped any more Americans from settling in Texas.

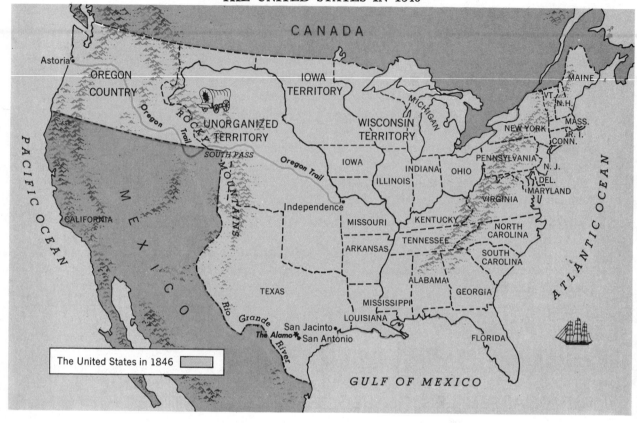

This law made the Americans who were already living in Texas very angry. Therefore in 1836, the Americans in Texas declared their independence. The Mexican ruler, General Santa Anna (SAHN-tah AH-nah), tried to put down this American revolt. But Sam Houston (HYOO-stun), the American leader, defeated Santa Anna and his army at the Battle of San Jacinto (SAN juh-SIN-toh). Texas now became an independent nation known as the **Lone Star Republic.**

Texas Remained an Independent Nation

The people of Texas wanted to join the United States. Most Southerners and Westerners wanted to have Texas join. But the people of the Northeast did not want Texas to become part of the United States. They knew that Southerners wanted to divide Texas into several slave states. Northerners did not want more slave states added to the United States because they did not want the South to have more votes in Congress. Northerners were also afraid that if Texas joined the United States, it might lead to a war with Mexico.

Neither President Andrew Jackson nor President Martin Van Buren wanted to stir up trouble between the Northern and Southern states by bringing Texas into the United States. For the time being, Texas stayed an independent nation. But when Great Britain and France showed an interest in Texas, the

United States became worried. In 1844, President John Tyler decided to act. He prepared a treaty to bring Texas into the United States. However, the Senate refused to approve this treaty.

Americans Settled in Oregon

At the same time that some Americans were settling Texas, thousands of other Americans were moving into Oregon. Some traveled by ship all the way around South America. But most traveled by land in covered wagons over the famous **Oregon Trail.** By 1845, over 5 thousand Americans had settled in Oregon. As you may remember, Oregon was claimed by both the United States and Great Britain. The American settlers in Oregon did not like this. They wanted Oregon to become part of the United States.

Texas and Oregon Joined the United States

In the election of 1844, Henry Clay of Kentucky was the candidate of the Whig Party for President. The Democrats chose James K. Polk of Tennessee as their candidate. Polk told the voters that he wanted both Texas and Oregon to become part of the United States. This pleased all the sections, because Texas was to be a slave state and Oregon was to be a free state. Polk was elected President.

Even before Polk took office, Congress voted to accept Texas as a slave state. After President Polk took office, he decided to try to make all of the Oregon Country part of the United States. However, part of the Oregon Country extended far north into British Canada. The United States and Great Britain were not able to agree on the boundary between Oregon and Canada. It looked as if the two nations might go to war. Finally, in 1846, the United States and Great Britain agreed to a boundary. The southern part of

MARCUS WHITMAN

Marcus Whitman is often called the "Father of Oregon." Whitman, a missionary doctor, decided to work with the Indians who lived in the Pacific Northwest. He and his wife, and several other missionaries, arrived in the Oregon Country in 1836. This small group built a mission at Walla Walla. Here, and in other missions, they worked with the Indians.

After a few years, Dr. Whitman returned to the East to interest other settlers in moving to the Oregon Country. He left Oregon in October, crossing the mountains and plains at the worst season, and reached Boston in April of 1843. Newspapers told of Whitman's trip and described the Northwest. Many settlers began to move to the Oregon Country.

Whitman returned to Oregon. In 1847 a terrible measles epidemic broke out. Dr. Whitman saved most of the white children. But the Indians had never had this disease, and the disease was worse for them. Although he worked tirelessly, many Indian children died. The Indians became bitter and blamed Whitman for these deaths. They turned against him, and in November of 1847, they killed Whitman, his wife, and twelve other settlers.

In this picture, a family moving West is having trouble on the trail. The oxen have collapsed from lack of food and water.

THE GROWING NATION 1836 to 1859

No.	State	Date Admitted
25.	Arkansas	June 15, 1836
26.	Michigan	January 26, 1837
27.	Florida	March 3, 1845
28.	Texas	December 29, 1845
29.	Iowa	December 28, 1846
30.	Wisconsin	May 29, 1848
31.	California	September 9, 1850
32.	Minnesota	May 11, 1858
33.	Oregon	February 14, 1859

Oregon then became a territory of the United States, and in 1859, it became a free state.

The United States Also Wanted California

Americans were also interested in California. As you may remember, California was part of the Spanish empire in America. Spaniards did not begin to settle California until 1769. In that year, under the leadership of

Father Junípero Serra (hoo-NEE-puh-roh SAIR-uh), the Spanish began to build a chain of twenty-one missions, or religious centers, from San Diego (SAN dee-AY-goh) northward to San Francisco. These missions were very successful. At the missions, the Indians learned about the Christian religion, and they also learned how to farm. However, when Mexico won its independence from Spain, California became a part of Mexico. The Spanish missions were then closed down.

Americans began to settle in California during the 1840's. Most of these American settlers wanted California to become part of the United States. In 1846, the Americans in California declared their independence from Mexico. One of the leaders of this Bear Flag Revolt was John C. Frémont (FREE-mahnt), an officer in the American army.

Summing Up

Most Americans wanted the United States to expand to the Pacific coast. Americans settled in Texas and Oregon. Both these areas soon became states. Americans also pushed into California. In the next chapter, you will find out how this westward movement led to a war with Mexico.

AFTER YOU READ THE CHAPTER

Do You Know These Important Terms?

For each sentence below, choose the term that best completes the sentence.

1. The wish of many Americans to have the United States take over all the land between the Atlantic and Pacific oceans was called (**Manifest Destiny/Territorial Expansion**).
2. The independent nation of Texas was called the (**Lone Star/Big Bear**) Republic.
3. The overland route by which many Americans traveled to Oregon was called the **Oregon/Rocky Mountain**) Trail.

Do You Remember These People?

Tell something about each of the following persons.

John Tyler   Sam Houston
James K. Polk   Henry Clay
Santa Anna   Junípero Serra
John C. Frémont

Can You Locate These Places?

Use the map on page 292 to do the following map work.

1. Locate the state of Texas. Near what city does the symbol for the Alamo appear? Why do you think San Jacinto appears on the map?
2. Locate the Oregon Trail. Where did the trail begin? end?

Do You Know When It Happened?

What are the years of this chapter? Place the following events in the order in which they occurred.

Texas became part of the United States.
California declared its independence.
Texas won its independence.
Oregon became a free state.
James K. Polk was elected President.

Discovering More About the Main Idea

Most Americans wanted the United States to reach all the way to the Pacific Coast. Americans settled in Texas, Oregon, and California.

Tell how each of the following developments is related to the MAIN IDEA.

Texas won its independence from Mexico and became the Lone Star Republic.

Thousands of American settlers moved into the Oregon Country. In 1846, the United States and Great Britain agreed on a boundary, and the Oregon Country became a territory of the United States.

Americans settled in California, and in 1846, they declared their independence.

Can You Discuss the Chapter?

Use the information you learned in this chapter to answer the following questions.

1. Why did many Americans in the early 1800's believe in Manifest Destiny?
2. Why was the United States unwilling to accept Texas as a new state for awhile?
3. How was President Polk able to please all the sections of the nation?
4. Why was there trouble over the settlement of Oregon? How was it settled?
5. If you were an American citizen of the 1840's, might you have favored Manifest Destiny? Why or why not?

Can You Connect the Past and the Present?

1. The United States has grown about as large as it possibly can. What United States territory might become a state in the future?
2. The Spanish and Mexican heritage can still be seen in the American nation. Are there any examples of this heritage in your community? Make a list of them.

CHAPTER 47

Winning the Mexican War

Courtesy Chicago Historical Society.

American army under General Scott enters Mexico City.

BEFORE YOU BEGIN THE CHAPTER

Know What to Look For

1. Many experts do not agree about whether Mexico or the United States started the Mexican War. Many people believe that the United States forced Mexico to fight by taking over its territory. On the other hand, some experts say that Mexico sent troops across the Rio Grande hoping to start a war with the United States.

Many Mexican leaders felt that Mexico was able to win a war with the United States. Although the leaders of Mexico knew that the United States was a much larger country than Mexico, they believed the Mexican army was strong. Their army had defeated the Spanish in Mexico and had put down a number of revolutions. In this chapter, you will read about the events and results of the Mexican War.

2. Read the title of the chapter. Then look through the chapter and read each heading. Can you tell what problems the new land taken in the Mexican War caused for the United States?

3. Look at the pictures in the chapter and read each caption. What is happening in the first chapter picture? Look at the maps on pages 298 and 299. What are the titles of these two maps? What is the name of the territory which was added to the United States? Note also the time line at the beginning of the chapter. What years are included in this chapter? Compare the years of this chapter time line to the years of the unit time line on page 289.

4. Read the last part of the chapter called Summing Up. What question came up over the new land the United States gained? What is the topic of the next chapter?

Know These Important Terms

Mexican War	Wilmot Proviso
Mexican Cession	Free-Soilers

Know the Main Idea

Here is the MAIN IDEA of this chapter.

The United States won a war with Mexico and gained new lands. Soon, the question of slavery in the new territory became a problem.

Keep this MAIN IDEA in mind as you study the chapter. Ask yourself the following questions as you read. They will help you remember the MAIN IDEA.

1. How much was the United States willing to pay for Mexican territory in 1845?

2. After the war, how much did the United States pay Mexico for the Mexican Cession?

3. Which political party lost many votes because of the Free-Soilers?

THE YEARS OF THIS CHAPTER ARE 1846 TO 1848

1820   1846   1848   1860

THE CHAPTER LESSON BEGINS HERE

American Problems with Mexico

In the 1840's, ill feeling grew up between Mexico and the United States. Mexico was angry at the United States for making Texas part of the United States. Mexico was also angry because the United States was encouraging American settlers in California to break away from Mexico. Also, the United States wanted New Mexico, the land between Texas and California. And the United States and Mexico disagreed over the southern boundary of Texas.

In 1845, President Polk sent John Slidell (sly-DELL) to Mexico to talk about these problems with the Mexican government.

Slidell was sent to ask the Mexican government to sell California and New Mexico to the United States and to accept the Rio Grande (REE-oh GRAND) River as the southern boundary of Texas. In return, the United States was willing to pay 40 million dollars.

War Between the United States and Mexico

But the Mexican government refused to see Slidell. They did not want to sell any part of their country. And Mexico did not agree to have the Rio Grande River as the boundary of Texas. The Mexican government claimed that

page 297

the Nueces (noo-AY-sus) River, located north of the Rio Grande River, was the boundary.

When President Polk learned that the Mexican government refused to talk to Slidell, he ordered the American army under General Taylor to move across the Nueces River. Mexican soldiers attacked the American troops led by General Taylor. President Polk then asked Congress to declare war on Mexico. On May 13, 1846, Congress voted to declare war, and the **Mexican War** began.

Neither Side Was Ready for War

Both Mexico and the United States ex-

pected to win the war quickly. Mexico expected to win because it had a large army and was fighting to defend its own land. Mexico also expected help from Great Britain and France. Although the Mexican army fought bravely, it was poorly trained and lacked supplies and leadership. And Great Britain and France did not help Mexico.

The United States was not prepared for war either. The American army had less than 8 thousand men when the war started. Also, the American army had to march hundreds of miles over rough country to fight the Mexicans. And finally, Congress was often slow in voting the money to pay for the war. The reason for this was that many Northern Congressmen were against the war.

The United States Won the War

In 1846, General Taylor won several battles in northeastern Mexico and became known as the hero of Buena Vista (BWEN-uh VEE-stuh). Another small American army, led by General Stephen Kearny (KAHR-nee), captured Santa Fé in New Mexico and then marched into California. Within a few months, Kearny and John C. Frémont, the leader of the Bear Flag Revolt, won control of all California.

The most important battles of the war were won by General Winfield Scott. In March, 1847, Scott's army captured the city of Vera Cruz (ver-uh KROOZ) on the east coast of Mexico. From Vera Cruz, Scott fought his way inland. In September, the American army under Scott captured Mexico City. The Mexican leaders now realized they could not win, and the war soon came to an end.

New Land Caused New Problems

The Treaty of Guadalupe Hidalgo (GWAH-dah-LOO-pay ee-DAL-goh) was the peace treaty that ended the war. In this peace treaty, the Rio Grande River was made the southern boundary of Texas. Mexico gave California and New Mexico to the United States in return for 15 million dollars. This new land was called the **Mexican Cession.** The United States now stretched all the way

THE GROWING UNITED STATES

CANADA

Columbia River

OREGON COUNTRY 1846

Missouri River

Lake Superior

MAINE

Lake Huron

Lake Ontario

VT.

N.H.

NEW YORK

MASS.

R.I.

CONN.

Lake Michigan

LOUISIANA PURCHASE 1803

Platte River

Missouri River

Lake Erie

PENNSYLVANIA

N.J.

THE UNITED STATES IN 1783

DEL.

MD.

MEXICAN CESSION 1848

Colorado River

Mississippi River

Ohio River

VIRGINIA

NORTH CAROLINA

SOUTH CAROLINA

GEORGIA

THE FIRST THIRTEEN STATES

PACIFIC OCEAN

ATLANTIC OCEAN

TEXAS 1845

Rio Grande River

FLORIDA TERRITORY 1819

The United States in 1848

GULF OF MEXICO

MEXICO

Here, American soldiers are storming Chapultepec Castle in Mexico City during the Mexican War.

from the Atlantic coast to the Pacific coast and all the way from Canada to the Rio Grande River.

The United States soon had to decide if slavery was to be allowed in the Mexican Cession. Even before the war ended, the House of Representatives approved the **Wilmot Proviso,** which said that slavery was not to be allowed in any new land won in the war. But

the Senate refused to agree. President Polk then suggested that the old Missouri Compromise Line of 1820 be extended to the Pacific coast. Slavery was to be forbidden in all the land north of the line. In all the land south of the line, slavery was to be allowed.

Very few Americans liked Polk's idea. Many Northerners did not want Congress to allow slavery in any new territory that became part of the United States. Many Southerners demanded that Congress allow slavery in all territories of the United States. A third group of Americans wanted Congress to allow the settlers in the new territories to decide for themselves if they wanted slavery or not.

General Taylor Was Elected President

The slavery question came up in the election of 1848. Because President Polk refused to run again, Lewis Cass, a Senator from Michigan, became the candidate of the Democratic Party. The Whigs picked General Zachary Taylor, a hero of the Mexican War. Neither Senator Cass nor General Taylor said clearly whether he was for or against the spread of slavery.

For this reason, many Northerners supported a new political party called the **Free-Soilers.** The Free-Soilers were strongly against the spread of slavery. The Free-Soilers received many votes from Northerners who usually voted for the Democratic Party. As a result, the Whig candidate, Zachary Taylor, won the election.

Summing up

In 1846, the United States went to war with Mexico. The United States won the war in 1847 and gained new land called the Mexican Cession. Soon the question of whether slavery was to be allowed in this new land came up. In the next chapter, you will find how the slavery problem was settled.

AFTER YOU READ THE CHAPTER

Do You Know These Important Terms?

For each sentence below, choose the term that best completes the sentence.

1. The war which began in 1846 with Mexico was called the (**Spanish-American/Mexican**) War.
2. The new territory of California and New Mexico was called the (**Arizona Territory/Mexican Cession**).
3. The (**Wilmot Proviso/Southwest Manifesto**) said that slavery was not to be allowed in any new land won in the war.
4. The (**Free–Soilers/Know Nothings**) were a new political party who were strongly against the spread of slavery.

Do You Remember These People?

Tell something about each of the following persons.

James Polk
Zachary Taylor
John C. Frémont
Lewis Cass

John Slidell
Stephen Kearny
Winfield Scott

Can You Locate These Places?

Use the maps in this chapter to do the following map work.

1. Map, page 298. Locate the Nueces and the Rio Grande rivers.
2. Map, page 299. What river flows through the Mexican Cession? Look at a map of the United States today. What states were once part of the Mexican Cession?

Do You Know When It Happened?

What are the years of this chapter? Place the following events in the order in which they occurred.

The Wilmot Proviso was turned down.
Scott's army captured Vera Cruz.
Zachary Taylor became President.

Discovering More About the Main Idea

The United States won a war with Mexico and gained new lands. Soon, the question of slavery in the new territory became a problem.

Tell how each of the following developments is related to the MAIN IDEA.

Both the United States and Mexico expected to win the war quickly. Both nations, however, were poorly prepared to fight a war.

The United States paid Mexico 15 million dollars after the war. As a result of the peace treaty, the United States gained California and New Mexico.

Free-Soilers took votes away from the Democratic Party in the election of 1848.

Can You Discuss the Chapter?

Use the information you learned in this chapter to answer the following questions.

1. Why did the United States and Mexico go to war in 1846?
2. How was the United States able to win the Mexican War?
3. What were the terms of the peace treaty that ended the Mexican War?
4. What were three views about slavery in the territories at this time? How did these views affect the election of 1848?

Can You Connect the Past and the Present?

1. War heroes often become Presidents. Name the most recent President who was also a war hero.
2. Whenever the two major political parties do not account for the beliefs of all the people, third parties are formed, like the Free-Soilers in this chapter. Was there a third party in the last major election in your community? Why was it necessary?

CHAPTER 48

The United States in the 1850's

Henry Clay explains the Compromise of 1850 to the Senate.

BEFORE YOU BEGIN THE CHAPTER

Know What to Look For

1. Many people did not think the first railroad locomotives would work. Many thought they were the work of the devil because they made so much noise and made great clouds of black smoke and fire. One afternoon near Baltimore, a horse-drawn railroad car challenged the new steam locomotive to a race. At the beginning of the race, the horse-drawn railroad car took the lead. But then, huge clouds of smoke came from the steam locomotive and the locomotive raced up to the horse and passed it. Suddenly, trouble developed in the steam engine and the locomotive slowed down. The horse raced ahead. Although the locomotive lost the race, the railroad had proved the great value of the steam locomotive. By 1850, rail lines joined most parts of the East. Lines were also planned to join the

West and the East. In this chapter, you will read about the United States in the early 1850's.

2. Read the title of the chapter. Then look through the chapter and read each heading. From the headings, what topics do you expect to read about in this chapter?

3. Look at the first chapter picture and read the caption. What is happening in the first chapter picture? Look at the map on page 304. What is the title of the map? Note also the time line at the beginning of the chapter. What years are included in this chapter? Compare this chapter time line to the unit time line on page 289.

4. Read the last part of the chapter called Summing Up. What helped to settle the slavery question for awhile?

Know These Important Terms

Forty-Niners   slums

Compromise of 1850   Know-Nothing Party
Gadsden Purchase

Know the Main Idea

Here is the MAIN IDEA of this chapter.

The Compromise of 1850 helped to settle the slavery question for awhile. The growth of the railroads and the large number of immigrants helped the nation to grow and change.

Keep this MAIN IDEA in mind as you study the chapter. Ask yourself the following questions as you read. They will help you remember the MAIN IDEA.

1. What kind of state did California wish to become?

2. Name the four ideas that made up the Compromise of 1850. Who drew up the Compromise of 1850?

3. What political party was against immigration?

THE YEARS OF THIS CHAPTER ARE 1848 TO 1860

1820   1848   1860

THE CHAPTER LESSON BEGINS HERE

California Wanted to Become a Free State

The slavery problem grew even more important after gold was discovered in California in 1848. Within a year, more than 80 thousand men called **Forty-Niners** arrived hoping to find gold and become rich. With the large number of people now in California, a government was necessary to protect life and property.

President Taylor encouraged the people of California to ask to become a state. In the year 1850, California asked to enter the United States as a free state. At the same time, New Mexico and Utah asked Congress to organize their areas into territories without slavery.

Clay Tried to Please Both Sides

The Southern states were very angry when they heard about California and the new territories. They talked about having their states withdraw from the United States. The Northern states were happy about California. They wanted Congress to stop slavery in all the lands taken after the Mexican War.

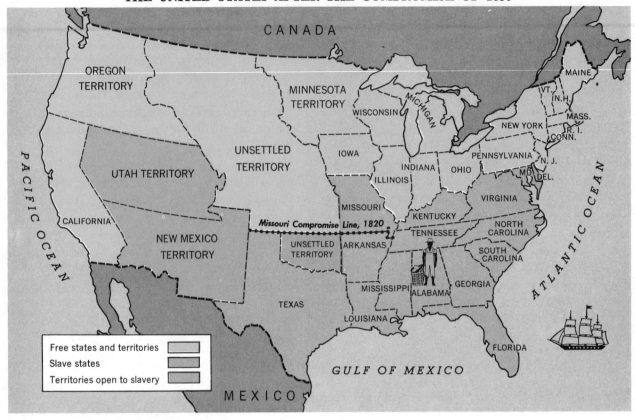

THE UNITED STATES AFTER THE COMPROMISE OF 1850

CANADA

OREGON TERRITORY

MINNESOTA TERRITORY

WISCONSIN

MICHIGAN

MAINE

VT.

N.H.

MASS.

NEW YORK

R. I.

CONN.

UNSETTLED TERRITORY

UTAH TERRITORY

IOWA

INDIANA

OHIO

PENNSYLVANIA

N. J.

MD.

DEL.

ILLINOIS

CALIFORNIA

MISSOURI

KENTUCKY

VIRGINIA

Missouri Compromise Line, 1820

NEW MEXICO TERRITORY

UNSETTLED TERRITORY

ARKANSAS

TENNESSEE

NORTH CAROLINA

SOUTH CAROLINA

TEXAS

MISSISSIPPI

ALABAMA

GEORGIA

LOUISIANA

FLORIDA

PACIFIC OCEAN

ATLANTIC OCEAN

Free states and territories
Slave states
Territories open to slavery

GULF OF MEXICO

MEXICO

Henry Clay, the great Senator from Kentucky, tried to settle the problem peacefully and fairly. Clay drew up a plan which became known as the **Compromise of 1850.** This Compromise of 1850 was made up of the following ideas:

1. California was to become a free state.

2. The rest of the lands taken from Mexico were to be divided into the territories of New Mexico and Utah. The people of these two territories were to decide if they wanted slavery or not.

3. The slave trade (but not slavery) was to be ended in Washington, D.C., the nation's capital.

4. Congress was to pass a strong law against runaway slaves to force Americans to return escaped slaves to their owners.

The Compromise of 1850 Was Accepted

Clay brought his compromise to Congress in January of 1850. Northern and Southern Congressmen fought over the Compromise for many months. Finally, both sides decided it was the best possible agreement, and Congress accepted the Compromise.

Millard Fillmore, who became President in July when President Taylor died, signed the Compromise into law in September of 1850. Some groups in both the North and the South were still unhappy. But most Americans were pleased that the slavery question was settled.

The Election of 1852

In the election of 1852, both political parties supported the Compromise of 1850. They knew that the Compromise settled the slavery question, and that it kept the country from being divided. The candidate of the Democratic Party was Franklin Pierce of New Hampshire. The Whig Party candidate, General Winfield Scott, was a Mexican War hero. Pierce won the election.

The United States Added New Land

While slavery was troubling the United States in the 1840's and 1850's, many changes were taking place in the country. In the 1850's, the United States began to grow into a great nation.

In the 1850's, some Americans wanted the United States to take over more land. They wanted Cuba, Central America, and even Hawaii. However, the United States only bought a small strip of land in the southern part of the Arizona Territory. This land, called the **Gadsden** (GADZ-dun) **Purchase,** was bought from Mexico in 1853 because the United States needed this land to build a railroad from New Orleans to California.

Railroads Joined the East and West

After 1850, railroads became very important to American life. The first important railroad in the United States, the Baltimore and Ohio, opened in 1830. By the 1850's, thousands of miles of tracks were built, and small railroads joined together to form railroad lines. These railroad lines ran from the cities along the Atlantic coast all the way to Chicago, St. Louis, and Memphis. They traveled at a speed of twenty to thirty miles an hour.

Many Newcomers Arrived

In the 1840's, and 1850's, many immigrants, or newcomers, came to the United States from foreign countries. Some immigrants came from England, Sweden, Norway, and Denmark. But most came from Germany or Ireland. In 1854 alone, over 400 thousand immigrants arrived in the United States.

Most of these immigrants settled in the North. Very few of them went to the South. The Irish stayed mainly in the cities of the Northeast. The Germans moved to the farms or cities of the Old Northwest. Wherever they settled, these immigrants helped to build America into a great country.

Some Americans Disliked Newcomers

Not all Americans welcomed these immigrants. They said that immigrants stayed together in their own group, and they did not dress or speak like other Americans. They blamed the growth of **slums,** or run-down city neighborhoods, and the increase of crime on immigrants. Some Americans were also frightened because many of the immigrants were Catholics.

In the 1850's, some Americans formed a political party called the **Know-Nothing Party.** It was called the Know-Nothing Party because its members answered "I know nothing" when asked about their party. The Know-Nothing Party tried to end immigration and make it hard for immigrants to become citizens. They also tried to keep immigrants from voting. The Know-Nothing Party was strong for a few years, but it soon died out.

Summing Up

After the discovery of gold in California, the slavery problem became important. The Compromise of 1850 settled the slavery problem for a while. After 1850, America grew and changed. In the next chapter, which begins Unit 13, you will see how slavery again caused trouble between the North and the South.

AFTER YOU READ THE CHAPTER

Do You Know These Important Terms?

For each sentence below, choose the term that best completes the sentence.

1. Settlers who rushed to California to look for gold were called (**prospectors/Forty-Niners**).
2. Henry Clay tried to settle the slavery question in 1850. The plan he drew up was called the (**Wilmot Proviso/Compromise of 1850**).
3. The (**Gila/Gadsden**) Purchase was a small strip of land in the southern part of the Arizona Territory.
4. Run-down city neighborhoods are often called (**tenements/slums**).
5. The (**Free-Soilers/Know-Nothing**) Party tried to end immigration.

Do You Remember These People?

Tell something about each of the following persons.

Zachary Taylor   Henry Clay
Millard Fillmore   Franklin Pierce
Winfield Scott

Can You Locate These Places?

Use the map on page 304 to do the following map work.

Find the Missouri Compromise line of 1820. Is California north or south of the line? Why were Southerners upset about California becoming a free state?

Do You Know When It Happened?

What are the years of this chapter? Tell why each of the following dates is important in American history.

1830   1848   1850   1853

Discovering More About the Main Idea

The Compromise of 1850 helped to settle the slavery question for awhile. The growth of the railroads and the large number of immigrants helped the nation to grow and change.

Tell how each of the following developments is related to the MAIN IDEA.

Southerners objected when California tried to enter the United States as a free state.

Railroads were being built or planned to join the East and the West. A small piece of land was purchased from Mexico in order to build a railroad from New Orleans to California.

Irish and German immigrants came to the United States in great numbers. These immigrants built the railroads, worked in factories, and farmed the land. Some Americans did not welcome the immigrants.

Can You Discuss the Chapter?

Use the information you learned in this chapter to answer the following questions.

1. Why did President Taylor encourage the people of California to ask for statehood?
2. How did the Compromise of 1850 help the South? the North?
3. Why did railroads become very important in American life after 1850?
4. Why did some Americans dislike the immigrants who came to the United States?

Can You Connect the Past and the Present?

Sometimes we blame people who happen to be different from us for many of our problems, just as some Americans blamed immigrants in the 1840's and 1850's for their problems. Do some people still think like this in your community? Explain.

Americans Fight a Terrible War

The War Between the North and South.

THE CHAPTERS IN UNIT 13 ARE

CHAPTER 49   A Nation Divided by Slavery
CHAPTER 50   Moving Toward War
CHAPTER 51   The War Between the North and the South
CHAPTER 52   Fighting the War

THE YEARS OF THIS UNIT ARE 1850 TO 1865

| 1800 | 1850 | 1865 | 1975 |

A Nation Divided by Slavery

Fighting in the Kansas Territory.

BEFORE YOU BEGIN THE CHAPTER

Know What to Look For

1. He was only five feet tall, but he had a loud, deep voice and was a good speaker. They called him the "Little Giant" because he had plenty of energy and was able to get things done. This was Stephen A. Douglas, the Senator from Illinois. At the age of twenty-three he was elected to the state legislature. When he was thirty years old, he was elected to Congress. Douglas was an important leader

of the Democratic Party, and he was against slavery. However, in this chapter, you will find out how Senator Douglas reopened the question of slavery in the territories. The slavery question continued to pull the North and the South farther apart.

2. Read the title of the chapter. Then look through the chapter and read each heading. Using information from the headings, tell where fighting over slavery first broke out.

3. Look at the pictures in the chapter and read each caption. What does the picture on page 310 show you about the lives of slaves? Look at the map on page 311. What territories were open to slavery? Note also the time line at the beginning of the chapter. What years are included in this chapter? Compare this time line to the unit time line on page 307.

4. Read the last part of the chapter called Summing Up. What caused many Northerners to turn against slavery?

Know These Important Terms

Fugitive Slave Act
personal liberty laws

Kansas-Nebraska Act
Republican Party

Know the Main Idea

Here is the MAIN IDEA of this chapter.

The slavery question again began to divide the North and the South. Many more Northerners turned against slavery, and fighting over slavery broke out in Kansas.

Keep this MAIN IDEA in mind as you study the chapter. Ask yourself the following questions as you read. They will help you remember the MAIN IDEA.

1. What were many leading citizens in the South trying to prove about slavery?
2. What book turned many Northerners against slavery?
3. What caused fighting to break out in the territory of Kansas?

THE YEARS OF THIS CHAPTER ARE 1850 TO 1861

1850   1861   1865

THE CHAPTER LESSON BEGINS HERE

Southerners Began to Strongly Defend Slavery

Until the 1830's, many Southerners were against slavery and thought that it was evil. They often called slavery the necessary evil. However, when the Northern abolitionists began to attack slavery, Southerners began to defend it. They claimed that slavery was good for both the slave owner and the slave. Many leading citizens in the South—ministers, scientists, and writers—tried to prove that slavery was good. Some of them even used history and science to try to show that slavery was both good and necessary. Also, Southerners talked of the poor conditions that the factory workers of the North lived under. They said that slaves were happier and better off than the Northern workers.

Northerners Disliked the Fugitive Slave Law

You may remember that many Northerners disagreed with the abolitionists when they first talked about ending slavery. In time, however, Northerners began to change their minds. One reason for this change was the **Fugitive Slave Act,** or runaway slave law, that was passed as a part of the Compromise of 1850. Under this law, Northerners were supposed to help capture runaway slaves and return them to their owners.

Most Northerners felt that the Fugitive Slave Act was very unfair. A man accused of being a runaway slave did not receive a jury trial. Under this law, free black men were often accused of being runaway slaves. Therefore, several Northern states passed **personal**

Slavery divided the North and the South as more Northerners turned against slavery. Above, slaves are sold at an auction.

liberty laws which stopped the arrest of free black people as runaway slaves and protected their right to a jury trial. These personal liberty laws made it difficult to enforce the Fugitive Slave Act in the North. And some Northerners even tried to rescue escaped slaves who were being returned to the South. All this greatly upset Southerners.

A Book Turned Northerners Against Slavery

Harriet Beecher Stowe, a Northern abolitionist, wrote a book called *Uncle Tom's Cabin,* which turned many Northerners against slavery. Mrs. Stowe showed slavery at its worst in *Uncle Tom's Cabin.* In the book,

Uncle Tom, a slave, is beaten to death by a cruel overseer named Simon Legree.

Uncle Tom's Cabin came out in 1852, and 300 thousand copies of the book were sold within one year. Thousands of people saw *Uncle Tom's Cabin* as a stage play. Because of *Uncle Tom's Cabin,* many Northerners decided that slavery must be ended. Southerners were shocked and angry because so many Northerners believed that slaves were treated as badly as those in *Uncle Tom's Cabin.*

Senator Douglas and the Railroad Route

In the 1850's, the question of building a railroad to connect the Atlantic coast and the

Pacific coast also helped divide the North and the South. Northerners wanted this railroad to begin at Chicago or St. Louis and then run west to California. Southerners wanted this railroad to begin at New Orleans and run through Texas and New Mexico to California.

Senator Stephen A. Douglas of Illinois was very interested in the northern railroad route. But he knew that this route ran through unsettled Indian lands. Douglas realized that the northern route was possible only if this unsettled land was organized into a territory and became settled. Therefore, Douglas asked Congress to make Nebraska a territory. To win Southern votes, he asked that the people who settled in Nebraska be allowed to decide if they wanted slavery or not.

The Kansas-Nebraska Act

Southern Congressmen agreed to accept Senator Douglas' plan only if Kansas, as well as Nebraska, was made into a territory. Kansas and Nebraska were both north of the Missouri Compromise line of 1820, where slavery was forbidden. Therefore, Congress repealed the Missouri Compromise, and in 1854, it passed the **Kansas-Nebraska Act.** This act organized Kansas and Nebraska as territories and allowed the settlers to decide if they wanted slavery or not. Southerners were very pleased with the Kansas-Nebraska Act because they saw a chance of spreading slavery into Kansas.

Northerners, however, were extremely angry. They did not want slavery to spread into

NEW TERRITORIES OPEN TO SLAVERY

Free states and territories
Slave states
Territories open to slavery

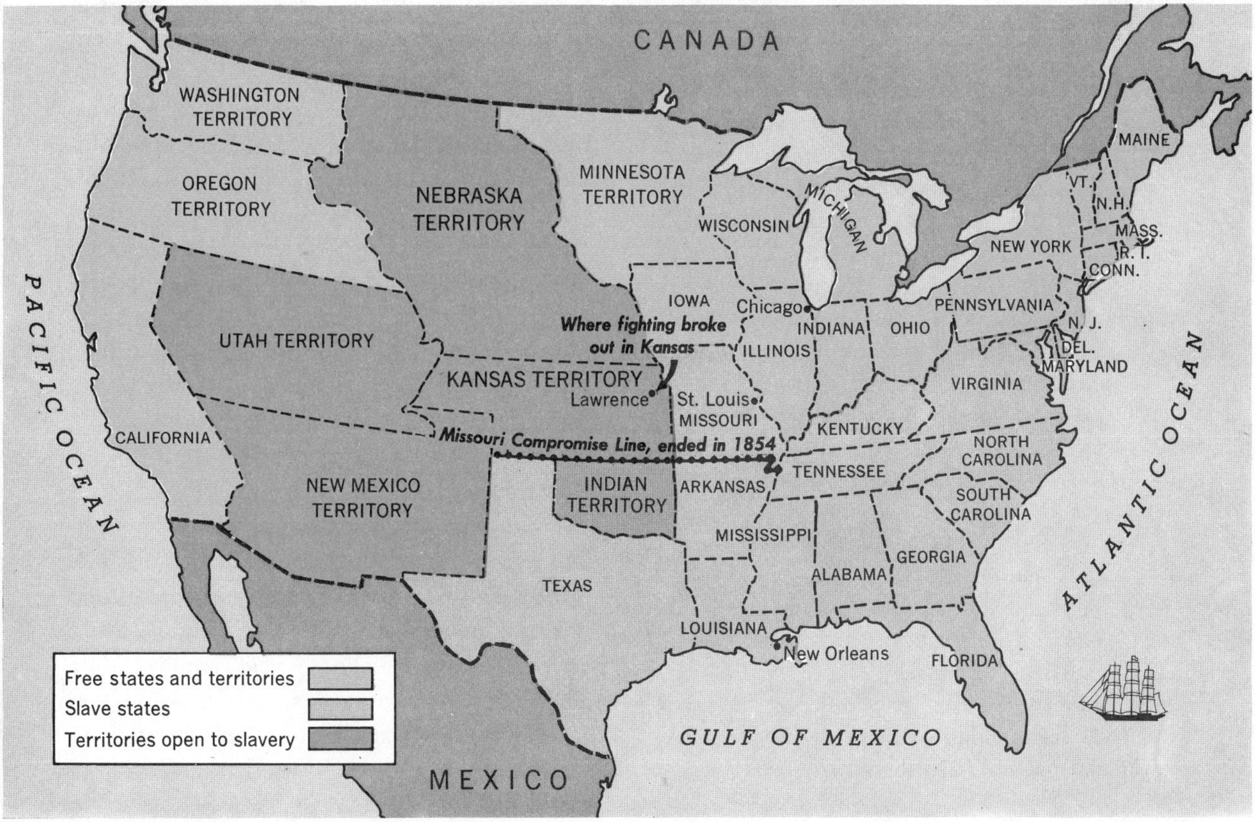

Crowd trying to free Burns.

ANTHONY BURNS—
A FUGITIVE SLAVE

Anthony Burns started life as a slave in Virginia. Burns had a quick mind and learned to read while he was a slave. His owner hired him out to work for a man in Richmond, Virginia. From here, Burns ran away from slavery and escaped to Boston, where he found a job.

One evening in 1854 as he left work, he was captured by slave catchers, who took him to prison. His owner wanted Burns returned to Virginia. Leading abolitionists tried to help Burns. They went to court to try to win his freedom. And some of the people of Boston tried to free him by using force.

Both attempts to gain Burns' freedom failed. The crowd that tried to free him was broken up. And the court decided that Burns must be returned to his owner. Burns was taken to an American navy ship by soldiers to make sure that he was not freed by a crowd.

The people of Boston were very upset. They decided to act to help Burns to gain his freedom. They collected money, which they paid to Burns' master for his freedom. After he was freed, Burns attended Oberlin College and became a minister. Later, he settled in Canada.

any new territory. Some people in the North and West who were against the spread of slavery organized a new party called the **Republican Party.** The Republican Party, which was formed in 1854, was not the Republican Party of Jefferson's time. This new Republican Party was made up of the Free-Soil Party, the Whigs, and other groups who were against slavery.

Northerners and Southerners Fought in Kansas

Everyone agreed that Nebraska was going to be free territory. But as soon as Kansas became a territory, both Northerners and Southerners rushed into the Kansas Territory. In the fall of 1854, an election was held in Kansas. Enough Southern settlers came in from the neighboring state of Missouri to elect a government favoring slavery. Northerners in Kansas then set up their own government which outlawed slavery.

Both sides soon used force. Southern settlers attacked the town of Lawrence, the capital of the "Northern" Kansas government. John Brown, a Northern abolitionist, led an attack against the Southern settlers. Soon fighting broke out all over Kansas. Federal troops had to be brought in to end the fighting. And not until 1861 did Congress finally settle the problem by allowing Kansas to become a free state.

Summing Up

During the early 1850's, the slavery problem again caused trouble between the North and the South. Many Northerners turned against slavery because of the Fugitive Slave law and a book called *Uncle Tom's Cabin*. The Kansas-Nebraska Act caused fighting in Kansas. In the next chapter, you will see how the slavery problem caused the Southern states to leave the United States.

AFTER YOU READ THE CHAPTER

Do You Know These Important Terms?

For each sentence below, choose the term that best completes the sentence.

1. The law that required Northerners to help catch runaway slaves and return them to their owners was the (**Slave Redemption/ Fugitive Slave**) Act.
2. (**Freedom's Code/Personal liberty laws**) helped stop the arrest of free black people as runaway slaves.
3. The (**Western Slave/Kansas-Nebraska**) Act opened up new territories and allowed settlers to decide if they wanted slavery.
4. A new political party formed in 1854 that was against slavery was named the (**Grand Old/Republican**) Party.

Do You Remember These People?

Tell something about each of the following persons.

Harriet Beecher Stowe   **John Brown**
Stephen A. Douglas

Can You Locate These Places?

Use the map on page 311 to do the following map work.

1. Locate the Missouri Compromise line of 1820. Locate also the Kansas and Nebraska territories.
2. Locate the cities of Chicago and St. Louis. Why do you think Northerners wanted the railroad to the Pacific Coast to begin in either of these cities?

Do You Know When It Happened?

Place the following events in the order in which they occurred.

Kansas-Nebraska Act was passed.
Kansas became a free state.
Fugitive Slave Act was passed.
Fighting broke out in Kansas.

Discovering More About the Main Idea

The slavery question again began to divide the North and the South. Many more Northerners turned against slavery, and fighting over slavery broke out in Kansas.

Tell how each of the following developments is related to the MAIN IDEA.

Southerners claimed that slavery was good and necessary, but the fugitive slave laws and *Uncle Tom's Cabin* turned many Northerners against slavery.

The Kansas-Nebraska Act was passed in order to build an East-West railroad. This reopened the question of slavery in the territories.

People in favor of slavery and people against slavery fought for control of Kansas.

Can You Discuss the Chapter?

Use the information you learned in this chapter to answer the following questions.

1. How did Southerners change their feelings about slavery between 1800 and 1860?
2. Why did many Northerners change their minds about slavery?
3. Why did Senator Douglas favor the Kansas-Nebraska Act?
4. How was the problem of Kansas settled?
5. How do you think you might have felt about the Fugitive Slave Act if you were a free black person? a runaway slave? a Southern slave holder? an abolitionist?

Can You Connect the Past and the Present?

A book or play can sometimes greatly influence the way people think, just as *Uncle Tom's Cabin* did in 1852. Do you know of any recent book, play, movie, or television program that has influenced the way people think?

CHAPTER 50

Moving Toward War

A Lincoln-Douglas debate.

BEFORE YOU BEGIN THE CHAPTER

Know What to Look For

1. In 1858, two men were candidates in the election for the Senator of Illinois. These two men were Stephen A. Douglas and Abraham Lincoln. Lincoln suggested that the two men hold a series of debates about slavery.

At the debates, Lincoln and Douglas could hardly have been less alike. Douglas, who was only five feet tall, was well dressed. He wore a fancy shirt, silk vest, and a wide brimmed

low hat. Lincoln stood six feet four inches tall. He wore a stovepipe hat which made him look even taller. And his clothes were wrinkled and did not fit.

Newspapers carried the news of the debates across the country. Stephen A. Douglas won the election, but Abraham Lincoln became known across the nation. In two years, this tall, thin man was elected President. In this chapter, you will read how his election caused seven states to leave the United States.

2. Read the title of the chapter. Then look through the chapter and read each heading. Using these headings only, list the events that divided the North and the South.

3. Look at the chapter pictures and read each caption. Find the pictures of Dred Scott and John Brown. Who were these men? Note also the time line at the beginning of the chapter. What are the years of this chapter? Compare the chapter time line to the unit time line on page 307.

4. Read the last part of the chapter called Summing Up. What led to the breakup of the United States in 1860?

Compare the chapter time line to the unit time line on page 307.

Know These Important Terms
Dred Scott Decision

Constitutional Union Party
Confederate States of America

Know the Main Idea
Here is the MAIN IDEA of this chapter.

In the late 1850's, events divided the North and the South even more. When Abraham Lincoln became President, seven Southern states seceded from the Union.

Keep this MAIN IDEA in mind as you study the chapter. Ask yourself the following questions as you read. They will help you remember the MAIN IDEA.

1. Which political party won the election of 1856?

2. Which section of the nation was most pleased by the Dred Scott Decision?

3. Which state was the first to secede? Name the six other states that seceded.

THE YEARS OF THIS CHAPTER ARE 1856 TO 1861

| 1850 | 1856 | 1861 | 1865 |

THE CHAPTER LESSON BEGINS HERE

The Democrats Won the Election of 1856

In the election of 1856, the new Republican Party chose as its candidate for President John C. Frémont, a hero of the Mexican War. The Republican Party came out against the spread of slavery into any new territories. The Democratic Party chose James Buchanan (byoo-KAN-un) of Pennsylvania. The Democrats said that the people of a territory had the right to decide if they wanted slavery or not. Buchanan won the election, but the election of 1856 showed how divided the North and South were over slavery. The Republicans won in eleven of the sixteen Northern states. Buchanan won in only five of the

Northern states, but he won in fourteen of the Southern states.

The Supreme Court and the Dred Scott Case

In 1857, the Supreme Court was asked to rule on an important case. The Court had to decide if a black man named Dred Scott was a slave or a free man. Dred Scott was a slave whose owner took him from Missouri into Illinois and the Wisconsin Territory, and then back to Missouri. Scott claimed that he was a free man because he lived in the free state of Illinois and in a free territory for four years.

page 315

Dred Scott claimed that living in a free state made him a free man. What did the Supreme Court decide?

Chief Justice Roger B. Taney (TAY-nee) gave the Court's decision. The Court ruled that since slaves were property Scott was still a slave. Even if a master took his slave to a free territory, he was still a slave. Living in a free territory did not give Scott his right to freedom. This **Dred Scott Decision** made slavery lawful any place in the United States. Southerners were very happy about the Dred Scott case. Northerners were angry and upset.

A Depression Helped Divide the Nation

The North and the South grew even further apart because of a depression that hit the United States in 1857. This depression hurt the North much more than it hurt the South. Many businessmen and farmers of the North blamed the Democratic Party for the depression because the Democrats lowered the tariff to help Southern planters. Northerners claimed that the lower tariff was the cause of the hard times in the North. As a result, more Northerners joined the Republican Party.

John Brown Tried to Start a Slave Revolt

John Brown's raid on Harpers Ferry, Virginia, in 1859, brought up the slavery problem once again. John Brown, the Northern abolitionist who fought against slavery in Kansas, planned to lead a slave revolt in Virginia. To get guns for this revolt, Brown tried to capture the government storehouse of weapons at Harpers Ferry, Virginia.

But Brown's plan failed, and after a short battle with United States troops, he and his followers were captured. John Brown was tried in court and hanged. Although his plan to lead a slave revolt failed, it frightened the South. For years, Southerners were frightened by the thought of slave revolts. Yet, many Northerners believed that John Brown was a hero. Many Southerners now feared that the North intended to use force to end slavery in the South.

The Candidates in the Election of 1860

The split between the North and South over slavery showed up very clearly in the election of 1860. The Democratic Party was not able to agree on a candidate, and the Party split into two groups—the Northern Democrats and the Southern Democrats. The Northern Democrats chose Stephen A. Douglas of Illinois as their candidate for President. The Southern Democrats chose John C. Breckinridge (BREK-un-rij) of Kentucky.

The Republican Party chose Abraham Lincoln of Illinois as their candidate. In the 1840's, Lincoln served in Congress and spoke out against slavery. In 1858, he ran for United States Senator against Stephen A. Douglas. Although Douglas won the election, Lincoln became known and respected throughout the

John Brown's raid further helped to divide the North and South. Below, John Brown is sentenced to death at his trial.

A depression which further divided the North and South hit the nation in 1857. Here, jobless men wait in line for dinner.

North. A fourth party, the **Constitutional Union Party,** named John Bell of Tennessee as its candidate.

Abraham Lincoln Was Elected President in 1860

The spread of slavery into the territories of the United States was the main question in the election. Stephen A. Douglas said that the settlers of a new territory must decide if they wanted slavery or not. Breckinridge said that slavery must be protected everywhere in the United States. Bell tried to avoid the slavery question in order to keep the nation together. And Abraham Lincoln said that slavery must not be allowed to spread into any of the new territories.

The Republicans developed several plans which pleased Northerners and Westerners. To please manufacturers, they favored a higher tariff. To please farmers, the Republicans came out for free land in the West. And to please immigrants, they favored laws to make it easier to become a citizen.

Seven Southern States Seceded

Lincoln won the election because of the votes of the Northern states. Douglas won in only two states. Breckinridge won in eleven of the fifteen slave states. Almost as soon as Lincoln was elected President, South Carolina seceded from, or left, the United States. Early in 1861, six more Southern states— Georgia, Florida, Alabama, Mississippi, Louisiana, and Texas—seceded. These seven Southern states formed their own nation, the **Confederate States of America.**

Summing Up

In the late 1850's, the Dred Scott case, John Brown's raid, and the depression of 1857 divided the North and the South even more. The election of Abraham Lincoln in 1860 led to the breakup of the United States. Seven Southern states seceded and formed their own nation, the Confederate States of America. In the next chapter, you will see how a war began between the United States and the Confederate States.

AFTER YOU READ THE CHAPTER

Do You Know These Important Terms?

For each sentence below, choose the term that best completes the sentence.

1. The (Stewart-Hayes/Dred Scott) Decision by the Supreme Court made slavery lawful any place in the United States.
2. The (Constitutional Union/Populist) Party was the fourth political party in the election of 1860.
3. The nation formed by the Southern states which seceded from the Union was called the (Columbian/Confederate) States of America.

Do You Remember These People?

Tell something about each of the following persons.

John C. Frémont	James Buchanan
Dred Scott	Roger B. Taney
John Brown	Stephen A. Douglas
John C. Breckinridge	Abraham Lincoln
John Bell	

Can You Locate These Places?

Use the map on page 311 to locate the following states. Tell how each state was related to the events in this chapter.

Virginia	Illinois
South Carolina	Georgia
Florida	Alabama
Mississippi	Louisiana
Texas	

Do You Know When It Happened?

Place the following events in the order in which they occurred.

The Confederate States were organized.

A depression hit the nation.

Lincoln was elected President.

Buchanan was elected President.

John Brown led a raid on Harpers Ferry.

Discovering More About the Main Idea

In the late 1850's, events divided the North and the South even more. When Abraham Lincoln became President, seven Southern states seceded from the Union.

Tell how each of the following developments is related to the MAIN IDEA.

The Dred Scott decision angered the North and pleased the South.

A depression hit the United States in 1857. Many Northerners blamed the Democratic Party for the depression.

Because of John Brown's raid, many Southerners feared that the North intended to use force to end slavery.

Can You Discuss the Chapter?

Use the information you learned in this chapter to answer the following questions.

1. Why were Northerners so upset by the Dred Scott decision?
2. Who were the four candidates in the election of 1860? What did each candidate say about slavery in the territories?
3. How was the Republican Party able to win the election of 1860?
4. Why do you think the Southern states seceded from the Union even before Lincoln took over his duties as President?

Can You Connect the Past and the Present?

1. The Supreme Court decision in the Dred Scott case was an important event in the late 1850's. What recent Supreme Court decisions have been important to you and your community?
2. Slavery helped to cause the split in the political parties in 1860. What recent issue, if any, has caused a split in a political party or the start of a new party?

CHAPTER 51

The War Between the North and the South

Southern troops fire on Fort Sumter.

BEFORE YOU BEGIN THE CHAPTER

Know What to Look For

1. At 4:30 in the morning on April 12, 1861, the loud burst of a cannon echoed across the waters of Charleston harbor. A cannon shell lit up the morning sky and exploded inside Fort Sumter. The shot was fired by Confederate forces across the harbor on the mainland.

Fort Sumter, a federal fort located on an island in Charleston harbor, was still held by Union troops even though it was almost completely surrounded by Confederate territory. Major Robert Anderson, the fort commander, refused to surrender. Then, General Pierre Beauregard, the Confederate general, ordered the Confederate guns to fire on the fort. Anderson lacked men, food, and ammunition, and the fort soon was forced to surrender. The War Between the North and South had begun.

In this chapter, you will read more about the beginning of the war.

2. Read the chapter title. Then look through the chapter and read each heading. From reading the headings, what topics do you expect to read about in this chapter?

3. Examine the pictures in the chapter and read each caption. What does the first picture show? Look at the map on page 322. What color symbol is used to show the Confederate States? the Union States? Note also the time line at the beginning of the chapter. What are the years of this chapter? Compare the chapter time line to the unit time line on page 307.

4. Read the last part of the chapter called Summing Up. What question was the Civil War fought to settle?

Know These Important Terms
Confederacy   Crittenden Compromise
Union   border states
Civil War   Copperheads
War Between the North and the South

Know the Main Idea
Here is the MAIN IDEA of this chapter.
The North and the South were unable to settle their problems, and war broke out in April, 1861. The war was fought to decide whether the Union was to stay together or be divided into two nations.

Keep this MAIN IDEA in mind as you study the chapter. Ask yourself the following questions as you read. They will help you remember the MAIN IDEA.

1. Who became President of the Confederate States of America?

2. Which Southern states decided not to join the Confederacy?

3. From which nations did the Confederate states expect aid?

THE YEARS OF THIS CHAPTER ARE 1860 TO 1861

| 1850 | 1860 | 1861 | 1865 |

THE CHAPTER LESSON BEGINS HERE

The Southern States Formed a New Government

What made the Southern states leave the United States? President Lincoln said he did not plan to free the slaves. The Supreme Court still sided with the South by claiming that all the territories were open to slavery. The Democrats, the party the South supported, still controlled the Senate.

The Southern states left the United States mainly because they wanted to protect slavery in their states. They were certain that Lincoln intended to end slavery in the South. The "Southern way of life" depended on slavery. Therefore, Southerners believed they had to form a new nation to protect their "Southern way of life."

The Confederate States of America, or the **Confederacy,** elected Jefferson Davis of Mississippi as President and Alexander H. Stephens of Georgia as Vice-President. The Confederate states approved a Constitution that was very much like the United States Constitution. But the eight other Southern states did not join the Confederacy. They wanted to see what was going to happen before they decided what to do.

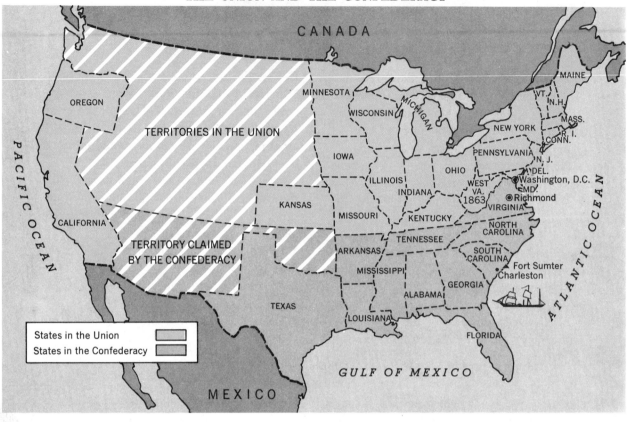

People Tried to Bring the North and the South Together

When the Confederacy was formed in February, 1861, President Buchanan was still in office. He did not believe that these states had the right to secede. But he also did not believe that the federal government had any right to force the Southern states to return to the **Union,** or the United States. Therefore, President Buchanan did almost nothing to stop the Southern states from leaving.

Before President Lincoln took office, many people tried to get the seven Southern states to return to the Union. Senator John Critten-

den (KRIT-un-dun) of Kentucky suggested that an amendment to the Constitution be passed to protect slavery in the South. He also wanted Congress to outlaw slavery north of the old Missouri Compromise line but to allow slavery in the territories south of the line. This plan became known as the **Crittenden Compromise.**

War Broke Out at Fort Sumter

But the Crittenden Compromise was not accepted by either the leaders of the North or the South. The Confederate states did not want to return to the United States. Instead, they wanted to build a new strong nation that might spread into Mexico and Central America. The Northern leaders were willing to protect slavery in the South, but they were not willing to let slavery spread into any new territories.

When Lincoln took office in March of 1861, he made it clear that he intended to keep the Union together. He was soon forced to prove that he intended to protect the Union. Fort Sumter, a United States fort in South Carolina, was almost out of food supplies. Unless the fort was supplied at once, it must be surrendered to the Confederacy. Lincoln sent word to South Carolina that he planned to send supplies to the fort. The Confederate states acted quickly. On April 12, 1861, even before the ships arrived, Fort Sumter was fired on by Southern troops. Two days later, Fort Sumter had to surrender to the Confederate troops. **The War Between the North and the South,** or the **Civil War,** now began.

Both Sides Prepared for War

Thousands of men joined the Northern armies and the Southern armies. Most Northerners agreed that the Union had to be kept together. If the Union was broken, Northerners felt the North and the South were certain to become two weak nations. Although both white men and black men asked to join the Northern army—the Union army—at first only white men were accepted into the Union army.

Now, the eight other Southern states had to decide if they were going to stay in the Union or join the Confederate states. Virginia, Arkansas, Tennessee, and North Carolina decided to join the Confederacy and fight to protect slavery. Maryland, Delaware, Missouri, and Kentucky, the **border states,** or the states between the North and the South, decided to remain in the Union. The

This photograph of President Lincoln was taken in 1863. He looks sad and troubled.

THE FIFTY-FOURTH MASSACHUSETTS REGIMENT

When the Civil War started, black Americans were not allowed to join the Union army. Many people urged President Lincoln to change this rule. Soon after he issued the Emancipation Proclamation in 1862, President Lincoln called for black troops to fight for the Union.

Black Americans answered the call by the thousands. Frederick Douglass, the black abolitionist, helped Governor John A. Andrew of Massachusetts to organize the 54th Massachusetts Regiment. So many black soldiers volunteered that another black regiment, the 55th Regiment, was formed. War Department rules said that the officers of the regiment had to be white Americans. Robert Gould Shaw, a white man from a New England family, became the Colonel of the regiment. Shaw worked well with his men. The 54th Regiment marched proudly out of Boston. Two months later, the 54th attacked Fort Wagner in South Carolina. The men of the 54th fought bravely, but they lost the battle. Colonel Shaw and over half the men of the regiment were killed.

Over 210 thousand black soldiers and sailors fought in the Civil War. Twenty-one of them received the Medal of Honor. President Lincoln said of America's black troops, "they proved their efficiency."

Confederacy had eleven states and the Union had twenty-three states.

The South Had Both Strengths and Weaknesses

Southerners expected to win the war by simply defending their own land. They believed that it was going to be easy to defend their land because they had trained fighting men and such outstanding generals as Robert E. Lee and Thomas "Stonewall" Jackson. The South also expected aid from Great Britain and France because it thought that these nations needed Southern cotton.

Yet the South also had weaknesses. The South did not have enough factories to supply its soldiers. Also, it did not have enough railroads to move troops and supplies where they were most needed. And the Confederate government was weak and did not have enough power over the states.

The North Had Both Strengths and Weaknesses

The North had more than twice as many people as the South. The North also had good railroads, big factories, and plenty of money. In addition, the North had a large navy. However, at first the North did not have good generals. And some Northerners did not support the war. One group of Northerners called **Copperheads** were against the war, and they tried to help the South.

Summing Up

The North and the South failed to settle their problems. And in April of 1861, when Southern troops fired on Fort Sumter, the war between the North and the South began. Both sides prepared for war. Was the Union to stay together or be divided into two nations? In the next chapter, you will read how the war was fought.

AFTER YOU READ THE CHAPTER

Do You Know These Important Terms?

For each sentence below, choose the term that best completes the sentence.

1. The Southern states that seceded from the Union formed the (**South/Confederacy**).
2. Another name for the United States was the (**Union/Confederation**).
3. The war which broke out in 1861 was called The War Between the (**Free and the Slave/North and the South**). The (**Five Years/Civil**) War is another name for the war.
4. The (**Davis/Crittenden**) Compromise was a plan to get the Southern states to return to the Union.
5. The states between the North and the South that remained in the Union were called (**traitor/border**) states.
6. Northerners who were against the war and who tried to help the South were called (**Rattlesnakes/Copperheads**).

Do You Remember These People?

Tell something about each of the following persons.

Abraham Lincoln   Jefferson Davis
Alexander H. Stephens   James Buchanan
John Crittenden   Robert E. Lee
Thomas "Stonewall" Jackson

Can You Locate These Places?

Use the map on page 322 to do the following map work.

1. Which states along the Pacific coast were loyal to the Union? How many states remained in the Union? How many joined the Confederacy?
2. Locate the states of Maryland, Delaware, Kentucky, and Missouri. Why do you think they were called border states?
3. Locate Fort Sumter near Charleston.

Do You Know When It Happened?

What are the years of this chapter? Why is the following date important?

April 12, 1861

Discovering More About the Main Idea

The North and the South were unable to settle their problems, and war broke out in April, 1861. The war was fought to decide whether the Union was to stay together or to be divided into two nations.

Tell how each of the following developments is related to the MAIN IDEA.

The Southern states that seceded from the United States formed the Confederacy.

The people who tried to bring the North and the South together again all failed.

When war broke out, four other Southern states joined the Confederacy.

Can You Discuss the Chapter?

Use the information you learned in this chapter to answer the following questions.

1. How did the Confederate states organize their government?
2. Why didn't the leaders of the North or South accept the Crittenden Compromise?
3. Why did the South expect to win the war?
4. Why did the North think it might defeat the Confederacy?

Can You Connect the Past and the Present?

1. Civil wars, or wars within a nation, are not too unusual in history. What nation is or was recently involved in a civil war?
2. People who are not in favor of a popular cause are frequently called names like Copperhead. Copperheads are deadly snakes. Can you give an example of this same idea in your community today?

CHAPTER 52

Fighting the War

The South surrenders at Appomattox.

BEFORE YOU BEGIN THE CHAPTER

Know What to Look For

1. The Civil War was one of the bloodiest wars in history. New weapons were beginning to appear. The automatic rifle, simple machine gun, observation balloon, telegraph, and railroad were all used in the war. However, the tactics, or the ways the war was fought, were old. They had been set up for wars in which simpler weapons were used. For example, soldiers still advanced in long, straight lines across open spaces. When weapons were not very accurate and only fired one shot at a time, few men were killed in this kind of advance. But with the new weapons, thousands of soldiers were killed or badly wounded as they advanced over open spaces. In the three days of battle at Gettysburg, almost one out of every three men in the Confederate army was killed or badly wounded. The Union

army lost even more men. In this chapter, you will read about the Civil War and the results of this war.

2. Read the title of the chapter. Then look through the chapter and read each heading. What happened when the South invaded the North?

3. Look at the pictures in the chapter and read each caption. What do the pictures show about the Civil War? Look at the map on page 328. What is the title of the map? What kind of information does the map show? Notice also the time line at the beginning of the chapter. What are the years of this chapter? Compare this chapter time line to the unit time line on page 307.

4. Read the last part of the chapter called Summing Up. What two things happened at the end of the war?

Know These Important Terms

blockade   Emancipation Proclamation

Know the Main Idea

Here is the MAIN IDEA of this chapter.

The Civil War lasted four long, terrible years. The war ended in a Northern victory, brought the Union together, and ended slavery.

Keep this MAIN IDEA in mind as you study the chapter. Ask yourself the following questions as you read. They will help you remember the MAIN IDEA.

1. What was the purpose of the Union blockade of Southern ports?
2. What Union general was made the chief commander of all the Union armies?
3. How did the North finally bring the war to an end? When did the war end?

THE YEARS OF THIS CHAPTER ARE 1861 TO 1865

1850   1861   1865

THE CHAPTER LESSON BEGINS HERE

The North Had to Fight a Long War

The North tried to win the war quickly by capturing Richmond, Virginia, the capital of the Confederacy. Richmond was only 100 miles from Washington, D.C. But a Confederate army met and defeated the Union army at Bull Run, a creek in northern Virginia. This defeat at the Battle of Bull Run taught the North a lesson. The North realized it was going to fight a long, hard war.

Therefore, the North decided to cut off the South's trade with Europe. The Union navy set up a **blockade** by placing ships around all Southern ports. At first, the Northern navy was too small to carry out a successful blockade. But as the war went on, the blockade became tighter. The blockade was very important in helping the North win the war. It stopped the South from getting war supplies.

The North Did Well in the West but Not in the East

In 1862, the North planned two main attacks in order to conquer the Confederacy. One attack was to come from the west. General Ulysses S. Grant led a Union army down the Mississippi River into Tennessee. Meanwhile, the Union navy under David Farragut (FAR-uh-guht) captured New Orleans. By the summer of 1862, the North controlled most of the Mississippi River.

Map: The Union War Plans

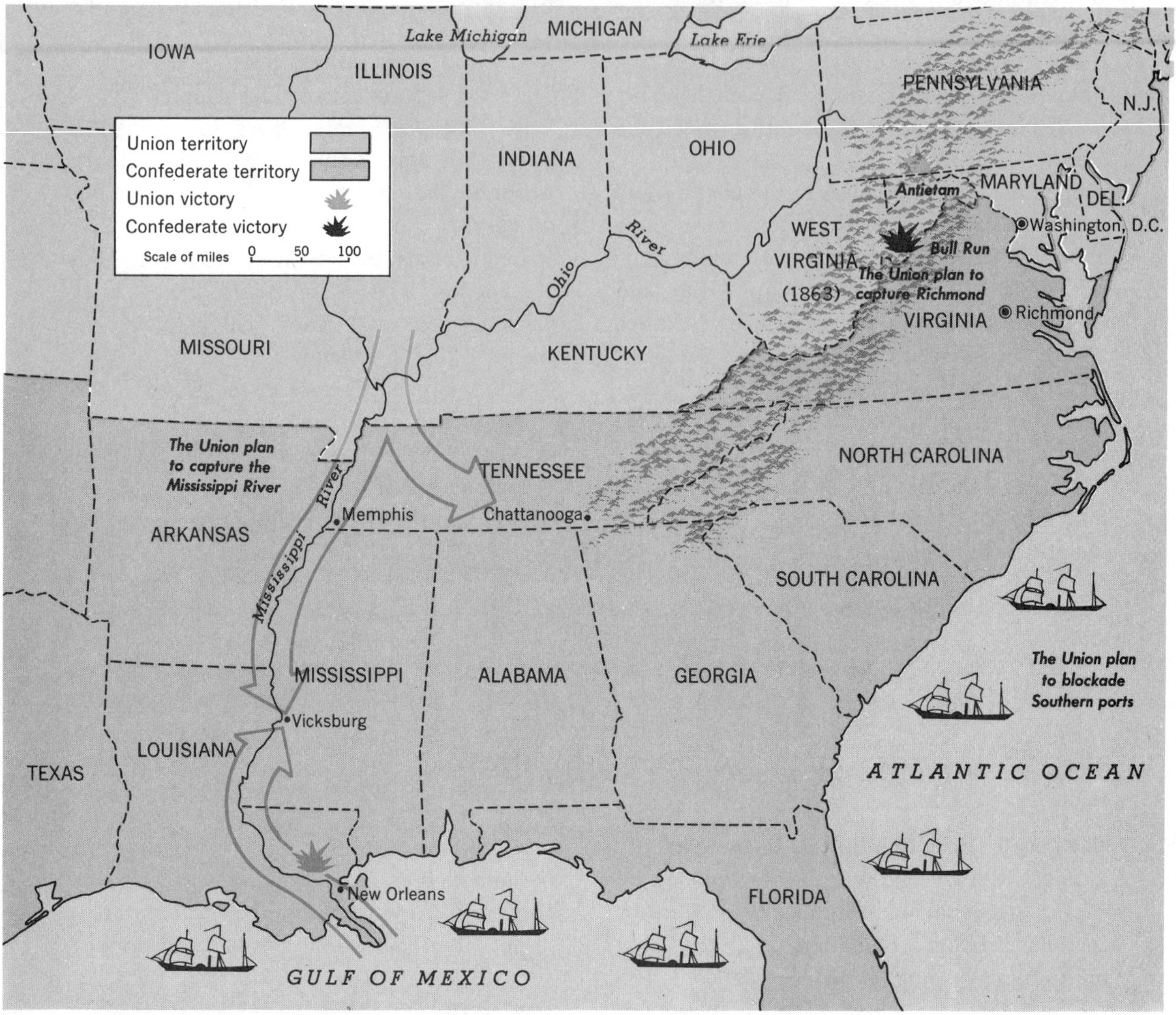

IOWA

ILLINOIS

MICHIGAN

Lake Michigan

Lake Erie

PENNSYLVANIA

N.J.

INDIANA

OHIO

MARYLAND

DEL.

Antietam

WEST
VIRGINIA
(1863)

Bull Run

The Union plan to capture Richmond

●Washington, D.C.

VIRGINIA

●Richmond

Union territory
Confederate territory
Union victory
Confederate victory
Scale of miles   0   50   100

River

Ohio

MISSOURI

KENTUCKY

The Union plan to capture the Mississippi River

Mississippi River

TENNESSEE

●Memphis

Chattanooga●

NORTH CAROLINA

ARKANSAS

SOUTH CAROLINA

The Union plan to blockade Southern ports

MISSISSIPPI

ALABAMA

GEORGIA

●Vicksburg

LOUISIANA

TEXAS

ATLANTIC OCEAN

●New Orleans

FLORIDA

GULF OF MEXICO

The second main attack against the South came from the east. General George McClellan (muh-KLEL-un) attacked Richmond, but he was not able to capture the city. After this attack failed, General Robert E. Lee's Confederate army marched north into Maryland. McClellan met Lee in Maryland and was barely able to defeat Lee at the Battle of Antietam (an-TEET-um).

The Emancipation Proclamation Was Signed

From the beginning of the war, many Northerners wanted Lincoln to free the slaves. At first, Lincoln wanted to free slaves only after paying slave owners for their loss. In April, 1862, Congress passed a law which freed the slaves in Washington, D.C., and allowed their owners to be paid. In June, Congress ended slavery in all the United States territories.

But in September, 1862, after the Battle of Antietam, President Lincoln wrote the **Emancipation Proclamation** (ih-MAN-suh-PAY-shun PRAHK-luh-MAY-shun). This Proclamation declared that all slaves in Confederate states were to be set free on January 1, 1863, unless these states surrendered before then. The Emancipation Proclamation turned the war into a fight to end slavery. It pleased many Northerners as well as people in Great Britain and France who disliked slavery. These people helped stop Great Britain and France from supporting the South.

Black Soldiers and Sailors Fought in the War

After the Emancipation Proclamation was signed, the Union army began to accept black soldiers. Over 180 thousand black soldiers served in the Union army. And about one fourth of all Union sailors were black.

Four black sailors won the Congressional Medal of Honor in the Civil War. Black soldiers also won medals and showed their bravery in battle. Some free Southern black men served in the Confederate army during the very last months of the war. And slave labor helped the South to hold out as long as it did in the war.

The South Invaded the North but Was Defeated

In 1863, General Grant's army was winning victories in the West. General Grant captured Vicksburg, Mississippi, which gave the North control of the entire Mississippi River. Later

This picture shows black Union soldiers from the Fourth United States Colored Infantry. Many black soldiers fought on the Union side.

In this drawing, a famous artist shows a young boy who fought on the Union side.

in 1863, Grant captured Chattanooga (CHAT-uh-NOO-guh), Tennessee, an important Southern railroad center. But in the East, the war was still not going well for the Union army.

In June of 1863, General Robert E. Lee tried to win the war for the South by invading the North. A large Union army met his Confederate army at Gettysburg (GET-eez-burg), Pennsylvania. The Battle of Gettysburg was the biggest battle of the war. For three days, both sides fought bravely. However, the Union army had more men, and it held a stronger position than General Lee's army. The Confederate army lost over 20 thousand men who were killed, wounded, or missing, and was forced to pull back into Virginia.

The War Came to an End

In 1864, President Lincoln made General Grant the chief commander of all the Union armies in the East and the West. General Grant was to lead the attack against the Confederate armies in the East. General William T. Sherman was to attack the Confederacy from the West. General Sherman fought his way from Chattanooga, Tennessee, to Atlanta, Georgia. From Atlanta, Sherman led his army through Georgia to the city of Savannah on the Atlantic coast. Sherman's army burned and destroyed everything in its path.

Meanwhile, General Grant slowly marched toward Richmond. Although he lost thousands of men against the Confederate army, Grant captured the city of Richmond in April, 1865. General Lee's army was trapped southwest of the city. The Confederacy was out of men and money and was not able to keep up the fight. On Sunday, April 9, 1865, General Lee surrendered to General Grant at Appomattox (AP-uh-MAT-uks) Court House in Virginia.

The War Had Two Main Results

The war was over. About 360 thousand Northerners and 258 thousand Southerners died on the battlefields. What results did this terrible war bring? First, the Union was back together. Never again did a state or group of states try to secede. And second, slavery was ended in the United States.

Summing Up

The war between the North and the South lasted four long, terrible years. In 1862, the Emancipation Proclamation turned the war into a fight to end slavery. Finally in 1865, the war was over. The war brought the Union together again and ended slavery. In the next chapter, which begins Unit 14, you will find out what the United States was like at the end of the war.

AFTER YOU READ THE CHAPTER

Do You Know These Important Terms?

For each sentence below, choose the term that best completes the sentence.

1. The placing of ships around an enemy's port cities is called a (**siege/blockade**).
2. The (**Anti-Slavery/Emancipation**) Proclamation declared that all slaves in the Confederate States were to be set free.

Do You Remember These People?

Tell something about each of the following persons.

Ulysses S. Grant   **David Farragut**
George McClellan   **Robert E. Lee**
William T. Sherman

Can You Locate These Places?

Use the map on page 328 to do the following map work.

1. Locate the Mississippi River. What Union victories were necessary for the Union to gain control of the river? Which Union officers won these victories?
2. Locate Richmond and Washington, D.C. Which battles were fought within a hundred or so miles of these cities? Which was the most important battle? Which battle ended the war?

Do You Know When It Happened?

What are the years of this chapter? Place the following events in the order in which they occurred.

Lee surrendered at Appomattox.

The Confederate army was defeated at Antietam.

Thousands of men were lost in the Battle of Gettysburg.

Union forces were defeated at Bull Run.

The Emancipation Proclamation was issued.

Discovering More About the Main Idea

The Civil War lasted four long, terrible years. The war ended in a Northern victory, brought the Union together, and ended slavery.

Tell how each of the following developments is related to the MAIN IDEA.

The North realized it was going to fight a long war after the defeat at Bull Run. The Union navy set up a blockade, which became tighter as the war went on.

After the Emancipation Proclamation, the war turned into a fight to end slavery. Many black Americans fought on the Union side.

Although General Grant lost thousands of men, he captured Richmond and trapped Lee's army southwest of the city.

Can You Discuss the Chapter?

Use the information you learned in this chapter to answer the following questions.

1. How did the North realize that it was going to fight a long war?
2. Why didn't Great Britain and France help the South?
3. How did the Civil War change from a war to keep the Union together to a war to end slavery?
4. How did black Americans help fight the Civil War?
5. What were the results of the Civil War?

Can You Connect the Past and the Present?

1. The draft was used for the first time during the Civil War to get soldiers for the army. How does the draft affect you and your community today?
2. In the Civil War, the black fighting men fought in separate black units. Are black Americans still placed in separate units?

PART III

The Nation Becomes A World Leader

1865 to 1919

THE UNITS IN PART III ARE

Unit 14 Americans Rebuild the Nation
Unit 15 America Becomes an Industrial Nation
Unit 16 Changes in American Life After 1865
Unit 17 Americans Try to Improve Their Life
Unit 18 The Progressives Reform the Nation
Unit 19 The United States and the World

Americans Rebuild the Nation

Badly wounded soldiers.

THE CHAPTERS IN UNIT 14 ARE

CHAPTER 53   Reconstruction of the Nation
CHAPTER 54   The End of Reconstruction
CHAPTER 55   The New South

THE YEARS OF THIS UNIT ARE 1864 TO 1900

1800	1864	1900	1975

Reconstruction of the Nation

The ruins of Richmond.

BEFORE YOU BEGIN THE CHAPTER

Know What to Look For

1. The end of the Civil War marked the beginning of a new period in the story of the American nation. In this new period, American industries which had grown during the Civil War continued to grow rapidly. This rapid growth of industry caused many changes and brought many new problems to the nation. The newly freed black Americans had to try to find their place in a rapidly changing

American nation. This, too, caused many problems. Today, Americans are still trying to solve these problems which started in the years after the Civil War.

The first job Americans had to turn to at the end of the war, however, was the rebuilding of the nation. Americans had to find a way to have the Confederate states return to the Union, to repair the damages of the war, and to provide aid to the freedmen and other Americans who needed help. In this chapter, you will read about the years immediately after the war, and the plans for rebuilding the Union.

2. Read the title of the chapter. Then look through the chapter and read each heading. Who was elected President in 1868?

3. Examine the chapter pictures and read each caption. What do the pictures show about the nation after the Civil War? Note also the time line at the beginning of the chapter. What are the years of this chapter? Compare this chapter time line to the unit time line on page 333.

4. Read the last part of the chapter called Summing Up. Who set up their own plan for Reconstruction in the South? What is the topic of the next chapter?

Know These Important Terms
Reconstruction
Thirteenth Amendment
Radical Republicans
Freedmen's Bureau
Fourteenth Amendment
Congressional Reconstruction
Fifteenth Amendment
impeach

Know the Main Idea
Here is the MAIN IDEA of this chapter.
Radical Republicans in Congress turned down the plans of President Lincoln and President Johnson to bring the North and South together. They set up their own Reconstruction plan for the nation.

Keep this MAIN IDEA in mind as you read the chapter. Ask yourself the following questions as you read. They will help you remember the MAIN IDEA.

1. Which section of the nation suffered the most damage from the war?

2. What group was set up to help former slaves?

3. What was the result of the trial of President Johnson?

THE YEARS OF THIS CHAPTER ARE 1864 TO 1868

1864   1868   1900

THE CHAPTER LESSON BEGINS HERE

The North and South After the War
Very little fighting took place in the North, and, therefore, the North suffered little damage during the war. In fact, at the end of the war, the North was enjoying good times. Factories were working at top speed, and factory workers were earning good wages. Farmers were able to sell their crops at high prices. But conditions were far different in the South.

Most of the fighting in the war took place in the South. As a result, the South suffered terrible damage. Southern farms, plantations, roads, and railroads were destroyed. Many Southern cities were ruined. Southern banks, businesses, and factories were closed.

Lincoln Planned to Rebuild the Nation
Abraham Lincoln was reelected President in 1864. His Vice-President was Andrew Johnson, a Democrat from Tennessee. President Lincoln wanted to make it as easy as possible

for the Southern states to return to the Union. His program for rebuilding the American nation was called **Reconstruction.**

Lincoln's plan for Reconstruction was simple. As soon as one tenth of the voters in each Southern state agreed to support the Constitution of the United States, that state was able to write a new state constitution and elect new state officials. Then the state was allowed to return to the Union.

The Death of President Lincoln

But on April 14, 1865—only five days after the war ended—President Lincoln was shot by John Wilkes Booth. Early the next morning, Lincoln died. Lincoln's death caused deep sorrow all over the nation. His death was a great blow to the nation. Lincoln's plans to rebuild the United States in friendship were not carried out.

Congress Refused to Back President Johnson's Reconstruction Plans

Vice-President Andrew Johnson became President after Lincoln's death. He followed most of Lincoln's Reconstruction plan. By the end of 1865, almost all the Southern states set up new state governments and elected new state officials. They also approved the **Thirteenth Amendment** to the Constitution, which ended slavery. These states promised to support the Constitution, and they asked to return to the Union.

But many Republican Congressmen from the North were against President Johnson's Reconstruction plan. They wanted the Congress to make Reconstruction plans for the South. As a result, they refused to allow the Southern states to return to the Union. One group of Republicans called **Radical Republicans** also wanted to punish the South because they blamed the South for starting the war.

The South Was Unfair to the Former Slaves

Congress also refused to let the South return because the Southern states were electing former Confederate leaders as their new officials. And the Southern states were not treating the former slaves fairly. Each Southern state passed Black Codes to control the black people living in the state. These codes forbade black Americans to vote, to serve on juries, or to carry guns.

Congress Tried to Protect Black Americans

Congress decided that it must help the black people of the South. Therefore, in 1865, Congress set up the **Freedmen's Bureau.** The Freedmen's Bureau helped find jobs for former slaves and gave them food, clothing, and medical treatment. The Freedman's Bureau opened up schools to help black Americans to get an education.

Congress also passed the Civil Rights Act of 1866, which gave black Americans all the rights of other United States citizens. Congress also approved what became the **Fourteenth Amendment** to the Constitution. This amendment made all black Americans citizens of the United States. It forbade certain Confederate leaders to serve in government offices, and it urged all states to allow their black citizens to vote. Tennessee was the only Southern state to approve this amendment.

Congress Drew up Its Own Reconstruction Plan

In the Congressional elections of 1866, the Radical Republicans gained control of the Congress. This meant that the Radical Republicans now had enough votes to pass any Reconstruction laws they wished. Congress now took over the Reconstruction of the South.

Schools were set up in the South after the war to educate the freed slaves. Pictured above is a primary school for freedmen.

The leaders of the Radical Republicans were Thaddeus Stevens of Pennsylvania and Charles Sumner of Massachusetts. Stevens and Sumner drew up a plan of **Congressional Reconstruction.** This plan included three main points:

1. The South was to be divided into five districts. Each district was to be governed by a Northern general and Northern troops.

2. The Southern states were to write new state constitutions that set up new state governments. These constitutions were also to give black citizens the right to vote.

3. The new Southern state governments were to approve the Fourteenth Amendment and the **Fifteenth Amendment** to the Constitution. The Fifteenth Amendment gave black Americans the right to vote.

Only after the Southern states carried out this plan were they to be allowed to rejoin the Union.

General Ulysses S. Grant Was Elected President in 1868

President Johnson was against the Congressional Reconstruction plan because he thought

Thaddeus Stevens makes the last speech in Congress on the impeachment of
President Johnson. How did the Senate vote in the trial?

it was too harsh. Finally, early in 1868, the Radical Republicans decided to **impeach** him, or charge him with misconduct and remove him from office. When the President is impeached, he is given a trial, and the Senate acts as his court. To remove him from office, two thirds of the Senate must vote against him. Congress failed to remove President Johnson by only one vote!

In 1868, however, the Republicans chose General Ulysses S. Grant as their candidate for President. They chose him because he seemed willing to go along with Congressional Reconstruction. The Democrats ran Governor Horatio Seymour (SEE-mor) of New York. Although the election was close, Grant won.

Summing Up

President Lincoln planned to bring the nation together again in friendship. After Lincoln was killed, President Andrew Johnson followed most of Lincoln's plans. However, the Radical Republicans gained control of Congress and set up their own plan for Reconstruction in the South. The next chapter tells about Reconstruction in the South.

AFTER YOU READ THE CHAPTER

In each of the sentences below, select the term that best completes the sentence.

1. The rebuilding of the nation after the Civil War was called (**Reconstruction/Renaissance**).
2. The (**Fourteenth/Thirteenth**) Amendment ended slavery in the United States.
3. The (**Northern/Radical**) Republicans wanted to punish the South.
4. The (**Black Brigade/Freedmen's Bureau**) was set up by Congress to help former slaves.
5. The (**Fourteenth/Fifteenth**) Amendment made all black Americans citizens.
6. The (**Radical/Congressional**) Reconstruction plan was the plan actually used to rebuild the nation.
7. The (**Fifteenth/Fourteenth**) Amendment gave black Americans the right to vote.
8. To (**reprimand/impeach**) a President means to charge him with a crime.

Do You Remember These People?

Tell something about each of the following persons.

Abraham Lincoln   Ulysses S. Grant
John Wilkes Booth   Andrew Johnson
Thaddeus Stevens   Charles Sumner
Horatio Seymour

Do You Know When It Happened?

What are the years of this chapter? Place the following events in the order in which they occurred.

Ulysses S. Grant was elected President.

Andrew Johnson was impeached.

Lincoln was reelected as President.

Congress drew up its own Reconstruction plan.

Andrew Johnson became President.

Discovering More About the Main Idea

Radical Republicans in Congress turned down the plans of President Lincoln and President Johnson to bring the North and South together. They set up their own Reconstruction plan for the nation.

Tell how each of the following developments is related to the MAIN IDEA.

President Lincoln drew up a simple and easy plan to rebuild the nation.

Radical Republicans in Congress were against President Johnson's Reconstruction plan. They wanted to punish the South. They drew up another plan of Reconstruction.

President Johnson was impeached and almost removed from office.

Can You Discuss the Chapter?

Use the information you learned in this chapter to answer the following questions.

1. What was Lincoln's Reconstruction plan?
2. Why were certain members of Congress worried that the South might be unfair to former slaves? How did they try to help?
3. Explain the Congressional Reconstruction plan.
4. Why did Congress impeach President Johnson? What were the results?

Can You Connect the Past and the Present?

1. The assassination, or murder, of the President of the United States is a tragic event. How many Presidents have been killed in this manner? Which was the most recent?
2. No President of the United States has yet been removed from office by impeachment and trial by the Senate. May officials of your local government be removed from office? For what reasons? Have any officials been removed from office?

CHAPTER 54

The End of Reconstruction

Needy Southerners receive food.

BEFORE YOU BEGIN THE CHAPTER

Know What to Look For

1. Robert Smalls of South Carolina served a longer time in Congress than any other black Reconstruction Congressman. Smalls was born a slave. During the Civil War, he became a crew member on the "Planter," a Confederate gunboat used in Charleston harbor.

While serving on the "Planter," Smalls thought of a daring plan to win his freedom. One night, when the officers of the ship went

ashore, he took over the "Planter." With his wife and children and twelve black crew members aboard, he sailed the ship out of Charleston harbor and turned it over to the Union navy. Smalls was made a member of the Union navy and commanded the "Planter" until 1866. In the years after the war, Smalls was elected to Congress four times. In this chapter, you will read more about Reconstruction.

2. Read the title of the chapter. Look through the chapter and read each heading. What states wrote new constitutions?

3. Look at the pictures in the chapter and read each caption. What do the pictures show about the South after the Civil War? Note also the time line at the beginning of the chapter. What years are included in this chapter? Compare this chapter time line to the unit time line on page 333.

4. Read the last part of the chapter called Summing Up. What happened during the Reconstruction period in the South?

Know These Important Terms
scalawags   Ku Klux Klan
carpetbaggers

Know the Main Idea
Here is the MAIN IDEA of this chapter.
During Reconstruction, new state governments were set up in the South. Most white Southerners, however, were against these governments, and in time they gained control of the state governments again.

Keep this MAIN IDEA in mind as you study the chapter. Ask yourself the following questions as you read. They will help you remember the MAIN IDEA.

1. Who were the people many white Southerners called scalawags?

2. How did the new state governments improve life in the South?

3. When did Reconstruction come to an end in the South?

THE YEARS OF THIS CHAPTER ARE 1865 TO 1877

1864   1865   1877   1900

THE CHAPTER LESSON BEGINS HERE

New Leaders Controlled the New Southern State Governments

By the end of 1870, all the Southern states were able to return to the Union. The Southern states wrote new state constitutions, which set up new Southern governments. The men who led the South before the war were not allowed to hold office in these new state governments. Many of the new Southern leaders had never before served in state governments. Southerners who supported the Confederacy believed that these new leaders were enemies of the South and called them **scalawags** (SKAL-uh-wagz). But most of them were farmers and businessmen who were not active in Southern government before the war.

Many Northerners moved to the South during the years of Reconstruction. Southerners called these Northerners **carpetbaggers** because some of them carried suitcases made of carpet cloth. A few of these carpetbaggers came to the South to get rich quick. But many of them were businessmen or teachers who planned to stay in the South and help build it up.

Black Leaders Served in the New Southern State Governments

The black citizens of the South also played an important part in the new Southern governments. Black men were elected to the state legislatures and held important offices in the state governments. The state of Mississippi elected two black men, Hiram Revels and

page 341

During Reconstruction several black Americans were elected to Congress. Pictured above are the first black Senator and Representatives.

Blanche K. Bruce, to the United States Senate. Fifteen other black men served in the House of Representatives during the Reconstruction period.

Most of the black leaders of the South in the Reconstruction period were either former slaves or came from the North. Many were teachers or ministers. Several were college graduates. Most of the black leaders worked hard to improve the condition of their own people as well as the whole South.

The Southern States Wrote New Constitutions

The new state constitutions written during the Reconstruction period improved the old Southern state constitutions in several ways. These new constitutions allowed more people to vote and to hold office. They improved city and town government in the South and made taxes fairer. Under these constitutions, farms, cities, and railroads were rebuilt.

But most important of all, these new constitutions set up free public schools for the first time in most Southern states. The black leaders of the South helped to bring about this public school system. However, except for New Orleans, all the public schools in the South were segregated.

Many Southerners Were Against the Reconstruction Governments

Most white Southerners refused to accept the rule of these Reconstruction governments. Southerners claimed that these new Southern governments were run by black people and

This picture shows black Americans voting for the first time. The Fifteenth Amendment gave black citizens the right to vote.

that they were very dishonest. But no Southern state was ever controlled by black people during the Reconstruction period. And most of the new Southern governments were not dishonest.

In some cases, money raised by the new Southern governments was wasted or spent foolishly. Also, some Southern leaders did spend the money raised by the state for themselves. But many of the governments which were set up in the South after the Reconstruction governments were far more dishonest than were any of the Reconstruction governments. And at this time, many state governments in the North were also dishonest.

However, the white Southerners tried to get rid of the Reconstruction governments. Most white Southerners tried to win control

of the governments peacefully, but some of them were willing to use force.

The Ku Klux Klan and the Reconstruction Governments

Many secret groups were formed in the South to get rid of the Reconstruction governments. The best known of these groups was the **Ku Klux Klan.** The members of the Ku Klux Klan wanted to keep black people, carpetbaggers, and scalawags from voting and taking part in Southern state governments. Klan members dressed in white sheets and white hoods in order to frighten these people. Soon, however, the Klan began to threaten or even kill black citizens who supported the Reconstruction governments.

The Ku Klux Klan was very successful, and

ROBERT BROWN ELLIOT—
BLACK STATESMAN

Not many American politicians can read French, German, Spanish, and Latin. One of the few who was able to do so was Robert Brown Elliot. Elliot was born in 1842, and his parents brought him to Boston from the West Indies when he was a young boy. Elliot was educated in Boston and in England, where he was trained as a lawyer.

When he finished his education in England, Elliot returned to the United States and settled in South Carolina. In 1868, he helped to rewrite the state constitution of South Carolina. Elliot was elected to the South Carolina legislature, and he also held several other important state offices. In 1870, he was elected to the United States House of Representatives.

In Congress, Elliot worked for civil rights laws for black Americans. Elliot's greatest speech in Congress was an answer to Alexander H. Stephens, the former Vice-President of the Confederacy. Stephens, who opposed all civil rights laws, was blasted by Elliot as a man who once "tried to break up the Union" and now was trying to "continue . . . the burdens" of black citizens. A civil rights bill was passed by Congress. Elliot later returned to private life, and he died in New Orleans in 1884.

it looked as if the Reconstruction governments were sure to fall. But the Radical Republicans in Congress passed several laws to stop the Klan's unlawful actions. Finally, in 1870 and 1871, Congress passed strong federal laws against the Klan. Under these laws, President Grant sent soldiers to the South to break up the Klan. Hundreds of Klan members were arrested. As a result, the once-strong Klan became weak in the South.

Reconstruction Came to an End

However, by the early 1870's, Northerners began to lose interest in Reconstruction. The death of Thaddus Stevens in 1868 and Charles Sumner in 1874 weakened the Radical Republicans' power in Congress. And in 1872, Congress gave the right to vote to thousands of Southerners who once supported the Confederacy. Within four years, white Southerners gained control of the state governments in all the Southern states except Louisiana, Florida, and South Carolina. In these states, Northern troops kept the Reconstruction governments in power. Finally, in order to elect Rutherford B. Hayes as President in 1876, the Republicans promised to take all the Northern troops out of the South. Hayes was elected President, and he removed the Northern troops from the South. By 1877, Reconstruction was ended.

Summing Up

Reconstruction in the South lasted from 1865 to 1877. During this period, new state governments were set up in the South. These Reconstruction governments made many improvements in the South, but most white Southerners refused to accept them. Some Southerners even used force to try to get rid of them. By 1877, Southerners again gained control of the state governments. The next chapter tells about the South after 1877.

AFTER YOU READ THE CHAPTER

Do You Know These Important Terms?

For each sentence below, choose the term that best completes the sentence.

1. Southerners who supported the Confederacy called the new white leaders from the South (**Copperheads/scalawags**).
2. Northerners who moved to the South during Reconstruction were called (**carpetbaggers/prospectors**).
3. The (**Flying Wedge/Ku Klux Klan**) was a secret group formed in the South to get rid of the Reconstruction governments.

Do You Remember These People?

Tell something about each of the following persons.

Hiram Revels   Blanche K. Bruce
Thaddus Stevens   Charles Sumner
Ulysses S. Grant   Rutherford B. Hayes

Can You Locate These Places?

Use the map on page 328 to locate the following places. Tell how each location is related to the events in this chapter.

Mississippi   New Orleans
Louisiana   Florida
South Carolina

Do You Know When It Happened?

What are the years of this chapter? Tell why each of the following dates is important.

1865   1872   1877

Discovering More About the Main Idea

During Reconstruction, new state governments were set up in the South. Most white Southerners, however, were against these governments, and in time they gained control of the state governments again.

Tell how each of the following developments is related to the MAIN IDEA.

Black leaders, scalawags, and carpetbaggers served in the new state governments in the South.

The new state governments improved the city and town governments in the South, made taxes fairer, rebuilt farms, cities, railroads, and factories, and set up a system of free public education.

By the early 1870's, Northerners began to lose interest in Reconstruction. In 1877, the last Northern troops were removed from the South.

Can You Discuss the Chapter?

Use the information you learned in this chapter to answer the following questions.

1. What kind of people were selected to run the new state governments in the South during Reconstruction?
2. Why did most white Southerners refuse to accept the rule of the new state governments? Were some of the things they claimed about these governments untrue?
3. Describe the purpose and actions of the Ku Klux Klan.
4. Why were the last Northern troops removed from the South in 1877?
5. What do you think of secret groups?

Can You Connect the Past and the Present?

1. Black Americans were active in the Reconstruction governments in the South. Not until recently have they been able to take a part in the governments of the Southern states. Name some important black American leaders from the South.
2. The Ku Klux Klan is still active today. Compare its purposes and methods today with its purposes and methods during the Reconstruction days.

CHAPTER 55

The New South

Coke ovens at Birmingham, Alabama.

BEFORE YOU BEGIN THE CHAPTER

Know What to Look For

1. Birmingham, Alabama, is one of the best locations in the world for the making of steel. The three main products used in steel-making—iron ore, coal, and limestone—are all found close together in the area around Birmingham. To make steel, coal is baked into a product called coke. Coke is used as fuel in the huge furnaces which melt the iron ore and turn it into steel. Limestone is put into the white-hot liquid iron ore to remove all the impurities. This stone acts like a great magnet and draws all the unwanted materials in the melted iron ore to the top where it can be separated from the metal.

The steel mills that have grown up around Birmingham are symbols of a new South. In this chapter, you will read about this new South. You will also discover that in many ways the South still followed its old ways.

2. Read the title of the chapter. Then look through the chapter and read each heading. What were some of the changes that took place in the South?

3. Look at the pictures in the chapter and read each caption. What does the opening picture show? Note also the time line at the beginning of the chapter. What years are included in this chapter? Compare this chapter time line to the unit time line on page 333.

4. Read the last part of the chapter called Summing Up. What changes in the South were really new?

Know These Important Terms

New South   share croppers
tenant farmers   Plessy against Ferguson

Know the Main Idea

Here is the MAIN IDEA of this chapter.

After Reconstruction, the South set up new governments, and manufacturing became important. Farming remained the most important business, however. Black people in the South lost many of their rights.

Keep this MAIN IDEA in mind as you study the chapter. Ask yourself the following questions as you read. They will help you remember the MAIN IDEA.

1. What activities did Southern leaders want to become even more important than farming?

2. What types of farming started in the South after the Civil War?

3. In what case did the Supreme Court rule that segregation was lawful? What was the result of this Supreme Court ruling in the Southern states?

THE YEARS OF THIS CHAPTER ARE 1877 TO 1900

1864	1877	1900

THE CHAPTER LESSON BEGINS HERE

The New Southern Leaders

After Reconstruction ended in 1877, white Southerners took control of the Southern state governments and elected Democrats to run these governments. But the leaders of the Democratic Party were no longer only the plantation owners who ruled the South before the Civil War. Many of these new leaders were businessmen, factory owners, and bankers.

These new Southern leaders did not want to bring back the "old days" when the South depended on farming. Instead, they wanted to build a **New South** in which manufacturing and trade were to be even more important

than farming. However, the South lacked the money to set up factories. Therefore, the new Southern leaders urged Northern businessmen to come to the South and to set up factories.

The New Southern Governments

To encourage Northerners to build factories in the South, the new Southern leaders lowered taxes. They also cut down on the amount of money the state governments spent. As a result, the public schools in the South lacked money.

Sometimes, the state governments set up by the new Southern leaders did not rule well.

Some of these governments were dishonest, and some Southern leaders took money from the state governments. However, many state governments in the North and West were also dishonest at this time.

The South Built Factories and Railroads

The new Southern leaders did succeed in building up Southern manufacturing. Railroads were built across the South. Iron and steel mills were also built all over the South. By the 1890's, Birmingham (BURR-meengham), Alabama, was one of the leading iron- and steel-making centers in the United States. Texas became the center of an oil industry. Tobacco products such as cigarettes and cigars were manufactured in North Carolina.

Other Southern factories made furniture, paper, and many other wood products. But the most important Southern industry was the manufacturing of cotton cloth. The South had the cotton, the water power and coal to run the machines, and many workers. By 1900, half of all the cotton-cloth mills in the United States were in the South.

Problems of Southern Manufacturing

Although many new factories were built in the South, the South was not able to catch up with Northern manufacturing. In fact, in 1900, the South was even farther behind the North in manufacturing than it was in 1860. Also, many of the new Southern factories were owned by Northerners. In many cases, these Northerners only let the Southern factories make part of the product. For example, Southern cotton mills did not finish making the cotton goods. Instead, they were finished in Northern cotton mills. The Southern iron and steel industry also had its problems. Because of higher shipping costs, Birmingham had to sell its steel products at higher prices than Pittsburgh, the Northern steel-making center.

Tenant Farming and Share Cropping in the South

The New South was still mainly a farming section, and cotton was still the main crop. After the war, many plantations were broken up, and some were sold to businessmen. Many land owners rented out small sections of land to tenant farmers. These tenant farmers paid rent to the land owners to use the land. But many tenant farmers were too poor to pay their rent in money. These tenant farmers paid their rent by giving the land owners a part of their crops.

Farmers who paid their rent in crops were known as share croppers. Share croppers had to pay from one third to one half of their crops as rent. Often, they also had to buy their food and their supplies from the land owner on credit. At the end of the planting season, most share croppers were in debt, and they owed more money to the land owner.

Black Citizens Lost the Right to Vote

After Reconstruction ended in 1877, black Americans in the South lost many of the rights they enjoyed during Reconstruction. This did not happen all at once. For more than twenty years after Reconstruction, black men were still able to vote and to hold office. But by the early 1900's, the Southern states passed laws which took the right to vote away from black citizens. One of these laws required all voters to pay a poll tax, or voting tax. But most black voters were too poor to pay this tax, and therefore, they were not allowed to vote. The Southern states also used literacy, or reading, tests and other ways to stop black citizens from voting. By 1900, very few black Americans were able to vote in the South.

Black Americans Were Separated from White Americans

In the 1890's, the Southern states began to

Separate schools for white and black students were set up in the South.
Pictured above is a class at the famous black school, Tuskegee Institute.

segregate, or separate, black Americans and white Americans. By 1900, black Americans were not allowed to sit in the same seats as white people on streetcars and railroads. They were not able to use the same restaurants, theaters, and hospitals as white Southerners. And separate schools were set up for black children and white children.

In 1896, in the case of **Plessy against Ferguson,** the Supreme Court ruled that segregation was lawful. As a result, Southern states continued to segregate black people from white people.

Summing Up

After Reconstruction ended, the South changed in many ways. These changes made a "New South." New Southern governments were set up. Manufacturing started to become important. However, farming was still the most important business, and cotton was the main crop. During these years, black Americans lost the right to vote in the South, and they were segregated, or separated, from white Americans. In the next chapters, which are in Unit 15, you will find out about changes in the West after the Civil War.

AFTER YOU READ THE CHAPTER

Do You Know These Important Terms?

For each sentence below, choose the term that best completes the sentence.

1. A South in which manufacturing and trade might be more important than farming was called the (**Industrial/New**) South.
2. Farmers who pay rent to land owners for the use of the land are called (**tenant/ gentlemen**) farmers.
3. Farmers who pay their rent in crops are known as (**migrant farmers/share croppers**).
4. In (**Plessy against Ferguson/Scott against Alabama**), the Supreme Court ruled that segregation was lawful.

Can You Locate These Places?

Use the map on page 366 to locate the following places. Tell how each location is related to the events in this chapter.

Birmingham   **Texas**
North Carolina   **Pittsburgh**

Do You Know When It Happened?

What are the years of this chapter? Tell how each of the following dates was important to the people of the South.

1877   1896

Discovering More About the Main Idea

After Reconstruction, the South set up new governments, and manufacturing became important. Farming remained the most important business, however. Black people in the South lost many of their rights.

Tell how each of the following developments is related to the MAIN IDEA.

The South lacked the money to set up factories so Southern leaders urged Northern businessmen to come to the South.

The South built up its manufacturing, especially of cotton textiles, iron and steel, oil, tobacco, and furniture. But the South was still mainly a farming section, and cotton was still the main crop.

The black people in the South lost their right to vote. Southern states also began to segregate, or separate, black people and white people.

Can Your Discuss the Chapter?

Use the information you learned in this chapter to answer the following questions.

1. Why was much Southern manufacturing controlled by Northern businessmen?
2. What were some problems of Southern manufacturing?
3. What is the difference between a tenant farmer and a share cropper?
4. How did black people in the South lose many of their rights?
5. How do you think the Supreme Court ruling in the case of Plessy against Ferguson might have affected the life of a white Southerner? a black Southerner? a white Northerner? a black Northerner?

Can You Connect the Past and the Present?

1. Manufacturing has grown in importance in the South. Are the manufactured products that were important in 1900 still important today?
2. What famous Supreme Court case changed the ruling in Plessy against Ferguson as far as public schools are concerned? Is segregation lawful today in any part of American life?

UNIT 15

America Becomes an Industrial Nation

Buffalo crossing railroad tracks stop a train.

THE CHAPTERS IN UNIT 15 ARE

CHAPTER 56   Settling the Last Frontier
CHAPTER 57   Farmers on the Last Frontier
CHAPTER 58   The Growth of Railroads
CHAPTER 59   The Growth of American Industries
CHAPTER 60   Problems of Industrial America

THE YEARS OF THIS UNIT ARE 1850 TO 1900

1800	1850	1900	1975

CHAPTER 56

Settling the Last Frontier

A young settler on the Great Plains.

BEFORE YOU BEGIN THE CHAPTER

Know What to Look For

1. The American buffalo once roamed the Great Plains in large herds. Some experts believe that there were about 75 million buffalo in 1860. The herds often held up travelers who just had to wait until the buffalo passed. For example, in 1869, a train in Kansas was held up for nine hours while a herd of buffalo crossed the tracks.

Within a period of about ten years, however, hunters almost wiped out the buffalo. Some hunted for sport. But most hunted as a business, killing the animals for meat and hides. By the 1880's, only a few small herds of buffalo were still alive. In this chapter, you will read about the settlement of the Great Plains and other parts of the last frontier. The last frontier was the unsettled western land located between the Mississippi River and California and Oregon.

2. Read the title of the chapter. Then look through the chapter and read each heading. Who helped open up the "last frontier"?

3. Look at the pictures in the chapter and read each caption. What do the pictures show you about life on the last frontier? Look at the map on page 354. What three important types of information does this map show? Note also the time line at the beginning of the chapter. What years are included in this chapter? Compare this chapter time line to the unit time line on page 351. How do the years of this chapter compare with the years of the unit?

4. Read the last part of the chapter called Summing Up. What movement brought an end to the days of the Cattle Kingdom?

Look at the map on page 354.

Know These Important Terms

Great Plains **Cattle Kingdom**
placer mining **long drives**

Know the Main Idea

Here is the MAIN IDEA of this chapter.

Settlement of the land west of the Mississippi River took place in the years between 1865 and 1900. This land was settled by miners, cattlemen, farmers, and sheep raisers.

Keep this MAIN IDEA in mind as you study the chapter. Ask yourself the following questions as you read. They will help you remember the MAIN IDEA.

1. What two towns grew rapidly in Nevada as a result of mining?

2. From whom did the American cowboy learn his trade of herding cattle to market?

3. Who caused problems for the cattlemen?

THE YEARS OF THIS CHAPTER ARE 1850 TO 1900

1850   1900

THE CHAPTER LESSON BEGINS HERE

America's Last Frontier Was Still Unsettled

After 1865, Americans were ready to settle the "last frontier" of their nation. The "last frontier" was the unsettled Western land located beyond the Mississippi River.

When American settlers pushed west of the Mississippi River during the 1840's, they reached a huge, flat, grassy land called the **Great Plains.** The Great Plains, which reached to the Rocky Mountains, was different from any land Americans had ever known. This land was very dry, covered with short grass, and had few trees.

Few Americans tried to settle on the Great Plains because the land seemed too dry for farming. And few Americans also settled on the Western lands between the Great Plains and the Pacific coast because this area was made up of mountains, hills, and deserts. Instead, settlers traveled across the Great Plains, and through the Rocky Mountains, and settled in Utah, Oregon, or California.

Miners Helped to Open Up the Unsettled Western Lands

For many years, it looked as if the unsettled parts of the West were never going to be settled. But during the 1850's, Americans began to move onto these unsettled Western lands.

THE WEST, 1865 TO THE 1890's

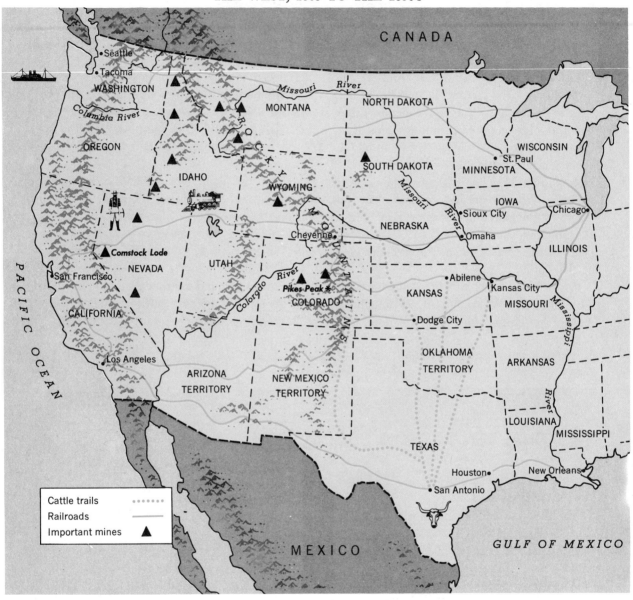

One of the important groups who opened the "last frontier" to settlement were the miners. The miners were looking for gold and silver. Most miners found no gold or silver, but in 1859, gold was discovered near what is now the city of Denver, Colorado.

Within a year, almost 100 thousand Americans rushed into Colorado to search for gold. However, very few settlers found gold in Colorado. Although gold was there, costly machinery was needed to get it out of the ground. Many of the settlers left when they failed to find gold. But thousands of people remained in Colorado, and it became a state in 1876.

Mining Became a Big Business in the West

In 1859, both gold and silver were discovered in Nevada. Thousands of settlers who hoped to get rich hurried into Nevada. Two towns, Virginia City and Carson City, grew up almost overnight, and Nevada became a state in 1864. Once again the gold and silver was hard to mine. But with drilling machines, the Comstock (KUM-stok) lode, or mine, produced about 300 million dollars worth of gold and silver between the years 1859 and 1879.

Many parts of the West, including the Great Plains and the lands of Western mountains, were settled because of gold rushes. Thousands of miners moved into what are now the states of Washington, Montana, Idaho, Wyoming, New Mexico, Arizona, North Dakota, and South Dakota. These men used a pick, a shovel, and a pan to mine for gold and silver. This type of mining is known as **placer mining**. By the 1870's, the placer miner was replaced by machines. Big mining companies were started, and many of the miners went to work for these companies.

The Cattle Industry Became Important on the Great Plains

From 1865 to about 1885, the Great Plains was known as the **Cattle Kingdom**. Millions of cattle ran loose and grazed freely on the grass land of the Great Plains. Texas was the center of this cattle industry. Before the Civil War, most Texas cattle were sold in the South.

But during the Civil War, Texas was cut off from the South. When Texans found that they were able to sell their cattle at high

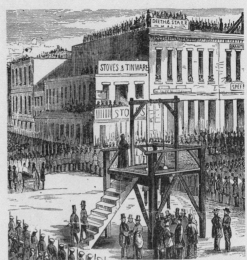

Vigilance committee hanging a criminal.

VIGILANTES

After gold was discovered in California in 1849, thousands of men rushed there. Mining camps sprang up overnight. Many of these mining camps were wild, lawless places where crimes such as stealing and murder were common. These mining camps had no regular government or police force. As a result, the miners themselves had to control crime. When a man was charged with a crime, the miners in the camp came together and gave him a trial. If he was found guilty, he was whipped, thrown out of the camp, or hanged. This rough type of justice worked fairly well in the mining camps.

In the growing cities of California, however, the problem of controlling crime was harder. Often the new city governments were not able to handle their crime problem. Therefore, citizens of San Francisco and other towns organized citizen police forces called vigilance committees during the 1850's. These committees captured criminals, tried them for their crimes, and punished them—often by hanging. Because of the efforts of vigilance committees, order was established in California in 1860.

Many early cowboys were black. Nat Love, above, was the famed "Deadwood Dick."

tected his eyes from the sun or the rain. The cowboy's high-heeled boots, spurs, and other parts of his outfit were all suited for life on horseback.

The cowboy's life was hard. Cowboys on the long drive often spent eighteen hours a day on horseback, and the long drive often lasted two or three months. Many of the early cowboys were former slaves who were first brought into Texas by their owners. A black cowboy named Bill Pickett developed the skill of "bulldogging," or steer wrestling, which became popular at Western rodeos.

The Cattle Kingdom Came to an End

By the 1880's, over 6 million cattle were driven north from Texas. Many men made fortunes in the cattle business. But the days of the long drive were almost over. Feeding so many cattle soon became a problem.

In the 1880's, cattlemen on the Great Plains also began to have troubles with sheep raisers and farmers, who started to settle on the Great Plains. Sheep ate the grass needed by the cattle. Farmers fenced in their lands and made it difficult for cattlemen to drive the cattle to market. By the 1890's, some cattlemen moved farther west and fenced in their lands. In time, all cattle were grazed on fenced-in ranches.

Summing Up

During the 1850's, Americans began to settle the "last frontier" of their nation. Miners in search of gold and silver started the settlement of the Great Plains and other Western lands. Then the cattlemen came, and the Great Plains became known as the Cattle Kingdom. And finally, farmers came and ended the days of the Cattle Kingdom. The next chapter tells about the farmers who settled on the Great Plains.

prices in the North, they began to make **long drives.** On a long drive, thousands of cattle grazed freely on the Great Plains. They were herded 1 thousand miles or more across the Great Plains to the railroad towns of Abilene (AB-uh-leen) and Dodge City in Kansas. At Abilene and Dodge City, the cattle were loaded into railroad cars and sent to Chicago, Illinois, which became the meat-packing center of the nation.

The Cowboy in the Cattle Kingdom

The hero of the Cattle Kingdom was the cowboy. The American cowboy learned his trade of herding cattle to market and borrowed much of his outfit from the Mexican cowboy. The cowboy's outfit was useful and suited to his life. His wide-brimmed hat pro-

AFTER YOU READ THE CHAPTER

Do You Know These Important Terms?

For each sentence below, choose the term that best completes the sentence.

1. The (**Columbia/Great**) Plains were the huge, flat, grassy lands west of the Mississippi River.
2. The use of a pick, shovel, and a pan to mine for gold is known as (**prospecting/placer mining**).
3. Between 1865 and 1885, the Great Plains was known as the (**Cattle/Ranchers'**) Kingdom.
4. On a (**roundup/long drive**) thousands of cattle were herded across the Great Plains to the railroad towns.

Can You Locate These Places?

Use the map on page 354 to do the following map work.

1. In what mountains were many mines located? In what state is the Comstock Lode located? Why was the Comstock Lode important?
2. Trace the railroads that cross the United States between the Mississippi River and the West coast. Trace also the cattle trails which go northward from Texas. Name the cattle towns located at points where cattle trails cross the railroads.

Do You Know When It Happened?

What are the years of this chapter? Place the following events in the order in which they occurred.

The Comstock Lode was discovered.

Texans began to make long drives to the railroads.

Colorado became a state.

The Cattle Kingdom came to an end.

Discovering More About the Main Idea

Settlement of the land west of the Mississippi River took place in the years between 1865 and 1900. This land was settled by miners, cattlemen, farmers, and sheep raisers.

Tell how each of the following developments is related to the MAIN IDEA.

Beginning in the late 1850's, miners began to open up the last frontier to settlement. Mining became a big business.

After the Civil War, cattlemen grazed large herds of cattle on the grass-covered Great Plains. They drove the cattle to railroad towns for shipment to market. Many former slaves became cowboys.

The arrival of sheep raisers and farmers who fenced their lands brought an end to the Cattle Kingdom.

Can You Discuss the Chapter?

Use the information you learned in this chapter to answer the following questions.

1. Why had earlier settlers bypassed the Great Plains to settle much farther west in California or Oregon?
2. How did mining in the West change during the 1870's?
3. Explain how a cowboy's outfit was useful and suited to his life.
4. Why did the Cattle Kingdom come to an end in the 1880's?
5. Which would you rather have been, in the early days of the West, a miner or a cowboy? Explain your answer.

Can You Connect the Past and the Present?

Mining is still very important in the West. Can you name some important mining centers and the minerals that are mined there?

CHAPTER 57

Farmers on the Last Frontier

Woman and girls on the plains picking flowers.

BEFORE YOU BEGIN THE CHAPTER

Know What to Look For

1. In 1969, the United States government put out a postage stamp in honor of Chief Joseph, a famous Indian Chief. In 1877, when the U.S. government ordered Chief Joseph's tribe to leave their land and move to a reservation, Chief Joseph refused. For two months, he was able to stay away from the army troops that were chasing his tribe of 200 warriors and 600 women and children. Chief Joseph had almost taken his tribe to safety in Canada when he and his tribe were captured in what is now Montana. The proud chief of the Nez Percé Indians stood and spoke boldly before his captors: "I am tired of fighting. Our chiefs are killed....It is cold and we have no blankets. The little children are freezing to death....My heart is sick and sad....I will fight no more, forever."

Chief Joseph and the army who captured him were part of the final settlement of the last frontier. You will read more about the last frontier in this chapter.

2. Read the title of the chapter. Then look through the chapter and read each heading. By using only the chapter headings, tell who moved to the West.

3. Look at the pictures in the chapter and read each caption. What do the pictures show about the lives of farmers on the frontier? Note also the time line at the beginning of the chapter. What years are included in this chapter? Compare this chapter time line to the unit time line on page 351. How do the years of this chapter compare to the years of the unit?

4. Read the last part of the chapter called Summing Up. What did the settlement of the Great Plains lead to? What is the topic of the next chapter?

Know These Important Terms

Homestead Act   dry farming
sod   reservations

Know the Main Idea

Here is the MAIN IDEA of this chapter.

Thousands of farmers settled on the Great Plains. However, the settlement of the Great Plains led to Indian wars in which the Indians were defeated and moved to reservations.

Keep this MAIN IDEA in mind as you study the chapter. Ask yourself the following questions as you read. They will help you remember the MAIN IDEA.

1. Why did many settlers buy railroad land in the West instead of accepting the free land?
2. What inventions helped to improve farming on the Great Plains?
3. When were all Indians made citizens of the United States?

THE YEARS OF THIS CHAPTER ARE 1860 TO 1900

1850   1860   1900

THE CHAPTER LESSON BEGINS HERE

Many Farmers Moved to the West and Settled on the Great Plains

In the year 1862, Congress passed the **Homestead Act.** This act gave 160 acres of land in the West free to any American who was willing to farm the land for five years. Many settlers rushed to accept this offer of free Western land and settled on the Great Plains.

Many other settlers bought land on the Great Plains from the railroad companies. This land was given to the railroad companies by the federal government and the state governments to encourage them to build rail-roads. The railroad companies then sold much of this land at low prices. In this way, the railroad companies gained money to build railroads. Many settlers bought land from the railroad companies instead of taking the free land because it was more valuable. They also bought railroad land because they were able to buy more than 160 acres of land. With so little rain on the Great Plains, farmers needed more than 160 acres to run a successful farm. During the 1870's, the government also made it possible for settlers to buy larger amounts of land.

Farmers on the Great Plains Had Many Troubles

Farming was very difficult on the Great Plains. Winters on the Great Plains were very cold, and summers were hot and dry. In the springtime, the melting snow and rains brought floods. And almost no rain fell for the rest of the year. Farmers on the Great Plains had to be prepared for dust storms, grass fires, blizzards, and grasshoppers. And since few trees grew on the Great Plains, farmers had no wood to build homes or fences. Finally, the thick, grassy soil of the Great Plains, called **sod**, was very difficult to plow.

The farmers of the Great Plains had still other problems. Cattle ranchers and sheep grazers disliked the farmers because they fenced in the land. In the early days of settlement, bitter fights broke out between cattlemen and farmers. Cattlemen drove many farmers off their land. And the Indians on the Great Plains were very dangerous because they disliked the settlers who were pushing them off their hunting grounds.

Farmers on the Great Plains Solved Their Problems

But in spite of all these difficulties, the farmers on the Great Plains were able to succeed. Instead of building wooden houses, the farmers built sod houses made out of bricklike chunks of sod, or earth. They used barbed wire fences instead of wooden fences. With the help of machines they dug deep wells to

A Nebraska family standing in front of their sod home. These houses were built with chunks of earth called sod.

get water for their crops. They used wind-mills to pump the water out of these wells and bring it to the land.

A new type of farming called **dry farming** was developed on the Great Plains. By plowing the earth deeply, farmers were able to bring up water. Then they broke the soil into very small bits which kept the water from evaporating (eh-VAP-uh-rayt-ing), or drying up. Farming on the Great Plains was also helped by the invention of such farming machines as the steel plow, the grain drilling machine, and the threshing machine.

The End of the Frontier

By the 1890's, the farms of the Great Plains were producing huge crops of corn and wheat. Thousands of settlers from the United States and Europe settled the Great Plains. Other parts of the West also were filling up with settlers. Only Oklahoma, Arizona, and New Mexico still did not have enough people to become states.

Many towns grew up in the West. San Francisco was the largest Western city. Denver, Colorado, and Omaha, Nebraska, were also very important. By the 1890's, the United States no longer had a frontier. Although there were still many empty spaces, America was settled from coast to coast.

The Indians on the Great Plains

The Indians who lived on the Great Plains made the settlement of the Great Plains difficult. After the Civil War, about 200 thousand Indians lived on the Great Plains. The Plains Indians hunted the buffaloes and depended on the buffaloes for their food, shelter, clothing, and tools. The Plains Indians were powerful hunters and warriors.

The United States government asked the Plains Indians to live on **reservations,** or lands which were promised to the Indians forever.

Thomas Gilcrease Institute, Tulsa, Oklahoma.

As the Great Plains were settled, Indian tribes were forced to move farther West.

THE GROWING NATION 1861 to 1896

No.	State	Date Admitted
34.	Kansas	January 29, 1861
35.	West Virginia	June 20, 1863
36.	Nevada	October 31, 1864
37.	Nebraska	March 1, 1867
38.	Colorado	August 1, 1876
39.	North Dakota	November 2, 1889
40.	South Dakota	November 2, 1889
41.	Montana	November 8, 1889
42.	Washington	November 11, 1889
43.	Idaho	July 3, 1890
44.	Wyoming	July 10, 1890
45.	Utah	January 4, 1896

Many Indian wars were fought after 1865 because the Indians did not want to give up their lands and move to reservations.

Thomas Gilcrease Institute, Tulsa, Oklahoma.

Many Indians agreed. But many Indians did not want to give up their way of life and settle on reservations.

The Indians Were Removed from the Great Plains

To protect their land, the Indians attacked the settlers. The United States government sent soldiers to fight the Indians. Between 1860 and 1890, many bloody Indian wars were fought. However, after a long hard fight, the Indians were defeated. By 1890, they were no longer a threat to the white settlers of the Great Plains.

One of the main reasons for the defeat of the Indians was the killing of the buffalo herds. By the 1880's, the huge buffalo herds were destroyed. Without the buffaloes, the Plains Indians had no food, clothing, or shelter.

After the 1880's, the Plains Indians were forced to move onto reservations. In 1887, Indians who owned their own land were allowed to become citizens of the United States. Indians were not given the right to vote until 1924, when all Indians were finally made citizens of the United States.

Summing Up

Thousands of farmers settled the Great Plains. Although they had many problems, farmers on the Great Plains learned how to make their farms successful. However, the settlement of the Great Plains led to Indian wars. In time, the Indians were forced to leave their hunting grounds. By the 1890's, the frontier was gone, and America was settled. In the next chapter, you will find out how the railroads helped the settlement of America.

AFTER YOU READ THE CHAPTER

Do You Know These Important Terms?

For each sentence below, choose the term that best completes the sentence.

1. The (**Agricultural/Homestead**) Act of 1862 gave 160 acres of land in the West free to any American who was willing to farm the land for five years.
2. The thick, short, grassy soil of the Great Plains is called (**sod/turf**).
3. A type of farming in which farmers plowed the earth deeply and then broke the soil into bits to keep the water from drying up is called (**dry/cultivated**) farming.
4. (**Stockades/Reservations**) were lands set aside which Indians were promised forever.

Can You Locate These Places?

Use the map on page 354 to do the following map work.

1. Locate the western railway lines. Why might lands located near these railroads be more valuable than other lands?
2. Locate Oklahoma, Arizona, and New Mexico. What made these places different from other states in 1890?

Do You Know When It Happened?

What are the years of this chapter? Place the following events in the order in which they occurred.

The Indian wars were ended.
The Homestead Act was passed.
The buffalo herds were killed off.
Settlers began to farm the Great Plains.

Discovering More About the Main Idea

Thousands of farmers settled on the Great Plains. However, the settlement of the Great Plains led to Indian wars in which the Indians were defeated and moved to reservations.

Tell how each of the following developments is related to the MAIN IDEA.

Settlers were able to get 160 acres of free western land from the government or buy land from the railroads at low prices.

Farmers learned to overcome some of the problems of farming the Great Plains. New inventions and new ways of doing things helped farmers overcome other problems.

The Indians fought to protect their land and to save the herds of buffalo on which they depended. By 1890, the Indian troubles had ended, and the last frontier was almost completely settled.

Can You Discuss the Chapter?

Use the information you learned in this chapter to answer the following questions.

1. Why did farmers who settled on the Great Plains need more than 160 acres of land?
2. Describe how farmers overcame some of the problems of farming on the Great Plains.
3. Why was there no frontier left by the year 1890?
4. Explain how the Indians depended on the buffalo herds.
5. Why do you think it took so long for the Indians to be made citizens? Explain your answer.

Can You Connect the Past and the Present?

1. Farming is still not easy on the Great Plains. Can you give some examples of recent events which show that farming the dry parts of the Great Plains is still difficult?
2. What are the problems of Indians who live on reservations today? How are they trying to solve these problems?

CHAPTER 58

The Growth of Railroads

Laying railroad tracks in the West.

BEFORE YOU BEGIN THE CHAPTER

Know What to Look For

1. When George Westinghouse spoke to a famous railroad owner about his idea for an air brake to stop railroad trains, the owner thought such a brake would never work. However, Westinghouse worked on the brake anyway. One day, Westinghouse's new brake was put in a locomotive, and the locomotive began a trial run to see how the brake worked. As

the locomotive came out of a tunnel, the engineer, or driver, saw a wagon and a team of horses crossing the tracks a short distance in front of him. The engineer quickly pulled the brake lever. The new air brake took hold and the train stopped just a few feet from the wagon. A train with the older brakes would never have stopped in time. In this chapter, you will read how this and other inventions helped the railroads develop a system of railroads across the nation.

2. Read the title of the chapter. Then look through the chapter and read each heading. What did the federal government try to do to the railroads?

3. Look at the pictures in the chapter and read each caption. What are the men doing in the first picture? Examine the map on page 366. What is the title of the map? Notice also the time line at the beginning of the chapter. What years are included in this chapter? Compare this chapter time line to the unit time line on page 351.

4. Read the last part of the chapter called Summing Up. How did the railroad help settlers?

Know These Important Terms
railroad rates   railroad systems

rebates   Wabash Railway Case
pools   Interstate Commerce Act

Know the Main Idea
Here is the MAIN IDEA of this chapter.

Between 1865 and 1900, the United States built many railroads which brought together all parts of the nation. Because of unfair practices, the government began to control the railroads.

Keep this MAIN IDEA in mind as you study the chapter. Ask yourself the following questions as you read. They will help you remember the MAIN IDEA.

1. Name the two railroads that met in Utah to complete the first railroad to connect the Atlantic coast and the Pacific coast.
2. How many railroads joined the East and the West in the 1890's?
3. What group was set up by the government to see that the railroads obeyed the law?

THE YEARS OF THIS CHAPTER ARE 1865 TO 1900

1850   1865   1900

THE CHAPTER LESSON BEGINS HERE

A Railroad Joins the Atlantic Coast and the Pacific Coast

Before the War Between the North and the South, many Americans wanted to have a railroad built to connect the Atlantic coast and the Pacific coast. During the war, Congress decided to build this railroad across the nation along a northern route.

Two railroad companies were chosen to build this east to west railroad. The Union Pacific Railroad built westward from Omaha in Nebraska. The Central Pacific Railroad built eastward from Sacramento (SAK-ruh-MENT-oh), California. The building of this

railroad across the nation began in 1863.

Thousands of Chinese workers were brought over to help build the railroad. And thousands of Irish workers helped build tracks across dangerous Indian territory. In 1869, the two railroads joined at Promontory (PRAHM-un-tor-ee), in Utah. The first east to west railroad that ran across the United States was finally completed.

Many Railroads Were Built
By the 1890's, four more railroads which

page 365

crossed the United States were built. Two of them, the Southern Pacific and the Santa Fé, followed southern routes across the nation. The other two railroads, the Northern Pacific and the Great Northern, ran across the northern part of the nation and ended in the far Northwest. These four railroads and other smaller railroads increased railroad mileage in America from 30 thousand miles in 1860 to about 200 thousand miles in 1900.

In the East, many smaller railroads were joined together to form **railroad systems,** or groups of railroad lines. The New York Central Railroad system went from New York to Chicago. The Pennsylvania Railroad system connected Philadelphia and the Pennsylvania coal fields with Chicago and St. Louis. The Illinois Central system went along the Mississippi River from Chicago to New Orleans. And the Southern Railway system connected the cities of the South.

Railroads Became Safer and Faster

Many inventions and improvements helped the growth of the railroads. Better roadbeds and the change from iron to steel rails made railroads safer. The invention of the air brake by George Westinghouse, the building of iron and steel bridges, and the invention of a better signal system made railroad travel faster and safer. And the Pullman sleeping car made travel more comfortable. Railroads were soon carrying most of the passengers and many of the products made in the nation.

RAILROADS BY THE EARLY 1900's

American railroads (R.R.) by the 1900's

A railroad station in Connecticut. Railroads were an important way to carry goods and passengers between the East and West.

Railroads Helped the East and the West

The railroads helped to open up the West. If you remember, railroads sold much of the land they received from the government to settlers at low prices. This sale of land helped to settle the West. Railroads made it easier to reach the West. Traveling by railroad was quicker and cheaper than any other type of travel. And the railroads carried the corn, wheat, and cattle that settlers raised in the West to markets in the East.

Railroads also helped the Eastern part of the United States. They brought products from the West to the people in the East. For example, raw materials like coal and iron were brought to the factories in the East. And railroads carried products manufactured in the East to the West and to all the other parts of the nation.

Railroads Used Unfair Practices

But railroads also caused the American people, especially Westerners, some trouble. When two cities were joined by several railroad lines, **railroad rates,** or prices, were very low. And railroad companies charged companies that sent large shipments of products low rates. Or they gave these companies a **rebate,** or money back, on the rates they paid. In this way, railroads often lost money. Railroads made up this money by charging very high rates in the West, where only one railroad line operated. Often they charged more money for a short haul, or trip, from one Western town to another than for a long trip between two large cities. Railroads also got together and formed **pools.** Pools were agreements between railroads to divide up the business in an area and to charge the same rates. These rates were usually very high.

Thomas Gilcrease Institute, Tulsa, Oklahoma.

Chinese railroad workers.

THE CHINESE AND THE RAILROAD

When gold was discovered in California, men from all over the world came to settle in California. Among these settlers were thousands of Chinese. At first, the Chinese were welcome because the nation needed many workers around the mines and in the new cities. Also, the Chinese worked well and were willing to work for low wages.

Ten thousand Chinese workers helped to build the Central Pacific Railroad. They prepared the road bed, blasted tunnels, and laid rails. Much of this work was done in the Sierra Nevada Mountains in fifteen- to eighteen-foot snows. The Chinese worked quickly and they set a "world record" by laying ten miles of track in one day.

But the railroad they helped to build hurt the Chinese. The railroad brought thousands of American workers to California. These workers disliked the Chinese because they worked for low wages. Also, many Americans felt the Chinese looked and acted differently. In the 1870's, riots against the Chinese broke out in Los Angeles, San Francisco, and Denver. And in the 1880's, Congress passed laws that no longer allowed the Chinese to come to America.

The Federal Government Tried to Control Railroads

Westerners felt that pools, rebates, and high rates for short hauls were unfair. Some Western states passed laws against these unfair railroad practices, and they tried to make the railroads charge fair rates. And several Western states tried to control the amount of money charged by the stockyards where cattle were kept and by grain storehouses, which were owned by the railroads. Although the railroads did not like these laws, they were not able to do anything about them.

However, in the **Wabash Railway Case** of 1886, the Supreme Court said that only Congress had the power to regulate railroads, or pass laws that controlled railroads. The Supreme Court made this ruling because the railroads passed through many states, not just one state. Then, in 1887, Congress passed the **Interstate Commerce Act.** This act tried to make railroads charge fair rates to everyone in all parts of the nation.

The Interstate Commerce Commission, a committee of five men, was formed to see that railroads obeyed the law. But the Commission had little power. If a railroad was not obeying the law, the Commission had to bring the railroad to court. And in almost every case, the courts sided with the railroads. Therefore, railroads were not brought under control for many years.

Summing Up

Between 1865 and 1900, the United States built many railroads which brought together all parts of the nation. These railroads helped open the West to settlers. But the railroads often charged unfair rates. In 1887, Congress passed the Interstate Commerce Act to regulate, or control, railroads. In the next chapter, you will read how other industries grew in the United States after 1865.

AFTER YOU READ THE CHAPTER

Do You Know These Important Terms?

For each sentence below, choose the term that best completes the sentence.

1. Prices charged by the railroads are called railroad (**rates/dues**).
2. Sometimes a shipper who sent a large shipment got money back on his charges. This was called a (**rebate/refund**).
3. Agreements between railroads to divide up the business in an area and to make the same charges were called (**conspiracies/pools**).
4. Railroad (**branches/systems**) were formed when many smaller railroads were joined.
5. In the (**Union Pacific/Wabash**) Railway Case, the Supreme Court ruled that Congress had the power to regulate the railroads.
6. The (**Interstate/Tristate**) Commerce Act tried to make railroads charge fair rates.

Can You Locate These Places?

Use the map on page 366 to do the following map work.

1. Locate the Central Pacific and Union Pacific railroads. Find Promontory in Utah where they met.
2. Name the four other railroad lines that cross the Western states.

Do You Know When It Happened?

What are the years of this chapter? Why is each of the following dates important?

1869   1886   1887

Discovering More About the Main Idea

Between 1865 and 1900, the United States built many railroads which brought together all parts of the nation. Because of unfair practices, the government began to control the railroads.

Tell how each of the following developments is related to the MAIN IDEA.

In 1869, the first railroad was completed joining the East coast with the West coast. Many small Eastern railroad lines joined together to form railroad systems.

New inventions and improvements made the railroads safer and faster. Soon they were carrying most of the goods and passengers.

When the railroads used unfair practices, especially in the West, the government attempted to control the practices of railroads.

Can You Discuss the Chapter?

Use the information you learned in this chapter to answer the following questions.

1. How did railroads become safer and faster in the years after 1865?
2. How did railroads help the people of the East and the West?
3. What were some of the unfair practices carried on by the railroads?
4. Why did many early government efforts to regulate the railroads through the Interstate Commerce Commission fail?
5. Do you think the government has the right to regulate privately owned businesses?

Can You Connect the Past and the Present?

1. How important is the railroad to your community today? What are some problems railroads face? How have they tried to meet competition and improve service?
2. The Interstate Commerce Commission has the power to regulate all companies that carry goods and passengers between states. What regulations are placed on companies that carry goods only within a state?

CHAPTER 59

The Growth of American Industries

Steel-making in the late 1800's.

BEFORE YOU BEGIN THE CHAPTER

Know What to Look For

1. A raw material only becomes important to people when they find a use for the material. Oil is a good example of this. Even before the European settlers arrived in America, the Indians knew about the oil that seeped from the ground into the streams. To them, the oil was not important for they had little or no use for it. In the early 1800's, farmers in

Pennsylvania knew about the same oil. Some used it to grease wagon wheels while others bottled it and sold it as medicine. But oil was still not an important resource.

However, in the 1850's, when people discovered that they were able to burn oil in lamps, it became an important resource. A new oil industry was started. In this chapter, you will read about the rapid growth of the oil industry, and other industries in the United States after 1865.

2. Read the title of the chapter. Then look through the chapter and read each heading. From the headings, can you tell what two industries grew rapidly?

3. Look at the pictures in the chapter and read each caption. What do the pictures show about American industries? Note also the time line at the beginning of the chapter. What years are included in this chapter? Compare this chapter time line to the unit time line on page 351.

4. Read the last part of the chapter called Summing Up. What helped industries to grow after 1865? What is the topic of the next chapter?

Know These Important Terms

consumer goods   open hearth
heavy industry

Know the Main Idea

Here is the MAIN IDEA of this chapter.

After 1865, industry grew rapidly, and the United States became a great industrial nation.

Keep this MAIN IDEA in mind as you study the chapter. Ask yourself the following questions as you read. They will help you remember the MAIN IDEA.

1. What type products did American industry make before 1865?

2. What fuel was used in the iron and steel industry after 1865?

3. What city became the flour-milling center?

THE YEARS OF THIS CHAPTER ARE 1865 TO 1900

1850   1865   1900

THE CHAPTER LESSON BEGINS HERE

The United States Had Two Types of Industries

Before 1865, most American factories made **consumer** (kuhn-soo-muhr) **goods,** or products that were sold directly to the people. Clothing factories, shoe factories, meat-packing plants, and flour mills made consumer goods needed by Americans. Most of the factories that made consumer goods were small and hired just a few workers.

During the 1850's, **heavy industry** began to grow rapidly in the United States. Heavy industry made such products as machinery, iron rails, and engines. These products were bought by other factories or other industries. Most heavy industry was located in the Northeastern part of the United States.

Why American Industries Grew

The Civil War helped both types of industry to grow in the United States. Factories became larger and needed many more workers. But the growth of industry in the United States was not caused by the Civil War alone. After the war, American industry grew larger and stronger than ever before. Six things helped the United States to grow into a great industrial nation, or a nation of factories and businesses.

1. The United States had large supplies of raw materials, or the things needed to make manufactured goods. These raw materials included coal, iron, oil, and lumber.

2. The United States had a large and growing population. As a result, industry had

JAN E. MATZELIGER—INVENTOR

Jan Ernst Matzeliger arrived in Lynn, Massachusetts, in 1876. He was a man that the city of Lynn was never to forget. Matzeliger was born in Dutch Guiana in 1852. He was the son of a Dutch father and an African mother. As a young man in Dutch Guiana he worked in a machine shop.

When he came to the United States, Matzeliger went to work in a shoe factory in Lynn, Massachusetts. Many machines were used in the making of shoes. But the final step in making shoes—attaching the sole to the upper part of the shoe—still was done by hand. This slowed down the making of shoes. Matzeliger decided to solve this problem.

Most people laughed at his idea of making a machine that was able to put shoes together. But Matzeliger kept on trying to build such a machine. By 1882, his efforts were successful. The United Shoe Company then bought Matzeliger's new machine. Using Matzeliger's machine, the United Shoe Company soon became one of the biggest shoe-making companies in the nation. However, Jan Matzeliger did not enjoy his success and good fortune for long. He died soon afterward at the age of 37.

plenty of workers and plenty of customers to buy the consumer goods they produced.

3. The United States had good railroad systems and river systems. Raw materials and manufactured products were shipped cheaply by railroads or by boats to all parts of the nation.

4. The people of the United States had the large amounts of money needed to build new industries and businesses.

5. The United States had many skilled inventors and scientists. These men were able to develop the machines and the manufacturing methods, or ways, to make American factories successful.

6. The United States government did many things to help American industry grow. The government passed a high tariff to keep foreign manufactured goods out of the country, and it kept taxes low to encourage people to build factories and businesses. And the government made it easy for immigrants to enter the United States because they worked in American factories for low wages.

The Iron Industry Grew and Changed

After 1865, iron and steel manufacturing became one of America's most important industries. Before 1865, iron mills used charcoal as fuel. This meant that iron mills had to be located near forests to get wood. After 1865, however, the iron industry's fuel was coal or coke, which is made from coal. Iron mills then moved to places like Pittsburgh, Pennsylvania, where coal and iron were located close together.

Iron broke easily. But steel, a harder metal which was made from iron ore, was too costly to make. Then, in the 1850's, William Kelly, an American, and Henry Bessemer, an Englishman, developed a new way of making steel cheaply. Later, another way, called the **open hearth** method, was developed which made

Many oil wells were drilled after Edwin L. Drake drilled the first oil well, shown here, near Titusville, in Pennsylvania.

steel-making even cheaper and easier. By 1890, the United States was the leading steel-making nation of the world.

The Oil Industry Developed Rapidly

One of the newest American industries was the oil industry. Before the Civil War, farmers in Pennsylvania used oil to grease their wagons. Other men put oil in bottles and sold it as a medicine. During the 1850's, people discovered that they were able to burn oil in lamps for lighting.

In 1859, the first oil well was drilled at Titusville (TY-tus-vill), Pennsylvania. Other oil fields were discovered in Ohio, West Virginia, and later in the southwestern part of the United States. Oil lamps soon were used to light American homes and cities. In later years, other important uses were found for oil. Oil was used in factories to oil machines, Soon, American oil was being sold all over the world.

Other Large Industries Developed

The meat-packing industry also grew into a large industry after 1865. The invention of the refrigerator car, a railroad car which was kept cold inside, helped the meat-packing industry to grow. Before the refrigerator car was invented, live animals had to be shipped to market. However, only part of the animal was used for food. The refrigerator car made it possible to kill the animal and to ship only the meat to market. Chicago and Kansas City became the leading meat-packing centers in the nation.

New inventions also changed the flour-milling industry. New ways of grinding grain

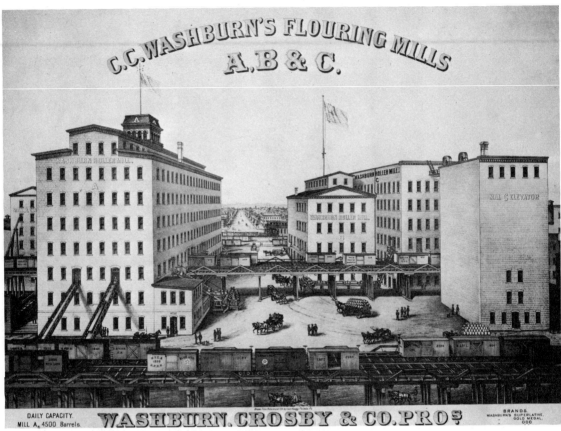

A large flour mill in Minneapolis, Minnesota. The railroads made possible the rapid growth of the milling industry in Minneapolis.

were discovered which produced a much finer flour. Minneapolis (MIN-ee-AP-uh-lis), Minnesota, became the flour-milling center of the United States. Other industries such as the shoe industry, the clothing industry, the sugar-refining industry, and the clock industry also grew rapidly. New machines and manufacturing ways helped these industries grow.

Inventions Helped America to Grow

Many other inventions changed American industries and American life. Alexander Graham Bell invented the telephone. Thomas A. Edison perfected the electric dynamo, which produced electric power, and the electric light. Christopher L. Sholes invented the typewriter. And Cyrus W. Field invented a cable, which was placed at the bottom of the Atlantic Ocean and allowed telegraph signals to be sent between the United States and Europe.

Summing Up

After 1865, industry grew rapidly, and the United States became a great industrial nation. Iron and steel, oil, and other industries became very important. Many inventions helped industry to grow. In the next chapter, you will read about the problems America's growing industries caused.

AFTER YOU READ THE CHAPTER

Do You Know These Important Terms?

For each sentence below, choose the term that best completes the sentence.

1. Products made to be sold directly to the people are called (**consumer/public**) goods.
2. (**Light/Heavy**) industry makes products which are sold to other factories.
3. The (**charcoal/open**) hearth method is a method of making steel.

Do You Remember These People?

Tell something about each of the following persons.

Alexander Graham Bell	William Kelly
Christopher L. Sholes	Henry Bessemer
Thomas A. Edison	Cyrus W. Field

Can You Locate These Places?

Use the map on page 366 to locate the following places. Tell how each location is connected to the events in this chapter.

Pittsburgh	Pennsylvania
Ohio	West Virginia
Chicago	Kansas City
Minneapolis	

Do You Know When It Happened?

Place the following events in the order in which they occurred.

The first oil well was drilled.

A new way of making steel cheaply was discovered.

The United States was the leading steel-making nation.

Most factories made consumer goods.

Coal became the main fuel for making steel.

Discovering More About the Main Idea

After 1865, industry grew rapidly, and the United States became a great industrial nation.

Tell how each of the following developments is related to the MAIN IDEA.

The Civil War helped industry to grow but six things helped industry to continue to grow. The United States had many raw materials, a growing population, good railroad and river systems, large amounts of money, skilled inventors, and a government willing to help industry.

Many industries developed rapidly when new machines and new ways of making products were found.

After 1865, many inventions helped change American industries and American life.

Can You Discuss the Chapter?

Use the information you learned in this chapter to answer the following questions.

1. Name the six things that helped the United States to grow into a great industrial nation.
2. How did the government help American industry to grow?
3. How did Chicago and Kansas City become the meat-packing centers of the nation?
4. If the United States did not have certain raw materials it needed for its industries how might the nation obtain these raw materials?

Can You Connect the Past and the Present?

1. A raw material only becomes important when a use is discovered for the material. Can you think of any material that has recently become valuable that was not important at all a few years ago?
2. Improving machines and the ways of making products is necessary for industry to grow. What industries are located in your community? What improvements have these industries made to continue to grow?

CHAPTER 60

Problems of Industrial America

A famous political cartoon from the late 1890's.

BEFORE YOU BEGIN THE CHAPTER

Know What to Look For

1. The story of Andrew Carnegie shows the opportunities that America offered to people in the 1800's. Andrew Carnegie came to the United States from Scotland when he was a young boy. At the age of thirteen he worked long hours in a textile factory. Later, he became a telegraph operator for the Pennsylvania Railroad. His work at the railroad

helped him to see that steel was going to become a very important product. Carnegie organized a large steel industry and became a very rich man. When he retired, he was worth about 225 million dollars. He then began to give his money away to worthy causes. In 1919, when he died, he had given most of his fortune away. In this chapter, you will read about Carnegie's steel industry. You will also read about the problems caused by big businesses.

2. Read the title of the chapter. Then look through the chapter and read each heading. What two monopolies were formed?

3. Look at the pictures in the chapter and read each caption. What does the cartoon on page 376 tell you about the monopolies, or trusts, in the United States? Note also the time line at the beginning of the chapter. What years are included in the chapter? Compare this chapter time line to the unit time line on page 351. How do the years of this chapter compare with the years of the unit?

4. Read the last part of the chapter called Summing Up. What did the government do about monopolies and trusts? What is the topic of the next chapter?

Know These Important Terms

integrated industry   trust

monopoly   Sherman Anti-Trust Act

Know the Main Idea

Here is the MAIN IDEA of this chapter.

Between 1865 and 1900, some companies gained control of entire industries. The government passed laws to try to control these powerful companies.

Keep this MAIN IDEA in mind as you study the chapter. Ask yourself the following questions as you read. They will help you remember the MAIN IDEA.

1. What man prevented Carnegie from controlling the entire steel industry?
2. Who built up a monopoly in the oil industry?
3. What happened to small businesses?

THE YEARS OF THIS CHAPTER ARE 1865 TO 1900

1850   1865   1900

THE CHAPTER LESSON BEGINS HERE

Andrew Carnegie Controlled the Steel Industry

In the years between 1865 and 1900, Andrew Carnegie (kahr-NAY-gee), who came to the United States from Scotland, gained control of much of the steel industry. Carnegie's company was larger than any other steel company. Because of its great size, Carnegie's company was able to make steel more cheaply than other companies. By lowering his prices and by receiving rebates, or refunds, from the railroad companies, Carnegie was able to sell his steel at lower prices than the other steel companies. As a result, Carnegie was able to force many other steel companies out of business.

Then, Carnegie began to buy companies that were connected with steel manufacturing. For example, he bought iron mines and coal mines, which supplied the raw materials he needed. He bought shipping lines and railroads to ship the steel, and he bought warehouses in which to store the steel. Carnegie soon controlled the factories that made the iron and steel from the iron ore and also the factories that turned the iron and steel into manufactured products such as rails and machines. This is called an **integrated industry,** or an industry that controls everything from the raw materials to the finished product.

Andrew Carnegie controlled much of the nation's steel industry in the late 1800's.

A Steel Monopoly Was Formed

When a company becomes strong enough to control an entire industry, it is called a **monopoly** (muh-NOP-uh-lee), or a **trust.** The Carnegie Steel Company was very powerful, but it did not have a monopoly of the iron and steel business in the United States. J. P. Morgan, the most important banker in the United States, backed several other big steel companies and prevented Carnegie from controlling the entire steel industry.

These steel companies and the Carnegie steel company struggled to gain control of the steel industry. Finally, J. P. Morgan bought Carnegie's steel company for 225 million dol-

lars. In 1901, the large steel companies were joined together into the United States Steel Corporation. The United States Steel Corporation was the first billion dollar business in America. It controlled about three fifths of all the steel business in the nation.

An Oil Monopoly Was Formed

In the 1870's, John D. Rockefeller, who owned the Standard Oil Company, gained control of most of the oil industry. Rockefeller built up a monopoly by lowering the price of his oil and also by getting rebates from the railroads. By 1879, about nine tenths of the oil industry was under Rockefeller's control.

In 1882, the Standard Oil Company became the Standard Oil Trust. A **trust** is a company that controls many smaller companies. The Standard Oil Trust controlled the oil business of the United States. Rockefeller owned the pipelines that carried the oil, the storage tanks that stored the oil, and the stores that sold the oil. Standard Oil even opened factories to build its own barrels to hold the oil. Rockefeller's Standard Oil Trust brought many improvements in the oil industry. However, it also gave Rockefeller a monopoly in the oil industry.

Bankers Took Over Many Companies

Many other American industries tried to copy Rockefeller's methods. Monopolies or trusts developed in the meat-packing industry, the sugar-refining industry, the coal-mining industry, and in many other industries. These trusts needed large amounts of money to carry on their business. Much of this money came from banker J. P. Morgan and other important bankers of the nation. These bankers had a great deal to say about how these companies carried on their business. J. P. Morgan was especially powerful, and his bank controlled many companies.

Trusts Hurt the United States

When a company controlled an entire industry, that company had great power. Sometimes these companies used this power to improve their product and their methods of making the product. But the trusts acted in unfair ways. For example, they often raised the prices of their products. Once a company controlled an industry, it was able to charge as much as it wanted for its product. Most people also felt that the trusts had too much power in the government.

The Government Tried to Control the Trusts

At first, the state governments tried to regulate or control the trusts, but this did not work too well. Therefore, in 1890, Congress passed the **Sherman Anti-Trust Act.** The Sherman Anti-Trust Act made it unlawful to organize a trust to gain a monopoly in any industry. However, the Sherman Anti-Trust Act was not able to prevent a company from controlling an industry. For example, new types of monopolies were formed which the Supreme Court said were not covered by the Sherman Anti-Trust Act. The Court also said that the manufacturing industries were not included in the Sherman Anti-Trust Act. Therefore, many companies continued to build up trusts.

Even though many monopolies grew up between 1865 and 1900, many small businesses were also started at this time. In 1880, there were about 750 thousand business companies in the United States. By 1900, the number of small businesses grew to over 1 million. These small companies were found in almost every industry except railroads and electric light and power production. Some of these small businesses manufactured products. Others sold products or provided services.

J. P. Morgan, an important banker, controlled many business companies.

Summing Up

Between 1865 and 1900, many American industries came to be controlled by one company. These companies were called monopolies or trusts. The government passed the Sherman Anti-Trust Act to control these powerful companies, but at first this law was not too successful. In the next chapters, which are in Unit 16, you will read about other changes in American life.

AFTER YOU READ THE CHAPTER

For each sentence below, choose the term that best completes the sentence.

1. An industry that controls everything from the raw material to the finished product is called (a total/an integrated) industry.
2. When a company becomes strong enough to control an entire industry, it is called a (monopoly/parent factory).
3. A company that controls many smaller companies is a (corporation/trust).
4. The (Dawes Trust/Sherman Anti-Trust) Act made it unlawful to organize a trust or monopoly.

Do You Remember These People?

Tell something about each of the following persons.

Andrew Carnegie   **J. P. Morgan**
John D. Rockefeller

Do You Know When It Happened?

What are the years of this chapter? Place the following events in the order in which they occurred.

Rockefeller gained control of nine tenths of the oil industry.

Carnegie organized an integrated company.

Andrew Carnegie sold his steel company.

The Standard Oil Trust controlled the oil business.

The Sherman Anti-Trust Act was passed.

Discovering More About the Main Idea

Between 1865 and 1900, some companies gained control of entire industries. The government passed laws to try to control these powerful companies.

Tell how each of the following developments is related to the MAIN IDEA.

Andrew Carnegie organized his steel company into a huge integrated industry, but he did not have a monopoly of the iron and steel business. When he sold his company, it became a part of a steel monopoly.

John D. Rockefeller developed the Standard Oil Company into a huge trust. Bankers usually gained control of industries and created great monopolies and trusts.

The government tried to control trusts and monopolies because of their unfair practices, but the government was not too successful.

Small businesses also grew rapidly between 1865 and 1900.

Can You Discuss the Chapter?

Use the information you learned in this chapter to answer the following questions.

1. How were men like Carnegie and Rockefeller able to form such large companies and gain monopolies?
2. Why were bankers able to take over or control many of the large monopolies and trusts?
3. How did monopolies and trusts hurt the people of the United States?
4. How were some companies able to get around the laws passed to regulate trusts and monopolies?
5. How might you have felt about the Sherman Anti-Trust Act if you had been the owner of a large factory? owner of a small business? a banker?

Can You Connect the Past and the Present?

1. Sometimes a monopoly is a good thing. Are there any monopolies in your community? Why are they good?
2. Do you have any integrated industry in or near your community? If so, explain how this industry operates.

Changes in American Life After 1865

The city of Pittsburgh in 1880.

THE CHAPTERS IN UNIT 16 ARE

CHAPTER 61   Problems of American Workers
CHAPTER 62   The Growth of American Cities
CHAPTER 63   Changes in American Life
CHAPTER 64   American Thought, 1865–1900

THE YEARS OF THIS UNIT ARE 1865 TO 1900

1800	1865	1900	1975

CHAPTER 61

Problems of American Workers

Workers in a locomotive factory.

BEFORE YOU BEGIN THE CHAPTER

Know What to Look For

1. Immigrants almost always increased the size of the labor force. At certain times, immigrants were encouraged to come to the United States because workers were needed. For example, after the Civil War, Chinese immigration was encouraged. At this time, workers were needed to build the railroads. Large numbers of Chinese came to the Pacific coast of the United States and by 1870, two out of

every ten workmen in California were Chinese.

Because they looked different, lived apart, and were willing to work for low wages, the Chinese immigrants were disliked by many other American workers. In fact, by 1882, American workers protested so much that Chinese were no longer allowed to come to the United States. In this chapter, you will find out about other immigrants and black workers. You will also learn about the problems faced by all workers.

2. Read the title of the chapter. Then look through the chapter and read each heading. Where did many new immigrants come from?

3. Look at the pictures in the chapter and read each caption. What do the pictures show you about American workers? Note also the time line at the beginning of the chapter. What years are included in this chapter? Compare this chapter time line to the unit time line on page 381.

4. Read the last part of the chapter called Summing Up. Which group of workers faced the most problems between 1865 and 1900?

Know These Important Terms
skilled workers   service trades
unskilled workers

Know the Main Idea
Here is the MAIN IDEA of this chapter.

Between 1865 and 1900, skilled workers did well but unskilled workers received low wages and had trouble finding jobs. Many immigrants and black workers were among these unskilled workers.

Keep this MAIN IDEA in mind as you study the chapter. Ask yourself the following questions as you read. They will help you remember the MAIN IDEA.

1. What skilled laborers found that machines were taking over their jobs?

2. What two groups of workers struggled against each other for jobs in the factories in the years between 1865 and 1900?

3. What black leader favored education and job training as ways that black people might win equal rights?

THE YEARS OF THIS CHAPTER ARE 1865 TO 1900

1865   1900

THE CHAPTER LESSON BEGINS HERE

America's Skilled Workers Did Well

American workers in the late 1800's were divided into two groups—**skilled workers** and **unskilled workers**. The skilled workers included printers, carpenters, bricklayers, masons, and machinists. Between 1865 and 1900, most skilled workers did well. They earned high wages and had good working conditions. However, some skilled workers such as tailors, shoemakers, and iron workers found that machines were beginning to take over their jobs.

America's Factory Workers Suffered

Unskilled workers did not do well in the years between 1865 and 1900. Most unskilled workers were factory workers who ran ma-chines. This required little skill, and most men were able to learn how to run a machine in a short time. Unskilled workers were paid by the hour, and they earned about 400 dollars a year. They usually worked ten hours a day for six days a week. But if business was slow, unskilled workers were the first workers to be fired.

Many Immigrants Came to the United States

One reason why unskilled workers did not do better in the years between 1865 and 1900 was that many immigrants, or newcomers, came to the United States during this period.

An immigrant family looks at the Statue of Liberty. Many immigrants came
to America in the late 1800's and worked in American factories.

Over 5 million immigrants entered the United States during the 1880's alone. Many of these immigrants were unskilled workers who came to America without their families. They were used to working for low wages, and they usually were not able to speak English. For these reasons, most immigrants were happy to take any job at any wage. They dug ditches and built railroads. They mined coal and did the heavy work in iron and steel mills.

Many New Immigrants Came from Southern and Eastern Europe

With more immigrants coming into the United States every year, unskilled workers were not able to get higher wages. Some fac-

tory owners tried to hire workers from many different countries because they were not able to understand each other. Therefore, the factory owner did not have to worry about his workers joining together in unions.

In the 1880's, more immigrants began to come from the countries of southern and eastern Europe—from Italy, Russia, Hungary, and Poland. Many of these immigrants were brought to the United States by factory owners, who hired them at very low wages while they were still living in Europe. The older group of workers from northern and western Europe—the Irish, the Germans, and the Scandinavians—disliked this newer group of immigrants. They felt that the newer immigrants were taking away their jobs and making wages lower.

Black Workers Faced Job Problems in the North

Besides the immigrants who were coming into the United States, black Americans in the North formed another large group of workers. Many of the black workers were also unskilled workers. They were often paid even lower wages than the unskilled workers from Europe.

The large group of immigrants and the black workers struggled against each other for jobs in the factories. Because of this struggle for jobs, white workers refused to work with black workers. And they refused to let black workers join the labor unions that were being formed in the years between 1865 and 1900. Only one labor union, the Knights of Labor, allowed black workers to become members.

Black Workers Also Had Job Problems in the South

Even though very few immigrants settled in the South, black workers also had problems finding jobs in the South. Before the Civil War, many free black men worked in the **service trades** and in the building trades. They were tailors, carpenters, cooks, and had many other skilled jobs. However, in the years after 1865, white skilled workers began to take over the jobs of black skilled workers. For example, in the late 1800's, black workers in the service trades—such as cooks and barbers—were replaced by white workers. Also the Southern trade unions in the building industry stopped accepting black workingmen, and by 1900, these unions were made up entirely of white members.

Often black workers were forced to accept lower wages, or they were pushed into jobs as

George Washington Carver.

THE WIZARD OF TUSKEGEE

George Washington Carver was born a slave in Missouri. When he was still a baby, he and his mother were kidnapped by a gang of slave stealers. Carver was recovered by his owner, but his mother was never seen again. Carver lived with his owner until several years after the Civil War. Then he left to try to get an education.

Carver found that getting an education was not easy, because many schools did not welcome black students. He was over twenty when he entered Simpson College in Indiana. From there, he went to Iowa State College. Carver worked his way through college. After he finished college, he was offered many jobs as a teacher. He decided to teach at Booker T. Washington's school, Tuskegee Institute, where he might be able to help black people.

Carver's work at Tuskegee helped both black and white Americans, and it changed farming in the South. He showed Southern farmers that the peanut and the sweet potato were better crops to grow than cotton. He discovered over 300 uses for the peanut and over 100 uses for the sweet potato. Carver's outstanding work won him the name the "Wizard of Tuskegee."

unskilled workers. Black workers were hired in Southern factories. But they were given the worst jobs and were paid the lowest wages.

Booker T. Washington, A Black Leader

Booker T. Washington became an important black leader in the late 1800's. During these years, black Americans in the South were losing their right to vote and their jobs, and they were being segregated. Booker T. Washington felt that the best way for black citizens to advance was to get an education and to train themselves to be good workers. After they were educated and became workers and businessmen, Washington felt that black Americans might be able to win equal rights, too. Therefore, his school, Tuskegee Institute, taught job skills to students.

Although Washington worked against segregation and tried to help form a class of black businessmen, many black Americans disagreed with his ideas. They felt that black people must struggle to gain equal rights as well as to improve their lives. Most white Americans, however, favored Washington's ideas. And many black Americans also agreed with his ideas because they felt that when black people gained a good education and jobs they then might win their equal rights.

Summing Up

In the years between 1865 and 1900, skilled workers did well in the United States. But unskilled workers received low wages and often had trouble finding jobs. The large number of immigrants who came to America during these years was one reason why unskilled workers did not do well. Black workers, too, had troubles in the North and the South. In the next chapter, you will find out about life in American cities.

Booker T. Washington set up Tuskegee Institute to help black Americans learn job skills.

AFTER YOU READ THE CHAPTER

Do You Know These Important Terms?

For each sentence below, select the term that best completes the sentence.

1. Workers like printers, carpenters, brick-layers, and machinists are called (**construction/skilled**) workers.
2. Workers whose job requires little or no skill are called (**unskilled/union**) workers.
3. Workers like cooks and barbers are said to be in the (**domestic/service**) trades.

Do You Remember This Person?

Tell something about Booker T. Washington.

Can You Locate These Places?

Use a map of Europe to do the following map work.

1. Locate the nations of Italy, Russia, Hungary, and Poland.
2. Locate Ireland, Germany, Norway, Sweden, and Denmark. When did people from these nations come to the United States?

Do You Know When It Happened?

What are the years of this chapter? Select the word which most correctly completes the sentence.

Immigrants came mainly from eastern and southern Europe (**before/after**) 1880.

Booker T. Washington was a black leader (**before/after**) 1880.

There were black skilled workers and black men in the service trades in the South (**before/after**) 1880.

Discovering More About the Main Idea

Between 1865 and 1900, skilled workers did well but unskilled workers received low wages and had trouble finding jobs. Many immigrants and black workers were among these unskilled workers.

Tell how each of the following developments is related to the MAIN IDEA.

Immigrants helped to increase the number of unskilled workers. The newer groups of immigrants were often disliked by the older groups of immigrants.

Black workers in the North were often paid even lower wages than the unskilled workers from Europe. In the South, they were given the worst jobs and paid the lowest wages.

Booker T. Washington thought that black citizens might be able to win their rights after they were educated and became workers and businessmen.

Can You Discuss the Chapter?

Use the information you learned in this chapter to answer the following questions.

1. Why did unskilled workers suffer during the late 1800's?
2. Explain the relationship between immigrants and unskilled workers.
3. Why did white workers in the North refuse to work with black workers?
4. What happened to the black workers in the South after 1865?
5. In the 1800's, there were not enough jobs for all the immigrants coming into the United States. Why do you think the United States did not put a stop to immigration?

Can You Connect the Past and the Present?

1. An unskilled laborer has always had a difficult time. How do unskilled workers do in your community today? What might be done to improve conditions for unskilled workers?
2. How do you think people in the civil rights movement today might feel about Booker T. Washington's views?

CHAPTER 62

The Growth of American Cities

An American city in the late 1800's.

BEFORE YOU BEGIN THE CHAPTER

Know What to Look For

1. On the night of October 8, 1871, fire broke out in the city of Chicago. Many people thought that this fire, which became known as the Great Chicago Fire, was started when a cow kicked over a lantern in Mrs. O'Leary's barn. A high wind spread the blaze from building to building until central Chicago was a mass of flames. The fire destroyed a large

part of Chicago. It destroyed 17 thousand buildings, and 250 persons lost their lives.

The great Chicago fire and fires in many other cities showed the danger of living in the crowded buildings of the city. These fires also showed that there were not enough firemen and that fire-fighting equipment was not good enough. In this chapter, you will read about the many other problems caused by the rapid growth of cities in the late 1800's.

2. Read the title of the chapter. Then look through the chapter and read each heading. From the headings, can you tell some of the problems of cities after 1865?

3. Look at the pictures in the chapter and read each caption. What do the pictures show you about life in the growing American cities? Examine the map on page 390. What information does this map show? Notice also the time line at the beginning of the chapter. What years are included in this chapter? Compare this chapter time line to the unit time line on page 381.

4. Read the last part of the chapter called Summing Up. What two serious problems were faced by many cities? What is the topic of the next chapter?

Know These Important Terms

tenements   political boss
political machine

Know the Main Idea

Here is the MAIN IDEA of this chapter.

Immigrants and Americans who moved away from the farms helped cities grow rapidly after 1865. The rapid growth of cities caused many city problems.

Keep this MAIN IDEA in mind as you study the chapter. Ask yourself the following questions as you read. They will help you remember the MAIN IDEA.

1. Which parts of the United States had the fastest growing cities?

2. What improvements made it possible for workers to get to their jobs in the city?

3. Who supported the political machines?

THE YEARS OF THIS CHAPTER ARE 1865 TO 1900

1865   1900

THE CHAPTER LESSON BEGINS HERE

Cities Were Growing Rapidly

In the years after 1865, American cities were growing rapidly. In 1850, about 2 million Americans lived in cities with a population of 100 thousand or more people. By 1890, over 9 million lived in cities with over 100 thousand people. And 22 million people lived in smaller cities.

Cities did not grow at the same rate all over the United States. The fastest growing cities were the cities in the Northeast and the Middle West. At this time, the Middle West included the states of Ohio, Indiana, Illinois, Michigan, Wisconsin, Minnesota, and Iowa. The Northeast and Middle West also had the largest number of cities. Although cities in the South and the West grew more slowly, by 1900 almost half of the American people lived in cities.

Two Groups Settled in the Cities

One group of people who were moving to the cities came from the farms of America. Many of these Americans felt that city life was easier than farm life. Also, fewer workers were needed on farms in the late 1800's because farm machines were replacing workers. And many young people wanted to leave the farm because they expected to make more money in the city.

The second group of people to settle in the

page 389

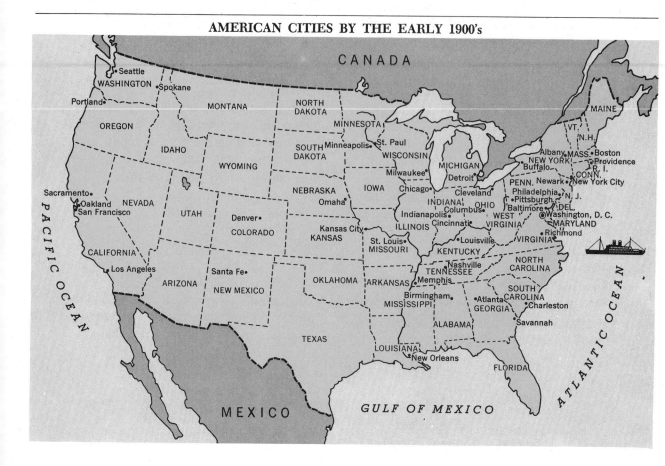

cities were the immigrants. In the years between 1870 and 1900, millions of immigrants arrived in the United States. Most of them settled in the cities of the Northeast or the Middle West.

Finding a Place to Live Was a Problem

The increase in the size of cities led to many problems. Many of these city problems were very much like the problems of American cities today. The main problem for most city people was finding a good place to live. Many city people were forced to live in slums, or run-down city neighborhoods. Most cities had slums before 1865. But in the years after 1865,

city slums began to grow and spread. These newer slums were caused by the building of **tenements** (TEN-uh-ments).

Tenements were apartment buildings about five or six stories high. People lived crowded together in these tenements, often without enough air, light, or heat. Many of these tenements lacked bathrooms and water. Tenement buildings helped to cause sickness, crime, and misery among the people who lived in the slums.

Of course, not all city people lived in slums. Many city people lived in good apartments or small homes on the outer edges of the city. And some rich people built huge homes for themselves in the cities.

This elevated train was built in New York City in the late 1800's. Such trains helped to solve the travel problems of cities.

Cities Solved Their Travel Problems

As cities grew, traveling around in the cities became a problem. Horse drawn streetcars were used by some people, but they were too slow and too small to carry large numbers of people. But the problem of travel was partly solved by the use of electric streetcars. During the 1890's, most of the large cities started to use electric streetcars. Also, in the 1890's and early 1900's, subways and elevated railway lines, called els, were put into use in some cities. These new forms of travel were fast and cheap. Cities began to spread out because it was now possible for workers to get to their jobs even if they lived far away from the city.

Cities Tried to Solve Their Other Problems

Other city problems were more difficult to solve. City-owned waterworks replaced wells, but city water was still not very healthy to drink. Police and fire protection was still a problem in most cities.

Many cities started to pave their streets with bricks or asphalt to make them smoother and cleaner. But the most important improvement in city life was in the lighting of city streets. Electric lighting came into use during the 1880's. Many cities started to replace the dim oil lamps in the streets with bright electric lights. Electric lights made city streets brighter and safer.

John L. Sullivan.

THE GREAT JOHN L.

John Lawrence Sullivan is still considered one of the greatest of all American boxers. The "Great John L." or the "Boston Strong Boy," as he was called, was born just outside Boston in 1858. Sullivan started boxing as a young man, and in 1882 he won the heavyweight championship.

For the next seven years, Sullivan fought and defeated all his opponents. He fought all his fights under the London Prize Ring rules. Under these rules, no boxing gloves were worn, and a round ended when a fighter was knocked down. The fighter had thirty seconds to rest and then eight more seconds to come out to the center of the ring. If he was not able to come to the center of the ring, the fight was over.

John L. Sullivan fought the last heavyweight championship fight under these rules in 1889. He won but did not fight for the next three years. Then, in 1892, he agreed to fight Jim Corbett. However, over the years, boxing rules had been changing. In this fight, gloves were worn and modern boxing rules were followed. Corbett defeated Sullivan. Sullivan only appeared in the boxing ring once more. In 1896, he fought in an exhibition fight.

Many City Governments Were Dishonest

In the years after 1865, many of America's city governments were dishonest. Many cities were taken over by a **political machine,** or a small group of political party leaders who completely controlled their political party in the city. The political machine was usually headed by a **political boss,** or a strong party leader. The boss and the machine often controlled the city's government. And the boss and the machine ran the city government for their own gains, rather than for the good of the people.

The machine was supported by businessmen who wanted favors from the city government. These businessmen wanted to be able to operate the city's streetcar lines, pave the city's streets, or put in the city's sewers. They paid large amounts of money to the machine in order to get the city's business.

Political machines depended on the votes of the immigrants to win elections and to control the cities. The machine was able to get the immigrants' votes by doing them favors. For example, the machine fed people when they were hungry. The machine found jobs for people who were out of work, and it even paid for boys from immigrant families to go to college. With all its money, votes, and power, the political machine was almost impossible to beat in elections in most cities.

Summing Up

After 1865, many people moved into America's cities. Some of these people came from the farms of America. Many others were immigrants from foreign nations. The growth of American cities led to many problems. The growth of slum neighborhoods and dishonest city governments were two important problems. In the next chapter, you will read about life in the American city.

AFTER YOU READ THE CHAPTER

Do You Know These Important Terms?

For each sentence below, choose the term that best completes the sentence.

1. Apartment buildings about five or six stories high were called (**tenements/ghettos**).
2. The small group of political party leaders who completely controlled their political party in the city was called a (**political machine/political banquet**).
3. The political (**chief/boss**), who was usually a strong party leader, headed the group.

Can You Locate These Places?

Use the map on page 390 to do the following map work.

1. Locate the Northeast and the Middle West. Name some large cities located in these sections of the nation. How can you tell the name of a city from the name of a state?
2. Name several cities in the western part of the nation and in the South. How can you tell the exact location of these cities?
3. According to this map, which section of the nation has the most cities?

Do You Know When It Happened?

What are the years of this chapter? What event during the 1880's made the streets of many cities safer? What new forms of travel did cities start to use in the years of the 1890's and 1900's? How did these new forms of travel help city workers?

Discovering More About the Main Idea

Immigrants and Americans who moved away from the farms helped cities grow rapidly after 1865. The rapid growth of cities caused many city problems.

Tell how each of the following developments is related to the MAIN IDEA.

By 1900 almost half of the American people lived in cities. The fastest growing cities were found in the Northeast and the Middle West.

Many city people were forced to live in slums. Improved city travel made it possible for city workers to live far away from the city.

Political machines controlled the governments in most cities. Businessmen, immigrants, and others supported these political machines even though the machines were dishonest.

Can You Discuss the Chapter?

Use the information you learned in this chapter to answer the following questions.

1. Why did people from farms and immigrants settle in the cities in the late 1800's?
2. How were the cities able to solve some of their problems? What problems did cities still have?
3. How were political machines able to stay in power?
4. How did city slums grow and spread?
5. If you had lived in a city of the late 1800's, which problem would you have thought was most serious? Why?

Can You Connect the Past and the Present?

1. In 1900, half the American people lived in cities. What percentage of the American people now live in cities?
2. Are political machines still active in the government of your community? If so, compare their method of operating with the political machines of the late 1800's.

CHAPTER 63

Changes in American Life

Americans riding bicycles in the late 1800's.

BEFORE YOU BEGIN THE CHAPTER

Know What to Look For

1. Football in the 1880's was a rough game with only a few simple rules. A report of the Yale and Princeton game appeared in a New York newspaper in 1884. The reporter described how the eleven men on each team threw themselves together and wound up in heaps on the ground. The people who watched the game applauded and cheered whenever the players shook their fists at one another or when one player tackled another. The people who were on the field, such as referees and reporters, saw how rough the game really was. They saw the players hit one another with blows strong enough to draw blood. Often when the players fell after being tackled it seemed they might break all their bones.

Football was one of the new sports that became popular in the late 1800's. In this chapter, you will read more about the many changes in American life.

2. Read the title of the chapter. Then look through the chapter and read each heading. From the headings, make a list of the things Americans enjoyed.

3. Look at the pictures in the chapter and read each caption. What do the pictures show you about American life after 1865? Note also the time line at the beginning of the chapter. What years are included in this chapter? Compare this chapter time line to the unit time line on page 381.

4. Read the last part of the chapter called Summing Up. How did city living change the way Americans lived? What will you read about in the next chapter?

Know These Important Terms

spectator sports   dime novels
vaudeville

Know the Main Idea

Here is the MAIN IDEA of this chapter.

City life caused important changes in the way Americans lived. Sports, shows, reading, and music became very popular.

Keep this MAIN IDEA in mind as you study the chapter. Ask yourself the following questions as you read. They will help you remember the MAIN IDEA.

1. Name some newer sports which became popular in the late 1800's.

2. Which was the first professional baseball team in the United States?

3. What new music with an African beat had its beginning in New Orleans?

THE YEARS OF THIS CHAPTER ARE 1865 TO 1900

1865   1900

THE CHAPTER LESSON BEGINS HERE

The City Changed American Family Life

City life changed the way Americans lived. City life especially brought important changes to American families. People in the city married later than people on farms. City families were smaller than farm families. City families broke up more often than farm families. And city families spent less time together than farm families.

City wives had more free time than farm wives. Inventions such as the carpet sweeper made work much easier for city wives. Ice boxes made it possible to store foods easily. City men spent many hours away from home working at their jobs. And city children spent many hours of the day away from home attending school.

Sports Became Very Popular

City people had more free time than farm families. Many city people spent this free time taking part in sports. Almost everybody began to ride bicycles. Hunting, fishing, hiking, and boating were also popular sports.

Some of the newer sports which became popular during the 1880's and 1890's were golf, tennis, and croquet (kroh-KAY). Football became the most popular college sport. Many other Americans took part in track

Above, men and women are shown playing lawn tennis. Tennis and many other sports were popular with Americans in the late 1800's.

meets and swimming meets. And the game of basketball, invented by Dr. James Naismith (NAY-smith) in 1891, soon was played all over the nation.

Baseball Became the National Game

Americans also enjoyed watching **spectator sports,** or popular games of sport. The most popular of these spectator sports was baseball. No one is sure exactly when baseball was first played. But it is known that the game was played in the Eastern part of the United States in the 1840's and perhaps even before.

The first professional baseball team, the Red Stockings, was organized in Cincinnati in 1869. The National League was formed in 1876, and the American League was formed a few years later in 1901. The first "world series" was played in 1903. Many great baseball players played in the 1880's and 1890's. Charles "Old Hoss" Radbourne, a famous pitcher, won sixty games in 1884. In 1888, Harry Stovey stole 156 bases. And Hugh Duffy had the highest batting average in baseball history, .438, in 1894. Baseball soon became America's great "national game."

Boxing Interested Many Americans

Boxing was also a popular American sport. Before the Civil War, many boxing champions were black. Boxers at this time fought with their bare fists, and a fight ended only when one of the boxers was knocked down.

During the 1880's, the most famous boxer was John L. Sullivan. In 1882, John L. Sullivan became heavyweight champion. In 1889, he beat Jake Kilrain in seventy-five rounds in the last of the bare-fisted championship fights. About this time, boxing rules were changed. And in 1892, Jim Corbett became heavyweight champion when he beat John L. Sullivan. This was the first championship fight in which boxing gloves were used. Among the heavyweight champions who followed Corbett was Jack Johnson, one of the greatest black fighters of all times.

Americans Enjoyed Theater Shows

In the years between 1865 and 1900, Americans enjoyed going to plays. Their favorite plays were melodramas. Melodramas always had a hero who was poor but honest, a heroine who was beautiful and brave, and a villain who was mean and rich. And they always had happy endings. Playgoers often cheered the hero and heroine and hissed at the villain in these plays.

A new type of theater show called **vaudeville** (VAWD-vill) also became popular during the 1880's. Vaudeville shows presented singers, dancers, comedians, magicians, and jugglers. Vaudeville remained an American favorite for many years.

Americans Enjoyed Reading Newspapers and Dime Novels

In 1896, the first comic strip character, a tough little slum boy called the Yellow Kid, appeared in a New York newspaper. The Yellow Kid was soon joined by many other

Baseball was the most popular sport in America in the late 1800's.

comic strip characters. These comic strip characters included Buster Brown, Happy Hooligan, the Katzenjammer Kids, and many others. Mutt and Jeff was the first comic strip to be printed in a newspaper every day.

Americans also enjoyed reading **dime novels,** or little books that cost about 10 cents. These dime novels contained exciting adventure stories, detective stories, and Western stories. The first dime novels came out in the 1860's. Dime novels, like the paperback books of today, were easy to carry around. Millions of Americans spent their free time reading about the adventures of Deadwood Dick, Nick Carter the detective, or Frank Merriwell the hero of Yale College.

By the late 1800's, most cities were well lit at night. This meant that more people were willing to go out at night.

Americans Listened to New Kinds of Music

Americans also liked to listen to music. Barbershop quartets sang the old favorite American songs. The player piano, or piano which played by itself, and Edison's new invention, the phonograph, helped bring music into many homes. Band concerts were popular in most towns. And the songs written in New York City's music section, Tin Pan Alley, were sold all over the nation.

At this time, Americans in New Orleans were beginning to play a new type of music called ragtime, or jazz. The black marching bands of New Orleans introduced a new rhythm—an African beat—to American music.

Ragtime piano players such as Scott Joplin, composer of the "Maple Leaf Rag," soon made ragtime the most popular type of music with young Americans. Jazz was the only form of music started in America.

Summing Up

City living caused important changes in the way Americans lived. City living changed family life and gave people more free time. Americans spent much of this free time enjoying sports. They also enjoyed going to shows, reading, and listening to music. In the next chapter, you will find out about new American writers and painters in the years after 1865.

AFTER YOU READ THE CHAPTER

Do You Know These Important Terms?

For each sentence below, choose the term that best completes the sentence.

1. Americans enjoyed watching popular games of sport called (**professional/spectator**) sports.
2. Shows which presented singers, dancers, comedians, magicians, and jugglers were called (**variety shows/vaudeville**).
3. Inexpensive little books that contained adventure stories, detective stories, and Western stories were called (**paperback/dime**) novels.

Do You Remember These People?

Tell something about each of the following persons.

Dr. James Naismith   **Charles Radbourne**
Harry Stovey   **Hugh Duffy**
John L. Sullivan   **Jake Kilrain**
Jim Corbett   **Jack Johnson**
Scott Joplin

Can You Locate These Places?

Use the map on page 390 to locate the following places. Tell how each location is related to this chapter.

Cincinnati   **New York City**
New Orleans

Do You Know When It Happened?

What are the years of this chapter? Place the following events in the order in which they occurred.

John L. Sullivan became heavyweight champion.

The American League was formed.

The first comic strip character appeared in a newspaper.

The National League was formed.

Basketball was invented.

Discovering More About the Main Idea

City life caused important changes in the way Americans lived. Sports, shows, reading, and music became very popular.

Tell how each of the following developments is related to the MAIN IDEA.

City life brought important changes to American families. City people had more free time. Many people spent their free time taking part in sports or watching spectator sports.

Comic strips and dime novels were enjoyed by many Americans.

Barber shop quartets, band concerts, and newly written songs played on the phonograph were popular. Ragtime began to grow in popularity.

Can You Discuss the Chapter?

Use the information you learned in this chapter to answer the following questions.

1. Why was city life so different from life on the farm?
2. How did many people use their free time during the last part of the 1800's?
3. What were some of the new types of reading materials that appeared?
4. Which types of music were enjoyed by many people?
5. Who is your favorite person from the late 1800's? Why?

Can You Connect the Past and the Present?

1. Compare the ways people spent their free time in the later part of the 1800's with the ways people in your community spend their free time. How are they alike? How are they different?
2. Tin Pan Alley was the music and recording center of the 1890's. Where is the music and recording center today?

CHAPTER 64

American Thought, 1865-1900

Courtesy of the Art Institute of Chicago.

"The Herring Net" by Winslow Homer.

BEFORE YOU BEGIN THE CHAPTER

Know What to Look For

1. After 1865, many Americans moved to the West. Life in the West was very difficult. Prairie fires, or grass fires, which were common on the Great Plains, were frightening experiences. Hamlin Garland, a famous writer at this time, described the horror of a prairie fire with great realism in one of his poems called "Prairie Songs."

A curling, leaping light,
A crackling roar from livid lungs,
A wild flush on the skies of night—
A force that gnaws with hot red tongues,
That leaves blackened, smoking sod—
A fiery furnace where the cattle trod.

In the years after 1865, realistic stories and poems became popular in America. Writers tried to describe life as it actually was. Hamlin Garland was a realistic writer who wrote about life on the Great Plains. In this chapter, you will read about other American writers, artists, and thinkers after 1865.

2. Read the title of the chapter. Then look through the chapter and read each heading. What did Americans write about?

3. Look at the pictures in the chapter and read each caption. Who painted the picture which is on the first page of this chapter? Note also the time line at the beginning of the chapter. What years are included in this chapter? Compare this chapter time line to the unit time line on page 381.

4. Read the last part of the chapter called Summing Up. In the years between 1865 and 1900, what did Americans become interested in?

Know These Important Terms

realistic novels   realistic painters
local-color stories   Chautauqua movement

Know the Main Idea

Here is the MAIN IDEA of this chapter.

Between 1865 and 1900, Americans became interested in books, art, and education. Many new American writers and artists became famous.

Keep this MAIN IDEA in mind as you study the chapter. Ask yourself the following questions as you read. They will help you remember the MAIN IDEA.

1. What European writers were popular in the United States during this period?
2. What American writer wrote *The Adventures of Huckleberry Finn?*
3. How was American education improved?

THE YEARS OF THIS CHAPTER ARE 1865 TO 1900

1865   1900

THE CHAPTER LESSON BEGINS HERE

American Writers Wrote About American Life

In the years after 1865, Americans were interested in books, education, and art. Americans continued to read the works of European writers. Charles Dickens and Sir Walter Scott, two British authors, were popular in America. Americans also enjoyed A. Conan Doyle's Sherlock Holmes detective stories and Jules Verne's science fiction stories. But as time went on, Americans began to read more of the books written by American writers. Many new American writers appeared after 1865.

Some of the new American writers wrote **realistic novels,** or books that tried to tell about American life as it really was in those years. One realistic novel, *The Red Badge of Courage* by Stephen Crane, gave a true-to-life account of a soldier's feelings during the Civil War. William Dean Howells also wrote realistic novels. In his books, he showed many of the problems of American life at this time.

Mark Twain Was a Great Writer

Another realistic writer was Mark Twain, whose real name was Samuel L. Clemens. Mark Twain described the mining camps of the West in his book *Roughing It,* and he described life on the steamboats that went

Mark Twain was an important American writer in the late 1800's.

up and down the Mississippi in his book *Life on the Mississippi.* He also wrote one of the most popular boys' books of all time, *The Adventures of Tom Sawyer.*

But Mark Twain's greatest book was *The Adventures of Huckleberry Finn.* In this book, Mark Twain described the friendship which grew up between a young boy called Huck and a runaway slave named Jim.

America Had Many Fine Writers

Other American writers wrote **local-color stories.** These were colorful stories about the past or about a particular section of the nation. One of the most popular local-color writers was Bret Harte, who wrote about the rough life in Western mining camps. And Hamlin Garland wrote about the hard life of farmers and their families on the Great Plains.

America Had Many Fine Artists

After 1865, many **realistic painters** also appeared. Thomas Eakins and George Bellows were realistic painters who liked to paint life as it was. They painted people at home and at work. Winslow Homer painted fishermen and sailors who made their living at sea. Another famous painter, Albert Ryder, was not a realistic painter. Instead, he painted imaginary scenes.

More Americans Received an Education

One reason that Americans read more and became interested in art was that they were getting more education. Between 1865 and 1900, more and more American children attended public elementary schools. In most states, the school year became longer, and children stayed in school for a greater number of years. Most states passed laws which required all children to attend elementary schools for a certain number of years. And most states began to spend more money on their schools.

One of the most important jobs of the schools was to prepare immigrants and their children for American life. Some schools had special classes to teach the immigrants the English language and to teach them the rights and duties of American citizens. The immigrants' children learned about American life when they attended school every day.

American Education Was Improved

Americans also realized that the nation needed more high schools. The nation's industries and businesses required better educated workers. Therefore, in the years after 1865, many high schools were built. In 1870, the United States had about 500 high schools. But by 1900, the United States had more than 6 thousand high schools. Vocational schools, or schools that trained workers for a job, and

A classroom in an American school in 1888. American education was greatly improved in the years after 1865.

night schools were also started during this period.

Children began to go to school at an earlier age. Many schools added kindergarten classes for young children. In these years, American children also began to receive a better education. Teachers were better trained for their job, and textbooks were improved.

American Colleges Improved and Expanded

Colleges also improved greatly in the years between 1865 and 1900. More science courses were taught in colleges. Students were allowed a greater choice in the courses they took. Many new state and private colleges were opened in these years. And more American men and even a few women were able to attend college.

In the years after 1865, universities were started. Universities trained students in special fields such as law and medicine, as well as going more deeply into all subjects. The students who graduated from the universities became the nation's leading teachers, doctors, scientists, and lawyers.

Americans Learned in Many Ways

Not all Americans were able to go to a college, or a university, or even to high school. But Americans read more books, newspapers, and magazines than they ever did before. They went to art museums and attended concerts. And they listened to lectures and took courses taught by the **Chautauqua** (shuu-TAW-kwuh) **movement.** The Chautauqua movement, which began in the 1870's, gave courses in art, music, plays, and other subjects. At one time, over 100 thousand Americans took the Chautauqua summer education courses.

Summing Up

In the years between 1865 and 1900, Americans became interested in books, art, and education. Many new American writers and artists became famous. Americans began to receive a better education. Many states required children to attend elementary school for a certain number of years. Many new high schools, colleges, and universities were opened. In the next chapters, which are in Unit 17, you will read about improvements in American life.

AFTER YOU READ THE CHAPTER

Do You Know These Important Terms?

For each sentence below, choose the term that best completes the sentence.

1. Books that tried to describe American life as it really was were called (**romantic/realistic**) novels.
2. Colorful stories about the past or about a particular section of the nation were called (**local-color/rural**) stories.
3. Artists who liked to paint life as it was were called (**realistic/abstract**) painters.
4. Lectures and courses given in the 1870's might have been part of the (**Chautauqua/Niagara**) movement.

Do You Remember These People?

Tell something about each of the following persons.

Charles Dickens	Sir Walter Scott
A. Conan Doyle	Jules Verne
Stephen Crane	Bret Harte
Mark Twain	Thomas Eakins
Hamlin Garland	Winslow Homer
George Bellows	William Dean
Albert Ryder	Howells

Do You Know When It Happened?

What are the years of this chapter? When was the Chautauqua movement popular?

Discovering More About the Main Idea

Between 1865 and 1900, Americans became interested in books, art, and education. Many new American writers and artists became famous.

Tell how each of the following developments is related to the MAIN IDEA.

Although Americans read books by European writers, many new American writers also became popular. The realistic novels and local-color stories captured the interest of Americans of this period. Realistic painters were also popular.

Americans began to receive a better education after 1865. One of the most important jobs of the schools was to teach immigrants the English language and to teach them the rights and duties of American citizens.

Colleges also improved greatly between 1865 and 1900. The students who graduated from colleges and universities became the nation's leading teachers, doctors, scientists, and lawyers.

Can You Discuss the Chapter?

Use the information you learned in this chapter to answer the following questions.

1. Who were some of the important American writers after 1865?
2. How did education in the public elementary schools change during this period?
3. What were some of the other changes made in American schools and colleges?
4. Why was the Chautauqua movement such a success?
5. Which do you think you like best, realistic novels or local-color stories? Why? What is the difference between the two?

Can You Connect the Past and the Present?

1. In this chapter, you read about the improvements in education and about the ways in which Americans who were not able to go to school learned. What opportunities are there for education in your community besides the public schools and colleges?
2. Educating the millions of immigrants was a great challenge for the public schools. Today there are few immigrants. What new challenges are the public schools facing?

Americans Try to Improve Their Life

William Jennings Bryan giving a campaign speech.

THE CHAPTERS IN UNIT 17 ARE

CHAPTER 65 American Government, 1865–1900
CHAPTER 66 American Workers Organize
CHAPTER 67 American Farmers Protest
CHAPTER 68 Progressives Work for a Better Nation
CHAPTER 69 Progressives Work for Better Government

THE YEARS OF THIS UNIT ARE 1865 TO 1920

1800	1865	1920	1975

American Government, 1865-1900

President McKinley meets with his Cabinet.

BEFORE YOU BEGIN THE CHAPTER

Know What to Look For

1. Did you ever hear of a candidate who received the largest number of the people's votes and still lost the election? This happened twice in the years after the Civil War. In the election of 1876, Samuel J. Tilden received a majority of the people's votes, but Rutherford B. Hayes became President. Again, in the Presidential election of 1888,

Grover Cleveland had the most votes, but Benjamin Harrison became President. As you read the chapter, you will find out what caused these two unusual elections. You will also read about the American government in the years after the Civil War and the role of businessmen in the government.

2. Read the title of the chapter. Then look

through the chapter and read each heading. What were two problems of the American government in the latter part of the 1800's?

3. Look at the pictures in the chapter and read each caption. What do the pictures show about American government after 1865? Note also the time line at the beginning of the chapter. What years are included in this chapter? Compare this chapter time line to the unit time line on page 405.

4. Read the last part of the chapter called Summing Up. What important new reform in the government was set up? What is the topic of the next chapter?

popular votes   hard money
Pendleton Civil Service Act   cheap money
merit system

Here is the MAIN IDEA of this chapter.

In the years after 1865, businessmen played an important part in government. The government was faced with the problems of the tariff, money, and civil service reform.

Keep this MAIN IDEA in mind as you study the chapter. Ask yourself the following questions as you read. They will help you to remember the MAIN IDEA.

1. Which group of Americans was most favored by the government between 1865 and 1900?

2. Why were the Southern electoral votes given to Hayes in the election of 1876?

3. What group of people wanted the government to increase the amount of money it put out?

THE YEARS OF THIS CHAPTER ARE 1865 TO 1900

1865   1900   1920

THE CHAPTER LESSON BEGINS HERE

Northern Businessmen and the Federal Government

After the Civil War, businessmen in the Northeast controlled most of the manufacturing, trading, and banking in the nation. They also had the most power in the nation's two main political parties, the Democratic Party and the Republican Party. As a result, the government often favored businessmen over American workers and farmers between 1865 and 1900.

Grant as President

If you remember, General Ulysses S. Grant, the great Northern war leader, was elected President in 1868. But President Grant was not a strong leader. He made poor choices in appointing men to fill government jobs. Several members of his Cabinet and many leaders of the federal, state, and city governments took part in dishonest business deals. However, President Grant was completely honest and was elected for a second term in 1872.

Hayes Won a Close Election in 1876

In the election of 1876, Samuel J. Tilden, the governor of New York, was chosen as the Democratic candidate for President. The Republicans chose Rutherford B. Hayes, the governor of Ohio, to run against Tilden. Tilden received the majority of the **popular votes,** or votes of the people. But if you remember, the President's election is decided by the electoral votes, not the popular votes. When the electoral votes were counted, twenty of them were undecided. All but one of these electoral votes were from three Southern states.

Congress set up a special commission, or group of men, to decide the election. This commission decided that the undecided electoral votes belonged to Hayes, and he became President. The Southern electoral votes were given to Hayes when the Republicans in Congress promised to remove the last federal troops from the South.

A President's Death
Led to an Important Reform

In 1880, James A. Garfield, a Republican Senator from Ohio, was elected President in a very close election. A few months after he became President, Garfield was killed by a job seeker who was refused a government job. As a result, Americans became concerned about finding a new way to fill government jobs.

Up to the time of President Garfield's death, most government workers were chosen by the spoils system. They received their jobs because they supported the winning political party.

In 1883, Congress passed the **Pendleton Civil Service Act.** This law set up a Civil

This picture shows the shooting of President Garfield at a railroad station in Washington, D.C., on July 2, 1881.

The men shown above are taking Civil Service tests for government jobs. This exam system replaced the spoils system.

Service Commission to test people for government jobs. Only people who passed Civil Service tests were to be given government jobs. This new plan for choosing government workers was called the **merit system**.

Cleveland Was Elected
President in 1884

In 1884, Grover Cleveland, the governor of New York, was elected President in a close election. Cleveland was the only Democrat to be elected President in the years between 1856 and 1912. However, between 1860 and 1900, the Democratic Party and the Republican Party were not very different.

One of the main differences between the two parties was over the tariff. Most Republicans favored a high tariff, or tax on goods brought in from other nations. The Republicans claimed a high tariff was needed to protect American industry against foreign goods. Most Democrats were against a high tariff, and they wanted the tariff to be lowered. They felt that American industries no longer needed protection and that the high tariff hurt the farmers of the South and West, who needed many goods which were manufactured in other countries.

The Problem of the Tariff

In the years after 1865, Congress kept on raising the tariff. When Cleveland became President, he tried to lower the tariff, but the Republicans in Congress refused to pass a lower tariff law. In the election of 1888, President Cleveland ran for a second term and

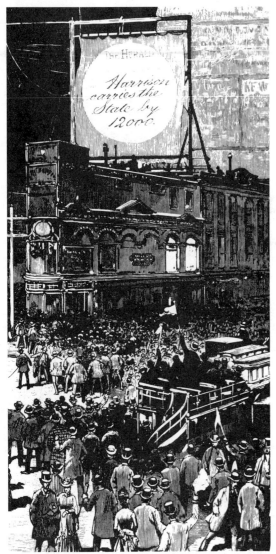

Voters gather to find out the results of the election of 1888.

won a majority of the popular votes, or the people's votes. But the Republican candidate, Benjamin Harrison of Indiana, won a majority of the electoral votes and became President.

Under President Harrison, the Republicans in Congress passed a still higher tariff. But by this time, many Americans began to believe that higher tariffs only meant higher

prices for the goods they bought. In the election of 1892, Grover Cleveland was again chosen by the Democrats for President. Cleveland defeated Harrison and again became President.

The Problem of Hard Money

Besides the tariff, the money affairs of the federal government were another important problem after the Civil War. Most businessmen favored **hard money,** or money backed by gold. However, most farmers and workingmen owed money. They felt that the reason they never had enough money was that the government did not issue enough money. Therefore, farmers and workingmen wanted the government to increase the amount of money it put out. Also, they wanted this money to be **cheap money,** or money not backed by gold.

Most farmers and workingmen wanted the government to issue more greenbacks, or cheap paper money not backed by gold. The government first printed greenbacks during the Civil War. Farmers and workingmen wanted to pay back the money they owed with these greenbacks. But the businessmen wanted to be paid back in hard money. Congress decided to stop issuing greenbacks and to replace them with hard money. This made it difficult for farmers to pay back their debts.

Summing Up

In the years after 1865, America's government had many problems to solve. The high tariff and the money question were among these problems. During this period, American businessmen played an important part in government. One important reform was the Pendleton Civil Service Act, which set up a new way of appointing workers to government jobs. In the next chapter, you will find out about American workers in these years.

AFTER YOU READ THE CHAPTER

Do You Know These Important Terms?

For each sentence below, choose the term that best completes the sentence.

1. In a Presidential election, the votes of the people are called the (**national/popular**) votes.
2. The (**Garfield/Pendleton**) Civil Service Act set up a commission to test people for government jobs.
3. The new plan for choosing government workers was called the (**merit/anti-spoils**) system.
4. Money backed by gold is called (**bullion/ hard money**).
5. Money not backed by gold is called (**gold certificates/cheap money**).

Do You Remember These People?

Tell something about each of the following persons.

Ulysses S. Grant   **Samuel J. Tilden**
Rutherford B. Hayes   **James A. Garfield**
Grover Cleveland   **Benjamin Harrison**

Do You Know When It Happened?

What are the years of this chapter? Place the following events in the order in which they occurred.

James A. Garfield was shot.

Tilden lost an election in which he had the most popular votes.

Benjamin Harrison became President.

The merit system was first used.

Grant was elected for a second term.

Discovering More About the Main Idea

In the years after 1865, businessmen played an important part in government. The government was faced with the problems of the tariff, money, and civil service reform.

Tell how each of the following developments is related to the MAIN IDEA.

President Garfield was killed by a job seeker who was refused a government job.

Businessmen had the most power in the nation's two main political parties. The government often favored businessmen over American workers and farmers.

The Democratic Party and the Republican Party were not very different. The Democrats wanted the tariff to be lowered while the Republicans favored a high tariff.

Businessmen favored hard money, while farmers and workers wanted the government to issue more greenbacks.

Can You Discuss the Chapter?

Use the information you learned in this chapter to answer the following questions.

1. How did Rutherford B. Hayes become President when he received less popular votes than Samuel Tilden?
2. Explain how the death of a President was related to an important reform in choosing government workers.
3. Why did most farmers and workers favor cheap money?
4. How can you prove that the government favored businessmen over farmers and workers in the years after 1865?
5. What was the main difference between the Republican Party and the Democratic Party?

Can You Connect the Past and the Present?

1. Is it still possible for a Presidential candidate to receive the largest number of popular votes and still not become President?
2. Does the United States have hard money or cheap money today?

CHAPTER 66

American Workers Organize

Workers demanding an eight-hour day.

BEFORE YOU BEGIN THE CHAPTER

Know What to Look For

1. The early labor unions were weak and had almost no power against the factory owners. Employers had weapons they were able to use against the unions. In some cases, they were even able to break up the unions in their factories. In order to gain better working conditions, unions had to find a weapon against employers.

After 1865, unions began to use the strike, or the stopping of work, to force factory owners to do what the unions wanted. A strike was a good weapon because it caused the employer to lose money. As unions learned to use this weapon, they gained more power. However, in the years between 1865 and 1900, the government favored businessmen and often helped them in their fight against labor unions and strikes. In this chapter, you will read more about the workers and their efforts to organize unions.

2. Read the title of the chapter. Then look through the chapter and read each heading. From the headings give the names of two labor unions.

3. Look at the pictures in the chapter and read each caption. What do the pictures show you about American workers? Note also the time line at the beginning of this chapter. What years are included in this chapter? Compare this chapter time line to the unit time line on page 405.

4. Read the last part of the chapter called Summing Up. How did American workers try to get better working conditions? What is the topic of the next chapter?

Know These Important Terms

Knights of Labor   yellow dog contract
Haymarket Riot   injunction
American Federation of Labor

Know the Main Idea
Here is the MAIN IDEA of this chapter.
The rapid growth of industry in the years after 1865 caused many problems for American workers. They formed labor unions to improve their working conditions.

Keep this MAIN IDEA in mind as you study the chapter. Ask yourself the following questions as you read. They will help you remember the MAIN IDEA.

1. Why were labor unions formed?
2. What union took in all workers?
3. Which union was the most successful in the years before 1900?

THE YEARS OF THIS CHAPTER ARE 1865 TO 1900

1865   1900   1920

THE CHAPTER LESSON BEGINS HERE

Working Conditions in Factories

In the years after 1865, many large business companies grew up in the United States. These companies hired many workers in their factories. This growth of American industry caused many problems for American workers.

If you remember, workers worked long, hard hours for very low pay in American factories. Many workers worked sixty hours or more a week and earned only about 8 to 10 dollars for this work. To get along, a worker's wife and older children often had to go to work. During these years many immigrants came to the United States. American workers and the new immigrants struggled for jobs in American factories.

Problems of Workers

Machines began to take over the jobs of many skilled workers. Often a machine was able to do the work of several workers. Therefore, many workers lost their jobs. In many large companies, the owner never met the workers. The owner hired a manager to run his factory. The manager often kept the workers working long, hard hours in order to make more money for the owner. The workers had to do as they were told or they lost their jobs.

In the years after 1865, a worker was not able to solve his job problem by himself. As a result, workers tried to join together to form labor unions. These labor unions were formed to try to get better working conditions.

Workers Began to Join Unions

Labor unions were not new to American workers. In the years before 1865, some American workers set up unions. But most of these early unions were weak, and they ended during the hard times of 1857.

In 1866, William H. Sylvis formed the National Labor Union. This union fought against monopolies and for an eight-hour working day. The National Labor Union won an eight-hour working day for federal government workers. But this union was never strong, and it soon ended.

The Knights of Labor

A more important union was the **Knights of Labor**. This union was the first to try to bring workers all over the nation into one large union. From its start in 1869, the Knights of Labor took in both skilled and unskilled workers, men and women, and black and white workers. The Knights of Labor worked for an eight-hour working day and for the end of child labor.

After Terence V. Powderly (POW-dur-lee) became the leader of the Knights of Labor in 1879, the union started to grow rapidly. Soon

A great demonstration of workingmen in New York City in the late 1800's. Workers began to organize to get better working conditions.

When policemen tried to break up a workers' protest meeting in Haymarket Square in Chicago, a bomb exploded among them.

the Knights of Labor had 700 thousand members. The Knights of Labor was usually against strikes, or stopping work, to force factory owners to do what the union wanted. But the Knights of Labor won a strike against a railroad in 1885, and this successful strike helped the union to grow.

The Haymarket Riot of 1886

In 1886, a labor union in Chicago went out on strike. During the strike, police attacked the strikers and shot several workers. The next day, a large group of workers held a meeting in Haymarket Square to protest against the shooting. Many of these workers were members of the Knights of Labor. The police tried to break up this meeting. But someone threw a bomb that killed or injured many policemen.

The Knights of Labor had nothing to do with the bomb throwing. But many people blamed the Knights of Labor for the **Haymarket Riot,** as it was called. Many people felt that labor unions caused trouble. As a result, the Knights of Labor lost most of its members.

The American Federation of Labor Was Formed

In 1881, however, the **American Federation of Labor,** or A.F. of L., was formed. The American Federation of Labor was a new kind of labor union. This union took in as members skilled workers such as machinists, carpenters, and cigar makers. The head of the A.F. of L. was Samuel Gompers. Under his leadership, the number of A.F. of L. members grew from 150 thousand in 1886 to over 500

State militia at Homestead mills.

THE HOMESTEAD STRIKE

In 1892, the Carnegie Steel Company cut the wages of the workers in its Homestead steel mills, located in Pennsylvania. Most of these workers belonged to a union. When the union objected to the wage cut and the workers went out on strike, the company closed down the mills.

The Carnegie Steel Company then sent 300 Pinkerton detectives to take over the mills and to break up the strike. The workers knew that once the detectives took over the mills, the company planned to hire non-union workers. When the Pinkerton detectives arrived, the union men attacked them. The battle lasted all day, and men on both sides were killed. Finally, the detectives surrendered and left the town.

Six days later, the governor of Pennsylvania sent the state militia to take over the Homestead mills. Soon after, non-union men were at work in the mills. Then, a man tried to kill Henry Frick, the general manager of the Carnegie Steel Company. Although he was not connected with the union, this act and the earlier violence turned the public against the union. The strike continued for several more months and finally collapsed. When it was over, the union was ruined, and over 3 thousand of the strikers lost their jobs.

thousand in 1900. However, its members were only skilled workers. Most American workers in these years were unskilled workers who did not belong to any labor union.

The American Federation of Labor worked for the eight-hour working day, higher wages, and an end to child labor. By using the strike, it was able to win higher wages and better working conditions for most of its members.

Unions Had Many Problems

In these years, unions still had many troubles. Some employers refused to hire union men. Many workers had to agree not to join unions before they were given a job. This agreement was called a **yellow dog contract.** When workers went out on strike, many owners hired strike breakers, or men who were not in the union, to break up the strike.

When labor unions were beginning, most state governments and the federal government backed the factory owners rather than the workers. For example, in the railroad strike of 1894, a federal court issued an **injunction** (in-JUNGK-shun), or a court order, against the strike. This injunction ordered the union not to strike. When the workers refused to obey the injunction, the government sent federal troops to keep the trains running. State courts also had the power to order a union not to strike.

Summing Up

In the years after 1865, American workers had many problems because of the rapid growth of industry. American workers tried to get better working conditions by forming unions. Most of these early unions were weak. However, the A.F. of L. succeeded even though both the factory owners and the government worked against unions. In the next chapter, you will find out about the problems of American farmers.

AFTER YOU READ THE CHAPTER

Do You Know These Important Terms?

For each sentence below, choose the term that best completes the sentence.

1. The (**Knights of Labor/Universal Union**) was the first to try to bring workers all over the nation into one large union.
2. The violence at the (**Pullman/Haymarket**) Riot was blamed on the union.
3. The (**International Workers of the World/ American Federation of Labor**) was a new kind of labor union made up of skilled workers.
4. When a worker signed a (**black ball/yellow dog**) contract, he agreed not to join the union.
5. A court order forbidding a strike is called an (**interdict/injunction**).

Do You Remember These People?

Tell something about each of the following persons.

William H. Sylvis   **Terence V. Powderly**
Samuel Gompers

Can You Locate These Places?

Use the map on page 390 to locate the following places.

Chicago   **Washington, D.C.**
New York City

Do You Know When It Happened?

What are the years of this chapter? How are the following dates important to the story of the labor movement?

1866   1869   1886   1894

Discovering More About the Main Idea

The rapid growth of industry in the years after 1865 caused many problems for American workers. They formed labor unions to improve their working conditions.

Tell how each of the following developments is related to the MAIN IDEA.

The large numbers of immigrants, machines, and the large size of industry caused problems for workers, but early unions were not very successful.

The Knights of Labor, a union for all workers, had many members and was successful until the Haymarket Riot caused it to lose many members.

The American Federation of Labor was the most successful union. Employers and the government worked against unions.

Can You Discuss the Chapter?

Use the information you learned in this chapter to answer the following questions.

1. Why did workers find it necessary to organize labor unions?
2. Why did the Knights of Labor lose most of its members after being the strongest union in the nation?
3. How was the American Federation of Labor different from the Knights of Labor?
4. How did the government and factory owners work against unions?
5. If you had lived in 1880, do you think you might have been on the side of labor unions or on the side of the factory owners? Why?

Can You Connect the Past and the Present?

1. Unions have continued to grow and become powerful. They still use the strike as their main weapon. When was the last strike in your community? How successful was it?
2. You read how the Knights of Labor were blamed for the Haymarket Riot even though they had nothing to do with it. Has anything like this ever happened in your community?

CHAPTER 67

American Farmers Protest

A reaping machine.

BEFORE YOU BEGIN THE CHAPTER

Know What to Look For

1. American politics seem to work best when there are only two political parties. It's almost like the old saying, "Two's a party. Three's a crowd." However, there have been times when three or more political parties were active. When there were more than two parties, one of three possible things happened. Sometimes, the third party grew so strong that it took the place of one of the two main parties. At other times, the ideas of the third party were taken over by one of the two parties, and there was no longer a need for the third party. Finally, the problems which brought about the start of the third party ended, and the need for another party also ended. In this chapter, you will read about a third political party which began to grow in the years of the 1890's.

page 418

2. Read the title of the chapter. Then look through the chapter and read each heading. What was the name of the new political party organized to solve some of the problems of the farmer?

3. Look at the pictures in the chapter and read each caption. What do the pictures show you about American farmers? Note also the time line at the beginning of the chapter. What years are included in this chapter? Compare the time line for this chapter with the unit time line on page 405.

4. Read the end of the chapter called Summing Up. What seems unusual about the main problem faced by the farmers?

Know These Important Terms
middlemen   Department of Agriculture
Grange   Colored Farmers Alliance
cooperatives   Northern Alliance
Populist Party   Southern Alliance

Know the Main Idea
Here is the MAIN IDEA of this chapter.

After 1865, farmers began to grow more crops but found it harder to make a living. They formed farmers' groups and a third political party to help solve their problems.

Keep this MAIN IDEA in mind as you study this chapter. Keep the following questions in mind as you read. They will help you remember the MAIN IDEA.

1. What helped farmers increase the amounts of crops they raised?

2. Whom did the farmer blame for most of his problems?

3. What were the demands of the Populist Party?

THE YEARS OF THIS CHAPTER ARE 1865 TO 1900

1865   1900   1920

THE CHAPTER LESSON BEGINS HERE

New Farm Machines
Changed the American Farm

By the year 1890, American farmers produced more than twice as much corn, wheat, and cotton as they did in 1860. The opening of new farm land in the West helped to increase the crops raised. But the main reason for the increase in crops was the use of farm machines. Farm machines helped farmers to grow much larger crops.

Another result of these new farm machines was that American farms became larger. This happened because many farmers who owned small farms were not able to afford farm machines. Without machines, small farmers were not able to raise enough crops. Many of these small farmers had to sell their land to a large farm owner, and they became tenant farmers.

Farming Became a Business

Another change in farming in the years after 1865 was the growth of commercial farming. Commercial farming meant that the farmer grew his crops to be sold, rather than for his own use. In other words, American farming was becoming a business very much like other businesses.

Because of the increase in the amount of crops, the supply of farm crops soon became larger than Americans needed. As a result,

Farmers and their wives attend a Grange meeting. The Grange provided a place for farmers to talk over their problems.

farmers were forced to sell their crops at very low prices. For example, the price for cotton dropped from about 15 cents a pound to about 5 cents a pound. Many farmers did not even make enough money to pay for the cost of growing and selling their crops.

The Farmers Had Many Problems

In the years after 1865, farmers had many problems. Farmers blamed most of their troubles on the **middlemen,** or the people who helped bring their farm products to the public. The railroad, the miller, the grain warehouse, the stockyard, and the banker who loaned farmers money, all made a great deal of money. Farmers felt that these middle-

men, especially the railroads, were taking too much money away from them.

Farmers also felt that the government was not doing anything to help them. The federal government set up the **Department of Agriculture** to help American farmers. But the government refused to regulate, or control, the railroads and the trusts. Also, the federal government refused to issue more cheap paper money.

Farmers Formed Farm Groups

Farmers began to form large farmers' groups in order to improve their conditions. The first of these farmers' groups was the **Grange.** The Grange was able to get many

Here, a Populist leader in the Kansas state legislature argues with another member of the legislature.

states to pass laws to regulate the railroads in the 1870's. The Grange also formed farmers' **cooperatives,** or groups of farmers who sold their farm products and bought manufactured goods together.

In the 1880's, the Grange was replaced by two new farmers' groups—the **Northern Alliance** and the **Southern Alliance.** In the South there was also a separate **Colored Farmers' Alliance** for black farmers. All these Alliances formed cooperatives and worked for laws to help the farmer.

The Populist Party Was Formed

About the year 1890, the Farmers' Alliances developed a third political party. They formed the People's Party, or the **Populist** (PAHP-yuh-list) **Party.** Most of the members of the Populist Party were farmers. But many workers also supported the new third party. And other Americans who felt that big business was too powerful also joined the Populist Party.

In 1892, the Populists decided to run a candidate for President. He received only about a million votes. But the Populists were able to elect ten members to the House of Representatives, five Senators, three governors, and hundreds of representatives to the state legislatures.

The Populists Had a Strong Program

The Populist Party wanted the federal government to do many things. Their most important demands were these.

1. Populists wanted the federal government to increase the amount of money in the nation by issuing more greenbacks or more silver dollars.

2. Populists wanted the federal government to set up storehouses for the farmers' crops and to loan farmers money on these crops.

3. Populists wanted an income tax law that required people with higher incomes to pay higher taxes.

4. Populists wanted United States Senators to be elected directly by the people. In many states, Senators were still elected by the state legislature.

5. Populists wanted a limit on the number of immigrants and an eight-hour working day for workers.

6. Populists wanted the federal government to own and operate all railroad, telephone, and telegraph systems in the nation.

The Populist Party Was Defeated in the Election of 1896

In 1894, the Populist Party ran many men for Congress. They were able to elect many Congressmen who favored their ideas. And in 1896, the Democratic Party took over some ideas of the Populist Party. The Democratic Party and the Populist Party both chose William Jennings Bryan, a young Nebraska lawyer, to run for President. The Republican candidate was William McKinley of Ohio.

The Republicans were backed by the businessmen and had more money to spend on the campaign. As a result, McKinley won the election of 1896. Once again, the businessmen defeated the farmers and the workers. But many ideas of the Populist Party were taken over by the two main political parties.

Above, William McKinley is making a speech. He was elected President in 1896.

Summing Up

After 1865, farmers greatly increased their crops because of new farm machines. At the same time, farmers found it harder to make a living. Because of their problems, farmers joined together in farmers' alliances, or groups. They also helped form a third political party—the Populist Party. The Populists backed many ideas to help all Americans. In the next chapter, you will read about Americans who tried to solve the nation's many problems.

AFTER YOU READ THE CHAPTER

Do You Understand These Important Terms?

For each sentence below, choose the term that best completes the sentence.

1. People who helped bring the farmers' products to the public were called (**wholesalers/ middlemen**).
2. The (**Wobblies/Grange**) was one of the first farmers' groups formed.
3. Groups of farmers who sold their farm products and bought manufactured goods together were called (**cooperatives/alliances**).
4. The (**Greenback/Populist**) Party was a third party, supported by many farmers.
5. The federal government set up the Department of (**the Interior/Agriculture**) to help American farmers.
6. The Northern, Southern, and Colored Farmers' (**Grange/Alliances**) formed cooperatives and worked for laws to help the farmer.

Do You Remember These People?

Tell something about each of the following persons.

William Jennings Bryan   William McKinley

Do You Know When It Happened?

What are the years of this chapter? Place the following events in the order in which they occurred.

The Grange was an active farmers' group.
William McKinley was elected President.
The Populist Party was formed.
The Northern Alliance was organized.

Discovering More About the Main Idea

After 1865, farmers began to grow more crops but found it harder to make a living. They formed farmers' groups and a third political party to help solve their problems.

Tell how each of the following developments is related to the MAIN IDEA.

New farm machines helped farmers to grow much larger crops. Some farmers increased the size of their farms. Many small farmers had to sell their land.

Farming grew into big business, but farmers usually faced hard times. The government provided little help to the farmers, so they organized farmers' groups to help themselves.

The two main political parties took over many of the ideas of the Populist Party.

Can You Discuss the Chapter?

Use the information you learned in this chapter to answer the following questions.

1. Why were many farmers not making enough money to pay for the cost of growing and selling their crops?
2. How were the farmers able to work together to help solve their problems?
3. What were the major demands made by the Populist Party?
4. Why did the Populist Party and the Democratic Party select the same Presidential candidate in the election of 1896?
5. With which demand of the Populist Party do you most agree? least agree? Why?

Can You Connect the Past and the Present?

1. In what recent elections have third parties been active? What has been the result of their activity?
2. Some present-day practices, especially in the area of politics, are left over from the time when most of the American population were farmers. They are old-fashioned now because most people live in cities. Can you name any of these old practices in your community?

CHAPTER 68

Progressives Work for a Better Nation

A Progressive leader demanding reform.

BEFORE YOU BEGIN THE CHAPTER

Know What to Look For

1. Dirty, filthy mud that is sometimes found along the sides and on the bottoms of streams is called muck. Most people dislike muck because it is dirty and unpleasant. In the early 1900's, Americans faced many serious problems. Because many of these problems were unpleasant, many Americans just wanted to forget about them. In some ways, the prob-

lems of American life were like the muck along a dirty stream—the people knew it was there, but they ignored it, or forgot about it.

However, not everyone ignored, or forgot about these problems. Some reformers began to show Americans the problems of American life. Because they raked, or searched, around in the muck of unpleasant problems, some people called these reformers muckrakers. Actually, the first man to use this term was Theodore Roosevelt. In this chapter, you will read about these reformers and some of the problems they uncovered. You will also find out how these reformers tried to solve these problems of American life.

2. Read the title of the chapter. Then look through the chapter and read each heading. What things did Progressives do to help improve the nation?

3. Look at the pictures in the chapter and read each caption. What do the pictures show you about the ways in which Progressives were trying to improve the nation? Note also the time line at the beginning of the chapter. What years are included in this chapter? Compare the chapter time line with the unit time line on page 405.

4. Read the last part of the chapter called Summing Up. Who were the Progressives? What is the topic of the next chapter?

Know These Important Terms

Progressives	settlement houses
Progressive Movement	child labor laws
muckrakers	

Know the Main Idea

Here is the MAIN IDEA of this chapter.

Progressives worked to improve American government and American life. They showed Americans the problems of American life and tried to solve them.

Keep this MAIN IDEA in mind as you study the chapter. Ask yourself the following questions as you read. They will help you remember the MAIN IDEA.

1. In what way were the Progressives different from the Populists?
2. Name the newspaper man who had a great deal to do with getting improvements in city housing.
3. What activities were carried on at a settlement house?

THE YEARS OF THIS CHAPTER ARE 1890 TO 1920

1865   1890   1920

THE CHAPTER LESSON BEGINS HERE

The Rapid Growth of Industry Caused Problems

If you remember, after 1865, the United States rapidly grew into an industrial nation. This rapid growth of industry caused many changes in the United States. Many Americans moved to the large cities. Many large business companies were formed. And some businessmen made huge amounts of money.

But these changes in America after 1865 also brought many problems to the nation. Many states and cities had dishonest governments. The federal government and the state governments favored businessmen over farmers and workers. A few businessmen became very rich, while most workers earned low wages. Some large business companies formed trusts or monopolies. Thousands of people were forced to live in city slums.

Progressives Worked to Improve America

You may remember that the Populist Party wanted to improve conditions in America.

page 425

COLLIER'S WEEKLY

AN ILLVSTRATED
JOVRNAL OF

ART LITERATVRE &
CVRRENT EVENTS

COPYRIGHT 1898 BY PETER FENELON COLLIER   ALL RIGHTS RESERVED

VOL. TWENTY-ONE NO. 20   NEW YORK AUGUST 20 1898   PRICE TEN CENTS

Above, a cover from "Collier's Weekly." Many muckrakers wrote for "Collier's."

However, the Populist Party ended after the election of 1896. But by the late 1890's, many Americans were worried about what was happening to the governments of their cities and states. A group of Americans called the **Progressives** (pruh-GRESS-ivz) decided to try to work for better government in America. Progressives wanted the workers and the farmers to have more power in the government. They wanted the federal government and the state governments to stop favoring businessmen.

Progressives also wished to improve conditions in America. They felt city life had to be made better. They thought that workers must be paid better wages and have better working conditions. This movement for reform, or improvement, in America became known as the **Progressive Movement.** The Progressives took over many of the demands of the Populist Party. But unlike the Populists, the Progressives never formed a political party. Instead of working through political parties, Progressives brought their program right to the people themselves.

Progressives Wrote About Problems in America

The Progressives included some well-known writers who were called **muckrakers** (MUK-rayk-urz). The muckrakers wrote on many subjects. These writers gathered facts to show Americans that some business leaders and government leaders in cities and states were dishonest. The muckrakers then wrote about these things in magazines such as *McClure's* (muh-KLURZ) and *Collier's.*

Ida M. Tarbell showed how the Standard Oil Trust took control of the oil industry. Lincoln Steffens wrote about dishonest leaders in city governments and state governments. Other muckrakers wrote about the unfair practices of the railroads, banks, insurance companies, and meat packers.

Millions of Americans read about these things in these magazines. For the first time, many Americans learned about some of the serious problems of American life.

Progressives Wrote Many Books

In these years, many books were written which also showed Americans some of the problems of American life. Among the writers of protest novels, as these books were called, were Theodore Dreiser (DRY-sur), Frank Norris, Jack London, and Upton Sinclair. They wrote about life among the poor and showed how the poor were hurt by dishonest business practices.

Progressives Worked to Improve Housing

Progressives found many things that needed to be improved in the cities. In 1890, Jacob Riis (REES), a newspaperman, wrote a book called *How the Other Half Lives*. This book described how poor people lived in the large cities. It helped many Americans to learn how terrible the living conditions were in large cities.

The Progressives demanded that state governments do something to improve housing conditions. In 1901, the state of New York passed the first state law to regulate the building of apartment houses. The new law required buildings to have more windows, more running water, and fire escapes. By 1910, most of the other states also passed laws to regulate the building of apartment houses.

Progressives Tried to Help Immigrants

Many immigrants were not used to American ways. They found living in the United States very difficult. To help the immigrants, some Progressives opened **settlement houses** in city neighborhoods. The most famous settlement house, Hull House, was started in 1889 in Chicago, Illinois, by Jane Addams. By 1900, over fifty settlement houses were open in the cities of the Northeast and the Middle West.

Settlement houses were buildings where immigrants and their children went to school to learn American ways. Settlement houses helped prepare immigrants for American life. They ran playgrounds, children's nurseries, and English classes. Settlement houses also worked to improve the health and working conditions of the immigrants.

Finley Peter Dunne.

FINLEY PETER DUNNE— MUCKRAKER

Most of the muckrakers wrote very serious articles about the problems of American life. However, one exception was a muckraker named Finley Peter Dunne who wrote humorous articles about American problems. Dunne was born in Chicago in 1867, and he became a successful newspaperman. In 1893, he started to use a make-believe character called "Mr. Martin Dooley" in his articles. Dunne wrote over 700 articles in which "Mr. Dooley" told his opinions to his friend "Hennessey," another make-believe character.

"Mr. Dooley" was an Irish bartender who had strong opinions on almost every issue in American life. At first, his comments were about politics and government in the city of Chicago. But, beginning with the Spanish-American War, "Mr. Dooley" spoke about the affairs of the nation as well. These articles were so popular that Dunne reprinted some of them in a book called *Mr. Dooley in Peace and in War*. Later, Dunne published several other books using his "Mr. Dooley" articles. After 1906, however, Dunne started to write more serious articles. Very few "Mr. Dooley" articles were written after this time.

This picture shows Hull House, America's first settlement house. It was set up in Chicago to help immigrants learn about American life.

Progressives Helped Workers

Progressives also worked to improve working conditions for workers. They were able to get some states to pass laws which cut the work-day for women from twelve or fourteen hours to ten hours a day. Progressives also wanted laws to protect children working at jobs. In the early 1900's, most states began to pass **child labor laws.** These laws made it unlawful for factory owners to hire children under twelve years old. Progressives also worked to pass laws requiring factory owners to use safer machines and to pay workers who were hurt on the job.

Summing Up

Progressives were a group of Americans who worked to improve American government and American life. Progressives, called muckrakers, wrote about the problems of American life and helped Americans to learn about these problems. Progressives worked to improve city life. They helped improve housing and the lives of immigrants. They also helped improve working conditions for women and children. In the next chapter, you will find out how the Progressives worked to improve American government, and how black Americans tried to improve their lives.

AFTER YOU READ THE CHAPTER

Do You Know These Important Terms?

For each sentence below, choose the term that best completes the sentence.

1. A group of Americans in the early 1900's who decided to work for better government and to improve conditions in America were called (**Reformers/Progressives**).
2. The (**ashcanners/muckrakers**) were writers who gathered facts to show that some business leaders and government leaders were dishonest.
3. The movement for improvement in America was called the (**Reform/Progressive**) Movement.
4. Buildings where immigrants and their children went to school and learned American ways were called (**new hope/settlement**) houses.
5. (**Child labor/Juvenile**) laws made it unlawful to hire children under twelve years old to work in factories.

Do You Remember These People?

Tell something about each of the following persons.

Ida M. Tarbell	**Lincoln Steffens**
Theodore Dreiser	**Frank Norris**
Jack London	**Upton Sinclair**
Jacob Riis	**Jane Addams**

Do You Know When It Happened?

What are the years of this chapter? Explain why each of the following dates is important to the Progressive Movement.

1890   1889   1901

Discovering More About the Main Idea

Progressives worked to improve American government and American life. They showed Americans the problems of American life and tried to solve them.

Tell how each of the following developments is related to the MAIN IDEA.

Progressives never formed a political party. They took over many of the demands of the Populist Party and brought their program right to the people.

For the first time, many Americans learned about some of the serious problems of American life through the Progressive writers.

Progressives brought about many changes. They helped improve housing and working conditions, helped immigrants, and worked to protect children who worked.

Can You Discuss the Chapter?

Use the information you learned in this chapter to answer the following questions.

1. How did the Progressives bring their program to the American people?
2. What was the role of the muckrakers in the Progressive Movement? What things did they attack?
3. How did the book, *How the Other Half Lives,* affect housing conditions?
4. How did the Progressive Movement help immigrants? factory workers?
5. Explain how you might have felt about Jacob Riis' book if you lived in an apartment, were an apartment owner, a New York law maker, or a farmer.

Can You Connect the Past and the Present?

1. Muckraking was a new thing in the early 1900's. Today it is rather common. Has a writer or a reporter written about any serious problems in your community recently?
2. Compare the work laws for women and children at the present time in your community with the work laws for women and children in the early 1900's.

CHAPTER 69

Progressives Work for Better Government

Men voting by secret ballot.

BEFORE YOU BEGIN THE CHAPTER

Know What to Look For

1. Because of the writings of a number of muckrakers, in 1906 the government passed the Pure Food and Drug Act. Before this law was passed, some manufacturers sold harmful foods and medicines to the American people. Canned vegetables were sometimes treated with dangerous chemicals to make them look fresh. Animals were slaughtered and meat was packed in the most unbelievably dirty conditions. Also, some companies allowed spoiled meat to be packaged and sold. Some medicines, many of which were given to babies, contained alcohol, opium, or other dangerous things. After the Pure Food and Drug Act was passed, people were able to be sure that their food and their drugs were safe. In this chapter, you will read about how the Progressives made reforms in city and state governments and began to work to solve other problems of American life.

2. Read the title of the chapter. Then look through the chapter and read each heading. What did the Progressives try to improve?

3. Look at the pictures in the chapter and read each caption. What do the pictures tell you about the way that Progressives were trying to improve American government? Note also the time line at the beginning of the chapter. What years are included in this chapter? Compare this chapter time line to the unit time line on page 405.

4. Read the last part of the chapter called Summing Up. What other group of Americans worked to improve their lives?

Know These Important Terms

secret ballot   direct primary election
initiative   Nineteenth Amendment
referendum   Niagara Movement
recall   National Urban League
National Association for the
    Advancement of Colored People

Know the Main Idea

Here is the MAIN IDEA of this chapter.

Progressives worked to improve city and state governments. Women gained the right to vote, and black Americans formed groups to improve their lives and to work for their rights.

Keep this MAIN IDEA in mind as you study the chapter. Ask yourself the following questions as you read. They will help you remember the MAIN IDEA.

1. What city was among the first to break the power of the political machine?

2. What laws were passed which helped improve state governments?

3. What black leader disagreed with the ideas of Booker T. Washington?

THE YEARS OF THIS CHAPTER ARE 1890 TO 1920

1865	1890	1920

THE CHAPTER LESSON BEGINS HERE

Progressives Wanted to Improve City Government

When the Progressives tried to improve conditions in the cities, they often ran into trouble with the political machines. If you remember, in the 1890's and 1900's, political machines and political bosses controlled many city governments.

The Progressives tried to end the power of these political machines. Progressives knew that political machines got most of their money from business companies that supplied the city with such services as gas, electricity,

water, and streetcars. Therefore, the Progressives felt that the way to beat the political machines was to have the city take over the running of these services itself. The Progressive mayor of Cleveland, Tom Johnson, tried this plan and it worked. Without money, the political machine in Cleveland lost much of its power. Many other cities followed Cleveland's example and took over the running of services. As a result, the power of political machines was weakened.

Women voting in Wyoming in 1888. Wyoming was the first state to allow women to vote.

Progressives Worked to Free Cities from State Control

Progressives often found that a dishonest state government stopped them from improving conditions in the city. One of the first things Progressives did, therefore, was to work to have the states give city governments more self-government. This made it possible for cities to manage their own affairs instead of taking orders from state governments.

By 1914, the Progressives succeeded in getting many states to give their large cities the right to manage their own affairs. Many cities took advantage of this new freedom by trying to improve their city government.

Progressives Improved State Governments

The Progressives also found that political machines controlled the governments in many states. Progressives such as Robert La Follette, the governor of Wisconsin, helped to pass

important laws to break the power of these political machines in state governments. One of these laws required the use of the **secret ballot** for voting. Before this law was passed, voters had to tell a voting official what their vote was.

Another law set up the **direct primary election.** This law gave the voters the power to choose their own candidates for office. In many states, a new law set up the **initiative,** which gave people the right to suggest new laws to the state legislature. Still another law set up the **referendum,** which made it necessary for certain important laws to be approved by the voters before the laws were passed by the state legislature. And the **recall** gave the people the right to remove dishonest officials from state governments.

These laws greatly improved most state governments, and they weakened the political machines in most states. Most states also passed civil service laws. These laws set up civil service commissions to test people for government jobs. And most states began to regulate big businesses and force them to pay their fair share of state taxes.

Women Won the Right to Vote

The Progressive Movement also helped women to gain important rights. In the 1900's, American women still did not have the right to vote. Progressives worked hard to change this. Wyoming was the first state to allow women to vote. Other Western states followed Wyoming's example. And in 1920, all American women gained the right to vote when the **Nineteenth Amendment** to the Constitution was approved.

Black Americans Faced Difficult Problems

For a few years during the early 1890's, when the Populist Party was strong in the

South, black and white farmers worked together to improve their condition.

But when the Populist Party ended in the 1890's, white Southerners went back to the Democratic Party. Black Southerners were worse off than ever before. Segregation became more strict, and most black citizens lost their right to vote. When black Americans tried to demand their rights, some white Americans used force to stop them. In the 1880's and 1890's, some black citizens were even hanged without a trial.

Black Americans Tried to Help Themselves

During the 1890's and 1900's, many black Americans were trying to help themselves. In 1890, the Afro-American Council was formed to work to build up the power of black people in America. It encouraged the founding of businesses owned by black Americans.

During these years, W. E. B. Du Bois (doo-BOYS) became an important black leader. Du Bois, an important thinker, was a graduate of Harvard University and a professor, or teacher, at Atlanta University. Du Bois disagreed with the ideas of Booker T. Washington, another important black leader. Du Bois believed that black Americans must struggle for their rights and also improve their lives at the same time. In 1905, Du Bois and other black leaders founded the **Niagara** (Neye-AG-ruh) **Movement.** The Niagara Movement worked for full equal rights for black Americans.

Black Americans Formed Groups to Struggle for Their Rights

W. E. B. Du Bois and his followers joined with a group of white Progressives in 1909 and formed the **National Association for the Advancement of Colored People,** or the N.A.A.C.P. By 1914, the N.A.A.C.P. had 6

W. E. B. Du Bois edited the N.A.A.C.P.'s magazine, the "Crisis", for many years.

thousand members. The N.A.A.C.P. worked hard to win full rights for black citizens. It fought hard in the nation's courts to improve the conditions of the black Americans.

In 1911, the **National Urban League** was started. The Urban League was formed to help black Americans who moved into Northern cities to find jobs and to make the change to city life. In these years, many black workers moved to the cities.

Summing Up

Progressives worked to improve American city and state governments. They succeeded in winning voting rights for women. In these years, black Americans also worked to improve their lives. In the next chapters, which are in Unit 18, you will find out how Progressives worked to improve the nation's government.

AFTER YOU READ THE CHAPTER

Do You Know These Important Terms?

For each sentence below, choose the term that best completes the sentence.

1. A new method of voting was called the (secret/closed) ballot.
2. The (suggestion box/initiative) gave people the right to suggest new laws.
3. The (referendum/trial period) made it necessary for certain important laws to be approved by the voters.
4. The (retreat/recall) gave the people the right to remove dishonest officials.
5. The (N.A.A.C.P./N.R.A.) was formed by black Americans and white Progressives to win full rights for black citizens.
6. The (convention system/direct primary) election gave the voters the power to choose their own candidates for office.
7. Women gained the right to vote when the (Thirteenth/Nineteenth) Amendment to the Constitution was approved.
8. The (Chautauqua/Niagara) Movement was founded by black leaders to fight for full equal rights for black Americans.
9. The National (City/Urban) League was founded to help black Americans who moved into Northern cities.

Do You Remember These People?

Tell something about each of the following persons.

Tom Johnson   Robert La Follette
W. E. B. Du Bois   Booker T. Washington

Do You Know When It Happened?

What are the years of this chapter? In what ways are the following dates important to the Progressive Movement?

1890   1905   1909   1911   1920

Discovering More About the Main Idea

Progressives worked to improve city and state governments. Women gained the right to vote, and black Americans formed groups to improve their lives and to work for their rights.

Tell how each of the following developments is related to the MAIN IDEA.

By 1914, Progressives succeeded in getting many states to give their large cities the right to manage their own affairs.

New laws helped break the power of political machines.

Wyoming was the first state to allow women to vote. Other states soon followed.

W. E. B. Du Bois helped to form groups to help black Americans to gain their full rights.

Can You Discuss the Chapter?

Use the information you learned in this chapter to answer the following questions.

1. How did the Progressives succeed in breaking the power of political machines?
2. How did Progressives improve state governments?
3. What happened to black Americans in the years between 1890 and 1900?
4. How did black Americans try to help themselves?
5. If you had lived in the early 1900's, do you think you might have favored the views of W. E. B. Du Bois or Booker T. Washington?

Can You Connect the Past and the Present?

1. Does your state have laws for initiative, referendum, or recall? Under what circumstances were they most recently used?
2. Are the N.A.A.C.P. and the National Urban League active in your community? What other newer groups have similar goals?

The Progressives Reform the Nation

Robert La Follette, a leader of the Progressive Movement.

THE CHAPTERS IN UNIT 18 ARE

CHAPTER 70   President Roosevelt and the Square Deal
CHAPTER 71   The Nation Under President Taft
CHAPTER 72   President Wilson and the New Freedom

THE YEARS OF THIS UNIT ARE 1900 TO 1920

1800	1900	1920	1975

CHAPTER 70

President Roosevelt and the Square Deal

Theodore Roosevelt giving a campaign speech.

BEFORE YOU BEGIN THE CHAPTER

Know What to Look For

1. John Muir was a strong believer in conservation. He helped to set up Yosemite National Park, a beautiful park in California. President Theodore Roosevelt spent several days camping with John Muir at Yosemite. The President was very interested in Muir's views about conserving, or taking care of, the natural wonders and beauty of the American nation. Later, President Roosevelt made sure

that the government began to pass conservation laws to safeguard the resources of the nation.

President Roosevelt was a great champion of the Progressive Movement. Under his leadership, many Progressive ideas were passed into law. In this chapter, you will read more about President Roosevelt and the Progressive Movement.

2. Read the title of the chapter. Then look through the chapter and read each heading. Using only the headings, list the goals of the Progressives which President Roosevelt was able to do something about.

3. Look at the pictures in this chapter and read each caption. What do the pictures show you about Theodore Roosevelt as President? Note also the time line at the beginning of the chapter. What years are included in this chapter? Compare the chapter time line to the unit time line on page 435.

4. Read the last part of the chapter called Summing Up. What information does this paragraph contain about this chapter?

Know These Important Terms

Square Deal	Pure Food and Drug Act
Elkins Act	Meat Inspection Act
Hepburn Act	conservation

Know the Main Idea

Here is the MAIN IDEA of this chapter.

President Roosevelt was a great national leader of the Progressives. He helped to pass laws to improve life for many Americans.

Keep this MAIN IDEA in mind as you study the chapter. Ask yourself the following questions as you read. They will help you remember the MAIN IDEA.

1. How did Theodore Roosevelt become President in 1901? What did Roosevelt mean when he said he wanted to give all Americans a Square Deal?

2. In which strike did President Roosevelt show that he was going to be fair to workers?

3. What actions did President Roosevelt take to guard against wasting America's resources?

THE YEARS OF THIS CHAPTER ARE 1901 TO 1908

1900   1901   1908   1920

THE CHAPTER LESSON BEGINS HERE

Theodore Roosevelt Was a Strong President

President William McKinley was elected to serve a second term in 1900. But in 1901, President McKinley was shot, and Vice-President Theodore Roosevelt became President. Roosevelt was a colorful and popular President. The Progressives found a strong national leader in President Roosevelt. He helped to lead the Progressives in working for laws that were important to all Americans.

Theodore Roosevelt was a strong President. Roosevelt believed that the President must serve all the people of the United States. He also believed that the President had the right to do anything except those things that the Constitution forbade a President to do. When he became President, Roosevelt said he wished to give all Americans a **Square Deal.** He meant that he wanted the federal government to pass laws to help all Americans, not just certain groups of Americans.

Roosevelt Worked to Control the Trusts

President Roosevelt became known as a "trustbuster." He was called that because he worked to control several of the nation's

This cartoon shows President Roosevelt trying to "clean up," or reform, the trusts.

that the government was able to regulate, or control, big businesses and stop them from becoming too powerful. A Bureau of Corporations was formed to gather information about businesses in order to find out what laws were necessary to regulate businesses.

Roosevelt Regulated the Railroads

President Roosevelt's main concern was the need to regulate the railroads. In the early 1900's, many railroads still charged unfair rates and gave rebates to certain large businesses. President Roosevelt wanted a new law to give the Interstate Commerce Commission the right to regulate, or control, railroad rates.

In 1903, Congress passed the **Elkins Act.** This law made rebates unlawful. And in 1906, Congress passed the **Hepburn Act,** which gave the Interstate Commerce Commission the right to regulate the rates that railroads were allowed to charge.

Roosevelt Treated Workers Fairly

President Roosevelt also showed that he was going to be fair to the workingmen. In the spring of 1902, the coal miners went on strike to win a nine-hour working day and a raise in pay. The railroad companies who owned most of the mines refused even to talk with the strikers. By October, the strike was still not settled, and the nation faced the coming winter without coal for heat.

The mine owners demanded that President Roosevelt send federal troops to break the strike. President Roosevelt refused. Instead, he wanted to form a commission, or group of men, to settle the strike. When the mine owners refused this commission, Roosevelt warned them that he might send soldiers to operate the mines and take the coal for the government. The owners then agreed to let the commission settle the strike. The workers got a raise and a nine-hour workday. This was

biggest trusts, or monopolies. Roosevelt was able to get laws passed which broke up several of the largest trusts and the railroad monopoly as well.

But President Roosevelt was not against all trusts. He felt that some trusts were good for the nation. Only those trusts that produced fewer products and then raised prices had to be broken up. The other trusts were to be controlled by the government. Roosevelt felt the first time the government had protected the workers in a strike.

Congress Passed Laws About Food and Drugs

President Roosevelt was also concerned about the food, drinks, and medicines that were being sold. Many of these products contained harmful things. Therefore, President Roosevelt asked Congress to do something about this problem.

In 1906, Congress passed the **Pure Food and Drug Act.** This law required food and drug manufacturers doing business in more than one state to show on each package what their products contained. Congress also passed a **Meat Inspection Act** requiring that all fresh meat and all canned meat be checked by federal inspectors to make sure the meat was safe to eat. The Pure Food and Drug Act and the Meat Inspection Act helped to protect the health of Americans.

Roosevelt Worked to Save America's Soil and Forests

Another problem facing President Roosevelt was the problem of **conservation** (KAHN-sur-VAY-shun), or the wise use of America's

This picture shows a meat-packing plant. Before the Meat Inspection Act was passed, bad meat was sometimes sold.

Theodore Roosevelt at Yosemite National Park. Roosevelt was a strong believer in conservation, and he set up national conservation forests.

soil, forests, and mines. For years, lumber companies cut down trees and forests without replacing them. Americans were wasting rich soil, too. For example, sheep and cattle ate away the grass of the Great Plains, and much Western land turned into "dust bowls." And many mining companies were wasting America's rich supplies of coal, iron ore, and oil.

President Roosevelt was very concerned about this waste of America's resources. He asked Congress to set aside 150 million acres of public land as national conservation forests. Congress also voted money to build several large dams to provide water for dry Western lands. President Roosevelt made Americans realize how important the conservation of the nation's natural resources was.

Roosevelt Served Two Terms as President

Theodore Roosevelt was easily elected President in the election of 1904. But President Roosevelt believed that two terms were enough for any President. Therefore, he refused to run again in the election of 1908.

Summing Up

The Progressives found a great national leader in Theodore Roosevelt. Under Roosevelt, Congress passed laws to control trusts, to regulate the railroads, to safeguard food and drugs, and to save America's natural resources. In the next chapter, you will find out what happened when William Howard Taft became President.

AFTER YOU READ THE CHAPTER

Do You Know these Important Terms?

For each sentence below, choose the term that best completes the sentence.

1. President Roosevelt's program to have the federal government pass laws to help all Americans was called the (New/Square) Deal.
2. The (Pennsylvania/Elkins) Act made railroad rebates unlawful.
3. The (Hepburn/Carrier Rate) Act gave the Interstate Commerce Commission the right to regulate the rates railroads might charge.
4. The (Pure Food and Drug/Sanitary Commodity) Act required food and medicine manufacturers to show what their products contained.
5. All fresh and canned meat had to be checked by federal inspectors to be sure it was safe to eat after the (Federal Inspection/Meat Inspection) Act was passed.
6. The wise use of America's soil, forests, and mines is called (preservation/conservation).

Do You Remember These People?

Tell something about each of the following persons.

William McKinley   Theodore Roosevelt
William Howard Taft

Do You Know When It Happened?

What are the years of this chapter? Place the following events in the order in which they occurred.

Theodore Roosevelt was elected President.
The Pure Food and Drug Act was passed by Congress.
The Square Deal program was begun.
President McKinley was shot.
The coal miners' strike was settled.

Discovering More About the Main Idea

President Roosevelt was a great national leader of the Progressives. He helped to pass laws to improve life for many Americans.

Tell how each of the following developments is related to the MAIN IDEA.

Theodore Roosevelt became President after President McKinley was shot and killed. Roosevelt started his Square Deal program.

President Roosevelt was able to control the trusts, regulate the railroads, and to help workers.

Under Roosevelt's leadership, food and drugs became safe to use, and a conservation program was started to safeguard American resources.

Can You Discuss the Chapter?

Use the information you learned in this chapter to answer the following questions.

1. Why didn't President Roosevelt break up all the trusts and monopolies?
2. How was President Roosevelt able to have the federal government get greater control over the railroads?
3. How did President Roosevelt show that he was going to be fair to workers?
4. Why was conservation necessary in a huge country with so many resources?

Can You Connect the Past and the Present?

1. Are there any conservation areas or projects near your community? Explain the purpose of these projects. Do you think they are successful?
2. America still has difficulty in the area of pure food and drugs. What recent incidents in your community or even in the nation have involved pure food or drugs?

CHAPTER 71

The Nation Under President Taft

William Howard Taft (at right) campaigning for the Presidency.

BEFORE YOU BEGIN THE CHAPTER

Know What to Look For

1. In many ways, Theodore Roosevelt was a remarkable man. As a young boy he was sickly and had poor eyesight. But Roosevelt rebuilt his body by will power. He taught himself how to ride a horse, shoot, and box. From 1882 to 1884, he served as a representative in the New York Assembly. After this, he bought a ranch in the West and learned to be a cowboy and buffalo hunter.

During the Spanish American War he commanded the famous Rough Riders. Roosevelt hunted big game in Africa and wrote over thirty books. He won the Nobel Peace Prize for helping to end a war. He started the United States Air Force in 1909 when he purchased an airplane for the army. He was the first President to ride in an automobile.

Roosevelt was a man of many talents and

page 442

interests. But he was also a man of action. When he was followed by William Howard Taft as President, many people felt that President Taft had let the Progressives down.

2. Read the title of the chapter. Then look through the chapter and read each heading. Who was elected President in 1912?

3. Look at the pictures in the chapter and read each caption. Name the Presidents who are shown in the chapter pictures. Note also the time line at the beginning of the chapter. What years are included in the chapter? Compare the time line for this chapter with the unit time line on page 435.

4. Read the last part of the chapter called Summing Up. Why did the Republicans lose the election of 1912?

Know These Important Terms
Mann-Elkins Act
Sixteenth Amendment
Seventeenth Amendment
Bull Moose Party

Know the Main Idea
Here is the MAIN IDEA of this chapter.
President Taft turned many Progressive ideas into law. However, he did not carry out enough of their ideas to please the Progressives.

Keep this MAIN IDEA in mind as you study the chapter. Ask yourself the following questions as you read. They will help you remember the MAIN IDEA.

1. What view did William Howard Taft have of the Presidency? Was this the same view that Theodore Roosevelt had?

2. What industries did the Mann-Elkins Act give the Interstate Commerce Commission the power to regulate?

3. Name the candidates in the election of 1912.

THE YEARS OF THIS CHAPTER ARE 1908 TO 1912

| 1900 | 1908 | 1912 | 1920 |

THE CHAPTER LESSON BEGINS HERE

Taft Was Elected President in 1908
Theodore Roosevelt suggested that the Republicans choose William Howard Taft, his Secretary of War, as their candidate for President in 1908. Roosevelt was sure that Taft believed in Progressive ideas. The Democratic candidate was once again William Jennings Bryan. During the campaign, the Republicans promised to lower the tariff, to regulate big businesses, and to continue the conservation of natural resources. In the election of 1908, Taft won over Bryan by more than 1 million votes.

William Howard Taft was not at all like Theodore Roosevelt. Taft was not a strong leader. He was slow in making up his mind. And most important of all, Taft had a different view of the Presidency from that of Roosevelt. Taft believed that the President must only do those things that the Constitution required a President to do. As a result, President Taft was not able to carry out all of the important ideas favored by Roosevelt and the Progressives.

Taft Let the Progressives Down
One of the first things the Progressives

page 443

This cartoon called "Mary had a Little Lamb" shows Roosevelt (Mary) choosing Taft (the lamb) as his candidate for the election of 1908.

tried to do was to lower the tariff. They succeeded in getting a lower tariff approved by the House of Representatives. But the Senate refused to accept this tariff law, and it passed a higher tariff. Although Taft talked the Senate into lowering the tariff on a few goods, the new tariff was higher than the old one. The Progressives felt Taft had let them down.

Many Progressives were also upset with President Taft because of the way he handled conservation. Taft allowed some valuable lands that President Roosevelt set aside as conservation forests to be sold. As a result, many Progressives believed that President Taft was not interested in conservation. However, during his term in office, President Taft

did help conservation. He stopped the federal government from selling public coal lands to business companies. He also added much land to the nation's conservation parks.

In 1910, the Progressives in the House of Representatives tried to end the great power of Joseph Cannon, the Speaker of the House of Representatives. Cannon used his power in the House of Representatives to fight most Progressive ideas and laws. The Progressives were not able to end Cannon's power completely, but they were able to take certain powers away from him. Once again, Progressives were angry at President Taft, because he had refused to support them in their effort to take away Cannon's power.

Progressive Laws Were Passed

In spite of the problems that developed between President Taft and the Progressives, many important laws were passed during Taft's term of office. Congress passed the **Mann-Elkins Act** giving the Interstate Commerce Commission the power to regulate telephone and telegraph companies. Congress also approved the **Sixteenth Amendment** and **Seventeenth Amendment** to the Constitution. The Sixteenth Amendment gave the federal government the right to pass an income tax law. The Seventeenth Amendment gave the voters, rather than the state legislatures, the power to elect United States Senators. President Taft backed both these amendments.

Taft Broke up Important Trusts

Under President Taft, many other Progressive ideas were passed into law. Congress passed a law to open postal savings banks for people with small savings accounts. Congress also passed a bill setting up the parcel post system of delivering packages. Parcel post was a cheap way for people to send packages.

More trusts were broken up by President Taft than by President Roosevelt. In 1911, two large trusts, the Standard Oil Company and the American Tobacco Company, were broken up. The government also brought almost eighty business companies to court because of unfair practices.

Roosevelt Broke with Taft

In the election of 1910, the Democrats won control of the House of Representatives and cut down the number of Republicans in the Senate. The Progressives—most of whom were Republicans—blamed these losses on President Taft. They formed the National Progressive Republican League to fight for a Progressive as the Republican candidate for President in 1912.

A cartoon about the Bull Moose Party.

STRONG AS A BULL MOOSE

By 1911, Theodore Roosevelt felt that his old friend, William Howard Taft, had let the Progressives down. Roosevelt was upset because he had helped to get Taft elected as President in 1908. Roosevelt felt that Taft had taken the side of the conservative Republicans rather than of the Progressive Republicans, especially on the issues of the tariff and conservation.

Theodore Roosevelt did not want to run for President, but he did not want Taft to be re-elected. As a result, Roosevelt decided to be a candidate in the election of 1912. Roosevelt felt that he had a better chance of winning the election than either Taft or Senator Robert La Follette, the other possible Republican candidate. But Roosevelt was too late. Taft was the leader of the Republican Party, and he won the Republican nomination at the convention in June, 1912.

Roosevelt then formed his own political party—the Progressive, or "Bull Moose" Party. It received this name because Roosevelt boasted that he was as strong as a "Bull Moose." Over 4 million Americans voted for Roosevelt. This was 600 thousand more votes than Taft received. But Woodrow Wilson, the Democrat, received over 6 million votes and was elected President.

Roosevelt giving a speech to a gathering of the Bull Moose Party. Roosevelt was the candidate of the Bull Moose Party in 1912.

At first, the Progressives backed Senator Robert La Follette of Wisconsin. However, Theodore Roosevelt was very unhappy with President Taft. He felt that Taft had not carried out enough Progressive ideas. Also, he was angry because Taft tried to break up the trusts instead of trying to regulate, or control, the trusts. Finally, Roosevelt agreed to be a candidate for President in the election of 1912.

Wilson Was Elected President in 1912

But President Taft wanted to run for another term. And the Republican Party chose Taft to run again. As a result, the Progressives left the Republican Party and formed a new party—the **Bull Moose Party,** or the Progressive Party. Roosevelt was the candidate of the Bull Moose Party. In the campaign, Roosevelt promised to regulate big businesses, to end child labor, to give all workers a fair wage, and to allow women to vote.

The Democrats chose Woodrow Wilson, the governor of New Jersey, as their candidate. He favored a lower tariff and the breaking up of trusts rather than regulating them. As a result of the split in the Republican vote, Woodrow Wilson was elected President in 1912.

Summing Up

President Taft turned many Progressive ideas into law. But he did not carry out enough of their ideas to please the Progressives. In the election of 1912, the Republican Party split, and the Progressives formed a new political party—the Bull Moose Party. Woodrow Wilson, a Democrat, defeated the regular Republican candidate, President Taft, and Theodore Roosevelt, the Progressive candidate. In the next chapter, you will find out about Wilson's years as President.

AFTER YOU READ THE CHAPTER

Do You Know These Important Terms?

For each sentence below, choose the term that best completes the sentence.

1. The (**Mann-Elkins/Federal Communications**) Act gave the Interstate Commerce Commission the power to regulate telephone and telegraph companies.
2. The (**Fifteenth/Sixteenth**) Amendment gave the federal government the right to pass an income tax law.
3. The (**Eighteenth/Seventeenth**) Amendment gave the voters the power to elect United States Senators.
4. The third party, which was made up mainly of Progressives who left the Republican Party, was called the (**Great Bear/Bull Moose**) Party.

Do You Remember These People?

Tell something about each of the following persons.

William Jennings Bryan   Joseph Cannon
William Howard Taft   Woodrow Wilson
Theodore Roosevelt   Robert La Follette

Can You Locate These Places?

Use the map on page 390 to locate the following places.

Wisconsin   **New Jersey**

How did these two states relate to the events of this chapter? Look at a map which shows some of the national parks of our nation.

Do You Know When It Happened?

What are the years of this chapter? Place the following events in the order in which they occurred.

Progressives tried to end the power of Joseph Cannon.

The Bull Moose Party was formed.

Woodrow Wilson was elected President.

Roosevelt completed his term as President.

Discovering More About the Main Idea

President Taft turned many Progressive ideas into law. However, he did not carry out enough of their ideas to please the Progressives.

Tell how each of the following developments is related to the MAIN IDEA.

President Taft was not as strong a leader as Roosevelt was. Progressives felt Taft let them down.

President Taft increased the powers of the Interstate Commerce Commission, supported the Sixteenth and Seventeenth Amendments, and broke up many trusts.

In the election of 1912, President Taft lost the support of the Progressives.

Can You Discuss the Chapter?

Use the information you learned in this chapter to answer the following questions.

1. Why did the Progressives feel that President Taft had let them down?
2. What were some of the Progressive laws that were passed under President Taft?
3. How was President Taft a greater trust buster than was Theodore Roosevelt?
4. Do you feel the Progressives were right in thinking President Taft let them down?

Can You Connect the Past and the Present?

1. In this chapter, you have seen the difference between a strong and a weaker leader in the Presidency. Have you ever been connected with an activity where the type of leader has made a difference?
2. The effect of a third political party was again shown in the election of 1912. Have splits in political parties ever had an effect on the elections in your community?

CHAPTER 72

President Wilson and the New Freedom

President Woodrow Wilson and Mrs. Wilson.

BEFORE YOU BEGIN THE CHAPTER

Know What to Look For

1. In the years after 1865, the Republican Party was the main political party in the nation. This means that more Republicans were elected to office in these years than Democrats. Of the ten men who served as President between 1865 and 1912, only Grover Cleveland was a Democrat. In 1912, another Democratic President was elected.

In the last two chapters, you have read about the Progressives and two Republican Presidents, Theodore Roosevelt and William Howard Taft, who worked to have the ideas of the Progressives passed into law. However, the Progressive Movement was not just a movement among Republicans. It was also supported by many Democrats . Woodrow

Wilson, a Democrat who was elected as President in 1912, continued to follow the ideas of the Progressives. In this chapter, you will read about Woodrow Wilson and his actions as President.

2. Read the title of the chapter. Then look through the chapter and read each heading. Using only the headings, what were some ideas of the Progressive Movement which President Wilson was able to help pass into law?

3. Look at the pictures in the chapter and read each caption. Who is shown in the opening chapter picture? Note also the time line at the beginning of the chapter. What are the years of this chapter? Compare the time line for this chapter with the unit time line on page 435.

4. Read the last part of the chapter called Summing Up. Make up a list of Wilson's plans for the nation that were passed into law between 1913 and 1917. What will you read about in the next chapters?

Know These Important Terms
New Freedom
Federal Reserve Act
Federal Reserve System
Clayton Anti-Trust Act
Federal Trade Commission Act
Federal Farm Loan Act

Know the Main Idea
Here is the MAIN IDEA of this chapter.

Most of President Woodrow Wilson's plans for the nation, called the New Freedom, were passed into law between 1913 and 1917.

Keep this MAIN IDEA in mind as you study the chapter. Ask yourself the following questions as you read. They will help you remember the MAIN IDEA.

1. Who had to pay the new federal income tax?

2. What two things did the Clayton Anti-Trust Act forbid big business companies to do?

3. What did President Wilson and the labor unions disagree about?

THE YEARS OF THIS CHAPTER ARE 1912 TO 1920

1900	1912	1920

THE CHAPTER LESSON BEGINS HERE

Wilson Was a Strong Leader

Woodrow Wilson's plans for the nation's government were named the **New Freedom**. The New Freedom called for lowering the tariff, improving the nation's money system, helping farmers and workers, and cutting down the power of big business companies.

President Wilson, like Theodore Roosevelt, believed that the President must be a strong leader. He often spoke directly to Congress to ask its members to pass laws that he felt to be important. Congress was now controlled

by Democrats and, therefore, most of Wilson's program was passed into law.

Congress Lowered the Tariff and Passed an Income Tax

In 1913, Wilson asked Congress to lower the tariff. Congress lowered the tariff, or tax on goods brought into the United States from other nations, for the first time since the Civil War. At the same time that the tariff was lowered, a federal income tax law was passed.

Americans getting information on how to fill out the first income tax forms.

This law required all Americans who earned over 3 thousand dollars a year to pay a federal income tax. Under this law, people with large incomes paid higher taxes than people with low incomes.

America's Banking System Was Improved

President Wilson felt that the banking system of the United States was not working well. The banking system was controlled by a few important bankers who controlled it for their own good rather than the good of the nation. To solve this problem, Wilson asked Congress to pass the **Federal Reserve Act.**

The Federal Reserve Act of 1913 set up the **Federal Reserve System** to regulate the nation's money and banking. Twelve Federal Reserve Banks were set up in the United States. These banks only did business with other banks. Banks were able to put money

into, or borrow money from, the Federal Reserve Banks. Federal Reserve Banks also issued paper money and handled the federal government's money affairs. A Federal Reserve Board regulated, or controlled, the entire system. The Federal Reserve Act greatly improved America's banking system and is still in operation today.

President Wilson Tried to Regulate the Trusts

President Wilson also took steps to regulate the trusts, or big business companies that controlled an entire industry. The Sherman Anti-Trust Act of 1890 was supposed to control trusts, but this law failed because it did not list clearly the things business companies were forbidden to do. Therefore, in 1914, Congress passed two laws, the **Clayton Anti-Trust Act** and the **Federal Trade Commission Act.** The purpose of these two acts was to end the control of any industry by a few business companies.

The Clayton Anti-Trust Act clearly listed the things big business companies were not allowed to do, such as fixing the prices for an entire industry. And it forbade one man to be head of two companies which were in the same business. The Clayton Act also limited the use of injunctions, or court orders, to stop strikes. Injunctions were only to be used to stop a strike if the strike was a danger to property.

The Federal Trade Commission Act set up a five-man commission to see that the Clayton Anti-Trust Act was obeyed. Any company that failed to obey the Clayton Anti-Trust Act was to be brought to court. The Federal Trade Commission was very active during its first few years. It forced many business companies to end their unfair practices. The Federal Trade Commission also helped to break up a few trusts.

Above, young workers in a textile factory are shown on strike. President Wilson tried to end child labor.

Wilson Helped the Farmers

President Wilson wanted to help the farmers solve their problems. The American farmers' greatest problem was their need for money to carry on their farm businesses. Most farmers were not able to borrow money from banks because banks charged very high rates of interest on loans. Interest is the fee charged for lending money. President Wilson asked Congress to pass the **Federal Farm Loan Act,** which set up special banks to provide easy loans to farmers.

Wilson Helped the Workers

President Wilson's New Freedom program also helped American workers. Earlier in this chapter, you read about the Clayton Act and how it limited the use of injunctions, or court orders, against unions. Later, Congress passed a law that improved working conditions for seamen. Congress also passed another law that gave railroad workers an eight-hour workday. This law helped to prevent a nationwide railroad strike.

President Wilson also tried to end the hiring of children in factories and mines. Congress passed a law against child labor, but the Supreme Court declared this law unconstitutional.

Wilson and the labor unions, however, differed on allowing immigrants into the United States. The unions wanted all immigrants to pass a literacy, or reading, test before they were allowed to enter the United States. Congress passed a law that made immigrants pass a literacy test before they were allowed into the United States in 1915. But President Wilson vetoed this law. However, in 1917, Congress passed this law over President Wilson's veto.

Summing Up

Most of Wilson's plans for the nation, called the New Freedom, were passed into law between 1913 and 1917. The tariff was lowered, and an income tax law was passed. A new banking system was set up. Laws were passed to control the power of the trusts. And American farmers and workers were helped. In the next chapters, which are in Unit 19, you will learn how the United States dealt with other nations between 1865 and 1920.

AFTER YOU READ THE CHAPTER

Do You Know These Important Terms?

1. President Wilson's plans for the nation's government were called the (Square Deal/New Freedom).
2. The (Federal Reserve/National Banking) Act greatly improved the banking system of the United States.
3. Twelve banks which serve as banks for all other banks are part of the (Federal Reserve/National Security)System.
4. The (Sherman/Clayton) Anti-Trust Act clearly listed the things business companies were not allowed to do.
5. The (Trust/Federal) Trade Commission Act set up a group of men to see that businesses obeyed the new anti-trust law.
6. The (Federal Farm Loan/Farmers' Trust) Act set up special banks to provide easy loans to farmers.

Do You Remember These People?

Tell something about each of the following persons.

Theodore Roosevelt   Woodrow Wilson
William Howard Taft

Do You Know When It Happened?

What are the years of this chapter? Place the following events in the order in which they occurred.

The Clayton Anti-Trust Act was passed by Congress.

President Wilson vetoed the immigrant literacy law.

The Federal Reserve System was established.

Congress passed a law that made immigrants pass a literacy test over President Wilson's veto.

President Wilson announced his New Freedom Program.

page 452

Discovering More About the Main Idea

Most of President Woodrow Wilson's plans for the nation, called the New Freedom, were passed into law between 1913 and 1917.

Tell how each of the following developments is related to the MAIN IDEA.

Congress lowered the tariff and passed a federal income tax law.

The Federal Reserve System was set up to regulate the nation's banking system.

New anti-trust laws helped regulate the big business companies that controlled an entire industry.

Can You Discuss the Chapter?

Use the information you learned in this chapter to answer the following questions.

1. How was the federal income tax different from most taxes that were in effect before 1913?
2. How did the Federal Reserve System improve America's banking system?
3. Why did the Sherman Anti-Trust Act of 1890 fail to control trusts? How was this corrected?
4. How did President Wilson try to help farmers and workers?
5. If you had lived in the early 1900's might you have favored the unions' or President Wilson's views on immigration? Why?

Can You Connect the Past and the Present?

1. Many Presidents have names for their plans for the nation such as Square Deal or New Freedom. Does the President's plan for the nation today have a name?
2. Do immigrants need to pass a literacy test today? Do you agree with this idea of a literacy test for immigrants?

The United States and the World

Theodore Roosevelt and the Rough Riders.

THE CHAPTERS IN UNIT 19 ARE

CHAPTER 73   The United States and the World, 1865–1900
CHAPTER 74   The Spanish-American War
CHAPTER 75   The United States and the World, 1900–1917
CHAPTER 76   The United States Enters World War One
CHAPTER 77   Fighting World War One
CHAPTER 78   Peace-Making After World War One

THE YEARS OF THIS UNIT ARE 1865 TO 1921

1800	1865	1921	1975

The United States and the World, 1865-1900

A cartoon about America and the Monroe Doctrine.

BEFORE YOU BEGIN THE CHAPTER

Know What to Look For

1. Many Americans laughed when the American Secretary of State William Seward purchased Alaska from Russia in 1867 for over 7 million dollars. They called Alaska "Seward's Folly" or "Seward's Icebox." About thirty years later, however, Americans began to realize what a great bargain they had made.

In 1897, gold was discovered in Alaska. A great gold rush started. Thousands of men came to Alaska and struggled across the dangerous Chilkoot Pass to get to the Yukon, where the gold was located. Many died on the way. Some struck it rich.

At this same time, some of the nations of Europe were building overseas empires. Some Americans now felt that the United States should also acquire overseas territories. In this chapter, you will read about the United States and its dealings with foreign nations in the years after the Civil War.

2. Read the title of the chapter. Then look through the chapter and read each heading. List some ways in which the United States became involved in world affairs.

3. Look at the pictures in the chapter and read each caption. What do the pictures show you about American dealings with foreign nations? Look at the map on page 456. What color is used to show overseas territories of the United States? Note also the time line at the beginning of the chapter. What years are included in this chapter? Compare this chapter time line to the unit time line on page 453.

4. Read the last part of the chapter called Summing Up. What territories did America acquire? What is the topic of the next chapter?

Know This Important Term
Pan-American Conferences

Know the Main Idea

Here is the MAIN IDEA of this chapter.

Between 1865 and 1900, the United States was becoming an important nation in the world. The nation gained new overseas territories and backed the Monroe Doctrine.

Keep this MAIN IDEA in mind as you study the chapter. Ask yourself the following questions as you read. They will help you remember the MAIN IDEA.

1. What action did the United States take toward the French in Mexico?

2. Why did the United States become interested in the islands in the Pacific Ocean?

3. When did Hawaii become a part of the United States?

THE YEARS OF THIS CHAPTER ARE 1865 TO 1900

1865   1900   1921

THE CHAPTER LESSON BEGINS HERE

The United States Helped Mexico

You may remember that in 1823 President Monroe warned the nations of Europe to stay out of the New World. Until the 1860's, the United States was able to back up this doctrine. But while the American nation was fighting the Civil War, France set up its own government in Mexico.

French troops overthrew the government of the Mexican leader Benito Juarez (HWAH-rays) and made the Austrian archduke Maximilian (MAX-suh-MIL-yun) the emperor, or ruler, of Mexico. President Lincoln did not try to stop France because American troops were needed in the Civil War. But as soon as the Civil War ended, the United States was ready to enforce the Monroe Doctrine. The United States sent 50 thousand American soldiers to the Mexican border. The French government did not want a war with the United States. Therefore, France removed its troops from Mexico, and in 1867, Mexico was again an independent nation.

The United States and Great Britain Settled a Problem

During the Civil War, Great Britain built several warships for the South. One of these warships, the "Alabama," destroyed many

Northern ships. After the war, the United States wanted Great Britain to pay for the damage done by the "Alabama." Both countries agreed to have a five-man commission decide how much money Great Britain was to pay to the United States. In 1872, the commission decided that Great Britain owed the United States over 15 million dollars.

The United States Bought Alaska

In 1865, the United States stretched from the Atlantic Ocean to the Pacific Ocean and from Canada to Mexico. Some Americans wanted the nation to grow even larger. They wanted the United States to take over Cuba and other islands in the Caribbean. But the American government did not do so.

However, in 1867, William Seward, the Secretary of State, was able to talk Congress into buying Alaska from Russia for over 7 million dollars. Many Americans felt this was a waste of money and called Alaska "Seward's Icebox." But buying Alaska turned out to be one of the best deals ever made by the United States. In the 1890's, gold was discovered in the area of the Yukon River in Alaska. And Alaska also has rich supplies of fish, furs, lumber, coal, and oil.

The United States Became More Friendly with Latin America

During the 1880's, the United States became interested in working together with the nations of Latin America. Latin America includes all the nations of Central America and South America. Several **Pan-American Conferences,** or meetings with the Latin American nations, were held after 1889. These meetings

NEW OVERSEAS TERRITORIES OF THE UNITED STATES

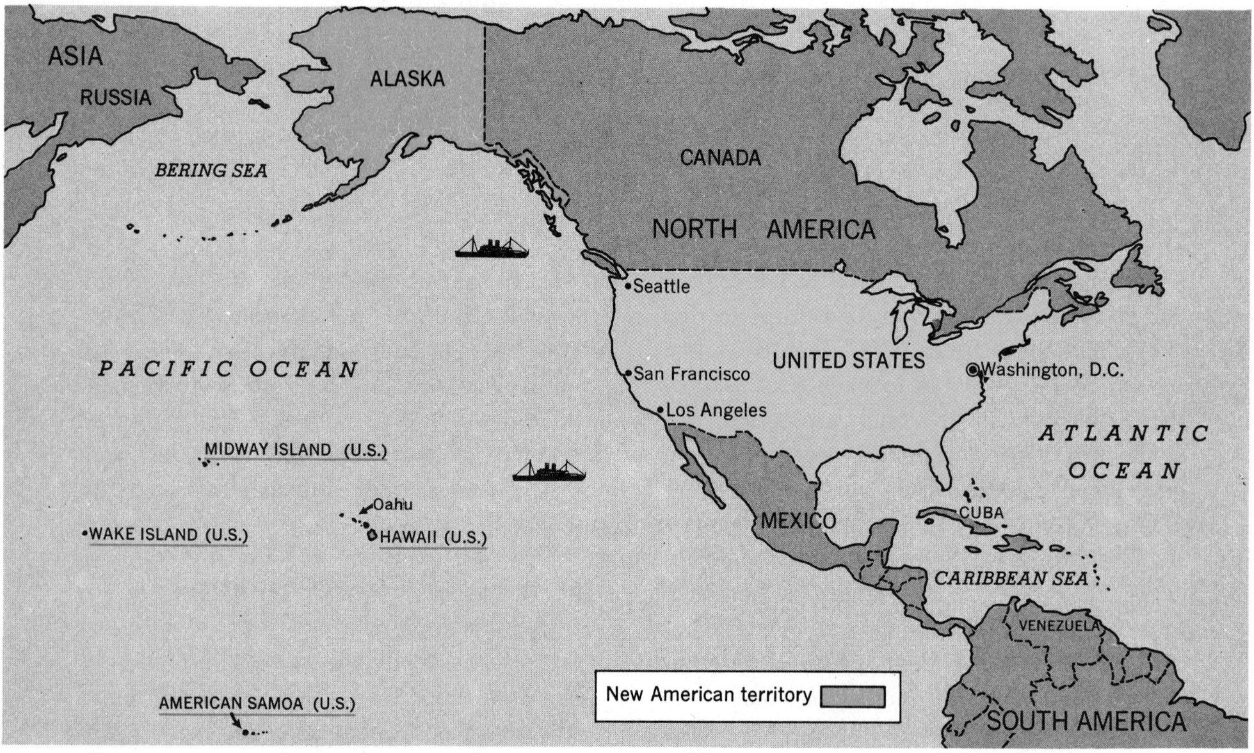

ASIA
RUSSIA
ALASKA
BERING SEA
CANADA
NORTH AMERICA
•Seattle
PACIFIC OCEAN
•San Francisco
UNITED STATES
⊙Washington, D.C.
•Los Angeles
ATLANTIC OCEAN
MIDWAY ISLAND (U.S.)
↗Oahu
•WAKE ISLAND (U.S.)
⬙HAWAII (U.S.)
MEXICO
CUBA
CARIBBEAN SEA
VENEZUELA
AMERICAN SAMOA (U.S.)
New American territory
SOUTH AMERICA

This picture shows the delegates to the first Pan-American Conference in 1889. This meeting was held to encourage friendship and trade.

helped to develop trade and friendship between the United States and the Latin American nations.

The United States Became Interested in the Pacific Ocean

In the late 1800's, the United States also became interested in the islands of the Pacific Ocean. Many of these islands were important to the United States because American trading ships and naval ships needed places where they were able to stop and pick up coal, water, and other supplies. During the 1870's, the United States won the right to have a naval base on the island of Samoa (suh-MOH-uh). And in 1899, the Samoan Islands were divided between the United States and Germany. The United States also took over Wake Island and Midway Island.

Hawaii Became a Part of the United States

Americans were also very much interested in the Hawaiian Islands. Many trading ships visited Hawaii, and as the years went by, the United States built up many ties with Hawaii. After 1865, thousands of Americans settled in the Hawaiian Islands. And American businessmen spent millions of dollars building up Hawaiian sugar plantations.

American businessmen became very important in the government of Hawaii. The Hawaiian people, however, were upset because much of the power and wealth of Hawaii was being taken by the Americans. Therefore, in 1893, Queen Liliuokalani (lee-LEE-woh-kah-LAH-nee) tried to force American businessmen to give up their sugar plantations.

Americans in Hawaii then revolted against

Queen Liliuokalani ruled Hawaii before it became part of the United States.

the queen. They asked the United States to take over Hawaii. However, President Grover Cleveland turned down their request. For several years, Americans in Hawaii tried unsuccessfully to have Hawaii become a part of the United States. Finally in 1898, Congress voted to bring Hawaii into the United States as a territory.

The United States Helped Venezuela Settle a Dispute with Great Britain

In 1895, the United States once again backed the Monroe Doctrine. The cause of the problem was the boundary between British Guiana (gee-AN-uh) and Venezuela (VEN-uh-ZWAY-luh). Great Britain and Venezuela had argued over this boundary ever since the British took over Guiana in 1814. Finally in 1895, Venezuela asked the United States for help. The United States wanted to form a commission to decide the boundary between British Guiana and Venezuela, but Great Britain refused.

President Cleveland threatened to appoint an American commission to decide the boundary. He made it clear that the United States was ready to fight for this new boundary if necessary. Great Britain gave in and agreed to allow a special commission to decide the boundary.

Summing Up

Between 1865 and 1900, the United States was becoming an important nation in the world. The United States backed the Monroe Doctrine in 1867 when it helped Mexico free itself from French control. America bought Alaska and also acquired Hawaii and some other Pacific islands. And the United States helped Venezuela with its boundary problem with Great Britain. The next chapter tells about a war between the United States and Spain.

AFTER YOU READ THE CHAPTER

Do You Know This Important Term?

Explain the meaning of the following term and use it in a sentence.

Pan-American Conferences

Do You Remember These People?

Tell something about each of the following persons.

Benito Juarez	Maximilian
Abraham Lincoln	William Seward
Liliuokalani	Grover Cleveland

Can You Locate These Places?

Use the map on page 456 to do the following map work.

1. Locate the United States. Also locate the nation of Mexico. Why should the United States be interested in what happens in Mexico?
2. Locate Alaska. Between what two large nations is it located? Compare the size of Alaska with that of the United States.
3. Locate American Samoa in the Pacific Ocean. What other islands or island groups are territories of the United States? Which group of islands appears to be the largest? Which is closest to the United States?
4. Locate Venezuela. What problem developed between Venezuela and Great Britain?

Do You Know When It Happened?

What are the years of this chapter? Place the following events in the order in which they occurred.

Gold was discovered in Alaska.

The United States established a naval base on Samoa.

Hawaii became a part of the United States.

The United States purchased Alaska.

Americans revolted against Queen Liliuokalani.

Discovering More About the Main Idea

Between 1865 and 1900, the United States was becoming an important nation in the world. The nation gained new overseas territories and backed the Monroe Doctrine.

Tell how each of the following developments is related to the MAIN IDEA.

The United States forced France to remove its troops from Mexico, made a settlement with Britain about war claims, and helped Venezuela settle a boundary dispute with Great Britain.

The United States purchased Alaska and took over several Pacific islands. In 1898, Hawaii became a part of the United States.

The United States became interested in working together with the nations of Latin America.

Can You Discuss the Chapter?

Use the information you learned in this chapter to answer the following questions.

1. How was France able to set up its own government in Mexico?
2. Why did the United States arrange to hold several Pan-American Conferences?
3. Why did Hawaii want to become a part of the United States?
4. How did the United States show that it was going to enforce the Monroe Doctrine?

Can You Connect the Past and the Present?

1. As you know, Alaska and Hawaii are now states in the United States. What is the present position of Samoa?
2. The Pan-American Conferences were early trys at developing friendship and cooperation among American nations. What group does this today?

CHAPTER 74

The Spanish-American War

American soldiers storming San Juan Hill in Cuba.

BEFORE YOU BEGIN THE CHAPTER

Know What to Look For

1. During the Spanish-American War, more American soldiers died from the disease yellow fever than they did from the fighting in the war. Dr. Walter Reed and three other army doctors were sent to Cuba to try to find out what caused this terrible disease. After some study, the doctors soon came to believe that the disease was carried by certain mos-

quitoes. Brave volunteers as well as two of the doctors allowed themselves to be bitten by the mosquitoes. All of them got the fever. All of them got well except for one of the doctors who died in a few days.

Once it was known that the mosquito caused the disease, a gigantic clean up plan to get rid of the mosquitoes began. Soon, yellow fever was almost wiped out. This victory was even greater than the victory in the Spanish-American War, which you will read about in this chapter.

2. Read the title of the chapter. Then look through the chapter and read each heading. Using only the headings, give a short account of the Spanish-American War.

3. Look at the pictures in the chapter and read each caption. What do the pictures show you about the fighting in the Spanish-American War? Look at the map in the chapter. What is the title of this map? Note also the time line at the beginning of the chapter. What years are included in the chapter? Compare this chapter time line to the unit time line on page 453.

4. Read the last part of the chapter called Summing Up. What were the results of the Spanish-American War?

Know These Important Terms

imperialism   Spanish-American War

Know the Main Idea

Here is the MAIN IDEA of this chapter.

In 1898, the United States fought and won the Spanish-American War. As a result, Cuba gained its independence, and the United States gained many new overseas territories.

Keep this MAIN IDEA in mind as you study the chapter. Ask yourself the following questions as you read. They will help you remember the MAIN IDEA.

1. Who was President of the United States when the Cuban revolt against Spain began?

2. What event caused many Americans to demand war with Spain?

3. What new territories did the United States gain as a result of the war?

THE YEARS OF THIS CHAPTER ARE 1895 TO 1902

| 1865 | 1895 | 1902 | 1921 |

THE CHAPTER LESSON BEGINS HERE

Some Americans Became Interested in Colonies

By the 1890's, Americans started to become interested in the world, and they began to believe in **imperialism** (ihm-PIHR-ee-ul-IZ-um). Imperialism is the idea that a nation needs many colonies and territories overseas in order to be rich and powerful. During the late 1800's, many nations of Europe became rivals for colonies and territories. These European nations took over some of the less powerful nations in Africa and Asia.

Some Americans wanted the United States to take over colonies and territories overseas. These Americans felt that the United States needed colonies in order to become a stronger nation. They also wanted colonies because colonies provided raw materials for American factories. And colonies provided a market, or selling place, for the products made in American factories.

Cuba Revolted Against Spain

In 1895, the people of Cuba revolted, or fought against, Spain, and a war began. Cuba was a Spanish colony, but the Cubans wanted their freedom. To crush the revolt, the Spanish government put many Cuban people into

THE SPANISH-AMERICAN WAR IN CUBA

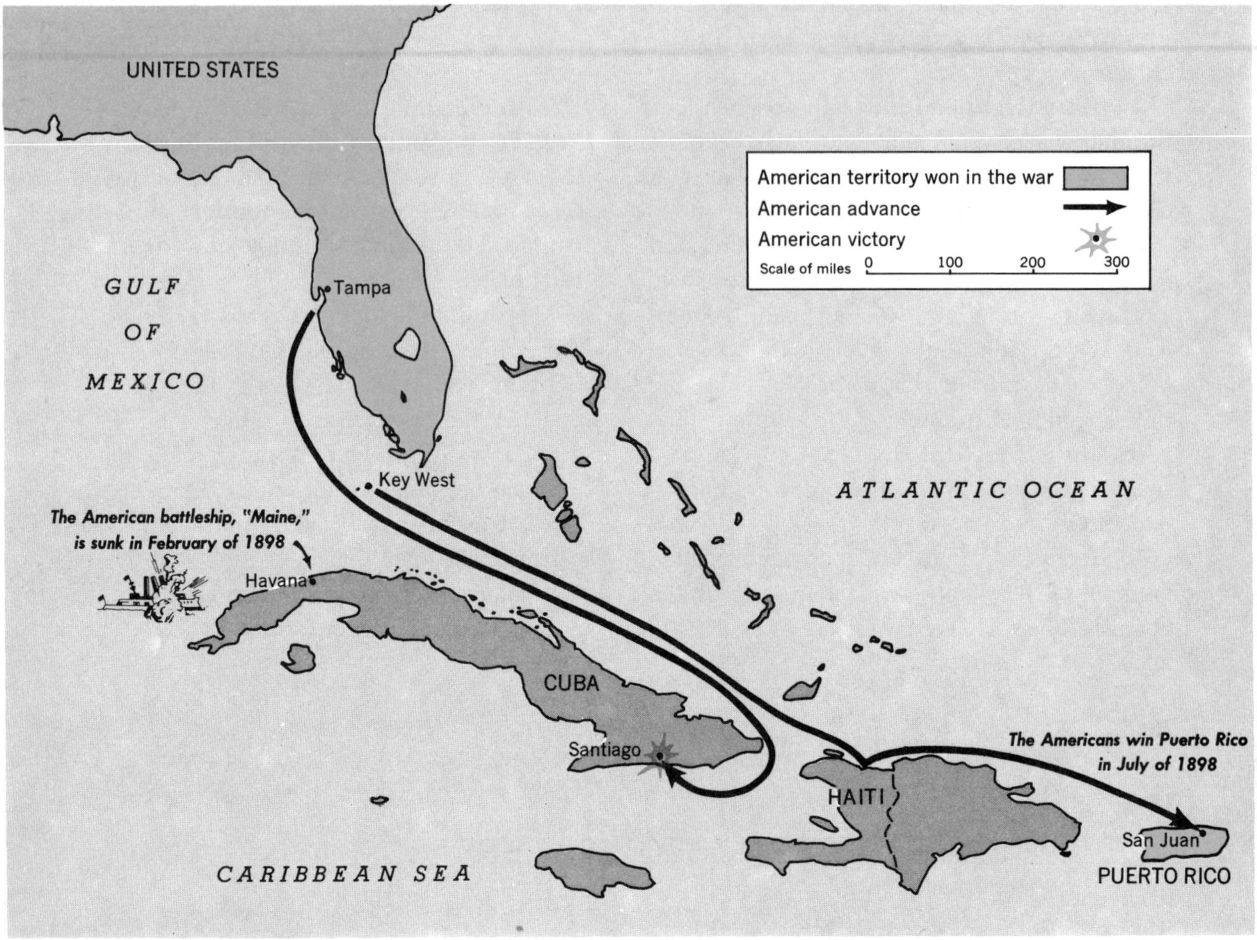
UNITED STATES
American territory won in the war
American advance
American victory
Scale of miles 0 100 200 300
GULF OF MEXICO
Tampa
Key West
ATLANTIC OCEAN
The American battleship, "Maine," is sunk in February of 1898
Havana
CUBA
Santiago
The Americans win Puerto Rico in July of 1898
HAITI
San Juan
PUERTO RICO
CARIBBEAN SEA

prison camps, where thousands died of sickness or lack of food. Spanish troops also killed Cubans and they burned many buildings in Cuba.

Americans read terrible stories in their newspapers about how cruelly Spain was treating the Cuban people. Some of these newspaper stories were false, but Americans did not know this. They demanded that the United States help Cuba in its fight against Spain. But President Grover Cleveland refused to allow the United States to get into this war.

Trouble Began Between the United States and Spain

William McKinley was elected President of the United States in 1896. President McKinley also thought that the United States must not enter the war between Cuba and Spain. But in 1898, the "Maine," a United States battleship, which was sent to Cuba to protect American lives and property, blew up and sank in the harbor of Havana, Cuba. More than 250 American navy men on the ship were killed. No one ever found what caused the "Maine" to blow up. But most

Americans blamed the Spanish government for causing it to happen. Angry Americans all over the United States were shouting the words "Remember the Maine!"

The Spanish-American War Began

Congress voted to use 50 million dollars to prepare for war. But President McKinley still tried to keep the United States out of war. In March of 1898, President McKinley demanded that Spain end the fighting in Cuba. In early April, the Spanish government agreed to do so because it feared a war with the United States. However, it was too late. Only two days later, President McKinley asked Congress to approve sending American troops to Cuba. President McKinley was no longer able to overcome the American people's demands to fight Spain. This war with Spain was called the **Spanish-American War.**

The War on Land

The American army was small and unprepared for war. Only 18 thousand soldiers— including four black regiments—were sent to Cuba. The Spanish army was much larger but very poorly organized. Within ten weeks, the United States army took over both Cuba and the island of Puerto Rico. Only a few hundred American soldiers were killed in the fighting. More died from yellow fever and malaria.

The War Was Won at Sea

The most important battles of the Spanish-American War took place at sea. The American navy in the Pacific Ocean was led by Commodore George Dewey. Commodore Dewey's ships destroyed Spain's Pacific navy at the Battle of Manila Bay in the Philippine (FILL-uh-PEEN) Islands. This American victory forced Spain to surrender all the Philippine Islands to the United States.

In Cuba, the Spanish fleet was trapped in the harbor of Santiago (SAN-tee-AH-goh), and it was completely destroyed by an American fleet. This naval victory made it possible for the United States to land troops in Cuba and to win the war.

This picture shows the battleship "Maine" being blown up in the harbor of Havana, Cuba. Many Americans lost their lives during the blast.

Courtesy Chicago Historical Society.

Battle of Manila Bay.

THE BATTLE OF MANILA BAY AND PHILIPPINE INDEPENDENCE

The Cubans were not the only people who wished to be independent from Spain in the 1890's. The people of the Philippine Islands also wanted their freedom. When the Spanish-American War started, the United States decided to help the Philippine people gain their independence. Commodore George Dewey, the commander of the American fleet in the Pacific, was ordered to attack the Spanish fleet in the Philippines.

The battle between the American and Spanish fleets took place in Manila Bay on the morning of May 1, 1898. The ships in the Spanish fleet were old and poorly equipped. Before noon, the battle was over, and the Americans won a great victory.

After the Battle of Manila Bay, Emilio Aguinaldo, the leader of the fight for Philippine independence, organized an army. This army conquered all of the main Philippine island of Luzon except for the city of Manila. Aguinaldo also wanted to capture Manila, but the American army decided to take the city. And when the war was over, the American government decided to make the Philippine Islands a territory of the United States. American leaders felt that the Philippine people needed more time to prepare for independence.

The United States Gained Many New Territories

In the peace treaty that ended the war, Spain gave Cuba its independence. Also, Spain gave the United States the island of Puerto Rico, the island of Guam, and the Philippine Islands. In return for the Philippine Islands, the United States paid Spain 20 million dollars.

Not all Americans favored the peace treaty with Spain. Many Americans felt that acquiring all these new territories was the first step toward imperialism. However, owning these new territories made the United States a powerful nation.

The United States Now Governed New Territories

The people who lived in the territories won in the Spanish-American War were not citizens of the United States. They enjoyed only those rights given to them by the American Congress. The island of Guam was governed by the navy. However, the island of Puerto Rico and the Philippine Islands were given some self-government.

After the Spanish-American War, the United States governed Cuba until 1902. During these years, an American army remained in Cuba and helped build new schools, roads, and hospitals. Living conditions in Cuba were improved, and yellow fever was almost wiped out.

Summing Up

In 1898, the United States fought the Spanish-American War to punish Spain and to help Cuba win its freedom. As a result of the war, Cuba gained its independence, and the United States gained many new overseas territories. In the next chapter, you will find out how the United States dealt with foreign nations between 1900 and 1914.

AFTER YOU READ THE CHAPTER

Do You Know These Important Terms?

For each sentence below, choose the term that best completes the sentence.

1. The idea that a nation needs many colonies and overseas territories in order to be rich and powerful is (imperialism/nationalism).
2. The war between the United States and Spain in 1898 is called the (Cuban-American/Spanish-American) War.

Do You Remember These People?

Tell something about each of the following persons.

Grover Cleveland   William McKinley
George Dewey

Can You Locate These Places?

Use the map on page 462 to do the following map work.

Locate the islands of Cuba and Puerto Rico. What event occurred in Havana? What American victory made it possible to land troops in Cuba?

Do You Know When It Happened?

What are the years of this chapter? Place the following events in the order in which they occurred.

Commodore Dewey won the battle at Manila Bay.

Cuba became an independent nation.

Cuba revolted against Spain.

The "Maine" was sunk.

Discovering More About the Main Idea

In 1898, the United States fought and won the Spanish-American War. As a result, Cuba gained its independence, and the United States gained many new overseas territories.

Tell how each of the following developments is related to the MAIN IDEA.

Some American people wanted the United States to practice imperialism. When Cuba revolted against Spain, Americans wanted to help Cuba.

After the sinking of the "Maine," the United States declared war against Spain. The war only lasted a short time, and most of the important battles were fought at sea. The United States easily defeated Spain.

The United States gained Puerto Rico, the Philippines, and Guam. American troops helped improve living conditions in Cuba before they were removed in 1902.

Can You Discuss the Chapter?

Use the information you learned in this chapter to answer the following questions.

1. Why did some Americans begin to believe in imperialism?
2. Why did most Americans take the side of Cuba in its revolt against Spain?
3. How was the United States able to defeat the Spanish so quickly?
4. How did the United States govern its newly acquired territories?
5. How do you think you might have felt about the conquest of the Philippines if you were a Spaniard? an American? a Filipino?

Can You Connect the Past and the Present?

1. Are any nations in the world today practicing the ideas of imperialism?
2. Which territories that you read about in this chapter are still part of the United States?

CHAPTER 75

The United States and the World, 1900-1917

American troops in Peking, China.

BEFORE YOU BEGIN THE CHAPTER

Know What to Look For

1. The building of the Panama Canal was a tremendous job. It took 50 thousand workers and some of the largest earth-moving machines built by man at that time, eight years to dig a fifty-mile ditch across the hot jungles and mountains of Panama. Six pairs of canal locks were built because the waters of the canal were on different levels. These canal locks helped the ships to move over the differ-

ent water levels from ocean to ocean.

When the canal was finished, it provided a great short cut between the Atlantic and Pacific coasts of the United States. The journey between New York and San Francisco was now 8 thousand miles shorter. The canal was important to a nation that now owned territories in both the Atlantic and Pacific oceans. In this chapter, you will read about the United

States and its part in world affairs during the early 1900's.

2. Read the title of the chapter. Then look through the chapter and read each heading. Where did the United States lose friends?

3. Look at the pictures in the chapter and read each caption. What do the pictures show you about the United States and its dealings with the world? Examine the map on page 469. What is the title of this map? Note also the time line on this page. What years are included in this chapter? Compare this chapter time line to the unit time line on page 453.

4. Read the last part of the chapter called Summing Up. Name some parts of the world that Americans became interested in during the early 1900's.

Know These Important Terms
Open Door Policy   Canal Zone
Boxers   Roosevelt Corollary
Boxer Rebellion   dollar diplomacy
Isthmus of Panama

Know The Main Idea
Here is the MAIN IDEA of this chapter.

In the early 1900's, Americans took an interest in the rest of the world. They were involved in China, built the Panama Canal, and were active in Latin America.

Keep this MAIN IDEA in mind as you study the chapter. Ask yourself the following questions as you read. They will help you remember the MAIN IDEA.

1. What nation did not want China to be divided into colonies?

2. Where did the United States decide to build a canal connecting the Atlantic and Pacific oceans?

3. Which Mexican leader gave the United States trouble in the months between 1916 and 1917?

THE YEARS OF THIS CHAPTER ARE 1900 TO 1917

1865   1900   1917 1921

THE CHAPTER LESSON BEGINS HERE

The United States Tried to Keep Chinese Trade Open

After the United States took over the Philippine Islands, Americans became interested in the affairs of countries in Asia. At this time, the nations of Europe were trying to take over Chinese territory. The United States did not want China to be divided into colonies by the nations of Europe. But the United States did not want to lose its trade with China.

In 1899, John Hay, the American Secretary of State, sent a note to the European nations. This note asked the European nations to allow all nations to have equal trading rights in China. This policy was called the **Open Door Policy.** Only Great Britain agreed to Hay's Open Door Policy. Most of the other European nations were not willing to agree completely. Nevertheless, John Hay hoped they might support his Open Door Policy.

The United States Tried to Keep China Independent

The Chinese people did not want to be ruled by European nations. Many of them formed a group called the **Boxers** to lead a

Theodore Roosevelt operating a steam shovel at the start of the Panama Canal.

After the Boxer Rebellion was over, several European nations wanted to take over China completely. But John Hay refused to agree to this. Instead, he suggested that China pay money to the European nations rather than give up its land. The European nations accepted Hay's suggestion, and China remained an independent nation.

The United States Decided to Build a Canal

After the Spanish-American War, the United States owned many new territories in both the Atlantic and Pacific oceans. But American ships had no way of sailing from one ocean to the other except by sailing around South America. Congress decided, therefore, to build a canal across the **Isthmus** (ISS-mus) **of Panama,** or the narrow strip of land that connects North America and South America.

Even before the 1890's, many people wanted a canal across the Isthmus of Panama. In 1850, the United States and Great Britain agreed to build a canal together. And in the 1880's, the French tried to build a canal, but they failed. However, by 1901, Great Britain was willing to let the United States build the canal alone. At this time, the Republic of Colombia (kuh-LUM-bee-uh) owned Panama. The United States offered to pay Colombia 10 million dollars plus a yearly rent of 250 thousand dollars for a strip of land across the isthmus.

The Panama Canal Was Built

Colombia refused this offer. However, a revolution soon broke out in Panama, and Panama declared its independence from Colombia. A few weeks later, early in 1904, the new government agreed to allow the United States to build the canal under the same terms that were offered to Colombia. The strip of land rented to the United States by Panama

movement against all foreigners in China. In 1900, the Boxers tried to force all foreigners to leave China. The United States and several European nations sent soldiers to China to end this **Boxer Rebellion,** as it was called.

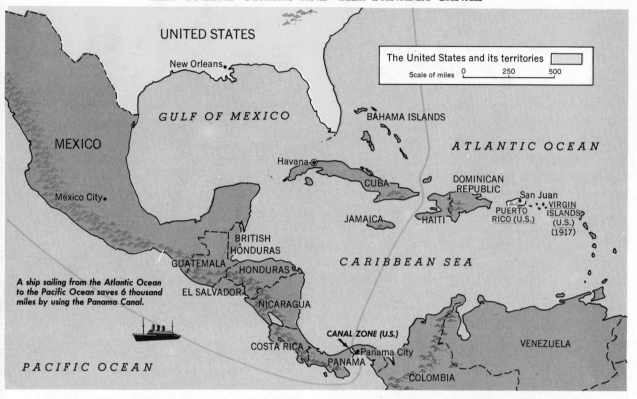

THE UNITED STATES AND THE PANAMA CANAL

UNITED STATES

New Orleans

GULF OF MEXICO

MEXICO

Mexico City

The United States and its territories

Scale of miles 0 250 500

BAHAMA ISLANDS

ATLANTIC OCEAN

Havana

CUBA

DOMINICAN REPUBLIC

San Juan

VIRGIN ISLANDS (U.S.) (1917)

PUERTO RICO (U.S.)

JAMAICA

HAITI

BRITISH HONDURAS

GUATEMALA

HONDURAS

A ship sailing from the Atlantic Ocean to the Pacific Ocean saves 6 thousand miles by using the Panama Canal.

EL SALVADOR

NICARAGUA

CARIBBEAN SEA

CANAL ZONE (U.S.)

COSTA RICA

Panama City

PACIFIC OCEAN

PANAMA

VENEZUELA

COLOMBIA

to build a canal was called the **Canal Zone.**

The great task of building the canal across the Canal Zone began in 1906. Before the canal was built, Dr. William Gorgas (GAWR-gus) had to wipe out malaria and ·yellow fever. Dr. Gorgas rid the Canal Zone of these diseases by destroying the mosquitoes that carried and spread them. The building of the canal was a tremendous job. Finally, in 1914, the canal was completed. The canal quickly proved to be very valuable to the United States and to many other nations of the world.

The United States Defended the Panama Canal

The Panama Canal immediately became important to the defense of the United States.

For this reason, the United States stood ready to prevent any nation from becoming a danger to the Canal Zone.

The nations of Latin America often owed money to European nations. When a Latin American nation was unable to pay back this money, many European nations wanted to send troops into the country to collect the money.

In order to prevent European nations from sending troops and to protect the Canal Zone, President Theodore Roosevelt suggested the **Roosevelt Corollary** (KAWR-uh-ler-ee), or an addition to the Monroe Doctrine. Under the Roosevelt Corollary, the United States agreed to send troops or to take over the affairs of Latin American nations if it became necessary. From time to time, the United States

President Wilson sent soldiers to capture Pancho Villa, pictured above. This action made the people of Mexico very angry.

sent American soldiers into several Latin American nations to keep European nations out.

The United States Lost Friends in Latin America

Many nations of Latin America were angry about American troops landing on their soil. They claimed that the United States was using **dollar diplomacy** (di-PLOH-muh-see). This meant that the United States sent American soldiers only because it wished to help American businessmen collect money that these countries owed them. Also, America was helping Americans carry on business there.

In 1916 and 1917, the United States had problems with Mexico. In 1916, Pancho Villa (VEE-yah), a Mexican leader, killed several Americans. President Wilson sent American troops into Mexico to capture Villa. Finally in 1917, the American troops were removed from Mexico, but the Mexican people remained angry at the United States for many years.

Summing Up

Between 1900 and 1917, Americans were very interested in the rest of the world. The United States tried to stop the nations of Europe from taking over China. The building of the Panama Canal helped to bring the United States closer to its overseas territories. And the United States became active in Latin America. In the next chapter, you will find out how the United States became involved in World War One.

AFTER YOU READ THE CHAPTER

Do You Know These Important Terms?

For each sentence below, choose the term that best completes the sentence.

1. The (**Fair Trade/Open Door**) Policy gave all nations equal trading rights in China.
2. Chinese who were against all foreigners in China were called (**Dragons/Boxers**).
3. The fight to force foreigners to leave China was called the (**Sin/Boxer**) Rebellion.
4. The land connecting North and South America is the (**Isthmus/Strait**) of Panama.
5. The strip of land rented to the United States to build a canal is called the (**Panama Republic/Canal Zone.**)
6. The (**Roosevelt/McKinley**) Corollary stated that the United States might send troops or take over the affairs of Latin American nations if it became necessary.
7. The claim by Latin American nations that the United States only sent troops to collect money for American businessmen was (**economic imperialism/dollar diplomacy**).

Do You Remember These People?

Tell something about each of the following persons.

John Hay　　　　**William Gorgas**
Theodore Roosevelt　　**Pancho Villa**
Woodrow Wilson

Can You Locate These Places?

Use the map on page 469 to do the following map work.

Locate the Panama Canal. What city is on the Pacific side of the canal?

Do You Know When It Happened?

What are the years of this chapter? Place the following events in the order in which they occurred.

The Panama Canal was completed.
Pancho Villa killed several Americans.
America set up the Open Door Policy.
Panama declared its independence.

Discovering More About the Main Idea

In the early 1900's, Americans took an interest in the rest of the world. They were involved in China, built the Panama Canal, and were active in Latin America.

Tell how each of the following developments is related to the MAIN IDEA.

The United States believed that all nations should have equal trading rights in China.

The United States built the Panama Canal and opened it to the entire world.

The United States wanted to prevent foreign nations from taking over Latin American nations, so it agreed to send troops or take over the affairs of Latin American nations.

Can You Discuss the Chapter?

Use the information you learned in this chapter to answer the following questions.

1. How did the United States help to stop the European nations from dividing up China?
2. Why do you think Panama declared its independence from Colombia in 1904?
3. Why was the Panama Canal so valuable to the United States and many other nations?
4. How did the United States try to manage the affairs of Latin America?
5. Do you agree with the ideas of the Roosevelt Corollary? Why or why not?

Can You Connect the Past and the Present?

1. When did the United States last take an active role in a Latin American nation?
2. What present-day engineering feat might be even greater than the building of the Panama Canal?

CHAPTER 76

The United States Enters World War One

President Wilson asks Congress to declare war.

BEFORE YOU BEGIN THE CHAPTER

Know What to Look For

1. A submarine is a ship that is designed and built to operate under water. The first submarine was a leather covered rowboat which was built by a Dutch scientist in 1620. Americans used a small, one-man submarine named the "Turtle" in the Revolutionary War. The "Turtle" rammed into a British warship in New York harbor but failed to sink it.

Robert Fulton, the inventor of the steamboat, made improvements in submarines in the early 1800's.

During the early 1900's, Germany succeeded in building large submarines which were powered by diesel engines. At about the same time, a new weapon was invented for use in the submarine. This weapon was a torpedo that steered itself toward the enemy's ship. In this chapter, you will read how the submarine played an important part in causing the United States to enter World War One.

2. Read the title of the chapter. Then look through the chapter and read each heading. From the headings, what topics do you expect to read about as you study this chapter?

3. Look at the pictures in the chapter and read each caption. What is happening in the first chapter picture? Study the map on page 476. Which color shows the Allies? Which color shows the Central Powers? Note also the time line at the beginning of the chapter. What years are included in this chapter? Compare this chapter time line to the unit time line on page 453.

4. Read the last part of the chapter called Summing Up. What actions caused the United States to enter World War One? What is the topic of the next chapter?

Know These Important Terms

Allies   **Central Powers**

Know the Main Idea

Here is the MAIN IDEA of this chapter.
When World War One broke out in Europe, the United States tried to remain neutral. Germany's sinking of American ships, however, forced the United States to enter the war.

Keep this MAIN IDEA in mind as you study the chapter. Ask yourself the following questions as you read. They will help you remember the MAIN IDEA.

1. Name the nations that made up the Allies. The Central Powers.
2. Which side did most Americans favor even though the American government was neutral?
3. Name the British passenger ship that was sunk by German submarines.

THE YEARS OF THIS CHAPTER ARE 1914 TO 1917

1865   1914   1917   1921

THE CHAPTER LESSON BEGINS HERE

The United States Tried to Stay Out of World War One

World War One broke out in Europe in 1914. The two main groups of nations in World War One were called the **Allies** and the **Central Powers**. Great Britain, France, and Russia made up the Allies. And the Central Powers included Germany, Austria-Hungary, and Turkey. Both the Allies and the Central Powers tried to win the support of the American people and government.

But as soon as war broke out in Europe, President Woodrow Wilson declared that the United States intended to remain neutral. To remain neutral meant that the United States was not going to favor either the Allies or the Central Powers. It also meant that the United States was willing to sell supplies to nations on both sides.

Most Americans Favored the Allies

The American government was neutral, but many Americans were not. Although Americans did not want to fight in World War One, most of them wanted the Allies to win. Americans felt this way because they shared the

page 473

President Woodrow Wilson.

THE ZIMMERMAN NOTE

The United States entered World War One for many reasons. One of the less important reasons for America's entry was the Zimmerman Note. This Zimmerman Note was actually a telegram sent by Arthur Zimmerman, a German leader, to the representative of Germany in Mexico City. The British captured this telegram and decoded the message it contained. In February, 1917, they sent a copy of the Note to the American government.

The Zimmerman Note shocked the American people. The Note contained orders to the German representative about what to do if war broke out between the United States and Germany. It stated that if the United States entered the war, Mexico was to be asked to attack the United States. In return, Germany promised to help Mexico reconquer the territory it lost in the Mexican War in the 1840's.

Soon after President Wilson received this Note, he announced that all American merchant ships sailing in the war zone were to be given weapons for defense against German submarines. A few days later, the President asked Congress to declare war against Germany.

same language and many ideas with the British people. They also remembered France's help during the Revolutionary War.

Another reason why most Americans backed the Allies was that Great Britain helped to spread many stories about the terrible way Germans treated their enemies. Many of these stories were not true, but Americans heard them so often that they believed them. Americans also backed the Allies because Great Britain and France had governments based on freedoms that were much like our own. But the governments in Germany and Austria-Hungary gave the people little freedom. Americans were afraid that a German victory was a danger to free governments all over the world.

The United States Had Problems with Great Britain

Selling goods to both the Allies and the Central Powers caused the United States a great deal of trouble. At first, most of the trouble was with Great Britain. The British navy stopped American ships to see if they were carrying war supplies, or even food, to Germany. However, Great Britain paid for all the supplies it took off American ships. And the British navy did not harm the American ships or the men on the ships that it stopped.

The United States Had Problems with Germany

The German navy also tried to stop American ships from carrying supplies to the Allies. But the German navy was not large enough to stop all the American ships from trading with Great Britain. Therefore, the German navy began to use submarines, which were more useful for sinking ships than for capturing them. Submarines depended on a surprise attack, and they gave no warning before attacking a ship. American lives as well as supplies were lost when German submarines attacked American ships.

President Wilson asked Germany to stop using submarines against American ships. However, Germany refused to stop using them. In 1915, the British passenger ship "Lusitania" (loos-uh-TAYN-yuh) was torpedoed and sunk by a German submarine. One hundred and twenty-eight Americans on this ship were killed. The American people were shocked and angry over the sinking of the "Lusitania." Some even wanted to go to war with Germany.

Germany Continued to Use Submarines

However, in 1915, most Americans hoped that the United States might be able to stay out of the war. President Wilson asked the German government for a money payment for the American lives lost on the "Lusitania." The President also demanded that Germany stop sinking passenger ships without warning them first to surrender. By February, 1916, the Germans agreed to all these demands. This promise kept President Wilson from asking Congress to declare war at that time.

But only one month later, a German submarine sank a French passenger ship, injuring several Americans. President Wilson again demanded that Germany stop sinking passenger ships. Once again the German government agreed not to sink any more ships without warning them first to surrender.

The United States
Entered World War One

In the election of 1916, the Republican candidate was Charles Evans Hughes, a Supreme Court judge. President Wilson was chosen to run for a second term by the Democrats. Many Americans supported Wilson because he promised to keep the United States out of the war. Many Americans also

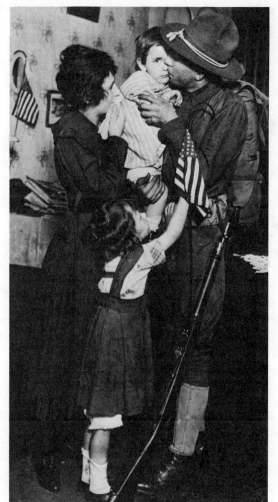

© International Film Service in the National Archives.

An American soldier says good-bye to his family before going off to war.

approved of the laws passed under Wilson's New Freedom Program. Wilson defeated Hughes, although the election was very close.

President Wilson tried hard to make peace between the Allies and the Central Powers, but his efforts failed. And President Wilson soon faced new problems in keeping the United States out of war. In 1917, Germany decided to try to end the war quickly by cutting off Great Britain's food supply until the British people were starved and forced to

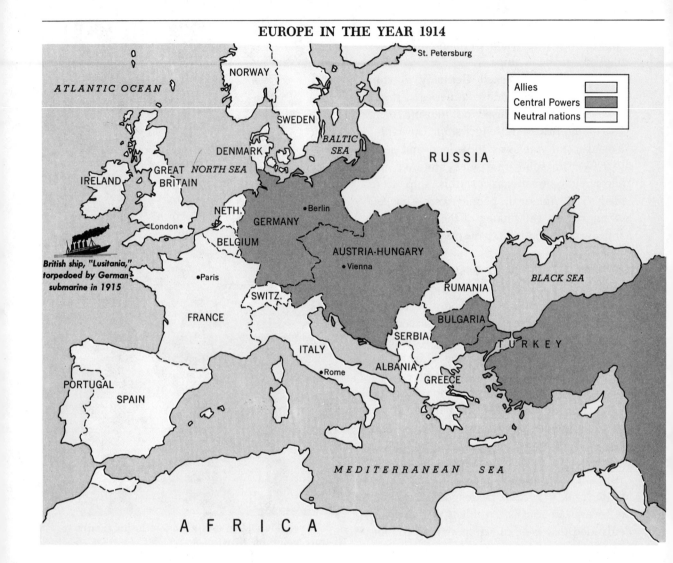

EUROPE IN THE YEAR 1914

Allies
Central Powers
Neutral nations

ATLANTIC OCEAN

NORWAY

SWEDEN

DENMARK

BALTIC SEA

RUSSIA

St. Petersburg

GREAT BRITAIN

NORTH SEA

IRELAND

London

NETH.

GERMANY

Berlin

BELGIUM

AUSTRIA-HUNGARY

Vienna

BLACK SEA

British ship, "Lusitania," torpedoed by German submarine in 1915

Paris

SWITZ.

FRANCE

RUMANIA

BULGARIA

SERBIA

TURKEY

ITALY

Rome

ALBANIA

GREECE

PORTUGAL

SPAIN

MEDITERRANEAN SEA

AFRICA

surrender. This meant that Germany was again going to sink all ships without warning them to surrender. The German government knew that sinking American ships might cause a war with the United States, but it was willing to take the chance.

Shortly after President Wilson began his second term, German submarines sank three American ships. Finally, President Wilson asked Congress to declare war on Germany. On April 6, 1917, Congress voted in favor of

war, and the United States entered World War One.

Summing Up

President Wilson tried hard to keep the United States out of World War One. However, most Americans wanted the Allies to win World War One. Finally, Germany's sinking of American ships forced the United States to declare war. In the next chapter, you will read about America in World War One.

AFTER YOU READ THE CHAPTER

Do You Know These Important Terms?

For each sentence below, choose the term that best completes the sentence.

1. Great Britain, France, and Russia made up the (Axis/Allies).
2. Germany, Austria-Hungary, and Turkey made up the (Eastern/Central) Powers.

Do You Remember These People?

Tell something about each of the following persons.

Woodrow Wilson

Charles Evans Hughes

Can You Locate These Places?

Use the map on page 476 to do the following map work.

1. Locate the Central Powers.
2. Name some European nations that were able to remain neutral during the war.
3. Name the nations that made up the Allies. Why do you think they might want to blockade the Central Powers?

Do You Know When It Happened?

What are the years of this chapter? Place the following events in the order in which they occurred.

Three American vessels were sunk by German submarines.

World War One broke out in Europe.

British and German vessels stopped American shipping.

The United States announced its neutrality.

German submarines sank the "Lusitania."

Discovering More About the Main Idea

When World War One broke out in Europe, the United States tried to remain neutral. Germany's sinking of American ships, however, forced the United States to enter the war.

Tell how each of the following developments is related to the MAIN IDEA.

Although the American government was neutral, most Americans wanted the Allies to win.

Both Germany and Great Britain stopped American ships on the seas to see if they were carrying supplies to the enemy.

President Wilson tried hard to make peace. When the Germans decided to starve the British into surrender, German submarines sank all ships going to Great Britain without warning.

Can You Discuss the Chapter?

Use the information you learned in this chapter to answer the following questions.

1. Why did many Americans want the Allies to win even though the American government was neutral?
2. Why did the German navy begin to use submarines?
3. Why do you think that the Germans agreed to all of President Wilson's demands after the sinking of the "Lusitania"?
4. What were Germany's plans to end the war quickly?
5. Do you think that nations at war have the right to stop neutral ships on the seas in order to search them for war supplies?

Can You Connect the Past and the Present?

1. What new developments have made the submarine a more dangerous weapon?
2. You probably have read how false newspaper stories have been used in the past to make people favor a certain point of view. Do newspapers still print false stories in order to make people favor a certain point of view? Can you find any recent examples?

CHAPTER *77*

Fighting World War One

Trench warfare on the Western front.

BEFORE YOU BEGIN THE CHAPTER

Know What to Look For

1. Perhaps you have heard the term "stalemate." It is used in the game of chess when neither player can win the game. This term also describes the situation in World War One in the year 1917. For three long years, the two sides, the Allies and the Central Powers, faced each other from trenches which ran along the Western front for 600 miles. Sometimes, one

side tried to attack the other side by crossing the area in between the two sets of trenches, called "no-man's" land. However, neither side was able to gain an advantage and win the war.

Then in 1917, Russia withdrew from the war. Soldiers of the Central Powers now stopped fighting on the Russian front in the war, and they were able to fight on the Western front. The stalemate in the war might have been broken by the Central Powers if American soldiers had not arrived in Europe in 1917. These fresh American troops were able to help the Allies win the war, instead.

2. Read the title of the chapter. Then look through the chapter and read each heading. How did the United States help the Allies?

3. Look at the pictures in the chapter and read each caption. What do the pictures tell you about the war? Look at the map on page 481. What information does the map show? Notice the time line at the beginning of this chapter. What years are included in the chapter? Compare the chapter time line to the unit time line on page 453. How do the years of this chapter compare with the years of the unit?

4. Read the last part of the chapter called Summing Up. How did Americans on the home front help to win the war?

Know These Important Terms

Selective Service Act	Liberty Bonds
War Industries Board	armistice
Committee on Public Information	convoys

Know the Main Idea

Here is the MAIN IDEA of this chapter.

The United States played an important part in winning World War One. American workers supplied weapons, food, and money. American soldiers helped to defeat the Germans on the battlefield.

Keep this MAIN IDEA in mind as you study the chapter. Ask yourself the following questions as you read. They will help you remember the MAIN IDEA.

1. Who was the head of the American army?
2. What happened to the American railroads during the war?
3. Name some battles in which American soldiers fought.

THE YEARS OF THIS CHAPTER ARE 1917 TO 1918

1865   1917   1918   1921

THE CHAPTER LESSON BEGINS HERE

The United States Raised an Army

The United States had to raise a large army of American soldiers to fight the war. In May of 1917, Congress passed the **Selective Service Act** to draft this large American army. Almost 3 million men were soon drafted. American soldiers were given six months of training at army bases in the United States before they were shipped overseas. A special three-month course was used to train some officers, who were called "90-day wonders." The head of the American army was General John J. Pershing (PURR-sheeng).

Providing Supplies for Europe

Getting troops and supplies to Europe was an important problem for the United States. The United States needed thousands of ships to carry soldiers and supplies to Europe. The American government built many ships and also used ships that it captured from Germany.

The use of **convoys** helped to protect American ships from submarine attacks. A convoy was a group of ten or twelve ships carrying men and supplies guarded by navy warships. The convoy system worked so well that not

This picture shows workers in an American factory making steel helmets for the army. Workers like these helped to make the war effort a success.

a single American troop ship was ever sunk by a German submarine.

American Factories Produced Supplies and Weapons for the War

American factories were put under the control of the **War Industries Board.** The War Industries Board was formed in July of 1917 to direct American factories in turning out war supplies and weapons. Within a year, nearly all American factories changed over to producing war supplies. Men and women worked long hours in these factories to produce the goods needed for the war.

During the war, the government also took over all American railroads and ran them as one large railroad system. After the war was over, the government returned the railroads to the companies that owned them.

American Farmers Helped the War Effort

Food was extremely important in World War One. The government set high farm prices which encouraged farmers to raise as much food as possible. At the same time, Americans were urged not to waste food. Americans saved food on "Wheatless Mondays," and "Meatless Tuesdays." In these ways, the United States was able to supply the food needed by American troops and the Allies in Europe.

Americans Were Expected to Support the War

To encourage all Americans to support the war effort, the American government set up the **Committee on Public Information.** This committee printed millions of booklets to explain why the United States was fighting the war.

Congress also passed four laws to stop anyone from working against the nation's war effort. As a result of these laws, any American who spoke out against the war or the government was in danger of being arrested.

The United States Raised Money for the War

Huge sums of money were needed to help the United States carry on the war. The American government raised money for the war from taxes. Congress passed many new taxes. And Congress also raised income taxes and taxes on businesses. Over 10 billion dollars were raised from taxes. Another way the government raised the money needed to pay for the war was by selling **Liberty Bonds.** By buying Liberty Bonds, Americans were lending their government the money it needed to fight the war. The United States loaned a great deal of this money to the Allies. The Allies bought war supplies with this money.

The American Army and Navy Arrived in France

Meanwhile, American soldiers and sailors were doing their part to help win the war. American navy ships destroyed many German submarines. The American navy also helped close off the North Sea by placing many underwater mines, or hidden bombs, in the North Sea. These mines prevented German submarines from getting from the North Sea into the Atlantic Ocean. The American navy also kept ships from carrying food and supplies to Germany. As a result, the German war effort was greatly weakened.

In November, 1917, a revolution broke out in Russia, and Russia stopped fighting and

page 481

Noble Sissle and Eubie Blake.

NOBLE SISSLE

Noble Sissle had a long career as a musician. He grew up in the state of Indiana, and he started his career in music by singing in a church choir. In World War One, he was the drum major of the 369th Regiment Band. This regiment was the first black combat unit to be sent to Europe.

The 369th Regiment became famous in Europe. The French government gave medals to every man in the regiment. So many people turned out to hear Sissle and the band play their jazz music that some people said that "Jazz won the war."

After the war, Sissle helped to write a musical revue called *Shuffle Along*. This show ran for more than two years. Later, Sissle wrote other shows and had a very successful band. One of the singers in Sissle's band was a young girl named Lena Horne. Sissle's style of music called "sophisticated swing" remained popular for many years. In 1952, Sissle and his band played at President Eisenhower's Inaugural Ball.

made peace with Germany. As a result, in 1918, Germany was able to move most of its soldiers from the Eastern front in Russia to the Western front in France. The German army now had more men on the Western front than the British and French armies did. Germany expected to win the war before American troops arrived in Europe. But American troops arrived in time to help Britain and France.

The War Came to an End in 1918

The Allies badly needed more soldiers. Therefore, in the spring of 1918, General Pershing agreed to send American troops into battle right away as part of one large Allied army. At the battles of Cantigny (kahn-teen-YEE), Chateau-Thierry (sha-TOH tye-REE), and Belleau (BEL-oh) Wood, American soldiers proved that they were among the finest in the world. With their help, the German armies in France were stopped.

Early in October of 1918, the German government asked the Allies for an **armistice** (AHR-muh-stuss), or an end to the fighting. But the Allies refused to agree to an armistice until November 11, 1918. By that time, the German army was badly defeated, and the German government was overthrown by the German people.

Summing Up

The United States played an important part in winning World War One. On the home front, American workers supplied the weapons, supplies, food, and money needed to fight the war. On the battlefield, American soldiers helped to defeat the German army. And the American navy made it possible for food, supplies, and American troops to reach Europe. In the next chapter, you will find out how the United States worked for a lasting peace.

AFTER YOU READ THE CHAPTER

Do You Know These Important Terms?

For each sentence below, choose the term that best completes the sentence.

1. The (**Free Enlistment/Selective Service**) Act was passed to draft soldiers for the army.
2. American factories were put under control of the (**War Industries/National Security**) Board.
3. The Committee on (**War Correspondence/Public Information**) was set up to encourage all Americans to support the war effort.
4. The government sold (**Liberty/Savings**) Bonds to raise money to pay for the war.
5. (**A peace treaty/An armistice**) marks the end of the fighting.
6. A (**convoy/dragnet**) was a group of ten or twelve ships carrying men and supplies guarded by navy warships.

Do You Remember These People?

Tell something about each of the following persons.

John J. Pershing   **Woodrow Wilson**

Can You Locate These Places?

Use the map on page 481 to do the following map work.

1. Locate the line of the farthest German advance by July, 1918. What Allied victories are near this line? Did Americans fight in these battles?
2. Locate the battle line when the armistice was signed on November 11, 1918.

Do You Know When It Happened?

What are the years of this chapter? Tell why each of the following dates is important in the story of World War One.

May, 1917   **July, 1917**
November, 1917   **November, 1918**

Discovering More About the Main Idea

The United States played an important part in winning World War One. American workers supplied weapons, food, and money. American soldiers helped to defeat the Germans on the battlefield.

Tell how each of the following developments is related to the MAIN IDEA.

The United States trained an army and sent men and supplies to Europe.

Americans worked together on the home front to turn out the machines and supplies, to grow the food, and to raise the money necessary to win the war.

American troops were able to join the Allied armies in time to stop the German armies in France.

Can You Discuss the Chapter?

Use the information you learned in this chapter to answer the following questions.

1. How was the United States able to solve the problem of getting troops and supplies to Europe?
2. How did the government make sure that American factories and railroads worked to help the war effort?
3. How did the American government raise the money for the war?
4. How did the American fighting forces help the Allies in their struggle with Germany?
5. Which part of the war effort do you think was most important? Why?

Can You Connect the Past and the Present?

Students today have never seen the United States prepare itself to fight a major war such as World War One. If a major war developed, what changes in your community do you think might be necessary?

CHAPTER 78

Peace-Making After World War One

Celebrating the end of World War One.

BEFORE YOU BEGIN THE CHAPTER

Know What to Look For

1. You may have heard the saying that winning the peace is often more difficult than winning the war. This was especially true after World War One. Most of the nations that fought the war had their own idea about the way they wanted the peace to work out. They were not willing to accept the plans of another nation.

The United States favored a fair peace for the world. It wanted the peace to be fair to both the losers of the war and the winners. But most of the other Allied nations wanted to punish the Central Powers and to gain some reward for winning the war. In this chapter, you will find out why America's efforts to set up a fair peace for the world were not completely successful. You will find out that most of President Wilson's plans for peace were turned down.

2. Read the title of the chapter. Then look through the chapter and read each heading. Using just the headings, can you tell how the American nation felt about the peace treaty that ended World War One?

3. Look at the pictures in the chapter and read each caption. What is happening in the first chapter picture? Examine the map on page 486. What is the title of the map? What information does the map show? Note also the time line at the beginning of the chapter. What years are included in the chapter? Compare this chapter time line to the unit time line on page 453.

4. Read the last part of the chapter called Summing Up. What happened to President Wilson's peace plan?

Know These Important Terms

Fourteen Points   reparations
League of Nations   Treaty of Versailles

Know the Main Idea

Here is the MAIN IDEA of this chapter.

The terms of the peace treaty were not as fair as President Wilson wanted. The American people refused to accept the Treaty of Versailles and the League of Nations.

Keep this MAIN IDEA in mind as you study the chapter. Ask yourself the following questions as you read. They will help you remember the MAIN IDEA.

1. What name was given to President Wilson's plan for peace?

2. Why did President Wilson accept most of the Allies' demands?

3. What treaty ended World War One?

THE YEARS OF THIS CHAPTER ARE 1918 TO 1921

1865   1918   1921

THE CHAPTER LESSON BEGINS HERE

President Wilson Made Plans for World Peace

President Wilson hoped to build a better world after World War One. Wilson believed that the peace terms must be fair to all nations, including the defeated nations. President Wilson's plan for peace was called the **Fourteen Points.** The most important of Wilson's Fourteen Points were these.

1. No nation was to be ruled by another nation if it did not want to be. This meant that the nations ruled before the war by Russia (now called the Soviet Union), Austria-Hungary, and Turkey were to become free nations.

2. The colonies in Asia and Africa that were ruled by European nations were to be prepared to govern themselves.

3. All nations were to lower their tariffs, or taxes on goods from other nations, to make it easier to trade with each other.

4. All nations were to cut down the sizes of their armies and navies. And all nations were to stop making secret agreements.

5. A **League of Nations** was to be formed to keep the peace and to settle problems between nations that might lead to war. Preventing another war was the main purpose of

this League of Nations. It was the most important part of President Wilson's peace plan.

Wilson Attended the Peace Conference

British and French leaders did not agree with Wilson's Fourteen Points. Britain and France wanted Germany to be punished for the losses their nations suffered in the war. They were determined to get money and territory from Germany and the other nations

President Wilson is greeted as he arrives in England in 1919. He was in Europe to attend the Paris peace conference.

that fought against the Allies. And many Americans did not like the peace plan. They felt that Wilson was not looking after the interests of the United States.

In December of 1918, President Wilson sailed to Paris to attend the peace conference, or peace meeting. Other leaders of the peace conference were David Lloyd George of Great Britain, Georges Clemenceau (KLEM-un-SOH) of France, and Vittorio Orlando (or-LAN-doh) of Italy.

Wilson Had to Give in to the Allied Demands

At the peace conference, President Wilson presented his Fourteen Points as a guide for the peace terms. But the Allies turned down most of his peace plan. They made many demands for money and territory from Germany and the other defeated nations.

France wanted to make Germany a weak nation and, therefore, make it impossible for Germany ever to start another war. Italy wanted to take over Austrian territory. Japan wanted to take over Chinese territory. Great Britain was interested in getting more colonies. And all these nations wanted **reparations** (REP-uh-RAY-shuns), or large amounts of money, from Germany to pay for the lives and property destroyed in the war. President Wilson had to accept most of their demands in order to get the Allies to form the League of Nations.

The Treaty of Versailles

The peace treaty that was written to end World War One was called the **Treaty of Versailles** (vur-SY). The Treaty of Versailles included the following peace terms.

1. The League of Nations was to be set up. The League was to include all nations. It was to try and solve peacefully any problems that were a danger to world peace.

2. German colonies in Asia and Africa were now to be governed by the League of Nations.

3. Poland, Yugoslavia (yew-goh-SLAHV-ee-uh), Czechoslovakia (CHEK-oh-sloh-VAHK-ee-uh), and several other nations once ruled by Russia (the Soviet Union) and Austria-Hungary became free nations.

Leaders sign the peace treaty to end World War One at the Palace of Versailles.

that without these changes the League might pull the United States into a new war.

But President Wilson refused to accept any of these changes. In September, 1919, he went on a trip across the United States to urge Americans to support the Treaty of Versailles and the League. During this trip, President Wilson became sick and was unable to work for several months. As a result, Wilson had to give up his efforts to get the Senate to approve the treaty and the League.

The Senate Refused to Approve the Treaty

While President Wilson was still sick, the Senate voted to turn down both the treaty and the League. But the fight was still not over. The treaty came up before the Senate again in March of 1920. However, the Senate turned down the treaty and the League again.

President Wilson expected the election of 1920 to show that the American people favored the treaty and the League. But instead, the American people showed that they were against the treaty and the League. The Democratic Party, which supported the League of Nations, lost the election to the Republicans. The United States never did join the League of Nations. In fact, the United States did not officially make peace with Germany until 1921.

4. Germany was required to pay reparations, or large amounts of money, to the Allies.

Wilson Urged Americans to Accept the League

President Wilson returned to the United States and asked Congress to approve the Treaty of Versailles. But Senator Henry Cabot Lodge and many other important Republican Senators did not agree with certain parts of the treaty. These Senators refused to approve the treaty unless changes were made in the plan for the League of Nations. They felt

Summing Up

President Wilson tried to plan a lasting peace for the nations of the world. However, the Allies turned down most of Wilson's peace plan, and the terms of the peace treaty were not as fair as President Wilson wanted. The American people refused to accept the Treaty of Versailles and the League of Nations. The next chapter, which begins Unit 20, tells you what America's government was like after World War One.

AFTER YOU READ THE CHAPTER

Do You Know These Important Terms?

For each sentence below, choose the term that best completes the sentence.

1. President Wilson's plan for peace was called the (**Verdun Pact/Fourteen Points**).

2. The most important part of Wilson's peace plan was a (**League of Nations/Security Council**) to be formed to keep peace and settle problems between nations.

3. Amounts of money to pay for the lives and property destroyed in the war were called (**blackmail/reparations**).

4. The Treaty of (**Versailles/Brussels**) was the peace treaty that ended World War One.

Do You Remember These People?

Tell something about each of the following persons.

Woodrow Wilson   **David Lloyd George**
Georges Clemenceau   **Vittorio Orlando**
Henry Cabot Lodge

Can You Locate These Places?

Use the map on page 486 to do the following map work.

1. Name the new nations formed after World War One.

2. Compare this map to the one on page 476. From what older nation was each made?

Do You Know When It Happened?

Tell how each of these dates was important in this chapter.

| 1918 | 1919 | 1920 | 1921 |

Discovering More About the Main Idea

The terms of the peace treaty were not as fair as President Wilson wanted. The American people refused to accept the Treaty of Versailles and the League of Nations.

Tell how each of the following developments is related to the MAIN IDEA.

Wilson had to give up many of his Fourteen Points and accept most of the Allies' demands in order to get the Allies to form the League of Nations.

The Treaty of Versailles formed new nations and set up the League of Nations, but it also required Germany to pay reparations.

The United States Senate refused to approve the Treaty of Versailles. The United States never joined the League of Nations, and it made a separate peace with Germany.

Can You Discuss the Chapter?

Use the information you learned in this chapter to answer the following questions.

1. What were the most important of President Wilson's Fourteen Points?

2. How did the views of the other Allied leaders differ from those of President Wilson?

3. Compare the Treaty of Versailles with Wilson's Fourteen Points. Which of his points can you recognize?

4. Why did the American people not approve the Treaty of Versailles and the League of Nations?

5. With which of Wilson's Fourteen Points do you most agree? least agree? Why?

Can You Connect the Past
and the Present?

1. Many people have called President Wilson a dreamer, or an idealist, because his ideas for making the peace did not work. Do you have any dreamers or idealists in your community today? Do you think such people are important?

2. What present-day group is somewhat like the League of Nations? Is the United States a member?

PART IV

Problems At Home And In The World
1920 to 1945

THE UNITS IN PART IV ARE

Unit 20 The American Nation in the 1920's
Unit 21 Changes in America in the 1920's
Unit 22 The American Nation in the 1930's
Unit 23 America Deals with Other Nations
Unit 24 America Fights in World War Two

The American Nation in the 1920's

Americans on the boardwalk in Atlantic City, New Jersey, in 1920.

THE CHAPTERS IN UNIT 20 ARE

CHAPTER 79   American Government in the 1920's
CHAPTER 80   American Problems in the 1920's
CHAPTER 81   American Life in the 1920's
CHAPTER 82   American Thought in the 1920's

THE YEARS OF THIS UNIT ARE 1920 TO 1930

1900   1920   1930   1975

American Government in the 1920's

President Harding (at left) and his Cabinet.

BEFORE YOU BEGIN THE CHAPTER

Know What to Look For

1. During World War One, many Americans found that their usual ways of living were greatly changed as a result of the war. After the war, many Americans wanted to get back to their own way of life, or as they said in 1919, "return to normalcy." However, conditions can never be the same as they were before. After all wars, great changes have taken place. After the Revolutionary War, the new American nation was formed. After the War of 1812, the country grew rapidly. And after the Civil War, industries grew rapidly in the United States.

Many changes also took place in the American nation after World War One. Exciting new inventions, such as the automobile, the airplane, and the radio, changed the way of life of the American people. However, in the election of 1920, American voters elected Warren Harding as President because he promised to bring a "return to normalcy."

2. Read the title of the chapter. Then look through the chapter and read each heading. What information about American government in the 1920's can you learn just by reading the headings?

3. Look at the pictures in the chapter and read each caption. What do the pictures show you about the American government in the 1920's? Note also the time line at the beginning of the chapter. What years are included in this chapter? Compare this chapter time line to the unit time line on page 491.

4. Read the last part of the chapter called Summing Up. Who were the three Republican Presidents during the 1920's?

Know This Important Term
Veterans' Bureau

Know the Main Idea
Here is the MAIN IDEA of this chapter.

During the 1920's, the United States had three Republican Presidents. The federal government favored big business, raised the tariff, and lowered taxes.

Keep this MAIN IDEA in mind as you study the chapter. Ask yourself the following questions as you read. They will help you remember the MAIN IDEA.

1. Who was elected President of the United States in 1920?

2. What other political party ran a candidate in the election of 1924? Who was their candidate?

3. What was held against Alfred E. Smith in the Presidential election campaign of 1928?

THE YEARS OF THIS CHAPTER ARE 1920 TO 1930

1920   1930

THE CHAPTER LESSON BEGINS HERE

Warren G. Harding Was Elected President in 1920

By 1920, most Americans were getting back to normal peace time living. And they wanted government leaders to bring back normal times to the nation. The days of Progressive reform were ended in the United States.

The Republican candidate in the election of 1920 was Warren G. Harding. Harding was a Republican Senator from Ohio. The Democrats ran James M. Cox, governor of Ohio. Harding promised to lower taxes and to raise the tariff. He also promised Americans a "return to normalcy" in the United States. This meant that he intended to lead the nation

back to the "good old days" before the war. Although Harding did not take a stand on the League of Nations, the American people approved the Republican plans for the nation, and he was elected President in the election of 1920.

Harding turned out to be a very weak President. He allowed Congress to run the nation. The Republican Congress under Harding favored big business. It raised the tariff, and it lowered the income tax. Congress also passed a law which set up the **Veterans' Bureau** to help soldiers and sailors who fought in World War One.

Calvin Coolidge became President in 1923 when President Harding died. He was later elected as President in the election of 1924.

Dishonest Government Officials Under Harding

President Harding chose high government officials on the basis of friendship rather than ability. He made the mistake of appointing several government officials who turned out to be dishonest.

In 1923, one of Harding's friends was caught taking large sums of money from the Veterans' Bureau. Two of the men who were dishonest were members of Harding's Cabinet. Their dishonest actions hurt the nation and caused Harding to become unpopular.

Harding was an honest man, and he was very angry at the way his friends acted. In 1923, Harding became ill, and he died early in August. Vice-President Calvin Coolidge (koo-lij) became President.

Coolidge Was Elected President in 1924

Coolidge finished out Harding's term, and in the election of 1924, the Republican Party chose him as their candidate for President. The Republicans told Americans to "Keep Cool with Coolidge." The Democrats ran John W. Davis, a rich lawyer from New York. The

page 494

Progressive Party appeared once again and ran as a third party against the Republicans and Democrats. The Progressive Party ran Senator Robert La Follette of Wisconsin as its candidate. The Progressives wanted the government to help the farmers, to place high taxes on large incomes and big businesses, and to take over the railroads. Coolidge won the election easily, but Senator La Follette received almost 5 million votes, mainly from farmers and workers.

Under President Coolidge, the government continued to favor big business. Laws to regulate big business, such as the Clayton Anti-Trust Act, were not enforced. Congress continued to raise the tariff and to lower income taxes. For these reasons, business grew rapidly during the 1920's.

Hoover Was Elected President in 1928

In 1928, President Coolidge decided not to run for another term. The Republicans chose Herbert Hoover, head of the World War One food program and Coolidge's Secretary of Commerce, as their candidate for President. The Democrats ran Alfred E. Smith, the governor of New York. The two men were very different. Hoover was a farm boy from Iowa who became a rich and successful mining engineer and businessman. Smith came from a slum neighborhood in New York City. But he worked hard and was elected governor of New York four times.

During the election campaign, Hoover promised to keep the tariff high and to support the prohibition law against alcoholic drinks. Smith was against the prohibition law, and he promised to help America's workers and farmers. Smith was the first Catholic to run for President of the United States, and his religion was held against him. Also in 1928, many Americans were enjoying good times, and they felt that Hoover was better able to

Alfred E. Smith, the Democratic candidate, campaigning in the election of 1928.

keep these good times. Hoover was elected President by a large number of votes.

All Three Republican Presidents Shared Similar Ideas

Harding, Coolidge, and Hoover were very different, but their ideas about government were very much alike. All of them believed

Herbert Hoover was elected President in the election of 1928. He was a farm boy who worked hard and became a successful businessman.

that it was all right for the government to help business. But they did not believe that the government had the right to regulate business. All three allowed Congress to run the nation. And they all felt that the states were better able to take care of most problems than the federal government.

The Government Helped Business

To help American business, Congress raised the tariff during the 1920's. By 1930, the tariff was higher than it ever was before in American history. Congress also believed that lower taxes encouraged industry to grow. Therefore, income taxes and taxes on businesses were lowered during the 1920's, and the government did not try to regulate big business. Very few cases against trusts or monopolies

were brought to court. Men who favored big business were appointed to the Interstate Commerce Commission and the Federal Trade Commission. And the government actually encouraged business activities that helped lead to the growth of trusts.

Summing Up

During the 1920's, the United States had three Republican Presidents—President Harding, President Coolidge, and President Hoover. The federal government favored big businesses in the 1920's. The government stopped trying to regulate big businesses, and Congress raised the tariff and lowered taxes. In the next chapter, you will find out about some important changes in America during the 1920's.

AFTER YOU READ THE CHAPTER

Do You Know This Important Term?

For the sentence below, choose the term that best completes the sentence.

The (**American Legion/Veterans' Bureau**) was set up to help soldiers and sailors who fought in World War One.

Do You Remember These People?

Tell something about each of the following persons.

Warren G. Harding   James M. Cox
Calvin Coolidge   John W. Davis
Robert La Follette   Herbert Hoover
Alfred E. Smith

Can You Locate These Places?

Use a map of the United States to do the following map work.

1. In the election of 1920, both the Republican and the Democratic candidates were from the same state. Name and locate this state.
2. The Progressive Party ran Senator Robert La Follette for President in 1924. Locate his home state of Wisconsin.
3. Which President grew up as a farm boy in Iowa? Locate the state of Iowa.

Do You Know When It Happened?

What are the years of this chapter? The main events in this chapter are the elections of 1920, 1924, and 1928. Who was elected President in each of these elections?

Discovering More About the Main Idea

During the 1920's, the United States had three Republican Presidents. The federal government favored big business, raised the tariff, and lowered taxes.

Tell how each of the following developments is related to the MAIN IDEA.

President Harding appointed several government officials who turned out to be dishonest.

The Progressive Party's candidate, Senator La Follette, received almost 5 million votes in the election of 1924.

Herbert Hoover defeated Alfred E. Smith in the election for President in 1928. By 1930, the tariff was higher than it ever was before, and the government actually encouraged business activities that helped lead to the growth of trusts.

Can You Discuss the Chapter?

Use the information you learned in this chapter to answer the following questions.

1. Why was President Harding considered a weak President?
2. In the election of 1924, what did the Progressive Party want the government to do?
3. Compare the backgrounds and views of the two major candidates in the Presidential election of 1928.
4. How were the ideas of the three Republican Presidents of the 1920's about government similar?
5. Do you think the religion of a Presidential candidate should be a campaign issue? Why or why not?

Can You Connect the Past and the Present?

1. Has the religion of a candidate ever had anything to do with the outcome of an election in your school or community?
2. Harding was an honest man who had some dishonest friends. Why are we sometimes judged by the friends we have? Do you think this is fair? Why or why not?

CHAPTER 80

American Problems in the 1920's

Immigrants arriving in 1920.

BEFORE YOU BEGIN THE CHAPTER

Know What to Look For

1. In 1915, a new Ku Klux Klan was started. The members of this new Klan, like the members of the old Ku Klux Klan, wore high, pointed hats and covered their heads with white pillow slips and their bodies with white sheets. The new Ku Klux Klan was very much like the old one, but members no longer came only from the South. Now, Klan members were in forty states.

By 1924, the Klan had over five million members. Like the old Klan, the new Klan burned crosses to frighten black Americans, Jews, and immigrants. If this did not work, they turned to kidnapping, whipping, and even killing. In this chapter, you will read more about the Klan and other problems the American nation faced in the 1920's.

2. Read the title of the chapter. Then look

through the chapter and read each heading What do these headings tell you about black Americans during the 1920's?

3. Look at the pictures in the chapter and read each caption. What do the pictures tell you about American problems in the 1920's? Note also the time line at the beginning of the chapter. What years are included in this chapter? Compare this chapter time line to the unit time line on page 491.

4. Read the last part of the chapter called Summing Up. What happened to American life during the 1920's? What is the topic of the next chapter?

Compare this chapter time line to the unit time line on page 491.

Know These Important Terms

quota system
Universal Negro Improvement Association

Know the Main Idea

Here is the MAIN IDEA of this chapter.

During the 1920's, the United States had many problems. In these years, immigration was sharply cut, a new Ku Klux Klan was started, and many black Americans moved to the North.

Keep this MAIN IDEA in mind as you study the chapter. Ask yourself the following questions as you read. They will help you remember the MAIN IDEA.

1. Who were the first immigrants to be kept out of the United States?
2. To which group of immigrants was the quota system unfair?
3. What made the Universal Negro Improvement Association different from the N.A.A.C.P. or the Urban League?

THE YEARS OF THIS CHAPTER ARE 1920 TO 1930

1920   1930

THE CHAPTER LESSON BEGINS HERE

The United States Tried to Cut Down Immigration

The American nation was started by immigrants, or newcomers. And millions of immigrants from all over the world helped the United States to grow and develop. However, immigrants were not always welcomed in the United States. For many years, the United States kept immigrants from Asia out of the country.

Some Americans also wanted to cut down the number of immigrants from Europe coming into the United States. Many of the new immigrants came from southern and eastern Europe. Many of these new immigrants spoke their own languages and still kept their European ways of living. Some Americans felt

these new immigrants did not mix well with the rest of the American population. Others were afraid that immigrants might take jobs away from American workers. And still others did not think that immigrants from southern and eastern Europe made good citizens.

The Gates Were Closed to Newcomers

In 1921, Congress passed a law setting up a **quota system** to limit the total number of immigrants to the United States each year. This quota system allowed more immigrants from northern and western Europe to enter the United States than immigrants from southern and eastern Europe. And immigrants from the rest of the world were kept out almost completely by this law.

In 1924, Congress passed an even stronger immigration law. This law only allowed 164 thousand new immigrants to enter the United States each year. And it set up an even smaller quota for immigrants from southern and eastern Europe than did the 1921 law. Later, in 1929, Congress passed a law which made the quota for immigrants from southern and eastern Europe fairer. But this law also cut down the number of immigrants allowed to enter the United States to 150 thousand persons each year.

The Ku Klux Klan Returned

During the 1920's, some Americans began to dislike immigrants as well as those Americans they thought were different from themselves. This led to the development of a new Ku Klux Klan. This new Klan was started in 1915, and by 1925, it had almost 5 million members all over the United States. Only white Americans who were Protestants and who were born in the United States were allowed to join the Klan.

Members of the Ku Klux Klan disliked black Americans, Jews, and Catholics. However, they especially disliked black Americans. The Klan used whippings, cross-burnings, and even murder to frighten the people it was against. The new Klan became important in several Southern states. But the Klan's goals and cruel methods were not accepted by most

Members of the Ku Klux Klan burning a cross. A new Ku Klux Klan was started in the United States in 1915.

Black soldiers who fought in World War One found they still did not have equal rights when they returned home.

Americans. By the end of the 1920's, the Klan lost most of its members and most of its power.

Black Americans Moved to the North

After World War One, black Americans continued to work to improve their lives and to gain the same rights as all other American citizens. During World War One, thousands of black Americans served in the armed forces. These black soldiers expected to be treated as equals when they returned to the United States. However, the black soldiers who returned found that they still did not have equal rights with white citizens.

Starting in the year 1915, many black Americans moved from the South to the North. This movement of people to the North continued through World War One and into the 1920's. Many of these black Americans left the South because the North offered better jobs and better wages for workers.

During World War One, Northern factories needed many workers to produce the supplies needed for the war. When the war was over, however, factories made fewer goods, and thousands of workers lost their jobs. Black workers and white workers struggled for the jobs that remained in Northern factories. When some white Americans tried to use force, black Americans fought back to protect their rights as free men. As a result, race riots broke out in some cities.

Black Americans Continued to Struggle for Their Rights

During the 1920's, groups such as the N.A.A.C.P. and the Urban League fought for

A silent march by the N.A.A.C.P. in 1917. The marchers are protesting against threats and violence against black Americans.

the rights of black Americans. But these groups were not too successful. Therefore, many black Americans turned to the **Universal Negro Improvement Association**, or U.N.I.A., which was led by Marcus Garvey. Garvey said it was not possible for black citizens to win their rights in America. For this reason, he suggested that some black Americans return to Africa. But most black Americans wanted to remain in America, and the U.N.I.A. soon came to an end.

Black Americans Find Problems and Opportunities

The black newcomers to the North found both problems and opportunities. A lack of housing led to the start of black ghettos, or all black neighborhoods, in northern cities. Black Americans often got the hardest jobs

and received the lowest pay. But many black workers found jobs in industry or became clerks in businesses. And some others set up their own businesses. Black Americans also found that they were able to vote in the North. In 1928, black voters in Chicago succeeded in electing Oscar De Priest, a black Representative, to Congress.

Summing Up

During the 1920's many changes took place in American life. Congress passed laws that sharply cut immigration to the United States. Some Americans joined a new Ku Klux Klan. Many black Americans from the South moved to the North. In the North, they found both problems and opportunities. The next chapter tells about changes in American life in the 1920's.

AFTER YOU READ THE CHAPTER

Do You Know These Important Terms?

For each sentence below, choose the term that best completes the sentence.

1. The (balance/quota) system limited the total number of immigrants to the United States each year.
2. The (Back to the Fatherland/Universal Negro Improvement Association) was a group that suggested that some black Americans return to Africa because it was not possible for black citizens to win their rights in America.

Do You Remember These People?

Tell something about each of the following persons.

Marcus Garvey   Oscar De Priest

Can You Locate These Places?

Use the maps in your classroom to locate the following places. Tell how each location is related to the events in this chapter.

Northern and Western Europe   Asia
Southern and Eastern Europe   Africa
Chicago

Do You Know When It Happened?

What are the years of this chapter? Tell why each of the following dates was important in this chapter.

1921   1924   1928   1929

Discovering More About the Main Idea

During the 1920's, the United States had many problems. In these years, immigration was sharply cut, a new Ku Klux Klan was started, and many black Americans moved to the North.

Tell how each of the following developments is related to the MAIN IDEA.

The quota system was started in 1921. This quota system allowed more immigrants from northern and western Europe to enter the United States than immigrants from eastern and southern Europe. Immigrants from the rest of the world were kept out.

The Ku Klux Klan gained many members but because of it's terrible methods, the Klan lost most of its power by the end of the 1920's.

Thousands of black Americans moved into Northern cities. They often had a hard time finding jobs and had other hardships. But even so, there were opportunities in the North.

Can You Discuss the Chapter?

Use the information you learned in this chapter to answer the following questions.

1. Why did many Americans want to cut down on the number of immigrants coming into the United States?
2. Why did the Ku Klux Klan lose most of its power by the end of the 1920's?
3. How were many black Americans disappointed after World War One?
4. Why didn't the U.N.I.A. last very long?
5. Why did black Americans from the South want to move to Northern cities?

Can You Connect the Past and the Present?

1. Is the Ku Klux Klan still active today? If so, how does it operate?
2. Is the quota system still in effect in the United States as it was in 1929? Do you think the quota system was fair? Why or why not? Were exceptions ever made in the quota system?

CHAPTER 81

American Life in the 1920's

Waiting in line to see the first talking motion picture.

BEFORE YOU BEGIN THE CHAPTER

Know What to Look For

1. On January 19, 1901, Guglielmo Marconi, an Italian inventor, sat waiting on the cold, wind-swept shores of Newfoundland. He was waiting to hear if his invention—the wireless telegraph—was able to send messages across the Atlantic Ocean without wires. An assistant in Great Britain was to send a message to Marconi. This message was to be sent through the air in a code made up of dots and dashes. The wireless method of sending messages through the air had already been tested for short distances. But was it able to send messages over thousands of miles? In his earphones, Marconi began to hear the dots and dashes. He was overjoyed.

With the invention of the wireless telegraph a new field of communication had been discovered. It led to the later invention of the radio and television. In this chapter, you will read how the radio and other new inventions began to change American life in the 1920's.

2. Read the title of the chapter. Then look through the chapter and read each heading. Besides the radio, what other types of amusements were popular during the 1920's?

3. Look at the pictures in the chapter and read each caption. What do the pictures tell you about American life in the years of the 1920's? Note also the time line at the beginning of the chapter. What years are included in this chapter? Compare this chapter time line to the unit time line on page 491.

4. Read the last part of the chapter called Summing Up. Why were the 1920's exciting years?

Know These Important Terms

flappers   nickelodeons
suburbs

Know the Main Idea

Here is the MAIN IDEA of this chapter.

During the 1920's, many changes in American life took place.

Keep this MAIN IDEA in mind as you study the chapter. Ask yourself the following questions as you read. They will help you remember the MAIN IDEA.

1. How did women show their new independence in the 1920's?

2. When were talking motion pictures developed?

3. What kinds of new amusements were introduced in the 1920's?

THE YEARS OF THIS CHAPTER ARE 1920 TO 1930

1920   1930

THE CHAPTER LESSON BEGINS HERE

The Roaring Twenties

So many changes took place in American life in the 1920's that the period is often called the "Roaring Twenties." These years were "roaring," or exciting, years in America's history. Many new things—movies, radio, and automobiles—were just becoming popular in the 1920's.

American Women Became More Independent

During the 1920's, American women became more independent than they ever were before. Women were now able to vote. A growing number of women were going out to work and earning their own living. And more women went to colleges.

To show that they were independent and equal with men, women learned how to drive automobiles and do many other things that men did. These modern American women of the 1920's were called **flappers**. The flapper wore a short skirt, cut her hair short, and used lipstick and rouge.

American Family Life Changed

American family life also changed in the 1920's. With the invention of machines such as vacuum cleaners and irons, housework took up much less of a woman's time. Many women were now able to go to work or to join clubs. Many more families broke up. And most families had fewer children.

page 505

Modern American women during the 1920's were called flappers. Above, two flappers walking down a city street.

In the cities, more and more people lived in apartment buildings. And many city people began to move from the city to the **suburbs,** or towns located near large cities. Before the 1920's, only rich people were able to live in the suburbs. But in the 1920's, many suburbs had large numbers of low-cost, one-story homes for sale. Workers were able to afford these homes and leave the crowded city.

The Automobile Changed American Life

In the 1920's, America became a nation of automobiles, or cars. The automobile was invented before the year 1900. But in 1914, only about 2 million automobiles were in use. By 1929, however, about 24 million automobiles were on the nation's roads. The growing use of automobiles improved life for Americans.

Automobiles made it possible for Americans to visit all parts of the United States. Many Americans were able to travel to beaches, or mountain resorts, or across the country on their summer vacation. Cars made it possible for people to work in the city but live outside the city in the suburbs. Suburbs grew as more and more people began to own cars. Automobiles made it possible for farmers and their families to drive to town to shop and enjoy themselves. And young people all over the United States welcomed the freedom that the automobile gave them.

Americans Enjoyed Movies and Radio Programs

Americans of the 1920's enjoyed going to the movies. Movies were first developed in the 1890's. The first movie theaters charged only 5 cents for admission and were called **nickelodeons** (NIK-ul-OH-dee-uhns). During the 1920's, nickelodeons were replaced by large movie theaters. These movie theaters were built in most large cities, and about 80 million Americans went to the movies every week to watch their favorite movie stars in silent pictures. And by the end of the 1920's, talking pictures, or movies with sound, were developed.

Radios first came into use in the 1920's. The first radio station, KDKA, was opened in Pittsburgh in 1920. Ten years later, almost 600 radio stations were offering radio programs. News reports, sports events, variety shows, and music programs were among the most popular programs on the radio stations. By the end of the 1920's, 12 million radios were already in use.

Sports Events Became Popular

During the 1920's, sports events became very popular. This happened because Americans had the free time and extra money to spend on watching sports. Baseball became especially popular, and "Babe" Ruth of the New York Yankees and other ball players attracted large crowds of sport fans into the baseball parks. "Red" Grange of the University of Illinois and other famous football stars helped Americans to become interested in football. And Johnny Weissmuller caused millions of boys and girls to want to learn to swim. During these years, golf and tennis also became popular sports.

Boxing was one of the most popular sports in America in the 1920's. Americans especially liked heavyweight championship fights. In 1919, Jack Dempsey became the heavyweight champion. His fights attracted the largest crowds ever to attend boxing matches. Boxing fans paid a total of almost 5 million dollars to watch two heavyweight championship fights between Jack Dempsey and Gene Tunney.

Charles Lindbergh.

THE LONE EAGLE

In 1919, a prize of 25 thousand dollars was offered to the first man to fly non-stop from New York to Paris. In 1927, this prize was still unclaimed. But in May of that year, Charles Lindbergh, a twenty-seven year old pilot, decided to try to make the flight. He took off from Roosevelt Field in New York on May 20, 1927, in his plane called the "Spirit of St. Louis."

Lindbergh's flight across the Atlantic was successful. He not only made the flight non-stop, he also made it alone. The flight of 3600 miles took thirty-three hours and thirty-nine minutes. Lindbergh, who came to be known as the "Lone Eagle," became a hero overnight. Over 100 thousand people greeted him when he landed in France. And the American government sent a navy ship to bring him and his plane home.

When he arrived in America, Lindbergh received a hero's welcome. He was given the Distinguished Flying Cross and the Congressional Medal of Honor. Cities all over the country gave him parades and held celebrations in his honor. Americans admired Lindbergh's great skill and courage in making his heroic solo flight across the Atlantic.

These three boys are listening to a crystal set with earphones. The crystal set was an early version of a radio.

Americans Found Many New Things to Do in Their Free Time

During the 1920's, Americans tried all kinds of new amusements. Some men tried to see how long they were able to sit on the top of flag poles. Dancing was especially popular in the 1920's. At special dances, dancers tried to see how many hours or days they were able to dance without stopping. Sometimes, these dances lasted as long as a week. The most popular dances of the 1920's were the Charleston, the black bottom, the varsity drag, and the lindy hop.

Theater shows were still very popular with Americans in the 1920's. Americans also continued to enjoy the vaudeville shows. These vaudeville shows were now shown along with movies at the movie theater. And for people who stayed at home, the popular amusements were crossword puzzles and card games.

Summing Up

The 1920's were exciting years when many changes in American life took place. American women became more independent. Automobiles gave Americans more freedom to travel. Movies, radio, and sports events became popular amusements. In the next chapter, you will find out about changes in American thought and education in the 1920's.

AFTER YOU READ THE CHAPTER

Do You Know These Important Terms?

For each sentence below, choose the term that best completes the sentence.

1. Modern women in the 1920's, who wore short skirts, short hair, and lipstick, were called (**flappers**/**pixies**).
2. Towns located near large cities are called (**suburbs**/**county seats**).
3. The first movie theaters, which charged only five cents for admission, were called (**silent flickers**/**nickelodeons**).

Do You Remember These People?

Tell something about each of the following persons.

"Babe" Ruth   **"Red" Grange**
Johnny Weissmuller   **Jack Dempsey**
Gene Tunney

Can You Locate These Places?

In this chapter, you read about the growth of the suburb. Use the maps in your classroom to locate some cities which started to develop large suburbs in the 1920's.

Do You Know When It Happened?

What are the years of this chapter? Place the following events in the order in which they occurred.

Talking motion pictures were developed.
Women gained the right to vote.
Movies were first developed.
The first radio station was opened in Pittsburgh.
Jack Dempsey became heavyweight boxing champion.

Discovering More About the Main Idea

During the 1920's, many changes in American life took place.

Tell how each of the following developments is related to the MAIN IDEA.

American family life changed. Women were more independent and had more free time. Many women went to work or joined clubs.

Automobiles made it possible for Americans to visit all parts of the United States. Cars also made it possible for people to work in the city but live in the suburbs.

New amusements like the movies and radio, as well as sports events, became popular. Some older kinds of amusements remained popular, but Americans also tried all kinds of new amusements.

Can You Discuss the Chapter?

Use the information you learned in this chapter to answer the following questions.

1. How did American family life change during the 1920's?
2. Explain how American women began to show their independence.
3. Why do you think that most Americans wanted to have an automobile?
4. Describe some popular amusements of the 1920's.
5. Of all the amusements of the 1920's, which do you think you might have liked the best? Why?

Can You Connect the Past and the Present?

1. What newer invention has limited the popularity of both radio and movies?
2. You have read how women of the 1920's tried to show their independence. How do young people today try to show their feelings of independence?

CHAPTER 82

American Thought in the 1920's

Sinclair Lewis and his wife in a Model T Ford.

BEFORE YOU BEGIN THE CHAPTER

Know What to Look For

1. Will Rogers was one of America's greatest humorists. Born in Oklahoma, he was proud of his Indian heritage. He once said, "My ancestors didn't come over on the Mayflower. They met the boat." Will Rogers was an actor, writer, and radio performer. He had the ability to make people laugh, and almost all Americans liked him.

Will Rogers criticized things that the government or people did which did not seem right to him. He did this by making fun of them. With his humor, he was able to criticize Presidents or kings, and millions of Americans turned on their radios to hear his funny but serious criticism. Humor is only one part of a nation's culture. In this chapter, you will read about other parts of American culture in the 1920's.

2. Read the title of the chapter. Then look through the chapter and read each heading. From reading the headings, tell what happened to American education in the 1920's.

3. Look at the pictures in the chapter and read each caption. Can you name the famous author shown in the first chapter picture? Note also the time line at the beginning of the chapter. What years are included in the chapter? Compare this chapter time line to the unit time line on page 491.

4. Read the last part of the chapter called Summing Up. Where did the changes in American thought show up?

Know These Important Terms
Harlem Renaissance
progressive education

Know the Main Idea
Here is the MAIN IDEA of this chapter.

Changes in American life during the 1920's brought changes in the way Americans thought. These changes in thought showed up in American writing, music, and education.

Keep this MAIN IDEA in mind as you study the chapter. Ask yourself the following questions as you read. They will help you remember the MAIN IDEA.

1. Who was the first musician to give a serious jazz concert?
2. What name was given to the excellent group of black writers who wrote about the life and problems of black Americans?
3. Who developed the ideas of progressive education?

THE YEARS OF THIS CHAPTER ARE 1920 TO 1930

1920

1930

THE CHAPTER LESSON BEGINS HERE

Important Writing Was Done During the 1920's

Many interesting novels, fine poems, and outstanding plays were written during the 1920's. Many writers in the 1920's wrote about machines and big businesses, and the changes that they were causing in American life. They showed that many Americans were only interested in becoming rich and owning many things. They felt that these Americans had false values. These writers tried to show that in some ways big businesses were causing serious problems in American life.

Sinclair Lewis attacked the false values of Americans who were only interested in making money. F. Scott Fitzgerald showed the problems that young people faced because of the changes in American life. In *A Farewell to Arms*, Ernest Hemingway attacked the evils of modern war. Theodore Dreiser's *An American Tragedy* described the life of a young man from the slums of Kansas City who tried to gain wealth and power. Eugene O'Neill, the most famous playwright of the 1920's, wrote about troubled people and their problems. And Robert Frost, Carl Sandburg, Stephen Vincent

Clarence Darrow and William Jennings Bryan.

THE MONKEY TRIAL

In 1925, the state of Tennessee passed a law making it unlawful to teach Darwin's theory of evolution in the schools. This theory of evolution said that it took thousands of years for modern man to fully develop. John T. Scopes, a young high-school biology teacher in Dayton, Tennessee, decided to teach Darwin's theory. He was immediately arrested and given a trial.

Scopes' trial was soon named the "monkey trial" because some people wrongly claimed that evolution meant man had developed from early apelike creatures. William Jennings Bryan, former Secretary of State and a three-time Presidential candidate, helped to represent the state of Tennessee at the trial. Clarence Darrow, the leading lawyer of the time, defended Scopes at the trial. The crowd attending the trial was so large that the judge moved the trial from the court house outside to the court-house lawn.

Scopes was found guilty and he was fined 100 dollars. Later, the Supreme Court of Tennessee overruled, or changed, this decision. But much more than one man was on trial in Tennessee. The main question was whether a state might pass a law to prevent certain new ideas from being taught.

Benét (bi-NAY), and T. S. Eliot wrote poetry which is still read and enjoyed today.

Jazz Became America's Most Popular Music

The period of the 1920's is often called the "Jazz Age," because jazz music became popular all over the nation. Jazz developed from the ragtime music played by black musicians in the South before World War One. Jazz was also played by black musicians, but many white bands took over this new kind of music and became famous. Young people went to hear jazz music played by Duke Ellington and Louis Armstrong. And many Americans enjoyed the music of Paul Whiteman or Guy Lombardo. In 1924, Whiteman played George Gershwin's "Rhapsody in Blue" at a jazz concert. This concert made jazz important. And many Americans now began to think of jazz as serious music.

Black Americans Made Important Contributions

In the 1920's, black Americans made many important contributions to American life. During the 1920's, black Americans produced outstanding books, poetry, and works of art. In the Harlem section of New York, an excellent group of black writers began to write about the life and problems of black Americans. This was called the **Harlem Renaissance** (REN-uh-SANS), or rebirth. However, many black writers and painters from other parts of America took part in the Harlem Renaissance. In their books and poems, black writers asked for an end to segregation and for equal rights for all Americans. They had a great effect on Americans.

Claude McKay's *Harlem Shadows* was one of the earliest works of this Renaissance. McKay was soon joined by such other great poets as Countee Cullen, James Weldon Johnson, and Langston Hughes. These black poets were probably the most important writers of this Renaissance. Their poems told of black life and problems in America and looked forward to a better way of life. Johnson and Hughes also wrote stories and movies about black Americans. In his book *The Walls of Jericho,* Rudolph Fisher described life in Harlem. Other well-known black writers were Jessie Fauset (FOH-set), Arna Bontemps, and Walter White.

Black painters were also a part of the Harlem Renaissance. Aaron Douglas' paintings are well known, and Richmond Barthe's sculptures, or figures made of wood, clay, or stone, are found in art museums all over the world. Many black Americans became actors, singers, and musicians in the 1920's. Among the black singers who became famous in the 1920's were Harry Burleigh (BUR-li), Roland Hayes, Paul Robeson, Bessie Smith, and Marian Anderson.

High School Education Was Improved in America

Americans were also very much interested in education during the 1920's. More children than ever before were going to school. And more children were now able to attend high school. Between 1920 and 1930, the number of students in high school went up from about 2 million to over 4 million. And the education these high school students received was also greatly changed.

During the 1920's, American high schools began to offer more vocational courses to students. Some of these vocational courses were typing, shorthand, the use of office machines, and other business skills. Other courses were given in cooking, sewing, and making things out of metal and wood. These vocational courses helped to prepare young Americans to get jobs when they finished school.

More Americans Attended College

The number of students who attended colleges in the 1920's also increased. Part of this growth was in the junior colleges, or colleges that offered two years of education beyond high school. Also, many students began to stay in college for more than four years. Students who stayed in college for an extra year received a master's degree. And students who stayed for two or three years more received a doctor's degree.

A New Type of Education Developed

During the 1920's, some elementary schools began to change their methods, or ways, of teaching children. Most of these changes were brought about because of the ideas of John Dewey. Dewey's ideas came to be called **progressive education.**

Dewey's progressive education taught that the two goals of education were to make better people and to make a better world in which to live. Dewey believed that schools might be able to reach both these goals if the students were allowed to work on things that they were interested in and able to do. Although Dewey's methods were never completely accepted, some schools began to use some of them.

Summing Up

In the 1920's, the changes in American life caused changes in the way Americans thought. These changes in thought showed up in American writing, music, and education. And many black Americans made important contributions to American life in the 1920's. In the next chapter, which begins Unit 21, you will read about the changes in America in the 1920's.

AFTER YOU READ THE CHAPTER

Do You Know These Important Terms?

For each sentence below, choose the term that best completes the sentence.

1. An excellent group of black writers and artists who used the life and problems of black Americans to write and paint about started the (**civil rights movement/Harlem Renaissance**).
2. The ideas of John Dewey became known as (**vocational/progressive**) education.

Do You Remember These People?

Tell something about some of these people.

Sinclair Lewis	Countee Cullen
F. Scott Fitzgerald	Langston Hughes
Ernest Hemingway	Rudolph Fisher
Theodore Dreiser	Jessie Fauset
Eugene O'Neill	Arna Bontemps
Robert Frost	Walter White
Carl Sandburg	Aaron Douglas
T. S. Eliot	Richmond Barthe
Duke Ellington	Harry Burleigh
Louis Armstrong	Roland Hayes
Paul Whiteman	Paul Robeson
Guy Lombardo	Bessie Smith
George Gershwin	Marian Anderson
Claude McKay	John Dewey
Stephen Vincent Benét	James Weldon Johnson

Do You Know When It Happened?

What are the years of this chapter?

Discovering More About the Main Idea

Changes in American life in the 1920's brought changes in the way Americans thought. These changes in thought showed up in American writing, music, and education.

Tell how each of the following developments is related to the MAIN IDEA.

Many writers wrote about the changes in American life. They showed that Americans who were only interested in becoming rich and successful had false values.

Black writers in Harlem and elsewhere began to write about the life and problems of black Americans.

Jazz music became popular all over the nation.

In 1924, Paul Whiteman played George Gershwin's "Rhapsody in Blue" in an important concert.

More students than ever before attended high school and college. American high schools began to offer vocational courses to help young Americans to get jobs.

Can You Discuss This Chapter?

Use the information you learned in this chapter to answer the following questions.

1. Who were some important writers during the 1920's? Name a work of each of these writers.
2. Explain how jazz music became popular across the nation.
3. Who are some black writers and artists who contributed to the Harlem Renaissance?
4. How did both high schools and elementary schools change during the 1920's?
5. Do you agree with John Dewey's two goals for education? Why or why not?

Can You Connect the Past and the Present?

1. Some writers, artists, musicians, and poets you read about in this chapter are still alive today. Do you know of any of their works? Which are your favorites?
2. In your school, which courses are set up to help you to get a job? go on to college? be a better citizen?

Changes in America in the 1920's

The Stock Market Crash on Wall Street.

THE CHAPTERS IN UNIT 21 ARE

CHAPTER 83   Changes in America in the 1920's
CHAPTER 84   Expansion of American Businesses
CHAPTER 85   The Great Depression

THE YEARS OF THIS UNIT ARE 1920 TO 1932

| 1900 | 1920 | 1932 | 1975 |

Changes in America in the 1920's

American soldiers returning from France.

BEFORE YOU BEGIN THE CHAPTER

Know What to Look For

1. In the 1920's, the prohibition law against the sale of alcoholic drinks led to lawlessness in many parts of the United States. Most of this lawlessness was centered around the unlawful sale of whisky. The gangs of gangsters who sold this bootleg liquor during the 1920's drove fast cars and fought with machine guns. Sometimes rival gangs almost

carried on open warfare to control the sale of bootleg liquor in a city.

In Chicago, on St. Valentine's Day in 1929, one gang shot down nine members of another gang in a garage. Chicago was especially troubled by these gangs of gangsters. But many other cities also had trouble with the gangsters who sold bootleg liquor. Cooperation between city police and federal police helped to bring this "gang era" to an end.

2. Read the title of the chapter. Next look through the chapter and read each heading. What were some problems in the 1920's?

3. Look at the pictures in the chapter and read each caption. What do the pictures tell you about problems in America during the 1920's? Notice also the time line at the beginning of the chapter. What years are included in this chapter? Compare this chapter time line to the unit time line on page 515.

4. Read the last part of the chapter called Summing Up. What group of Americans faced hard times during the 1920's?

Know These Important Terms

McNary-Haugen Bill
Eighteenth Amendment

Know the Main Idea

Here is the MAIN IDEA of this chapter.

During the 1920's, many changes took place in the United States. Farmers and unskilled workers did not share in the good times of the 1920's. Prohibition led to lawlessness in many areas.

Keep this MAIN IDEA in mind as you study the chapter. Ask yourself the following questions as you read. They will help you remember the MAIN IDEA.

1. What was the result of the coal and steel workers' strike in 1919? What did this show about government policy toward workers?

2. What law which promised help to the farmer was vetoed, or turned down, by President Coolidge?

3. What types of crime were encouraged by the prohibition law?

THE YEARS OF THIS CHAPTER ARE 1920 TO 1930

1920   1930   1932

THE CHAPTER LESSON BEGINS HERE

The Nation Went Back to Peace Time Living

Right after World War One, the United States cut down the size of the army and navy. This was done so quickly that many soldiers and sailors who returned from the war were not able to find jobs right away. Government control of American factories and railroads ended, and these businesses were returned to their owners.

Many Strikes Were Called After World War One

During World War One, workers in factories earned high wages. After the war, however, factories made fewer goods and

thousands of workers lost their jobs. Also, wages did not increase as fast as did the prices of food and clothing. In 1919, many groups of workers went on strike for higher wages and better working conditions. At first, these strikes were successful. But then factory owners began to feel that unions were becoming too strong.

In 1919, the government used its power to help end strikes against the coal and steel industries. Workers in these two industries went on strike to win shorter hours and higher wages. However, the owners refused even to talk with the unions. Instead, the

page 517

Workers on strike against the steel industry in 1919. Many workers went on strike after World War One to demand higher wages.

companies were able to get injunctions, or court orders, to end these two strikes. Once again, the government returned to favoring big business over workers.

Unions Grew Weaker During the 1920's

In the 1920's, many skilled workers lost their interest in unions, and the American Federation of Labor and other unions lost members. One reason for this lack of interest was that good times returned to the nation during the 1920's. In these years, skilled workers were able to find plenty of jobs, and they earned high wages. Also, many owners refused to hire union men.

Labor unions also lost the support of many skilled workers because many large companies started to treat their workers better. Many companies began to pay higher wages and to give their workers a shorter workday. And some companies began to give their workers paid vacations and pension plans. However, unskilled workers did not share in these improved working conditions. Many unskilled workers still worked twelve hours a day and earned low wages.

Farmers Faced Hard Times During the 1920's

You may remember that American farmers

Above, a farm family who left their farm in Oklahoma. Many such families traveled to California hoping to find a better life.

enjoyed good times during World War One. But after the war, the demand for farm crops decreased, because Great Britain and France now were able to supply their own food. Farm prices fell sharply as American farmers grew more crops than they were able to sell. But the prices of manufactured goods farmers needed went up in these years.

Also, many farmers bought extra land at high prices during the war. After the war, many farmers were unable to pay for this new land. As a result, large numbers of farmers went into debt, and many of them lost their farms. Many of these farmers were forced to become tenant farmers. But many others gave up farming and moved to the cities.

The Government Did Not Help the Farmer

At first, farmers hoped that a high tariff might help them sell more of their crops because a high tariff kept the prices for farm crops from Europe very high. But the high tariff did not help improve prices for American farm crops. Then in 1924, the **McNary-Haugen** (mak-NAR-i HOU-gen) **Bill** came before Congress. This bill suggested that the federal government buy the farm crops that American farmers were unable to sell. Then,

Federal agents pouring whisky into a sewer after the Prohibition Amendment was passed.

the government was to sell these farm crops to foreign countries.

At first, Congress turned down the McNary-Haugen Bill. Later, Congress passed the bill twice, but President Coolidge vetoed it, or turned down the bill, both times.

Alcoholic Drinks Were Made Unlawful

In 1919, the **Eighteenth Amendment**, often called the Prohibition Amendment, was approved by Congress. The Eighteenth Amendment made it unlawful to sell or buy alcoholic drinks. This amendment was passed because

many Americans were against the use of alcoholic drinks.

If you remember, several states in the 1800's passed prohibition laws which made it unlawful to buy or sell alcoholic drinks. Then in World War One, many Americans gave up drinking. Grain, which is used to make alcoholic drinks, was needed to supply the nation with food during the war. Also, many Americans began to believe that alcoholic drinks harmed people's health. For these reasons, many Americans wanted a Constitutional amendment against alcoholic drinks.

Prohibition Led to Lawlessness

However, many Americans were against the Eighteenth Amendment, and they did not obey this law. These Americans felt that the government did not have the right to tell people they were not allowed to drink.

Some of them bought "bootleg liquor," or alcohol produced or sold unlawfully. Bootlegging, or the unlawful making of alcohol, became a big business. In some cities, gangsters who distributed alcohol unlawfully became very powerful. Sometimes, gangs of gangsters fought one another to control the bootleg business in a city. Many Americans believed that the repeal of the prohibition law might help cut down on crime.

Summing Up

After World War One, many changes took place in the United States. Right after the war, many workers went out on strike. But by 1920, factories were busy, and skilled workers got better working conditions. But farmers and unskilled workers faced hard times. The Eighteenth Amendment, which outlawed the making or using of alcoholic drinks, was passed in 1919. In the next chapter, you will read about growing American industries in the 1920s.

AFTER YOU READ THE CHAPTER

Do You Know These Important Terms?

For each sentence below, choose the term that best completes the sentence.

1. The (McNary-Haugen/Farm Loan) Bill was designed to help farmers, but it was vetoed by the President.
2. The (Eighteenth/Nineteenth) Amendment made it unlawful to sell or buy alcoholic drinks.

Can You Locate These Places?

Use a map of the United States to locate the following places. Tell in which state each place is located.

Chicago	**New York**
Boston	**San Francisco**
Kansas City	**Washington, D.C.**

Do You Know When It Happened?

What are the years of this chapter? Tell how each of the following dates is connected to the events in this chapter.

1919   **1924**

Discovering More About the Main Idea

During the 1920's, many changes took place in the United States. Farmers and unskilled workers did not share in the good times of the 1920's. Prohibition led to lawlessness in many areas.

Tell how each of the following developments is related to the MAIN IDEA.

Unions grew weaker during the 1920's because skilled workers were able to find plenty of jobs, and they earned high wages. Unskilled workers did not share in the improved working conditions.

The prices of farmers' crops dropped, but the prices of manufactured goods that farmers needed went up. Congress tried to help the farmer by passing the McNary-Haugen Bill, but the President vetoed the bill.

The Eighteenth Amendment led to lawlessness. Sometimes gangs of gangsters fought one another to control the bootleg business in a city.

Can You Discuss the Chapter?

Use the information you learned in this chapter to answer the following questions.

1. Why did unions grow weaker during the 1920's?
2. Why did farmers face hard times when most of the nation was enjoying good times?
3. How did the government try to help farmers? What happened?
4. How did prohibition lead to lawlessness in some areas?
5. Why do you think the prohibition law did not work too well?

Can You Connect the Past and the Present?

1. Many Americans were against the Prohibition Amendment, and they refused to obey it. Today, Americans sometimes disagree with laws that are passed. Instead of breaking these laws, what can Americans do to try and change these laws? Can you give any example of laws that Americans have been able to change?
2. Is there a difference in the number of jobs or the working conditions for skilled and unskilled workers in your community today? Explain the differences, if there are any.

CHAPTER 84

Expansion of American Businesses

A blast furnace in a Pittsburgh steel mill.

BEFORE YOU BEGIN THE CHAPTER

Know What to Look For

1. Have you ever been to a drag strip? Sleek, high-powered cars roll to the starting line. Each driver guns his engine waiting for the "Christmas tree" lights, a series of lights that give the green light to go. Then, with a squeal and burning of tires, each car leaps from the starting line, racing the quarter mile track with engine wide open.

Drag racing is a favorite sport of many young men. Drag racers can be the boy next door in his "souped up" car or a professional in a specially made car. Automobiles and speed are important to young people today. In this chapter, you will read about some developments that made all of this possible.

2. Read the title of the chapter. Then look through the chapter and read each heading. Using the headings, can you tell if all types

of manufacturing grew during the 1920's?

3. Look at the pictures in the chapter and read each caption. What do the pictures show you about American industries in the 1920's? Note also the time line at the beginning of the chapter. What years are included in this chapter? Compare this chapter time line to the unit time line on page 515.

4. Read the last part of the chapter called Summing Up. What new industries developed in the United States? What is the topic of the next chapter?

Know These Important Terms

mass production   Federal Power Commission
standard parts   chain stores
assembly line   trade associations

Know the Main Idea

Here is the MAIN IDEA of this chapter.
American business and industry enjoyed good times during the 1920's. Many new industries developed, and new methods of manufacturing helped many businesses and industries to grow.

Keep this MAIN IDEA in mind as you study the chapter. Ask yourself the following questions as you read. They will help you remember the MAIN IDEA.

1. Name some of the new jobs that the automobile industry provided for workers.

2. How were most American homes lighted by the end of the 1920's?

3. Name some industries that became less important in the 1920's.

THE YEARS OF THIS CHAPTER ARE 1920 TO 1930

1920   1930   1932

THE CHAPTER LESSON BEGINS HERE

Automobile Manufacturing Became America's Largest Industry

In the 1920's, automobile manufacturing became America's largest industry. The automobile industry provided thousands of new jobs for workers. Many thousands of workers were needed to help make cars and to work in the new industries that made parts for cars. And many other workers were needed to service and repair cars in gasoline stations and garages. Other workers found jobs building roads and working in the roadside inns, restaurants, and motels that soon opened everywhere to serve Americans.

New Methods of Manufacturing Helped Industries Grow

Several things helped the growth of the automobile industry and other industries in the 1920's. One thing was **mass production.** Mass production means that large amounts of a product are made. Usually, when a product is mass produced, its price is lower, and therefore, large amounts of the product can be sold. For example, in 1908, when Henry Ford made his first Model T Ford automobile, it sold for 950 dollars. But mass production made it possible for him to sell his Model T for 290 dollars in 1925.

Another thing that helped the growth of the automobile industry and other industries was **standard parts.** When parts are standard, a part made for one machine—such as a car—fits any other machine of the same type and

This picture shows an assembly line in a Ford plant. Workers are adding bolts and other parts to the Model T Ford.

model. The use of standard parts was not new. Eli Whitney used standard parts to manufacture guns in the 1800's. But in the 1920's, the use of standard parts became necessary for mass production.

The **assembly line** also was necessary for mass production. On the assembly line, machine parts were moved along from worker to worker. These parts were put together by the workers who were trained to do only one particular job on the assembly line. The assembly line cut the time needed to put an automobile together from twelve hours to about an hour and a half. And the assembly line worked just as well in other industries.

Most Americans Now Used Electricity

The electrical industry also grew very rapidly during the 1920's. Very few American homes were lighted by electricity at the end of World War One. But by the end of the 1920's, almost two thirds of American homes used electricity. And the Americans soon started to use many electrical appliances such as irons and vacuum cleaners.

All this electric power was produced by a

This picture shows the first airplane ever to be flown. It was flown by the Wright brothers at Kitty Hawk, North Carolina in 1903.

few very large electric power companies. Congress formed the **Federal Power Commission** to regulate, or control, these companies, but during the 1920's, this commission was very weak. Some Congressmen wanted the government to own some electric power companies. They believed the government might force the other power companies to lower their prices. But this idea was not accepted by most Americans during the 1920's.

Many New Industries Became Important

Many new industries developed and grew rapidly in the 1920's. The movie industry and the radio industry developed into large industries during the 1920's. Bus companies and trucking companies also started to become important, and they grew rapidly. And the chemical industry was helped by the development of rayon, plastics, and other man-made materials.

The airplane industry started to become important in the 1920's. The Wright brothers flew their first plane in 1903. And by 1918, the American government was already beginning to send mail by airplane. This was

One of Woolworth's early chain stores, located in Lancaster, Pennsylvania, is shown here.

known as air mail service. During the 1920's, airplanes carried very few passengers.

Some Industries Became Less Important

Not all industries enjoyed good times during the 1920's. The coal industry became less important as more electrical power was used. The cotton industry also began to decrease in importance, because many foreign nations now grew cotton, and materials such as silk and rayon became popular. American shipping lines began to lose business. Many people started to travel on foreign ships because they were often faster and charged lower

prices than many of the American ships.

During the 1920's, American railroads began to lose business to the trucking companies and the bus companies. In order to gain business, the railroads tried to make their trains more modern and faster. Many railroad companies joined together and formed one large company. In this way, the railroads did not fight one another for business, and they were able to charge lower prices and provide better service.

Businesses Grew Larger

In the 1920's, business companies started to grow larger. When the United States Steel Corporation was formed in 1901, it was the only company in America that made a billion dollars. However, by the end of the 1920's, many companies became billion dollar companies. Also, some companies began to open many stores called **chain stores.** Chain stores, such as Woolworth's and the Great Atlantic and Pacific Tea Company (A&P), grew up almost everywhere in the United States.

Some industries were controlled by a few very large companies. These companies decided how to run the industry. They set prices and regulated how much was produced each year. In other industries, **trade associations,** or groups of businessmen, also decided how the industry must be run. Usually this kind of control led to higher prices.

Summing Up

During the 1920's, most American businesses and industries enjoyed good times. Many new industries developed in the United States. These included automobile manufacturing, electrical power production, movies, and radio. New methods, or ways, of manufacturing helped many businesses to grow. The next chapter tells how the United States faced hard times in the 1930's.

AFTER YOU READ THE CHAPTER

Do You Know These Important Terms?

For each sentence below, choose the term that best completes the sentence.

1. (Mass/Wholesale) production means that large amounts of a product are made.
2. (Multiple/Standard) parts means that the part made for one machine will fit any other machine of the same type and model.
3. On the (power/assembly) line, parts were moved along from worker to worker, and each worker did only one particular job on the product.
4. The (Federal Power/Trans Power) Commission was supposed to regulate, or control, the electric power companies.
5. Many stores in various locations, that are operated by one large company, are called (super markets/chain stores).
6. (Secret lodges/Trade associations) were groups of businessmen who decided how a certain industry must be run.

Do You Remember These People?

Tell something about each of the following persons.

Henry Ford   **Eli Whitney**
Wright brothers

Do You Know When It Happened?

What are the years of this chapter? Place the following events in the order in which they occurred.

United States Steel Corporation was the only company to make a billion dollars.

The United States started the first air mail service.

Henry Ford's Model T sold for 290 dollars.

Eli Whitney used standard parts.

The Wright brothers flew their first plane.

Discovering More About the Main Idea

American business and industry enjoyed good times during the 1920's. Many new industries developed, and new methods of manufacturing helped many businesses and industries to grow.

Tell how each of the following developments is related to the MAIN IDEA.

New methods such as mass production, the assembly line, and the use of standard parts cut the time needed to put machines together and lowered the prices of goods.

New industries like the automobile and electrical industry often provided many new jobs for workers and led to new businesses.

Some industries like the railroads, the cotton industry, and shipping lines lost business.

Can You Discuss the Chapter?

Use the information you learned in this chapter to answer the following questions.

1. How can you prove that new manufacturing methods used during the 1920's helped to lower prices on manufactured goods?
2. How can an industry like the automobile industry provide jobs for many workers and lead to the start of new businesses?
3. Why did some businesses become less important during the 1920's?
4. Explain how the growth of larger and larger businesses might cause problems for the people who bought products.

Can You Connect the Past and the Present?

1. Can you think of any recently invented product or material that has caused some other material or product to be useless?
2. Chain stores are still around today. Do you think they have grown more or less popular since the 1920's? Why?

CHAPTER 85

The Great Depression

Jobless men waiting on a breadline in the 1930's.

BEFORE YOU BEGIN THE CHAPTER

Know What to Look For

1. Early in the 1930's, a type of railroad freight car had a series of steel rods underneath the car. By placing a board across these rods, a person was able to ride along on the board which was between the bottom of the car and the rails. This was called "riding the rods." Many young men who did not have the money to pay the railroad fare used this method of travel.

In the early 1930's, thousands of young men had no money because they were unemployed. And, no matter how hard they searched, they were not able to find jobs during the Great Depression of the 1930's. As a result, many young men "rode the rods" all over the United States, living on charity or on money earned from odd jobs. In this chapter, you will read more about the Great Depression that left millions of men without jobs during the 1930's.

2. Read the title of the chapter. Then look through the chapter and read each heading. From the headings, tell what event helped lead to the Depression.

3. Look at the pictures in the chapter and read each caption. What do the pictures tell you about the Great Depression? Note also the time line at the beginning of the chapter. What years are included in this chapter? Compare this chapter time line to the unit time line on page 515.

4. Read the last part of the chapter called Summing Up. What did the Great Depression do to the American nation?

Know These Important Terms

stock market   Great Depression
stock market crash   public works

unemployed

Reconstruction Finance Corporation

Know the Main Idea

Here is the MAIN IDEA of this chapter.

The Great Depression, which began in 1929, brought the most serious hard times America ever faced. The federal government was not able to end the Depression.

Keep this MAIN IDEA in mind as you study the chapter. Ask yourself the following questions as you read. They will help you remember the MAIN IDEA.

1. What advantages did Americans gain by buying stock?

2. What event helped bring on the Great Depression?

3. How many workers were unemployed by 1932?

THE YEARS OF THIS CHAPTER ARE 1929 TO 1932

1920   1929   1932

THE CHAPTER LESSON BEGINS HERE

Times Were Not as Good as They Seemed

When Herbert Hoover became President early in 1929, the United States seemed to be enjoying good times. Workers were receiving high wages. Businesses were making large amounts of money. But at the same time, many workers lost their jobs because machines took over their jobs. And if you remember, some industries, such as the coal industry, were not doing well. Some people began to feel that perhaps most American businesses were not really doing well.

By the summer of 1929, it looked as if these people were right. The building of new homes slowed down. Many people began to spend their money more carefully. Prices began to fall, and in many businesses many workers lost their jobs.

Stock Prices Kept Going Up

During the 1920's, the **stock market,** or the place where people were able to buy and sell stock in American business companies, did especially well. Many Americans began to buy stock in business companies in the 1920's. Owning this stock made them part owners of these companies, and allowed them to share some of the money earned by these companies. If a company did well, then its

Shacks, such as the ones above, provided shelter for jobless workers in many cities.

The Stock Market Crashed in 1929

By September, 1929, stocks were selling for much higher prices than they were really worth. And yet, still more Americans bought stock. But in October, 1929, stock prices fell sharply. This was known as the **stock market crash** of 1929.

People who owed money on their stocks were forced to sell them right away. This large sale of stock pushed stock prices down even more. By 1930, many stocks were worth almost nothing.

The Stock Market Crash Helped Lead to the Depression

This stock market crash helped to lead to the **Great Depression,** or the most serious hard times that America ever faced. After the crash, millions of Americans lost all the money they put into stock because this stock was now worthless. Without money, Americans were not able to buy things they needed. Soon factories were not able to sell their products, and they were forced to let their workers go. Some workers were able to keep their jobs, but they often had to take a cut in pay and work fewer hours. Many businesses closed down. By 1932, 11 million workers were **unemployed,** or without jobs.

The Depression Hurt Millions of Americans

The Depression brought hard times to Americans. Millions of farmers lost their farms. Millions of workers lost their jobs. And millions of Americans lost their savings when many banks were closed. Many families even lost their homes. Thousands of Americans were hungry and stood for hours in bread lines to get something to eat. And thousands of young men without jobs moved from town to town looking for any kind of work.

stock went up in price. Stock owners were then able to make money from their stock by selling it for higher prices than they paid for it.

However, many people did not have enough money to buy all the stock they wanted. Therefore, they only paid part of the stock's price. When they sold their stock at a higher price, they paid for the rest of it. This system worked well as long as stock prices kept going up.

The Federal Government Failed to End the Depression

President Hoover thought that helping American businesses get started again was the best way to end the Depression. Therefore, Congress set up the **Reconstruction Finance Corporation** (R.F.C.) to lend money to railroads, banks, and other businesses. Taxes were cut, and the government made it easier for businessmen to borrow money. Money was also loaned to state and local governments for building roads, bridges, and buildings. President Hoover hoped to provide many jobs for Americans by this building program. A Farm Board was set up to buy farm crops from American farmers and to try to keep farm prices up.

Congress also passed a new tariff law which raised the tariff. But this high tariff only made the Depression worse because other nations also passed high tariff laws. These high tariff laws hurt the sale of American goods and farm products in the rest of the world. None of the government's efforts succeeded in ending the Depression.

President Hoover Became Very Unpopular

The Depression was not President Hoover's fault, but many Americans blamed him for the Depression. Many Americans also felt that President Hoover did not do enough to help the people who suffered because of the Depression. Although Hoover did begin some **public works,** or government building projects, he was not able to provide enough jobs for the millions of unemployed Americans.

And President Hoover refused to allow the federal government to provide any relief, or help, to the millions of Americans who were without jobs, money, and food. He felt that relief, or help, should be provided by private charities or by the cities and states. But the

A jobless worker stands outside a vacant store during the Depression.

cities, states, and charities were not able to provide relief to the millions of Americans suffering hard times.

Summing Up

The Great Depression began in 1929. This Depression brought very hard times to America. President Hoover and Congress tried to help businessmen, farmers, and jobless workers, but they did not succeed. In the next chapter, which begins Unit 22, you will find out how Franklin D. Roosevelt dealt with the Depression in the years after he became President.

AFTER YOU READ THE CHAPTER

Do You Know These Important Terms?

For each sentence below, choose the term that best completes the sentence.

1. The (broker/stock) market is the place where people are able to buy and sell stock in American business companies.
2. When stock prices fell very sharply in 1929, it was called the (doom's day/stock market) crash.
3. When someone is without a job, he is (unskilled/unemployed).
4. The (National Recovery/Reconstruction Finance) Corporation was set up to lend money to businesses to help them get started again.
5. The (Great Depression/Depression of the 1920's) was the most serious hard times the nation ever faced.
6. Government building projects are called (welfare/public) works.

Do You Remember This Person?

President Hoover has sometimes been unjustly blamed for the Great Depression. What was his background before he became President? How did he think the federal government should help to end the Depression?

Do You Know When It Happened?

What are the years of this chapter? Place the following events in the order in which they occurred.

Factories began to shut down because they were not able to sell their products.

Stock prices reached an all-time high.

Eleven million American workers were unemployed.

Many Americans invested their money in stocks.

Stock prices fell sharply.

Many stocks were worth almost nothing.

Discovering More About the Main Idea

The Great Depression, which began in 1929, brought the most serious hard times America ever faced. The federal government was not able to end the Depression.

Tell how each of the following developments is related to the MAIN IDEA.

Millions of Americans lost all the money they put into stocks in the stock market crash in 1929. Without money, Americans were not able to buy products. Many businesses closed.

Millions of farmers and workers were hurt by the Depression.

The government felt that relief, or help, should be provided by the states or private charities. But they did not have the money to provide relief. None of the government's efforts succeeded in ending the Depression.

Can You Discuss the Chapter?

Use the information you learned in this chapter to answer the following questions.

1. Why did some people begin to feel that businesses were not really doing well?
2. Why were many people forced to sell their stocks when the price of stock went down? How did this add to the stock market crash?
3. Explain how the stock market crash helped lead to the Depression.
4. How did President Hoover try to get business started again?

Can You Connect the Past and the Present?

1. How has the attitude of the federal government changed toward giving relief to needy citizens? Give a recent example.
2. A certain number of workers are always unemployed. How does this unemployment today differ from unemployment during the Great Depression?

The American Nation in the 1930's

President Franklin D. Roosevelt talking to reporters.

THE CHAPTERS IN UNIT 22 ARE

CHAPTER 86   Franklin D. Roosevelt and the New Deal
CHAPTER 87   New Laws Under the New Deal
CHAPTER 88   The Last Years of the New Deal
CHAPTER 89   American Life in the 1930's
CHAPTER 90   American Thought in the 1930's

THE YEARS OF THIS UNIT ARE 1930 TO 1940

1900	1930	1940	1975

Franklin D. Roosevelt and the New Deal

President Herbert Hoover (left) and President Franklin D. Roosevelt.

BEFORE YOU BEGIN THE CHAPTER

Know What to Look For

1. Franklin D. Roosevelt was born into a well-to-do family. As a young man he had a successful career in government. During World War One, he served as Assistant Secretary of the Navy. Then, in the summer of 1921, Franklin Roosevelt suffered an attack of polio, which crippled both his legs so badly that he was not able to walk. It looked as if his promising career in government was over.

But Roosevelt refused to give up. He spent long hours learning to stand and to walk in leg braces. Before long, Roosevelt returned to politics. In 1928, he was elected Governor of New York State. In this chapter, you will read about how he was elected as the President of the United States in 1932.

2. Read the title of the chapter. Then look through the chapter and read each heading.

page 534

From the headings, list some of the things Roosevelt did to help the Americans who were suffering from the Great Depression.

3. Look at the chapter pictures and read each caption. What is happening in the picture on page 536? Note also the time line at the beginning of the chapter. What years are included in this chapter? Compare this chapter time line to the unit time line on page 533.

4. Read the last part of the chapter called Summing Up. Why was Franklin Roosevelt elected as President in 1932?

Know These Important Terms

New Deal
Twentieth Amendment
Agricultural Adjustment Act
National Recovery Administration
Public Works Administration
Civilian Conservation Corps
Home Owners Loan Corporation

Know the Main Idea

Here is the MAIN IDEA of this chapter.

President Roosevelt's New Deal, or plan to end the Depression, made it possible for banks to reopen, helped business and industry, and provided relief and jobs for workers.

Keep this MAIN IDEA in mind as you study the chapter. Ask yourself the following questions as you read. They will help you remember the MAIN IDEA.

1. What government job did Franklin Roosevelt hold before he became President of the United States?

2. Under the Agricultural Adjustment Act, what did the government do for farmers who agreed to cut down the number of acres they planted?

3. What program did the New Deal provide for unemployed young men between the ages of eighteen and twenty-five?

THE YEARS OF THIS CHAPTER ARE 1932 TO 1936

| 1930 | 1932 | 1936 | 1940 |

THE CHAPTER LESSON BEGINS HERE

Roosevelt Ran Against Hoover

In the election of 1932, the Republicans chose Hoover to be their candidate again. Hoover promised to continue his plans of the past four years because he believed they were beginning to help the country. He also promised to let the states decide if they wanted prohibition laws. The Democrats chose Franklin D. Roosevelt, the governor of New York, to run against President Hoover.

Roosevelt Won the Election of 1932

In the campaign of 1932, Roosevelt promised voters a **New Deal,** or a plan to lead the nation out of the Depression. This New Deal program included: (1) a large program of public works, or government building projects to provide jobs, (2) federal relief payments, or help, for Americans without jobs, (3) old age pensions, or payments, (4) a lower tariff, and (5) higher prices for farm products. Roosevelt also promised to regulate, or control, banks and the stock market, and to end the prohibition law. Roosevelt won the election by more than 7 million votes. And the Democrats won control of both houses of Congress.

page 535

A group of people gather in front of a closed bank. By 1933, hundreds of banks all over the country had gone out of business.

The Twentieth Amendment to the Constitution Was Passed

Franklin Roosevelt was elected in November, 1932, but under the Constitution he was not able to take office until March, 1933. During these four months, President Hoover was not able to do much to help the American people. And Franklin Roosevelt was not able to do anything until he was inaugurated as President.

To solve this problem, Congress passed the **Twentieth Amendment** to the Constitution. This amendment moved up the beginning of the President's term in office from March to January. But this amendment was not passed in time for Roosevelt to become President on January 20, 1933.

Congress Passed Many New Laws

The day after Franklin Roosevelt became President, he called Congress into special session. This special session of Congress lasted more than three months. The President asked the Congress to pass many new laws. During this three-month period, which became known as the "Hundred Days," Congress passed some of the most important laws in America's history.

Roosevelt Dealt with the Bank Problem

Early in 1933, hundreds of banks were going out of business. Many of these banks were still strong banks, but they were forced to close because Americans were taking their money out of them. By March of 1933, most

These young men were given jobs by the Civilian Conservation Corps. They did useful work all over the United States.

states closed their banks in order to keep them from being completely ruined by people taking their money out.

One of the first laws passed during the "Hundred Days" made it possible for strong banks to reopen again. Soon after this law was passed, many banks reopened, and Americans started to put their money back into banks. Under the banking law, the government promised to pay back the money Americans put in the bank, in case the bank closed.

Roosevelt's Plans to Help the Farmer

Farmers suffered badly in the Depression. By 1933, prices for farm products were so low that many farmers were not able to pay to the banks the money they owed on their farms. As a result, many farmers lost their farms. To help the farmers, Congress passed a law which made it possible for farmers to borrow money from the government and pay what they owed to the banks.

To help the farmers get higher prices for their crops, Congress passed the **Agricultural Adjustment Act** (A.A.A.) in 1933. This act limited the amount of crops that farmers were to grow. The act gave cash payments to farmers who agreed to cut down the number of acres they planted. Farmers began to grow smaller amounts of crops, and as a result, prices for corn, wheat, and other crops went up. However, the Supreme Court later ruled that the A.A.A. was unconstitutional.

These farmers are dumping milk to protest the low prices for farm products.

Roosevelt Tried to Help Industry

President Roosevelt wanted to help American businesses and industries. Therefore, he asked Congress to pass a law that set up the **National Recovery Administration** (N.R.A.). The N.R.A. set up codes, or sets of rules, for each industry. These codes cut down working hours, raised wages and prices, and

limited the amount of goods produced. However, the N.R.A. came to an end in 1935, when the Supreme Court ruled that it was unconstitutional.

Roosevelt Provided Relief

Millions of Americans were unemployed, or without jobs. President Roosevelt had to find ways to help these millions of unemployed Americans. Roosevelt asked Congress to set up the **Public Works Administration** (P.W.A.), to provide jobs for thousands of workers. These workers helped to build government projects such as government buildings, bridges, and dams. The government also set up the **Civilian Conservation Corps** (C.C.C.) to provide jobs for young men between the ages of eighteen and twenty-five. The men in the C.C.C. lived in camps. They planted trees, built roads, and did many other kinds of useful work all over the country.

To provide relief, or help, for the many Americans who were still unemployed, the government passed a law to provide relief payments. And home owners were helped by the **Home Owners Loan Corporation** (H.O.L.C.). Home owners borrowed money from the H.O.L.C. and paid off the loans on their homes. Then they were able to pay back the government loan slowly and at a low rate of interest.

Summing Up

Franklin D. Roosevelt was elected President in 1932, after he promised Americans a New Deal, or a plan to end the Depression. The New Deal made it possible for banks to reopen, helped American businesses and industries, and provided relief and jobs for workers. In the next chapter, you will find out about other important laws passed during the New Deal.

AFTER YOU READ THE CHAPTER

For each sentence below, choose the term that best completes the sentence.

1. Roosevelt's plan to lead the nation out of the Depression was called the (Square/New) Deal.
2. The (Eighteenth/Twentieth) Amendment moved up the beginning of a new President's term from March to January.
3. The (Agricultural Adjustment/Farmers Relief) Act was passed to help farmers get higher prices for their crops by limiting the amounts of crops the farmers grew.
4. The (National Industrial Act/National Recovery Administration) set up codes, or sets of rules, to be followed by each industry.
5. The (Public Assistance Program/Public Works Administration) was set up to provide jobs for thousands of workers.
6. The (Youth Employment Program/Civilian Conservation Corps) was set up to provide jobs for young men between eighteen and twenty-five years of age.
7. The (Home Owners Loan/Property Loan) Corporation helped home owners borrow money at low interest in order to save their homes.

Do You Remember These People?

Tell something about each of the following persons.

Herbert Hoover   **Franklin D. Roosevelt**

Do You Know When It Happened?

What are the years of this chapter? Place the following events in the order in which they occurred.

The Agricultural Adjustment Act was passed.

Most states closed their banks.

Franklin D. Roosevelt became President.

The National Recovery Administration was declared unconstitutional.

Discovering More About the Main Idea

President Roosevelt's New Deal, or plan to end the Depression, made it possible for banks to reopen, helped business and industry, and provided relief and jobs for workers.

Tell how each of the following developments is related to the MAIN IDEA.

During the "Hundred Days," Congress passed some of the most important laws in America's history.

The New Deal included plans to help farmers, workers, home owners, and young men without jobs.

Can You Discuss the Chapter?

Use the information you learned in this chapter to answer the following questions.

1. In the campaign of 1932, what did the New Deal program include?
2. Why was Roosevelt not able to do anything to help the American people right after he was elected in November, 1932?
3. How did the government hope to raise the income of farmers?
4. In an emergency such as the great Depression, do you think the federal government should be given unlimited powers?

Can You Connect the Past
and the Present?

1. The practice of calling laws and government agencies by initials is still used. Can you name some now in common use?
2. What groups do we have today that are somewhat similar to the Civilian Conservation Corps? How are the present groups different?

CHAPTER 87

New Laws under the New Deal

A dam built by the Tennessee Valley Authority.

BEFORE YOU BEGIN THE CHAPTER

Know What to Look For

1. During the Depression, farmers living on the Great Plains became victims of a double disaster. Like other Americans, they all suffered from the Depression. At the same time, some people on the Great Plains watched helplessly as their farms blew away.

During the 1930's, the Great Plains had a bad drought, and rain did not fall for months. Everything dried up, and winds began to blow

away the rich topsoil. Great clouds of dust blew across the country, burying farms, fences, and roads. Many farms in this "Dust Bowl," as it was called, were ruined. Some farmers abandoned their farms and never returned.

At this same time, farmers in the Tennessee Valley, who were suffering from the Depression, also faced the problem of floods. Each year, the Tennessee River overflowed its banks and the waters flooded the land, ruining crops and carrying away the topsoil. The "Dust Bowl" and the Tennessee Valley floods were only two problems facing President Roosevelt.

2. Read the title of the chapter. Then look through the chapter and read each heading. From the headings, tell some ways that workers were helped.

3. Look at the pictures in the chapter and read each caption. What does the first chapter picture show? Look at the map on page 542. What is the title of this map? What states are part of the Tennessee Valley? Note also the time line at the beginning of the chapter. Compare this chapter time line to the unit time line on page 533.

4. Read the last part of the chapter called Summing Up. List some ways in which the New Deal hoped to return America to better times.

Know These Important Terms
Tennessee Valley Authority
Securities Exchange Act
gold standard
Works Progress Administration
National Labor Relations Act
Congress of Industrial Organizations
Wages and Hours Law
Social Security Act of 1935

Know the Main Idea
Here is the MAIN IDEA of this chapter.

The New Deal continued to pass many new laws to help America to return to better times.

Keep this MAIN IDEA in mind as you study the chapter. Ask yourself the following questions as you read. They will help you remember the MAIN IDEA.

1. What was the purpose of the Tennessee Valley Authority?

2. How did the New Deal help labor unions?

3. What shift in votes helped Franklin Roosevelt to be elected to a second term as President in 1936?

THE YEARS OF THIS CHAPTER ARE 1933 TO 1938

1930   1933   1938   1940

THE CHAPTER LESSON BEGINS HERE

The Government Improved the Tennessee Valley

One New Deal law formed the **Tennessee Valley Authority** (T.V.A.). The purpose of the T.V.A. was to improve living conditions for people in the Tennessee Valley, the area including parts of seven states through which the Tennessee River flows. The T.V.A. improved farming, planted forests, and built dams along the river. These dams helped to improve travel on the river and to control floods.

But the main purpose of the T.V.A. was to use the waters of the Tennessee River to provide electric power. The T.V.A. was able to sell electrical power at lower rates than the electric power companies. These low rates made it possible for thousands of homes and factories in the Tennessee Valley to use electrical power. And it also helped cut the rates for electrical power all over the United States. The T.V.A. also provided many jobs.

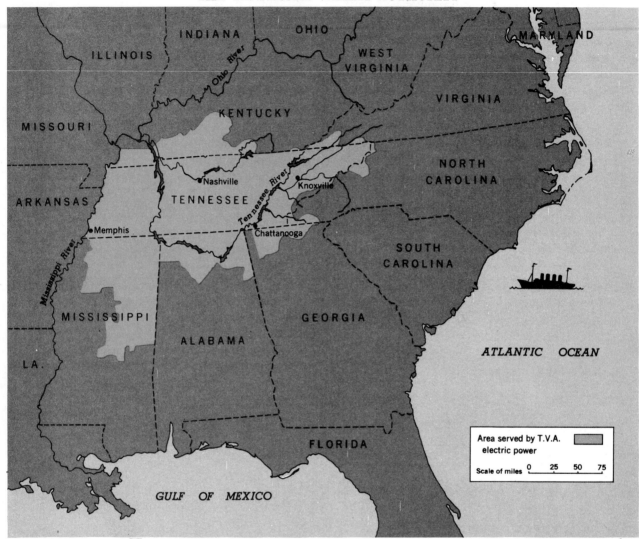

The New Deal Made Changes in the Money System

The New Deal also tried to improve the financial, or money, system of the United States. In 1934, Congress passed the **Securities Exchange Act.** This act set up a commission to regulate, or control, the stock market in order to prevent any future stock market crash.

In 1933, the United States went off the gold standard. This meant that Americans were no longer able to exchange a dollar in paper money for a dollar's worth of gold. In fact, gold money was not to be used any more. All Americans had to turn in their gold coins to the federal government. In return, they received paper money. The government also cut the worth of a dollar to fifty-nine cents. This meant that a dollar was only backed by fifty-nine cents in gold instead of 100 cents in gold. Going off the gold standard improved trade with foreign nations, but it did not help to bring good times back to the nation.

Public Works Provided Many Jobs

In the election of 1934, American voters elected Congressmen who favored the New Deal. After this election, President Roosevelt had more support in Congress for his New Deal program. Roosevelt first asked Congress to set up the **Works Progress Administration** (W.P.A.) to provide jobs for workers on government projects. These W.P.A. projects built schools, museums, roads, and bridges, and provided jobs for millions of Americans. Other W.P.A. projects provided work for writers, artists, musicians, and other talented people.

A New Law Helped Unions

In 1935, Congress passed the **National Labor Relations Act.** This act made it unlawful for a business company to refuse to deal with a labor union. It also said that if most of the workers in a company voted to join a union, all the workers in the company had to join the union. A National Labor Relations Board was set up to make sure that this law was obeyed. The National Labor Relations Act gave labor unions the protection they needed to grow stronger.

The C.I.O. Labor Union Was Formed

After the National Labor Relations Act was passed, the American Federation of Labor (A.F. of L.) began to take in more skilled workers as members. But some labor leaders, such as John L. Lewis, wanted to bring unskilled workers into unions, too. In 1936, Lewis and other leaders formed a union that

Marian Anderson.

A VICTORY FOR DEMOCRACY

In 1939, Washington, D.C., had only one large concert hall—Constitution Hall. Howard University planned to have Marian Anderson sing at a concert in this hall. However, Howard University was not able to obtain the use of Constitution Hall for the concert. Finally, the university discovered that black artists were not allowed to perform there.

Many Americans became concerned about the incident. Eleanor Roosevelt, the President's wife, was especially interested in helping black Americans, and she became greatly upset. She resigned from the Daughters of the American Revolution, the group that owned Constitution Hall.

Finally, Harold Ickes, the Secretary of the Interior, arranged for an outdoor concert at the Lincoln Memorial. The concert was held on Easter Sunday, and 75 thousand people came to hear Miss Anderson sing. She sang both operatic music and black spirituals. A few weeks later, Miss Anderson sang at the White House for the Roosevelts and the king and queen of England. And within a few years, she and other black artists were able to sing at Constitution Hall.

John L. Lewis, pictured above, helped to form the C.I.O. labor union.

later became known as the **Congress of Industrial Organizations** (C.I.O.).

The C.I.O. formed unions of all the workers in an industry including both skilled and unskilled workers. By 1940, the C.I.O. had 4 million members in the automobile industry, the steel industry, the coal mining industry, and many other industries. And the A.F. of L. had almost 5 million members.

The Wages and Hours Law Helped Workers

In 1938, workers gained better working conditions from a law called the **Wages and Hours Law.** This law set the minimum, or lowest, hourly wage for most jobs at 25 cents and limited the work week to forty-four hours. If a worker worked more than forty-

four hours, he had to be paid overtime pay. In later years, the Wages and Hours Act was changed many times.

The Social Security Law of 1935

One of the most important of all New Deal laws was the **Social Security Act of 1935.** The Social Security Act provided for monthly payments, called pensions, to be paid to most American workers who were sixty-five years old and over. The money for these pensions was to be raised by taxes on employers and workers. The Social Security Act also provided weekly payments to workers who lost their jobs.

Roosevelt Was Reelected in 1936

Franklin Roosevelt ran for a second term in the election of 1936. The Republicans ran Governor Alfred M. Landon of Kansas. The American people showed that they favored the New Deal by reelecting Roosevelt by over 11 million votes.

One reason for Roosevelt's great victory in the election of 1936 was that black Americans shifted their vote from the Republican Party to the Democratic Party. Black Americans were hit harder than anyone else by the Depression. They were helped by many of the New Deal laws, and in return, they voted for Roosevelt.

Summing Up

The New Deal continued to pass many new laws to help America to return to better times. The Tennessee Valley Authority was set up to improve the Tennessee Valley. The nation's money system was changed. Conditions for workers were improved, and the Social Security Act set up payments for jobless workers and workers over sixty-five. The next chapter tells about the problems of the New Deal.

AFTER YOU READ THE CHAPTER

Do You Know These Important Terms?

For each sentence below, choose the term that best completes the sentence.

1. The (Tennessee Valley Authority/Flood Control Act) was set up to help improve living conditions in the Tennessee Valley.
2. The law to control the stock market and prevent any future stock market crash was the (Securities Exchange/Wall Street) Act.
3. When a dollar in paper money is worth a dollar in gold, the nation is on the (legal/gold) standard.
4. The (Works Progress Administration/Government Project Act) provided jobs for workers on government projects.
5. The (Union Recognition/National Labor Relations) Act made it unlawful for a company to refuse to deal with a labor union.
6. A new union, the (Congress of Industrial Organizations/Order of Industrial Laborers) was formed to include all workers in an industry.
7. The (Minimum Wage/Wages and Hours) Law set a minimum wage and limited the hours of the work week.
8. The (Pension Plan/Social Security) Act of 1935 provided for monthly payments to workers who were over sixty-five years old.

Can You Locate These Places?

Use the map on page 542 to do the following map work.

Locate the Tennessee Valley. What states are in the valley? How did the T.V.A. control floods on the Tennessee River?

Do You Remember These People?

Tell something about each of the following persons.

Franklin D. Roosevelt   John L. Lewis
Alfred M. Landon

Do You Know When It Happened?

What are the years of this chapter? In what years were each of the following acts passed?
National Labor Relations Act
Social Security Act
Securities Exchange Act

Discovering More About the Main Idea

The New Deal continued to pass many new laws to help America to return to better times.

Tell how each of the following developments is related to the MAIN IDEA.

The government set up the T.V.A. to improve the Tennessee Valley.

The nation went off the gold standard and tried to control the stock market.

The government encouraged unions. It helped workers by providing jobs on government projects, establishing minimum wages and hours, and providing pensions for workers over sixty-five.

Can You Discuss the Chapter?

Use the information you learned in this chapter to answer the following questions.

1. How did the Tennessee Valley Authority help the people in the Tennessee Valley?
2. How did the government try to improve the financial, or money, system of the nation?
3. How was the C.I.O. different from the A.F. of L.?
4. Why did many black Americans change from the Republican Party?

Can You Connect the Past and the Present?

1. What is the minimum wage paid in your community today?
2. Has anyone you know ever benefited from the Social Security Act? Explain how.

CHAPTER 88

The Last Years of the New Deal

President Franklin D. Roosevelt shaking hands with a coal miner.

BEFORE YOU BEGIN THE CHAPTER

Know What to Look For

1. Some Americans who favored the New Deal spoke of the Supreme Court as the "Nine Old Men." They used this unfavorable term for two reasons. The first reason was that the Court had declared so many New Deal laws unconstitutional. The second reason was that most of the judges on the Court were quite old. Six of the judges were over seventy, which was the usual age to retire.

Between 1935 and 1936, the Supreme Court declared seven out of the nine New Deal laws it ruled on unconstitutional. Some Americans thought this was unfair. However, the judges were only doing what they thought was right. They felt that these New Deal laws were against the Constitution. In this chapter, you will read more about the New Deal and the Supreme Court and how the New

Deal came to an end in the years after 1938.

2. Read the title of the chapter. Then look through the chapter and read each heading. From the headings, can you tell how the Supreme Court changed its mind about the New Deal?

3. Look at the pictures in the chapter and read each caption. What does the picture on page 549 tell you about the "Dust Bowl"? Note also the time line at the beginning of the chapter. What years are included in this chapter? Compare this chapter time line to the unit time line on page 533.

4. Read the last part of the chapter called Summing Up. When did the New Deal finally come to an end? What is the topic of the next chapter?

Know These Important Terms
Agricultural Adjustment Act
Farm Security Administration

Know the Main Idea
Here is the MAIN IDEA of this chapter.

Between 1935 and 1936, the Supreme Court declared many New Deal laws unconstitutional. However, after 1937, the Court became more favorable to New Deal laws. After 1938, good times began to return, and the New Deal came to an end.

Keep this MAIN IDEA in mind as you study the chapter. Ask yourself the following questions as you read. They will help you remember the MAIN IDEA.

1. Which New Deal laws did the Supreme Court declare unconstitutional between 1935 and 1936?
2. What plan did President Roosevelt have to change the Supreme Court? Was his plan approved by Congress?
3. How did President Roosevelt spend most of his time after the New Deal was ended in 1938?

THE YEARS OF THIS CHAPTER ARE 1935 TO 1938

| 1930 | 1935 | 1938 | 1940 |

THE CHAPTER LESSON BEGINS HERE

The Supreme Court Declared
New Deal Laws Unconstitutional

You may remember that the Supreme Court has the right to declare a law passed by Congress unconstitutional. The Court first used this power in the case of Marbury against Madison in 1803. And after 1803, the Court ruled many laws passed by Congress unconstitutional. But the Court never declared as many laws unconstitutional as it did in the years between 1935 and 1936. In these years, the Court ruled that the National Recovery Act was unconstitutional. The Court also declared that the Agricultural Ad-justment Act and other important New Deal laws were unconstitutional.

Roosevelt Tried to Add More Judges
to the Supreme Court

President Roosevelt was afraid that the Supreme Court also might rule against the Social Security Act and the National Labor Relations Act. Therefore, in 1937, Roosevelt asked Congress for the power to add more judges to the Supreme Court. He wanted to be able to appoint six new judges.

ALL I SAID WAS "GIMME SIX MORE JUSTICES!"

This cartoon shows the unfavorable reaction caused by Roosevelt's plan for the Court.

Roosevelt's Plan to Change the Court Was Not Popular

The nation was divided over Roosevelt's plan for the Court. Many Americans who usually supported President Roosevelt were not in favor of his Court plan. They felt that Roosevelt was trying to "pack" the Court with judges who might take orders from him rather than use their own judgment. The members

of the Supreme Court were against Roosevelt's Court plan.

The Supreme Court Became More Favorable to the New Deal

In the spring of 1937, a new group of New Deal laws reached the Supreme Court. However, this time the Court was more favorable to the New Deal laws. The Supreme Court approved the National Labor Relations Act and the Social Security Act. And a few months later, one of the justices who was against the New Deal resigned from the Court.

President Roosevelt still felt his plan to add judges to the Court was necessary, but Congress refused to approve it. Although he was defeated in Congress, Roosevelt gained most of the things he wanted. The Court was now more favorable to the New Deal laws. And in a few years, almost all the older members of the Supreme Court left the Court. Therefore, President Roosevelt was able to appoint to the Court many new justices who favored the New Deal.

The Depression Returned in 1937

After the fight over the Supreme Court, President Roosevelt had to deal with other problems. Business began to improve in the nation between 1936 and 1937. Congress, therefore, cut down the amount of money to be spent in public works and relief. However, this cut in government spending hurt American businesses. Businesses were not strong enough to give jobs to all the people who were no longer working on government projects. And in October, 1937, the Depression again returned in the United States. At the beginning of 1938, 10 million workers were unemployed, or without jobs.

In April, President Roosevelt asked Congress to increase the amount of money to be spent

A farmer and his sons walking in a dust storm. Strong winds turned many acres of dry farm land in the West into "dust bowls."

for public works and relief. Congress voted to raise more money for public works and relief, and soon more people were working on W.P.A. projects. Congress also made it possible for businessmen to take out loans to carry on their businesses. Business began to improve again, and by the end of 1938, the worst of the Depression was over.

The Government Helped Farmers

The farmers also were hit by the hard times of 1937 and 1938. When the Supreme Court ruled that the Agricultural Adjustment Act was unconstitutional in 1936, Congress passed another law to help farmers. Under this new law, farmers were paid by the federal government not to grow more than a certain amount of a crop. As a result, farm production of some crops was cut down. However, prices for farm crops were still not high enough.

Therefore, in 1938, Congress passed a second **Agricultural Adjustment Act.** This act allowed the government to limit the production of certain farm crops and, therefore, keep the prices for these crops high. Congress also passed a law which set up the **Farm Security Administration** (F.S.A.). The F.S.A. loaned money to tenant farmers in order to help them buy their own farms.

This picture shows a grocery store in the 1930's. The low prices for food show the effects of the Depression.

The New Deal Comes to an End

In 1938, American businesses began to improve again. The Depression was coming to an end, and the nation was beginning to enjoy good times again. As a result, after 1938, no more New Deal laws, or laws to lead the nation out of the Depression, were passed. Although the New Deal was ended, President Roosevelt was reelected as President two more times. He was elected President in 1940 and again in 1944. In the years after 1938, President Roosevelt spent most of his time dealing with foreign nations.

Summing Up

Between 1935 and 1937, the Supreme Court ruled that many of the New Deal laws were unconstitutional. Therefore, President Roosevelt tried to add more judges to the Supreme Court. This plan failed, but the Supreme Court became more favorable to New Deal laws. In 1937 and 1938, more New Deal laws were passed to help the farmers. But after 1938, good times returned in the nation, and the New Deal came to an end. In the next chapter, you will find out what American life was like during the years of the 1930's.

AFTER YOU READ THE CHAPTER

For each sentence below, choose the term that best completes the sentence.

1. The second (Famers Aid/**Agricultural Adjustment**) Act allowed the government to limit the production of certain farm crops in order to keep the prices for these crops high.
2. The law that was passed to help tenant farmers to obtain loans to buy their own farms was called the (**Farmers' Loan/Farm Security**) Administration.

Can You Locate These Places?

The "Dust Bowl" was located in the states of Kansas, Colorado, Oklahoma, New Mexico, and Texas. Locate these states on a map of the United States. How did the dust storms affect farming in this area?

Do You Know When It Happened?

What are the years of this chapter? Place the following events in the order in which they occurred.

The Depression again returned in the United States.

President Roosevelt was elected for a third term.

The Supreme Court declared many New Deal laws unconstitutional.

The New Deal came to an end.

The Supreme Court approved the Social Security Act.

Discovering More About the Main Idea

Between 1935 and 1936, the Supreme Court declared many New Deal laws unconstitutional. However, after 1937, the Court became more favorable to New Deal laws. After 1938, good times began to return, and the New Deal came to an end.

Tell how each of the following developments is related to the MAIN IDEA.

President Roosevelt wanted to add more judges to the Supreme Court, but many Americans were not in favor of his Court plan.

Business was not quite strong enough to withstand the cut in government spending, and the Depression returned again in 1937.

The government tried to help the farmer by passing new laws to help keep the prices of crops high and to help farmers to buy their own farms.

Can You Discuss the Chapter?

Use the information you learned in this chapter to answer the following questions.

1. Why was President Roosevelt's plan to add more judges to the Supreme Court unpopular?
2. How was President Roosevelt able to gain most of the things he wanted regarding the Supreme Court?
3. Why did the Depression return again in 1937?
4. How did the government try to help the farmers of the nation?
5. Would you have agreed with the President's plan to add more judges to the Supreme Court if you were a citizen in the years of the 1930's?

Can You Connect the Past and the Present?

1. When Roosevelt was President, there were nine judges on the Supreme Court. How many judges are there today?
2. Are farmers still paid *not* to grow certain crops?

CHAPTER 89

American Life in the 1930's

Tommy Dorsey and his band.

BEFORE YOU BEGIN THE CHAPTER

Know What to Look For

1. On the evening of October 30, 1938, the power of the radio was clearly shown. Million of radio listeners had turned on the CBS station to listen to a show which was presenting a play called *The War of the Worlds*. The CBS radio station stated at four different times during the hour long show that this was only a radio play. But the play, which was

about men from Mars landing on earth, was so real that an untold number of listeners became scared. They believed that men from Mars had actually landed in New Jersey and were making war against the people living on earth with deadly ray guns. Some people rushed from their homes and fled on foot or by car.

Radio had become an important part of life in America by the 1930's. In this chapter, you will read about radio and other parts of everyday American life.

2. Read the title of the chapter. Then look through the chapter and read each heading. How did people spend their free time during the 1930's?

3. Look at the pictures in the chapter and read each caption. What do the pictures tell you about American life in the 1930's? Note also the time line at the beginning of the chapter. What years are included in this chapter? Compare this chapter time line to the unit time line on page 533. How do the years of this chapter compare to the years of the unit?

4. Read the last part of the chapter called Summing Up. How did Americans enjoy themselves during the 1930's?

Know This Important Term
fireside chats

Know the Main Idea
Here is the MAIN IDEA of this chapter.
During the Depression, Americans found many ways to forget their troubles and enjoy themselves. Movies, sports events, radio, and inexpensive amusements were popular.

Keep this MAIN IDEA in mind as you study the chapter. Ask yourself the following questions as you read. They will help you remember the MAIN IDEA.

1. What kinds of movies were popular during the 1930's?

2. Who was the heavyweight boxing champion?

3. How were many artists, actors, and writers employed during the 1930's?

THE YEARS OF THIS CHAPTER ARE 1930 TO 1940

1930   1940

THE CHAPTER LESSON BEGINS HERE

Movies Remained Popular

During the Depression, people wanted to forget their troubles, but they needed entertainment that cost little money. Many Americans went to the movies because they were popular and cheap. Movie theaters cut their prices, offered "double features," and gave away free prizes to get people to attend.

During the 1930's, Americans especially enjoyed comedies, or funny movies with happy endings, and action movies. These two kinds of movies soon became their favorites. Movies made by Charlie Chaplin were especially popular. Walt Disney's cartoons and his movie *Snow White and the Seven Dwarfs* also be-came very popular. However, a few movies made during the 1930's did deal with the problems of American life. The movie *Dead End* was about life in city slums. *The Grapes of Wrath* showed the troubles of a farm family who lost its farm.

People Listened to Their Radios

Millions of Americans spent much time listening to radio programs. Comedians such as Fred Allen, Jack Benny, and Eddie Cantor were popular. Americans also liked programs that offered variety shows, children's shows, news reports, and sports events.

page 553

Above, Charlie Chaplin is shown in the film "City Lights." It was made in 1931.

President Roosevelt often used the radio to speak to the American people. These talks to the American people over the radio were known as fireside chats. During these radio programs, the President explained his plans for the American nation to the people. Most Americans felt that President Roosevelt was interested in telling them about his plans, and they usually gave him their full support.

Alcoholic Drinks Were Made Lawful Again

The Prohibition Amendment, or the law against the making or selling of alcoholic drinks, was repealed, or ended, in December of 1933. At first, only certain wines and beer were sold. Later, the sale of all types of alcoholic drinks was allowed. Cocktail lounges and taverns opened in most cities and towns. But a few states passed their own prohibition laws against making or selling alcoholic drinks.

Americans Enjoyed Sports

Sports of all types remained popular during the 1930's. However, spectator sports that people had to pay to see, such as boxing or football, became less popular during the Depression because tickets were too expensive. But new sports heroes were able to bring many people to sports events again. Lou Gehrig, "Dizzy" Dean, and Joe DiMaggio in baseball, Don Budge in tennis, Jesse Owens in track, and heavyweight boxing champion Joe Louis were some of the great sports heroes of the 1930's.

Instead of just watching sporting events, many Americans began to take part in sports. Bicycling became very popular again, and skiing also began to catch on. Many Americans took part in sports and games in the parks, baseball fields, golf courses, and tennis courts built as public works by the government during the 1930's. These sports cost little money, and they helped people forget about the troubles of the Depression.

Americans Enjoyed Reading Newspapers and Magazines

During the 1930's, Americans enjoyed reading newspapers and magazines. However, Americans had fewer newspapers to read because many newspapers joined together. Soon,

Jesse Owens was a popular sports hero in the 1930's. In the 1936 Olympic games, he won three gold medals in track events.

readers in many cities had only one morning newspaper and one evening newspaper to choose from. Most newspapers printed a large Sunday paper with the comics in color and a special magazine section.

Many Americans read magazines during the 1930's. *Reader's Digest* became one of the most widely read magazines. *Time* and *Newsweek* told Americans about the news. *Life* and *Look* had stories and many pictures. But many

Americans also enjoyed reading mystery magazines, Western adventure magazines, and movie magazines.

Americans Enjoyed Dancing and Listening to Music

The 1930's was the time of the "big bands." During these years, Americans enjoyed listening and dancing to the music played by big bands. Jazz was still popular, but it had

William C. Handy.

THE FATHER OF THE BLUES

William C. Handy was born in Alabama in 1873. As a young man he played the cornet in a minstrel show. Then in 1903, he formed his own band. Handy became famous for playing a new kind of jazz music called the "blues." He took black spirituals and work songs, added an African rhythm to them, and developed these songs into the blues.

In 1909, Handy wrote a song to be used in Mayor E. H. Crump's election campaign in Memphis. Three years later, this song was published as the "Memphis Blues." This was the first blues song to be published in America. Handy also wrote the "St. Louis Blues" and the "Beale Street Blues." Blues songs are made up of three lines. The first two lines are the same, and the third line rhymes with the first two. The mood of a blues song is usually sad but still hopeful.

In his later years, W. C. Handy became a successful music publisher. He continued to try to popularize black music such as the blues and jazz. By the time of his death in 1958, W. C. Handy was known as the "Father of the Blues."

a "sweeter" sound and was easier to dance to. However, a new band leader, Benny Goodman, started to play the older type of "swing" jazz. Goodman borrowed much of his style from black musicians, and he hired several black musicians to play in his band.

During the 1930's, Americans enjoyed going to see musical comedies, or shows with music. Americans were able to see musical comedies both in the theater and in the movies. They especially enjoyed movies with Ginger Rogers and Fred Astaire, a famous dancing team. George Gershwin's musical play *Porgy and Bess* was also very popular. And *As Thousands Cheer* (1933), starring Ethel Waters, was one of the first plays in which black and white actors appeared together.

The Government Started Programs to Help Artists, Actors, and Musicians

During the 1930's, the Works Progress Administration provided work for the many artists, actors, and musicians who were unable to find jobs because of the Depression. Members of the Federal Art Project painted thousands of pictures which were loaned to schools and libraries. Other artists made art works for public buildings. Fifteen thousand musicians in the Federal Music Project put on music concerts and gave music lessons to children. The Federal Theater Project gave jobs to over 12 thousand actors who put on plays seen by millions of Americans.

Summing Up

During the Depression, Americans found many ways to forget their troubles and enjoy themselves. They went to movies and sports events, listened to radio programs, and read newspapers and magazines. Americans also listened to music, danced, and went to see plays. In the next chapter, you will read more about American life during the 1930's.

AFTER YOU READ THE CHAPTER

Do You Know This Important Term?

For the sentence below, choose the term that best completes the sentence.

The radio talks of President Roosevelt to the American people were called (**fireside chats/people press conferences**).

Do You Remember These People?

Tell something about some of the following persons.

Charlie Chaplin   Don Budge
Walt Disney   Jesse Owens
Fred Allen   Joe Louis
Jack Benny   Benny Goodman
Eddie Cantor   Ginger Rogers
Lou Gehrig   Fred Astaire
"Dizzy" Dean   George Gershwin
Joe DiMaggio   Ethel Waters

Do You Know When It Happened?

What are the years of this chapter? In the year 1933, the musical play *As Thousands Cheer* was produced. Why was this an unusual play for the time?

Discovering More About the Main Idea

During the Depression, Americans found many ways to forget their troubles and enjoy themselves. Movies, sports events, radio, and inexpensive amusements were popular.

Tell how each of the following developments is related to the MAIN IDEA.

Many Americans attended the movies each week. They enjoyed comedies, action movies, cartoons, musicals, and stories about American life.

Millions of Americans listened to radio programs. They liked radio programs that offered variety shows, children's shows, news reports, and sports events.

Spectator sports were still popular, but fewer people were able to afford to attend them. Many Americans began to take part in sports themselves.

Reading newspapers and magazines and listening and dancing to music were popular and did not cost too much money. The federal government put on concerts, plays, and art exhibits for many Americans.

Can You Discuss the Chapter?

Use the information you learned in this chapter to answer the following questions.

1. How did movie theaters encourage more people to attend the movies during the 1930's?
2. How did President Roosevelt make use of the radio?
3. What effect did the repeal of the prohibition law have on the nation?
4. Why did many Americans take part in sports rather than just watching sporting events?
5. Describe the developments in popular music during the 1930's.
6. Do you think the government's programs in art, music, and the theater might be a good thing today? Why or why not?

Can You Connect the Past and the Present?

1. Some of the sports heroes or other people you read about in this chapter are still alive today. Choose one of them and find out what he is doing today.
2. Does your community have any projects like those provided by the Works Progress Administration for artists, writers, actors, or musicians?

CHAPTER 90

American Thought in the 1930's

"The Homesteader" by American artist Harvey Dunn.

BEFORE YOU BEGIN THE CHAPTER

Know What to Look For

1. A person who likes to make candid pictures takes pictures of anything, anywhere, at any time. He wants to catch the person or the scene he sees as it actually is. The candid-picture taker is only interested in how realistic the picture is.

The writers, artists, painters, and poets of the 1930's were like candid-picture takers. Most of them wanted to show realistically the terrible effects of the Great Depression. More than ever before, writers wrote with complete realism. Often the stories they wrote were powerful. One of the most powerful and realistic books written at this time was *The Grapes of Wrath*. Some people compared this book with *Uncle Tom's Cabin* because of the powerful effect it had on Americans.

2. Read the title of the chapter. Then look

through the chapter and read each heading. From the headings, can you tell some changes in American thought?

3. Look at the pictures in the chapter and read each caption. What do the pictures tell you about American thought in the 1930's? Note also the time line at the beginning of the chapter. What years are included in this chapter? Compare this chapter time line to the unit time line on page 533.

4. Read the last part of the chapter called Summing Up. What were most writers and artists trying to show in the 1930's? What is the topic of the next unit?

Know This Important Term

dictatorship

Know the Main Idea

Here is the MAIN IDEA of this chapter.

During the 1930's, American life changed and showed the hardships of the Depression. These changes in American life showed up in population growth, education, painting, poems, books, and plays.

Keep this MAIN IDEA in mind as you study the chapter. Ask yourself the following questions as you read. They will help you remember the MAIN IDEA.

1. What effect did the Depression have on schools?

2. Name writers or artists who showed the problems of the Depression in their works.

3. Who helped to change American building styles in the 1930's?

THE YEARS OF THIS CHAPTER ARE 1930 TO 1940

1930   1940

THE CHAPTER LESSON BEGINS HERE

America's Population Growth Slowed Down

Many men did not earn enough money during the Depression to be able to support a wife and family. Therefore, not as many marriages took place among Americans in these years. And many marriages broke up. At the same time, only about half as many babies were born during the 1930's as were born during the 1920's.

As a result, America's population did not increase during the 1930's as fast as it did in earlier years. And America's population became an older population because Americans lived longer than they ever did before.

Education Became More Important

Schools were especially hard hit by the Depression. They had very little money to spend during the Depression years. Some schools even had to close. To save money, most schools were forced to have larger classes, fewer courses, and shorter school years. Teachers worked for low wages and sometimes for no pay at all. However, more students stayed in school than ever before because jobs were scarce. And many older people returned to school during the Depression to take courses to improve themselves and prepare for a better job.

In the elementary schools, progressive education became even more popular. Children spent less time reading books and spent more time studying the world around them. Many

Carl Sandburg was an important American writer of poems and books.

small high schools joined together during the 1930's, and therefore, they were able to provide a better education for their students.

Painters and Poets Dealt with Problems of American Life

During the 1930's, many artists felt that their work must show the problems of the Depression. Grant Wood and Thomas Hart Benton painted pictures of the life and people of the Middle West. Other painters tried to show the troubles of city life. And Robert Gwathmey painted some outstanding pictures which showed the life of black Americans.

During the Depression, poets also wrote about the problems of American life. In many of his poems, Archibald MacLeish (mak-LEESH) described the troubles of unemployed workers and poor farmers. Carl Sandburg, in a poem called "The People, Yes," called for

improvements in American life. And Stephen Vincent Benét (bi-NAY) wrote about the hardships of city life in a book of poems called *Burning City*.

Plays Showed the Problems of American Life

Many of the plays written in the 1930's were also about the problems in America which were caused by the Depression. Clifford Odets (oh-DETZ) dealt with labor unions in the play *Waiting for Lefty*. Erskine Caldwell's *Tobacco Road* showed the terrible living conditions of poor Southern farmers. And *Winterset*, by Maxwell Anderson, was about a murder trial in which a man was unjustly tried and put to death for a murder he did not do.

Other playwrights attacked the evils of war and **dictatorship,** or government in which the ruler has complete power to govern a nation and to order the people to obey him. In 1934, in a play called *Judgment Day*, Elmer Rice warned America about Adolf Hitler, who set up a dictatorship in Germany. One of the most popular plays put on by the Federal Theater Project of the W.P.A. was *It Can't Happen Here*. This play was taken from a book against dictatorship written by Sinclair Lewis.

Many fine books were written in the 1930's. Ernest Hemingway was a famous writer during these years. In his book *For Whom the Bell Tolls*, Hemingway described the Spanish Civil War. And in his book *To Have and Have Not*, he described the trouble caused by the Depression. John Dos Passos (dohs PAS-ohs) attacked American life in a three-volume book called *U.S.A.* And John Steinbeck described the hard times suffered by American farmers in two famous books, *The Grapes of Wrath* and *Of Mice and Men*.

James T. Farrell wrote about the lives of young Irish-Americans in a Chicago slum in

The rocks, trees, and water on this piece of land were used by Frank Lloyd Wright to build this modern style home.

his Studs Lonigan books. Meyer Levin and Henry Roth described Jewish life in American cities. William Faulkner (FAWK-nur) wrote about life in the South. And Richard Wright in *Native Son* described the lives of black Americans who lived in a Chicago slum. One of the few great writers who did not write about the problems of American life in the 1930's was Thomas Wolfe.

New Building Styles Were Used

Even American building styles changed during the 1930's. This change began when Frank Lloyd Wright began building homes which were planned to fit into the land area on which they were built. For example, large stones or trees on a piece of land were often used to build the house. The new building style was called "modern."

Modern buildings were plain and simple.

The furniture used in these buildings was often made of metal instead of wood. Large windows called "picture windows" were also part of this modern style. After a while, Americans began to learn to like this new modern style of building.

Summing Up

During the 1930's, American life showed the hardships of the Depression. Fewer Americans married during these years, and fewer babies were born. In these years, Americans took a greater interest in getting an education. American writers, poets, and painters all tried to show the problems caused by the Depression. And many plays showed the hardships of American life. In the next chapters, which are in Unit 23, you will find out how the United States dealt with other nations between 1920 and 1940.

AFTER YOU READ THE CHAPTER

Do You Know This Important Term?

For the sentence below, choose the term that best completes the sentence.

A government in which a ruler has complete power to govern a nation and to order the people to obey him is a (**dictatorship**/**matriarchy**).

Do You Remember These People?

Tell something about some of the following persons.

Grant Wood	Sinclair Lewis
Thomas Hart Benton	Ernest Hemingway
Robert Gwathmey	John Dos Passos
Archibald MacLeish	John Steinbeck
Carl Sandburg	James T. Farrell
Clifford Odets	Meyer Levin
Erskine Caldwell	Henry Roth
Maxwell Anderson	William Faulkner
Elmer Rice	Richard Wright
Stephen Vincent Benét	Thomas Wolfe
	Frank Lloyd Wright

Can You Locate These Places?

Each of these places was mentioned in the chapter. See if you can find them on a map in your classroom.

Germany	Spain
Chicago	

Do You Know When It Happened?

What are the years of this chapter? How did the changes in American life show up in the years of the 1930's?

Discovering More About the Main Idea

During the 1930's, American life changed and showed the hardships of the Depression. These changes in American life showed up in population growth, education, painting, poems, books, and plays.

Tell how each of the following developments is related to the MAIN IDEA.

American's population did not increase during the 1930's as fast as it did in earlier years. The population became an older population because Americans lived longer than they ever did before.

Many high schools were able to provide a better education for their students during the 1930's.

Frank Lloyd Wright helped to begin a new building style which was called modern. Modern buildings were plain and simple.

Can You Discuss the Chapter?

Use the information you learned in this chapter to answer the following questions.

1. What did the Depression do to the population growth of the United States?
2. Why did some American high schools become better during the Depression?
3. Although most writers wrote about Depression problems, what other problem did some writers write about?
4. What is meant by the modern style of building?
5. Do you like modern buildings? Explain why or why not.

Can You Connect the Past and the Present?

1. When the nation faces a serious problem, the artists and writers often try to show this problem in their works. Can you give an example of this in the work of any writer or painter today?
2. Compare the size of the population of the United States in the 1930's with the population today.

America Deals with Other Nations

German soldiers marching in a parade.

THE CHAPTERS IN UNIT 23 ARE

CHAPTER 91 The United States and the World, 1920–1930
CHAPTER 92 The United States and the World, 1930–1940
CHAPTER 93 Moving Toward World War Two
CHAPTER 94 World War Two Begins

THE YEARS OF THIS UNIT ARE 1920 TO 1940

| 1900 | 1920 | 1940 | 1975 |

The United States and the World, 1920–1930

The Washington Naval Conference.

BEFORE YOU BEGIN THE CHAPTER

Know What to Look For

1. The battleship was supposed to be a ship that was almost impossible to destroy. It was the most important ship in every nation's navy. In July, 1921, a German battleship captured during World War One was anchored off the coast of Virginia. This battleship, which had a triple steel hull and eighty-five watertight compartments, was supposed to be unsinkable. The new American air force, which was part of the army, had promised to sink the vessel. But no one believed that airplanes would be able to sink the huge battleship.

The planes flew over the ship and bombed it. The people who were watching the bombing saw the ship sink under water within a half-hour. A new period had begun. In the future, airplanes would become an important new weapon. In the same year, as you will read in this chapter, nations of the world met to limit the size of their navies. They did not think to limit air power, however.

2. Read the title of the chapter. Then look through the chapter and read each heading. With what part of the world did the United States become friendly in the 1920's?

3. Look at the pictures in the chapter and read each caption. What do the pictures show you about American dealings with foreign nations during the 1930's? Note also the time line at the beginning of the chapter. What years are included in this chapter? Compare this chapter time line to the unit time line on page 563.

4. Read the last part of the chapter called Summing Up. What problem did the United States have with European nations?

Know These Important Terms
Kellogg-Briand Pact   Young Plan
Dawes Plan
Washington Naval Conference

Know the Main Idea
Here is the MAIN IDEA of this chapter.
The United States worked hard to maintain peace during the 1920's.

Keep this MAIN IDEA in mind as you study the chapter. Ask yourself the following questions as you read. They will help you remember the MAIN IDEA.

1. Why was the Washington Naval Conference not as successful as it seemed?

2. What event in the early 1930's kept Germany from paying its reparations to European nations?

3. What action helped the dealings between the United States and Latin America?

THE YEARS OF THIS CHAPTER ARE 1920 TO 1930

1920   1930   1940

THE CHAPTER LESSON BEGINS HERE

The United States Agreed to Cut Down Its Navy

In 1921, the United States, Great Britain, Japan, and six other nations met in Washington, D.C., to find a way to limit the size of their navies. At this **Washington Naval Conference,** the nine nations agreed not to build any more large warships for ten years. They also agreed to destroy some of the ships already built.

However, the Washington Naval Conference was not as successful as it seemed. At the conference, the nations only limited the number of large warships that were to be built. Nations were still able to build as many small ships such as destroyers, cruisers, and submarines as they wanted.

The United States Helped Develop a New Peace Plan

Although the United States never joined the League of Nations, it was very much interested in working for world peace. In 1928, the French leader, Aristide Briand (bree-AHN), suggested that the United States and France sign an agreement promising never to go to war against each other. The American Secretary of State, Frank Kellogg (KELL-aug), in-

American Secretary of State Frank Kellogg (left) and the French leader
Aristide Briand (right) sign the Kellogg-Briand Pact.

vited other nations to sign this agreement called the **Kellogg-Briand Pact.** The Kellogg-Briand Pact was signed by sixty other nations. The nations that signed the pact promised to settle all their problems peacefully.

European Nations Owed War Debts to the United States

During World War One, the United States loaned the European nations that fought on America's side almost 10 billion dollars. They owed this huge amount of money as war debts to the United States. Because these European nations used most of this money to buy weapons and supplies in the United States, they wanted the American government to cancel, or wipe out, these war debts. However, the American government agreed to cut only the interest, or the fee charged for lending money, on the loans and to give the European nations more time to pay.

In order to pay their war debts, the European nations had to be able to sell their products to the United States. However, during the 1920's, the United States raised its tariff, or tax on goods from other nations. This high tariff made it hard for Europeans to sell their goods in the United States. And it also made it hard for the European nations to pay the debts they owed to America.

Germany Owed War Debts to European Nations

The European nations wanted to use the reparations, or payments, they were receiving from Germany to pay their war debts to the United States. Under the Treaty of Versailles, Germany was to pay large amounts of money to the European nations for the damage that the German armed forces caused during the war. However, in the early 1920's, Germany was suffering from hard times and was unable to pay its reparations to the European nations.

The United States knew that the other European nations needed these reparations to pay their war debts to the United States. Therefore, the United States helped to develop two plans, the **Dawes Plan** and the **Young Plan,** to help Germany to pay its reparations. Under these two plans, the United States agreed to loan money to Germany. These loans made it possible for Germany to pay its reparations and for the European nations to pay their war debts during the 1920's.

However, by the early 1930's, Germany was suffering from a depression and was not able to keep up its payments to the European nations. As a result, these nations were not able to pay their debts to the United States.

The United States Became Friendly with Latin America

If you remember, before the United States entered World War One, it had troubles with Mexico. After the war, these troubles con-

Herbert Hoover visits the country of Nicaragua in Latin America.

tinued. The main problem concerned the right of American companies to own land and oil wells in Mexico. Finally, the Mexican government agreed to protect the rights of Americans in Mexico. In the late 1920's, the United States succeeded in becoming friendly with Mexico.

The United States was not well liked by the nations of Latin America. The Latin American nations were angry with the United States because from time to time the United States sent troops into the Latin American nations to protect American citizens and the Panama Canal.

During the 1920's, when revolutions broke out in some Latin American countries, the

Before the 1930's, the United States sent troops to some Latin American countries to protect the Panama Canal, pictured above.

United States sent troops to these countries. The Latin American nations felt the United States had no right to send troops into these nations. Then, in 1930, the United States promised to stop sending troops into the Latin American nations. This improved dealings between the United States and Latin America.

United States Territories Wanted More Self-Government

During the 1920's, the people of Puerto Rico wanted more self-government. They especially wanted the right to elect their own governor. However, the United States government refused to agree to this request. And during the 1920's, the people of the Philippine Islands demanded complete independence from the United States. The United States promised to give the Philippine Islands their independence.

Summing Up

During the 1920's, the United States and other nations agreed to limit their navies. And the United States worked with other nations to prevent war. But the European nations did not pay the war debts they owed to the United States. The American government became more friendly with the nations of Latin America. In the next chapter, you will find out how the United States dealt with foreign nations during the 1930's.

AFTER YOU READ THE CHAPTER

Do You Know These Important Terms?

For each sentence below, choose the term that best completes the sentence.

1. At the (Washington/London) Naval Conference, nine nations agreed not to build any more large warships for ten years.
2. Almost all nations of the world signed the (Post-Armour/Kellogg-Briand) Pact promising to settle their problems peaceably.
3. The (Harper/Dawes) Plan and the (Elder/Young) Plan were developed by the United States to help Germany to pay its reparations.

Do You Remember These People?

Tell something about each of the following persons.

Aristide Briand   **Frank Kellogg**

Can You Locate these Places?

Use the maps in your classroom to locate the following places. Tell how each location is connected to the events in this chapter.

Japan   **Great Britain**
France   **Germany**
Mexico   **Puerto Rico**
Philippine Islands

Do You Know When It Happened?

What are the years of this chapter? Tell why each of the following dates is important to the developments in this chapter.

1921   **1928**   **1930**

Discovering More About the Main Idea

The United States worked hard to maintain peace during the 1920's.

Tell how each of the following developments is related to the MAIN IDEA.

The United States agreed to limit the size of its navy and signed the Kellogg-Briand Pact.

European nations were unable to pay their war debts. They blamed the high tariff of the United States and the inability of Germany to pay reparations.

After the United States agreed to stop sending troops into Latin America, dealings between the United States and Latin America improved.

Can You Discuss the Chapter?

Use the information you learned in this chapter to answer the following questions.

1. How did the United States show that it was working for peace in the 1920's?
2. Why were the European nations not able to pay their war debts to the United States by the early 1930's?
3. Why did Germany have trouble keeping up its reparations payments to the European nations?
4. How did the United States improve its dealings with the Latin American nations?
5. Do you think that European nations should have paid their war debts to the United States? Why or why not?

Can You Connect the Past and the Present?

1. How was the Washington Naval Conference similar in many ways to efforts being made today to limit nuclear weapons?
2. Puerto Rico wanted more self-government during the 1920's. What is the present state of Puerto Rico today?

CHAPTER 92

The United States and the World, 1930-1940

President Franklin D. Roosevelt speaking in Latin America.

BEFORE YOU BEGIN THE CHAPTER

Know What to Look For

1. If you went to school during the 1930's, you would have studied a great deal about Latin America. In social studies classes, pupils learned about Latin American countries and about American dealings with them. High school students were encouraged to study Spanish because many Americans felt that much of America's future business was to be with the Latin American nations. Airlines

scheduled airplane flights to many Latin American cities. All of this was part of America's Good Neighbor Policy.

The United States was trying to show the people of Latin America that it wanted to be friendly. Americans also wanted to overcome the fear and dislike many people of Latin America had for the United States. In this chapter, you will read about American dealings with Latin America and other nations in the world.

2. Read the title of the chapter. Then look through the chapter and read each heading. What do the headings tell you about the United States and its dealings with other nations in the 1930's?

3. Look at the pictures in the chapter and read each caption. What do the pictures tell you about American dealings with the world? Note also the time line at the beginning of the chapter. What years are included in the chapter? Compare this chapter time line to the unit time line on page 563.

4. Read the last part of the chapter called Summing Up. What policy did the United States follow toward Latin America? What is the topic of the next chapter?

Know These Important Terms
reciprocal trade agreements
Good Neighbor Policy

Know the Main Idea
Here is the MAIN IDEA of this chapter.
During the 1930's, America tried to improve its dealings with other nations.

Keep this MAIN IDEA in mind as you study the chapter. Ask yourself the following questions. They will help you remember the MAIN IDEA.

1. How did the United States increase its trade with other nations?

2. Which European nation was the only one to pay its war debt in full?

3. What was the greatest test of the Good Neighbor Policy in 1938?

THE YEARS OF THIS CHAPTER ARE 1930 TO 1940

1920   1930   1940

THE CHAPTER LESSON BEGINS HERE

World Trade Began to Improve

In the early 1930's, the United States tried to increase its trade with other nations. The American government agreed to lower its tariff, or tax on goods coming from other nations, if these nations agreed to lower their tariffs on American goods. These trade agreements were called **reciprocal trade agreements**. The United States signed reciprocal trade agreements with Great Britain, Canada, and many other nations. These agreements helped to rebuild trade between the nations of the world.

The United States and the Soviet Union

If you remember, in 1917 a revolution broke out in Russia, and the Communists took over Russia, which then became known as the Soviet Union. After the Communist Revolution of 1917, the United States refused to recognize, or to deal with, the Soviet Union. However, by 1933, the United States and the Soviet Union agreed that they must begin to work and trade together. Therefore, in 1933, the United States agreed to recognize the Soviet Union, and the two nations once again began dealing with each other.

But this new agreement did not work out as well as the United States hoped. The Soviet Union refused to pay the money that the old Russian government owed to the United States. Also, trade between the United States

Philippine soldiers march in the ceremonies in Manila on July 4, 1946, the day the Philippine Islands gained their independence.

and the Soviet Union did not increase very much, and the two nations never became very friendly.

European War Debts Still Caused Trouble

You may remember that the United States refused to cancel, or wipe out, the war debts owed to the nation by many European nations. Because of the Great Depression, many European nations were not able to keep up their debt payments to the United States. By 1934, almost all the European nations that owed war debts to the United States had stopped making debt payments. As it turned out, Europe never paid off its debts to the United States, and the whole problem of war debts remained unsolved during the 1930's.

The only nation that paid off its war debt in full was Finland.

The Philippine Islands Won Their Independence

If you remember, during the 1920's, the United States agreed to give the Philippine Islands their independence. Finally, in 1933, during President Hoover's term in office, Congress passed a law that gave independence to the Philippine Islands. However, the Philippine people refused to accept this plan because the law placed a high tariff on goods made in the Philippine Islands. This high tariff was certain to make it hard for the Philippine Islands to sell their goods in the United States. Therefore, in 1934, Congress passed another law to give the Philippine

Islands independence. This law agreed to give the Philippines full independence in 1946. It also set up lower tariffs on Philippine goods. The Philippine people accepted this plan for independence.

The United States Followed the Good Neighbor Policy

In the 1930's, the United States continued to improve its dealings with the Latin American nations. Under President Roosevelt, the American government followed the **Good Neighbor Policy,** a plan to have friendly dealings with Latin American nations. The United States promised never again to send American troops or to become involved in the affairs of any Latin American nation unless it was asked to do so by a Latin American nation.

In 1934, as part of the Good Neighbor Policy, President Roosevelt ordered that American troops be removed from Haiti. These troops were in Haiti because of a revolution that broke out there. After the American troops left, Haiti and the United States signed a reciprocal trade agreement.

The United States also followed the Good Neighbor Policy toward Cuba. In 1933, a revolution broke out in Cuba. This time, however, the United States did not send American troops to Cuba. And in 1934, the United States promised never again to become involved in the affairs of the Cuban nation. The United States and Cuba also signed a reciprocal trade agreement. And the Cuban government allowed the United States to keep a naval base located at Guantanamo (gwahn-TAH-nuh-moh) Bay in Cuba.

The Good Neighbor Policy Improved Dealings with Latin America

The greatest test of the Good Neighbor Policy came in 1938, when the Mexican government took over all the oil lands that be-

President Franklin D. Roosevelt.

THE GOOD NEIGHBOR POLICY

When Franklin D. Roosevelt became President, he said that he wanted the United States to follow "the policy of the good neighbor— the neighbor who . . . respects the rights of others." This speech was the beginning of a new American policy toward the nations of Latin America. The policy became known as the "Good Neighbor Policy."

To prove that the United States intended to be a good neighbor, President Roosevelt promised never to send American troops into any Latin American nation. He also promised never to interfere in the affairs of Latin American nations in any way. And he agreed to lower tariffs on the goods of any Latin American nation that lowered its tariffs on United States goods.

The Good Neighbor Policy was tested in the 1930's. During these years, some Latin American nations took over property in their countries that belonged to American businessmen. During the early 1900's, the United States might have sent troops into these nations to stop the takeover of American property. But no American troops were sent during the 1930's. For this reason, the nations of Latin America came to believe that the United States wanted to be a "Good Neighbor."

A view from the air of the American naval base located at Guantanamo Bay in Cuba. Cuba agreed to let America keep this base in 1934.

longed to American oil companies. Although the American oil companies demanded action from the United States government, President Roosevelt refused to send American troops to Mexico. Instead, President Roosevelt encouraged the American oil companies to work out their problems with the Mexican government. As a result, the Mexican government and the American oil companies worked out an agreement. In this agreement, Mexico promised to pay the American oil companies part of the value of the oil lands.

The Good Neighbor Policy was very successful. This plan helped to improve dealings between the United States and the nations of Latin America. Also, the Latin American nations began to think of the United States as a friend.

Summing Up

In the 1930's, America tried to improve its dealings with other nations. The United States increased its trade with other nations and began to deal with the Soviet Union. America agreed to give the Philippine Islands their independence. And the United States began to follow the Good Neighbor Policy toward Latin America. In the next chapter, you will find out about troubles in Europe and Asia during the 1930's.

AFTER YOU READ THE CHAPTER

Do You Know These Important Terms?

1. The agreement in which two nations decide to lower their tariff on goods coming from the one nation to the other nation is called a (**two-way/reciprocal**) trade agreement.

2. The (**Good Neighbor/New Image**) Policy was a plan to have friendly dealings with Latin American nations.

Do You Remember These People?

Tell something about each of the following persons in connection with the events in this chapter.

Herbert Hoover   **Franklin D. Roosevelt**

Can You Locate These Places?

Use the maps in your classroom to locate the following places. Tell how each location was related to the chapter.

Great Britain	**Canada**
Soviet Union	**Finland**
Philippine Islands	**Haiti**
Cuba	**Mexico**

Do You Know When It Happened?

What are the years of this chapter? Place the following events in the order in which they occurred.

American troops were removed from Haiti.

America recognized the Soviet Union.

Mexico and American oil companies worked out their problems.

Russia had a revolution and became a Communist nation, called the Soviet Union.

The United States was able to keep a naval base at Guantanamo Bay.

Discovering More About the Main Idea

During the 1930's, America tried to improve its dealings with other nations.

Tell how each of the following developments is related to the MAIN IDEA.

The United States established reciprocal trade agreements with many nations. America also agreed to recognize the Soviet Union, but war debts still caused trouble.

The United States agreed to give the Philippine Islands independence and set up low tariffs on Philippine goods.

The United States followed the Good Neighbor Policy in the Cuban revolution in 1933 and in the disagreement between American oil companies and Mexico in 1938.

Can You Discuss the Chapter?

Use the information you learned in this chapter to answer the following questions.

1. Why do you think that reciprocal trade agreements increase trade?

2. Describe the dealings between the Soviet Union and the United States after the United States recognized the Soviet Union in 1933.

3. Why did the Philippine Islands refuse to accept the independence plan Congress passed in 1933?

4. Can you name some times when the Good Neighbor Policy worked well?

5. Do you think the Philippines were right to expect special treatment when they became an independent nation? Explain.

Can You Connect The Past and the Present?

1. Describe America's present relationship with Cuba. Does the United States still have a naval base at Guantanamo Bay?

2. In the 1930's, the United States followed the Good Neighbor Policy toward Latin America. Does the United States have a plan for dealing with Latin America today?

CHAPTER 93

Moving Toward World War Two

Japanese soldiers in China.

BEFORE YOU BEGIN THE CHAPTER

Know What to Look For

1. By the fall of 1937, President Roosevelt was very concerned about the troubles of the world. He told the American people of his concern in a speech in 1937. In this speech, President Roosevelt suggested that the United States must help the other nations of the world to keep the peace.

However, most Americans did not realize that Japan, Germany, and Italy wanted to

conquer other nations. Several months after President Roosevelt's speech, Japanese planes bombed a United States gunboat, the "Panay," and three American oil tankers in the Yangtze River near China. Even after this, most Americans still did not want to get involved in the troubles in Europe and Asia. In this chapter, you will read about the world events which caused President Roosevelt and others to believe the world was moving toward war.

2. Read the title of the chapter. Then look through the chapter and read each heading. From the headings, tell how Americans felt about getting involved with world problems.

3. Look at the pictures in the chapter and read each caption. What do the pictures tell you about what was happening in the world in the 1930's? Note also the time line at the beginning of the chapter. What years are included in this chapter? Compare this chapter time line to the unit time line on page 563.

4. Read the last part of the chapter called Summing Up. What three nations took over other countries' territory?

Know These Important Terms
isolation movement   isolate

Neutrality Act of 1935   **Rhineland**
Neutrality Act of 1937   **Axis Powers**

Know the Main Idea

In the 1930's, Germany, Italy, and Japan began to conquer other nations, but the United States cut itself off from the troubles of the world.

Keep this MAIN IDEA in mind as you study the chapter. Ask yourself the following questions as you read. They will help you remember the MAIN IDEA.

1. What did Japan do about the League of Nations' warning to get out of China?

2. Who became the dictator of Germany in 1933?

3. Which nations signed an alliance and made up the Axis Powers?

THE YEARS OF THIS CHAPTER ARE 1930 TO 1937

1920   1930   1937   1940

THE CHAPTER LESSON BEGINS HERE

Japan Attacked China in 1931

In the 1930's, Japan was ruled by a small group of army men who decided to conquer China in order to gain certain raw materials Japan needed. In 1931, the Japanese army attacked Manchuria (man-CHOOR-ee-uh) in the northeastern part of China. The Japanese soon took over all of Manchuria.

China asked the League of Nations for help against Japan. A committee of League members met to discuss this problem. The United States government promised to help the League. However, the League of Nations did not take action, but only warned Japan that it must get out of China. Japan paid no attention to this warning and soon quit the League of Nations.

The Race to Build Weapons Continued

During the early 1930's, the United States met with Japan and the leading nations of Europe to talk about cutting down their armies and navies. Although these nations agreed to stop building large warships, none of the larger European nations was willing to cut down the size of its armies. They also were not willing to limit the use of weapons. Instead, nations were building larger armies and bigger and better weapons. Many people feared that this arms-building race, or build-up of armies and weapons, was leading to another war.

Then in 1933, Adolf Hitler (AY-dawlf HIT-lur), the leader of the Nazi Party in Germany, became the dictator of Germany. Hitler was

Adolf Hitler is saluted by German soldiers. Hitler became the dictator of Germany in 1933 and started to build up the armed forces.

determined to conquer Europe, and he began building up the German army, navy, and air force. When the world learned that Hitler was building up his armed forces, the other nations of Europe began to build up their armed forces.

Many Americans Wanted to Stay Out of Europe's Troubles

Many Americans felt that the United States must **isolate** (EYE-suh-layt) itself, or cut itself off from the world. This **isolation** (EYE-suh-LAY-shun) **movement** had several causes. One reason was that European nations refused to pay the war debts they owed to the United States. Another reason was that many Americans did not think the League of

Nations was able to prevent war among the nations. But the most important cause of the isolation movement was that many Americans were unhappy with the results of World War One. The war had not brought peace and free governments to nations everywhere.

Italy Attacked Ethiopia

In the 1890's, Italy tried but failed to take over the African nation of Ethiopia. During the 1920's, Benito Mussolini (bun-NEET-oh MOO-soh-LEE-nee) became the dictator of Italy. When he became dictator, Mussolini took away the freedom of the Italian people. In 1935, Mussolini attacked Ethiopia. The people of Ethiopia fought bravely against the

Soldiers of the Italian army march into Ethiopia. Italian armies conquered the African nation of Ethiopia in 1936.

Italian armies, but by 1936, Ethiopia was conquered.

Haile Selassie (HY-lee suh-LASS-ee), the emperor of Ethiopia, asked the League of Nations for help against Italy. The League ordered its members to stop selling war supplies to Italy. However, oil was not included in this list of war supplies not to be sold. This meant that Italy was able to buy the oil it needed for Italian tanks and planes attacking Ethiopia.

The United States Tried to Keep Out of War

After Italy attacked Ethiopia, the United States Congress decided to pass a law to keep the United States from becoming involved in any new war. This **Neutrality Act of 1935** set up certain rules for the United States to follow in dealing with nations at war.

1. American factories were forbidden to sell weapons to any nation at war.

2. American ships were forbidden to carry weapons to any nation at war.

3. American citizens were forbidden to travel on ships that belonged to any nation at war.

The United States Passed Another Neutrality Law

In 1936, Hitler was ready to begin his first move toward conquering Europe. He sent the German army to take over the **Rhineland,**

Senator Gerald P. Nye.

THE NYE COMMITTEE

During the 1930's, many Americans said that the United States was wrong to fight in World War One. People who believed this were called isolationists.

Many isolationists also believed that American weapons-making companies had forced the United States into the war. Senator Gerald P. Nye of North Dakota asked Congress to set up a committee to look into these charges. Congress agreed, and Senator Nye became the ·chairman of this committee. The Nye Committee, as it was called, went over the records of many of the larger weapons-making companies. The Committee found that these companies made huge profits during the war. But it was not able to prove that these companies were responsible for the United States entering World War One. These charges were just not true.

Many Americans, however, were still not convinced. They continued to believe that the large companies had forced America into the war. These Americans felt that laws must be passed to keep the United States out of any future wars. Such laws were soon passed. The Neutrality Acts of the late 1930's, forbidding the shipment of weapons to European nations, were intended to keep America out of World War Two.

or the territory along the Rhine River in western Germany. Then, Hitler and Mussolini signed an alliance, or an agreement, and called themselves the **Axis Powers.** And later the same year, the Axis Powers sent troops into Spain to fight on the side of General Francisco Franco (FRAHN-koh) during the civil war in Spain.

In 1937, Congress decided to pass another **Neutrality Act.** This law allowed a nation at war to buy non-military goods in the United States if it paid cash for the goods and carried them away in its own ships. This was called the "cash and carry" rule, and it helped nations that had ships and money.

Americans Did Not Want to Fight

In 1937, trouble broke out in the Far East. Japan once again attacked China. However, President Roosevelt did not apply the Neutrality Act rules because he wanted to be able to help China. But the American people strongly favored staying out of all wars. When the Japanese bombed an American gunship in China, the American government accepted an apology and a money payment from Japan.

By 1937, lands in Europe and Asia were being conquered. But the American people still believed it was possible to remain isolated.

Summing Up

In the 1930's, troubles broke out in Europe and Asia. In 1931, Japan attacked Manchuria in China. Italy, led by Benito Mussolini, conquered Ethiopia in 1936. And in 1936, Germany, led by Adolf Hitler, took over the Rhineland. During these years, the United States wanted to cut itself off from the troubles of the world. The United States passed Neutrality Acts in order to keep out of any new wars. The next chapter tells about the start of World War Two.

AFTER YOU READ THE CHAPTER

Do You Know These Important Terms?

For each sentence below, choose the term that best completes the sentence.

1. Americans who felt the United States must stay out of other nations' troubles were part of the (isolation/insulation) movement.
2. The Neutrality Act (of 1935/of 1933) forbade Americans to have any dealings with nations at war.
3. The Neutrality Act of (1935/1937) allowed a nation at war to buy non-military goods in the United States on a "cash and carry" basis.
4. (Infringe/Isolate) means to cut one's self off from the world.
5. The (Sudetenland/Rhineland) was the territory along the Rhine River in western Germany.
6. Hitler and Mussolini signed an alliance and called themselves the (Big Two/Axis Powers).

Do You Remember These People?

Tell something about each of the following persons.

Adolf Hitler   Benito Mussolini
Haile Selassie   Francisco Franco
Franklin D. Roosevelt

Can You Locate These Places?

Use the maps in your classroom to do the following map work.

1. Locate the Axis Powers in Europe. By the Treaty of Versailles, Germany was not to enter the Rhineland. When did Germany take over the Rhineland?
2. Locate the nation of Japan. Where did Japan first attack China?

Do You Know When It Happened?

What are the years of this chapter? Tell how each of the following dates was important.

1931   1933   1935   1936   1937

Discovering More About the Main Idea

In the 1930's, Germany, Italy, and Japan began to conquer other nations, but the United States cut itself off from the troubles of the world.

Tell how each of the following developments is related to the MAIN IDEA.

Japan paid no attention to the warning given by the League of Nations and continued to take over parts of China.

Germany took over the Rhineland, and Italy conquered the African nation of Ethiopia.

The United States passed two Neutrality Acts, and most Americans felt the United States must isolate itself.

Can You Discuss the Chapter?

Use the information you learned in this chapter to answer the following questions.

1. Why did many nations of Europe begin to build up their armed forces during the 1930's?
2. Why did many Americans believe in the isolation movement?
3. How effective was the League of Nations in solving world problems?
4. Why was the German takeover of the Rhineland in 1936 so important?
5. Do you think world events might have been different if the United States had taken an active part in world affairs during the 1930's? Why or why not?

Can You Connect the Past and the Present?

Why is it no longer possible for the United States to isolate itself?

CHAPTER 94

World War Two Begins

The Munich Conference.

BEFORE YOU BEGIN THE CHAPTER

Know What to Look For

1. In the early summer of 1939, a great World's Fair opened in New York. The flags of almost all the nations of the world waved above "The World of Tomorrow," as the fair was called. Over sixty nations set up exhibits to show the progress that had been made in industry, education, science, building, and art.

The thousands of visitors who came to the

fair were impressed by the beautiful buildings each country had built. The most outstanding sights at the fair were the Trylon, a tall needle-like pyramid, and the Perisphere, a large white sphere, which were the symbols of the fair.

The thousands of visitors were amazed at what the world of the future held in store for them. But shortly after the fair opened, World War Two began. The future shown at the fair was to be put off, while nations fought a long, terrible war. In this chapter, you will read about the beginning of World War Two.

2. Read the title of the chapter. Then look through the chapter and read each heading. What do the headings tell you about America's role in World War Two even though it was not fighting in the war?

3. Look at the picture in the chapter and read the caption. Can you name any of the world leaders in the picture? Look at the map on page 584. What do the black arrows show on the map? Note also the time line at the beginning of the chapter. What years are included in this chapter? Compare this chapter time line to the unit time line on page 563.

4. Read the last part of the chapter called Summing Up. How successful was Germany at the beginning of World War Two?

Know These Important Terms

Munich Conference	draft law
racism	Lend-Lease Act
Allies	

Know the Main Idea

Here is the MAIN IDEA of this chapter.

World War Two broke out in 1939, because Germany, Italy, and Japan began to take over other nations. Although Americans wanted to stay out of the war, the United States aided Great Britain.

Keep this MAIN IDEA in mind as you study the chapter. Ask yourself the following questions as you read. They will help you remember the MAIN IDEA.

1. What agreement was made at the Munich Conference?

2. What countries did Germany take over?

3. What steps did the United States take to prepare for war?

THE YEARS OF THIS CHAPTER ARE 1938 TO 1940

1920   1938   1940

THE CHAPTER LESSON BEGINS HERE

Germany Took Over More Territory in Europe

In March, 1938, the German army took over Austria. Later in the same year, Hitler demanded the Sudetenland (soo-DAYT-un-land), a rich industrial part of Czechoslovakia where many Germans lived. Czechoslovakia wanted to fight to protect its territory. However, Great Britain and France believed that if Hitler's demands were satisfied war might be prevented. At the **Munich Conference,** in September, 1938, British and French leaders met with Hitler and agreed to let Germany have the Sudetenland. In return, Hitler then promised not to take over any more territory.

The United States Began to Increase Its Armed Forces

By 1938, many Americans began to realize how dangerous it was to let Japan, Italy, and Germany continue to take over other countries' territory. Many Americans were also upset by Hitler's **racism,** or the false belief that one race, or group of people, is better than all other races. The arrest and torture of the Jews who lived in Germany showed what

THE AXIS POWERS BY 1939

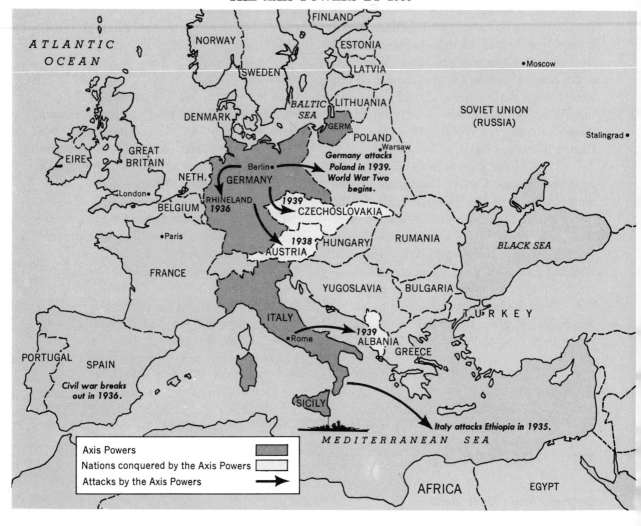

might happen to any group of people whom Hitler wished to mistreat or punish.

President Roosevelt realized that to protect the American nation the United States must make its armed forces stronger. Therefore, he asked Congress to raise the money to build up the American army, navy, and air force.

World War Two Began

As it turned out, the United States began

to build up its armed forces just in time. In March of 1939, Hitler took over all the rest of Czechoslovakia. In April, Italy attacked Albania (al-BAY-nee-uh). And in August of 1939, Germany signed a treaty with the Soviet Union. In this treaty, the two nations agreed not to fight each other and to divide up the nations of eastern Europe.

Hitler was now ready to take over Poland. On September 1, 1939, German troops marched into Poland. Great Britain and France now realized that only a war was going to stop Hitler from taking over all of Europe. On September 3, 1939, Great Britain and France declared war on Germany, and World War Two began. Almost all of the American people wanted to stay out of the war in Europe. Yet, almost all of them wanted the **Allies** (Great Britain and France) to defeat Germany.

The United States Strengthened Itself

After World War Two began, President Roosevelt decided to help Great Britain and France by changing the Neutrality Act of 1937. Congress passed another neutrality law in 1939. This law allowed any nation to buy American war weapons if the nation paid cash and carried the weapons away in its own ship. This new law helped Great Britain.

In 1940, Congress passed the first peacetime **draft law** in American history. This draft law required all men between the ages of twenty-one and thirty-five to serve in the army. These men were to serve in the army for one year only and were not to be sent outside the United States.

The United States Aided Great Britain

Congress passed these laws because it seemed as if Hitler was going to conquer all of Europe. By the end of June of 1940, Germany conquered Norway, Denmark, the Netherlands, Belgium, and France. Only Great Britain was still left to fight against Germany.

The American people realized that the United States also faced a great danger if Germany defeated Great Britain. Therefore, the United States decided to give more aid to Great Britain. In 1940, the United States traded fifty warships to Great Britain in exchange for leases on British naval bases.

Roosevelt Was Elected to a Third Term

The election of 1940 was held during World War Two. The Republicans ran Wendell L. Willkie, a rich businessman from Indiana. The American people reelected Roosevelt by almost 5 million votes. Franklin Roosevelt became the first American President to be elected for a third term.

The United States Increased Its Aid to Great Britain

At the end of 1940, Germany began a series of terrible air attacks against Great Britain. Great Britain needed help badly but no longer had the cash to pay for war supplies. Therefore, in 1941, Congress passed the **Lend-Lease Act.** This law made it possible for the United States to lend war supplies to Great Britain (and later to other nations fighting Germany). These supplies were to be paid back to the United States at the end of the war.

In 1941, the American navy began to guard and protect merchant ships that were delivering war supplies to Great Britain. And after several American merchant ships were attacked, Congress allowed merchant ships to be armed. The United States was no longer neutral, but it was still not at war.

Summing Up

In 1938, Germany took over more territory. Then in 1939, Hitler attacked Poland, and Great Britain and France declared war on Germany. After World War Two began, the United States began to increase its armed forces. In 1940, German armies conquered all the nations of western Europe except Great Britain. The United States now increased its aid to Great Britain, but the American people wanted to stay out of the war. In the next chapter, which begins Unit 24, you will find out how the United States was finally forced to fight in World War Two.

AFTER YOU READ THE CHAPTER

Do You Know These Important Terms?

For each sentence below, choose the term that best completes the sentence.

1. Germany agreed not to take over any more European territory at the (Berlin/Munich) Conference.
2. The false belief that one race, or group of people, is better than other groups is called (discrimination/racism).
3. The nations fighting against the Axis Powers in World War Two were called the (Allies/Freedom Fighters).
4. The law requiring young men to serve in the army was called the (draft/induction) law.
5. The (War Materials/Lend-Lease) Act made it possible for the United States to provide war supplies to nations fighting Germany.

Do You Remember These People?

Tell something about each of the following persons.

Adolf Hitler   Franklin D. Roosevelt
Wendell L. Willkie

Can You Locate These Places?

Use the map on page 584 to locate the following places. Tell how each location was related to World War Two.

Austria	Poland
Albania	Denmark
Norway	Belgium
The Netherlands	Great Britain
France	

Do You Know When It Happened?

What are the years of this chapter? Explain why the following date is important in American history.

September 3, 1939

Discovering More About the Main Idea

World War Two broke out in 1939, because Germany, Italy, and Japan began to take over other nations. Although Americans wanted to stay out of the war, the United States aided Great Britain.

Tell how each of the following developments is related to the MAIN IDEA.

German armies attacked Poland after Germany agreed not to take over any more European territory at the Munich Conference.

The United States began to build up its army, navy, and air force.

Most Americans favored aiding the Allies, but they wanted the United States to stay out of the war.

Can You Discuss the Chapter?

Use the information you learned in this chapter to answer the following questions.

1. Why did the United States begin to increase its armed forces?
2. Why did Great Britain and France realize that war was the only way to stop Germany?
3. How did the United States strengthen itself after World War Two began?
4. Explain the following statement. "The United States was no longer neutral, but it was still not at war."

Can You Connect the Past and the Present?

1. President Roosevelt served four terms as President. The Twenty-Second Amendment passed in 1951 only allows a President to serve two terms. Do you think a President should be able to serve more than two terms? Why or why not?
2. Adolf Hitler believed in racism. Why is racism a false belief?

UNIT 24
America Fights in World War Two

American soldiers in the Pacific.

THE CHAPTERS IN UNIT 24 ARE

CHAPTER 95   The United States in World War Two
CHAPTER 96   The Home Front in World War Two
CHAPTER 97   The Battle Fronts in World War Two
CHAPTER 98   Planning for Peace After the War

THE YEARS OF THIS UNIT ARE 1940 TO 1945

1900	1940	1945	1975

CHAPTER 95

The United States in World War Two

The Japanese attack on Pearl Harbor.

BEFORE YOU BEGIN THE CHAPTER

Know What to Look For

1. In 1940, Hitler decided to bomb Great Britain until it was forced to surrender. Night after night for months, the German air force bombed British cities and factories. At first, the British Royal Air Force was not able to defend Britain against these terrible German bombing attacks. But in a short time, British fighter planes started to shoot down hundreds of German bombing planes. In just one night,

the Royal Air Force shot down 100 German planes. As a result, Hitler was forced to give up the "Battle of Britain," as this was called.

This brave deed was the work of the 15 hundred pilots in the British Royal Air Force. One third of these men gave up their lives to save Britain. After the battle was won, the leader of Great Britain, Winston Churchill, honored these brave men by saying, "Never in the field of human conflict was so much owed by so many to so few." In this chapter, you will read about the events that led the United States to join the Allies in World War Two.

2. Read the title of the chapter. Then look through the chapter and read each heading. How did the war start for the United States?

3. Look at the pictures in the chapter and read each caption. What do the pictures tell you about the fighting in World War Two? Look at the map on page 590. What is the title of the map? Note also the time line at the beginning of the chapter. What years are included in this chapter? Compare this chapter time line to the unit time line on page 587.

4. Read the last part of the chapter called Summing Up. Who was winning when the United States entered World War Two?

Battle of the Coral Sea
Battle of Midway Island
Office of Production Management

Know the Main Idea
Here is the MAIN IDEA of this chapter.

After Japan attacked Pearl Harbor on December 7, 1941, the United States entered World War Two on the side of the Allies.

Keep this MAIN IDEA in mind as you study the chapter. Ask yourself the following questions as you read. They will help you remember the MAIN IDEA.

1. Why did the United States cut off its trade with Japan?

2. What event caused the United States to declare war?

3. In what ways had the United States prepared for war?

THE YEARS OF THIS CHAPTER ARE 1940 TO 1942

1940   1942   1945

THE CHAPTER LESSON BEGINS HERE

Japan Sided with Germany and Italy in World War Two

Many Americans were so concerned about the war in Europe that they almost forgot about the war that was still going on between China and Japan. But in September of 1940, Japan signed a treaty of alliance with Germany and Italy and joined the Axis Powers. In this treaty, all three nations agreed to fight together if any one of them was attacked by a nation not already fighting either in the war in Europe or the war in Asia. This treaty was a warning to the United States not to try and stop Japan from taking over China and other nations in Asia.

The United States government still hoped to settle its problems with Japan peacefully. But in 1941, Japan took over French Indo-China in Asia. Japan also intended to take over nearby British and Dutch colonies. President Roosevelt realized that Japan was a danger to all the countries of Asia. Therefore, the United States stopped sending shipments of raw materials such as gasoline, iron, and steel to Japan. Soon, all trade between the two nations was cut off. In March of 1941, leaders of the United States and Japan began a series of talks to try to solve their troubles.

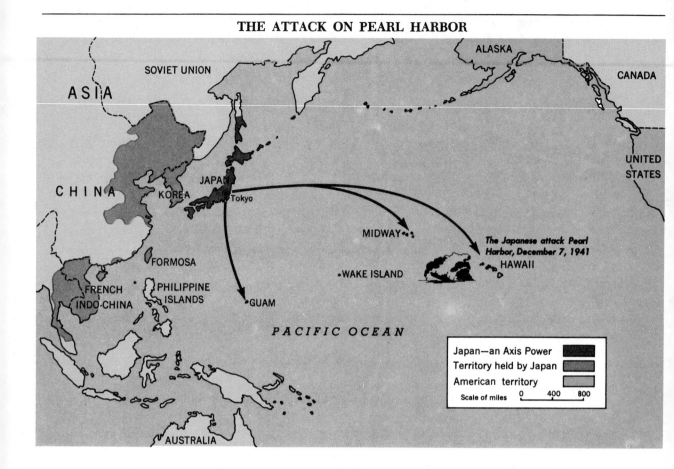

Japan Prepared to Attack the United States

These talks between the United States and Japan lasted for many months. In November, 1941, Japan promised not to attack British Malaya and the Dutch East Indies in Asia if the United States agreed to trade with Japan again and to give Japan a free hand in China. However, the United States refused to accept this agreement. After the United States turned down this agreement, the Japanese government believed that the United States might try to stop Japan from taking more territory. Japan decided, therefore, to attack the United States. Japan felt an attack might end the power of America in the Pacific.

Japan Attacked Pearl Harbor in 1941

The Japanese decided to try to attack the great American navy and air force base at Pearl Harbor to destroy the American planes and ships there. Japanese planes suddenly bombed Pearl Harbor, America's main Pacific naval base, early on Sunday morning, December 7, 1941. Over 2 thousand American soldiers and civilians were killed and 1 thousand more were wounded. Many American planes were destroyed, and most of the American ships in the Pacific fleet were sunk or damaged.

On the next day, President Roosevelt asked Congress to declare war on Japan. On December 11, Germany and Italy declared war

...we here highly resolve that these dead shall not have died in vain...

REMEMBER DEC. 7th!

This picture shows a poster from World War Two. It tells Americans not to forget the Japanese attack on Pearl Harbor.

---

on the United States. Later that day, Congress declared war on Germany and Italy. The United States was now fighting in World War Two.

The War Started Badly for the United States

When the United States entered World War Two, Germany, Italy, and Japan (the Axis Powers) were winning. Japan soon captured much American territory in the Pacific —the Philippine Islands, Guam, the Gilbert Islands, and Wake Island. Hong Kong, Malaya, Burma, and most of the Dutch East Indies were also taken over by Japan. The valuable raw materials of these areas were now under Japanese control. And Japan was getting ready to attack the countries of Australia and India next.

In Europe, the situation was just as bad. Great Britain was still under heavy air attack by German bombers. Greece and Yugoslavia were occupied by Germany. In June of 1941, Hitler attacked his ally, the Soviet Union. By early 1942, the German armies held most of western Europe and were occupying a large part of the Soviet Union. And the German armies in North Africa were preparing to capture Egypt, the Suez (soo-EZ) Canal, and the Middle East.

The war at sea in the Atlantic Ocean was also going badly for the United States and its

Navy base at Pearl Harbor.

PEARL HARBOR

Many Americans still wonder why the American armed forces were caught by surprise at Pearl Harbor. As early as January, 1941, Joseph C. Grew, the American ambassador to Japan, reported that the Japanese might attack Pearl Harbor. But American military leaders did not expect an attack against the United States. Instead, military experts thought Japan planned to attack European colonies in the Far East to gain needed raw materials. As a result, the United States followed a policy of delaying Japan until American armed forces were strong enough to prevent any such Japanese attacks. But Japan needed the raw materials of the European colonies in the Far East. Only the United States stood in Japan's way.

General Tojo, the head of the Japanese government, set November 25 (later November 29) as the deadline. If the United States did not agree to allow Japan to take over the European colonies in the Far East, war was to begin. The American government learned of this plan by intercepting some secret Japanese messages. But still the American government did not think that American territory was in danger. Then on December 7, the attack on Pearl Harbor came.

allies. German submarines were sinking many American ships carrying war supplies to Great Britain and the Soviet Union. However, the United States fleet started to do better against the Japanese in the Pacific. American victories in the **Battle of the Coral Sea** and in the **Battle of Midway Island,** in May and June of 1942, stopped any more Japanese conquests in the Pacific.

The United States Had Started to Prepare for a Possible War

The United States was more prepared for World War Two than it was for World War One. When Japan attacked Pearl Harbor, the United States already had about 2 million men in its armed forces. Later, Congress changed the draft law and men between the ages of eighteen and forty-five were open to be drafted to serve in the army. More than 16 million Americans including about 1 million black Americans served in the armed forces.

The **Office of Production Management** (O.P.M.) was formed early in 1941 to help American industry change over from peace time to war time production. By the end of the year, many American factories had started to turn out war supplies. However, many more factories had to change over to producing weapons and war supplies needed by the United States.

Summing Up

On December 7, 1941, Japan attacked Pearl Harbor, and the United States was forced to enter World War Two. When the United States started fighting in the war, the Axis Powers were winning. However, the United States had begun to prepare for war even before it started to fight. In the next chapter, you will find out how the American people worked on the home front to win the war.

AFTER YOU READ THE CHAPTER

Do You Know These Important Terms?

For each sentence below, choose the term that best completes the sentence.

1. The Battles of (**the Coral Sea and Midway Island/Guam and Pearl Harbor**) stopped any more Japanese conquests in the Pacific Ocean.
2. The Office of (**Price Fixing/Production Management**) helped American industry change over from peace time to war time production.

Can You Locate These Places?

Use the map on page 590 to do the following map work.

Locate Pearl Harbor. Why was this attack important? Name some of the lands in Asia and the Pacific held by the Japanese during World War Two.

Do You Know When It Happened?

What are the years of this chapter? Tell why the following date is important in American history.

December 7, 1941

Discovering More About the Main Idea

After Japan attacked Pearl Harbor on December 7, 1941, the United States entered World War Two on the side of the Allies.

Tell how each of the following developments is related to the MAIN IDEA.

The United States stopped sending shipments of raw materials to Japan because Americans realized that Japan was a danger to all the countries of Asia. The United States refused to give Japan a free hand in China.

By early 1942, the Axis Powers held all of western Europe and were occupying a large part of the Soviet Union. They controlled most of North Africa and were preparing to capture Egypt, the Suez Canal, and the Middle East.

The United States had started to build up its armed forces, and in early 1941, had started to change many of its factories from peace time to war time production.

Can You Discuss the Chapter?

Use the information you learned in this chapter to answer the following questions.

1. Why didn't the United States accept the agreement suggested by Japan in November, 1941?
2. What territories and countries was Japan able to take over in Asia and the Pacific?
3. How was the war going in Europe in early 1942?
4. What stopped the Japanese conquests in the Pacific?
5. Do you think that the attack on Pearl Harbor might have been prevented? Why or why not?

Can You Connect the Past and the Present?

1. Trade can be very important in world affairs. At the present time, are there any countries that the United States refuses to trade with? Why does the United States refuse to trade with these countries?
2. Pearl Harbor Day is a day that many Americans remember. What does your school or community do to remember this day?

CHAPTER 96

The Home Front in World War Two

Women workers in World War Two.

BEFORE YOU BEGIN THE CHAPTER

Know What to Look For

1. Americans on the home front in World War Two worked together to produce the food, weapons, and other supplies needed in the war. They also had to make sacrifices, or give up certain things, in order to help win the war. People were only allowed to buy limited amounts of shoes, sugar, meat, and many other items. Most car owners were al-

lowed to buy only about four gallons of gas a month. Women found it difficult to get silk stockings. And many other luxury items were in short supply because factories were only making war supplies. Often during World War Two, Americans stood in line for hours outside of stores to buy hard-to-get items like silk stockings or coffee. In this chapter, you will read more about Americans on the home front in World War Two.

2. Read the title of this chapter. Then look through the chapter and read each heading. What do the headings tell you about the home front in World War Two?

3. Look at the pictures in the chapter and read each caption. What do the pictures tell you about Americans on the home front? Note also the time line at the beginning of the chapter. What are the years of this chapter? Compare this chapter time line to the unit time line on page 587.

4. Read the last part of the chapter called Summing Up. How did the American people work together to win World War Two?

Know These Important Terms
War Production Board
Executive Order 8802
Fair Employment Practices Committee
Office of Price Administration
rationing system
Nisei

Know the Main Idea
Here is the MAIN IDEA of this chapter.
The American people worked together to help win World War Two.

Keep this MAIN IDEA in mind as you study the chapter. Ask yourself the following questions as you read. They will help you remember the MAIN IDEA.

1. How many war supplies were the Americans producing by the end of the war?

2. What event made it unlawful for factories producing war supplies to refuse to hire workers because of their race, color, or religion?

3. How did Japanese-Americans prove their loyalty to the United States during World War Two?

THE YEARS OF THIS CHAPTER ARE 1942 TO 1945

1940   1942   1945

THE CHAPTER LESSON BEGINS HERE

American Industry Produced War Supplies

After the United States entered World War Two, American industries had to produce weapons and war supplies to fight the powerful Axis Powers. The **War Production Board** was set up in January, 1942 to help direct industry to change over to producing weapons and war supplies. By 1943, American factories were turning out thousands of tanks, guns, ships, and airplanes. By the end of the war, American industry was producing twice as many war supplies and weapons as all its enemies put together.

American Workers Helped the War Effort

American workers worked hard to produce this huge amount of war supplies. During World War Two, American workers did everything possible to help the war effort. Labor unions promised not to slow down the production of war supplies by going on strike. Except for a long strike by the coal miners, most unions kept this promise and settled their problems without going on strike.

When the war started, many workers were unemployed. However, the great increase in the production of war supplies soon led to

Workers in an American factory work on tanks. During the war, American factories produced huge supplies of war weapons.

many jobs for workers in factories. In fact, many factories were not able to find enough workers. With most American men in the armed forces, many jobs in the factories that made war supplies were taken over by women.

Black Workers Won Jobs During the War

Many black workers worked in American factories to help the war efforts. During World War Two, thousands of black Americans left the South and moved to the cities of the Northeast and Middle West to find jobs. But at first, many factories refused to hire black workers, or they only gave them unskilled jobs.

A. Philip Randolph, head of the Brotherhood of Sleeping Car Porters union, planned an all black march on Washington in July of 1941, to try to help black workers to get jobs in factories. However, the march was called off when President Roosevelt issued **Executive Order 8802.** This order made it unlawful for any factory producing war supplies to refuse to hire workers because of their race, color, or

This picture shows black soldiers guarding a bridge over the Rhine River in Germany in 1945. The army still had segregated units.

religion. A **Fair Employment Practices Committee** was formed to see that this order was carried out. By the end of the war, 2 million black Americans were working in war-production factories.

American Farmers Helped the War Effort

Just as in World War One, a tremendous amount of food was needed to supply the United States army and the armies of its allies. Once again the American farmers worked hard to supply this food. In spite of a lack of farm workers and parts for farm machines, American farmers grew the largest crops in America's history.

During the war, prices for farm products increased. Many farmers made enough money to pay off the money they owed on their farms. Other farmers were able to buy more land and increase the size of their farms. And some farmers bought new farm machines in order to grow even larger crops.

The Government Raised Money to Pay for the War

World War Two cost more than any other war in American history. From 1941 to 1945, the United States government spent about 400 billion dollars to pay for fighting the war. This huge amount of money was more than twice the amount spent by the American government during all the years from 1789 to 1941. The government raised much of this money from taxes. The government raised taxes to the highest level in America's history. Another way the government raised money for the war was by selling war bonds.

The Government Set Up War Controls

One of the most important war time problems was the control of prices. The **Office of Price Administration** (O.P.A.) was set up to keep prices from increasing sharply as they did during World War One. The O.P.A. fixed prices, wages, and rents.

The O.P.A. also had the job of setting up

Japanese in relocation camp.

JAPANESE-AMERICANS DURING WORLD WAR TWO

During the first half of 1942, the American government moved over 70 thousand Japanese-Americans from their homes in the states of California, Oregon, Washington, and Arizona. Most of these Japanese-Americans were American citizens. None of them were accused of any crime. But the American nation was nervous after the attack on Pearl Harbor, and it feared that Japanese-Americans might help Japan if that nation ever attacked the Pacific coast.

Japanese-Americans were moved to "relocation centers" in states far from the Pacific coast. Here, they lived in buildings in fenced-in camps much like army barracks. Beginning in 1943, many were allowed to resettle in various cities of the Middle West. After the war ended, they were able to settle where they wished.

Several legal cases resulted from the removal of Japanese-Americans from the Pacific coast. In these cases, it was argued that moving them was against their rights as citizens. Although the Supreme Court decided that this action was not unlawful, after the war many Americans realized that the Japanese had been treated unfairly. Many of them lost their homes, businesses, and property. And in 1948, Congress passed a law to help these Japanese-Americans recover their property losses.

a **rationing** (RASH-uh-neeng) **system.** This rationing system allowed Americans to buy only small amounts of hard-to-get products. Various kinds of products—including shoes, tires, sugar, gasoline, coffee, and meat—were rationed. Most Americans agreed to these wartime controls because they realized that such controls were necessary to help win the war.

Japanese-Americans Were Mistreated

During World War Two, the **Nisei** (NEE-say), or American citizens of Japanese parents, were treated unfairly. In 1942, over 70 thousand Nisei were taken from their homes on the Pacific coast of the United States and sent to special camps. Later, when the nation's fears were calmed, the Nisei were allowed to return to their homes. Before the war ended, thousands of these Nisei proved their loyalty to the United States by fighting bravely.

Roosevelt Was Elected to a Fourth Term

While the United States was fighting in World War Two, the election of 1944 was held. The Republicans ran Thomas E. Dewey, the governor of New York. Franklin D. Roosevelt ran for a fourth term as the Democratic candidate. And once again, Roosevelt was reelected as President. The Vice-President elected with Roosevelt in 1944 was Harry S. Truman, a Senator from Missouri.

Summing Up

The American people worked together to win World War Two. American workers produced huge amounts of war supplies. Farmers grew tremendous amounts of food. And all Americans accepted wage, price, and rent controls as well as rationing. In the next chapter, you will find out how American fighting men helped win World War Two on the battlefields.

AFTER YOU READ THE CHAPTER

Do You Know These Important Terms?

For each sentence below, choose the term that best completes the sentence.

1. The (**Works Progress/War Production**) Board helped industry change over to the production of weapons and war supplies.
2. (**Anti-discrimination Order 401/Executive Order 8802**) made it unlawful for a factory producing war supplies to refuse to hire workers because of their race, color, or religion. The (**Fair Employment/Job Equalization**) Practices Committee was formed to see that the order was carried out.
3. The (**Price Regulation/Office of Price**) Administration fixed prices, wages, and rents.
4. A (**quota/rationing**) system allowed Americans to buy only small amounts of hard-to-get products.
5. American citizens of Japanese parents were called (**Nisei/Yakashima**).

Do You Remember These People?

Tell something about each of the following persons.

Harry S. Truman   **Franklin D. Roosevelt**
Thomas E. Dewey   **A. Philip Randolph**

Do You Know When It Happened?

What are the years of this chapter? Place the following events in the order in which they occurred.

Over 70 thousand Nisei were removed from their homes.

The President issued Executive Order 8802.

American industry was producing twice as many war supplies as all its enemies.

The War Production Board was established.

Franklin Roosevelt ran for a fourth term.

Discovering More About the Main Idea
The American people worked together to help win World War Two.

Tell how each of the following developments is related to the MAIN IDEA.

American industry was able to produce twice the amount of war supplies and weapons as all its enemies put together. Black workers and women worked in American factories to help the war effort.

Prices were strictly controlled, and hard-to-get products were rationed. Most Americans agreed that these wartime controls were necessary. They paid the highest taxes ever.

President Roosevelt was elected for a fourth term in 1944.

Can You Discuss the Chapter?

Use the information you learned in this chapter to answer the following questions.

1. How was America able to produce so many war supplies?
2. How did black workers and women help in the war effort?
3. How did the United States raise the money to pay for the war?
4. Why were price controls necessary?
5. Do you agree that the Nisei were treated unfairly? Give reasons for your answers.

Can You Connect the Past and the Present?

1. Do you know of any other Executive Orders issued by a President which have helped black Americans?
2. When people get upset or excited, they often do strange things. This can be seen in American treatment of the Nisei in 1942. Have you ever seen an incident in which people who were excited or upset treated other people unfairly?

CHAPTER 97

The Battle Fronts in World War Two

American soldiers invading Europe in 1944.

BEFORE YOU BEGIN THE CHAPTER

Know What to Look For

1. "Nuts!" That was the one-word reply of an American general who was asked by the Germans to surrender during the Battle of the Bulge. This is one of many sayings that became famous during World War Two. Another famous saying from the early days of the war was "Sighted ship sank same." This message was sent by a navy pilot before he crashed his plane, which was filled with bombs, into a

Japanese warship. He sank the Japanese ship.

The most famous of all the sayings from the war, however, was "Kilroy was here." This saying appeared wherever American fighting men went. Some Americans swear that this saying was written on the walls and buildings of towns even before American troops arrived. No one knew who Kilroy was, but his message helped to cheer up American soldiers. In this chapter, you will read about the fighting in World War Two.

2. Read the title of the chapter. Then look through the chapter and read each heading. By using the chapter headings, what can you tell about the fighting in World War Two?

3. Look at the pictures in the chapter and read each caption. What do the pictures tell you about the fighting in World War Two? Examine the two maps on page 602 and on page 603. What information does each map show? Note also the time line at the beginning of the chapter. What years are included in the chapter? Compare this chapter time line to the unit time line on page 587.

4. Read the last part of the chapter called Summing Up. When was World War Two finally over? What is the topic of the next chapter?

Know These Important Terms

Battle of the Bulge   atomic bomb
concentration camps

Know The Main Idea
Here is the MAIN IDEA of this chapter.
The United States and the Allies fought against the Axis Powers all over the world. They finally won the war in 1945.

Keep this MAIN IDEA in mind as you study the chapter. Ask yourself the following questions as you read. They will help you remember the MAIN IDEA.

1. Which enemy did the Allies decide must be defeated first?
2. Where did the Allied invasion of Europe take place?
3. What action by the United States made the Japanese decide to surrender?

THE YEARS OF THIS CHAPTER ARE 1942 TO 1945

1940   1942   1945

THE CHAPTER LESSON BEGINS HERE

The Allies Won in North Africa

The United States had to fight on two battle fronts—in Asia against Japan, and in Europe against Germany and Italy. The United States and its allies decided that Germany and Italy must be defeated first. They decided to strike their first blow at the German and Italian armies in Africa. In November of 1942, a large army of American, Canadian, and British troops led by General Dwight D. Eisenhower (I-zun-HOW-ur) landed on the northern coast of Africa.

By May, 1943, the Allied army forced the German and Italian armies in Africa to surrender. The Suez Canal and the Middle East were now safe. And the Allied armies were now able to attack along the coast of Europe.

Sicily and Italy Were Attacked

However, before the Allies were able to attack Europe, they had to win control of the Atlantic Ocean. In the first few months of 1943, over 200 German submarines in the Atlantic were sinking American ships faster than the United States was able to build them. However, the Allies began to use radar and radio-wave warning systems on their ships to warn them of German submarines. By 1943, the Allies won the Battle of the Atlantic, and American ships were arriving safely in Europe.

Axis Powers

Territory held by Axis Powers by 1942

Allied attacks on Axis Powers

After the Allies won control of the Atlantic, they were able to attack Europe. In July of 1943, Allied troops from northern Africa captured Sicily, the island at the tip of Italy. Early in September, Allied troops landed in southern Italy, and the Italian government surrendered. However, German troops were rushed into Italy, and hard fighting continued there until 1945.

The War in the Soviet Union

The Allies also began to do better on the eastern front in the Soviet Union. In Sep-

tember 1942, the German armies attacked the city of Stalingrad (STAHL-un-grad). Stalingrad had to be held or all of the Soviet Union might be conquered. The Russians held the city, and slowly but surely the Soviet troops began to push back the German armies.

The Allies Invaded Europe in 1944

Meanwhile, the Allies were planning to invade western Europe. In 1944, the United States and Great Britain felt they were ready to begin the attack. First, the Allies bombed Germany until its air force, factories, and transportation system were greatly weakened. Then on June 6, 1944, the Allied army under General Eisenhower landed in Normandy, in northern France.

In August of 1944, another American army landed in southern France. By the end of 1944, these Allied armies drove the German armies out of France and Belgium. And on the eastern front, the Soviet armies captured Rumania, Bulgaria, and Hungary.

The War Ended in Europe in May of 1945

At the **Battle of the Bulge** in December, 1944, the German army tried to stop the Allies' advance in Europe, but failed. In March of 1945, the Allied armies invaded Germany. Soon, the American, British, and Soviet armies closed in on all sides. On May 8, 1945, Germany surrendered to the Allies. President Roosevelt did not live to see this great victory in Europe. He died in April, 1945. Harry S. Truman, the Vice-President, became President of the United States.

The United States Began to Defeat Japan

The United States was now ready to end the war in the Pacific. In 1942, American armies started to win victories over the Japanese forces. In August of 1942, American marines landed on Guadalcanal (GWAHD-ul-

WORLD WAR TWO—VICTORY IN ASIA

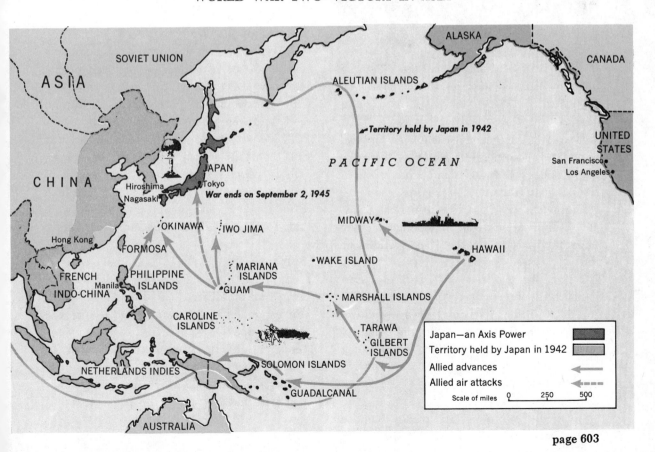

Ruins in Nagasaki after an atomic bomb was dropped on the city.

kuh-NAL) in the Solomon Islands. By the end of 1943, American forces captured the Solomon Islands, Midway Island, and much of New Guinea (GHIN-ee).

During 1944 and 1945, the American army, navy, and marines worked together to win important victories in the Pacific. American forces captured Saipan (Seye-PAN), Guam, Iwo Jima (EE-wo JEE-mah), and the Japanese island of Okinawa (OH-kuh-NAH-wuh). And in 1945, the Americans succeeded in recapturing the Philippines. But the Japanese government still was not willing to surrender.

War in Asia Ended in September of 1945

In June, 1945, American planes bombed

Japan heavily, but Japan still did not give up. An attack on Japan was certain to cost the lives of thousands of American soldiers. In order to save the lives of thousands of American soldiers, President Harry S. Truman ordered that the **atomic bomb** be dropped on Japan. The atomic bomb was the most powerful weapon ever developed.

On August 6, 1945, an atomic bomb was dropped on the Japanese city of Hiroshima (HIR-uh-SHEE-muh). The bomb destroyed most of the city and killed almost 80 thousand people. Still the Japanese government refused to surrender. Three days later, a second atomic bomb was dropped on Nagasaki (NAHG-uh-SAHK-ee), killing another 70 thousand people. Finally, the Japanese government surrendered. World War Two ended in Asia on September 2, 1945.

Results of the War

World War Two was over, but its cost was terrible. Over 20 million people died during the war. Over 1 million Americans were either killed or wounded. Large parts of Europe and Asia were completely destroyed.

The most shocking discovery of the war was the terrible German **concentration camps.** These were special prison camps where prisoners were tortured and killed. More than 6 million Jews and many other people were killed in these German concentration camps.

Summing Up

By 1943, the Allies began to win World War Two on all fronts. In June, 1944, Allied armies landed in France and began to reconquer Europe. On May 8, 1945, Germany surrendered, and the war in Europe ended. In Asia, the war ended on September 2, 1945, when Japan surrendered. In the next chapter, you will find out about the peace that followed World War Two.

AFTER YOU READ THE CHAPTER

Do You Know These Important Terms?

For each sentence below, choose the term that best completes the sentence.

1. In 1944, the German army tried to stop the Allied advance at the (**Salerno Beach line/ Battle of the Bulge**).
2. (**Stalag/Concentration**) camps were prisons where prisoners were tortured and killed.
3. The most powerful weapon ever developed was called the (**atomic/radar**) bomb.

Do You Remember These People?

Tell something about each of the following persons.

Dwight D. Eisenhower
Harry S. Truman
Franklin D. Roosevelt

Can You Locate These Places?

Use the map on page 602 to follow the fighting in Europe. Locate the following places and tell why they are important.

Egypt	**Normandy**
Sicily	**Berlin**
Stalingrad	

Use the map on page 603 to follow the fighting in Asia. Locate the following places and tell why they are important.

Guadalcanal	**Guam**
Iwo Jima	**Okinawa**
Hiroshima	**Nagasaki**

Do You Know When It Happened?

What are the years of this chapter? Can you give the dates of the following events?

German and Italian armies in North Africa surrendered.
American marines landed on Guadalcanal.
Allied troops landed in Normandy.
Germany surrendered.
Two atomic bombs were dropped on Japan.

Discovering More About the Main Idea

The United States and the Allies fought against the Axis Powers all over the world. They finally won the war in 1945.

Tell how each of the following developments is related to the MAIN IDEA.

The Allies decided that Germany and Italy must be defeated first. The turning points in the war were at Stalingrad and in North Africa.

The long battle from island to island in the Pacific began with Guadalcanal in 1942 and ended at Okinawa. Japan surrendered after two atomic bombs were dropped.

Over 20 million people died during the war. The most shocking discovery, however, were the concentration camps where 6 million Jews and many other people were killed.

Can You Discuss the Chapter?

Use the information you learned in this chapter to answer the following questions.

1. How were the Allies able to overcome German submarines in the North Atlantic?
2. How did the Allied armies invade Europe in 1944?
3. Why did President Truman decide to drop the atomic bomb on Japan?
4. What were the results of World War Two?
5. Do you think it was right for President Truman to order that the atomic bomb be dropped on Japan? Why or why not?

Can You Connect the Past and the Present?

In 1945, President Truman had to decide whether to send American soldiers to attack Japan or drop the atomic bomb. He chose to drop the bomb to save American lives. Have you ever been faced with a difficult choice in your life?

CHAPTER 98

Planning for Peace After the War

Japan surrenders to General MacArthur.

BEFORE YOU BEGIN THE CHAPTER

Know What to Look For

1. You may remember reading about how difficult it was to set up a lasting peace after World War One. The League of Nations was too weak to prevent World War Two. And the United States refused to join the League and to accept the Treaty of Versailles. Most Americans remembered that America's efforts to set up a fair peace for the world after World War One were not completely successful.

They hoped that this time a fair peace would be set up. In order to set up a fair peace, the leaders of the United States, Britain, and the Soviet Union met even before the war was over. At these meetings they made plans to win the war. And they also made plans for the peace after the war. In this chapter, you will find out about these plans and how they were put into operation after the war.

2. Read the title of the chapter. Then look through the chapter and read each heading. What do the chapter heads tell you about the plans made for peace after the war?

3. Look at the pictures in the chapter and read each caption. Who are the three world leaders in the picture on page 609? Look at the map on page 608. What is the title of this map? Note also the time line at the beginning of the chapter. What years are included in this chapter? Compare this chapter time line to the unit time line on page 587.

4. Read the last part of the chapter called Summing Up. What group was set up to keep peace in the world?

Know These Important Terms
Atlantic Charter
Big Three nations

United Nations
General Assembly
Security Council
International Court of Justice

Know the Main Idea
Here is the MAIN IDEA of this chapter.

The United States, Great Britain, and the Soviet Union made plans for peace after World War Two.

Keep this MAIN IDEA in mind as you study the chapter. Ask yourself the following questions as you read. They will help you remember the MAIN IDEA.

1. What nations were called the Big Three nations?

2. Why was the United Nations set up?

3. What happened to the leaders of the Nazi government in Germany?

THE YEARS OF THIS CHAPTER ARE 1941 TO 1945

1940   1941   1945

THE CHAPTER LESSON BEGINS HERE

The Allies Were Fighting for Freedom

As early as August of 1941, President Roosevelt and Winston Churchill, the Prime Minister, or leader, of Great Britain, met and drew up a statement of their war aims. This **Atlantic Charter,** as it was called, was very much like President Wilson's Fourteen Points of World War One. The most famous part of the Atlantic Charter called for certain important freedoms for all the people of the world. These freedoms included freedom from want and freedom from fear. President Roosevelt also said that all people should have freedom of religion and freedom of speech.

The Atlantic Charter was signed by twenty-

six nations. These nations promised to work together to win the war. But it was up to the **Big Three nations**—the United States, Great Britain, and the Soviet Union—to see that the Charter was carried out. During the war, the leaders of the Big Three nations, President Roosevelt of the United States, Prime Minister Churchill of Great Britain, and the leader of the Soviet Union, Joseph Stalin, met several times to plan for the war and to plan for the peace after the war.

The Big Three Met Together

At a meeting at Casablanca (KAS-uh-BLANG-ka) in North Africa, in January of 1943,

A DIVIDED GERMANY

Map labels: NORTH SEA, BALTIC SEA, NETHERLANDS, U.S., BRITISH ZONE, Berlin, SOVIET ZONE, POLAND, G E R M A N Y, BELGIUM, LUX., FRENCH ZONE, CZECHOSLOVAKIA, U.S. ZONE, FRANCE, AUSTRIA, SWITZERLAND

The Allies' zones
The Soviet zone
Scale of miles 0 50 100 150 200

Roosevelt and Churchill decided that the Allies must demand the "unconditional surrender" of their enemies. This meant that the Axis Powers must give up completely. Later, Stalin also agreed to this policy of unconditional surrender.

In November of 1943, the leaders of the Big Three nations, Roosevelt, Churchill, and Stalin, met for the first time in Teheran, Iran. At this meeting, they decided to start a Second Front in the war at Normandy, France. The Soviet Union agreed to declare war on Japan as soon as Germany was defeated.

Plans for Peace Were Made

In 1944, the leaders of the United States, Great Britain, China, and the Soviet Union met to make plans to organize the **United Nations.** The Allies agreed that the United Nations organization was necessary to keep

peace in the world after the war ended.

The Big Three nations met for the second time at Yalta, in southern Russia, early in 1945. At Yalta, Roosevelt, Churchill, and Stalin agreed to call a meeting in San Francisco, in April of 1945, to draw up plans for the United Nations. They also made plans to occupy Germany after the war. They decided to divide Germany and the city of Berlin into four zones, or parts. The United States, Great Britain, the Soviet Union, and France were each to occupy and control one of the four zones. The Big Three also decided that free elections were to be held in the nations of eastern Europe in order for the people to choose their own governments.

The United Nations Was Formed

In April of 1945, the leaders of fifty nations met in San Francisco, California, and drew up the Charter, or constitution, of the United Nations (U.N.). The purpose of the United Nations organization was to keep peace in the world. The Charter was completed in June, and the United Nations was officially started in October of 1945.

Under the United Nations Charter, the **General Assembly,** an agency, or part, of the U.N., was made up of all the member nations. Five nations—the United States, Great Britain, the Soviet Union, France, and China were regular members of the main agency of the United Nations, the **Security Council.** Six other nations ° were elected to the Security Council for a period of two years by the General Assembly. The Security Council had the power to use armed force, if necessary, to keep peace among nations. However, each of the five permanent nations on the Security Council had to agree before the Council took any action.

° Later, four more nations were added, making a total of ten nonpermanent members.

Pictured above, from the left, are Winston Churchill, Franklin Roosevelt, and Joseph Stalin, the leaders of the Big Three nations.

The United Nations was also made up of other agencies, or parts, that tried to improve health, education, working conditions, and money conditions all over the world. The United Nations also had an **International Court of Justice.** This court settles legal disputes between nations.

Germany's Future Was Decided

In the summer of 1945, the leaders of the United States, Great Britain, and the Soviet Union met again. Stalin was still the head of the Soviet Union, but Harry S. Truman was now President of the United States, and Clement Attlee (AT-lee) replaced Churchill as Prime Minister of Great Britain. By this time, the Soviet Union was becoming a danger to world peace. The Soviet Union did not want to keep its promise to allow free elections in the nations of eastern Europe.

This picture shows the meeting in San Francisco in 1945 at which leaders of fifty nations set up the United Nations.

However, the United States, Great Britain, and the Soviet Union were still able to reach some agreement on the treatment of Germany. Territory in the eastern part of Germany was given to Poland and the Soviet Union. The rest of Germany was divided into four zones, or parts. These zones were each occupied by one of the allied nations. Hitler's government was completely done away with, and the leaders of this Nazi government were tried as war criminals.

Summing Up

During World War Two, the Big Three nations, or the United States, Great Britain, and the Soviet Union, worked closely together. Leaders of these nations held meetings to make plans to win the war and to make plans for peace after the war. In 1945, the United Nations was set up to keep peace in the world. The next chapter, which begins Unit 25, tells how the United States returned to peacetime living.

AFTER YOU READ THE CHAPTER

Do You Know These Important Terms?

For each sentence below, choose the term that best completes the sentence.

1. The war aims drawn up by President Roosevelt and Winston Churchill were called the (**Atlantic Charter/Declaration of Human Rights**).
2. The United States, Great Britain, and the Soviet Union were called the (**Big Three/Solid Trio**) nations.
3. The (**Court of Peace/United Nations**) was the organization formed to keep peace in the world after the war ended.
4. The (**Congress/General Assembly**) is made up of all the member nations.
5. The (**Closed Council/Security Council**) has the power to use armed force, if necessary, to keep peace among nations.
6. The International (**Court of Justice/Supreme Bench**) settles legal disputes between nations.

Do You Remember These People?

Tell something about each of the following persons.

Franklin D. Roosevelt   Clement Attlee
Joseph Stalin   Harry S. Truman
Winston Churchill

Can You Locate These Places?

Use the map on page 608 to locate the following places.
Zones of Germany   Berlin

Do You Know When It Happened?

What are the years of this chapter? Place the following events in the order in which they occurred.

The United Nations was formed.
The Atlantic Charter was drawn up.
The Big Three met in North Africa.

Discovering More About the Main Idea

The United States, Great Britain, and the Soviet Union made plans for peace after World War Two.

Tell how each of the following developments is related to the MAIN IDEA.

The Atlantic Charter stated the war aims of the Allies. The Charter called for certain important freedoms for the people of the world.

The Security Council of the United Nations has the right to use armed force to keep peace as long as each of the five permanent nations on the Security Council agree.

The Soviet Union became a danger to world peace when it did not keep its promise to allow free elections in the nations of eastern Europe.

Can You Discuss the Chapter?

Use the information you learned in this chapter to answer the following questions.

1. What were the freedoms for all people of the world included in the Atlantic Charter?
2. How did the leaders of the Big Three nations make their plans for the war and for the peace after the war?
3. What are the main agencies, or parts, of the United Nations?
4. How did the Big Three nations decide to divide Germany and the city of Berlin?
5. Do you think the leaders of a defeated government should be tried as war criminals? Why or why not?

Can You Connect the Past and the Present?

1. The United Nations was founded in San Francisco. Where is it located today?
2. Has the Security Council had to use armed force recently to keep the peace in the world? If so, explain the circumstances.

page 611

PART V

The Nation In The Modern Age

1945 to 1970

THE UNITS IN PART V ARE

Unit 25 The American Nation After the War

Unit 26 The United States As a World Leader

Unit 27 American Life Changes

Unit 28 Changes in American Government

Unit 29 America in the Space Age

Unit 30 The American Nation Today

The American Nation After the War

Harry S. Truman (left) taking oath as President.

THE CHAPTERS IN UNIT 25 ARE

CHAPTER 99 The United States After the War
CHAPTER 100 President Truman's Fair Deal
CHAPTER 101 The Nation Under President Eisenhower

THE YEARS OF THIS UNIT ARE 1945 TO 1960

| 1900 | 1945 | 1960 | 1975 |

The United States After the War

An American factory making cars.

BEFORE YOU BEGIN THE CHAPTER

Know What to Look For

1. On December 2, 1942, an event took place in Chicago which changed the world. This event began the Atomic Age. A group of scientists under the leadership of Enrico Fermi, a famous Italian scientist, were making tests to see if man was able to control the power of the atom. They had built the world's first atomic reactor in a handball court beneath the football stadium at the University of Chicago.

Fermi ordered the control rods to be pulled out of the reactor. As the rod came out, the first man-made atomic chain reaction in history was produced. Fermi then ordered the rod to be put back in the reactor. The atomic chain reaction stopped. Man had learned to control atomic power! You already know about the role of the atomic bomb in World War Two. In this chapter, you will read about peace time uses of atomic energy and about America's return to peace time living.

2. Read the title of the chapter. Then look through the chapter and read each heading. From the headings, list some of the things that happened in the United States after the war.

3. Look at the pictures in the chapter and read each caption. What do the pictures show about the United States after World War Two? Note also the time line at the beginning of the chapter. What years are included in this chapter? Compare this chapter time line to the unit time line on page 613.

4. Read the last part of the chapter called Summing Up. Who was elected President in 1948?

Know These Important Terms
G.I. Bill of Rights
Taft-Hartley Act

Employment Act
Council of Economic Advisers
Atomic Energy Act
National Security Act
Twenty-Second Amendment
Fair Deal

Know the Main Idea
Here is the MAIN IDEA of this chapter.

After 1945, the American nation changed back again to peace time living, and Congress passed some important new laws.

Keep this MAIN IDEA in mind as you study the chapter. Ask yourself the following questions as you read. They will help you remember the MAIN IDEA.

1. What law helped veterans to continue their education or loaned them money to buy a home or business?
2. Who controls the development of atomic energy?
3. What did the Fair Deal program of Harry Truman promise?

THE YEARS OF THIS CHAPTER ARE 1945 TO 1948

1945   1948   1960

THE CHAPTER LESSON BEGINS HERE

American Troops Returned Home
The Americans who were in the greatest hurry to go back to peace time living were the men in the armed forces. Americans made it clear to Congress that they expected the men and women in the armed forces to return home from Europe and Asia right away. The government allowed American troops to return home as quickly as possible. By the end of 1946, the American armed forces were down to a little more than a million men.

However, the United States still felt that it needed to draft men into the armed forces. Therefore, Congress passed a new peace time draft law. Congress also passed a law known as the **G.I. Bill of Rights.** This law helped veterans to continue their education, loaned them money to buy a home or business, and gave them pensions and hospital care.

American Business and Industry Returned to a Peace Time Basis
American industry was also in a hurry to

After the war, American workers went back to producing peace time goods.

During World War Two, the prices of food, housing, and most products were controlled, or fixed, by the federal government. In 1946, however, Congress ended all price controls, except for the price controls on rent and a few products that were still hard to get. After price controls were ended, the prices of most products went up.

Congress Passed a Law to Control Unions

Right after World War Two, many strikes took place. These strikes were caused by the loss in pay resulting from a cutback from a forty-eight-hour to a forty-hour work week in most industries. After price controls were removed in 1946, prices for goods rose sharply. More strikes took place because workers needed higher wages to pay for the goods they needed. Strikes took place in the automobile industry, the steel industry, the coal industry, and the railroad industry. In all these strikes, the workers won wage increases.

Because of these strikes, Congress began to feel that unions must be controlled. Therefore, in 1947, Congress passed the **Taft-Hartley Act** over President Truman's veto. This law required labor unions to give sixty days' notice before they started a strike. The law also allowed the President to get an injunction, or a court order, to stop a strike that was a danger to the nation's safety.

Congress Dealt with the Problems of Unemployment and Atomic Energy

Two important laws were passed by Congress in 1946. One was the **Employment Act.** This law made it the government's duty to try to prevent unemployment. Also a **Council of Economic Advisers** was set up to help the President improve the American economy and, therefore, provide more jobs.

return to peace time production. As soon as World War Two was over, America's factories went back to making the goods that Americans needed in peace time. As millions of soldiers returned home, and as factories stopped making war materials, many American workers were afraid that they might be without jobs. However, the demand for goods was so great that few workers lost their jobs.

Above, steel workers on strike are picketing. Many workers went on strike after World War Two to gain higher wages.

Another important law passed by Congress was the **Atomic Energy Act.** This act dealt with the development and use of atomic energy. Atomic energy is the powerful force that is set off when atoms are split in a "chain reaction." Atomic energy is used in atomic bombs. The law set up the Atomic Energy Commission and put the development of atomic energy under civilian control.

Congress Passed Many Important Laws in 1947

In the Congressional election of 1946, the Republican Party won control of both houses of Congress. The Republican Congress soon

passed a new tax law that cut taxes by twenty percent.

Congress passed three other important bills during 1947. The **National Security Act** set up the Department of Defense, headed by the Secretary of Defense, to join together all the nation's armed forces. Another law stated that in case of the death of the President and the Vice-President, the Speaker of the House of Representatives was to become President. If he died or was unable to take office, the next in line to become President was the pro tempore President of the Senate. Finally, Congress suggested that a President be allowed to serve only two full terms in office. This

Many newspapers incorrectly reported that Dewey won the election of 1948. Here, President Truman holds up one of those newspapers.

plan later became the **Twenty-Second Amendment** to the Constitution.

Truman Won the Election of 1948

The Republicans were certain that their candidate was going to win the election for President in 1948. The Republicans chose Thomas E. Dewey, the governor of New York, as their candidate for President. President Truman was the Democratic candidate.

However, two groups in the Democratic Party refused to support President Truman in the election of 1948. One group was made up of Southerners who were against President Truman. The other group disagreed with President Truman's policy toward Europe after World War Two. President Truman seemed to have little chance of being elected.

But Truman had a program of change and reform, which appealed to many Americans. He called this program the **Fair Deal.** The Fair Deal promised laws to enforce equal rights for all Americans, more public housing, aid to education by the federal government, a health insurance plan, and repeal of the Taft-Hartley Act. President Truman won the election of 1948, and the Democrats won back control of Congress.

Summing Up

After 1945, the American nation changed back to peace time living. American troops returned home quickly. American business and industry enjoyed good times. In the election of 1948, the American people elected President Truman. In the next chapter, you will find out about Truman's years as President.

AFTER YOU READ THE CHAPTER

For each sentence below, choose the term that best completes the sentence.

1. The (**Veterans Loan Law/G.I. Bill of Rights**) helped veterans to continue their education, loaned them money to buy a home or business, and provided other benefits.
2. The (**Taft-Hartley/Harley-Smoot**) Act was to control the growing power of unions.
3. The law which made it the government's duty to try to prevent unemployment was the (**Employment/Wages and Hours**) Act.
4. The Council of (**Economic Security/Economic Advisers**) was set up to help the President improve the American economy.
5. The (**Nuclear Power/Atomic Energy**) Act set up the Atomic Energy Commission and put the development of atomic energy under civilian control.
6. The (**National Security/Armed Forces**) Act set up the Department of Defense and joined together all the armed forces.
7. The (**Twenty-Second/Twenty-Fifth**) Amendment allows a President to serve only two full terms in office.
8. In the election of 1948, President Truman's program of change and reform was called the (**Real Deal/Fair Deal**).

Tell something about each of the following persons.

Harry S. Truman   Thomas E. Dewey

What are the years of this chapter? Place the following events in the order in which they occurred.

Strikes took place in many industries.

President Truman was elected as President.

The G.I. Bill of Rights was passed.

The Taft-Hartley Act was passed.

After 1945, the American nation changed back again to peace time living, and Congress passed some important new laws.

Tell how each of the following developments is related to the MAIN IDEA.

The demand for peace time goods was so great that few workers lost their jobs. Prices of most products went up, however, when price controls were lifted.

Because of strikes after the war, Congress began to feel that unions must be controlled. In 1947, Congress passed the Taft-Hartley Act.

Although the Democratic Party was split into three separate groups, President Truman won the election of 1948.

Use the information you learned in this chapter to answer the following questions.

1. Why did prices of most products go up after the war?
2. Name some important laws passed in the years immediately after the war.
3. Why did it seem that President Truman had little chance to be elected in 1948?
4. Do you think that the development of atomic energy should be under civilian control? Explain your answer.

1. Do you know of anyone who has received benefits from the G.I. Bill of Rights? In what way was this person helped?
2. Describe any peace time uses of atomic energy that may be in operation in or near your community.

CHAPTER 100

President Truman's Fair Deal

President Truman celebrating his election victory.

BEFORE YOU BEGIN THE CHAPTER

Know What to Look For

1. In the election of 1948, most Americans thought that President Truman was going to be defeated. Because two groups in the Democratic Party refused to support him, and because Thomas E. Dewey, the Republican candidate, was very popular, no one thought President Truman had a chance. President Truman, however, believed he was able to

win the election, and during the campaign, he made speeches all over the United States.

Early on election night, President Truman seemed to be losing. Most Americans heard over their radios that President Truman was defeated. And some newspapers even had headlines that said Dewey had won the election. But later on election night, Truman began to gain votes. And when all the votes were in and counted, President Truman was the winner of the election. In this chapter, you will read about the Fair Deal program of President Truman.

2. Read the title of the chapter. Then look through the chapter and read the headings. Using only the headings, tell what happened to President Truman's Fair Deal program in Congress.

3. Look at the pictures in the chapter and read each heading. What do the pictures tell you about the United States in the years between 1948 and 1952? Note also the time line at the beginning of the chapter. What years are included in the chapter? Compare this chapter time line to the unit time line on page 613.

4. Read the last part of the chapter called Summing Up. What problem did President Truman have to face during his term in office? What is the topic of the next chapter?

Know These Important Terms
National Housing Act of 1949
Internal Security Act

Know the Main Idea
Here is the MAIN IDEA of this chapter.
Between 1948 and 1952, Congress refused to pass many parts of President Truman's Fair Deal plan into law, but it did pass some important new laws.

Keep this MAIN IDEA in mind as you study the chapter. Ask yourself the following questions as you read. They will help you remember the MAIN IDEA.
1. What happened to President Truman's laws designed to enforce equal rights for all Americans?
2. How was the immigration law passed in 1952 different from the 1924 immigration law?
3. Who made some unfair charges about Communists in the government?

THE YEARS OF THIS CHAPTER ARE 1948 TO 1952

| 1945 | 1948 | 1952 | 1960 |

THE CHAPTER LESSON BEGINS HERE

Congress Refused to Pass Many Fair Deal Laws

The new Congress did not pass many of the Fair Deal laws favored by President Truman. Southern Democrats refused to vote in favor of laws to enforce equal rights for all Americans. The Southern Democrats and the Republicans in Congress joined together to vote against and defeat many other parts of President Truman's Fair Deal program. Only a few parts of the Fair Deal program were passed into law by Congress. This disappointed many Americans.

President Truman Tried to End Segregation

President Truman asked Congress to pass laws to enforce equal rights for all Americans. He asked for a federal law to make lynching, or hanging someone without a trial, unlawful. President Truman also wanted laws to open jobs to everyone on a fair basis, to end segregation on all travel systems that went from one state to another, and to forbid the use of the poll tax as a voting requirement. Congress did not pass any of these laws favored by President Truman.

Polish immigrants arriving in America after World War Two.

However, on his own, President Truman did much to bring about equal treatment for all Americans. He ended unfair practices in hiring government workers in the federal civil service system. President Truman also ended segregation in the armed forces. As late as World War Two, black soldiers fought in segregated units. However, by the time the Korean War broke out in 1950, black Americans and white Americans fought side by side in the army, navy, and air force.

Other Parts of the Fair Deal Were Defeated

The President failed to get Congress to repeal the Taft-Hartley law. Also, President Truman's plan for aid to education by the

federal government was defeated in Congress. And Congress also turned down a government health insurance plan.

Some Parts of the Fair Deal Were Passed

Congress was willing to improve the Social Security system. The Social Security program was made larger, to include over 10 million more Americans, and the monthly payments to American workers over sixty-five were increased. Congress also agreed to raise the minimum wage for workers from 40 cents an hour to 75 cents an hour. Over 1 million workers benefited from this increase.

Congress also passed the **National Housing Act of 1949.** This law made it possible to clear slums and to build public housing. The public housing projects built under this law helped to improve the living conditions of many Americans.

Congress Passed New Immigration Laws

If you remember, Congress passed laws in the 1920's that cut down the number of immigrants who were allowed to come to the United States. During the Great Depression and the years of World War Two, few immigrants came to the United States. However, after the war, many homeless Europeans wished to enter the United States. Therefore, in 1948, Congress passed a law that allowed about 200 thousand Europeans to enter the United States.

President Truman felt that this law favored Europeans from western Europe and kept homeless Europeans from southern and eastern Europe out of the United States. In 1950, Congress agreed to change the law. The new law allowed 415 thousand Europeans from all parts of Europe to enter the United States.

But in 1952, Congress passed a new immi-

This picture shows a segregated army unit. President Truman issued an executive order ending segregation in the armed forces in 1948.

gration law over President Truman's veto. This new law kept the quota system set up in 1924 to limit the number of immigrants entering the United States. This quota system favored immigrants from northern and western Europe. A very small quota was set up for immigrants from southern and eastern Europe. However, for the first time since 1924, immigrants from Asia were allowed to enter the United States and to become citizens of the United States.

The Problem of Communists in the National Government

President Truman had to face the problem of the loyalty of government officials. If you remember, the Soviet Union became a danger to world peace right after World War Two. As relations grew worse between the United States and the Soviet Union, the American people's fear of Communism increased. The United States government became careful about checking the loyalty of the people it hired. A few Communists were found in government jobs. Some Soviet spies were successful in stealing atomic bomb secrets. These few cases greatly upset the American people.

At the same time, Senator Joseph McCarthy of Wisconsin made unfair charges against many Americans. He said he had a list of

In 1947, President Truman visited Latin America. Above, he is greeted by American children living in Latin America.

Communists who worked for the American government. These unfair charges greatly increased America's fear of Communism.

As a result, Congress passed the **Internal Security Act** over President Truman's veto. This act required all Communist groups to file their membership lists with the government. However, many Americans felt that the Truman administration was not hard enough on Communists.

Some Government Officials Were Dishonest

Between 1950 and 1952, a problem over the honesty of some important government officials developed. These officials accepted gifts in return for doing special favors for their friends. These actions caused Americans to

wonder whether these officials were honest. President Truman was not involved in any of these deals. But the question raised about the honesty of these officials caused him trouble.

Summing Up

Congress refused to pass many parts of President Truman's Fair Deal plan into law. However, Congress did agree to improve the Social Security system, to raise the minimum hourly wage, and to build public housing. Congress also passed a new immigration law. President Truman had to face the problem of the loyalty and honesty of government officials during his term in office. In the next chapter, you will read about General Dwight D. Eisenhower's years as President.

AFTER YOU READ THE CHAPTER

Do You Know These Important Terms?

For each sentence below, choose the term that best completes the sentence.

1. The (**National Housing/Urban renewal**) Act of 1949 made it possible to clear slums and to build public housing.
2. The (**Internal Security/Alien Communist**) Act required all Communist groups to file their membership lists with the government.

Do You Remember These People?

Tell something about each of the following persons.

Harry S. Truman   **Joseph McCarthy**

Can You Locate These Places?

Use a map of Europe to do the following map work.

1. Locate southern and eastern Europe. Name some countries in this part of Europe. Why did President Truman feel that the new immigration law of 1948 was unfair to this area?
2. Locate northern and western Europe. Name some nations located there. Which immigration law favored people from this part of Europe?

Do You Know When It Happened?

What are the years of this chapter? Tell why each of the following dates is important in this chapter.

1924   1948   1949   1950   1952

Discovering More About the Main Idea

Between 1948 and 1952, Congress refused to pass many parts of President Truman's Fair Deal plan into law, but it did pass some important new laws.

Tell how each of the following developments is related to the MAIN IDEA.

President Truman tried to end segregation. He was able to end unfair practices in hiring government workers in the civil service and segregation in the armed forces.

More immigrants were allowed to enter the United States after the war. In 1952, a new immigration law was passed. It kept the quota system set up in 1924 but allowed immigrants from Asia to enter the United States.

A few Communists were found in the government, and some spies were successful in stealing secrets. But Senator McCarthy made unfair charges against many Americans.

Can You Discuss the Chapter?

Use the information you learned in this chapter to answer the following questions.

1. How did President Truman try to end segregation?
2. Which parts of the Fair Deal did Congress pass? Which parts did it change? Which parts did Congress refuse to pass?
3. How did Communism become a problem within the government?
4. Compare the immigration law Congress passed in 1948 with the immigration law passed in 1950.
5. Do you think that the quota system set up in 1924 is a fair way to control immigration?

Can You Connect the Past and the Present?

1. What parts of President Truman's Fair Deal that were turned down in the years between 1948 and 1952 are now laws?
2. Senator McCarthy sometimes called people Communists just because they disagreed with him. Have you heard people make unfair charges against someone because they disagreed with that person? Explain the circumstances.

CHAPTER 101

The Nation Under President Eisenhower

President Eisenhower with supporters.

BEFORE YOU BEGIN THE CHAPTER

Know What to Look For

1. As a general in the army, Dwight D. Eisenhower was used to making decisions. However, on June 5, 1944, he had to make a very difficult and important decision. The plans to invade Europe were made. The success of the invasion depended upon the tide at the landing site at Normandy Beach. Many soldiers were waiting aboard ships ready to go.

But on the evening planned for the invasion the weather was very bad.

General Eisenhower held a meeting with other army leaders to talk about the situation. Not to go meant that the invasion would be delayed at least a month until the tide was right again. During this time, the well-kept secret of the invasion might get out. To go on with the invasion with bad weather conditions might mean the failure of the invasion. Eisenhower listened to the advice of his staff. Then he thought for a minute and said, "We go!" D-Day, which was on June 6, 1944, was a success. In this chapter, you will read about Dwight Eisenhower's actions as President in the years from 1953 to 1961.

2. Read the title of the chapter. Then look through the chapter and read each heading. From the headings, tell what Congress did.

3. Look at the pictures in the chapter and read each caption. What does the chapter opening picture tell you about President Eisenhower? Note also the time line at the beginning of the chapter. What years are included in this chapter? Compare this chapter time line to the unit time line on page 613.

4. Read the last part of the chapter called Summing Up. Who took the lead in government when Eisenhower was President? What is the topic of the next chapter?

Know These Important Terms
budget
Department of Health, Education, and Welfare
National Defense Education Act

Know the Main Idea
Here is the MAIN IDEA of this chapter.
Under President Eisenhower, no new plans for reform and change were started, but many old laws were improved.

Keep this MAIN IDEA in mind as you study the chapter. Ask yourself the following questions as you read. They will help you remember the MAIN IDEA.

1. What did President Eisenhower think the role of the President should be?

2. Which party controlled Congress during most of the time Eisenhower was President?

3. What event caused Americans to believe that American education had to be made better?

THE YEARS OF THIS CHAPTER ARE 1952 TO 1960

1945   1952   1960

THE CHAPTER LESSON BEGINS HERE

Eisenhower Was Elected President in 1952

In the election of 1952, the Democratic candidate for President was Governor Adlai Stevenson of Illinois. However, the American people elected a Republican President, Dwight D. Eisenhower. President Eisenhower was the most famous American general of World War Two.

President Eisenhower's background as a general helped shape the way he acted as President. Instead of trying to handle all the nation's problems, he allowed the members of his Cabinet to make many plans and decisions. President Eisenhower himself helped to solve only the nation's more important problems. This plan often worked out well. But under this plan, the President often did not know enough about certain important problems, and this made it difficult for him to try to solve these problems.

Eisenhower's Ideas as President
President Eisenhower believed that it was

THE GROWING NATION 1907 to 1959

No.	State	Date Admitted
46.	Oklahoma	November 16, 1907
47.	New Mexico	January 6, 1912
48.	Arizona	February 14, 1912
49.	Alaska	January 3, 1959
50.	Hawaii	August 21, 1959

up to Congress, not the President, to decide what laws to pass for the nation. Unlike President Roosevelt and President Truman, President Eisenhower did not try to force Congress to pass many laws. He felt that Congress knew what laws the American people wanted.

President Eisenhower also had different ideas about the duties of the federal government. He did not believe that the federal government was supposed to try to solve all the nation's problems. He believed that state governments were often able to handle many problems faced by the nation.

President Eisenhower and the Republican Party were very interested in balancing the federal government's **budget.** This meant that President Eisenhower tried to make sure that the federal government collected as much money as it spent. President Eisenhower also tried to lower the cost of government. Because of President Eisenhower's ideas as President, few new laws were passed in the years between 1952 and 1960.

President Eisenhower Was Reelected in 1956

Even though President Eisenhower did not have a plan of change and reform for the nation, he was very popular with the American people. In the Presidential election of 1956, President Eisenhower again defeated Adlai

Stevenson by an even larger vote than in 1952. However, the Republican Party lost seats in Congress in the elections of 1954, 1956, and 1958, and the Democrats won control of both houses of Congress.

President Eisenhower Tried to Balance the Government's Budget

President Eisenhower found that it was very difficult to balance the federal government's budget. Some parts of the budget were fixed, or unchangeable. For example, a certain amount of money had to be set aside to pay the wages of the people who worked for the government. Much of the government's money was spent for the nation's defense or for foreign aid. Most Americans felt that these two things were very important. Therefore, they did not want the amount of money spent for them cut too much.

However, President Eisenhower was able to balance three of the government's budgets during his years as President. Also, under President Eisenhower, the government lowered taxes. New tax laws passed in 1954 saved Americans over 7 billion dollars.

Congress Passed New Laws to Help Americans

President Eisenhower did not want to end the laws passed under the New Deal and the Fair Deal to help the American people. Instead, he tried to improve some of these laws. President Eisenhower asked Congress to raise the minimum wage to one dollar an hour. Congress also made the Social Security program larger, to include over 10 million more Americans, and monthly payments were increased. President Eisenhower set up the **Department of Health, Education, and Welfare** to look out for the needs of the American people.

The President also asked Congress to raise

money to build more public housing. By 1960, many slums were cleared, and many public housing projects were built. Laws were also passed that made it easier for Americans to get loans to buy houses.

Congress Helped American Education

During the 1950's, many Americans wanted the federal government to help improve education. But President Eisenhower and most Congressmen felt that the states were able to take care of education.

Then, in 1957, the Soviet Union put Sputnik 1, the first man-made satellite, into orbit around the earth. After this, all Americans began to believe that American education had to be made better. For this reason, Congress passed the **National Defense Education Act** in 1958. This law provided federal money to help improve the teaching of science, mathematics, and foreign languages. The law also provided loans to help needy college students pay for their education.

Congress Censured Senator McCarthy

As you may remember, Senator Joseph McCarthy said that many Americans who worked for the government were Communists. President Eisenhower and many Congressmen were against McCarthy's unfair methods of accusing people of being Communists. But at first they did nothing about it. However, in 1954, Senator McCarthy began an attack on the army.

A series of hearings was held to look into Senator McCarthy's charges against the army. These hearings were shown on television. Americans soon began to see that McCarthy was not able to prove his charges. Before long, the American people turned against Senator McCarthy's unfair methods. And finally, the Senate voted to censure, or officially criticize, Senator McCarthy.

Senator McCarthy used unfair methods to accuse some Americans of being Communists.

Summing Up

Dwight D. Eisenhower was President from 1953 to 1961. He let Congress and the states take the lead in government. Under President Eisenhower no new plans for reform and change were started, but many old laws were improved. And, for the first time, the federal government began to aid education. In the next chapter, which begins Unit 26, you will find out how the United States dealt with foreign nations after World War Two.

AFTER YOU READ THE CHAPTER

Do You Know These Important Terms?

For each sentence below, choose the term that best completes the sentence.

1. To balance the (**budget, treasury**) the federal government must collect as much money as it spends.
2. President Eisenhower set up the Department of (**Urban Affairs/Health, Education, and Welfare**) to look out for the needs of the American people.
3. Congress passed the (**Elementary-Secondary/National Defense**) Education Act in 1958 to help make education better.

Do You Remember These People?

Tell something about each of the following persons.

Adlai Stevenson   **Dwight D. Eisenhower**
Joseph McCarthy

Can You Locate These Places?

Use the maps in your classroom to locate the following places. Tell how each location is connected to the events in this chapter.

Illinois   **Soviet Union**

Do You Know When It Happened?

What are the years of this chapter? Place the following events in the order in which they occurred.

Eisenhower was elected President.

The Soviet Union put Sputnik 1 into orbit.

President Eisenhower defeated Adlai Stevenson for the second time.

The National Defense Education Act was passed.

Discovering More About the Main Idea

Under President Eisenhower, no new plans for reform or change were started, but many old laws were improved.

Tell how each of the following developments is related to the MAIN IDEA.

President Eisenhower believed it was up to Congress to decide what laws to pass. He also thought that state governments were often able to handle many problems.

President Eisenhower raised the minimum wage, made the Social Security program larger, continued to build public housing, and set up the Department of Health, Education, and Welfare.

Congress passed the National Defense Education Act after the Soviet Union put the first man-made satellite into orbit around the earth.

Can You Discuss the Chapter?

Use the information you learned in this chapter to answer the following questions.

1. Explain the advantages and disadvantages of the way President Eisenhower used his Cabinet.
2. What were President Eisenhower's views on the duties of the President and the duties of the federal government?
3. How did the laws passed under President Eisenhower help the nation?
4. Why did Americans come to believe that American education had to be made better?
5. Why was Senator McCarthy censured by the United States Senate?

Can You Connect the Past and the Present?

1. President Eisenhower wanted to balance the federal government's budget. Does your city always balance its budget? What happens when a family is unable to balance its budget?
2. Try to find out from your teacher how your school has benefited from the National Defense Education Act.

The United States As a World Leader

President Eisenhower with President and Mrs. De Gaulle.

THE CHAPTERS IN UNIT 26 ARE

CHAPTER 102 The Cold War in Europe
CHAPTER 103 The Cold War in Asia
CHAPTER 104 The United States and the World, 1952–1960

THE YEARS OF THIS UNIT ARE 1945 TO 1960

1900	1945	1960	1975

The Cold War in Europe

Berlin children watching for planes during the Berlin airlift.

BEFORE YOU BEGIN THE CHAPTER

Know What to Look For

1. Night and day, in rain, snow, or sunshine, American and British airplanes landed at Templehof Airport in Berlin at the rate of almost one every minute. For nearly a year, these airplanes kept the people who lived in West Berlin alive. In 1948, the Soviet Union blocked all routes into the city. No one was able to get in or out of the city. And all shipments of goods into Berlin stopped completely.

The American and British planes began to fly in all necessary supplies from meat and milk to coal and oil. They brought almost three million tons of food and supplies to the city. American and British pilots flew more than 100 million miles in the largest air delivery service ever operated. In this chapter, you will read more about the struggle that developed in Europe between the Soviet Union and the nations of the free world.

2. Read the title of the chapter. Then look through the chapter and read each heading. From the headings, list some steps in the development of the Cold War.

3. Look at the pictures in the chapter and read each caption. What do the pictures tell you about the Cold War in Europe? Examine the map on page 634. What is the title of the map? Note also the time line at the beginning of the chapter. What years are included in the chapter? Compare this chapter time line to the unit time line on page 631.

4. Read the last part of the chapter called Summing Up. What three things were successful against the spread of Communism in Europe?

Know These Important Terms
Cold War   Marshall Plan

Berlin blockade   North Atlantic Treaty
Berlin airlift   Organization
Truman Doctrine

Know the Main Idea
Here is the MAIN IDEA of this chapter.

After 1945, the United States and other free nations worked to stop the Soviet Union from spreading Communism in the world.

Keep this MAIN IDEA in mind as you study the chapter. Ask yourself the following questions as you read. They will help you remember the MAIN IDEA.

1. Which three parts of Germany were joined together in 1948? How did the Soviet Union react to this?

2. What is unusual about the location of the city of Berlin?

3. To what part of the United Nation's atomic control plan did the Soviet Union refuse to agree?

THE YEARS OF THIS CHAPTER ARE 1945 TO 1950

1945   1950   1960

THE CHAPTER LESSON BEGINS HERE

The Cold War

After World War Two ended, the Soviet Union set up Communist governments in the nations of eastern Europe. The Soviet Union was mainly interested in increasing its power and spreading Communism to other nations of the world. However, the United States was determined to stop the Soviet Union from spreading Communism in the world. As a result, a **Cold War** between the Soviet Union and the United States began after 1945. This Cold War was a new kind of war—a war without weapons.

The United States and the Soviet Union Disagreed About Germany

After World War Two, the Allies signed treaties with most of their former enemies. However, the United States and the Soviet Union were unable to agree on a treaty with Germany. The United States, France, and Great Britain—the Allies—were not able to agree with the Soviet Union on how to govern Germany. The Allies wanted to rebuild Germany into a strong, free nation. But the Soviet Union wanted to keep Germany a weak and divided nation.

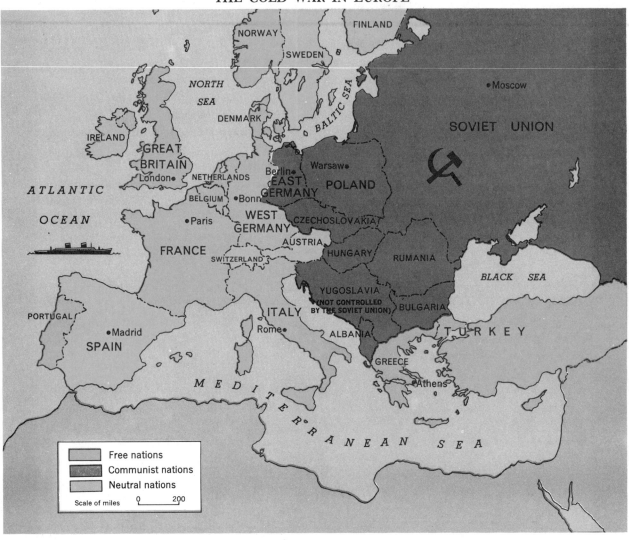

Therefore, in 1948, the United States, Great Britain, and France joined together their three zones of Germany. Their plan was to rebuild this western part of Germany and allow it to govern itself. This plan made the Soviet Union very angry.

Germany Was Split into Two Parts

The city of Berlin was also divided into four zones. Berlin was now located within the Soviet zone, or eastern part, of Germany. To get from western Germany to Berlin, it was necessary to enter the Soviet-controlled part of Germany. But from June 1948 to May 1949, the Soviet Union set up a blockade—that is, it cut off all travel and all shipments of food and supplies between western Germany and Berlin.

The United States, France, and Great Britain knew that if the **Berlin blockade** succeeded, the Soviet Union was certain to take over all of Berlin. However, the United States refused to be forced out of Berlin. Soon, American and British planes began flying all the supplies that were needed in Berlin—everything from flour to coal. The **Berlin airlift**, as it was called, forced the Soviet Union to lift the blockade and prevented the Soviet Union from taking over Berlin. Later, in 1949, Germany was split into two parts, and each part formed a separate government.

The Truman Doctrine Helped to Stop the Spread of Communism

You may remember that the Soviet Union set up Communist governments in all the nations of eastern Europe. The United States was not able to stop this. In 1947, the Soviet Union tried to set up a Communist government in Greece. The Soviet Union also tried to take control of Turkey's water passage from the Black Sea to the Mediterranean Sea.

But President Truman was determined to stop the Soviet Union from spreading Communism further. Therefore, in 1947, he asked Congress for 400 million dollars to help Greece and Turkey defend themselves. He also promised to help any other European nation to protect itself against the Soviet Union. This plan of opposing the spread of Communism was called the **Truman Doctrine.** It was successful in preventing the Soviet Union from setting up Communist governments in Greece and Turkey.

The Marshall Plan Helped to Fight Communism

But as long as many Europeans were poor and hungry, Communism was a danger to all European nations. In several European nations, Communist leaders were winning many

Signing the N.A.T.O. alliance.

THE NORTH ATLANTIC TREATY ORGANIZATION

Up until the year 1949, the United States never signed a peace time alliance with a European nation. But on April 4, 1949, the United States signed an alliance with ten European nations and Canada. This alliance is known as the North Atlantic Treaty Organization, or N.A.T.O., as it is often called. Later, three more European nations joined the alliance.

N.A.T.O. was formed because the Soviet Union became a danger to peace in the years after World War Two. During these years, the Soviet Union took over most of the nations in central and eastern Europe and set up Communist governments in them. The nations of western Europe were afraid that the Soviet Union might try to take them over next. To prevent this, they promised to help defend each other if any one of them was attacked.

However, the nations of western Europe were not strong enough to defend themselves against the Soviet Union. For this reason, the United States joined the N.A.T.O. alliance. America wanted to help defend Europe against Communism. Each nation contributed troops and weapons to N.A.T.O., and it soon developed into a strong military force.

This picture shows an atomic bomb test explosion on Bikini Island in 1946. Control of the atomic bomb was a serious problem after the war.

votes by promising these nations food and better times. The only way to prevent the Communists from taking over the nations of Europe was to help Europe recover from the war and return to better times.

To do this, the United States developed the **Marshall Plan**, named after American Secretary of State George C. Marshall. The purpose of the Marshall Plan was to send money and goods to the European nations to help them build up their cities, farms, and factories. The Marshall Plan helped many European nations to recover from the war and return to better times.

The North Atlantic Treaty Organization Was Formed

In 1949, the United States and the other free nations took another important step to protect themselves against a Soviet attack. The United States, Canada, and ten European nations formed the **North Atlantic Treaty Organization** (N.A.T.O.). The N.A.T.O. nations agreed to build up their armed forces to protect themselves from attack by any enemy. Each N.A.T.O. nation promised to help defend any other N.A.T.O. nation if it was attacked. General Dwight D. Eisenhower was chosen as the commander of these forces.

Atomic Control Failed

One of the most serious problems facing the world after World War Two was the control of the atomic bomb. Therefore, early in 1946, the United Nations set up an Atomic Energy Commission. At the first meeting of this commission, the United States, the only nation that had atomic bombs at that time, suggested that complete control of atomic energy be taken over by the United Nations.

But the United States felt that the United Nations must have the power to inspect, or check, atomic energy plants in every nation to make sure that these nations were not making atomic bombs. The Soviet Union refused to agree to this plan. Three years later, in 1949, when the Soviet Union exploded its first atomic bomb, its reason for refusing to agree to the plan became clear.

Summing Up

After 1945, the United States and other free nations worked to stop the Soviet Union from spreading Communism in the world. The Truman Doctrine, the Marshall Plan, and N.A.T.O. were successful American efforts against the spread of Communism in Europe. The next chapter tells you about efforts to prevent the spread of Communism in Asia.

AFTER YOU READ THE CHAPTER

Do You Know These Important Terms?

For each sentence below, choose the term that best completes the sentence.

1. The new kind of war without weapons between the United States and the Soviet Union was called the (**Talk/Cold**) War.
2. The Berlin (**blockade/rampart**) cut off all travel and all shipments of supplies between western Germany and Berlin.
3. The flying of supplies into Berlin was called the Berlin (**lifeline/airlift**).
4. The plan to help nations to protect themselves against the spread of Communism was called the (**Berkeley Plan/Truman Doctrine**).
5. The (**Marshall/Stevenson**) Plan was to send money and goods to European nations to help them build up again.
6. The United States, Canada, and ten European nations formed the (**North American Tactical Operation/North Atlantic Treaty Organization**) to protect themselves.

Do You Remember These People?

Tell something about each of the following persons.

Harry S. Truman   **George C. Marshall**

Can You Locate These Places?

Use the map on page 634 to do the following map work.

1. Locate East Germany, West Germany, and the city of Berlin.
2. Locate each of the following places.
   Greece   **Turkey**

Do You Know When It Happened?

What are the years of this chapter? Place the following events in the order in which they occurred.

N.A.T.O. was formed.

The Berlin airlift began to supply Berlin.

The United Nations set up an Atomic Energy Commission.

The Truman Doctrine was started.

Discovering More About the Main Idea

After 1945, the United States and other free nations worked to stop the Soviet Union from spreading Communism in the world.

Tell how each of the following developments is related to the MAIN IDEA.

Germany was split into two separate nations. Berlin was a divided city located inside East Germany.

The Truman Doctrine succeeded in stopping the spread of Communism into Greece and Turkey. Many European nations were able to rebuild because of the Marshall Plan.

The free nations formed N.A.T.O. to protect themselves from attack by any enemy.

Can You Discuss the Chapter?

Use the information you learned in this chapter to answer the following questions.

1. Why was Germany split into two nations?
2. How did the free nations show the Soviet Union that they were not going to be forced out of Berlin?
3. How did the Truman Doctrine help to stop the spread of Communism?
4. What was the purpose of the Marshall Plan? What effect did the Marshall Plan have?

Can You Connect the Past and the Present?

1. Do you think the United States and the Soviet Union are still fighting a Cold War? Use examples to prove your point of view.
2. How far has the world gone in solving the problem of controlling atomic weapons?

CHAPTER 103

The Cold War in Asia

General MacArthur in Japan.

BEFORE YOU BEGIN THE CHAPTER

Know What to Look For

1. During the last part of World War Two, the Japanese government knew it was losing the war. As a result, Japanese leaders used propaganda, or false stories, to stir up the people to fight harder. They trained hundreds of Japanese pilots, called kamikazes, to crash their airplanes filled with bombs into American ships. These pilots were told that by dying

for Japan they would become heroes. Japanese leaders told the people untrue stories about how the American army tortured its prisoners.

At the end of the war, when the Americans landed in Japan, the Japanese were very frightened. They thought they would be tortured or killed. However, under the leadership of General MacArthur, the Americans helped to rebuild Japan instead. In this chapter, you will read about Japan and other nations in Asia after the war.

2. Read the title of the chapter. Then look through the chapter and read each heading. From the headings, tell what happened in Korea.

3. Look at the pictures in the chapter and read each caption. What do the pictures tell you about the Cold War in Asia? Study the map on page 640. What is the title of the map? Note also the time line at the beginning of the chapter. What years are included in this chapter? Compare this chapter time line to the unit time line on page 631.

4. Read the last part of the chapter called Summing Up. In what way did the United States try to stop the spread of Communism in Asia?

Know These Important Terms

Chinese Nationalist government
Korean War

Know the Main Idea

Here is the MAIN IDEA of this chapter.
During the Cold War, the United States tried to stop the spread of Communism in Asia.

Keep this MAIN IDEA in mind as you study the chapter. Ask yourself the following questions as you read. They will help you remember the MAIN IDEA.

1. What changes were made in Japanese farming and industry?
2. Whom did the United States still accept as the ruler of all of China?
3. What did General MacArthur and President Truman disagree about during the Korean War?

THE YEARS OF THIS CHAPTER ARE 1945 TO 1952

1945   1952   1960

THE CHAPTER LESSON BEGINS HERE

Japan Became a Democratic Nation

From 1945 to 1947, the United States army ruled Japan. General Douglas MacArthur was the leader of the American army in Japan. During these years, the United States helped Japan to become a peaceful and free nation. The business life of Japan was improved. Large farms were divided and sold to small farmers. The power of the few rich families who once controlled most of Japan's industry ended. American troops continued to occupy Japan until 1951, but the American army no longer ruled Japan after the year 1947.

The United States helped to set up a democratic government in Japan. In 1947, Japan adopted a constitution. Under this constitution, the Japanese emperor remained the head of the government, but he now had very little power. The real power of the Japanese government was given to a two-house legislature. All Japanese citizens were given the right to vote. And a bill of rights was written to protect the freedoms of the Japanese people. Under this new constitution, Japan once again became the richest nation of Asia.

Many New Nations of Asia Tried to Stay Out of the Cold War

After World War Two, many nations in

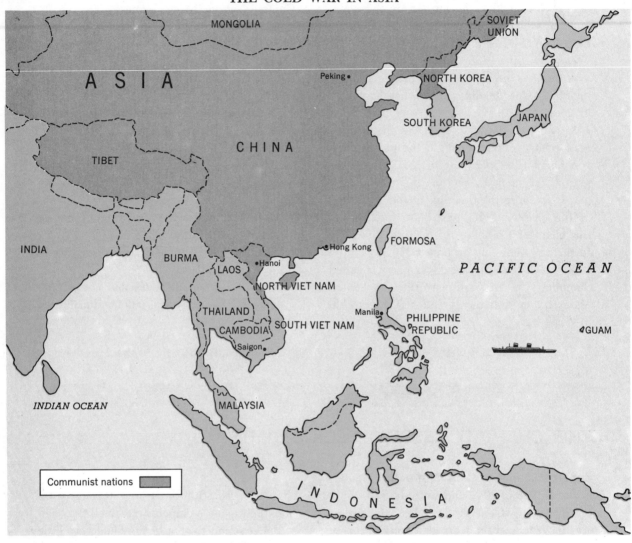

MONGOLIA

SOVIET UNION

A S I A

Peking •

NORTH KOREA

SOUTH KOREA

JAPAN

CHINA

TIBET

INDIA

BURMA

LAOS

•Hanoi

Hong Kong

FORMOSA

PACIFIC OCEAN

NORTH VIET NAM

THAILAND

Manila•

PHILIPPINE REPUBLIC

GUAM

CAMBODIA

SOUTH VIET NAM

Saigon•

INDIAN OCEAN

MALAYSIA

I N D O N E S I A

Communist nations

Asia gained their freedom. The United States gave the people of the Philippine Islands their independence in 1946. Great Britain also allowed its colonies in Asia to become independent nations. France and the Netherlands (Holland), however, were slower to free their colonies. The Dutch gave up their fight to hold Indonesia (in-duh-NEE-zhuh) in 1949. And the French finally left Viet Nam in 1954, after a long, hard war in this Asian country.

The leaders of the fight for independence in Asia disliked the European nations that once ruled their countries. These European nations were now the allies of the United States, and therefore, many of these Asian leaders did not trust the United States. Some of them were Communists or had been trained by Communists. For these reasons, it is not surprising that many new nations in Asia, such as India, Pakistan (PAH-kih-STAN), and Indonesia, tried to stay out of the Cold War.

The Communists Took Over in China

Communism did begin to spread in Asia during the Cold War. When World War Two ended, most of China was under the control of Chiang Kai-shek (CHYAHNG KY-SHEK), the leader of the Chinese government. However, one section of China was under the control of Mao Tse-tung (MAOW TSAY-TOONG), the leader of the Chinese Communists. By 1945, the Chinese Communists were strong enough to start a revolt against the government of Chiang Kai-shek.

The United States tried to bring peace between Chiang Kai-shek's armies and the Communist forces, but American efforts failed. Then the United States started to send supplies and weapons to Chiang Kai-shek. But by 1949, the Communists controlled nearly all of China, and Chiang Kai-shek was forced to move his **Chinese Nationalist government** to the island of Formosa, off the mainland of China. However, the United States government still accepted Chiang Kai-shek as the ruler of all of China. America never recognized, or agreed to deal with, the Communist government in China.

War Broke Out in Korea

Their victory in China encouraged the Communists to try to take over Korea, another country in Asia. At the end of World War Two, Korea was divided into two parts. The southern part of Korea was occupied by American troops, and the northern part was occupied by Soviet troops. Free elections were held in South Korea, but a Communist government was set up in North Korea.

In June of 1950, the North Korean army suddenly invaded South Korea. The United

President Truman with General MacArthur.

PRESIDENT TRUMAN AND GENERAL MACARTHUR

The President of the United States is also the commander in chief of the nation's armed forces. During the Korean War, President Truman proved that commander in chief is not just a title but an important responsibility of the President.

General Douglas MacArthur was the commander of the United Nations army in Korea. He believed that the only way to win the Korean War was to attack Communist China. President Truman and the leaders of many of the other nations fighting with the United States in Korea disagreed with MacArthur. They were afraid that an attack on Communist China might start another world war.

President Truman, as commander in chief of the American armed forces, ordered General MacArthur not to attack China. But General MacArthur disagreed with President Truman's policy in Korea, and he began to openly work against it. As a result, President Truman removed MacArthur as commander of the United Nations troops. At first General MacArthur received support from many Americans. But as time passed, Americans realized that in a democracy, military leaders must follow the orders of the officials elected by the people.

was led by General Douglas MacArthur, and it was made up mostly of American soldiers.

Neither Side Was Able to Win in Korea

At first, the United Nations army was almost pushed out of Korea by the North Korean army. But by October of 1950, the United Nations army began to win victories, and it pushed into North Korea. General MacArthur was sure that the **Korean War,** as the struggle was called, was almost over. But the attack on North Korea frightened the Chinese Communists. They sent hundreds of thousands of soldiers to help North Korea fight the United Nations army. With the help of the Chinese, the North Korean army drove the United Nations army back into South Korea once again.

General MacArthur now felt that the only way to win the war was to attack Communist China. However, President Truman believed that an attack on China might bring the Soviet Union into the war and lead to a new world war. MacArthur disagreed with President Truman and spoke out against the President to the American people. Finally, President Truman removed MacArthur from command in Korea. But President Truman was not able to end the war in Korea, and the fighting continued during 1951 and 1952.

Summing Up

The United States tried to stop the spread of Communism in the nations of Asia. Americans helped Japan to set up a strong, free government. However, in the other nations of Asia, the United States was not as successful. China became a Communist nation. And the United States fought in Korea to prevent the Communists from taking over South Korea. In the next chapter, you will find out about some events in the Cold War while Eisenhower was President.

American troops near the Naktong River during the Korean War.

Nations asked the North Korean government to end its attack, but North Korea refused. The United Nations quickly formed an army and sent it to help South Korea. This army

AFTER YOU READ THE CHAPTER

Do You Know These Important Terms?

For each sentence below, choose the term that best completes the sentence.

1. The Chinese government on the island of Formosa is called the (**Chinese Nationalist/People's Republic**) government.
2. The war between the United Nations Army and North Korea was called the (**Asian Police Action/Korean War**).

Do You Remember These People?

Tell something about each of the following persons.

Douglas MacArthur   **Chiang Kai-shek**
Mao Tse-tung   **Harry S. Truman**

Can You Locate These Places?

Use the map on page 640 to do the following map work.

1. Locate the Japanese islands. Also locate Korea. Why do you think having American troops in Japan during the Korean War was an advantage?
2. Locate some other new nations in Asia. Name the Communist nations. Name the non-Communist nations.

Do You Know When It Happened?

What are the years of this chapter? Place the following events in the order in which they occurred.

The French finally left Viet Nam.
Chiang Kai-shek moved to Formosa.
The United States army occupied Japan.
The Korean War broke out.
The Philippines became independent.

Discovering More About the Main Idea

During the Cold War, the United States tried to stop the spread of Communism in Asia.

Tell how each of the following developments is related to the MAIN IDEA.

In 1947, Japan adopted a new democratic constitution. Under this constitution, Japan once again became the richest nation of Asia.

In the years after World War Two, Great Britain, France, and the Netherlands allowed their colonies in Asia to become independent nations. Many of these new nations tried to stay out of the Cold War.

The Communists took over in China. But when North Korea attacked South Korea, the United Nations sent an army to help South Korea.

Can You Discuss the Chapter?

Use the information you learned in this chapter to answer the following questions.

1. Describe some changes the United States helped Japan to make.
2. Why did many new Asian nations want to stay out of the Cold War?
3. Why did war break out between North Korea and South Korea in 1950?
4. Why did President Truman remove General MacArthur from command in Korea?
5. Do you think that President Truman was right to remove General MacArthur from command in Korea? Why or why not?

Can You Connect the Past and the Present?

1. The United States has still not recognized, or agreed to deal with, the government of Communist China. Do you think that the United States should continue not to recognize the Communist government in China? Why or why not?
2. Compare the economy of present-day Japan with other nations of the world. In which areas does Japan rank very high?

CHAPTER 104

The United States and the World, 1952-1960

President Eisenhower in Korea.

BEFORE YOU BEGIN THE CHAPTER

Know What to Look For

1. Dr. Ralph J. Bunche, the grandson of a slave, was born in a Detroit ghetto. He went to the University of California and later attended Harvard University. He was a teacher until World War Two, when he joined the armed forces. After the war, the United States government appointed Ralph Bunche as a representative to the United Nations.

When the British left the Middle East in 1948, fighting broke out between the new nation of Israel and some Arab nations. As a United Nations representative, Dr. Bunche was given the assignment of ending the fighting in the Middle East. He was able to do this, and as a result, Dr. Bunche received the Nobel Peace Prize. In this chapter, you will read more about the Middle East and other trouble areas of the world during the 1950's.

2. Read the title of the chapter. Then look through the chapter and read each heading. What areas of the world will you read about in this chapter? Which of these areas were trouble spots?

3. Look at the pictures in the chapter and read each caption. What do the pictures show you about the United States and the world? Note also the time line at the beginning of the chapter. What years are included in this chapter? Compare this chapter time line to the unit time line on page 631.

4. Read the last part of the chapter called Summing Up. What things did President Eisenhower do? What is the topic of the next chapter?

Know These Important Terms
Vietcong
Southeast Asia Treaty Organization

Eisenhower Doctrine
Central Treaty Organization

Know the Main Idea
Here is the MAIN IDEA of this chapter.

After the Korean War ended, the United States tried to stop the spread of Communism in China, Southeast Asia, and the Middle East.

Keep this MAIN IDEA in mind as you study the chapter. Ask yourself the following questions as you read. They will help you remember the MAIN IDEA.

1. In what way did President Eisenhower keep the Chinese Communists from attacking Formosa?

2. What defeat in the Cold War did the United States suffer in Europe in 1956?

3. What Soviet ruler visited the United States in 1959?

THE YEARS OF THIS CHAPTER ARE 1952 TO 1960

1945   1952   1960

THE CHAPTER LESSON BEGINS HERE

President Eisenhower
Ended the Korean War

During the election campaign of 1952, President Eisenhower promised to go in person to Korea to try to end the war there. President Eisenhower kept his promise and went to Korea right after his election. This trip showed the President that it was impossible to drive the Communists completely out of Korea. Peace talks, which began when Truman was President, were started again by President Eisenhower. Finally in July of 1953, an armistice, or an end to the fighting, was arranged.

Under this armistice agreement, Korea was still to be divided into two parts. A two and a half mile zone was set up between North Korea and South Korea. Neither side was to station any troops in this zone.

The United States Protected
Chiang Kai-shek

President Eisenhower, like President Truman earlier, promised to protect Chiang Kai-shek's Nationalist Chinese government on the island of Formosa from any possible Communist attack. In 1958, it looked as if the Chinese Communists were going to attack the island of Formosa. But President Eisenhower

This picture shows French soldiers in trenches at Dien-Bien-Phu in Viet Nam. The French were defeated here and left Indo-China.

kept his promise to defend Formosa by sending a fleet of ships to the island. This stopped the Chinese from attacking Formosa.

Trouble Developed in Viet Nam

You may remember that the people who lived in Indo-China fought against France to gain their freedom. Both President Truman and President Eisenhower helped France in this war by sending war supplies and weapons, because they were afraid that Indo-China might be taken over by the Communists. In 1954, however, the French were defeated, and they gave up the fight in Indo-China.

When France left Indo-China, the land was divided into four separate countries—

Cambodia, Laos, North Viet Nam, and South Viet Nam. North Viet Nam became a Communist nation. South Viet Nam remained a free nation.

In 1958, the **Vietcong,** or Communist-led rebels in South Viet Nam supported by North Viet Nam, started to fight to take over South Viet Nam. In order to prevent the Communists from taking over South Viet Nam, President Eisenhower sent money, war supplies, and American army advisers to the South Viet Nam government to help it fight the Vietcong.

In 1954, the United States helped to form the **Southeast Asia Treaty Organization** (S.E.A.T.O.) to fight Communism in Asia. However, India and other important Asian nations refused to join S.E.A.T.O., and it was never as strong as N.A.T.O.

Efforts to Try to End the Cold War

During the 1950's, the Cold War between the Soviet Union and the United States and its N.A.T.O. allies kept on in Europe. But in 1955, the leaders of the United States, the Soviet Union, Great Britain, and France met at Geneva, Switzerland. At this meeting, they did not settle any problems. However, the meeting seemed to show that the free nations and the Communist nations might work together and be able to live together in peace.

The Revolt in Hungary Failed

In 1956, the Hungarian people revolted against the Communist government in Hungary. But the United States was unable to give Hungary any help. When troops from the Soviet Union crushed the Hungarian revolt, the people of eastern Europe learned that the United States was not able to liberate, or free, them. This was a defeat for the United States in the Cold War.

War Broke Out in the Middle East

During the Hungarian revolt, a war broke out in the Middle East. This war started because President Nasser of Egypt took control of the Suez Canal, which had been controlled by Great Britain and France. Great Britain and France sent troops into Egypt to try to retake the Suez Canal. Israel also invaded Egypt.

The United States and the United Nations forced these three nations to withdraw their troops from Egypt. But this war led to bad feelings between the United States and its allies. It also strengthened the Soviet Union in the Middle East because the Soviet Union threatened to fight Britain, France, and Israel if they did not withdraw their troops.

To make sure that the Soviet Union did not become too strong in the Middle East, President Eisenhower promised to send aid and to help defend any Middle Eastern nation against Communism. This policy was called the **Eisenhower Doctrine.**

In 1958, the country of Lebanon asked for help against rebels. President Eisenhower sent American troops to help Lebanon fight these rebels. The United States also helped form the **Central Treaty Organization** (C.E.N.T.O.) to defend the Middle East. But some nations in the Middle East refused to join this group, and therefore, it was never very strong.

The Cold War in the Late 1950's

By the end of the 1950's, dealings between the United States and the Soviet Union began to improve. The new Soviet ruler, Nikita Khrushchev (ne-KY-ta kroosh-CHOFF), visited the United States in 1959. At this time, President Eisenhower and Premier Khrushchev agreed to set up a meeting between American leaders and European leaders.

Just before the meeting was to take place, however, an American military plane was caught taking pictures over the Soviet Union. Premier Khrushchev was very angry with President Eisenhower. As a result, the meeting broke up, and the Cold War continued.

Summing Up

President Eisenhower ended the Korean War, and he tried to stop the spread of Communism in the world. He agreed to defend Chiang Kai-shek's government in Formosa, and sent supplies to South Viet Nam to help fight the Communists there. President Eisenhower also agreed to help any nation in the Middle East defend itself. The next chapter, which begins Unit 27, tells about life in the United States between 1945 and 1960.

AFTER YOU READ THE CHAPTER

Do You Know These Important Terms?

For each sentence below, choose the term that best completes the sentence.

1. Communist-led rebels in South Viet Nam are called the (**Vietcong/Vietminh**).
2. The nations united to fight Communism in Asia are called the (**South Pacific Treaty/ Southeast Asia Treaty**) Organization.
3. The promise of President Eisenhower to send aid and to help defend any Middle Eastern nation against Communism was the (**Middle East/Eisenhower**) Doctrine.
4. The United States helped form the (**Central Eastern Nations'/Central Treaty**) Organization to defend the Middle East.

Do You Remember These People?

Tell something about each of the following persons.

Dwight D. Eisenhower   Chiang Kai-shek
Harry S. Truman   Gamal Abdel Nasser
Nikita Khrushchev

Can You Locate These Places?

Use a world map to do the following map work.

1. Locate Formosa and China.
2. Locate the new nations in Southeast Asia formed from Indo-China.
3. Locate the Suez Canal. Why do you think the Middle East is always a trouble spot?

Do You Know When It Happened?

What are the years of this chapter? Place the following events in the order in which they occurred.

The Hungarian people revolted.
Eisenhower sent ships to protect Formosa.
S.E.A.T.O. was formed.
C.E.N.T.O. was formed.
Nikita Khrushchev visited the United States.

Discovering More About the Main Idea

After the Korean War ended, the United States tried to stop the spread of Communism in China, Southeast Asia, and the Middle East.

Tell how each of the following developments is related to the MAIN IDEA.

President Eisenhower sent a fleet of ships to protect Formosa. He also sent money, war supplies, and American army advisers to help the South Viet Nam government.

Hard feelings developed between the United States and its allies when the United States and the United Nations forced Great Britain, France, and Israel to withdraw their troops from Egypt.

Can You Discuss This Chapter?

Use the information you learned in this chapter to answer the following questions.

1. Why did President Eisenhower agree to help both Chiang Kai-shek and South Viet Nam?
2. Why did hopes for world peace look a little brighter in 1955?
3. Why did the war in the Middle East lead to bad feelings between the United States and its allies?
4. Why did the meeting which was to be held between American leaders and European leaders in 1960 break up?
5. Do you think the United States had the right to send a spy plane over the Soviet Union? Why or why not?

Can You Connect the Past and the Present?

You saw how the United States first became involved in South Viet Nam. Is the United States still involved in South Viet Nam today?

American Life Changes

A rocket is launched from Cape Kennedy.

THE CHAPTERS IN UNIT 27 ARE

CHAPTER 105 American Life, 1945–1960
CHAPTER 106 Changes in America, 1945–1960
CHAPTER 107 The Civil Rights Movement Begins

THE YEARS OF THIS UNIT ARE 1945 TO 1963

1900   1945   1963   1975

American Life, 1945-1960

A science classroom in a high school.

BEFORE YOU BEGIN THE CHAPTER

Know What to Look For

1. During the 1950's, most Americans looked forward to Tuesday evening. Tuesday evening was the night that the Texaco Star Theater, starring the comedian Milton Berle, was shown on television. For one hour, Americans were entertained by the gags, slap-stick humor, songs, and short, funny skits. Reruns of these shows today might seem old fashioned or corny. But in the 1950's, this was the

most popular show on television. Some people thought that the show would be popular forever. But finally, after many years, the show lost its popularity.

Today, television is a part of America's life. In the years between 1945 and 1960, television was an exciting new development. This chapter tells you about other changes that were important in these years.

2. Read the title of the chapter. Then look through the chapter and read each heading. List some topics you will expect to read about as you study this chapter.

3. Look at the pictures in the chapter and read each caption. What do the pictures tell you about American life between 1945 and 1960? Note also the time line at the beginning of the chapter. What years are included in this chapter? Compare this chapter time line to the unit time line on page 649.

4. Read the last part of the chapter called Summing Up. How did Americans make use of their free time during the 1950's?

Know This Important Term
beatniks

Know the Main Idea
Here is the MAIN IDEA of this chapter.
After World War Two, American life changed. Americans had more free time, and they spent this time watching television, reading, going to museums, libraries, and concerts, and in traveling.

Keep this MAIN IDEA in mind as you study the chapter. Ask yourself the following questions as you read. They will help you remember the MAIN IDEA.

1. What helped increase the number of students in colleges during the 1950's?

2. What invention greatly changed American life after World War Two?

3. What goals did most young Americans seem to share during the 1950's?

THE YEARS OF THIS CHAPTER ARE 1945 TO 1960

1945   1960   1963

THE CHAPTER LESSON BEGINS HERE

Americans Improved Their Schools and Colleges

In the years between 1945 and 1960, more American children were in school than ever before. Almost every child finished elementary school, and nine out of ten American students went to high school for at least a year. The number of students attending college more than doubled between 1945 and 1960. Much of this increase in the number of students in colleges was the result of the G.I. Bill of Rights, which made it possible for veterans of World War Two and the Korean War to go to college.

This increase in the number of students caused many problems for America's schools and colleges. Many more teachers were needed. New schools, larger classrooms, and better teaching tools also were needed. Educational television, team teaching, teaching machines, and other teaching methods were developed to help the schools solve these problems. And during the late 1950's, Congress passed the National Defense Education Act, which provided money to help education.

More Americans Became Church Members

During and after World War Two, church membership increased. By 1960, more Americans were members of a church than ever before. However, many people seemed to join churches to meet people and to attend such church events as parties and picnics. Although

page 651

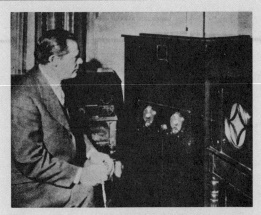

An early television set.

THE DEVELOPMENT OF TELEVISION

No one person can be considered the inventor of television. Instead, modern television is the result of many men's discoveries in electricity and electronics.

The first workable television system was set up by an inventor in Germany in 1884. However, this early television showed only light and shadows. In the 1920's, several American radio stations tried to set up television systems. But these television systems were only able to show pictures which were very small and not clear enough. By the late 1930's, television was improving, and a few test television stations broadcasted shows several hours a day. Many Americans became interested in television when they saw it for the first time at the World's Fair held in New York in 1939. And finally on July 1, 1941, regular television shows began. Soon after, World War Two began, and the growth of television was all but stopped for several years.

After World War Two, the television industry grew rapidly. Manufacturers turned out millions of television sets. Hundreds of new television stations started to broadcast shows. And Americans soon spent many hours a day watching their favorite shows.

church membership was high, fewer people attended religious services than ever before.

Americans Had Much Free Time

After World War Two, Americans had more free time than ever before. Most Americans now worked only about forty hours a week. And almost all Americans were able to take a vacation every year. Many people were now able to drive around the country and see many parts of the United States.

New machines made the lives of American women easier. Housewives were able to use steam irons, electric mixers, and many other new appliances to make housework easier. Frozen foods and freezers made cooking much easier and faster.

Americans now had to find things to do with all their free time. Movies were not as popular as before the war. However, many Americans began to watch television. Many others found new activities to enjoy. Boating, skiing, and camping became popular free-time activities. And more Americans traveled around the United States or traveled to foreign nations.

Americans Enjoyed Television, Books, Art, and Music

The invention of television greatly changed American life after World War Two. Television became very popular, and by 1960, nine out of ten American families had a television set. Many Americans spent as much as five hours a day watching television programs. Most television programs were watched as good family entertainment. But some television programs helped Americans to enjoy fine plays, to learn about world news, and to see and hear interesting people.

In the years between 1945 and 1960, more and more Americans began to enjoy art, music, and good books. Americans went to see

Above, city families are shown spending their free time rowing boats on a lake in a city park.

many plays. They listened to concerts, visited museums and libraries, and attended lectures. More and more Americans also began to read good books. One reason was the great increase in the number of paperback books printed after 1945. Thousands of the world's finest books were now available to Americans as low-cost paperback books.

Outstanding Books and Plays Were Written

Many fine books were written about World War Two. Two of the most famous were *The Naked and the Dead* by Norman Mailer and *From Here to Eternity* by James Jones. During the 1950's, many other important American writers appeared. Saul Bellow's books were widely read. J. D. Salinger (SAL-in-jur),

who wrote *The Catcher in the Rye,* became very popular with young people. Two well-known black writers were Ralph Ellison, who wrote *The Invisible Man,* and James Baldwin, who wrote *Go Tell It on the Mountain* and other popular books.

After World War Two, some fine plays were written about the problems people face in everyday life. Arthur Miller wrote the famous play *Death of a Salesman.* Tennessee Williams' plays *A Streetcar Named Desire* and *Cat on a Hot Tin Roof,* and William Inge's (INGH) plays *Come Back Little Sheba* and *Picnic* dealt with important problems. Plays were also written to amuse and entertain people. Americans enjoyed such entertaining musical plays as *Oklahoma, South Pacific,* and *My Fair Lady.*

James Baldwin (left) and Norman Mailer (right) become well-known American writers during the years of the 1950's.

Young Americans During the 1950's

During the 1950's, most young Americans seemed to share the same goals in life. They wanted to go to school, to get a good job, and to settle down to raise a family. They read the same books, listened to the same records, and dressed in the same way. These young Americans were not active in government, and they were not interested in solving the many problems of American life.

Some other young Americans believed that the rules and customs most Americans followed had to be changed. They felt that a person must live his own life just the way he wished to, in order to be free and happy.

Those who lived this type of life were called **beatniks**. But the beatniks did not work to solve America's many problems.

Summing Up

American life changed after World War Two. Many more Americans attended schools and colleges. Americans had more free time than ever before. They spent this free time watching television, reading, and going to museums, libraries, and music concerts. Many fine books and plays were written in the 1950's. In the next chapter, you will find out about other changes in American life between 1945 and 1960.

AFTER YOU READ THE CHAPTER

Do You Know This Important Term?

For the sentence below, select the term that best completes the sentence.

Those who felt a person must live his own life just the way he wished to in order to be free and happy were called (**beatniks/ hippies**).

Do You Remember These People?

Tell something about some of the following persons.

Norman Mailer	**James Jones**
Saul Bellow	**J. D. Salinger**
Ralph Ellison	**James Baldwin**
Arthur Miller	**Tennessee Williams**

Do You Know When It Happened?

What are the years of this chapter? Why do you think the year 1945 might be used as the starting date of any new period of history? In what ways did American life change in the years after 1945?

Discovering More About the Main Idea

After World War Two, American life changed. Americans had more free time, and they spent this time watching television, reading, going to museums, libraries, and concerts, and in traveling.

Tell how each of the following developments is related to the MAIN IDEA.

After World War Two, more American children were in school than ever before. This increase in the number of students caused many problems for American schools and colleges. Many more teachers, schools, and larger classrooms were needed.

Television became very important to most Americans. Mainly, it was used for good family entertainment, but it also helped Americans to enjoy fine plays and to learn about world news.

Many outstanding books, plays, and musicals were written.

Most young Americans seemed to share the same goals in life. They wanted to go to school, to get a good job, and to settle down to raise a family.

Can You Discuss the Chapter?

Use the information you learned in this chapter to answer the following questions.

1. Why did America's schools and colleges face many new problems in the years after 1945?
2. Why did Americans have more free time after World War Two?
3. What were some ways that Americans used their new free time?
4. What were some famous books written in the years between 1945 and 1960?
5. What were some famous plays?
6. What do you think of the goals of most young Americans during the 1950's? Explain your answer.

Can You Connect the Past and the Present?

1. Television is still a very popular form of entertainment. What types of shows are the most popular today?
2. What group of young people has taken the place of beatniks in America today? How are they like the beatniks? How are they different from the beatniks?

CHAPTER 106

Changes in America, 1945-1960

New houses in a suburb.

BEFORE YOU BEGIN THE CHAPTER

Know What to Look For

1. During the 1930's, the average person in the United States expected to live about sixty years. Today, the average person expects to live about seventy years. This increase in the number of years that Americans can expect to live is due mainly to the great achievements of medical science.

One of these important achievements came in the year 1953. Before 1953, the terrible disease of polio killed or crippled thousands of children and adults. You may remember that Franklin Roosevelt got this disease. But in 1953, Dr. Jonas Salk developed a vaccine that prevented people from getting polio. Soon this disease was almost wiped out. Since Americans were living longer than ever before, the population of the United States was increasing. In this chapter, you will read about the growing population and other changes in America in the years between 1945 and 1960.

2. Read the title of the chapter. Then look through the chapter and read each heading. From the headings, can you name some changes that took place in America?

3. Look at the pictures in the chapter and read each caption. What do the pictures tell you about the changes in the United States? Note also the time line at the beginning of the chapter. What years are included in the chapter? Compare this chapter time line to the unit time line on page 649.

4. Read the last part of the chapter called Summing Up. Who did not share in the good times in the years after 1945? What is the topic of the next chapter?

Know These Important Terms

automation   poverty
fringe benefits

Know the Main Idea

Here is the MAIN IDEA of this chapter.

Between 1945 and 1960, many changes took place in the United States. In these years, most Americans enjoyed good times.

Keep this MAIN IDEA in mind as you study the chapter. Ask yourself the following questions as you read. They will help you remember the MAIN IDEA.

1. What problem developed when many people moved out of the cities into the suburbs?

2. What were some industries that grew rapidly after 1945?

3. What groups of Americans especially were the victims of poverty?

THE YEARS OF THIS CHAPTER ARE 1945 TO 1960

1945   1960   1963

THE CHAPTER LESSON BEGINS HERE

America's Population Grew Rapidly

America's population grew rapidly after World War Two ended. Between the years 1945 and 1960, America's population grew from 140 million to 180 million people. Part of this increase resulted from earlier marriages and a large number of babies being born. Also, Americans were living longer than ever before, and after World War Two many immigrants came to the United States.

Americans Moved to the Cities and the Suburbs

After World War Two, many Americans began to move to different parts of the United States. Black Americans continued to leave the South and to settle in the cities of the Northeast and Middle West. And many Americans moved to the Western states—especially to California.

Americans also continued to move to the cities. By 1960, only three out of every ten Americans still lived on farms or in rural areas. Suburbs grew even faster than large cities in the years after 1945.

As cities grew larger, more and more city families moved to the suburbs. Most of these families bought homes in the suburbs. The new super highways built during the 1950's

Above, boats sailing on San Francisco Bay in California. Many Americans moved to California in the years after 1945.

made it possible for them to drive to work every day, in some nearby city. This movement of people out of the city made it more difficult for many cities to pay for the services that they had to provide for their citizens.

America's large cities faced many growing problems. The older, downtown parts of the cities often needed rebuilding. New housing was needed to replace slums and rundown apartments. Traffic jams, dirty air, and overcrowded schools were problems in most cities, too.

Most Americans Enjoyed Good Times in the 1950's

Most Americans enjoyed good times during the 1950's. Although prices were high, wages were good, and wages kept on going up. More people had jobs than ever before.

However, unskilled workers did not share in the good times of the 1950's. Unskilled workers found fewer jobs because of **automation** (AW-tuh-MAY-shun). Automation is the use of automatic, or self-operating, machines to do many jobs. Automation made it clear that Americans had to go to school and learn skills in order to get a job. Many black workers, who found it difficult to find jobs as skilled workers, were especially hard hit by automation.

Many farmers also suffered hard times during the 1950's. Farmers found that it cost them more and more money to raise their crops. As a result, they were not able to buy

This picture shows an automated rolling-mill. Automatically controlled machines roll out sheets of aluminum in this factory.

the farm machines and supplies that were needed to grow large crops cheaply. Thousands of smaller farmers were forced to sell their farms and move to the cities to find jobs.

American Industry Grew Rapidly

At the end of the 1950's, automobile manufacturing was still America's largest industry, but the chemical industry was growing rapidly. The use of plastics, detergents, and new types of drugs caused this rapid growth of the chemical industry. The electrical industry and the electronics industry, which made parts for televisions, radios, and computers, also grew rapidly during and after World War Two. And the airplane industry also became an important industry in the 1950's. Jet planes began to carry passengers and goods to all parts of the world. These industries provided many new jobs for American workers.

Unions Grew Larger and Stronger

Unions continued to grow in size and to become stronger in the 1950's. In 1955, the two main labor unions, the American Federation of Labor (A.F. of L.) and the Congress of Industrial Organizations (C.I.O.), joined

George Meany and Walter Reuther were the leaders of the new A.F.L.-C.I.O. labor union.

Most strikes were no longer started because workers wanted a shorter working day or higher wages. During the 1950's, labor unions began to strike to gain **fringe benefits** for American workers. Fringe benefits are special benefits such as paid vacations, health insurance, and pension plans given to workers by the company they work for. But the most important cause of strikes in the 1950's was automation. Unions wanted companies to retrain and to find jobs for men who were replaced by machines. Several bitter strikes were caused by automation.

Many Americans Were Still Poor

Although many Americans enjoyed good times during the 1950's, some American families had low incomes and lived in **poverty.** Poverty means that these American families were so poor that they were not able to afford proper food, clothing, or a place to live. In the 1950's, 25 million American families lived on an income of less than 4 thousand dollars a year. Many black, Puerto Rican, and Mexican-American families in the United States were living on less than 2 thousand dollars a year. And many American farm families had even lower incomes. Also, many Americans over sixty-five had barely enough money to live on. Nearly one out of every five Americans had a low income and lived in poverty.

Summing Up

After 1945, America's population increased rapidly. Many Americans continued to move to the cities, and the suburbs grew rapidly. The years after 1945 brought good times for American businesses and for most workers. Unskilled workers and small farmers did not share in these good times. And many Americans had to live on very low incomes. In the next chapter, you will find out how black Americans began to win their equal rights.

together and formed the A.F.L.-C.I.O. labor union. Almost nine out of ten American workers belonged to this combined labor union. During the 1950's, more and more problems between workers and employers were settled by talks and meetings rather than by strikes.

AFTER YOU READ THE CHAPTER

Do You Know These Important Terms?

For each sentence below, choose the term that best completes the sentence.

1. The use of self-operating machines to do many jobs is called (**mechanization/automation**).
2. Special benefits such as paid vacations, health insurance, and pension plans given to workers by the company for which they work are called (**bonuses/fringe benefits**).
3. (**Poverty/Charity**) means that families are so poor that they are not able to afford proper food, clothing, or a place to live.

Can You Locate These Places?

Use the map of the United States on pages 14-15 to locate the following cities. These cities have large populations and many suburbs.

New York	Boston
Philadelphia	Baltimore
Washington, D.C.	Detroit
Cleveland	Chicago
Pittsburgh	St. Louis
New Orleans	San Francisco
Los Angeles	Seattle
Portland	

Do You Know When It Happened?

What are the years of this chapter? Why is the following date important for labor unions?

1955

Discovering More About the Main Idea

Between 1945 and 1960, many changes took place in the United States. In these years, most Americans enjoyed good times.

Tell how each of the following developments is related to the MAIN IDEA.

Many city families moved to the suburbs. The movement of people out of the city made it more difficult for cities to pay for the services they had to provide. Cities faced many growing problems.

American industry grew rapidly. Older industries expanded and many new industries were founded. Automation began to take over the jobs of many unskilled workers.

Although many Americans enjoyed good times, some American families lived in poverty. Black, Puerto Rican, and Mexican-American families, and Americans over sixty-five, were very poor. Nearly one out of every five Americans lived in poverty.

Can You Discuss the Chapter?

Use the information you learned in this chapter to answer the following questions.

1. What were the problems that large American cities faced?
2. Why did unskilled workers and small farmers not share in the good times of the 1950's?
3. Why did unions grow larger and stronger during the 1950's?
4. What American families lived in poverty in America in the 1950's?
5. What do you think can be done to end poverty in America?

Can You Connect the Past and the Present?

1. Compare the problems of American cities that you read about in this chapter with the problems faced by your city or community. Can you add any new ones? Are there problems listed that are not present in your community?
2. How has automation affected the businesses and workers in your community?

CHAPTER 107

The Civil Rights Movement Begins

Dr. Martin Luther King, Jr., speaks for civil rights.

BEFORE YOU BEGIN THE CHAPTER

Know What to Look For

1. In April of 1962, five college students entered a restaurant in a small Southern town. They sat at the counter and waited to order. After half an hour, no one had taken their order, but they continued to sit and wait. The five students were finally told that they would not be served. However, they refused to leave and continued to sit at the counter. A short time later, the police arrived

at the restaurant and ordered the five students to leave. When they refused, they were arrested.

These five students were holding a sit-in to protest against segregation in restaurants and other public places in the South. In the early 1960's, sit-ins were held all over the South to force an end to segregation. In this chapter, you will read about sit-ins and the other methods Americans used to end segregation and to gain equal rights for all.

2. Read the title of the chapter. Then look through the chapter and read each heading. What can you tell about the civil rights movement from reading the headings?

3. Look at the pictures in the chapter and read the captions. What do the pictures tell you about the civil rights movement? Note also the time line at the beginning of the chapter. What years are included in the chapter? Compare this chapter time line with the unit time line on page 649.

4. Read the last part of the chapter called Summing Up. How did black Americans work to end segregation? What is the topic of the next chapter?

Know These Important Terms

civil rights   bus boycott
civil rights movement   sit-in

separate but equal   freedom rides
Brown against the Board
  of Education of Topeka

Know the Main Idea

Here is the MAIN IDEA of this chapter.

During the 1950's, black Americans began to work for equal rights in many ways. This effort to gain equal rights was called the civil rights movement.

Keep this MAIN IDEA in mind as you study the chapter. Ask yourself the following questions as you read. They will help you remember the MAIN IDEA.

1. What groups of Americans did not enjoy all their civil rights?

2. What was the separate but equal practice? When was this practice ruled unlawful by the Supreme Court?

3. What were the purposes of freedom rides in the South?

THE YEARS OF THIS CHAPTER ARE 1950 TO 1963

1945   1950   1963

THE CHAPTER LESSON BEGINS HERE

The Civil Rights of Americans

To most Americans, **civil rights** include such rights, or freedoms, as the right to vote, the right to a good education, the right to any job for which a worker is qualified, the right to buy or rent housing that a person wants and can afford, the right to a fair trial, and the right to be admitted to all public places. Some of these rights are guaranteed by the Constitution. Some of these rights Americans enjoy as part of the American way of life.

However, some groups of Americans did not enjoy all these civil rights. These groups included black Americans, Puerto Ricans, Mexican-Americans, Chinese-Americans, Japanese-Americans, and the Indians. But starting in the 1950's, black Americans, supported by many white Americans, demanded equal civil rights for all Americans. The efforts to gain equal civil rights for all Americans became known as the **civil rights movement**.

The Beginning of the
Civil Rights Movement

Black Americans worked for equal rights long before the 1950's. The National Association for the Advancement of Colored People

Federal troops sent by President Eisenhower are escorting black students into a high school in Little Rock, Arkansas.

(N.A.A.C.P.), set up in 1909, went to the nation's courts to try to end segregation and to gain equal rights for black Americans.

The N.A.A.C.P. attacked the **separate but equal** practice in education. This was the practice of having black students and white students attend segregated, or separate, schools, as long as their schools were equally good. Most black Americans felt that segregation in public schools was wrong, even if the schools were equal. And in most cases, black schools and white schools were not equal.

The Supreme Court Ruled
Against School Segregation

The Supreme Court made a very important decision in 1954 in the case of **Brown against the Board of Education of Topeka.** In the Brown case, the Supreme Court ruled that segregation in public schools was unlawful and must be ended. The Supreme Court declared that all children—both black children and white children—had an equal right to a good education. And the Court ruled that segregated schools for black children were not equal schools.

Some Southern Schools Refused
to End Segregation

Most of the public schools in the South were segregated into all-black or all-white schools. Some Southern states obeyed the Supreme Court's ruling. They began to allow both black children and white children to attend the same schools. In many Southern states, however, schools refused to obey the Supreme Court's ruling.

In September of 1957, the Arkansas national guard was used to prevent nine black students from entering an all-white high school in Little Rock. Then President Eisenhower decided he must act to enforce the Supreme Court's ruling against segregated schools. After the President sent federal troops to Little Rock, the black students were able to attend this high school in Little Rock.

However, most black students in the South continued to attend segregated schools in the 1950's. And most black students in the North also attended segregated schools. The North did not have laws requiring segregated schools as the South did. But in the North, most black Americans lived in all-black neighborhoods and, therefore, most black students attended the all-black schools in their own neighborhoods.

The End of Bus Segregation

One of the first important events in the civil rights movement began on December 1, 1955. On this day, Rosa Parks, a black woman, sat in the white section of a bus in Montgomery, Alabama, and refused to move. After Mrs. Parks was arrested, the black citizens of Montgomery decided to boycott the city buses, or refuse to ride them, as long as they remained segregated. The leader of this **bus boycott** was Dr. Martin Luther King, Jr., a young minister from Georgia.

The black citizens of Montgomery strongly supported the bus boycott. Finally, the city of Montgomery agreed to end segregation on the buses. And in 1956, the Supreme Court ruled that segregation on buses, trains, planes, or other public vehicles was unlawful.

Sit-Ins Helped to End Segregation at Lunch Counters

Another important event in the civil rights movement began in February of 1960, when a **sit-in** protest was started by black students. Four black college students sat down at a lunch counter in Greensboro, North Carolina, to force an end to segregation in public eating places. When they were refused service, they remained seated and refused to leave. Soon, thousands of black citizens and white citizens were holding sit-ins at eating places all over the South. The sit-ins finally led to the end of segregation at lunch counters, hotels, and theaters in many Southern cities.

Freedom Riders Helped to End Segregation in Travel

In 1961, black citizens and white citizens began **freedom rides** in the South. The pur-

Black Americans holding a sit-in protest at a segregated lunch counter.

pose of freedom rides was to end segregation in Southern bus and train stations. "Freedom riders" traveled to many cities of the South until they won their fight. In November of 1961, the Supreme Court ruled that segregation was unlawful in bus, plane, or train stations.

Summing Up

During the 1950's, black Americans began to work for equal civil rights in many ways. They began to win many of their rights in this civil rights movement. In 1954, the Supreme Court ruled against segregated public schools. Black Americans then worked to end other forms of segregation. They used boycotts, sit-ins, and freedom rides in many Southern states to help end these other kinds of segregation. In the next chapter, which begins Unit 28, you will read about President Kennedy's efforts to improve life for all Americans.

AFTER YOU READ THE CHAPTER

Do You Know These Important Terms?

For each sentence below, choose the term that best completes the sentence.

1. (Civil/Political) rights include such rights as the right to vote, the right to a good education, the right to buy or rent a house that a person wants and can afford, the right to any job for which a worker is qualified, and the right to be admitted to all public places.

2. The efforts to gain equal civil rights for all Americans became known as the (Declaration of Human Rights/civil rights movement).

3. The practice in education of having black and white students attend segregated schools that were equally good is (racial imbalance/separate but equal).

4. The Supreme Court ruled in (Brown/Greene) against the Board of Education of Topeka that segregation in the public schools was unlawful and must be ended.

5. Refusing to ride on the buses of Montgomery, Alabama, was called the (transportation strike/bus boycott).

6. A (lunch-in/sit-in) was a protest method used to force an end to segregation in public eating places.

7. Black and white citizens used (freedom/glory) rides to help end segregation.

Do You Remember These People?

Tell something about these people.

Dwight D. Eisenhower   Rosa Parks
Dr. Martin Luther King, Jr.

Do You Know When It Happened?

What are the years of this chapter? Place the following events in order.

Freedom rides began in the South.
Sit-ins were used in the South.
The Supreme Court ruled segregation unlawful in public schools.
The bus boycott in Montgomery began.

Discovering More About the Main Idea

During the 1950's, black Americans began to work for equal rights in many ways. This effort to gain equal rights was called the civil rights movement.

Tell how each of the following developments is related to the MAIN IDEA.

The N.A.A.C.P. attacked the separate but equal practice in education, and the Supreme Court ruled that segregation in public schools was unlawful.

As a result of the bus boycott, the city of Montgomery agreed to end segregation on the buses.

Sit-ins finally led to the end of segregation at lunch counters, hotels, and theaters.

Can You Discuss the Chapter?

Use the information you learned in this chapter to answer the following questions.

1. How did black Americans work for equal rights before the 1950's?

2. How did segregation come to an end in most schools?

3. How did segregation come to an end on buses, trains, planes, and other public vehicles?

4. What methods did Americans use to end segregation in restaurants, railroads, and bus stations?

Can You Connect the Past and the Present?

1. Was there ever legal segregation in your school system?

2. What methods are Americans using in your community to gain equal civil rights?

UNIT 28

Changes in American Government

The White House.

THE CHAPTERS IN UNIT 28 ARE

CHAPTER 108 President Kennedy and the New Frontier
CHAPTER 109 The Nation Under President Kennedy
CHAPTER 110 President Johnson's Great Society
CHAPTER 111 The Nation Under President Johnson

THE YEARS OF THIS UNIT ARE 1960 TO 1968

1900   1960   1968   1975

President Kennedy and the New Frontier

President Kennedy speaking at his inauguration.

BEFORE YOU BEGIN THE CHAPTER

Know What to Look For

1. The day before John F. Kennedy's inauguration as President, a snow storm hit Washington, D.C. Throughout the day and night the wind howled and the snow fell. By morning, the snow stopped, and the day for the inauguration dawned cold and clear. At twelve noon, John F. Kennedy appeared at the Capitol building for his inauguration. As he walked down the steps of the Capitol to the platform which had been built for the ceremony, the band played "Hail to the Chief." The new President took the oath of office and then gave his inauguration speech. He spoke of freedom for all men and urged Americans to become more involved in their nation's government. "Ask not what your country can do for you—ask what you can do for your country."

President Kennedy was the youngest elected President of the United States. His youth, spirit, and style made him a very popular President. In this chapter, you will read about the nation under President Kennedy.

2. Read the title of the chapter. Then look through the chapter and read each heading. In what ways did President Kennedy try to help Americans?

3. Look at the pictures in the chapter and read each heading. What do the pictures tell you about President Kennedy and his New Frontier program? Note also the time line at the beginning of the chapter. What years are included in the chapter? Compare this chapter time line with the unit time line on page 667.

4. Read the last part of the chapter called Summing Up. What happened to President Kennedy's New Frontier program? What is the topic of the next chapter?

Know These Important Terms
New Frontier
Manpower Development and Training Act
Civil Rights Act of 1957
Civil Rights Act of 1960
Twenty-Fourth Amendment

Know the Main Idea
Here is the MAIN IDEA of this chapter.
President Kennedy called his plan to improve the American nation the New Frontier. He was only able to get part of his plan passed into law.

Keep this MAIN IDEA in mind as you study the chapter. Ask yourself the following questions as you read. They will help you remember the MAIN IDEA.

1. What part of the campaign most helped John F. Kennedy to become President?

2. What parts of the New Frontier plan did Congress refuse to pass into law?

3. What voting requirement was outlawed by the Twenty-Fourth Amendment?

THE YEARS OF THIS CHAPTER ARE 1960 TO 1962

1960   1962   1968

THE CHAPTER LESSON BEGINS HERE

John F. Kennedy Won the Election of 1960

In the Presidential election of 1960, the Republican candidate was Richard M. Nixon, who served as Vice-President under President Eisenhower. The Democratic candidate was John F. Kennedy, a Senator from Massachusetts. Senator Kennedy was the first Catholic to run for President since Alfred E. Smith ran and lost in 1928.

Senator Kennedy campaigned hard and successfully. Americans were impressed by his youth and energy. Television played an important part in the campaign. Special television debates were held between Vice-President Nixon and Senator Kennedy. These debates greatly helped Senator Kennedy, and he won a great deal of attention because of them. Still, John F. Kennedy was elected President by only 118 thousand votes. This was one of the closest elections ever held. Lyndon B. Johnson of Texas became Vice-President.

James Meredith.

JAMES MEREDITH AND THE UNIVERSITY OF MISSISSIPPI

In 1962, James Meredith, a twenty-nine-year-old black college student, decided to transfer from Jackson State College to the University of Mississippi. At this time, no black students attended the university. Governor Ross Barnett of Mississippi refused to allow Meredith to attend the university. Since this action was unlawful, Meredith went to court. A federal court ordered the University of Mississippi to admit Meredith.

President John F. Kennedy sent federal marshals, or law enforcing officers, to Mississippi to make sure that the law was obeyed. These marshals brought James Meredith to the university. When Meredith arrived on campus, rioting broke out. It took the army fifteen hours to clear the campus. During the rioting, two men were killed, and many people were hurt.

James Meredith was finally admitted to the University of Mississippi. But United States marshals had to protect Meredith for the entire year he attended the university. In 1963, Meredith graduated from the University of Mississippi. In the later 1960's, other black students attended and graduated from southern colleges.

Kennedy as President

John F. Kennedy was forty-three years old when he became President. He was the youngest man ever elected President. He had many new ideas and great energy. President Kennedy brought well-educated men with fresh ideas into the government. He had great style as President, and he encouraged Americans to take a greater interest in the government.

President Kennedy's New Frontier Plan

President Kennedy called his plan to help improve the American nation the **New Frontier.** The New Frontier promised civil rights laws, health insurance for Americans over sixty-five, federal aid to education, more public housing, and better conditions for farmers and workers. Although the Democratic Party controlled both houses of Congress, President Kennedy had a hard time trying to get Congress to pass his New Frontier plan into law.

Part of the New Frontier Plan Was Passed into Law

President Kennedy did get Congress to pass some parts of his New Frontier plan. The minimum wage was raised from $1.00 an hour to $1.25 an hour. Social Security payments to older Americans were increased. And Congress voted to raise over 6 billion dollars to clear slums and to build public housing for families with low incomes.

Congress passed the **Manpower Development and Training Act.** This law set up a training program to help teach new job skills to unemployed workers so that they might find jobs. Money was voted by Congress to be loaned or given to sections of the country that were suffering from bad times. This money was to be used to help businesses and to retrain unemployed workers.

Congress also passed the Trade Expansion

This picture shows John F. Kennedy standing on top of a car and campaigning during the election campaign of 1960.

Act, which gave President Kennedy the power to lower American tariffs in order to increase American trade with foreign nations.

Congress Refused to Pass
Many New Frontier Laws

But several of the most important parts of the New Frontier plan were not passed into law. Congress refused to grant any money for aid to education. Congress also refused to pass a law to provide health insurance for Americans over sixty-five years old. President Kennedy asked Congress to set up a Department of Urban Affairs to help solve the problems of American cities. The head of this department was to be a member of the President's Cabinet. However, Congress refused to set up a Department of Urban Affairs.

President Kennedy Believed in
Equal Job Opportunities

President Kennedy was interested in helping all Americans to enjoy equal rights. Therefore, one of his first acts as President was to appoint several black Americans as judges and ambassadors. President Kennedy also ordered all government departments and all business companies that did work for the federal government to hire workers on the basis of their ability, regardless of their color or race. Vice-President Johnson took charge of this program of equal job opportunity.

Better Housing and Education
for Black Americans

President Kennedy helped black Americans to gain their equal rights in many other ways.

President Kennedy talking with civil rights leaders. Kennedy's New Frontier
program promised civil rights laws for all Americans.

In 1962, he issued an order making segregation unlawful in housing that was built with federal government money. And he sent federal troops to the states of Mississippi and Alabama to make sure that black students were allowed to register at and to attend the University of Mississippi and the University of Alabama.

President Kennedy Protected the Right to Vote

President Kennedy believed that it was necessary to protect the black citizen's right to vote. He worked hard to enforce two civil rights laws passed during President Eisenhower's second term. The **Civil Rights Act of 1957** gave federal judges the right to jail anyone who stopped a qualified person from voting. And the **Civil Rights Act of 1960** gave the federal government the power to appoint officials to register qualified voters if state or local officials refused to register these voters.

President Kennedy believed that poll taxes and literacy, or reading, tests were still being used in some states to prevent black Americans from voting. Congress refused to outlaw literacy tests. But Congress agreed to outlaw poll taxes as a requirement for voting in Presidential elections. In 1964, such poll taxes were outlawed by the **Twenty-Fourth Amendment** to the Constitution.

Summing Up

John F. Kennedy was elected President in 1960. He called his plan to improve the American nation the New Frontier. However, President Kennedy was able to get only certain parts of his New Frontier plan passed into law. President Kennedy worked hard to help all Americans gain their equal rights. In the next chapter, you will read about the last years of President Kennedy's term in office.

AFTER YOU READ THE CHAPTER

Do You Know These Important Terms?

For each sentence below, choose the term that best completes the sentence.

1. President Kennedy's plans to help improve the American nation were called the (**New Frontier/New Freedom**).
2. The law that set up a training program to help teach new job skills to unemployed workers so that they might find jobs was called the (**Skill-Tool Project/Manpower Development and Training Act**).
3. The Civil Rights Act of (**1963/1957**) gave federal judges the right to jail anyone who stopped a qualified person from voting.
4. The Civil Rights Act of (**1964/1960**) gave the federal government power to appoint officials to register qualified voters if state or local officials refused to register these voters.
5. The amendment to the Constitution that outlawed the poll tax as a voting requirement in Presidential elections was the (**Twenty-Fourth/Twenty-Fifth**) Amendment.

Do You Remember These People?

Tell something about each of the following persons.

Richard M. Nixon   **John F. Kennedy**
Alfred E. Smith   **Lyndon B. Johnson**

Can You Locate These Places?

Use a map of the United States to locate the following states. Explain how they were connected to the events in this chapter.

Mississippi   **Alabama**

Do You Know When It Happened?

What are the years of this chapter? Explain how each of the following dates was important in this chapter.

1957   1960   1962   1964

Discovering More About the Main Idea

President Kennedy called his plan to improve the American nation the New Frontier. He was only able to get part of his plan passed into law.

Tell how each of the following developments is related to the MAIN IDEA.

The election of 1960 was one of the closest elections ever held. Television debates helped John F. Kennedy become President.

The Congress under the New Frontier passed a new minimum wage law, agreed to build public housing, and passed the Manpower Development and Training Act and the Trade Expansion Act.

President Kennedy sent federal troops into Mississippi and Alabama to make sure black students registered at the state universities.

Can You Discuss This Chapter?

Use the information you learned in this chapter to answer the following questions.

1. How did John F. Kennedy win the Presidential election of 1960?
2. What was the purpose of the Manpower Development and Training Act?
3. Which parts of the New Frontier program did Congress refuse to pass into law?
4. How did President Kennedy work for equal rights for all Americans?
5. How do you think the winner in the closest election in the nation's history might feel about his plans for the nation?

Can You Connect the Past and the Present?

1. Do you know about any Manpower Development and Training Act programs in your community? If so, describe some of them.
2. What are the requirements for voting in your state? Who sets up these qualifications?

CHAPTER 109

The Nation Under President Kennedy

The March on Washington in 1963.

BEFORE YOU BEGIN THE CHAPTER

Know What to Look For

1. For most Americans it was a Friday like any other Friday in the fall. Then suddenly radio and television announcers interrupted the regular radio and television shows. Americans listened in disbelief. President John F. Kennedy had been shot while visiting in Texas. A little while later, Americans heard that the President was dead.

Not since President McKinley was killed in 1901 had an American President been assassinated. Americans knew that such events took place in other countries, but they did not think it could happen in the United States. Americans were shocked. Many burst into tears when they heard the news. One television announcer cried as he reported the

page 674

death of President Kennedy. In this chapter, you will read about the period before the President's death, and the effect of his death on his New Frontier program. You will also read about Lyndon Johnson as President.

2. Read the title of the chapter. Then look through the chapter and read each heading. What were the main concerns of the President that you will read about in the chapter?

3. Look at the pictures in the chapter and read each caption. What important event is shown in the first picture? Note also the time line at the beginning of the chapter. What years are included in this chapter? Compare this chapter time line with the unit time line on page 667.

4. Read the last part of the chapter called Summing Up. What happened to the New Frontier program after the death of President Kennedy? What will you find out about in the next chapter?

Know These Important Terms
Alliance for Progress
March on Washington
Civil Rights Act of 1964

Know the Main Idea
Here is the MAIN IDEA of this chapter.
After President Kennedy's death, President Johnson carried out President Kennedy's New Frontier program.

Keep this MAIN IDEA in mind as you read the chapter. Ask yourself the following questions as you read. They will help you remember the MAIN IDEA.

1. Which nations of North and South America are not members of the Alliance for Progress?

2. Why did the March on Washington take place?

3. What job did President Johnson have during the 1950's?

THE YEARS OF THIS CHAPTER ARE 1962 TO 1964

| 1960 | 1962 | 1964 | 1968 |

THE CHAPTER LESSON BEGINS HERE

President Kennedy Tried to Build Up Latin America

President Kennedy wanted to help improve life for the people of the Latin American nations. Therefore, he helped form the **Alliance for Progress,** a ten-year plan to improve life in Latin America. All the nations of North and South America, except Canada and Cuba, are members of this Alliance. The Alliance for Progress planned to spend billions of dollars to help solve the many problems of the Latin American nations.

The nations of Latin America used money from the Alliance for Progress to build homes, schools, and hospitals. They also tried to build up manufacturing and to improve farming in their nations. Many people hoped that the Alliance for Progress might bring peace and prosperity to Latin America.

President Kennedy Had Plans for His Last Two Years in Office

In the Congressional elections of 1962, Americans showed that they favored President Kennedy's New Frontier program by electing many Democrats to the Congress.

President Kennedy visiting a low-cost housing project in Mexico City.

President Kennedy believed he might be able to get the rest of his New Frontier program passed by Congress during the second half of his term. He still hoped to talk Congress into passing laws to give federal aid to public schools and to set up a health insurance plan for Americans over sixty-five.

President Kennedy also felt that stronger laws were necessary to help black Americans enjoy all their civil rights. He wanted black Americans to be able to vote and to get jobs they were qualified for. He also wanted to end segregation in schools and to make segregation unlawful in hotels, restaurants, and all other public places. For these reasons, in 1963 he asked Congress to pass a new civil rights law.

Black Americans Demanded Their Equal Rights

The year 1963 was the one hundredth anniversary of Abraham Lincoln's Emancipation Proclamation. Black Americans felt that 100 years was a long time for a people to wait to gain their equal rights. Therefore, many black Americans held protest marches all over the South to demand equal civil rights.

An important protest march took place in Birmingham, Alabama, in 1963. Dr. Martin Luther King, Jr., led this peaceful march to protest against the unfair way many black citizens were treated in Birmingham. The Birmingham police used police dogs and water hoses against the marchers. Dr. King and hundreds of black marchers were arrested. Then, a few months later, a black church in Birmingham was bombed, killing four school girls.

Americans Demanded a Civil Rights Bill

These terrible events in Birmingham angered many Americans. Then two civil rights leaders, William Moore and Medgar W. Evers, were murdered. But still Congress did not act on the civil rights bill President Kennedy asked it to pass. This led to a protest march in the nation's capital in August of 1963.

This **March on Washington** was an important event in the civil rights movement. Over

200 thousand Americans took part in the March on Washington, D.C., in support of President Kennedy's civil rights bill. Although the civil rights movement was becoming stronger, Congress still did not pass the civil rights bill.

President Kennedy Was Killed

Several months later, on November 22, 1963, President Kennedy was shot and killed in Dallas, Texas. The American people were shocked and saddened by President Kennedy's death. Lee Harvey Oswald was accused as the assassin, or murderer. A few days later, Oswald himself was murdered as he was being moved from one prison to another prison in Dallas.

President Johnson Carried on the New Frontier

President Kennedy's New Frontier plan to improve America was taken over by the new President, Lyndon B. Johnson. He promised the American people to carry on President Kennedy's program. President Johnson was the majority leader, or the Democratic Party leader in the Senate, during the 1950's. He knew Congress well, and he was able to get Congress to pass most of the laws that President Kennedy had requested Congress to pass earlier.

Early in 1964, Congress passed a law giving the American people an income tax cut. Congress also agreed to provide more money to aid education. Also, Congress promised to

President Kennedy was assassinated on November 22, 1963. Here, the funeral procession makes its way to Arlington National Cemetery.

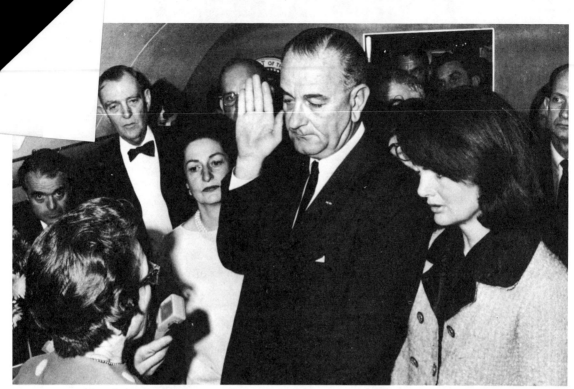

Lyndon Johnson is sworn in as President in the cabin of the Presidential plane shortly after the death of President Kennedy.

raise money to help American cities solve their transportation problems. And Congress voted to build more public housing. President Johnson also was able to get Congress to pass many other parts of President Kennedy's New Frontier program into law.

The Civil Rights Act of 1964

But one of the most important laws of the New Frontier, the Civil Rights Act, was still not passed into law. In June, President Johnson succeeded in getting Congress to pass the **Civil Rights Act of 1964.** This law forbade segregation in hotels, restaurants, and other public places. The law required all states to allow qualified voters to register and to vote. The law gave the government the power to ask the courts to force segregated schools to admit black children. It forbade

employers, labor unions, or job agencies to treat anyone unfairly because of his race, color, or religion. And the law allowed the government to take away the federal government's money from any state programs in which all citizens were not treated fairly.

Summing Up

In November of 1963, President Kennedy was murdered, and Vice-President Lyndon B. Johnson became President. President Johnson carried out President Kennedy's New Frontier program. Congress passed the Civil Rights Act of 1964 to end segregation in public places. President Johnson was also able to get Congress to pass many other New Frontier laws. In the next chapter, you will find out about President Johnson's own program for the American nation.

AFTER YOU READ THE CHAPTER

page 679

Do You Know These Important Terms?

For each sentence below, choose the term that best completes the sentence.

1. The (**Pan-American Union/Alliance for Progress**) was a ten-year plan to improve life in Latin America.
2. The (**March in Birmingham/March on Washington**) was an important event in the civil rights movement in support of President Kennedy's civil rights bill.
3. The Civil Rights Act of (**1964/1960**) forbade segregation in hotels, restaurants, and other public places. The law also acted against discrimination in other areas. And it allowed the federal government to take away its money from any state program in which all citizens were not fairly treated.

Do You Remember These People?

Tell something about each of the following persons.

John F. Kennedy   Martin Luther King, Jr.
William Moore   Lee Harvey Oswald
Medgar W. Evers   Lyndon B. Johnson

Can You Locate These Places?

Each of the following places is related to the events of this chapter. Locate each place on maps in your classroom.

Latin America   Birmingham, Alabama
Washington, D.C.   Dallas, Texas

Do You Know When It Happened?

What are the years of this chapter? Tell something about each of the following dates.

August, 1963   November 22, 1963   1964

Discovering More About the Main Idea

After President Kennedy's death, President Johnson carried out President Kennedy's New Frontier program.

Tell how each of the following developments is related to the MAIN IDEA.

President Kennedy asked Congress to pass laws to give federal aid to public schools and to end segregation in schools and in all public places.

Peaceful protest marchers were arrested in Birmingham, Alabama, and two civil rights workers were murdered.

The March on Washington was held to support President Kennedy's request for a new civil rights bill.

President Kennedy was shot and killed.

Lyndon B. Johnson then became President of the United States.

Can You Discuss the Chapter?

Use the information you learned in this chapter to answer the following questions.

1. How did the Alliance for Progress plan to improve life for the people of Latin America?
2. What did many black Americans do on the one hundredth anniversary of the Emancipation Proclamation?
3. Why was the March on Washington held?
4. How did President Johnson carry out the plans of the New Frontier?
5. Do you think the federal government should take away its money from any project in which all citizens are not treated fairly? Explain your answer.

Can You Connect the Past and the Present?

1. Have any more civil rights laws been passed recently?
2. Has the federal government needed to take away money from any projects in your community because it did not follow the Civil Rights Act of 1964?

CHAPTER 110

President Johnson's Great Society

President Johnson campaigning.

BEFORE YOU BEGIN THE CHAPTER

Know What to Look For

1. Jonathan is forty-two years old. He is married and has seven children who range in age from three to seventeen years old. His elderly mother also lives with the family in an unpainted shack in the mountains. The family is poorly clothed and fed because they have very little money. Jonathan is a miner. However, the coal mines are closed and he cannot work. With odd jobs and welfare checks, he

manages to earn about 2 thousand dollars a year.

Jonathan's family is typical of the many poor families who live in America. In the late 1960's, one out of every five American families was living in poverty. These poor Americans included unskilled workers who lived in crowded city ghettos, migrant farm workers who picked crops all over the country, rural farmers, and many Americans over sixty-five. In this chapter, you will read how President Johnson tried to attack the problem of poverty and other American problems.

2. Read the title of the chapter. Then look through the chapter and read each heading. Besides poverty, what other problems did President Johnson try to solve?

3. Look at the pictures in the chapter and read each caption. What do the pictures show you about President Johnson's plans for the nation? Note also the time line at the beginning of the chapter. What years are included in the chapter? Compare this chapter time line to the unit time line on page 667.

4. Read the last part of the chapter called Summing Up. How did President Johnson's Great Society plan help Americans?

Know These Important Terms

Great Society	Job Corps
Economic Opportunity Act	Vista

Voting Rights Act of 1965   Medicare Act
Elementary and Secondary Education Act
Department of Housing and
    Urban Development

Know the Main Idea

Here is the MAIN IDEA of this chapter.

President Johnson called his plans to improve the American nation the Great Society. He worked to end poverty and to help black Americans.

Keep this MAIN IDEA in mind as you study the chapter. Ask yourself the following questions as you read. They will help you remember the MAIN IDEA.

1. Who was the Republican candidate for President in the election of 1964?

2. What new department was added to the President's Cabinet?

3. Which children did the Elementary and Secondary Education Act help provide a better education for?

THE YEARS OF THIS CHAPTER ARE 1964 TO 1965

1960   1964   1965   1968

THE CHAPTER LESSON BEGINS HERE

President Johnson's Program Was Called the Great Society

After President Johnson carried out much of John F. Kennedy's New Frontier program, he developed his own plans to help improve the American nation. President Johnson called this program the **Great Society.** Important parts of President Johnson's Great Society program were health insurance for Americans over sixty-five, federal aid to education, stronger civil rights laws, jobs for all workers, and plans to end poverty. President Johnson hoped to improve life for all Americans.

President Johnson Won the Election of 1964

In the election of 1964, President Johnson was the Democratic Party's choice for President. The Republican candidate for President was Barry Goldwater, a Senator from Arizona. Both candidates spoke to Americans in all parts of the nation during the campaign. However, Senator Goldwater did not have the support of all the Republican leaders. This hurt him in the election. Lyndon Johnson won the election by more than 15 million votes, and the Democrats won control

Here, a young girl works with two city children. Many young Americans joined Vista to help poor people in the cities.

of Congress. Hubert Humphrey was elected Vice-President.

President Johnson's "War on Poverty"

One of the most important parts of President Johnson's Great Society program was a plan to end poverty. He wanted every American family to be able to afford enough food, proper clothing, and a comfortable place to live. In the 1960's, nearly one out of every five American families had an income of less than 3 thousand dollars a year and was living in poverty.

Even before he won the election of 1964, President Johnson began to try to aid these low-income families by starting a "war on poverty." In August of 1964, Congress passed

the **Economic Opportunity Act.** This law set up the **Job Corps** to give job training to young Americans from low-income families who had left school but were not able to find work. It also formed **Vista** (Volunteers in Service to America), a group of Americans who worked to help poor people in the cities of the United States.

Congress Passed Laws to Help End Poverty in America

After his great victory in the election of 1964, President Johnson felt that it was time to step up the war on poverty. He asked Congress to pass the Appalachian (AP-uh-LAY-chee-un) Regional Development Act. This law provided for a large sum of money

President Johnson talks to a family during his visit to Appalachia. Large sums of money were spent to fight poverty in this region.

to be spent to fight poverty in Appalachia, a large but poor region stretching from Pennsylvania all the way down to Alabama.

Congress also passed the Housing and Urban Development Act to help American cities solve their growing problems. This law allowed the government to give large sums of money to cities to build public housing. Also, money was to be given to poor people to help them pay their rent if they did not live in public housing. This act also set up the **Department of Housing and Urban Development** to work to solve city problems. Robert C. Weaver, the head of this new department, became the first black man ever to be a member of the President's Cabinet.

A Health Insurance Plan for Older Americans

Congress next turned to President Johnson's request to provide health insurance for Americans over sixty-five. In 1965, Congress passed the **Medicare Act,** as part of the Social Security program. This health insurance plan provided for free hospital care for people over sixty-five. It also provided for low-cost insurance to help older persons pay doctor bills.

Congress Voted Money to Help Education

Because President Johnson realized the importance of a good education for all Americans, he made aid to education an important part of his Great Society program. In 1963, Congress passed a law which provided help to colleges to build the new buildings they needed. And in 1965, Congress passed another law to lend money or give scholarships to needy students who were not able to afford to go to college.

But the most important education law proposed by President Johnson and passed by Congress was the **Elementary and Secondary**

This picture shows a classroom in a city school. The Elementary and Secondary Education Act of 1965 helped many city schools.

Education Act of 1965. For the first time, the federal government provided several billion dollars to help improve American elementary schools and high schools. Much of this money was given to city schools to help provide a better education for children from low-income families.

A Stronger Voting Rights Bill Was Passed

Even after the Civil Rights Act of 1964 was passed, many black Americans still had trouble voting in certain parts of the South. Officials in Selma, Alabama, refused to register black voters and to allow them to vote. The federal government had to protect Dr. Martin Luther King, Jr., and other Americans who marched from Selma to Montgomery to protest against this unfair treatment.

President Johnson and Congress realized that action had to be taken. Therefore, Congress passed the **Voting Rights Act of 1965.**

This law forbade the use of literacy, or reading, tests to prevent Americans from voting. This law also gave the government the power to register black voters when local officials refused to register these voters. This law greatly increased the number of black voters in the South.

Summing Up

President Johnson called his plans to improve the American nation the Great Society. President Johnson began a "war on poverty," or a plan to end poverty in America. Congress voted large amounts of money to help low-income families and to improve American education. A health insurance program was set up for older persons. The Voting Rights Act of 1965 helped many black Americans in the South to be able to vote. In the next chapter, you will read about other changes during the years of President Johnson's term in office.

AFTER YOU READ THE CHAPTER

Do You Know These Important Terms?

For each sentence below, choose the term that best completes the sentence.

1. President Johnson's plans to help improve the nation were called the (**Renewed Frontier/Great Society**).
2. The (**Economic Opportunity/Welfare Administration**) Act started the "war on poverty."
3. The (**Literacy/Voting Rights**) Act of 1965 forbade the use of literacy tests to prevent Americans from voting.
4. To provide a better education for children from low-income families the (**School Equipment and Lunch/Elementary and Secondary Education**) Act was passed.
5. The (**Department of Cities/Department of Housing and Urban Development**) was set up to solve city problems.
6. The (**Civilian/Job**) Corps was formed to give job training to young Americans from low-income families who had left school and were unable to find work.
7. A group of Americans who worked to help poor people in cities was called (**Service for Cities/Vista**).
8. A health insurance plan that provides for hospital care for people over sixty-five was set up in the (**Social Security/Medicare Act**).

Do You Remember These People?

Tell something about each of the following persons.

Lyndon B. Johnson   Barry Goldwater
Hubert Humphrey   Robert C. Weaver
Martin Luther King, Jr.

Do You Know When It Happened?

What are the years of this chapter? When did the "war on poverty" begin?

Discovering More About the Main Idea

President Johnson called his plans to improve the American nation the Great Society. He worked to end poverty and to help black Americans.

Tell how each of the following developments is related to the MAIN IDEA.

Lyndon Johnson won the Presidential election by more than 15 million votes because Senator Goldwater did not have the support of all the Republican leaders.

The Job Corps and Vista provided many new opportunities for young Americans.

The Department of Housing and Urban Development was set up. It was headed by Robert C. Weaver, the first black American ever to be a member of the President's Cabinet.

Can You Discuss the Chapter?

Use the information you learned in this chapter to answer the following questions.

1. How did President Johnson attack the problem of poverty in America?
2. How did the Great Society program help cities to solve their problems?
3. Describe the health insurance plan for older Americans.
4. Why was it necessary to pass the Voting Rights Act of 1965?
5. Do you think the federal government should try to help American cities to solve their problems? Why or why not?

Can You Connect the Past and the Present?

1. Has anyone you know been helped by the Medicare plan? How have they benefited from this health insurance plan?
2. Is there a Job Corps center in or near your community? What does it do?

The Nation Under President Johnson

President Johnson signing a law.

BEFORE YOU BEGIN THE CHAPTER

Know What to Look For

1. During the 1960's, many young Americans became interested in what was happening in America. These young people, many of them students, had new ideas and wanted these ideas to be heard. Some of them became involved in the civil rights movement and worked to gain equal rights for all Americans. Later in the 1960's, many young Americans became discouraged with the war in Viet Nam.

They held protest marches and other demonstrations to try to urge President Johnson to end the war.

In the Presidential election of 1968, many young people became involved in the campaigns of Senators Eugene McCarthy and Robert F. Kennedy. These young people did all kinds of work in the campaigns, and they tried to convince other Americans to vote for the candidate that they favored. So many students took part in Senator McCarthy's campaign that it became known as the "Children's Crusade." In this chapter, you will read about the nation under President Johnson and the election of 1968.

2. Read the title of the chapter. Then look through the chapter and read each heading. From the headings, tell some things that happened in the nation under President Johnson.

3. Look at the pictures in the chapter and read each caption. What does the first chapter picture show you? Note also the time line at the beginning of the chapter. What years are included in the chapter? Compare the time line for this chapter with the unit time line on page 667.

4. Read the last part of the chapter called Summing Up. Who became President after Lyndon B. Johnson?

Know These Important Terms
Department of Transportation
Immigration and Nationality Act
Twenty-Fifth Amendment

Know the Main Idea
Here is the MAIN IDEA of this chapter.
Not all of President Johnson's program was passed into law. The Supreme Court helped to bring about many changes in American life.

Keep this MAIN IDEA in mind as you study the chapter. Ask yourself the following questions as you read. They will help you remember the MAIN IDEA.

1. What new department was added to the President's Cabinet in 1966?

2. In what ways was the immigration law changed in 1965?

3. What were the issues in the election campaign of 1968?

THE YEARS OF THIS CHAPTER ARE 1965 TO 1968

1960   1965   1968

THE CHAPTER LESSON BEGINS HERE

President Johnson's Program Slowed Down

In his last two years in office, President Johnson still had many plans to improve the American nation. However, Congress did not act favorably on all of President Johnson's plans for new laws. In 1966, Congress did agree to set up the **Department of Transportation** in the President's Cabinet. And Congress passed an income tax increase, but only after the President promised to cut down the amount of money the government spent.

Congress also passed a gun control law to try to end the increasing crime and violence

of the 1960's. This law made it unlawful for a person to buy a handgun in a state other than the one he lived in.

A New Immigration Law Was Passed

In 1965, Congress passed a new immigration law called the **Immigration and Nationality Act.** Since the 1920's, American immigration laws had been based on a quota system which favored newcomers from the nations of northern or western Europe. The 1965 law ended the quota system. Although the law still limited the number of immigrants allowed to enter the United States, it now allowed people from all over the world to enter the United States.

The Twenty-Fifth Amendment Was Approved

In 1967, the **Twenty-Fifth Amendment** to the Constitution was passed. This Amendment solved the problem of who was to run the government if the President became sick or unable to carry out his duties for a long period of time. The Twenty-Fifth Amendment allowed the Vice-President to take over the duties and powers of the President, if the President became too ill to continue his duties.

The Supreme Court Made Many Important Decisions

The Supreme Court helped to bring about important changes in American life during the 1960's. The Supreme Court had to decide if some of the civil rights laws passed by Congress were against the Constitution. In a series of cases, the Supreme Court ruled in favor of the civil rights laws passed by Congress. The Court also tried to speed up the end of segregation in schools in both the North and the South. And the Court ruled that Bible reading and prayers in the public schools were unlawful.

The Supreme Court also helped to protect the rights of people who were accused of breaking the law. The Court ruled that the police must tell a person accused of breaking the law what his rights were. Also, a person accused of a crime must be able to have a lawyer present when he was questioned by the police. And the Supreme Court ruled that the states must provide a lawyer for anyone accused of a crime if he was not able to afford a lawyer.

The Supreme Court Helped City Voters

The Supreme Court also made several rulings which changed voting in the United States. For many years, large cities with many voters were not given enough Congressmen or state legislators to represent them. Instead, small towns and farming areas with small populations had the largest numbers of Congressmen and state legislators.

However, between 1962 and 1964, the Supreme Court made a number of rulings which helped city voters. In its "one man, one vote" decision, the Court ruled that all voters must be equally represented. Therefore, state legislatures had to set up new election districts in which all the people in the state were equally represented. Cities now got more representatives in Congress and in the state legislatures.

New Leaders Within the Democratic Party

Most Americans expected President Johnson to run for a second term in the Presidential election of 1968. But two other men tried to become the Democratic candidate for President. The first was Senator Eugene J. McCarthy of Minnesota. Senator McCarthy had won an unexpected victory over President Johnson in the New Hampshire primary election in March, 1968. This victory also encouraged Senator Robert F. Kennedy of New York to also try to become the Democratic candidate.

President Johnson surprised everyone in March of 1968 when he decided not to be a candidate for President. After President Johnson stepped aside, Vice-President Hubert H. Humphrey decided to try to become the Democratic candidate for President. Both Senator McCarthy and Senator Kennedy spoke out strongly against the war in Viet Nam. They also felt that President Johnson was not doing enough to help black Americans and the poor people in America. Vice-President Humphrey defended President Johnson's policies.

The Presidential Election of 1968

In June of 1968, Robert F. Kennedy was assassinated, or murdered, after he won the California primary election. His followers split between Senator McCarthy and Vice-President Humphrey. At the Democratic Party's convention in Chicago, Humphrey was chosen to be the Democratic candidate. But his choice as candidate divided the Democratic Party, and many of Senator McCarthy's backers refused to support Humphrey in the election.

The Republican Party chose Richard M. Nixon to be its candidate for President. Governor George C. Wallace of Alabama formed a third party and also became a candidate for President.

The election campaign of 1968 was not as exciting as most Americans expected it to be. The major issues in the campaign were "law and order" in America and the war in Viet Nam. President Richard M. Nixon won the election, but only by about 300 thousand votes. This was one of the closest Presidential elections in America's history.

Summing Up

Not all of President Johnson's Great Society program was passed into law. However, Congress did pass a gun control law and a new immigration law which ended the quota system. The Supreme Court also helped to bring important changes to American life in the 1960's. In the election of 1968, Americans elected a Republican President, Richard M. Nixon. In the next chapter, which begins Unit 29, you will read about America's dealings with foreign nations in the early 1960's.

President Nixon with Earl Warren and Warren Burger.

WARREN BURGER—FIFTEENTH CHIEF JUSTICE

The Chief Justice of the United States Supreme Court is one of the most important leaders in the nation. The decisions he helps to make can affect the nation for many years. For this reason, Americans were very interested in Warren Burger, who was appointed Chief Justice by President Nixon in 1969.

Warren Burger was born in Minnesota in 1908. His family was not rich, and he had to work his way through the University of Minnesota and the St. Paul College of Law. After he graduated from law school, Burger built up a successful law practice in St. Paul, Minnesota. President Eisenhower asked Warren Burger to work for the Justice Department in Washington, D.C., in 1952. In 1956, Burger became a judge of the United States Court of Appeals for the District of Columbia.

As a federal judge, Warren Burger usually took a sound position in cases. He was an able, hard-working judge, who was respected by other judges and lawyers. Both Democrats and Republicans in Congress quickly approved him as the new Chief Justice in 1969. As Chief Justice, Warren Burger will play an important role in shaping the Supreme Court's rulings in the 1970's.

AFTER YOU READ THE CHAPTER

Do You Know These Important Terms?

For each sentence below, choose the term that best completes the sentence.

1. The Department of (**Transportation/Urban Affairs**) was added to the President's Cabinet in 1966.
2. The (**New Entrants/Immigration and Nationality Act**) did away with the old quota system but still limited the number of immigrants allowed to enter the United States.
3. The problem of who was to run the government if the President became sick or unable to carry out his duties for a long time was solved by the (**Twenty-Fifth Amendment/Succession in Office Act**).

Do You Remember These People?

Tell something about each of the following persons.

Lyndon B. Johnson	**Eugene McCarthy**
Robert F. Kennedy	**Hubert H. Humphrey**
Richard M. Nixon	**George Wallace**

Can You Locate These Places?

Use the maps in your classroom to locate the following places. Tell how each location is related to the events in the chapter.

Minnesota	**New Hampshire**
New York	**Viet Nam**
California	**Chicago**

Do You Know When It Happened?

What are the years of this chapter? Place the following events in the order in which they occurred.

Robert Kennedy was assassinated.

A new immigration law was passed.

Richard Nixon was elected President.

Department of Transportation was set up.

The Democratic Party selected a candidate in Chicago.

Discovering More About the Main Idea

Not all of President Johnson's program was passed into law. The Supreme Court helped to bring about many changes in American life.

Tell how each of the following developments is related to the MAIN IDEA.

Congress set up the Department of Transportation, passed an income tax increase, a gun control law, and a new immigration law.

The Supreme Court ruled in favor of the civil rights laws passed by Congress. The Court also ruled against prayers and Bible reading in the public schools. It ruled that all voters must be equally represented.

Can You Discuss the Chapter?

Use the information you learned in this chapter to answer the following questions.

1. How did the new immigration law differ from the older immigration laws?
2. How did the Supreme Court help the cause of civil rights?
3. What was the Supreme Court's "one man, one vote" decision?
4. Who were the candidates in the Presidential election of 1968?
5. Do you think the Court's rulings about people who were accused of breaking the law are fair? Why or why not?

Can You Connect the Past and the Present?

1. The Constitution says that Americans have the right to carry guns. However, in 1966, a gun control law was passed. Do you think there is any contradiction between this gun control law and the Constitution?
2. Have the election districts in your state been changed as a result of the Supreme Court rulings in 1962 and 1964?

America in the Space Age

Astronaut Edward White walks in space.

THE CHAPTERS IN UNIT 29 ARE

CHAPTER 112 The United States and the World, 1961–1963
CHAPTER 113 The United States and the World, 1963–1970
CHAPTER 114 America's Adventure in Space

THE YEARS OF THIS UNIT ARE 1957 TO 1970

| 1900 | 1957 | 1970 | 1975 |

CHAPTER 112

The United States and the World, 1961-1963

Khrushchev meets with Castro.

BEFORE YOU BEGIN THE CHAPTER

Know What to Look For

1. American U-2 airplanes were made of plywood and carried only one crew member. U-2 planes were able to fly very high and very fast. They flew so high and so fast that it was almost impossible to locate them on radar screens. For this reason, the United States used U-2 planes as spy planes. They carried complex camera equipment, which took very clear photographs.

In the early 1960's, the United States used U-2 airplanes to fly over Cuba to keep an eye on things. During the rainy season in the summer of 1962, most of Cuba was covered with clouds. No photographs could be taken. When the clouds cleared in the fall, photographs taken by U-2 planes showed that missile bases to launch Soviet rockets had been built in Cuba. In this chapter, you will read about the missile crisis this discovery caused. You will also read about how the United States continued to work against the spread of Communism.

2. Read the title of the chapter. Then look at the chapter and read each heading. Using the headings, tell what nations the United States had dealings with between 1961 and 1963.

3. Look at the pictures in the chapter and read each caption. What do the pictures show you about the United States and world affairs between 1961 and 1963? Note also the time line at the beginning of this chapter. What years are included in the chapter? Compare this chapter time line to the unit time line on page 691.

4. Read the last part of the chapter called Summing Up. From what country did the Soviet Union remove its missile bases?

Know These Important Terms
Berlin Wall   test ban treaty

Know the Main Idea
Here is the MAIN IDEA of this chapter.
Under President Kennedy, the United States continued to try to stop the spread of Communism in the world.

Keep this MAIN IDEA in mind as you study the chapter. Ask yourself the following questions as you read. They will help you remember the MAIN IDEA.

1. Why did the United States support Fidel Castro when he first became the leader of Cuba in 1959?

2. Why did the Russians build the Berlin Wall in 1961?

3. What type of atomic testing was allowed to continue under the test ban treaty? What type of testing was banned?

THE YEARS OF THIS CHAPTER ARE 1960 TO 1963

1957	1960	1963	1970

THE CHAPTER LESSON BEGINS HERE

The United States Had Troubles with Cuba

Soon after John F. Kennedy became President in 1961, he grew worried about events in Cuba. In 1959, when Eisenhower was President, a new Cuban leader named Fidel Castro overthrew Colonel Batista, the dictator of Cuba. At first, the United States supported Premier Castro because he promised to build a democratic government in Cuba.

But Castro soon showed that he was a dictator too and that he favored Communism. The United States stopped supporting Castro after he set up a dictatorship.

Under President Eisenhower, the United States started to train and equip a group of anti-Castro Cubans to attack Cuba. In April, 1961, President Kennedy and his advisers decided to allow this group of anti-Castro Cubans to invade Cuba from the United States. About a thousand Cubans landed at the Bay of Pigs on the southern coast of Cuba. However, the Cuban people did not support the anti-Castro Cubans, and the invaders were soon defeated by Castro's army. The failure of this invasion was a defeat for the United States. And afterward, Premier Castro turned even more strongly to the Soviet

This picture shows a part of the Berlin Wall. This wall was built by the Russians to prevent East Germans from escaping to West Berlin.

Union for support and aid for his country.

Soviet Weapon Bases in Cuba

In the fall of 1962, the United States discovered that the Soviet Union was building missile (MISS-ul) bases, or rocket-launching bases, in Cuba. President Kennedy felt that these missile bases were a danger to the United States, and he acted quickly to end this danger. In October of 1962, President Kennedy warned the Soviet Union to remove the Soviet bases in Cuba. And he ordered the American navy to stop any Soviet ships carrying missiles to Cuba.

For a few days, it seemed as if the United States and the Soviet Union might go to war. But Premier Khrushchev, the Soviet leader, finally agreed to remove the missile bases in

Cuba. In return, the United States promised not to attack Cuba.

The United States Protected West Berlin

Although the Soviet Union backed down in Cuba, the danger of war between the United States and the Soviet Union was still far from ended. In 1961, Premier Khrushchev demanded that the United States and its allies leave West Berlin. West Berlin, you may remember, was the free part of Berlin that belonged to West Germany.

The Soviet Union wanted to take over all of Berlin because hundreds of Germans living in East Germany (Communist Germany) were escaping into West Berlin. The Communists wanted to stop the East Germans

A group of Cuban refugees display the Free Cuba flag. They escaped from Cuba on this sailing ship and were picked up at sea.

from escaping. Therefore, they threatened to block all food and supplies from entering West Berlin.

But President Kennedy refused to give up West Berlin. He sent troops to West Berlin to prevent a Communist blockade being set up. When Khrushchev saw that the United States was not going to give up West Berlin, he backed down. But to make sure that no more East Germans escaped to West Berlin, the Russians built the **Berlin Wall** in 1961 to cut off East Berlin from West Berlin. Over the years, they made the wall stronger.

President Kennedy and the War in Viet Nam

President Eisenhower, you may remember, tried to help the government of South Viet Nam defeat the Vietcong, or the Communist-led forces supported by North Viet Nam. But by 1961, the efforts to stop the Communists from taking over Viet Nam were going badly. Therefore, in 1962, President Kennedy tried to help South Viet Nam by sending a few thousand American military advisers to help train South Viet Nam's army. By 1963, 16 thousand American troops were in South Viet Nam.

However, the war continued to go badly for South Viet Nam. Many people in South Viet Nam refused to support their own government. Finally, in 1963, a new government was formed, but army leaders ruled South Viet Nam for the next two years. During these years, South Viet Nam was still not able to defeat the Communist forces.

A Peace Corps worker in Bolivia.

THE PEACE CORPS

On October 14, 1960, while he was running for President, John F. Kennedy suggested the idea of a Peace Corps to a group of students at the University of Michigan. After his election, President Kennedy proposed the idea to Congress, and Congress set up the Peace Corps in 1961. Kennedy named Sargent Shriver as the head of this program. The Peace Corps had three main goals: 1. to build up foreign nations; 2. to encourage good will for the United States; 3. to give young Americans a chance to use their skills to help others. During its first few years, over 100 thousand Americans volunteered to join the Peace Corps.

The Peace Corps is made up of Americans who want to help the people of other nations help themselves. Americans who join the Peace Corps serve as teachers, nurses, and farm laborers in more than fifty nations of Asia, Africa, and South America. They must learn the language of the nation they serve in, and they must follow the same ways of living as the people of the nation. The Peace Corps is doing an important job all over the world. It has shown that Americans care about the other peoples of the world.

A Treaty Stopped Some Atomic Testing

In 1963, President Kennedy thought that it was time to stop testing atomic bombs on the earth's surface because these tests were dangerous. Therefore, President Kennedy proposed a **test ban treaty**, or an agreement to stop certain kinds of atomic bomb testing. By this treaty, atomic bomb tests on the earth's surface and in the skies were not allowed. Only underground and underwater atomic testing were allowed to continue. The Soviet Union and many other nations signed this treaty in 1963.

Communism Was Kept Out of the Congo

In 1960, the Republic of the Congo, once a colony of Belgium, became an independent nation. But when a civil war broke out in the Congo in 1960, the Soviet Union tried to set up a government favorable to Communism. However, the United States supported the United Nations army that was sent to the Congo. This United Nations army finally defeated the government favorable to Communism and brought peace to the Congo.

Summing Up

Under President Kennedy, the United States continued to try to stop the spread of Communism in the world. In 1961, an American-supported invasion of Cuba by anti-Castro Cubans failed. But in 1962, the United States demanded that the Soviet Union remove its missile bases in Cuba. The Soviet Union finally was forced to agree to this demand. The United States also helped to protect West Berlin against the Soviet Union. President Kennedy was able to stop certain kinds of atomic bomb tests. In the next chapter, you will find out how the United States dealt with foreign nations under Presidents Johnson and Nixon.

AFTER YOU READ THE CHAPTER

Do You Know These Important Terms?

For each sentence below, choose the term that best completes the sentence.

1. The Russians built the (**Berlin Wall/ Brandenburg Gate**) to cut off East Berlin from West Berlin.
2. The agreement signed in 1963 to stop certain kinds of atomic bomb tests was called the (**arms ban/test ban**) treaty.

Do You Remember These People?

Tell something about each of the following persons.

John F. Kennedy   **Fidel Castro**
Fulgencio Batista   **Nikita Khrushchev**
Dwight D. Eisenhower

Can You Locate These Places?

Use the maps in your classroom to do the following map work.

1. Locate the island of Cuba. Why do you think missile bases on this island might be a danger to the United States?
2. Locate South Viet Nam and North Viet Nam. Which of these nations is a Communist nation? What other Communist nation is nearby?
3. Locate the Republic of the Congo. What nation formerly controlled the Congo?

Do You Know When It Happened?

What years are included in this chapter? Place the following events in the order in which they occurred.

The Berlin Wall was built.

The United States supported Fidel Castro.

The test ban treaty was signed.

United Nations army brought peace to the Congo.

The United States discovered missile bases in Cuba.

Discovering More About the Main Idea

Under President Kennedy, the United States continued to try to stop the spread of Communism in the world.

Tell how each of the following developments is related to the MAIN IDEA.

The United States supported Fidel Castro at first, but when he set up a dictatorship in Cuba the United States stopped supporting him. President Kennedy warned the Soviet Union to remove the Soviet missile bases from Cuba.

Because so many East Germans were escaping into West Berlin, the Soviet Union threatened to set up a blockade. The Russians built the Berlin Wall, instead.

President Kennedy continued to help South Viet Nam in its fight against the Vietcong.

Can You Discuss the Chapter?

Use the information you learned in this chapter to answer the following questions.

1. Why did Castro turn more strongly toward the Soviet Union after the Bay of Pigs invasion?
2. What happened when the United States discovered missile bases in Cuba in 1962?
3. Why did the Soviet Union decide to build the Berlin Wall?
4. How did the United States continue to help South Viet Nam?
5. Some people thought the Bay of Pigs invasion was a bad mistake. What do you think?

Can You Connect the Past and the Present?

1. Is the Berlin Wall still standing? Did it accomplish the purpose for which it was built?
2. Is the United States still trying to stop the spread of Communism in the world? in what ways?

CHAPTER 113

The United States and the World, 1963-1970

American tanks pass an ox cart in Viet Nam.

BEFORE YOU BEGIN THE CHAPTER

Know What to Look For

1. The war in Viet Nam differs in many ways from most wars. For example, it is impossible to draw a line on the map and say that the Vietcong occupy the land on one side of the line while the government of South Viet Nam occupies the land on the other side. In the war in Viet Nam, the battle front lines are never clear.

The soldiers of the Vietcong are experts in

jungle warfare. They hide during the day and come out to fight at night. Land that may belong to South Viet Nam during daylight hours may be taken over by the Vietcong after dark without even a battle. The Vietcong frequently strike in small forces and then, after a short battle, seem to disappear into the rice fields or the jungle. In this chapter, you will read about the war in Viet Nam, and other world problems the United States faced during the late 1960's.

2. Read the title of the chapter. Then look through the chapter and read each heading. From the headings, tell what nations the United States had dealings with in the years of the 1960's.

3. Look at the pictures in the chapter and read each caption. What do the pictures show you about the United States and the world in the 1960's? Note also the time line at the beginning of the chapter. What years are included in this chapter? Compare this chapter time line to the unit time line on page 691.

4. Read the last part of the chapter called Summing Up. What difficult problem faced both President Johnson and President Nixon? What is the topic of the next chapter?

Know This Important Term
National Liberation Front

Know the Main Idea
Here is the MAIN IDEA of this chapter.

President Johnson and President Nixon faced the difficult problem of ending the war in Viet Nam and of dealing with other nations.

Keep this MAIN IDEA in mind as you study the chapter. Ask yourself the following questions as you read. They will help you remember the MAIN IDEA.

1. Who operates the Panama Canal today?
2. What action by the Soviet Union helped to strengthen N.A.T.O. in 1968?
3. When did North Viet Nam agree to start peace talks in Paris? When did the American bombing of North Viet Nam stop?

THE YEARS OF THIS CHAPTER ARE 1963 TO 1970

1957   1963   1970

THE CHAPTER LESSON BEGINS HERE

The Alliance for Progress Was Continued

The Alliance for Progress formed by President Kennedy did not build up Latin America as quickly as he had hoped. But President Johnson decided to continue the Alliance for Progress because he hoped that it might help the nations of Latin America.

Panama Regained Control of the Canal Zone

In 1964, trouble broke out in the Latin American nation of Panama. Many of the people of Panama were angry at the United States because the United States controlled the Panama Canal Zone. They wanted Panama to be able to control the Canal Zone.

President Johnson agreed that the people of Panama should have control of the Canal Zone. Therefore, he agreed to make a new treaty with Panama, which gave Panama control of the Canal Zone. However, the United States and Panama were to operate the Panama Canal together.

American Troops Were Sent to the Dominican Republic

In 1965, a civil war broke out in the Dominican Republic, a small nation in the Caribbean Sea. President Johnson was afraid

Czechoslovakian youths carry the Czech flag past a burning Soviet tank after troops from the Soviet Union invaded Czechoslovakia in 1968.

that this civil war might make it possible for Communists to take over the Dominican government. Therefore, he sent 20 thousand American soldiers to the Dominican Republic.

Most Latin American nations were unhappy about President Johnson's action. They were afraid that the use of American troops might be the start of a new American plan to become involved in the affairs of Latin American nations. Some Latin American leaders were angry because they believed the United States was breaking its promise never to interfere in the affairs of the nations of Latin America.

However, President Johnson agreed to remove the American troops as soon as the Latin American nations joined in keeping the peace in the Dominican Republic. Four Latin American nations sent troops and formed a peace-keeping army there. In 1966, free elections were held, and soon all the troops left the Dominican Republic.

The Cold War in Europe

The Cold War in Europe remained fairly quiet during President Johnson's term in office. The Soviet Union usually seemed to want to get along with the United States. However, in 1968, when Czechoslovakia granted its people more freedom, Soviet troops took over Czechoslovakia. This Soviet invasion of Czechoslovakia encouraged the European nations to strengthen the N.A.T.O. forces.

North Viet Nam Invaded
South Viet Nam

In 1963, you may remember, during President Kennedy's term, a new government was formed to strengthen South Viet Nam's efforts to defeat the Communists. South Viet Nam was fighting the Vietcong alone. American troops served only as advisers to South Viet Nam's army.

However, in 1964, large numbers of soldiers from North Viet Nam invaded South Viet

These marines are leaving Viet Nam. They were the first American troops to be withdrawn under President Nixon's withdrawal program.

Nam. These Communist troops from North Viet Nam began to help the Vietcong's fight to take over South Viet Nam.

The United States Entered the Viet Nam War

In August of 1964, North Viet Nam's gunboats attacked American navy ships in the Gulf of Tonkin, about thirty miles off the coast of North Viet Nam. Congress then gave President Johnson the power to "take all necessary measures" to protect American armed forces in Viet Nam and also to protect South Viet Nam against invading armies. By February of 1965, it looked as if South Viet Nam's army was in danger of being defeated. In order to prevent this, President Johnson ordered the American air force to begin to bomb certain targets in North Viet Nam. And in March of 1965, American combat soldiers were sent into battle against the Vietcong and North Viet Nam's troops.

The United States Tried to End the War

President Johnson still hoped to settle the war and gain an early peace. In April, 1965, he promised over 1 billion dollars in aid to the countries of Southeast Asia—including North Viet Nam—as soon as the war was ended. In May, 1965, the President ordered the bombing of North Viet Nam to stop. But the **National Liberation Front** (the official name of the Vietcong), and the North Viet Nam government refused to end the fighting.

The United States started to bomb North Viet Nam again, and more American soldiers entered the fighting. By the end of 1965, 125 thousand American troops were fighting in South Viet Nam. The United States tried to make peace in December, 1965, but once again failed. Many more peace offers were made by the United States during the next three years. But North Viet Nam refused to consider any peace offers unless the American

Delegates from North and South Viet Nam, the National Liberation Front, and the United States at the Viet Nam peace talks in Paris.

bombing of North Viet Nam stopped completely and unless all American troops left South Viet Nam.

The Viet Nam War Continued

By 1968, most Americans were discouraged by the war in Viet Nam. More than 540 thousand American soldiers were fighting in South Viet Nam. About 30 thousand Americans had been killed and more than 100 thousand wounded. The war was costing the United States more than 25 billion dollars a year. Besides, neither side was winning, and South Viet Nam was being destroyed by this terrible war.

In March of 1968, President Johnson again tried to make peace. He ordered American planes to limit the bombing of North Viet Nam. Soon after, North Viet Nam agreed to start peace talks in Paris. In November of 1968, all American bombing of North Viet

Nam was ended. President Nixon, too, continued to try to end the war. In the summer of 1969, the fighting in Viet Nam slowed down, and President Nixon began to withdraw the first American troops. Then in the autumn of 1969, Ho Chi Minh, the leader of North Viet Nam, died. Many Americans wondered how or if his death might affect the war.

Summing Up

During Lyndon Johnson's years as President, Panama was given control of the Canal Zone. A civil war started in the Dominican Republic, and President Johnson sent American troops to prevent a Communist takeover of this country. By 1965, the United States was involved in the terrible war in Viet Nam. President Johnson and President Nixon faced difficult problems in trying to end this war. The next chapter tells about space exploration.

AFTER YOU READ THE CHAPTER

Do You Know This Important Term?

In the sentence below, select the term that best completes the sentence.

The official name of the Vietcong is the (**Peoples Freedom Movement/National Liberation Front**).

Do You Remember These People?

Tell something about each of the following persons.

John F. Kennedy   Lyndon B. Johnson
Richard M. Nixon   Ho Chi Minh

Can You Locate These Places?

Use the map of the world to do the following map work.

1. Locate the nation of Panama.
2. Locate the Dominican Republic.
3. Locate the nation of Czechoslovakia in Europe. What country invaded Czechoslovakia in 1968?
4. Locate North Viet Nam, South Viet Nam, Saigon, and Hanoi.

Do You Know When It Happened?

What are the years of this chapter? Place the following events in the order in which they occurred.

Soviet troops invaded Czechoslovakia.

American troops were sent to the Dominican Republic.

Viet Nam peace talks were begun.

Panama gained control of the Canal.

Some American troops were withdrawn from Viet Nam.

Discovering More About the Main Idea

President Johnson and President Nixon faced the difficult problem of ending the war in Viet Nam and of dealing with other nations.

Tell how each of the following developments is related to the MAIN IDEA.

When American troops were sent to the Dominican Republic, some Latin American nations believed the United States broke its promise never to interfere in the affairs of Latin American nations.

In 1964, soldiers from North Viet Nam began to help the Vietcong. In 1965, when it looked as if South Viet Nam's army was in danger of being defeated, the United States sent American combat troops into battle.

North Viet Nam demanded an end to American bombing and the total withdrawal of American troops before it considered any peace offers.

Can You Discuss This Chapter?

Use the information you learned in this chapter to answer the following questions.

1. How did the United States solve the trouble that broke out in Panama in 1964?
2. Why were some Latin American nations unhappy about the United States sending troops into the Dominican Republic?
3. Why did President Johnson send many American combat soldiers to Viet Nam?
4. Why were Americans discouraged by the war in Viet Nam?
5. Do you think that the United States should have become involved in the war in Viet Nam? Why or why not?

Can You Connect the Past and the Present?

1. What were the results of the Paris peace talks?
2. Do you know anyone in the American armed forces who fought in Viet Nam? What did he say about his experiences in the war?

CHAPTER 114

America's Adventure in Space

Astronaut Edwin Aldrin walking on the moon.

BEFORE YOU BEGIN THE CHAPTER

Know What to Look For

1. During the 1930's, an American scientist named Robert Goddard made experiments with rockets. In his experiments, Goddard discovered that rockets were able to work in a vacuum. Since outer space was a vacuum, he believed that rockets might be made to travel through space.

Goddard was ahead of his time. Although he built successful rockets, no one was willing

to use them. However, in the late 1950's, the United States and the Soviet Union started to use rockets in space exploration. Goddard's experiments with rockets helped lead to the building of modern rockets and to the exploration of space. In this chapter, you will read about man's exciting explorations in space.

2. Read the title of the chapter. Then

look through the chapter and read each heading. What do the headings tell you about America's space program?

3. Look at the pictures in the chapter and read each caption. What do the pictures tell you about America's achievements in space? Note also the time line at the beginning of the chapter. What years are included in the chapter? Compare this chapter time line to the unit time line on page 691.

4. Read the last part of the chapter called Summing Up. When did the race to explore space begin? What is the topic of the next chapter?

Know These Important Terms

space satellite   soft landing

Know the Main Idea

Here is the MAIN IDEA of this chapter.

The United States and the Soviet Union were in a race to explore space. In 1969, the United States won the space race when two American astronauts were first to land on the moon.

Keep this MAIN IDEA in mind as you study the chapter. Ask yourself the following questions as you read. They will help you remember the MAIN IDEA.

1. What nation was the first to put a space satellite into orbit around the earth?

2. What historic event occurred during the summer of 1969?

3. Name some ways outer space is already being used to serve peaceful purposes.

THE YEARS OF THIS CHAPTER ARE 1957 TO 1970

1957   1970

THE CHAPTER LESSON BEGINS HERE

The Beginning of the Space Race

You probably remember the names of Leif Ericson, Christopher Columbus, and other early explorers of America. But you are probably even more familiar with such names as Neil Armstrong, John Glenn, Frank Borman, Edwin Aldrin, and other modern explorers of space.

Many people date the beginning of the Space Age from October 4, 1957. On that day, the Soviet Union sent Sputnik 1, the first **space satellite,** or man-made moon, into orbit around the earth. Early in 1958, the United States sent up its first space satellite, Explorer 1. In the years following, the United States and the Soviet Union became rivals in space as well as on earth.

One of the main aims of the space race was to land a man on the moon and to return him safely to earth. In 1959, an unmanned Soviet spaceship reached the moon. Two years later, Yuri Gagarin of the Soviet Union became the first man to orbit the earth. John Glenn was the first American to orbit the earth, in 1962. In that same year, an unmanned United States spaceship, Ranger 4, landed on the moon.

Key Events in Exploring Space

In 1965, Aleksei Leonov of the Soviet Union and later, Edward White of the United States, walked in space outside their space capsules. Later that same year, two American

Astronauts John Young (left) and Gus Grissom (right) are shown in their spacecraft just before blastoff.

ships, Gemini 6 and Gemini 7, met in space. At times, these two spaceships were less than ten feet apart while moving at a speed of 17 thousand miles an hour. This flight proved that spaceships can refuel in space.

In 1966, a Soviet spaceship made the first **soft landing** on the moon. A soft landing is one in which the spaceship lands safely and is not destroyed. An American spaceship also made a soft landing on the moon later that same year.

American Space Men Explored the Moon

By 1968, the United States was moving ahead in the race to the moon. In December of 1968, American astronauts Frank Borman, James Lovell, and William Anders flew their spaceship, Apollo 8, around the moon. They were the first men ever to see the dark side of the moon. Early in 1969, the Apollo 9 space

mission tested out a special space vehicle designed to explore the moon. Soon after this, Thomas Stafford, John Young, and Eugene Cernan circled the moon in Apollo 10. On this flight, the special space vehicle was used to explore the moon's surface. The Apollo spaceship came within ten miles of the moon. This prepared the way for landing on the moon.

Americans Landed on the Moon

On July 20, 1969, the Apollo 11 space mission achieved one of the greatest scientific successes in all of history. American astronauts Neil Armstrong and Edwin Aldrin landed their space vehicle on the moon while Michael Collins continued to orbit the space ship around the moon. They spent several hours exploring the moon's surface and collecting moon rock samples, as men back on earth watched this history-making event on television. Man had proved that he was able to live in another world—in space! An endless, unknown world in outer space now awaited earth's explorers.

America's moon landing had very important scientific results as well. Scientists studied the moon rocks and moon soil to learn how the moon was formed. These studies also helped scientists to learn important new facts about the earth itself. The moon landing marked the beginning of man's greatest adventure. As Neil Armstrong said during his moon walk, the moon landing was "one small step for a man, one giant leap for mankind."

Outer Space Can Help or Hurt

Exploring space is an exciting challenge to all men. It also creates difficult new problems. For example, what might happen if nations began to set up military bases on the moon to attack other nations on earth? To solve this problem, the United States, the Soviet Union, and many other nations agreed in 1966 not to use outer space for purposes of war. No atomic weapons are to be allowed in space, and no military bases will be set up on the moon.

Outer space is already serving many peaceful purposes. Satellites with television cameras help to predict the weather. Other satellites help ships and planes to travel safely. Satellites with telescopes are teaching us much about the stars and planets. And satellites make it possible for television programs to be sent all over the world.

Summing Up

The race to explore space began in 1957. At first, the Soviet Union's great successes put that nation ahead in the space race. But by the mid-1960's, the United States' achievements enabled it to lead this race. In 1969, the United States' victory in space was won when two United States astronauts landed

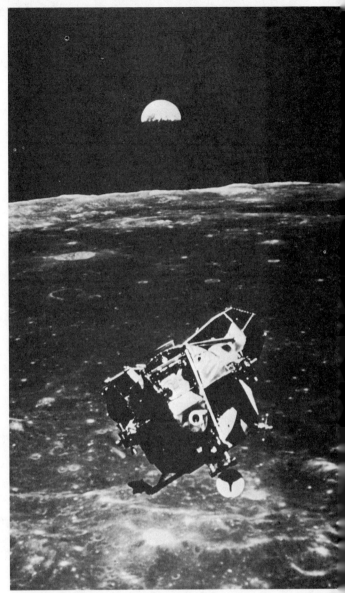

The Apollo 11 lunar module is making its docking approach to the command spaceship.

on the moon. With this moon landing, man proved that he can live in another world. The vast, unknown world of space now waited to be explored. In the next chapter, which begins Unit 30, you will read about the nation under President Nixon.

AFTER YOU READ THE CHAPTER

Do You Know These Important Terms?

In the sentences below, select the term that best completes the sentence.

1. A man-made moon that orbits the earth is called a (**space satellite/space station**).
2. A landing in which the space ship lands safely and is not destroyed is called a (**lunar landing/soft landing**).

Do You Remember These People?

Tell something about some of the following persons.

John Glenn
Edwin Aldrin
Aleksei Leonov
James Lovell
Thomas Stafford
Eugene Cernan
Michael Collins

Frank Borman
Yuri Gagarin
Edward White
William Anders
John Young
Neil Armstrong

Can You Locate These Places?

All space flights have been launched from Cape Kennedy in Florida. On a map of the United States locate Florida.

Do You Know When It Happened?

What are the years of this chapter? Place the following events in the order in which they occurred.

The first man walked in space.

Astronauts walked on the moon's surface.

Soviet Union sent Sputnik 1 into orbit.

A Soviet spaceship and an American spaceship made soft landings on the moon.

Discovering More About the Main Idea

The United States and the Soviet Union were in a race to explore space. In 1969, the United States won the space race when two American astronauts were first to land on the moon.

Tell how each of the following developments is related to the MAIN IDEA.

The Soviet Union sent Sputnik 1 into orbit in October, 1957. Early in 1958, the United States sent up its first space satellite, Explorer 1.

Spacemen were soon able to orbit the earth in their spaceships, walk in space, and move two spaceships so that they might meet in space.

Scientists studied the moon rocks and moon soil to learn how the moon was formed. These studies helped scientists to learn important new facts about the moon and also about the earth itself.

Can You Discuss the Chapter?

Use the information you learned in this chapter to answer the following questions.

1. What was the main aim of the space race between the Soviet Union and the United States?
2. What were some of the important events in the exploration of space?
3. Why was the landing of American astronauts on the moon of such historic importance?
4. How can outer space be used for the benefit of mankind?
5. Do you think the money spent on putting a man on the moon might have been spent in a better way? Explain your answer.

Can You Connect the Past and the Present?

1. What are the latest achievements in the exploration of space?
2. What television programs have you watched recently which would not have been possible without space communication satellites?

The American Nation Today

The city of San Francisco.

THE CHAPTERS IN UNIT 30 ARE

CHAPTER 115 The Nation Under President Nixon
CHAPTER 116 The Black Power Movement
CHAPTER 117 America's Modern Economy

THE YEARS OF THIS UNIT ARE 1960 TO 1970

1900		1960	1970	1975

The Nation Under President Nixon

President and Mrs. Nixon in India.

BEFORE YOU BEGIN THE CHAPTER

Know What to Look For

1. In the election of 1960, Richard M. Nixon ran for President and was defeated. Two years later, he was defeated in the election for governor of California. After losing these two elections, it seemed as if Nixon's political career was over.

Although he was no longer a candidate for any political office, Nixon remained an important member of the Republican Party.

Working behind the scenes, he helped to elect Republican candidates all over the country. When it came time to choose a candidate for President in 1968, the Republican Party once again turned to Richard Nixon. This was truly an amazing comeback for Richard Nixon. Only six years before, most people thought his political career was over. Now he was the Republican Party's candidate for President. And in a few months, he was elected President of the United States. In this chapter, you will read about the many problems President Nixon had to face.

2. Read the title of the chapter. Then look through the chapter and read each heading. From the headings, what were some of the important problems President Nixon had to face?

3. Look at the pictures in the chapter and read each caption. What do the pictures tell you about the nation under President Nixon? Note also the time line at the beginning of the chapter. What years are included in the chapter? Compare this chapter time line with the unit time line on page 709.

4. Read the last part of the chapter called Summing Up. What serious problems did President Nixon face when he began his term in office? What is the topic of the next chapter?

Know These Important Terms
anti-ballistic missile system
urban nation

Know the Main Idea
Here is the MAIN IDEA of this chapter.
The main problem facing President Nixon was the Viet Nam War. He also had to deal with problems of defense and the growing problems of American cities.

Keep this MAIN IDEA in mind as you study this chapter. Ask yourself the following questions as you read. They will help you to remember the MAIN IDEA.

1. What did President Nixon expect North Viet Nam to do after he promised to withdraw American troops from Viet Nam?

2. What is the purpose of the anti-ballistic missile system?

3. What are some of the difficulties of living in cities?

THE YEARS OF THIS CHAPTER ARE 1968 TO 1970

1960   1968   1970

THE CHAPTER LESSON BEGINS HERE

President Nixon Tried to End the Viet Nam War

As soon as his term began, President Nixon tried hard to end the Viet Nam War. In the early months of 1969, the peace talks in Paris continued. But little progress was made. North Viet Nam insisted that the United States withdraw all its troops from Viet Nam. North Viet Nam also demanded that the United States end its support of the South Viet Nam government.

In May of 1969, President Nixon proposed an end to the war, based on withdrawal of all foreign troops from Viet Nam. As a start, he promised to pull out 25 thousand American troops. Soon after, President Thieu (THE-u) of South Viet Nam offered to hold free elections in which the Communists could take part. President Nixon also stated that he was considering withdrawing 100 thousand more American troops by the end of 1969. But he expected North Viet Nam also to begin to withdraw its troops. In the summer of 1969, the level of fighting in Viet Nam fell off. Americans hoped that this marked the beginning of the ending of the war.

President Nixon talks with troops during his visit to South Viet Nam in 1969.

The Senate and President Nixon

In June of 1969, the Senate passed a recommendation asking President Nixon not to send troops overseas without the approval of Congress. The President did not have to accept this recommendation. But it did help to remind him that many Americans wanted an end to the Viet Nam War as soon as possible. In July of 1969, President Nixon traveled to several Asian nations. In the Philippines, he pledged that the United States never again would become involved in another war in Asia like the one in Viet Nam.

A Treaty Limiting Nuclear Weapons

Earlier in 1969, the Senate approved a treaty to limit the use of nuclear weapons. In the treaty, the United States, the Soviet Union, and eighty other nations agreed not to help any other nation build up its nuclear power. Many Americans hoped that this treaty might soon lead to other disarmament agreements between the United States and the Soviet Union. And in November of 1969, the United States and the Soviet Union began talks about nuclear disarmament.

Congress Approved a Missile Defense System

Congress had trouble making up its mind about an **anti-ballistic missile system** called A.B.M. The purpose of the defense weapon system was to protect America from atomic attack. In 1968, Congress approved the building of a "thin" A.B.M. missile system. This system was planned to be strong enough to protect the United States from Communist China but not from the Soviet Union.

Some members of Congress felt that this "thin" missile system must be expanded so that American cities might be protected from attack. The estimated cost of this new expanded missile system was 100 billion dollars.

Here, automobiles are stuck in a city traffic jam. Traffic tie-ups are one of the many problems facing American cities.

Other Congressmen felt that the A.B.M. system did not really provide the United States with effective protection. They also felt that the huge cost of this system might leave the federal government with little money to spend on many other important needs.

President Nixon tried to compromise by suggesting that A.B.M. sites be built only to protect important American military bases and Washington, D.C. The cost of this system was to be about 7 billion dollars. It was to be built and ready by 1975. After much debate, Congress approved this plan.

Serious Problems in America's Cities

President Nixon also faced many serious problems at home. The most difficult of these problems concerned America's cities. The United States was now an **urban nation**—a nation where nearly two out of every three persons lived in cities. Life in an urban nation was filled with difficulties. City houses and apartments often were crowded, and many city dwellers lived in slums. Too many automobiles created traffic tie-ups. Crime increased rapidly in most American cities. City air often was smoky and harmful to breathe.

To escape these problems, many white city dwellers moved from the cities to the suburbs. At the same time, many black Americans, Puerto Ricans, and Mexican-Americans moved to the cities. As a result, cities had fewer sources of tax money at a time when they needed more money to provide welfare for the poor and many other services.

Workers in a Post Office.

THE POST OFFICE DEPARTMENT

During colonial days, colonists did not receive regular mail service. However, when Benjamin Franklin became Postmaster General of the colonies in 1751, he set up an improved mail service. When the United States was established, the Founding Fathers realized that mail delivery was important. Therefore, the Constitution gave Congress the power "to establish Post Offices and Post Roads." The federal government has run the Post Office Department ever since.

Today, the Post Office Department is headed by the Postmaster General, who is a member of the President's Cabinet. However, Congress also helps run the department. It fixes postage rates and salaries of post office workers.

The Post Office today is a big business. But it costs the federal government many millions of dollars each year. And as more mail is sent each year, mail service faces more and more problems. For this reason, President Johnson set up a commission to study ways to improve the Post Office. This commission suggested that the Post Office be turned into a public business corporation and run as a business corporation. A law passed in 1970 ended Congress' control over the Post Office and made it an independent agency.

President Nixon and Congress began to plan major programs to help America's cities solve their problems in the 1970's. New ways to share taxes between cities, states, and the federal government were discussed. New ideas were discussed to improve city schools and to provide better housing and living conditions in America's cities. By the 1970's, the American people were beginning to work together to improve city life.

A New Program to Help the Poor

President Nixon sent Congress a plan to improve government programs of aid to poor Americans. He proposed giving 1,600 dollars a year in federal money to families in which no one had a job. State governments were going to continue to help support these families, too. President Nixon also asked Congress to set up a program to help train jobless workers in poor families to find new jobs. He proposed that Congress set up day care centers to care for children in poor families while their parents were away at work. With this plan, the federal government hoped to help solve the difficult problem of poverty in America.

Summing Up

As soon as President Nixon began his term in January of 1969, he faced the serious problem of the Viet Nam War. The new President worked to try to bring an end to this conflict. By the summer of 1969, the fighting in Viet Nam had slowed down, but the war continued. In the United States, Congress approved a missile defense system after long debate. The problems of cities and how to solve them became the most serious task facing President Nixon at home. In the next chapter, you will learn about the problems of black Americans and the black power movement in the 1960's.

AFTER YOU READ THE CHAPTER

Do You Know These Important Terms?

In the sentences below, select the term that best completes the sentence.

1. The defense weapon-system designed to protect America from atomic attack was called the (**Apollo-Zeus/anti-ballistic missile**) system.
2. An (**urban/rural**) nation is a nation where most people live in cities.

Do You Remember This Person?

Tell something about the following person.

Richard M. Nixon

Can You Locate These Places?

On a map of Asia, do the following map work.

Locate Viet Nam and the Philippines. What promise did President Nixon make when he visited the Philippines? Why do you think he chose this place to make the announcement?

Do You Know When It Happened?

What are the years of this chapter? When is the A.B.M. system supposed to be completed?

Discovering More About the Main Idea

The main problem facing President Nixon was the Viet Nam War. He also had to deal with problems of defense and the growing problems of American cities.

Tell how each of the following developments is related to the MAIN IDEA.

Some American troops were pulled out of Viet Nam in 1969. President Nixon pledged that the United States would never again become involved in another war in Asia like the one in Viet Nam.

The United States, the Soviet Union, and eighty other nations signed a treaty to limit the use of nuclear weapons.

At the same time many white families moved from cities to the suburbs, many black Americans, Puerto Ricans, and Mexican-Americans moved to the cities. As a result, cities had fewer sources of tax money.

Can You Discuss the Chapter?

Use the information you read in this chapter to answer the following questions.

1. How did President Nixon go about trying to end the war in Viet Nam?
2. Why did Congress have trouble making up its mind about an anti-ballistic missile system?
3. What are some of the problems of an urban nation?
4. What was President Nixon's new program to help the poor?
5. Do you think the United States should pull its troops out of South Viet Nam if North Viet Nam does not withdraw its troops? Why or why not?

Can You Connect the Past and the Present?

1. Which of the urban problems listed in this chapter are also problems in your community?
2. What projects have recently been set up in your community to help poor people?

CHAPTER 116

The Black Power Movement

Malcolm X speaking in Harlem in New York City.

BEFORE YOU BEGIN THE CHAPTER

Know What to Look For

1. Dr. Martin Luther King, Jr., was one of the leaders of the civil rights movement in the 1960's. He believed in non-violent methods, such as protest marches, to win equal rights for all Americans. In 1964, he was awarded the Nobel Peace Prize for his work in the civil rights movement.

In 1968, Dr. King went to Memphis, Ten-

nessee, to lead a non-violent march in support of some striking workers. On the evening of April 4, while standing on the balcony of a motel talking with friends, Dr. King was shot. He died within minutes. Dr. King gave his life for a cause in which he believed. On his gravestone these words which he spoke in one of his last speeches are carved.

Free at last.

Free at last.

Thank God Almighty, I'm free at last. In this chapter, you will read about the civil rights movement in the 1960's.

2. Read the title of the chapter. Then look through the chapter and read each heading. From the headings, tell some ways that black Americans tried to gain their rights.

3. Look at the pictures in the chapter and read each caption. What do the pictures tell you about black Americans in the 1960's? Next look at the time line at the beginning of the chapter. What years are included in the chapter? Compare this chapter time line to the unit time line on page 709.

4. Read the last part of the chapter called Summing Up. What aims did the black power leaders have for black Americans?

Know These Important Terms
Kerner Report
Poor People's Campaign
black power movement
Black Muslims
Civil Rights Act of 1968

Know the Main Idea
Here is the MAIN IDEA of this chapter.
As peaceful efforts to improve the lives of black Americans slowed down, the black power movement developed.

Keep this MAIN IDEA in mind as you read the chapter. Ask yourself the following questions as you read. They will help you remember the MAIN IDEA.

1. Where were the effects of discrimination most clearly seen?
2. What program was organized to influence Congress to pass laws for the benefit of poor Americans?
3. What organization wants to establish a separate nation for black Americans within the United States?

THE YEARS OF THIS CHAPTER ARE 1963 TO 1970

| 1960 | 1963 | 1970 |

THE CHAPTER LESSON BEGINS HERE

Black Americans Still Faced Discrimination

During the 1950's and 1960's, black Americans won many civil rights. More black citizens were voting than ever before. Segregation in public places was outlawed. But most black students still attended segregated schools. Most black Americans still lived in segregated, or separate, communities apart from white Americans. And most black Americans still suffered from economic discrimination. That is, they often did not have an equal opportunity to work at many jobs.

And many black Americans worked at low-paying jobs and did not share in the nation's rich economy.

Part of the economic problem was due to the fact that black workers often were unskilled workers. But even more important was the slowness of businesses and labor unions to give equal opportunities to black workers. Black workers were often limited to the least skilled and least interesting jobs. And unemployment among black workers was much

Dr. Martin Luther King, Jr., stands on the balcony of the motel where he was shot.

more serious riot broke out in the Watts neighborhood in Los Angeles. In the next few years, other serious riots took place in the ghettos of Detroit, Cleveland, Newark, and many other cities.

These riots shocked the American nation. The federal government formed a commission, or group of experts, to study the causes of the riots. This commission wrote a thorough report—often called the **Kerner Report.** The Kerner Report made many suggestions for the improvement of housing, education, jobs, and welfare services for black Americans. However, little immediate progress was made in carrying out these suggestions.

Dr. King and His Dream for America

Martin Luther King, Jr., still believed that non-violence, or a peaceful effort, was the most effective way to improve life for all Americans. In 1966, he tried without much success to improve housing conditions for the black people of Chicago. And in 1968, he organized the **Poor People's Campaign.** The purpose of this campaign, or program, was to influence Congress to pass laws for the benefit of poor Americans.

Dr. King hoped that a march on Washington, D.C., might help the poor people of America, many of whom were black. Unfortunately, Dr. King met his tragic death before the "army of the poor" reached Washington, D.C.

The Poor People's Campaign Failed

The Reverend Ralph D. Abernathy, one of Dr. King's co-workers, took over the leadership of the Poor People's Campaign. Not only black Americans, but also Spanish-Americans, Indians, Puerto Ricans, and some poor white Americans joined in the campaign. They built housing for themselves in the park near the Washington monument, and they called this

higher than unemployment among white workers.

Riots in the Ghettos

The effects of discrimination were most clearly seen in the ghettos, or black neighborhoods, of many large American cities. Black people living in these ghettos felt that they were not sharing in many of the benefits of American life. They saw little hope of improving their lives or the lives of their children.

In 1964, a riot broke out in New York City's Harlem ghetto. In the following year, an even settlement in Washington Resurrection City.

The Poor People's Campaign reminded the American people that poverty still existed in America. But Congress failed to pass new laws to help the poor. In June of 1968, the poor people left Resurrection City and returned to their homes. The failure of the Poor People's Campaign made some black Americans feel that peaceful efforts were no longer useful in bringing about improvement and change in their lives.

The Civil Rights Act of 1968

A short while after Dr. King's death, Congress passed the **Civil Rights Act of 1968.** This law, known as the open housing act, was a memorial to Dr. King. The law forbade discrimination in the sale or rental of housing. This meant that it was unlawful to refuse to rent or sell housing to any American because of his race, color, or religion. Only homes in which the owner lived and which the owner himself sold were not covered by this law. The act also gave federal protection to civil rights workers.

The Black Power Movement Developed

In the late 1960's, the **black power movement** began to develop. The black power movement aimed at getting black Americans to depend more on working together to improve their own lives. The black power movement hoped to encourage new businesses owned and operated by black people. It hoped to work for the election of black candidates to public government offices. It tried to establish community control of the schools in the black ghettos. And the black power movement worked to develop black Americans' pride in their history and in the achievements of black people everywhere.

During the late 1960's, the term "black

Dr. King receives the Nobel Peace Prize.

DR. KING'S "DREAM"

Dr. Martin Luther King, Jr., was the minister of a church in Montgomery, Alabama, in 1955 when Mrs. Rosa Parks was arrested for refusing to give up her seat in the white section of a bus. After her arrest, the black citizens of Montgomery decided to boycott, or refuse to ride, city public buses. Dr. King led this bus boycott, which resulted in an end to segregation on buses in Montgomery. After this, Dr. King became an important leader in the civil rights movement.

Dr. King believed in non-violent protest, or peaceful action, to gain equal rights. The high point of non-violent protest in the civil rights movement was the March on Washington in 1963. At this march, over 200 thousand Americans gathered at the Lincoln Memorial. There, Dr. King told them of his "dream" of freedom and equality for all Americans.

"I have a dream that my little children will one day live in a nation where they will not be judged by the color of their skin, but by the content of their character.

"This is our hope . . . with this faith we will be able to hew out of the mountain of despair a stone of hope."

The three black mayors of major American cities, Carl Stokes, Walter Washington, and Richard Hatcher, speak with Robert Weaver (left).

power" was used by many black Americans. But the goals of the black power movement were not new. Marcus Garvey, W. E. B. Du Bois, and Booker T. Washington supplied many of its basic ideas. Today, the black power movement is strongest among young black Americans who feel that the progress of black people in the United States must depend on the efforts of black Americans themselves.

Some Black Groups Worked for Separation

Other groups of black Americans have gone beyond black power. The best known example of such a group is the **Black Muslims.** The Black Muslim movement was organized by Elijah Muhammad (moo-HA-mud) during the 1930's. The Black Muslims want to establish a separate nation for black Americans within the United States. A belief in hard work and in strict discipline are extremely im-

portant parts of the Black Muslim movement.

One of the best known of the Black Muslims was Malcolm X. At the end of 1963, Malcolm X left the Black Muslims because he felt their teachings were wrong. Malcolm X then formed his own group. Two years later, Malcolm X was murdered, but his influence among young black people remained strong. His emphasis on black pride was taken over by the black power movement. Another well-known group is the Black Panther party.

Summing Up

As peaceful efforts to improve the lives of black Americans slowed down, the black power movement developed. Black power leaders aimed to have black Americans gain greater economic, political, and social power by their own efforts. The Black Muslims began to work for complete separation. In the next chapter, you will read about America's economy, its successes and failures.

AFTER YOU READ THE CHAPTER

Do You Know These Important Terms?

In each of the sentences below, select the term that best completes the sentence.

1. The report of the commission which studied the causes of riots was called the (**Kerner/ Watts**) Report.
2. The (**March on Poverty/Poor People's**) Campaign was set up to influence Congress to pass laws for poor Americans.
3. The (**Civil Rights Act of 1968/Housing Act of 1968**) forbade discrimination in the sale or rental of housing.
4. The movement that aimed at getting black Americans to work together to improve their lives was the (**black power/black imperialism**) movement.
5. A group that wants to establish a separate nation for black Americans is called the (**Black United Front/Black Muslims**).

Do You Remember These People?

Tell something about each of the following persons.

Elijah Muhammad   Marcus Garvey
Ralph D. Abernathy   Malcolm X
Martin Luther King, Jr.   W. E. B. Du Bois
Booker T. Washington

Can You Locate These Places?

Use a map of the United States to locate the following places.

New York City   Los Angeles
Detroit   Cleveland
Newark   Washington, D.C.

Do You Know When It Happened?

What are the years of this chapter?

Arrange the following events in the order in which they occurred.

A riot broke out in Harlem in New York City.

Dr. King was shot and killed.

The Black Muslim movement was organized.

A riot broke out in Watts.

The poor people left Resurrection City.

Discovering More About the Main Idea

As peaceful efforts to improve the lives of black Americans slowed down, the black power movement developed.

Tell how each of the following developments is related to the MAIN IDEA.

Segregation and economic discrimination continued in many areas. Riots took place in many ghettos in American cities.

The Poor People's Campaign was organized to help poor people, but it failed to convince Congress to pass new laws.

Some groups of black Americans believed in the separation of black and white Americans.

Can You Discuss the Chapter?

Use the information you learned in this chapter to answer the following questions.

1. What kinds of discrimination did black Americans still face in the 1960's?
2. What dream did Martin Luther King, Jr., have for America?
3. Explain what is meant by the black power movement.
4. Why do you think that some groups of black Americans have begun to work for separation?

Can You Connect the Past and the Present?

1. How has the black power movement operated in your community?
2. What labor unions are active in your community? Do they accept black members?

America's Modern Economy

Industry on Lake Michigan.

BEFORE YOU BEGIN THE CHAPTER

Know What To Look For

1. A computer is a complex machine that is able to do many jobs. This machine has almost completely changed our lives. Today, businesses would be lost without computers. If you look at one of your parents' monthly bills, you will probably find that it was calculated and prepared by a computer. In large schools, computers are used to schedule pupils' classes.

Computers can store vast amounts of information. These machines then use this stored information to work out complex mathematical problems in seconds. The same problems might take a man hours or even days to figure out. In this chapter, you will read more about computers. You will also read about the modern economy of America.

2. Read the title of this chapter. Then

look through the chapter and read each heading. Judging by the headings, how would you rate the present-day economy of the nation?

3. Look at the pictures in the chapter and read each caption. What do the pictures tell you about America's economy? Note also the time line at the beginning of the chapter. What years are included in this chapter? Compare this chapter time line to the unit time line on page 709.

4. Read the last part of the chapter called Summing Up. What problem do most Americans believe must soon be solved?

Know These Important Terms
computers   computer programmers

Know the Main Idea

Here is the MAIN IDEA of this chapter.

Today, the United States is the richest nation in the world. Although most Americans enjoy good times, one out of every five Americans still lives in poverty.

Keep this MAIN IDEA in mind as you study this chapter. Ask yourself the following questions as you read. They will help you remember the MAIN IDEA.

1. What new industry now provides jobs for 5 million workers?

2. What two facts help explain the increase in farm production?

3. What problem do many Americans still suffer from in spite of good times?

THE YEARS OF THIS CHAPTER ARE 1960 TO 1970

1960   1970

THE CHAPTER LESSON BEGINS HERE

Times Are Good in the United States

The United States is today the richest nation in the world. Its factories produce almost as many goods as the rest of the world's factories put together. Most of its workers have jobs. These workers produce more goods and buy more than ever before. And workers' wages and businesses' profits both continue to increase.

Most industries are sharing in these good times. But the biggest gainers are the newer industries, such as aviation and electronics. An entirely new industry—the space industry—has developed in recent years. The space industry alone now provides jobs for 5 million workers.

Government Spending Affects Business

One of the reasons for the rapid growth of the space and electronics industries is the huge amount of money spent by the federal government. Each year, the American government spends billions of dollars to buy products for both peaceful and military uses. This high rate of government spending does a great deal to keep American businesses operating.

Profitable companies often try to merge, or join together. Sometimes, these mergers can form a company so large that it might control an entire industry. In these cases, the government enforces anti-trust laws to prevent such a merger. Although the government tries to stop unfair mergers, it does not limit the size of businesses. Today, many American business companies continue to grow larger and larger.

Americans have more money to spend than ever before. Here, cars are parked at a large suburban shopping center.

Automation Has Increased

Another reason for the growth in American industry is the increase in automation. As you read, automation, or the use of automatically controlled machines, began in the 1950's. Today, these machines regulate themselves through the feedback of information. This feedback is done by the use of **computers.**

Fifteen years ago, 500 computers were in use in the United States. Today, many thousands of computers are in operation. Large companies own their own computers. Smaller companies rent them. Computers are used to keep business office records, control factory machinery, run oil refineries and steel mills, and to solve complex engineering and business problems.

Automation Affects Workers

Automation makes it possible for an industry to make better and cheaper products. Usually, automation also cuts down on the number of workers needed in a factory. If properly retrained, some of these workers can be used to operate and service the new automatic machines. But others are no longer needed, and they are without jobs.

But automation also creates many new jobs. Many thousands of workers are needed to make automatic machines and the computers which operate them. Large numbers of office workers called **computer programmers** are needed to collect and organize, or program, information to be used by computers in solving problems and keeping records. But the unskilled worker often lacks a job in the age of automation.

Farming Has Changed Greatly

American farming today is far different from what it used to be. Farming, too, is becoming a big business. The number of farms keeps growing smaller while the size of each farm keeps increasing. Also, the size of the total crop grown keeps increasing each year at the same time that the number of farmers decreases.

Two facts help to explain this greatly increased farm production by an ever smaller number of farmers. One is the greatly increased use of large farm machinery. Today, mechanical cotton pickers are common in the South, and mechanical corn pickers are common in the Middle West. The second fact is the greater use of scientific farming methods. Farmers now use chemicals to kill insect pests, to fertilize the soil, and to improve the kinds of crops they grow.

The farm policies of the federal government also help to explain the changes in the number and size of farms. The government keeps farm prices from dropping below a certain level. These prices are not high enough for a small, inefficient farmer to make a profit. Therefore, he sells his farm. But these prices are high enough to make it worthwhile for an efficient, large farmer to buy the small farm. He then adds it to his own land, and this increases his own crop and his profits.

Some Americans Are Poor

In spite of the generally good times today, many Americans are still poor. Poverty is hard to define, but most experts agree that at least one fifth of all American families still fall below the poverty level. These families are made up largely of older couples, poor farm families, handicapped and jobless workers, and black Americans, Mexican-Americans, and Puerto Ricans. The problems of each of

These farm machines are cutting wheat. Today, farmers use many farm machines and scientific farming methods.

This picture shows a poor area in Appalachia. Many American families in this region still live in poverty.

these groups of families are different, of course. Therefore, different solutions are needed for each group. Increased Social Security pension benefits may be the answer for the older group. Vocational training may be the answer for the jobless and the handicapped. Higher minimum wages and job relocation may be the answer for farm families. And fair treatment in hiring and promotion practices may be the answer for black Americans, Mexican-Americans, and Puerto Ricans.

New Solutions for Poverty

Many Americans agree with President Nixon that the federal government must improve the system of welfare payments to the poor. If you remember, President Nixon, in August, 1969, asked Congress to improve America's welfare system. Many Americans believe that Congress should try to keep each family's income above a certain level, just as it does with farm prices. If the head of the family does not earn an income equal or greater than this minimum income level, the federal government must help the state governments to pay the difference.

Summing Up

Times are generally good in the United States today. Businesses are growing larger and more profitable. Farms, too, are becoming bigger as the number of farms decreases. But despite the good times, one fifth of all Americans today suffer from poverty, and the problem is one that most Americans believe must soon be solved. New ways to solve this problem are being considered.

AFTER YOU READ THE CHAPTER

Do You Know These Important Terms?

In the sentences below, select the term that best completes the sentence.

1. A (feed-back/**computer**) is a complex machine used to keep records and to solve engineering and business problems.
2. Workers who collect, organize, and plan information for use in computers are called computer (operators/**programmers**).

Do You Remember These People?

Tell something about each of the following persons, including their names.
the President of the United States
the Vice-President of the United States
the Secretary of State
the Governor of your state
the chief executive of your town or city

Can You Locate These Places?

Use a map of the United States to do the following map work.

1. Find the approximate location of your home. How would you describe its location in the United States?
2. Do you live in an urban, suburban, or rural community? How does this location relate to the problems of your community?

Do You Know When It Happened?

What are the years of this chapter? When did automation in industry begin?

Discovering More About the Main Idea

Today, the United States is the richest nation in the world. Although most Americans enjoy good times, one out of every five Americans still lives in poverty.

Tell how each of the following developments is related to the MAIN IDEA.

New industries, growth in businesses, and government spending have helped bring about good times in the United States.

Automation and computers have hurt unskilled workers, but they have also created many new jobs for other workers. Automation has also been an important reason for the growth in American industry.

The size of farms and the size of the total farm crop keeps growing while the number of farms and farmers keeps growing smaller. In spite of good times, many Americans are still poor. Americans believe that this problem of poverty must be solved.

Can You Discuss the Chapter?

Use the information you learned in this chapter to answer the following questions.

1. How does government spending affect business in the United States?
2. What are computers used for? How do they affect workers?
3. Why does farm production continue to increase even though the number of farms and farmers continues to decrease?
4. Which groups of Americans still face the problem of poverty?
5. Would you be in favor of a minimum income level? Why or why not?

Can You Connect the Past and the Present?

1. How does the change in the kinds of jobs affect you as a student?
2. Are any new types of industries located in your community? What kinds of jobs do they provide?

Glossary

This glossary contains the meanings of special terms in American history that you will learn in the chapters of this book. Use this glossary to study and review these important historical terms.

abolition movement: the efforts of many Americans to end slavery in the 1800's.

abolitionists: a group of Americans in the 1800's who worked to end slavery.

Adams-Onís (oh-NEES) **Treaty:** an agreement between the United States and Spain in 1819, in which Spain agreed to sell Florida to the United States.

Agricultural Adjustment Act: a law passed by Congress in 1933 to help farmers suffering from the Great Depression to get higher prices for their crops. A second Agricultural Adjustment Act was passed in 1938.

Albany Congress: a meeting held at Albany, New York, in 1754 at which colonial leaders and Iroquois Indians promised to help Great Britain fight against the French forces in America.

Albany Plan: a plan proposed by Benjamin Franklin in 1754 to unite the colonies to fight against the French.

Alien Acts: laws passed by Congress in 1798, which made it more difficult for aliens to become American citizens and which gave the President power to force aliens to leave the United States.

aliens (AY-lee-unz): people who live in the United States but who are citizens of another nation.

Alliance for Progress: a plan to improve living conditions and businesses in Latin America.

Allies: the name given to Great Britain, France, Russia, the United States, and other nations that fought against the Central Powers in World War One.

Allies: the name given to Great Britain, France, the United States, the Soviet Union, and other nations that fought against the Axis Powers in World War Two.

amendments (uh-MEND-munts): changes or additions made in the Constitution of the United States.

American Federation of Labor: a labor union formed in 1881 to include only skilled workers.

American System: the name given by Republican Congressmen in the early 1800's to their plan for helping the United States to grow.

anti-ballistic missile system: the defense weapon system approved by Congress in 1969 to protect our nation from atomic attack.

Anti-Federalists (AN-ti-FED-uh-ruhl-ists): those Americans who did not want the Constitution of the United States to be approved.

armistice (AHR-muh-stuss): the official end of fighting in a war.

Articles of Confederation (kun-FED-uh-uh-RAY-shun): the first plan of government for the new American nation, which lasted from 1781 to 1789.

assembly: the name given to the lower house, or elected members, of the legislature in each of the English colonies.

assembly line: a line of workers who are trained to do particular jobs in putting together a product or machine as the parts move past them in the factory.

Atlantic Charter: a statement of the Allies' war aims in World War Two.

Atomic Energy Act: a law passed by Congress in 1946 to regulate the development and use of atomic energy.

Attorney (uh-TUR-nee) **General:** the member of the President's Cabinet who serves as the chief law officer of the government.

automation (AW-tuh-MAY-shun): the use of automatic, or self-operating, machines in modern factories and offices.

Axis Powers: the name given to Germany, Italy, and Japan when they fought against the Allies in World War Two.

Aztec (AZ-teck) **Indians:** Indians who built a great nation in Mexico and were conquered by explorers in the early 1500's.

Bacon's Rebellion: an uprising in Virginia in which Western settlers demanded that the Eastern colonists provide protection against Indian attacks and allow Westerners to elect members to the legislature.

Berlin airlift: the flying in of needed supplies to Berlin during the Berlin blockade of 1948 and 1949.

Berlin blockade: the Soviet Union's attempt in 1948 and 1949 to cut off all travel and all shipments of food and supplies between West Germany and Berlin.

Berlin Wall: a wall built in 1961 by the Communist government of East Germany to prevent people from escaping from East Berlin to West Berlin.

Big Three nations: the United States, Great Britain, and the Soviet Union—the three Allies that fought together and planned for peace during World War Two.

bill of rights: a list of important freedoms included in the new state constitutions that were written during and after the Revolutionary War.

Bill of Rights: the name given to the first ten amendments to the Constitution of the United States, which promise important freedoms to all American citizens.

black codes: state laws that ruled the lives of slaves during the 1800's.

black conventions: meetings held in the 1830's and 1840's by black Americans who joined together to work for equal rights.

black power movement: the efforts to have black Americans gain greater economic, political, and social power by their own actions and by working together.

blockade: the placing of armed ships around a seaport in order to cut off trade.

border states: the four states located between the North and the South which remained in the Union in 1861—Maryland, Delaware, Missouri, and Kentucky.

Boxer Rebellion: an uprising in China in 1900 in which a group called the Boxers tried to force all foreigners to leave China.

boycotted: refused to use the services of a person or business to force them to do something.

breadbasket colonies: the name given to the Middle colonies because they grew and sold so much wheat, which is used in making bread.

Brown against the Board of Education of Topeka: an important law case in 1954 in which the Supreme Court ruled that segregation in public schools was unlawful and must be ended.

Bull Moose Party: a third political party formed in 1912 by Republicans who broke away from their party because they wanted to continue the Progressive programs of Theodore Roosevelt.

Cabinet: the group of men chosen by the President to head the executive departments and to help him carry out his job.

carpetbaggers: Northerners who moved to the South during the years of Reconstruction and who took an active part in rebuilding the South.

Central Powers: the name given to Germany, Austria-Hungary, Bulgaria, and Turkey when they fought against the Allies in World War One.

Central Treaty Organization: an agreement among several free nations against the spread of Communism.

Chautauqua (shuh-TAW-kwuh) **movement:** an educational movement that began in the 1870's, which taught art, music, plays, and other subjects to Americans in many parts of the nation.

Church of England: the church formed in 1534 by King Henry the Eighth of England as the official church for all Englishmen.

civil rights: all the rights, or freedoms, which the Constitution and its amendments guarantee to all American citizens.

Civil Rights Act of 1957: a law passed by Congress which gave federal judges the right to jail anyone who stopped a qualified person from voting.

Civil Rights Act of 1960: a law passed by Congress which gave the federal government the power to help register voters who are unlawfully prevented from voting by state or local officials.

Civil Rights Act of 1964: a law passed by Congress which ended segregation in public places.

Civil Rights Act of 1968: a law passed by Congress which forbade discrimination in the sale or rental of housing.

civil rights movement: the efforts of black Americans, supported by other Americans, to gain equal rights for all American citizens.

Civil War: another name for the War Between the North and the South.

Clayton Anti-Trust Act: a law passed by Congress in 1914 that forbade certain unfair practices by big business companies.

Cold War: the struggle between the free nations and the Communist nations of the world that began after 1945.

colonies: settlements that a nation makes in a new land overseas.

colonists: people who leave their own country to settle in a new or unsettled land.

Colored Farmers' Alliance: a black farmers' group formed in the South in the 1800's to get laws passed to help farmers and improve farm life.

commercial farming: farming in which crops are grown to be sold rather than to be used by the farmer and his family.

commercial industry: manufacturing in which products are made in order to be sold.

Committee of Public Information: a group set up by the federal government during World War One to encourage all Americans to support the war effort.

Committees of Correspondence: organized groups of colonists who wrote letters to each other shortly before the Revolutionary War, to exchange information on what the British were doing in their colonies.

Communism: a form of government in which the government owns everything in the nation, and in which people are told where to work, what to do, and whom to vote for in elections.

Compromise of 1850: the agreement reached by Congress in 1850 that settled the slavery question in the new Western lands.

compromises: agreements between two sides in which each side gives up part of what it wants.

computers: electronic machines which handle information with great speed and accuracy and which are used in many industries and businesses to solve problems and to control other machines.

Confederacy: another name for the Confederate States of America.

Confederate States of America: the name used by the eleven Southern states that seceded from the United States in 1860 and 1861 to form a separate nation.

Congress: the national law-making group of the United States.

Congress of Industrial Organizations: a labor union formed in the 1930's which included both skilled and unskilled workers in an industry.

Congressional Reconstruction: the program worked out by Congress to rebuild the South after the War Between the North and the South.

conservation (KAHN-sur-VAY-shun): the wise use of soil, forests, mines, and other natural resources.

constitution: a written plan of government.

Constitution of the United States: the new and stronger plan of government for the United States that was drawn up at Philadelphia in 1787.

Constitutional Convention: the meeting of American leaders at Philadelphia in 1787, at which they worked out a new and stronger plan of government for the United States.

Constitutional Union Party: a political party formed in 1860 whose chief aim was to keep the nation united.

Copperheads: Northerners who tried to help the South during the War Between the North and the South.

Crittenden (KRIT-un-dun) **Compromise:** a plan suggested in 1861 to bring the Southern states back into the Union.

Crusades (kroo-SADES): religious wars that began in 1096 and lasted for 200 years, in which Europeans failed to capture the Holy Land from the Moslems.

Declaration of Independence: the famous document of July 4, 1776, which stated the American colonists' reasons for wanting to be independent from Great Britain.

Declaratory (di-KLAR-uh-tor-ee) **Act:** a British law of 1766 that gave Parliament the right to pass laws for the colonies.

Democratic Party: a political party which was formed during the 1820's by Andrew Jackson and his followers.

Department of Agriculture: a department of the federal government that gives useful information to farmers and advises the President about farm problems.

Department of Health, Education, and Welfare: a department of the federal government set up in 1953 to look out for the needs of the American people.

Department of Housing and Urban Development: a department of the federal government set up in 1965 to help American cities solve their problems.

Department of Transportation: a department of the federal government set up in 1966 to help improve the nation's highway, railroad, sea, and air travel systems.

dictatorship: a government in which one man, or a small group of men, has complete power to govern a nation and to order the people to obey.

direct primary election: a special election in which American voters have the right to choose their own candidates for office.

domestic industry: the making of products, such as furniture and tools, for a family's own use rather than for sale.

Eastern Woodland Indians: Indians who lived in the forests along the eastern coast of North America.

Economic Opportunity Act: a law passed by Congress in 1964 to give job training to young Americans from low-income families.

Eighteenth Amendment: the amendment to the Constitution, approved in 1919, which made it unlawful to sell or buy alcoholic drinks.

Eisenhower Doctrine: a plan announced by President Dwight D. Eisenhower in 1957 to send aid to and to help defend any Middle Eastern nation against Communism.

electoral votes: the votes of members of the electoral college that officially elect the President and Vice-President of the United States.

Elementary and Secondary Education Act of 1965: a law passed by Congress to enable the federal government to provide money to help improve American elementary schools and high schools.

Elkins Act: a law passed by Congress in 1903 that made the accepting of rebates unlawful.

Emancipation Proclamation (ih-MAN-suh-PAY-shun PRAHK-luh-MAY-shun): President Abraham Lincoln's order that all slaves in Confederate States were to be set free on January 1, 1863.

Embargo Act: a law passed by Congress in 1807 which forbade American ships to sail to any foreign ports and also closed American ports to all foreign ships.

executive branch: that part of the federal government which carries out our laws and is headed by the President.

Fair Deal: President Harry S. Truman's program of change and reform for the American nation.

Farewell Address: George Washington's last speech as President, in which he advised Americans about matters that were important to the nation's future.

Farm Security Administration: a federal agency set up during the 1930's which loaned money to tenant farmers to help them buy their own farms.

Federal Farm Loan Act: a law passed by Congress in 1916 which set up special banks to help farmers borrow money more easily.

federal government: a government in which the powers are divided between the national government and the state governments; another name for the national government of the United States.

Federal Reserve System: a federal banking system set up in 1913 to regulate the nation's banking and money.

Federal Trade Commission Act: a law passed by Congress in 1914 which set up a federal commission to enforce the anti-trust laws.

Federalist Party: an early political party led by Alexander Hamilton which was made up of large land owners, merchants, and bankers who favored a strong federal government.

Federalists (FED-uh-ruhl-ists): those Americans who wanted the Constitution of the United States to be approved.

Fifteenth Amendment: the amendment to the Constitution, approved in 1870, which gave black Americans the right to vote.

First Continental (KAHN-tuh-NEN-tul) **Congress:** a meeting of colonial leaders held at Philadelphia in 1774 to demand that Great Britain stop punishing Massachusetts and stop taxing the colonies.

Founding Fathers: the men who wrote the Constitution of the United States in Philadelphia in 1787.

Fourteen Points: President Woodrow Wilson's plan for making a lasting peace after World War One.

Fourteenth Amendment: the amendment to the Constitution, approved in 1868, which made all black Americans citizens of the United States.

Freedmen's Bureau: an agency set up by the federal government in 1865 to help the former slaves in the South after the Civil War.

freedom rides: a method used by black Americans and white Americans as part of the civil rights movement to help end segregation in Southern bus and train stations.

Free-Soilers: a political party which was formed in 1848 by Americans who were strongly against the spread of slavery.

French and Indian War: a war between Great Britain and France that was fought in North America from 1754 to 1763.

frontier: the unsettled land in the colonies just beyond the settled areas.

Fugitive Slave Act: a law passed by Congress as part of the Compromise of 1850, which required all Americans to help capture runaway slaves and return them to their owners.

Gadsden (GADZ-dun) **Purchase:** a small strip of land in the southwestern part of the United States that was bought from Mexico in 1853.

Good Neighbor Policy: President Franklin D. Roosevelt's plan in the 1930's for improving United States relations with Latin American nations.

gradual abolition: the program favored by some Americans in the 1800's to end slavery slowly by first working out a plan to pay slave owners for their slaves.

Granges: farmers' groups formed in the 1870's to help farmers improve their way of life.

Great Awakening: a new interest in religion that started in the colonies in the 1730's.

Great Depression: the period of very hard times which our nation faced during the 1930's, when many businesses closed and millions of workers were without jobs.

Great Society: President Lyndon B. Johnson's plan to help improve the American nation.

hard money: money backed by gold.

Harlem Renaissance (REN-uh-sans): a period beginning in the 1920's when black Americans produced outstanding books, poetry, and works of art that described the life and problems of black Americans.

Hepburn Act: a law passed by Congress in 1906 that gave the Interstate Commerce Commission the power to regulate railroad rates.

Home Owners Loan Corporation: a federal agency set up in 1933 to help home owners suffering from the Great Depression to keep their homes.

Homestead Act: a law passed by Congress in 1862 that gave 160 acres of Western land free to any American who was willing to farm the land for five years.

House of Burgesses (BURR-juh-suz): the law-making group in the Virginia colony.

immediate abolition: the program favored by some Americans in the 1800's to end slavery quickly by making slave owners free their slaves without being paid for them.

immigrants (IM-uh-grunts): people who come to the United States from other nations and settle here.

Immigration and Nationality Act: a law passed by Congress in 1965 which replaced the quota system with an immigration system that allowed people from all over the world to enter the United States.

impeach: to accuse a government official of misconduct or unlawful acts, for which he must stand trial.

imperialism (ihm-PIRH-ee-ul-IZ-um): a belief held by many Americans in the late 1800's and early 1900's that a nation needs many overseas colonies and territories in order to be powerful.

impressed: forced to serve in a foreign army or navy.

Inca (INK-uh) **Indians:** Indians who developed a large and rich empire in the western part of South America.

indentured (in-DEN-churd) **servants:** people who agreed to work for a master for a certain number of years in order to pay for their journey to America.

Indians: the name that Columbus gave to the people living in the new land that he discovered in 1492.

initiative: the right of the people of a state to suggest new laws to the state legislature.

injunction (in-JUNGK-shun): an order issued by American courts to stop union workers from striking.

integrated industry: an industry that controls everything from the raw materials to the finished product.

internal improvements: roads, canals, and other improvements made by the federal government.

Internal Security Act: a law passed by Congress in 1950 requiring all Communist groups to file their membership lists with the government.

Interstate Commerce Act: a law passed by Congress in 1887 to control the way that the railroad companies did business.

Iroquois (EER-ur-kwoy): the most powerful group of Eastern Woodland Indians.

isolation (EYE-suh-LAY-shun) **movement:** an attempt by many Americans during the 1930's to get the United States to cut itself off from the problems of the rest of the world.

Job Corps: an agency of the federal government set up in 1964 to give job training to young Americans from low-income families.

judicial branch: that part of the federal government which is made up of the federal courts, whose duty it is to interpret the laws.

judicial (joo-DISH-uhl) **review:** the power of the Supreme Court to decide when a law of Congress is unconstitutional.

Judiciary (joo-DISH-e-er-ee) **Act:** one of the first laws passed by Congress which set up the system of federal courts.

Kansas-Nebraska Act: a law passed by Congress in 1854 that allowed the settlers in the Western territories to decide whether they wanted to become free states or slave states.

Kellogg-Briand (KELL-aug bree-AHN) **Pact:** an agreement signed in 1928 by the United States, France, and many other nations promising to settle all future problems peacefully.

Kerner Report: the report of the commission that was formed to study the causes of the riots that broke out in the ghettos of large American cities in the 1960's.

Knights of Labor: a labor union formed in 1869 to bring skilled and unskilled workers from all parts of the nation into one large union.

Know-Nothing Party: a political party which was formed in the 1850's by Americans who wanted to end immigration.

Korean War: the struggle between United Nations troops and Communist forces in Korea between 1950 and 1953.

Ku Klux Klan: a secret group formed by Southerners during the Reconstruction years to keep black people, carpetbaggers, and scalawags from voting and taking part in Southern state governments.

labor unions: groups of workers who join together in order to improve their working conditions.

League of Nations: an organization of nations set up after World War One to keep world peace and to settle disputes between nations.

legislative branch: that part of the federal government which makes our laws and which consists of the Congress of the United States.

legislature (LEJ-uh-SLAY-chur): a law-making group.

Lend-Lease Act: a law passed by Congress in 1941 permitting the United States to lend war supplies to Great Britain to help it fight against the Axis Powers during World War Two.

Lone Star Republic: the name of the independent nation of Texas after it won its independence from Mexico in 1836.

Louisiana Purchase: the large territory between the Mississippi River and the Rocky Mountains, which the United States bought from France in 1803.

lower house: the assembly, or that part of a colony's legislature whose members were elected by the voters of the colony.

Loyalists: American colonists who were against independence from Great Britain and who helped the British during the Revolutionary War.

lyceum (ly-SEE-um) **lectures:** public talks given all over the United States in the 1800's by famous writers, scientists, and government leaders.

McCulloch against Maryland: an important law case in 1819 which helped strengthen the federal government because it decided that the Supreme Court has the power to declare a state law unconstitutional.

McNary-Haugen (mak-NAR-i HOU-gen) **Bill:** a bill proposed during the 1920's that asked the federal government to buy the farm crops that farmers could not sell and then sell them to foreign countries.

Manifest Destiny (MAN-uh-fest DES-tuh-nee): the name used in the 1840's to describe the belief of

many Americans that the United States should expand all the way to the Pacific coast.

Mann-Elkins Act: a federal law of 1910 that gave the Interstate Commerce Commission the power to regulate telephone and telegraph companies.

Manpower Development and Training Act: a law passed by Congress in 1962 which set up a training program to help teach new job skills to unemployed workers.

Marbury against Madison: an important law case in the early 1800's which decided that the Supreme Court has the power to declare a law of Congress unconstitutional.

March on Washington: a protest march in the nation's capital in 1963 by 200 thousand Americans in support of President John F. Kennedy's proposed civil rights bill.

Marshall Plan: a program of the United States to send goods and money to European nations to help them rebuild their cities, farms, and factories after World War Two.

mass production: the manufacture of products in huge amounts at low costs.

Maya (MY-yuh) **Indians:** Indians of Central America who developed a great culture which lasted for more than a thousand years.

Mayflower Compact: an agreement signed by the Pilgrims aboard the ship "Mayflower" in which they set down rules for forming their own government in the Plymouth Colony.

Meat Inspection Act: a law passed by Congress in 1906 which required that all fresh and canned meat must be checked by federal inspectors.

Medicare Act: a law passed by Congress in 1965, as part of the Social Security system, to set up a program of health insurance for American citizens over sixty-five years of age.

merit system: a method of choosing people for government jobs on the basis of their scores on Civil Service tests rather than on the basis of their political party.

Mexican Cession: the Western land, including California and New

Mexico, that the United States won from Mexico as a result of the Mexican War.

Mexican War: the war between the United States and Mexico that was fought from 1846 to 1848.

Middle colonies: the name given to the colonies of New York, New Jersey, Pennsylvania, and Delaware.

Minutemen: colonists who were trained to be ready to fight at a minute's notice if war broke out with Great Britain.

Missouri Compromise: the agreement reached by Congress in 1820 that settled the slavery question for a few years by keeping the number of free states and slave states equal.

monopoly (muh-NOP-uh-lee): a business company that controls an entire industry.

Monroe Doctrine: a speech by President Monroe in 1823, in which he warned European nations to stay out of the affairs of the nations of North America and South America.

Mormons (MORE-muns): members of a religious group founded in the 1820's that settled around the Great Salt Lake in what is now the state of Utah.

Mountain Men: American fur trappers who explored the Rocky Mountains during the 1820's.

muckrakers (MUK-rayk-urz): American writers during the Progressive Movement who presented facts to show that some business leaders and government leaders were dishonest.

National Association for the Advancement of Colored People: an organization formed by black leaders and white Progressives in 1909 to work for equal rights for black Americans.

National Defense Education Act: a law passed by Congress in 1958 to help improve the teaching of science, mathematics, and foreign languages in America's schools.

national government: another name for the federal government of the United States.

National Housing Act of 1949: a law passed by Congress to clear slums and build public housing.

National Labor Relations Act: a law passed by Congress in 1935 to protect labor unions and enable them to grow stronger.

National Liberation Front: the official name of the Vietcong, the Communist-led rebels in South Vietnam.

National Recovery Administration: a federal agency set up in 1933 to help American businesses and industries suffering from the Great Depression.

National Road: a road built by the federal government in the 1800's to link the Eastern states with settlements west of the Appalachian Mountains.

National Security Act: a law passed by Congress in 1947 that set up the Department of Defense, to join together all the nation's armed forces.

National Urban League: an organization formed in 1911 to help black Americans who moved into Northern cities.

natural resources: soil, forests, coal, oil, and other products found in nature.

Navigation (NAV-uh-GAY-shun) **Acts:** laws passed by the English government to control the trade of the English colonies.

neutral (NOO-trul): refusing to take sides in a war or dispute between other nations.

Neutrality Act: a law passed by Congress in 1935 to keep the United States from becoming involved in a war. A second Neutrality Act was passed in 1937; a third in 1939.

New Deal: President Franklin D. Roosevelt's plan to lead the American nation out of the Great Depression in the 1930's.

New England colonies: the name given to the colonies of Massachusetts, Rhode Island, Connecticut, and New Hampshire.

New France: the name given to the French settlements in the New World.

New Freedom: President Woodrow Wilson's plans for the American nation.

New Frontier: President John F. Kennedy's plan to help improve the American nation.

New World: the name given to the new lands discovered by Columbus and later called America.

Niagara (neye-AG-ruh) **Movement:** a movement started by black leaders in 1905 to work for equal rights for black Americans.

Nineteenth Amendment: the amendment to the Constitution, approved in 1920, which gave American women the right to vote.

Norsemen: sailors from northern Europe who discovered North America in the year 1000.

North: the northern part of the United States.

North Atlantic Treaty Organization: an agreement among several free nations, signed in 1949, to defend each other against a Communist attack.

Northeast: the name given to that part of the United States which includes the New England states and the Middle states.

Northern Alliance: a Northern farmers' group formed in the 1880's to get laws passed to help farmers and improve farm life.

Northwest Ordinance (OR-duh-nuns): a law passed by Congress in 1787, which set up a plan for settling and governing the Northwest Territory and for organizing new states.

Northwest Indians: Indians who lived along the Pacific coast of North America.

nullify (NUL-uh-fy): to refuse to obey a law.

Office of Price Administration: a federal agency set up during World War Two to control prices, wages, and rents.

Office of Production Management: a federal agency set up in 1941 to help American industry change over from peace time to war time production during World War Two.

Old Northwest: the name given to the lands north of the Ohio River —what are now the states of Ohio, Indiana, Illinois, Wisconsin, and Michigan.

Old South: the name given to the original Southern states along the Atlantic coast—Maryland, Virginia, North Carolina, South Carolina, and Georgia.

Old Southwest: the name given to the lands south of the Ohio River —what are now the states of Kentucky, Tennessee, Alabama, and Mississippi.

Open Door Policy: a plan proposed by the United States in 1899 to allow all nations to have equal trading rights in China.

Oregon Trail: the most famous route used by settlers traveling by land, in covered wagons, to Oregon.

Pan-American Conferences: meetings attended by the United States and Latin American nations after 1889.

Parliament: the law-making group of England.

peace treaty: an agreement that ends a war.

Pendleton Civil Service Act: a law passed by Congress in 1883 which set up a Civil Service Commission to test people for government jobs.

personal liberty laws: laws passed by several Northern states in the 1850's to stop the arrest of free black people as runaway slaves.

Pilgrims: a group of English people who started the Plymouth Colony in America in 1620.

pioneer farmers: farmers who moved into the frontier lands and cleared these lands for farming and settlement.

Plains Indians: Indians who lived by hunting buffalo on the Great Plains of North America.

plantations: very large farms in the South on which such crops as tobacco, rice, indigo, and cotton were grown.

Plessy against Ferguson: an important law case in 1896 in which the Supreme Court decided that segregation was lawful.

political boss: a strong party leader who heads a political machine.

political machine: a small group of political leaders who completely control their political party within a city or state.

political parties: organizations made up of groups of people who share the same ideas about government.

poll tax: a tax that had to be paid before a person could vote, used in some states in the past to keep black Americans from voting.

Poor People's Campaign: the program organized in 1968 by Dr. Martin Luther King, Jr., to influence Congress to pass laws to help poor Americans.

popular votes: the votes of the people in a national election.

Populist (PAHP-yuh-list) **Party:** a third political party formed about the year 1890 to help American farmers and workers.

Proclamation (prahk-luh-MAY-shun) **of 1763:** a law passed by the British government that made it unlawful for any colonists to settle on land west of the Appalachian Mountains.

Progressive Movement: a movement to bring about reforms in American government and American life during the early 1900's.

Progressives (pruh-GRESS-ivz): a group of Americans who worked to bring about reforms in government and living conditions during the early 1900's.

proprietary (pruh-PRY-uh-TERR-ee) **colonies:** those English colonies in which the owners had the power to rule as they wished.

proprietor (pruh-PRY-uh-tur): an owner of an English colony.

Public Works Administration: a federal agency set up in 1933 to plan government building projects in order to provide jobs for unemployed workers during the Great Depression.

Pueblo (PWEB-low) **Indians:** Indians who lived in villages in the southwestern part of North America.

Pure Food and Drug Act: a law passed by Congress in 1906 that required food and drug manufacturers to list on each package what their products contained.

Puritans: a group of English people who started the Massachusetts Bay Colony in America in 1630.

Quaker: a member of the group of English people who started the colony of Pennsylvania in 1682.

quota system: a system set up by Congress in the 1920's to limit the total number of immigrants allowed to enter the United States each year.

Radical Republicans: a group of Republican Congressmen who were against President Andrew Johnson's plans for Reconstruction and who wanted to punish the South for starting the Civil War.

raw materials: products from na-ture, such as animal hides, lumber, and furs.

rebate: money given back to a person or company that has already paid a particular price.

recall: the right of the people of a state to remove dishonest officials from state governments.

reciprocal trade agreements: trade agreements between nations in which each nation agrees to lower its tariffs on goods coming from the other nation.

Reconstruction: the program for making the North and the South into one nation again after the War Between the North and the South. Reconstruction lasted from 1865 to 1877.

Reconstruction Finance Corporation: a federal agency set up by Congress in the early 1930's to lend money to American railroads, banks, and other businesses.

referendum: the right of the people of a state to vote on certain important laws before the laws are voted on by the state legislature.

reform: to improve living conditions and make the world a better place to live in.

reparations (REP-uh-RAY-shuns): large amounts of money that a nation must pay to other nations for the lives and property it has destroyed during a war.

Republican Party: an early political party led by Thomas Jefferson and James Madison, which was made up of planters, small farmers, and city workers who wished to limit the power of the federal government.

Republican Party: a political party formed in 1854 to prevent the spread of slavery.

Revolutionary War: the war in which the thirteen colonies fought for and won their independence from Great Britain.

Roosevelt Corollary (KAWR-uh-ler-ee): President Theodore Roosevelt's plan to keep European nations out of Latin America and to protect the Panama Canal.

royal colonies: those English colonies that were ruled directly by the king of England.

scalawags (SKAL-uh-wagz): Southerners who held office in the new state governments of the South during the years of Reconstruction.

secede (suh-SEED): to break away from a nation, as the South broke away from the United States during the War Between the North and the South.

Second Continental Congress: a meeting of colonial leaders held at Philadelphia in 1775 to carry on the fight for independence from Great Britain.

secret ballot: the right of Americans to cast their votes in private.

Secretary of State: the Cabinet member who advises the President on foreign affairs.

Secretary of the Treasury: the Cabinet member who advises the President on money matters.

Secretary of War: the Cabinet member, now called the Secretary of Defense, who advises the President in planning the defense of the nation.

sections: different parts of the nation, where the people share certain ways of making a living and doing things.

Securities Exchange Act: a law passed by Congress in 1937 which set up a commission to regulate the stock market in order to prevent any future stock market crash.

Sedition (seh-DISH-un) **Act:** a law passed by Congress in 1798 that made it a crime to write or say anything against the government or President of the United States.

segregated: separated, or set apart, from other people because of race or color.

Selective Service Act: a law passed by Congress in 1917 to draft men for the American army in World War One.

self-governing colonies: those English colonies that governed themselves and were almost free from English control.

separate but equal: in education, the practice of having black students and white students attend separate but equally good schools.

separation of powers: the division of powers among the three branches of the federal government.

Seventeenth Amendment: the amendment to the Constitution, approved in 1913, which gave the voters, rather than the state legislatures, the power to elect United States Senators.

Shays' Rebellion: an armed uprising of Massachusetts farmers in 1786 and 1787 against the state government of Massachusetts.

Sherman Anti-Trust Act: a law passed by Congress in 1890 that made it unlawful for a company to form a trust in order to win control of an industry.

sit-in: a method used by black Americans as part of the civil rights movement to help end segregation in eating places and other public places in the South.

Sixteenth Amendment: the amendment to the Constitution, approved in 1913, which gave the federal government the power to pass an income tax law.

slave: a person who is treated like property and who is forced to work for a master.

slave codes: strict laws passed in the colonies to control the lives of the slaves.

slave revolt: an uprising of slaves against their masters.

smuggling: unlawful trade

social classes: the groups into which Americans were divided in the colonies, according to their wealth or occupations.

Social Security Act: a law passed by Congress in 1935 to provide monthly payments for older workers and payments for workers who lost their jobs.

Sons of Liberty: groups of colonists who joined together to fight the Stamp Act and other British tax laws.

South: that part of the United States which in early times was made up of the Southern states along the Atlantic coast and, later, the Old Southwest and some lands west of the Mississippi River.

Southeast Asia Treaty Organization: an agreement among several free nations, signed in 1954, to fight the spread of Communism in Asia.

Southern Alliance: a Southern farmers' group formed in the 1880's to get laws passed to help farmers and improve farm life.

Southern colonies: the name given to the colonies of Maryland, Virginia, North Carolina, South Carolina, and Georgia.

Southwestern Indians: Indians who lived on the lands of the southwestern part of North America.

Spanish-American War: a war between the United States and Spain in 1898.

Spanish Armada (ar-MAH-duh): a large fleet of Spanish ships sent to conquer England, which the English fleet defeated in 1588.

spoils system: the practice of rewarding friends and political party members with government jobs.

Square Deal: President Theodore Roosevelt's plan in the early 1900's to help all Americans, not just certain groups.

squatters: people who settled on Western land before it was put up for sale by the federal government.

Stamp Act: a law passed by the British government in 1765 that taxed newspapers, books, legal papers, calendars, and playing cards sold in the colonies.

Stamp Act Congress: a meeting held at New York City in 1765, at which leaders from nine colonies joined together to fight the Stamp Act.

standard parts: parts that will fit all machines of the same make and model.

stock market: the place where people buy and sell shares of ownership, called stocks, in business companies.

stock market crash: a sharp fall in the price of stocks in October, 1929, which helped to bring on the Great Depression.

strike: workers' refusal to work in order to force factory owners to meet their demands.

subsistence (sub-SIS-tens) **farming:** farming, usually on small farms, where families raise just enough crops and animals for their own use rather than for sale.

suburbs: towns located near large cities, where many city workers live.

Sugar Act: a law passed by the British government in 1764 that taxed sugar, molasses, and other products brought into the colonies from other countries.

Supreme Court: the highest court in the United States, which has the power to judge laws passed by Congress.

Taft-Hartley Act: a law passed by Congress in 1947 to control labor unions.

tariff: a tax, or duty, collected on goods brought into a country from other nations.

Tariff Act of 1816: a law passed by Congress to keep foreign manufactured goods out of the United States in order to protect American manufacturing.

Tariff of 1828: a law passed by Congress which set very high taxes on goods brought into the United States from other countries.

Tea Act: a British law of 1773 that enabled the British East India Company to sell its tea in America at a very low price without paying a tea tax.

temperance movement: the efforts of reformers to stop the use of alcoholic drinks in the United States in the mid-1800's.

Tennessee Valley Authority: a company run by the federal government, set up in 1933 to build dams, provide electric power, and improve living conditions for people in the Tennessee Valley.

territory: land owned by the United States which was later able to become a state or states.

test ban treaty: an agreement signed by many of the world's nations in 1963 to stop certain kinds of atomic bomb testing.

Thirteenth Amendment: the amendment to the Constitution, approved in 1865, which freed the slaves and made slavery unlawful in the United States.

Toleration (TAHL-ur-RAY-shun) **Act:** a law passed in the Maryland colony in 1649 that allowed all Christians to worship as they wished.

town meetings: meetings held in colonial New England towns in which all the citizens met together to discuss and settle important matters.

Townshend (TOUN-zend) **Acts:** laws passed by the British government in 1767 that taxed all glass, lead, paper, paint, and tea brought into the colonies.

trade routes: trade paths.

trading company: a group of European businessmen who were given the right to trade and start colonies in the New World.

Treaty of Ghent: the agreement between the United States and Great Britain that ended the War of 1812.

Treaty of Paris: the agreement between the United States and Great Britain in 1783 that ended the Revolutionary War.

Treaty of Versailles (vur-SY): the peace treaty that was written to end World War One.

triangular trade: the most important colonial trade that followed a trade route shaped like a triangle.

Truman Doctrine: a plan announced by President Harry S. Truman in 1947 to help nations defend themselves against the spread of Communism.

trust: a business company that controls many smaller companies in order to win control of an entire industry.

Twentieth Amendment: the amendment to the Constitution, approved in 1933, which moved back the beginning of the President's term of office from March to January.

Twenty-Fifth Amendment: the amendment to the Constitution, approved in 1967, which allows the Vice-President to take over the duties and powers of the President if the President dies, resigns, or becomes too ill to continue his duties.

Twenty-Fourth Amendment: the amendment to the Constitution, approved in 1964, which forbids the collection of taxes as a requirement for voting in Presidential elections.

Twenty-Second Amendment: the amendment to the Constitution, approved in 1951, which limits to two terms the number of terms a President can be elected to office.

unconstitutional: not approved or within the powers granted by the Constitution of the United States.

Underground Railroad: the name of the system that was set up to help runaway slaves escape to the North and to Canada.

Union: another name for the United States used especially during the War Between the North and the South.

United Nations: an organization of most of the nations of the world formed in 1945 to keep peace and to improve the lives of peoples everywhere.

Universal Negro Improvement Association: an organization formed during the 1920's to encourage black Americans to return to Africa.

upper house: that part of a colony's legislature whose members were rich and important men and that served as the governor's council.

urban nation: a nation where nearly two out of every three persons live in cities.

Veterans Bureau: an agency of the federal government set up after World War One to help soldiers and sailors who fought in the war.

veto: to turn down, or refuse to approve, a law.

Vietcong: Communist-led rebels in South Vietnam who are supported by the Communist government of North Vietnam.

Vista: the short name for Volunteers in Service to America, a group of Americans who work to help poor people in the cities of the nation.

Voting Rights Act of 1965: a law passed by Congress that forbids the use of literacy tests as a requirement for voting.

Wabash Railway Case: a law case in 1886 in which the Supreme Court ruled that only the federal government, and not the states, had the power to regulate railroads.

Wages and Hours Law: a law passed by Congress in 1938 which helped workers to get higher wages and fewer working hours.

War Between the North and the South: the war that was fought between the Southern states and the Northern states from 1861 to 1865. Also called the Civil War.

War Hawks: the name given to members of Congress in 1811 who wanted to go to war against Great Britain.

War Industries Board: a federal agency set up during World War One to direct American factories in turning out war supplies and weapons.

War of 1812: the war between the United States and Great Britain fought from 1812 to 1815.

War Production Board: a federal agency set up in 1942 to help American industry to change over to producing weapons and war supplies during World War Two.

Washington Naval Conference: a meeting of leaders from nine nations held at Washington, D.C., in 1921 to find a way to limit their navies.

Webster-Ashburton Treaty: an agreement between the United States and Great Britain in 1842, which fixed the boundary between Maine and Canada.

West: that part of the United States which in early times was the land west of the Appalachian Mountains, later, was the land between the Mississippi River and the Rocky Mountains, and now is the land between the Great Plains and the Pacific coast.

Whig Party: a political party formed in the 1830's by people who did not like the ideas of the Democratic Party.

Wilmot Proviso: a plan suggested during the Mexican War which said that slavery was not to be allowed in any new land won by the United States in the war.

Works Progress Administration: a federal agency set up in 1935 to provide work for millions of jobless Americans during the Great Depression.

World War One: the great war between the Central Powers and the Allies fought between 1914 and 1918. The United States entered the war in 1917 on the side of the Allies.

World War Two: the great war between the Axis Powers and the Allies fought from 1939 to 1945. The United States entered the war in 1941 on the side of the Allies.

writs of assistance (RITZ of uh-SIS-tunts): court orders that gave British officials the right to enter a colonist's house, ship, or warehouse to search for smuggled goods.

yellow dog contract: an agreement by workers not to join a union if they are hired for jobs.

THE DECLARATION OF INDEPENDENCE

The United States of America was born on July 4, 1776, when members of the Second Continental Congress signed a statement declaring their independence from Great Britain. Although this statement was short, it contained many important ideas. What were the important ideas in the Declaration of Independence?

The Declaration of Independence may be divided into four parts: (1) The Preamble, (2) The American Idea of Government, (3) The Reasons Why the Colonists Wanted Independence, and (4) The Declaration of American Independence. As you read the Declaration of Independence, use the notes written at the side to help you better understand the important ideas it contains.

The Preamble

When, in the course of human events, it becomes necessary for one people to dissolve the political bands which have connected them with another, and to assume, among the powers of the earth, the separate and equal station to which the laws of nature and of nature's God entitle them, a decent respect to the opinions of mankind requires that they should declare the causes which impel them to the separation.

> When people decide to form their own nation, it is right for them to explain to other nations why they wish to do so.

The American Idea of Government

We hold these truths to be self-evident: That all men are created equal; that they are endowed by their Creator with certain unalienable rights; that among these are life, liberty, and the pursuit of happiness.

> All men are born equal, and all men have certain rights which cannot be taken away from them. These rights are the rights to live, to be free, and to try to be happy.

That to secure these rights, governments are instituted among men, deriving their just powers from the consent of the governed; that, whenever any form of government becomes destructive of these ends, it is the right of the people to alter or to abolish it, and to institute a new government, laying its foundation on such principles, and organizing its powers in such form, as to them shall seem most likely to effect their safety and happiness. Prudence, indeed, will dictate that governments long established should not be changed for light and transient causes; and accordingly, all experience hath shown that mankind are more disposed to suffer while evils are sufferable, than to right themselves by abolishing the forms to which they are accustomed. But when a long trial of abuses and usurpations, pursuing invariably the same object, evinces a design to reduce them under absolute despotism, it is their right, it is their duty, to throw off such government, and to provide new guards for their future security.

> The purpose of a government is to protect the rights of men.

> When a government does not protect the rights of men, the peope have the right to end this government and to set up a new government.

The King of Great Britain tried in many ways to take away the freedom of the colonies. This is proved by the King's actions.

The British King refused to pass laws to help the colonies.

The King made it difficult for the colonists to pass their own laws for the colonies.

The King tried to prevent the growth of the colonies.

The King prevented the colonies from having their own judges and courts of law.

The King sent too many officials to rule the colonies.

The King sent British troops to the colonies without the agreement of the colonists.

The King and Parliament forced the colonists to provide shelter for British troops.

These British soldiers were free from trial by the colonists even if they were guilty of crimes.

The King and Parliament cut off colonial trade with other nations, taxed the colonists without their agreement, refused to allow the colonists the right to trial by jury, and harmed the colonies.

Such has been the patient sufferance of these colonies; and such is now the necessity which constrains them to alter their former systems of government. The history of the present King of Great Britain is a history of repeated injuries and usurpations, all having in direct object the establishment of an absolute tyranny over these states. To prove this, let facts be submitted to a candid world.

He has refused his assent to laws the most wholesome and necessary for the public good.

He has forbidden his governors to pass laws of immediate and pressing importance, unless suspended in their operation till his assent should be obtained; and, when so suspended, he has utterly neglected to attend to them.

He has refused to pass other laws for the accommodation of large districts of people, unless those people would relinquish the right of representation in the legislature, — a right inestimable to them, and formidable to tyrants only.

He has called together legislative bodies at places unusual, uncomfortable, and distant from the depository of their public records, for the sole purpose of fatiguing them into compliance with his measures.

He has dissolved representative houses repeatedly, for opposing, with manly firmness, his invasions on the rights of the people.

He has refused, for a long time after such dissolutions, to cause others to be elected, whereby the legislative powers, incapable of annihilation, have returned to the people at large for their exercise; the state remaining, in the mean time, exposed to all the dangers of invasions from without and convulsions within.

He has endeavored to prevent the population of these states; for that purpose obstructing the laws for the naturalization of foreigners, refusing to pass others to encourage their migration hither, and raising the conditions of new appropriations of lands.

He has obstructed the administration of justice, by refusing his assent to laws for establishing judiciary powers.

He has made judges dependent on his will alone for the tenure of their offices, and the amount and payment of their salaries.

He has erected a multitude of new offices, and sent hither swarms of officers to harass our people and eat out their substance.

He has kept among us in times of peace standing armies, without the consent of our legislatures.

He has affected to render the military independent of, and superior to, the civil power.

He has combined with others to subject us to a jurisdiction foreign to our constitutions and unacknowledged by our laws, giving his assent to their acts of pretended legislation:

For quartering large bodies of armed troops among us;

For protecting them, by a mock trial, from punishment for any murders which they should commit on the inhabitants of these states;

For cutting off our trade with all parts of the world;

For imposing taxes on us without our consent;

For depriving us, in many cases, of the benefits of trial by jury;

For transporting us beyond seas, to be tried for pretended offenses;

For abolishing the free system of English laws in a neighboring province, establishing therein an arbitrary government, and enlarging its boundaries, so as to render it at once an example and fit instrument for introducing the same absolute rule into these colonies;

For taking away our charters, abolishing our most valuable laws, and altering, fundamentally, the forms of our governments;

For suspending our own legislatures, and declaring themselves invested with power to legislate for us in all cases whatsoever.

He has abdicated government here, by declaring us out of his protection and waging war against us.

He has plundered our seas, ravaged our coasts, burned our towns, and destroyed the lives of our people.

He is at this time transporting large armies of foreign mercenaries to complete the works of death, desolation, and tyranny already begun with circumstances of cruelty and perfidy scarcely paralleled in the most barbarous ages, and totally unworthy the head of a civilized nation.

He has constrained our fellow-citizens, taken captive on the high seas, to bear arms against their country, to become the executioners of their friends and brethren, or to fall themselves by their hands.

He has excited domestic insurrection among us, and has endeavored to bring on the inhabitants of our frontiers the merciless Indian savages, whose known rule of warfare is an undistinguished destruction of all ages, sexes, and conditions.

In every stage of these oppressions we have petitioned for redress in the most humble terms; our repeated petitions have been answered only by repeated injury.

A prince whose character is thus marked by every act which may define a tyrant is unfit to be the ruler of a free people.

Nor have we been wanting in our attentions to our British brethren. We have warned them, from time to time, of attempts by their legislature to extend an unwarrantable jurisdiction over us. We have reminded them of the circumstances of our emigration and settlement here. We have appealed to their native justice and magnanimity; and we have conjured them, by the ties of our common kindred, to disavow these usurpations, which would inevitably interrupt our connections and correspondence. They, too, have been deaf to the voice of justice and consanguinity. We must, therefore, acquiesce in the necessity which denounces our separation, and hold them, as we hold the rest of mankind, enemies in war, in peace friends.

The Declaration of American Independence

We, therefore, the representatives of the United States of America, in General Congress assembled, appealing to the Supreme Judge of the world for the rectitude of our intentions, do, in the name and by the authority of the good people of these colonies, solemnly publish and declare, That these united colonies are, and of right ought to be, free and independent states; that they are absolved from all allegiance to the British crown, and that all political connections between them and the state of Great Britain is, and ought to be, totally dissolved; and that, as free and independent states, they have full power to levy war, conclude peace, contract alliances, establish commerce, and do all other acts and things which independent states may of right do. And, for the support of this declaration, with a firm reliance on the protection of Divine Providence, we mutually pledge to each other our lives, our fortunes, and our sacred honor.

The King and Parliament took away the colonists' laws and right to govern themselves.

The King of Great Britain can no longer be the colonists' king. He does not protect the colonists, but instead wages war on them. (The colonies and Great Britain were already at war. Fighting broke out at Lexington and Concord in April of 1775.)

The colonists asked the King of Great Britain many times to stop his unlawful acts.

The colonists asked Parliament not to pass laws without the agreement of the colonies.

The colonists declare that the United States of America is an independent nation, and no longer a part of Great Britain.

The United States of America has all the rights of a free nation.

The men who signed the Declaration of Independence promise to do everything in their power to support the Declaration.

THE CONSTITUTION OF THE UNITED STATES OF AMERICA

The Constitution of the United States provides the basis of our American form of government. Perhaps the most important thing to remember about the Constitution is how it divides the powers of our government. The Constitution divides the powers of the national government among three branches — the legislative branch, the executive branch, and the judicial branch. The Constitution also separates the powers of the national government and the powers of the state governments.

As you study the Constitution, use the notes at the side of each page to help you better understand the important ideas it contains. Use these notes also to help you understand the Amendments that have been added to the Constitution. The lines in color drawn through some parts of the Constitution show that these parts are out of date or have been changed by amendment.

The Preamble

The Preamble lists the reasons for writing the Constitution.

We the people of the United States, in order to form a more perfect union, establish justice, insure domestic tranquillity, provide for the common defence, promote the general welfare, and secure the blessings of liberty to ourselves and our posterity, do ordain and establish this CONSTITUTION for the United States of America.

Article 1. The Legislative Branch

Section 1. Congress

The power to make laws is given to a Congress of two houses.

All legislative powers herein granted shall be vested in a Congress of the United States, which shall consist of a Senate and a House of Representatives.

Section 2. The House of Representatives

1. Members of the House of Representatives are chosen every two years. They are elected by the voters who are qualified to vote for members of the state legislatures.

1. ELECTION OF MEMBERS AND TERM OF OFFICE. The House of Representatives shall be composed of members chosen every second year by the people of the several States, and the electors in each State shall have the qualifications requisite for electors of the most numerous branch of the State Legislature.

2. A member of the House of Representatives must be at least 25 years old, a United States citizen for 7 years, and living in the state that he represents.

2. WHAT PERSONS ARE QUALIFIED TO BE MEMBERS. No person shall be a Representative who shall not have attained to the age of twenty-five years, and been seven years a citizen of the United States, and who shall not, when elected, be an inhabitant of that State in which he shall be chosen.

3. The number of Representatives for each state is based on the state's population.

3. HOW THE NUMBER OF MEMBERS FOR EACH STATE IS DECIDED. Representatives and direct taxes shall be apportioned among the several States

page 740

which may be included within this Union, according to their respective numbers, which shall be determined by adding to the whole number of free persons, including those bound to service for a term of years, and excluding Indians not taxed, three fifths of all other persons. The actual enumeration shall be made within three years after the first meeting of the Congress of the United States, and within every subsequent term of ten years, in such manner as they shall by law direct. The number of Representatives shall not exceed 1 for every 30,000, but each State shall have at least one representative; and until such enumeration shall be made, the State of New Hampshire shall be entitled to choose three, Massachusetts eight, Rhode Island and Providence Plantations one, Connecticut five, New York six, New Jersey four, Pennsylvania eight, Delaware one, Maryland six, Virginia ten, North Carolina five, South Carolina five, and Georgia three.

4. FILLING EMPTY SEATS. When vacancies happen in the representation from any State, the Executive authority thereof shall issue writs of election to fill such vacancies.

5. OFFICERS OF THE HOUSE; THE POWER OF IMPEACHMENT. The House of Representatives shall choose their Speaker and other officers; and shall have the sole power of impeachment.

Section 3.   The Senate

1. NUMBER OF MEMBERS AND TERM OF OFFICE. The Senate of the United States shall be composed of two Senators from each State, chosen by the Legislature thereof, for six years; and each Senator shall have one vote.

2. ELECTION OF MEMBERS; FILLING EMPTY SEATS. Immediately after they shall be assembled in consequence of the first election, they shall be divided as equally as may be into three classes. The seats of the Senators of the first class shall be vacated at the expiration of the second year, of the second class at the expiration of the fourth year, and of the third class at the expiration of the sixth year, so that one third may be chosen every second year; and if vacancies happen by resignation, or otherwise, during the recess of the Legislature of any State, the Executive thereof may make temporary appointments until the next meeting of the Legislature, which shall then fill such vacancies.

3. WHAT PERSONS ARE QUALIFIED TO BE MEMBERS. No person shall be a Senator who shall not have attained to the age of thirty years, and been nine years a citizen of the United States, and who shall not, when elected, be an inhabitant of that State for which he shall be chosen.

4. PRESIDENT OF THE SENATE. The Vice-President of the United States shall be President of the Senate, but shall have no vote, unless they be equally divided.

5. OTHER SENATE OFFICERS. The Senate shall choose their other officers, and also a President *pro tempore,* in the absence of the Vice-President, or when he shall exercise the office of President of the United States.

6. TRIAL OF IMPEACHMENT CASES. The Senate shall have the sole power to try all impeachments. When sitting for that purpose, they shall be on oath or affirmation. When the President of the United States is tried, the Chief Justice shall preside; and no person shall be convicted without the concurrence of two thirds of the members present.

7. PUNISHMENT IN CASES OF IMPEACHMENT. Judgment in cases of impeachment shall not extend further than to removal from office, and disqualification to hold and enjoy any office of honor, trust, or profit un-

[This was changed by Amendment 14.]

A national census, or an official count of the population, must be taken every ten years.

4. Empty seats in the House of Representatives must be filled by special elections.

5. The House of Representatives has the power of impeachment, or the power to accuse a federal official of wrongdoing in office.

1. In the Senate, each state is represented equally by two Senators. [The way of electing Senators was changed by Amendment 17.]

2. One third of the Senators are elected every two years. Each Senator serves a six-year term.

[This way of filling empty seats in the Senate was changed by Amendment 17.]

3. A Senator must be at least 30 years old, a United States citizen for 9 years, and living in the state that he represents.

4. The Vice-President is the officer in charge of the Senate, but he may vote only in the case of a tie.

5. The Senate elects a temporary officer in charge from among its members to serve when the Vice-President is absent or when he becomes President.

6. The Senate has power to hold a trial in cases of impeachment. A two-thirds vote is needed to declare an impeached official guilty.

7. The Senate can remove from office officials found guilty on impeachment charges. These officials also may have a court trial if they have broken any laws.

der the United States; but the party convicted shall nevertheless be liable and subject to indictment, trial, judgment, and punishment, according to law.

Section 4. Elections and Meetings of Congress

1. HOLDING ELECTIONS. The times, places, and manner of holding elections for Senators and Representatives shall be prescribed in each State by the Legislature thereof; but the Congress may at any time by law make or alter such regulations, except as to the places of choosing Senators.

2. MEETINGS. The Congress shall assemble at least once in every year, and such meeting shall be on the first Monday in December, unless they shall by law appoint a different day.

1. Election rules are set by the states. But Congress may pass laws that set new election rules.

[2. The meeting time of Congress was changed by Amendment 20. Congress now meets January 3.]

Section 5. The Rules of Congress

1. ORGANIZATION. Each House shall be the judge of the elections, returns, and qualifications of its own members, and a majority of each shall constitute a quorum to do business; but a smaller number may adjourn from day to day, and may be authorized to compel the attendance of absent members, in such manner, and under such penalties, as each House may provide.

2. RULES OF MEETING. Each House may determine the rules of its proceedings, punish its members for disorderly behavior, and, with the concurrence of two thirds, expel a member.

3. PUBLIC RECORD. Each House shall keep a journal of its proceedings, and from time to time publish the same, excepting such parts as may in their judgment require secrecy; and the yeas and nays of the members of either House on any question shall, at the desire of one fifth of those present, be entered on the journal.

4. ADJOURNMENT. Neither House, during the session of Congress, shall, without the consent of the other, adjourn for more than three days, nor to any other place than that in which the two Houses shall be sitting.

1. Each house of Congress decides whether its members are qualified and were elected fairly. A majority (more than half) of the members, or a quorum, must be present before each house may carry on its work.
Members of either house of Congress may be required to attend meetings in order that Congress can carry on its activities.

3. Each house of Congress must print an official record of its activities.

4. Neither house of Congress may adjourn, or put off meeting, for more than three days unless the other house agrees to it.

Section 6. Special Rules for Congressmen

1. SALARY AND SPECIAL RIGHTS. The Senators and Representatives shall receive a compensation for their services, to be ascertained by law, and paid out of the treasury of the United States. They shall in all cases, except treason, felony, and breach of the peace, be privileged from arrest during their attendance at the session of their respective Houses, and in going to and returning from the same; and for any speech or debate in either House they shall not be questioned in any other place.

2. MEMBERS CANNOT HOLD OTHER OFFICES. No Senator or Representative shall, during the time for which he was elected, be appointed to any civil office under the authority of the United States, which shall have been created, or the emoluments whereof shall have been increased, during such time; and no person holding any office under the United States shall be a member of either House during his continuance in office

1. Members of Congress are paid salaries and receive extra sums of money for certain things they must do.
Members of Congress cannot be arrested for anything they say in Congress. But they can be arrested for serious crimes while Congress is meeting.

2. A member of Congress cannot hold any other federal office while he serves in Congress.

Section 7. The Way Laws are Passed

1. TAX BILLS. All bills for raising revenue shall originate in the House of Representatives; but the Senate may propose or concur with amendments as on other bills.

2. HOW A BILL BECOMES A LAW. Every bill which shall have passed the House of Representatives and the Senate shall, before it become a law, be presented to the President of the United States; if he approve he

1. All tax bills must be started in the House of Representatives, but the Senate can suggest changes.

2. A bill passed by Congress must be sent to the President. If the President signs the bill, it becomes a law. If the President vetoes, or refuses to sign, the bill, it returns to the house where it was started.

shall sign it, but if not he shall return it with his objections to that House in which it shall have originated, who shall enter the objections at large on their journal, and proceed to reconsider it. If after such reconsideration two thirds of that House shall agree to pass the bill, it shall be sent, together with the objections, to the other House, by which it shall likewise be reconsidered, and, if approved by two thirds of that House, it shall become a law. But in all such cases the votes of both Houses shall be determined by yeas and nays, and the names of the persons voting for and against the bill shall be entered on the journal of each House respectively. If any bill shall not be returned by the President within ten days (Sundays excepted) after it shall have been presented to him, the same shall be a law, in like manner as if he had signed it, unless the Congress by their adjournment prevent its return, in which case it shall not be a law.

The President's veto may be overcome by a two-thirds vote of each house of Congress.

3. PRESIDENTIAL APPROVAL OR VETO. Every order, resolution, or vote to which the concurrence of the Senate and House of Representatives may be necessary (except on a question of adjournment) shall be presented to the President of the United States; and, before the same shall take effect, shall be approved by him, or, being disapproved by him, shall be repassed by two thirds of the Senate and House of Representatives, according to the rules and limitations prescribed in the case of a bill.

The President can let a bill become a law without signing it. But a bill sent to the President during the last 10 days when Congress is meeting does not become law if the President does not sign it.

3. The President must either sign or veto everything passed by Congress, except when Congress votes to put off meeting.

Section 8. Powers Given to Congress

[The Congress shall have power,]

① To lay and collect taxes, duties, imposts, and excises, to pay the debts and provide for the common defense and general welfare of the United States; but all duties, imposts, and excises shall be uniform throughout the United States; *(By Passing Laws)*

2. To borrow money on the credit of the United States;

3. To regulate commerce with foreign nations, and among the several States, and with the Indian tribes;

4. To establish a uniform rule of naturalization, and uniform laws on the subject of bankruptcies throughout the United States;

5. To coin money, regulate the value thereof, and of foreign coin, and fix the standard of weights and measures;

6. To provide for the punishment of counterfeiting the securities and current coin of the United States;

7. To establish post offices and post roads;

8. To promote the progress of science and useful arts, by securing for limited times to authors and inventors the exclusive right to their respective writings and discoveries;

9. To constitute tribunals inferior to the Supreme Court;

10. To define and punish piracies and felonies committed on the high seas, and offences against the law of nations;

11. To declare war, grant letters of marque and reprisal, and make rules concerning captures on land and water;

12. To raise and support armies, but no appropriation of money to that use shall be for a longer term than two years;

13. To provide and maintain a navy;

14. To make rules for the government and regulation of the land and naval forces;

15. To provide for calling forth the militia to execute the laws of the Union, suppress insurrections, and repel invasions;

16. To provide for organizing, arming, and disciplining the militia, and for governing such part of them as may be employed in the service

The powers given to Congress are:

① to vote for and collect equal taxes, to pay debts, and to provide for the defense and general welfare of the nation

2. to borrow money

3. to make rules for trade between the states and with other nations

4. to set up rules on how foreign-born persons become citizens, and rules about failure to pay debts

5. to coin money and to decide what weights and measures shall be used

6. to fix rules for punishing any person who makes false money

7. to establish post offices and roads for carrying mail

8. to prevent the works of writers and inventors from being copied by others unlawfully

9. to set up federal courts

10. to punish piracy, or robbery at sea

⑪ to declare war *(only cong can)*

⑫ to raise and support armies

⑬ to support a navy

⑭ to make rules for the armed forces

⑮ to provide for calling out the militia (the National Guard)

⑯ to help states support their militia

of the United States, reserving to the States respectively, the appointment of the officers, and the authority of training the militia according to the discipline prescribed by Congress;

17 to set up and govern the District of Columbia (Washington, D.C.), and to govern other federal property

17. To exercise exclusive legislation, in all cases whatsoever, over such district (not exceeding ten miles square) as may, by cession of particular States, and the acceptance of Congress, become the seat of the government of the United States; and to exercise like authority over all places purchased by the consent of the Legislature of the State in which the same shall be, for the erection of forts, magazines, arsenals, dock-yards, and other needful buildings; and

18. to make all "necessary and proper" laws. Number 18 is called the "elastic clause," because it allows Congress to stretch its powers and to take many actions not named in the Constitution.

18. To make all laws which shall be necessary and proper for carrying into execution the foregoing powers, and all other powers vested by this Constitution in the government of the United States, or in any department or officer thereof.

The powers forbidden to Congress are:

Section 9. Powers Forbidden to Congress

[1. to try to stop the slave trade before the year 1808]

1. The migration or importation of such persons as any of the States now existing shall think proper to admit, shall not be prohibited by the Congress prior to the year one thousand eight hundred and eight, but a tax or duty may be imposed on such importation, not exceeding ten dollars for each person.

2 to refuse to allow a prisoner to hear the charges against him, except when the nation is in danger

2. The privilege of the writ of *habeas corpus* shall not be suspended, unless when in cases of rebellion or invasion the public safety may require it.

3. to take away a guilty person's property, or to punish a person for doing something that was not yet against the law when he did it

3. No bill of attainder or *ex post facto* law shall be passed.

4. to vote for direct taxes, except taxes based on a state's population. [This was changed by Amendment 16, the Income Tax Amendment.]

4. No capitation or other direct tax shall be laid, unless in proportion to the census or enumeration herein before directed to be taken.

5. to tax goods sent out of a state

5. No tax or duty shall be laid on articles exported from any State.

6. to pass a law that favors the trade of one state over another state

6. No preference shall be given by any regulation of commerce or revenue to the ports of one State over those of another; nor shall vessels bound to, or from, one State, be obliged to enter, clear, or pay duties in another.

7. to spend money without voting for it in both houses

7. No money shall be drawn from the treasury, but in consequence of appropriations made by law; and a regular statement and account of the receipts and expenditures of all public money shall be published from time to time.

8. to give or accept any title of nobility (favored high position)

8. No title of nobility shall be granted by the United States; and no person holding any office of profit or trust under them shall, without the consent of the Congress, accept of any present, emolument, office, or title, of any kind whatever, from any king, prince, or foreign state.

The powers forbidden to the states are:

Section 10. Powers Forbidden to the States

1. to make treaties, to coin money, and to do certain things also forbidden to the federal government

1. No State shall enter into any treaty, alliance, or confederation; grant letters of marque and reprisal; coin money; emit bills of credit; make anything but gold and silver coin a tender in payment of debts; pass any bill of attainder, *ex post facto* law, or law impairing the obligation of contracts, or grant any title of nobility.

2. to vote for taxes on goods sent in or out of a state, unless Congress agrees

2. No State shall, without the consent of the Congress, lay any imposts or duties on imports or exports, except what may be absolutely necessary for executing its inspection laws; and the net produce of all duties and imposts, laid by any State on imports or exports, shall be for the use of the treasury of the United States; and all such laws shall be subject to the revision and control of the Congress.

3. No State shall, without the consent of Congress, lay any duty of tonnage, keep troops or ships of war in time of peace, enter into any agreement or compact with another State, or with a foreign power, or engage in war, unless actually invaded, or in such imminent danger as will not admit of delay.

③ to keep troops or warships in peacetime or to deal with another state or a foreign nation, unless Congress agrees

Article 2. The Executive Branch

Section 1. The President and Vice-President

1. TERM OF OFFICE. The executive power shall be vested in a President of the United States of America. He shall hold his office during the term of four years, and, together with the Vice-President, chosen for the same term, be elected as follows:

2. THE ELECTORAL SYSTEM. Each State shall appoint, in such manner as the Legislature thereof may direct, a number of Electors equal to the whole number of Senators and Representatives to which the State may be entitled in the Congress; but no Senator or Representative, or person holding an office of trust or profit under the United States, shall be appointed an Elector.

An Old Way of Using the Electoral System. The electors shall meet in their respective States, and vote by ballot for two persons, of whom one at least shall not be an inhabitant of the same State with themselves. And they shall make a list of all the persons voted for, and of the number of votes for each; which list they shall sign and certify, and transmit sealed to the seat of the government of the United States, directed to the President of the Senate. The President of the Senate shall, in the presence of the Senate and House of Representatives, open all the certificates, and the votes shall then be counted. The person having the greatest number of votes shall be the President, if such number be a majority of the whole number of electors appointed; and if there be more than one who have such majority, and have an equal number of votes, then the House of Representatives shall immediately choose by ballot one of them for President; and if no person have a majority, then from the five highest on the list the said House shall in like manner choose the President. But in choosing the President, the votes shall be taken by States, the representation from each State having one vote; a quorum for this purpose shall consist of a member or members from two thirds of the States, and a majority of all the States shall be necessary to a choice. In every case, after the choice of the President, the person having the greatest number of votes of the electors shall be the Vice-President. But if there should remain two or more who have equal votes, the Senate shall choose from them by ballot the Vice-President.

3. TIME OF ELECTIONS. Congress may determine the time of choosing the electors, and the day on which they shall give their votes; which day shall be the same throughout the United States.

4. WHAT PERSONS ARE QUALIFIED TO BE PRESIDENT. No person except a natural-born citizen, or a citizen of the United States at the time of the adoption of this Constitution, shall be eligible to the office of President; neither shall any person be eligible to that office who shall not have attained to the age of thirty-five years, and been fourteen years a resident within the United States.

5. FILLING THE EMPTY OFFICE OF PRESIDENT. In case of the removal of the President from office, or of his death, resignation, or inability to dis-

1. Executive power, or the power to carry out laws, is given to the President. The President serves in office for a four-year term.

2. The President is elected by electors, or representatives, chosen by the people.

[This way of electing the President and Vice-President was changed by Amendment 12.]

3. Today, Presidential elections are held on the first Tuesday after the first Monday in November. Electoral votes are cast on the first Monday after the second Wednesday in December.

4. The President must be a citizen born in the United States, at least 35 years old, and living in the United States for at least 14 years.

5. If the President dies, or for any reason cannot carry out his duties, the Vice-President will act as President. If the Vice-President also is unable to serve, Congress has voted that the Speaker of the House, and, after him, the temporary President of the Senate, will serve as President.

charge the powers and duties of the said office, the same shall devolve on the Vice-President, and the Congress may by law provide for the case of removal, death, resignation, or inability, both of the President and Vice-President, declaring what officer shall then act as President, and such officer shall act accordingly, until the disability be removed, or a President shall be elected.

6. The President must be paid a salary, and the amount he is paid cannot be changed during his term in office.

6. SALARY. The President shall, at stated times, receive for his services a compensation, which shall neither be increased nor diminished during the period for which he shall have been elected, and he shall not receive within that period any other emolument from the United States, or any of them.

7. The President takes an oath of office, or is "sworn in," before he begins his duties.

7. THE OATH OF OFFICE. Before he enter on the execution of his office, he shall take the following oath or affirmation: — "I do solemnly swear (or affirm) that I will faithfully execute the office of President of the United States, and will, to the best of my ability, preserve, protect, and defend the Constitution of the United States."

Section 2. The Powers of the President

The powers of the President are:

1. to act as commander in chief of the armed forces. The President may ask for help from the heads of each federal goverment department, who make up the President's Cabinet.
The President may give pardons to, or set free, persons who acted against the United States, except in cases of impeachment.

① MILITARY POWERS. The President shall be commander-in-chief of the army and navy of the United States, and of the militia of the several States, when called into the actual service of the United States; he may require the opinion, in writing, of the principal officer in each of the executive departments, upon any subject relating to the duties of their respective offices, and he shall have power to grant reprieves and pardons for offences against the United States, except in cases of impeachment.

2. to make treaties and to appoint federal officials, with the agreement of the Senate.

2. POWER TO MAKE TREATIES; POWER TO APPOINT OFFICIALS. He shall have power, by and with the advice and consent of the Senate, to make treaties, provided two thirds of the Senators present concur; and he shall nominate, and, by and with the advice and consent of the Senate, shall appoint ambassadors, other public ministers, and consuls, judges of the Supreme Court, and all other officers of the United States, whose appointments are not herein otherwise provided for, and which shall be established by law; but the Congress may by law vest the appointment of such inferior officers, as they think proper, in the President alone, in the courts of law, or in the heads of departments.

3. to appoint temporary officials to fill empty federal offices, without the agreement of the Senate when Congress is not meeting

3. POWER TO FILL EMPTY OFFICES. The President shall have power to fill up all vacancies that may happen during the recess of the Senate, by granting commissions which shall expire at the end of their next session.

Section 3. Duties of the President

The President must send or read a report on the "state of the Union"—the condition of the nation—at each opening meeting of Congress. He also may send special messages to Congress.
The President may call special meetings of Congress.
The President must meet with foreign ambassadors, carry out the laws of the nation, and sign orders appointing new officers in the armed forces.

He shall from time to time give to the Congress information of the state of the Union, and recommend to their consideration such measures as he shall judge necessary and expedient; he may, on extraordinary occasions, convene both Houses, or either of them, and in case of disagreement between them, with respect to the time of adjournment, he may adjourn them to such time as he shall think proper; he shall receive ambassadors and other public ministers; he shall take care that the laws be faithfully executed, and shall commission all the officers of the United States.

Section 4. Impeachment

The President and other federal officials may be removed from office if they are found guilty in cases of impeachment.

The President, Vice-President, and all civil officers of the United States, shall be removed from office on impeachment for, and conviction of, treason, bribery, or other high crimes and misdemeanors.

Article 3. The Judicial Branch

Section 1. The Federal Courts

THE SUPREME COURT AND LOWER FEDERAL COURTS. The Judicial power of the United States shall be vested in one Supreme Court, and in such inferior courts as the Congress may from time to time ordain and establish. The judges, both of the Supreme and inferior courts, shall hold their offices during good behavior, and shall, at stated times, receive for their services a compensation, which shall not be diminished during their continuance in office.

Judicial power, or the power to judge the law, is given to a Supreme Court and to lower federal courts set up by Congress.

Federal judges serve in office for life, but they may be removed in cases of impeachment.

Section 2. What Cases Are Tried in Federal Courts

1. FEDERAL COURT CASES. The judicial power shall extend to all cases, in law and equity, arising under this Constitution, the laws of the United States, and treaties made, or which shall be made, under their authority; to all cases affecting ambassadors, other public ministers and consuls; to all cases of admiralty and maritime jurisdiction; to controversies to which the United States shall be a party; to controversies between two or more States, between a State and citizens of another State, between citizens of different States, between citizens of the same State claiming lands under grants of different States, and between a State, or the citizens thereof, and foreign states, citizens, or subjects.

1. Federal courts judge cases that concern the meaning of the Constitution, federal laws, and treaties. They also judge cases that concern the United States, a state, citizens of different states, and citizens of foreign nations.

2. SUPREME COURT CASES. In all cases affecting ambassadors, other public ministers, and consuls, and those in which a State shall be party, the Supreme Court shall have original jurisdiction. In all the other cases before mentioned, the Supreme Court shall have appellate jurisdiction, both as to law and fact, with such exceptions, and under such regulations, as the Congress shall make.

2. Cases that concern ambassadors or other officials of foreign nations, and cases that concern states, are judged by the Supreme Court. Other cases begin in lower courts, but they may sometimes be judged again in the Supreme Court.

3. THE WAY FEDERAL TRIALS ARE HELD. The trial of all crimes, except in cases of impeachment, shall be by jury; and such trial shall be held in the State where the said crimes shall have been committed, but when not committed within any State, the trial shall be at such place or places as the Congress may by law have directed.

3. All federal crimes, except cases of impeachment, are to be judged in trials in the states where the crimes took place.

Section 3. Treason

1. THE MEANING OF "TREASON." Treason against the United States shall consist only in levying war against them, or in adhering to their enemies, giving them aid and comfort. No person shall be convicted of treason unless on the testimony of two witnesses to the same overt act, or on confession in open court.

1. Treason is carefully explained as making war against the United States or helping its enemies.

2. PUNISHMENT. The Congress shall have power to declare the punishment of treason, but no attainder of treason shall work corruption of blood, or forfeiture, except during the life of the person attainted.

2. The family of a person found guilty of treason cannot also be punished.

Article 4. Relations Between the States

Section 1. Respect for Other States

Full faith and credit shall be given in each State to the public acts, records, and judicial proceedings of every other State. And the Congress may by general laws prescribe the manner in which such acts, records, and proceedings shall be proved, and the effect thereof.

All states must respect each other's laws, records, and lawful decisions.

Section 2. Rights of Citizens of a State

1. RIGHTS OF CITIZENS. The citizens of each State shall be entitled to all privileges and immunities of citizens in the several States.

1. Each state must treat citizens of other states as it treats its own citizens.

2. A person accused of a crime who runs away to another state must be returned to the state where the crime took place.

2. THE RETURN OF PERSONS ACCUSED OF CRIMES. A person charged in any State with treason, felony, or other crime, who shall flee from justice, and be found in another State, shall, on demand of the executive authority of the State from which he fled, be delivered up, to be removed to the State having jurisdiction of the crime.

[3. This rule about runaway slaves was not used after Amendment 13 ended slavery in 1865.]

3. THE RETURN OF RUNAWAY SLAVES. ~~No person held to service or labor in one State, under the laws thereof, escaping into another, shall, in consequence of any law or regulation therein, be discharged from such service or labor, but shall be delivered up on claim of the party to whom such service or labor may be due.~~

Section 3. New States and Territories

1. New states cannot be formed by dividing or joining present states, unless the state legislatures and Congress agree. New states may be admitted into the Union by Congress.

1. HOW NEW STATES ENTER THE UNION. New States may be admitted by the Congress into this Union; but no new State shall be formed or erected within the jurisdiction of any other State; nor any State be formed by the junction of two or more States, or parts of States, without the consent of the Legislatures of the States concerned, as well as of the Congress.

2. Congress has power to make laws for the territories and for federal property.

2. POWERS OF CONGRESS OVER TERRITORIES AND OTHER PROPERTY. The Congress shall have power to dispose of and make all needful rules and regulations respecting the territory or other property belonging to the United States; and nothing in this Constitution shall be so construed as to prejudice any claims of the United States, or of any particular State.

Section 4. Rights Promised to the States

Each state is promised a republican form of government, or a government in which the people elect their representatives. The federal government must protect states against foreign attack or trouble within the state.

The United States shall guarantee to every State in this Union a republican form of government, and shall protect each of them against invasion; and on application of the Legislature, or of the Executive (when the Legislature can not be convened), against domestic violence.

Article 5. How Amendments Are Made

Amendments may be suggested by a two-thirds vote of each house of Congress or at the request of two-thirds of the states. Amendments must be ratified, or approved, by the legislatures of three fourths of the states or by voters in three fourths of the states.

The Congress, whenever two thirds of both houses shall deem it necessary, shall propose amendments to this Constitution, or, on the application of the Legislatures of two thirds of the several States, shall call a convention for proposing amendments, which, in either case, shall be valid to all intents and purposes, as part of this Constitution, when ratified by the Legislatures of three fourths of the several States, or by conventions in three fourths thereof, as the one or the other mode of ratification may be proposed by the Congress; provided ~~that no amendment which may be made prior to the year one thousand eight hundred and eight shall in any manner affect the first and fourth clauses in the ninth section of the first article; and~~ that no State, without its consent, shall be deprived of its equal suffrage in the Senate.

No amendment may take away from a state its right to an equal vote in the Senate.

Article 6. General Provisions

1. The federal government must respect all debts and agreements of the United States made before the adoption of the Constitution.

1. PUBLIC DEBT. All debts contracted and engagements entered into, before the adoption of this Constitution, shall be as valid against the United States under this Constitution as under the Confederation.

2. The Constitution, laws, and treaties of the United States are the highest law of the nation. No state or local laws may disagree with them.

2. THE HIGHEST LAW OF THE NATION. This Constitution, and the laws of the United States which shall be made in pursuance thereof, and all treaties made, or which shall be made, under the authority of the United

States, shall be the supreme law of the land; and the judges in every State shall be bound thereby, anything in the constitution or laws of any State to the contrary notwithstanding.

3. OATHS OF OFFICE. The Senators and Representatives before mentioned, and the members of the several State Legislatures, and all executives and judicial officers, both of the United States and of the several States, shall be bound by oath or affirmation to support this Constitution; but no religious test shall ever be required as a qualification to any office or public trust under the United States.

> 3. All federal and state officials must promise to support the Constitution.
>
> Religion is not important in deciding if a person is qualified to serve in a federal office.

Article 7. The Adoption of the Constitution

The ratification of the conventions of nine States shall be sufficient for the establishment of this Constitution between the States so ratifying the same.

> The Constitution was to become the law of the nation when it was ratified, or approved, by nine states.

Done in Convention, by the unanimous consent of the States present, the seventeenth day of September, in the year of our Lord one thousand seven hundred and eighty-seven, and of the Independence of the United States of America the twelfth. *In Witness* whereof we have hereunto subscribed our names.

THE BILL OF RIGHTS
(Amendments 1 to 10, Adopted in 1791)

Amendment 1. Freedom of Religion, Speech, the Press, Assembly, and Petition

Congress shall make no law respecting an establishment of religion, or prohibiting the free exercise thereof; or abridging the freedom of speech, or of the press, or the right of the people peaceably to assemble, and to petition the government for a redress of grievances.

> Congress may not set up an official church or pass laws that limit freedom of religion, speech, the press, assembly (public meeting), and petition (asking the government to do certain things).

Amendment 2. Right to Keep Weapons

A well regulated militia being necessary to the security of a free state, the right of the people to keep and bear arms shall not be infringed.

> Citizens have the right to keep weapons.

Amendment 3. Right to a Private Home

No soldier shall, in time of peace, be quartered in any house, without the consent of the owner, nor in time of war, but in a manner to be prescribed by law.

> Military troops may not take over private houses in peace time.

Amendment 4. Limits on Government Search and Taking of Property

The right of the people to be secure in their persons, houses, papers, and effects, against unreasonable searches and seizures, shall not be violated, and no warrant shall issue but upon probable cause, supported by oath or affirmation, and particularly describing the place to be searched, and the persons or things to be seized.

> The government is limited in its right to search and take hold of persons and property.

A person cannot be put on trial for a serious crime unless he is accused by a grand jury. He cannot be tried for the same crime twice. He cannot be forced to give evidence against himself. No person's right to life, liberty, or property can be taken away except by lawful means.

No person shall be held to answer for a capital, or otherwise infamous crime, unless on a presentment or indictment of a grand jury, except in cases arising in the land or naval forces, or in the militia, when in actual service in time of war or public danger; nor shall any person be subject for the same offence to be twice put in jeopardy of life or limb; nor shall be compelled in any criminal case to be a witness against himself, nor be deprived of life, liberty, or property, without due process of law; nor shall private property be taken for public use without just compensation.

A person accused of a crime has the right to a fair, public trial by a jury in the state where the crime took place. He must be told the charges against him. He has the right to have a lawyer defend him, to question people who speak against him, and to call people to speak in his favor.

In all criminal prosecutions, the accused shall enjoy the right to a speedy and public trial, by an impartial jury of the State and district wherein the crime shall have been committed, which district shall have been previously ascertained by law, and to be informed of the nature and cause of the accusation; to be confronted with the witnesses against him; to have compulsory process for obtaining witnesses in his favor, and to have the assistance of counsel for his defence.

A person has a right to a jury trial in most cases that concern him.

In suits at common law, where the value in controversy shall exceed twenty dollars, the right of trial by jury shall be preserved, and no fact tried by a jury shall be otherwise reexamined in any court of the United States, than according to the rules of the common law.

Prison bails, fines, and punishments must be fair.

Excessive bail shall not be required, nor excessive fines imposed, nor cruel and unusual punishments inflicted.

The promise of certain rights in the Constitution does not mean that these rights are the only rights the people have. The people have other rights that may not be taken away or limited by the government.

The enumeration in the Constitution of certain rights shall not be construed to deny or disparage others retained by the people.

All powers not given to the federal government are left to the states and to the people.

The powers not delegated to the United States by the Constitution, nor prohibited by it to the States, are reserved to the States respectively, or to the people.

OTHER AMENDMENTS TO THE CONSTITUTION

No state may have a law case brought against it by a citizen of another state or of a foreign nation.

The judicial power of the United States shall not be construed to extend to any suit in law or equity, commenced or prosecuted against one of the United States by citizens of another State, or by citizens or subjects of any foreign state.

Amendment 12. Election of President and Vice-President (1804)

The Electors shall meet in their respective States, and vote by ballot for President and Vice-President, one of whom, at least, shall not be an inhabitant of the same State with themselves; they shall name in their ballots the person voted for as President, and in distinct ballots the person voted for as Vice-President; and they shall make distinct lists of all persons voted for as President, and of all persons voted for as Vice-President, and of the number of votes for each, which lists they shall sign and certify, and transmit sealed to the seat of the government of the United States, directed to the President of the Senate; — the President of the Senate shall, in the presence of the Senate and House of Representatives, open all the certificates, and the votes shall then be counted; — the person having the greatest number of votes for President shall be the President, if such number be a majority of the whole number of Electors appointed; and if no person have such majority, then from the persons having the highest numbers not exceeding three on the list of those voted for as President, the House of Representatives shall choose immediately, by ballot, the President. But in choosing the President, the votes shall be taken by States, the representation from each State having one vote; a quorum for this purpose shall consist of a member or members from two thirds of the States, and a majority of all the States shall be necessary to a choice. And if the House of Representatives shall not choose a President, whenever the right of choice shall devolve upon them, before the fourth day of March next following, then the Vice-President shall act as President, as in the case of the death or other constitutional disability of the President. The person having the greatest number of votes as Vice-President shall be the Vice-President, if such number be a majority of the whole number of Electors appointed, and if no person have a majority, then from the two highest numbers on the list the Senate shall choose the Vice-President; a quorum for the purpose shall consist of two thirds of the whole number of Senators, and a majority of the whole number shall be necessary to a choice. But no person constitutionally ineligible to the office of President shall be eligible to that of Vice-President of the United States.

Electors (members of the Electoral College) shall vote separately for President and Vice-President.

Amendment 13. Slavery Is Ended (1865)
Section 1.

Neither slavery nor involuntary servitude, except as a punishment for crime whereof the party shall have been duly convicted, shall exist within the United States, or any place subject to their jurisdiction.

Slavery is ended. Congress is given power to enforce the ending of slavery.

Section 2.

Congress shall have power to enforce this article by appropriate legislation.

Amendment 14. Rights of Citizens (1868)
Section 1. The Rights and Meaning of "Citizenship"

All persons born or naturalized in the United States, and subject to the jurisdiction thereof, are citizens of the United States and of the State wherein they reside. No State shall make or enforce any law which shall abridge the privileges or immunities of citizens of the United States; nor shall any State deprive any person of life, liberty, or property, without due process of law; nor deny to any person within its jurisdiction the equal protection of the laws.

Citizenship is given to Negroes. The states cannot pass laws that take away the rights and protections promised to all United States citizens by the Constitution.

Section 2. Representation in Congress

A state's representation in Congress may be made less if the state refuses the right to vote to any citizen who is qualified.*

Representatives shall be apportioned among the several States according to their respective numbers, counting the whole number of persons in each State, excluding Indians not taxed. But when the right to vote at any election for the choice of Electors for President and Vice-President of the United States, Representatives in Congress, the executive and judicial officers of a State, or the members of the Legislature thereof, is denied to any of the male inhabitants of such State, being twenty-one years of age and citizens of the United States, or in any way abridged, except for participation in rebellion or other crime, the basis of representation therein shall be reduced in the proportion which the number of such male citizens shall bear to the whole number of male citizens twenty-one years of age in such State.

Section 3. Persons Who May Not Serve in the Federal Government

Any United States government official who later became an officer of the Confederate States of America may not hold federal or state office.

No person shall be a Senator or Representative in Congress, or Elector of President and Vice-President, or hold any office, civil or military, under the United States, or under any State, who, having previously taken an oath, as a member of Congress, or as an officer of the United States, or as a member of any State Legislature, or as an executive or judicial officer of any State, to support the Constitution of the United States, shall have engaged in insurrection or rebellion against the same, or given aid or comfort to the enemies thereof. But Congress may, by a vote of two thirds of each House, remove such disability.

Section 4. Public Debt

All debts of the federal government connected with the War Between the North and the South must be paid. All debts of the Confederate states are unlawful and will not be paid by the federal government.

The validity of the public debt of the United States, authorized by law, including debts incurred for payment of pensions and bounties for services in suppressing insurrection or rebellion, shall not be questioned. But neither the United States, nor any State shall assume or pay any debt or obligation incurred in aid of insurrection or rebellion against the United States, or any claim for the loss or emancipation of any slave; but all such debts, obligations, and claims shall be held illegal and void.

Section 5. Enforcement

The Congress shall have power to enforce, by appropriate legislation, the provisions of this article.

Amendment 15. The Right to Vote (1870)

Section 1.

No citizen can be refused the right to vote because of his race or color, or because he was once a slave.

The right of citizens of the United States to vote shall not be denied, or abridged by the United States, or by any State, on account of race, color, or previous condition of servitude.

Section 2.

The Congress shall have power to enforce this article by appropriate legislation.

Amendment 16. Taxes on Income (1913)

Congress is given the power to pass a law to tax incomes (the money people earn).

The Congress shall have power to lay and collect taxes on incomes, from whatever source derived, without apportionment among the several States, and without regard to any census or enumeration.

Amendment 17.   Election of Senators (1913)

Section 1.

The Senate of the United States shall be composed of two Senators from each State, elected by the people thereof, for six years; and each Senator shall have one vote. The electors in each State shall have the qualifications requisite for electors of the most numerous branch of the State legislatures.

Senators are to be elected by the voters of each state.

Section 2.

When vacancies happen in the representation of any State in the Senate, the executive authority of such State shall issue writs of election to fill such vacancies: Provided, that the Legislature of any State may empower the executive thereof to make temporary appointment until the people fill the vacancies by election as the Legislature may direct.

An empty seat in the Senate may be filled by a special election. Or, the legislature of a state may ask the Governor to appoint someone to fill the empty seat until the next election.

Section 3.

This amendment shall not be so construed as to affect the election or term of any Senator chosen before it becomes valid as part of the Constitution.

Amendment 18.   Prohibition of Alcoholic Drinks (1919)

Section 1.

After one year from the ratification of this article the manufacture, sale, or transportation of intoxicating liquors within, the importation thereof into, or the exportation thereof from the United States and all territory subject to the jurisdiction thereof, for beverage purposes is hereby prohibited.

The making, sale, and carrying of alcoholic drinks in the United States are prohibited, or outlawed. [This amendment was ended by Amendment 21.]

Section 2.

The Congress and the several States shall have concurrent power to enforce this article by appropriate legislation.

Section 3.

This article shall be inoperative unless it shall have been ratified as an amendment to the Constitution by the Legislatures of the several States as provided in the Constitution within seven years from the date of the submission hereof to the States by the Congress.

Amendment 19.   The Right of Women to Vote (1920)

Section 1.

The right of citizens of the United States to vote shall not be denied or abridged by the United States or by any State on account of sex.

The right to vote is given to women. Congress is given the power to enforce this right.

Section 2.

Congress shall have power to enforce this article by appropriate legislation.

Section 1. When the President Takes Office

The President and Vice-President are to take office on January 20. Members of Congress are to take office on January 3.

The terms of the President and Vice-President shall end at noon on the 20th day of January, and the terms of Senators and Representatives at noon on the 3d day of January, of the years in which such terms would have ended if this article had not been ratified; and the terms of their successors shall then begin.

Section 2. When Congress Meets

Congress is to meet at least once every year.

The Congress shall assemble at least once in every year, and such meeting shall begin at noon on the 3d day of January, unless they shall by law appoint a different day.

Section 3. Filling the Presidential Office

If the newly-elected President dies before January 20 or fails to qualify for office, the office of President is to be filled in the order given here.

If, at the time fixed for the beginning of the term of the President, the President-elect shall have died, the Vice-President-elect shall become President. If a President shall not have been chosen before the time fixed for the beginning of his term, or if the President-elect shall have failed to qualify, then the Vice-President-elect shall act as President until a President shall have qualified; and the Congress may by law provide for the case wherein neither a President-elect nor a Vice-President-elect shall have qualified, declaring who shall then act as President, or the manner in which one who is to act shall be selected, and such person shall act accordingly until a President or Vice-President shall have qualified.

Section 4. Filling the Empty Office of President

The Congress may by law provide for the case of the death of any of the persons from whom the House of Representatives may choose a President whenever the right of choice shall have devolved upon them, and for the case of the death of any of the persons from whom the Senate may choose a Vice-President whenever the right of choice shall have devolved upon them.

Section 5. When This Amendment Becomes Law

Sections 1 and 2 shall take effect on the 15th day of October following the ratification of this article.

Section 6. Limit on Time for Approval of This Amendment

This article shall be inoperative unless it shall have been ratified as an amendment to the Constitution by the legislatures of three-fourths of the several States within seven years from the date of its submission.

Section 1.

Amendment 18 is repealed, or ended.

The eighteenth article of amendment to the Constitution of the United States is hereby repealed.

Section 2.

The states have the right to outlaw the sale of alcoholic drinks.

The transportation or importation into any State, Territory, or possession of the United States for delivery or use therein of intoxicating liquors, in violation of the laws thereof, is hereby prohibited.

Section 3.

This article shall be inoperative unless it shall have been ratified as an amendment to the Constitution by conventions in the several States, as provided in the Constitution, within seven years from the date of the submission hereof to the States by Congress.

Amendment 22.   Two-Term Limit for Presidents (1951)

Section 1.

No person shall be elected to the office of the President more than twice, and no person who has held the office of President, or acted as President, for more than two years of a term to which some other person was elected President, shall be elected to the office of the President more than once. But this article shall not apply to any person holding the office of President when this article was proposed by the Congress, and shall not prevent any person who may be holding the office of President, or acting as President, during the term within which this article becomes operative from holding the office of President, or acting as President, during the remainder of such term.

A President may only serve two full terms in office. If a Vice-President has already served more than two years as President, he may be elected President only once.

Section 2.

This article shall be inoperative unless it shall have been ratified as an amendment to the Constitution by the legislatures of three-fourths of the several states within seven years from the date of its submission to the states by the Congress.

Amendment 23.   Presidential Electors for District of Columbia (1961)

Section 1.

The District constituting the seat of Government of the United States shall appoint in such manner as Congress may direct: A number of electors of President and Vice-President equal to the whole number of Senators and Representatives in Congress to which the District would be entitled if it were a State, but in no event more than the least populous State; they shall be in addition to those appointed by the States, but they shall be considered, for the purposes of the election of President and Vice-President, to be electors appointed by a State; and they shall meet in the District and perform such duties as provided by the twelfth article of amendment.

People who live in the District of Columbia (Washington, D.C.) are given the right to vote for President and Vice-President. The District of Columbia is given three electoral votes.

Section 2.

The Congress shall have power to enforce this Article by appropriate legislation.

Amendment 24.   A Tax on Voters Is Unlawful in National Elections (1964)

Section 1.

The right of citizens of the United States to vote in any primary or other election for President or Vice-President, for electors for President

A poll tax, or a tax on voters, cannot be required in elections for federal officials.

or Vice-President, or for Senator or Representative in Congress, shall not be denied or abridged by the United States or any state by reason of failure to pay any poll tax or other tax.

Section 2.

The Congress shall have power to enforce this Article by appropriate legislation.

Amendment 25. Filling the Empty Offices of President and Vice-President (1967)

Section 1. Filling the Empty Office of President

If a President dies or resigns from office, the Vice-President becomes President.

In case of the removal of the President from office by his death or resignation, the Vice-President shall become President.

Section 2. Filling the Empty Office of Vice-President

If the office of Vice-President becomes empty, the President may appoint someone to fill this office, with the agreement of Congress.

Whenever there is a vacancy in the office of the Vice-President, the President shall nominate a Vice-President who shall take the office upon confirmation by a majority vote of both houses of Congress.

Section 3. When the Vice-President Acts as President

If the President feels unable to carry out the duties of office, he shall tell Congress so in a written message. The Vice-President shall act as President until the President declares that he is again able to carry out his duties.

Whenever the President transmits to the President pro tempore of the Senate and the Speaker of the House of Representatives his written declaration that he is unable to discharge the powers and duties of his office, and until he transmits them a written declaration to the contrary, such powers and duties shall be discharged by the Vice-President as Acting President.

Section 4. When Congress Decides Who Shall Be President

If the Vice-President and a majority of the Cabinet members feel that the President is unable to carry out the duties of office, they shall tell Congress so in a written message. The Vice-President shall act as President. When the President feels ready to carry out his duties again he shall declare so to Congress. But if the Vice-President and a majority of the Cabinet members do not agree with him, then Congress must decide by a two-thirds vote within 21 days who is President.

Whenever the Vice-President and a majority of either the principal officers of the executive departments, or of such other body as Congress may by law provide, transmit to the President pro tempore of the Senate and the Speaker of the House of Representatives their written declaration that the President is unable to discharge the powers and duties of his office, the Vice-President shall immediately assume the powers and duties of the office as Acting President.

Thereafter, when the President transmits to the President pro tempore of the Senate and the Speaker of the House of Representatives his written declaration that no inability exists, he shall resume the powers and duties of his office unless the Vice-President and a majority of either the principal officers of the executive department, or of such other body as Congress may by law provide, transmit within four days to the President pro tempore of the Senate and the Speaker of the House of Representatives their written declaration that the President is unable to discharge the powers and duties of his office. Thereupon Congress shall decide the issue, assembling within 48 hours for that purpose if not in session. If the Congress, within 21 days after receipt of the latter written declaration, or, if Congress is not in session, within 21 days after Congress is required to assemble, determines by two-thirds vote of both houses that the President is unable to discharge the powers and duties of his office, the Vice-President shall continue to discharge the same as Acting President; otherwise, the President shall resume the powers and duties of his office.

See Amendment 26 on page 769.

A Time Line of American History

The Discovery of America

1000	Norsemen discover America.
1096	The Crusades to the Holy Land begin.
1492	Columbus discovers America.
1497–98	Cabot explores the coast of North America for England.
1498	Vasco da Gama reaches India.
1500	Cabral claims Brazil for Portugal.
1513	Balboa discovers the Pacific Ocean.
1519	Cortés conquers the Aztecs of Mexico.
1519–22	Magellan's ships sail around the world.
1531	Pizarro conquers the Incas of Peru.
1588	England defeats the Spanish Armada.

The Colonial Years

1607	English start colony at Jamestown.
1608	Champlain founds Quebec.
1619	The Virginia House of Burgesses meets.
1619	The first Africans arrive in America as indentured servants.
1620	The Pilgrims start Plymouth Colony.
1624	The Dutch form the colony of New Netherland.
1630	The Puritans start the Massachusetts Bay Colony.
1634	The Maryland Colony is settled.
1636	Roger Williams begins the colony of Rhode Island.
1636	Thomas Hooker starts a colony in Connecticut.
1636	Harvard College is started.
1638	Settlers from Massachusetts begin a new colony in New Hampshire.
1639	The first written constitution in America is drawn up in Connecticut.
1643	The New England Confederation is formed.
1647	Massachusetts passes a school law.
1649	The Maryland Toleration Act is passed.
1663	The Carolinas are started as one colony.
1664	English take New Netherland.
1676	Bacon's Rebellion in Virginia.
1682	William Penn begins the colony of Pennsylvania.
1730's	The Great Awakening takes place.
1732	The colony of Georgia is started.
1754	The French and Indian War begins.

1759	General Wolfe captures Quebec.
1763	A peace treaty between Great Britain, France, and Spain.

The Colonies Win Their Independence

1763	The Proclamation of 1763.
1764	The Sugar Act is passed by Parliament.
1765	The Stamp Act is passed.
1765	The Stamp Act Congress meets.
1766	The Stamp Act is ended.
1767	The Townshend Acts are passed.
1770	The Boston Massacre takes place.
1772	The Committees of Correspondence are formed.
1773	The Tea Act is passed by Parliament.
1773	The Boston Tea Party takes place.
1774	The First Continental Congress meets.
1775	Fighting at Lexington and Concord starts the Revolutionary War.
1775–76	The Second Continental Congress meets.
1776	Thomas Paine's *Common Sense* appears.
1776	The Declaration of Independence is signed.
1777	The colonists win the Battle of Saratoga. France decides to help the colonists.
1781	The British surrender at Yorktown.

Building the New American Nation

1781	The Articles of Confederation become the first plan of American government.
1783	The Treaty of Paris guarantees the independence of the United States.
1786–87	Shays' Rebellion takes place.
1787	The Northwest Ordinance is passed.
1787	The Constitutional Convention meets.
1788	The Constitution of the United States is approved.
1788	**George Washington is elected the first President of the United States.**
1789	President Washington takes office.
1791	The Bill of Rights is approved.
1792	**President Washington is reelected.**

The Early Years of the Nation

1793	Eli Whitney invents the cotton gin.

1794	The Whisky Rebellion takes place.
1796	**John Adams is elected President.**
1798	The Eleventh Amendment is approved.
1798	American and French ships battle at sea.
1798	The Alien and Sedition Acts.
1800	**Thomas Jefferson is elected President.**
1801	John Marshall is appointed Chief Justice of the Supreme Court.
1803	The Louisiana Purchase.
1804	**President Jefferson is reelected.**
1807	The Embargo Act is passed.
1807	The steamboat "Clermont" makes its first trip.
1808	**James Madison is elected President.**
1808	Congress makes it unlawful to bring any more slaves into the nation.
1811	The Battle of Tippecanoe.
1811	The National Road is begun.
1812	**President Madison is reelected.**
1812	The War of 1812 begins.
1814	The British burn Washington, D.C.
1814	A peace treaty ends the War of 1812.
1816	A new tariff protects American factories.
1816	**James Monroe is elected President.**
1819	The United States buys Florida.
1820	The Missouri Compromise is accepted.
1820	**President Monroe is reelected.**
1821	Mexico wins independence from Spain.
1823	The Monroe Doctrine is announced.
1824	**John Quincy Adams is elected President.**
1824	The Democratic Party is formed.

The Growing Nation

1828	**Andrew Jackson is elected President.**
1831	Nat Turner leads a slave revolt.
1831	William L. Garrison prints *The Liberator*.
1832	Congress passes a new tariff.
1832	South Carolina threatens to secede.
1832	President Jackson vetoes the Bank law.
1832	**President Jackson is reelected.**
1833	President Jackson forces South Carolina to accept a compromise tariff.
1834	The Whig Party is formed.
1836	Texas wins independence from Mexico.
1836	**Martin Van Buren is elected President.**
1837	Hard times come to the nation.
1837	Horace Mann leads the movement for free public schools.
1840	**William Henry Harrison is elected President.**
1841	President Harrison dies. **Vice-President John Tyler becomes President.**

1844	**James K. Polk is elected President.**
1846	The Bear Flag Revolt in California.
1846	The Mexican War begins.
1848	A peace treaty ends the Mexican War.
1848	**Zachary Taylor is elected President.**
1849	The California gold rush begins.

A Nation Divided

1850	President Taylor dies. **Vice-President Millard Fillmore becomes President.**
1850	The Compromise of 1850 is accepted.
1852	*Uncle Tom's Cabin* become a best seller.
1852	**Franklin Pierce is elected President.**
1853	The Gadsden Purchase.
1853	Perry opens Japan to trade with America.
1854	The Kansas-Nebraska Act is passed.
1854	The Republican Party is formed.
1856	**James Buchanan is elected President.**
1857	The Dred Scott case.
1859	John Brown raids Harpers Ferry.
1860	**Abraham Lincoln is elected President.**
1860	South Carolina secedes from the Union.
1861	The Confederate States of America is formed.
1861	The firing on Fort Sumter begins the War Between the North and the South.
1862	President Lincoln issues the Emancipation Proclamation.
1864	**President Lincoln is reelected.**
1865	The South surrenders at Appomattox.

Rebuilding the Nation

1865	President Lincoln is killed. **Vice-President Andrew Johnson becomes President.**
1865	The Freedmen's Bureau is set up.
1865	The Thirteenth Amendment is approved.
1865	The National Labor Union is formed.
1867	The United States buys Alaska.
1867	Congress passes a plan for Reconstruction.
1868	The Fourteenth Amendment is approved.
1868	President Johnson is accused of misconduct in office. He is not found guilty.
1868	Ulysses S. Grant is elected President.

1869	The first railroad to cross the nation is completed at Promontory, Utah.
1869	The Knights of Labor is formed.
1870	The Fifteenth Amendment is approved.
1871	The Ku Klux Klan is outlawed.
1872	Former Confederate officials are given the right to vote again.
1872	**President Grant is reelected.**
1870's	The Chautauqua movement begins.
1876	**Rutherford B. Hayes is elected President.**
1877	Northern troops leave the South.
1880	**James A. Garfield is elected President.**
1881	President Garfield is killed. **Vice-President Chester A. Arthur becomes President.**
1883	The Pendleton Civil Service Act.
1884	**Grover Cleveland is elected President.**
1886	The American Federation of Labor (A. F. of L.) is formed.
1886	The Haymarket Riot takes place.
1887	The Interstate Commerce Act is passed.
1888	**Benjamin Harrison is elected President.**
1889	Jane Addams opens a settlement house.
1889	The first Pan-American Conference.

The Nation Becomes a World Leader

1890	The frontier ends.
1890	The Sherman Anti-Trust Act is passed.
1891	The Populist Party is formed.
1892	**Grover Cleveland is again elected President.**
1890's	Progressives work for reform in government and business.
1890's	Many immigrants enter the nation from southern and eastern Europe.
1896	**William McKinley is elected President.**
1898	The Spanish-American War is fought.
1898	Hawaii becomes a United States territory.
1899	The Open Door Policy for China.
1900	**President McKinley is reelected.**
1901	President McKinley is killed. **Vice-President Theodore Roosevelt becomes President.**
1903	The Elkins Act is passed.
1904	**President Roosevelt is reelected.**
1906	The Pure Food and Drug Act.
1906	The Meat Inspection Act is passed.
1906	The Hepburn Act is passed.

1908	**William Howard Taft is elected President.**
1909	The N.A.A.C.P. is formed.
1911	The National Urban League is formed.
1912	The Bull Moose, or Progressive, Party is formed.
1912	**Woodrow Wilson is elected President.**
1913	The Sixteenth Amendment is approved.
1913	The Seventeenth Amendment is approved.
1913	The Federal Reserve System is set up.
1914	The Clayton Anti-Trust Act is passed.
1914	The Federal Trade Commission Act.

The United States and World War One

1914	World War One begins in Europe.
1914	The Panama Canal opens.
1915	German submarines sink the "Lusitania."
1916	**President Wilson is reelected.**
1917	United States enters World War One.
1918	American soldiers fight in Europe.
1918	World War One ends.
1919	President Wilson suggests the Fourteen Points at the Paris peace conference.
1919	The European Allies sign the Treaty of Versailles with Germany.
1919	The Eighteenth Amendment is approved.

The Years After World War One

1920	The United States votes not to join the League of Nations.
1920	The Nineteenth Amendment is approved.
1920	**Warren G. Harding is elected President.**
1921	The United States signs a peace treaty with Germany.
1921	The Washington Naval Conference.
1921–29	Congress sets up limits on immigration.
1923	President Harding dies. **Vice-President Calvin Coolidge becomes President.**
1924	**President Coolidge is reelected.**
1928	The Kellogg-Briand Pact.
1928	**Herbert Hoover is elected President.**

The Great Depression

1929	The stock market crash takes place. The Great Depression begins.

1932	Franklin D. Roosevelt is elected President.
1933	The Twentieth Amendment is approved.
1933	The C.C.C. is set up by Congress.
1933	The Agricultural Adjustment Act.
1933	The N.R.A. is set up by Congress.
1933	The T.V.A. is formed.
1933	The Twenty-First Amendment is approved.
1930's	The Good Neighbor Policy is adopted.
1935	The National Labor Relations Act.
1935	The Social Security Act is passed.
1936	**President Roosevelt is reelected.**
1936	The Congress of Industrial Organizations (C.I.O.) is formed.
1938	A new Agricultural Adjustment Act.
1938	The Wages and Hours Law is passed.

The United States and World War Two

1939	World War Two begins in Europe.
1940	**President Roosevelt is elected to a third term.**
1940	Germany conquers western Europe.
1941	The Lend-Lease Act is passed.
1941	Japan attacks Pearl Harbor. The United States enters World War Two.
1944	An Allied army invades Europe.
1944	**President Roosevelt is elected to a fourth term.**
1945	President Roosevelt dies. **Vice-President Harry S. Truman becomes President.**
1945	The United Nations (U.N.) is formed.
1945	World War Two ends in Europe (May).
1945	The United States drops atomic bombs on Japan.
1945	World War Two ends in Asia (September).

The Nation After the War

1946	The Philippine Islands become independent.
1947	The Truman Doctrine is announced.
1947	The Taft-Hartley Act is passed.
1948–49	The Berlin airlift takes place.
1948	**President Truman is reelected.**
1949	The Marshall Plan is put into action.
1949	The North Atlantic Treaty Organization (N.A.T.O.) is formed.

1950–53	The Korean War is fought.
1951	The Twenty-Second Amendment is approved.
1952	**Dwight D. Eisenhower is elected President.**
1954	The Supreme Court declares school segregation unlawful.
1954	The Southeast Asia Treaty Organization (S.E.A.T.O.) is formed.
1956	**President Eisenhower is reelected.**
1957	Federal troops help black students enter Little Rock High School.
1957	The Civil Rights Act of 1957 is passed.
1957	The Soviet Union launches "Sputnik."
1958	The United States launches a space satellite.

America in the Space Age

1960	The Civil Rights Act of 1960 is passed.
1960	**John F. Kennedy is elected President.**
1961	The Peace Corps is started.
1961	The Alliance for Progress is formed.
1961	The Berlin Wall is built.
1961	The Twenty-Third Amendment is approved.
1962	The Soviet Union tries to build missile bases in Cuba.
1963	An atomic test-ban treaty is signed.
1963	The March on Washington takes place.
1963	President Kennedy is killed. **Vice-President Lyndon B. Johnson becomes President.**
1964	The Economic Opportunity Act is passed.
1964	The Civil Rights Act of 1964 is passed.
1964	The Twenty-Fourth Amendment is approved.
1964	**President Johnson is reelected.**
1965	The Voting Rights Act of 1965.
1965	Health insurance for older persons (Medicare) is added to the Social Security system.
1965	American soldiers fight in South Viet Nam.
1965	The Elementary and Secondary Education Act is passed.
1967	The Twenty-Fifth Amendment is approved.
1968	The Civil Rights Act of 1968 is passed.
1968	The Poor People's Campaign is held.
1968	**Richard M. Nixon is elected President.**
1969	American astronauts land on the moon.
1969	President Nixon begins to withdraw troops from Viet Nam.

Index

Page numbers in italics that have *f*, *m*, or *p* written before them refer to features (*f*), maps (*m*), or pictures (*p*). Page numbers in **boldface** show that the word's meaning is given on this page.

Abolition movement, 275–76, *p 276*, *p 278*, 281–82, *f 281*, *p 282*, 286, 316–17
Academies, 121
Adams, John, *f 152*, 159, 166, 191–92, *p 192*, 195–96, 239
Adams, John Quincy, 214, 245, *p 245*
Adams, Samuel, 152, 153–54
Adams-Onís Treaty, 213
Addams, Jane, 427
A.F.L.-C.I.O., 660
Africa, 26–27, *m 27*, 38–39, 86–87, 104–6, *p 106*, 280–81, *p 280*, 461, 485, 487, 591, 601, *m 602*
Afro-American Council, 433
Agricultural Adjustment Act, 537, 549
Agriculture, 38, 40, 127–29, 171–72, 190, 196, *m 220*, 222, 225–28, *m 226*, *p 228*, 233, 238, 244–45, 256–57, *p 260*, 261, 285, 348, 355–56, 359–61, 367, 389, 409, 410, *p 418*, 419–22, 432–33, 440, 451, 480, 518–20, 530–31, 537, *p 538*, 549, *p 549*, 557, 657–59, 725, *p 725*; colonial, 56–58, *m 57*, *p 58*, 62, 74, 75, *p 78*, 79–82, *p 81*, *p 82*, 98, *f 99*, 103–4, 109–11, *p 111*; European, 19–20, *p 20*, 22, 50
Agriculture, Department of, 420
Alabama, 226, 318, *p 346*, 348, 665, 672, 676
Alaska, 456, *m 456*
Albany Congress, 140
Albany Plan, 140
Alien Acts, 196
Alliance for Progress, 675, 699
Allies, *see* World War One, World War Two
Almanacs, 122
America, 27, 28; discovered, *p 17*, *p 18*, 19, 20, 28

American Colonization Society, 281
American Federation of Labor, 415–16, 518, 543, 544, 659–60
American System, 239
Amusements and recreation, 39, 118, *p 118*, 123, 262–63, *p 262*, 356, 395–98, *p 491*, 506–8, 553, 554–56, 652–53, *p 653*
Anderson, Marian, 513, *f 543*
Anthony, Susan B., *f 274*
Anti-Ballistic Missile System, 712
Anti-Federalists, 183
Appalachian Mountains, 127, 231
Appomattox, *p 326*, 330
Arizona, 355, 361
Arkansas, 226, 231, 323, 664, *p 664*
Art, *p 106*, 124, 270, *p 400*, 402, 513, 556, *p 558*, 560, 652
Articles of Confederation, 172–73, 174, 177, 179
Asia, 21, *m 21*, *m 26*, *m 27*, 461, 485, 487; Cold War, 639–42, *m 640*, 645–46; immigrants from, 365, *f 368*, 499, 623; trade with, 22, 25–27, *m 26*, *m 27*; World War Two, 589–92, 603–4, *m 603*, 639–40
Assembly, colonial, 134–35, *p 136*
Astronauts, *p 704*, 705–7, *p 706*
Atlantic Charter, 607
Atomic bomb, 604, *p 604*, 623, 636, *p. 636*, 696
Atomic Energy Act, 617
Attucks, Crispus, *f 152*
Automation, 658, *p 659*, 723–24
Automobiles and automobile industry, 506, *p 510*, 523–24, *p 524*, *p 614*, 616, 659
Axis Powers, 580, *m 584*, 589
Aztec Indians, 32, *m 32*, *p 33*, *f 34*, *p 36*, 37

Bacon's Rebellion, 129
Balboa, Vasco de, 37, *m 38*
Baltimore, Maryland, *p 90*, *m 208*, 209
Bank of the United States (first), 185, 196, 222, 238–39, *p 240*; (second), 238–39, 251–52, 256
Banking, *m 220*, 222, 257, 374, 445, 450, 451; in Depression, 530, 536–37, *p 536*; state banks, 252, 256, 257
Barnum, Phineas T., 263
Belgium, 585, *m 602*, 603
Benefit societies, 281
Berlin, *m 602*, 608, *m 608*, *p 632*, 634–35; Wall, *p 694*, 695
Big Three Nations, 607–10
Bill of Rights, 172; in Constitution, 184
Birmingham, Alabama, *p 346*, 348, 676

Black Americans, 115, *p 356*, *f 386*, 397, 500, 556, 717–20; abolitionists, *p 278*, 281–82, *f 281*, *p 282*; in armed forces, *f 152*, 163, 208, 209, 323, *f 324*, 329, *p 329*, 463, 501, *p 501*, *p 597*, 612, *p 623*; artists and writers, 512–13, 560, 561, 653; in Civil War, 323, *f 324*, 329, *p 329*; education, *see* Education; in government, 341–44, *p 342*, *f 344*, 348, 502, 671, 683; groups of, 280, 282, 433, 501–2, 663–64, 719–20; music and performers, 398, 512, 513, *f 543*, 556; Reconstruction and, 336–37, 341–44; return to Africa, 280–81, *p 280*, 502; rights of, 135, 280–81, 282, 309–10, 336, 337–48, 433, 501–2, 544, 663–65, 671–72, 676–78, 684, 717; in South, 228, 336, 341–44, 348–49, 385–86, 421, 433; workers, *see* Labor; *see also* Slavery
Black Codes, 336
Black conventions, 282
Black Muslims, 720
Black power movement, 719–20
Bolívar, Símon, 213, *p 214*
Books, 26, 122–23, 267–69, *f 269*, 397, 401–2, 426–27, 511–13, 560–61, 652–53
Border states, 323
Boston, 88, 93, *p 93*, *f 151*, 152–53, 163, 219, 222, 280, *f 312*
Boston Massacre, *f 152*
Boston Tea Party, *p 150*, 153
Boundaries, of United States, 166, 209, 215, *m 292*, 293, 297–98, 299–300, *m 299*, 456, *m 456*
Boxer Rebellion, 467–68
Boycotts, 280, 665, *f 719*
Braddock, Edward, 140–41
Bradford, William, 62
Briand, Aristide, 565, *p 566*
Breckinridge, John C., 317, 318
Brown against the Board of Education of Topeka, 664
Brown, John, 312, 316–17, *p 317*
Bruce, Blanche K., 342
Bryan, William Jennings, *p 405*, 422, 443, *f 512*
Buchanan, James, 315, 322
Bull Moose Party, *f 445*, 446, *p 446*
Bull Run, Battle of, 327, *m 328*
Bunker Hill, Battle of, 158, *p 158*, 159, 163
Burger, Warren, *f 689*
Burgoyne, John, 163–64
Burns, Anthony, *f 312*
Business, *p 316*, 379, 407, 470, 495, 496, 526, 723; *see also* Industries

Cabinet, President's, **184**
Cabot, John, 49
Cabral, Pedro, 43
Calhoun, John C., 250–51
California, 38, 294, *m 298,* 303–4, 353, *f 355, f 368, p 519,* 657, *p 658*
Cambodia, *m 640,* 646
Canada, 43–45, 142, 203–4, 209, 210, 215, 571; American Revolution, 157–58, *p 159,* 163; French and Indian War, *f 140,* 141; War of 1812, 207, 208
Canals, *p 217,* **232**–33, *p 242,* 243–45, *m 244,* 249–50, 468–69, *p 468, m 468*
Cannon, Joseph, 444
Carnegie, Andrew, 377, *p 378*
Carnegie Steel Company, 378, *f 416*
Carpetbaggers, 341, 343
Cartier, Jacques, *p 42,* 43–44
Carver, George Washington, *p 385*
Cass, Lewis, 300
Castro, Fidel, *p 692,* 693
Catholics, 39, *p 40,* 41, 45, 51–52, 135, 294, 305, 495, 500, 669
Cattle, *f 99, m 220,* 222, 233, *m 354,* 355–56, 360, 440; *see also* Agriculture
Central America, 37–39, *m 38,* 213, 305; Indians of, 31–32, *m 32, p 33, f 34, p 36,* 37
Central Pacific Railroad, 365, *m 366, f 368*
Central Powers, 473, *m 476, m 481*
Central Treaty Organization, 647
Champlain, Samuel de, 44, *m 44*
Charleston, South Carolina, 74, 93, *p 105, m 164,* 251, 286
Chautauqua movement, 403
Cheap money, **410**
Chiang Kai-shek, 641, 645–46
Chicago, 233, 305, 311, 356, 366, 373, 415, *p 415,* 427, *p 428,* 502
Child labor, 221, 413, 414, 415, 451, *p 451;* laws, **428,** 451
China, 26, 467–68, 487, 608; immigrants from, 365, *f 368;* Japanese war with, *p 576,* 577, 580, 589; trade with, 215, 219, 291, 467
Church of England, 51–52, 61, 62, 99
Churchill, Winston, 607–8, *p 609*
Cincinnati, 233, 396
Cities and towns, 219, 222, 233, 305, *p 388,* 389–92, *m 390,* 427, 506, 596, 657–58, 659, 670, 678, 683, 688; colonial, 64, 93; early European, 20, 22, *p 22;* government of, 392, 407, 426, 431–32; life in, 261–63, *p 262,* 395–98, 713–14; oldest United States city, 40; riots

in, 718; transportation, 391, *p 391,* 678, *p 713*
Civil Rights Act (1957, 1960), **672;** (1964), **678;** (1968), 719
Civil rights movement, *p 662,* 663–65, 671–72, *p 672, p 674,* 676–78, 684, 718–19, *f 719*
Civil Service, 408–9, *p 409,* 432, 622
Civil War, *p 307, m 322,* 323–24, *f 324, p 326,* 327–30, *m 328, p 333,* 355–56, 365, 371, 455–56
Civilian Conservation Corps, *p 537,* 538
Clark, George Rogers, *m 164,* 165
Clark, William, 233
Clay, Henry, 239, 245, 293, *p 302,* 304
Clayton Anti-Trust Act, **450,** 495
Cleveland, Grover, 409, 410, 458, 462
Clothing, 110, 116, 128, 262, *p 264,* 356, 505; factories, 220, 371, 374
Coal industry, 372, 378, 438–39, 517, 526, 595, 616
Cold War, *see* Communism
Colleges and universities, 39, 122, *f 123,* 171, *p 266,* 274, 403, 505, 513, 651, *f 670,* 683
Colombia, 468–69, *m 469*
Colonial America, 55–159, *f 88, f 116, f 124;* "American" thinking, 146; amusements and recreation, 118, *p 118,* 123; armed forces in, 133, 147, 151; art in, 124; books and newspapers, 122–23; British laws disliked in, 85–86, 91–92, 142, 151–53; family life, *p 114,* 116; foods and drink, 34, 116; French and Indian War, *p 138,* **140**–42; frontiers of, 69, *p 95, p 98, m 100, p 126,* 127–29, *m 128,* 142; government of, 56–57, 58, 62, 63–64, *f 64,* 68, 69, 73–75, 129, 133–36, 145–48; immigrants to, **97**–100; Indians and, 34, 62, 69, 70; landholding in, 57, 58, 67, 69, 75; Pilgrims, *p 60,* 61–62, *p 62, p 113;* Puritans, 62–64, 67, 69, *p 70;* Quakers, **75,** 135; Revolutionary War, 154, *p 154,* 157–60; social classes, **115;** travel, 34, *p 117*
Colorado, 354–55
Columbus, Christopher, *p 17,* 27–28, *m 27, p 28*
Commercial industries, 92
Committees of Correspondence, 152
Common Sense (Paine), 159
Communism, 623–24, 629; Cold War, *p 632,* 633–36, *m 634,* 640–42, *m 640,* 645–47, 693–96, 699–702
Compromise of 1850, *p 302,* 304, *m 304,* 305

Concentration camps, 604
Concord, Battle of, *p 153,* 154, *m 154,* 163
Confederate States of America (Confederacy), **318,** 321–24, *m 322,* 327–30, 455
Congo, 696
Congress: black Americans in, 342, *p 342, f 344,* 502; Constitutional powers of, 179, 185, 239; "Hundred Days," 536; judicial review of laws passed by, **239;** petitions to end slavery, **286;** Reconstruction and, 336–38, 344; representation in, 178, 688; under Articles of Confederation, 173–74; *see also* House of Representatives; Senate
Congress of Industrial Organizations, 544, 659–60
Connecticut (colonial), 68–70, *m 68,* 80–81, 122, 133–37, *p 367*
Conservation, 439–40, 444
Constitution, 69; *see also* states
Constitution of United States, *p 169,* 178–80, *p 178, p 180,* 183, 227; amendments, **184,** 336, 337, 432, 445, 520, 536, 554, 618, 689
Constitutional Convention, 177–80
Constitutional Union Party, 318
Continental Congresses, **153,** 157, 159, 163, 173
Coolidge, Calvin, 494–96, *p 494,* 520
Copperheads, 324
Corbett, Jim, *f 392,* 397
Cornwallis, Charles, *m 164,* 166, *p 166*
Cortés, Hernando, *p 36,* 37, *m 38*
Cotton, *p 224,* 225–28, *m 226, p 228, m 232,* 243–44, **285;** gin, 172, **225;** manufacturing, 220, 226, *f 227,* 348, 526
Council, colonial, **63,** 134
Courts, 179, 184, 239, 256; colonial, 134, 146; *see also* Supreme Court
Cowboys, *f 99,* 356
Cox, James M., 493
Crawford, William H., 245
Crime, 93, *f 116,* 171, 273, *f 355,* 520, 687, 688
Crittenden Compromise, 322
Crusades, 21, *m 21*
Cuba, 213, 305, 456, *p 460,* 461–64, *m 461,* 573, *p 574,* 693–94, *p 695*
Cuffe, Paul, 280
Cushing, Thomas, *f 172*
Czechoslovakia, *m 486,* 487, 583, 584, *m 584,* 700, *p 700*

Da Gama, Vasco, 27, *m 27*
Darrow, Clarence, *f 512*
Davis, Jefferson, 321
Davis, John W., 494
Dawes, William, 154

Declaration of Independence, *p 131, p 156,* 159
Declaratory Act, 151
Defense, Department of, 617
Delaware, 323; colonial, 45, *m 74,* 75, 80, 81
Democratic Party, 245, 255–57, 315–17, 347, 407, 409, 422, 433, 488, 544, 618
Depressions, 256–57, 316, *p 318,* 567, 572; Great Depression, *p 528,* 530–31, 535–38, 541–44, *p 550,* 553–56, 559–61, 572, 622
De Priest, Oscar, 502
Dewey, George, 463, *p 464*
Dewey, John, 513
Dewey, Thomas E., 598, 618, *p 618*
Dias, Bartholomeu, 27
Douglas, Stephen A., 311, *p 314,* 317–18
Douglass, Frederick, 281–82, *p 282,* 287, *f 324*
Drake, Francis, 49
Dred Scott Decision, 316
Du Bois, W. E. B., 433, *p 433*
Dunne, Finley Peter, *f 427*
Dutch colonies, 45, 73
Dutch (Netherlands) East Indies, 590, 591, *m 603*

Eastern Woodland Indians, *m 32,* 33
Economic Opportunity Act, 682
Edison, Thomas A., 374, 398
Education, 39, 171, 264, 269, 274, 347, 402–3, *p 403,* 505, *f 512,* 513, 559–60, 622, 629, *p 650,* 651, 658, 677; of black Americans, 280, 336, *p 337,* 342, 349, *p 349,* 386, 644, 664–65, *f 670,* 672, 678, 688, 717; colonial, 121–22, *p 122, f 123,* 124, 683–84; free, 255, 264, 342; schoolbooks, 264, *f 269,* 403
Eighteenth Amendment, 520
Eisenhower Doctrine, 647
Eisenhower, Dwight D., 601, 603, *p 626,* 627–29, *p 631,* 636, *p 644,* 645–47, 664, 672, 693
Elementary and Secondary Education Act of 1965, 683–84
Elkins Act, 438
Elliott, Robert Brown, *f 344*
Emancipation Proclamation, 328–29
Embargo Act, 202
Emerson, Ralph Waldo, 267, 268, *p 268*
Employment Act, 616
England, 25, *p 48,* 49–50, *p 50,* 61, *p 96,* 121; colonies of (*see also* Colonial America; names of colonies), 45, 49–52, 55–58, *m 57, m 68,* 73–75, *m 74, m 80,* 133; religion in, 51–52, *p 51,* 61, 62, 75, 99; *see also* Great Britain

Ericson, Leif, 18, 20
Erie Canal, 232, *m 244*
Ethiopia, 578–79, *p 579, m 584*
Europe, 19–20, *m 21, m 26, m 27,* 461, 567, 572, 577; China and, 467–68; Cold War and Communism in, 633, 635–36, *m 634,* 647, 700; immigrants from, 97–100, 293, 361, 384–85, 499–500, 622–23; Monroe Doctrine and, 214–15, 469–70; trade, 20, 22, *p 22,* 219; war debts, 566–67, 572, 578; World Wars, *see* World War One, World War Two; *see also* countries
Explorers, 26–28, *m 27,* 37–38, *m 38,* 43–44, *m 44,* 49, 233

Fair Deal, 618, 621–22, 628
Fair Employment Practices Committee, 597
Fallen Timbers, Battle of, 186
Farm Security Administration, 549
Farmers and farming, *see* Agriculture
Farragut, David, 327
Federal Farm Loan Act, 451
Federal Power Commission, 525
Federal Reserve Act, 450
Federal Reserve System, 450
Federal Trade Commission, 450, 496
Federalist Party, 191, 192, 195–96, 203, 257
Federalists, 183
Fifteenth Amendment, 337
Fillmore, Millard, 304
First Continental Congress, 153
Fishing and Fisheries, 86, 140, 166
Florida, 195, 203, 213, 249, *m 299,* 318, 344; Spain and, 37, 38, *m 38,* 40, 142, 166
Food, 21, 34, 110, 116, 128, 261, 373, 652; Indian, 31, 33, 361, 362; industries, 355–56, 371, 373–74, *p 374,* 439, *p 439;* laws, 439; in wartime, 480, 520, 597, 598
Fort Sumter, *p 320,* 323
Fort Ticonderoga, 157, *m 164*
Founding Fathers, *p 169,* 177–80, *p 178*
Fourteen Points, 485–86, 487
Fourteenth Amendment, 336
France, 25, *p 42,* 43–45, *m 44,* 70, 100, 140, 195–97, 215, 292, 468, 565–66, 583, 640, 647; and American Revolution, 160, 164, *m 164,* 165, 166; British and, *p 138,* 139–42, *f 140,* 189–90, 197, 201; Civil War (American) and, 324, 329; Cold War, 633–35, 646–47; Indo-China, 646, *p 646;* Mexico and, 455; trade with, 201, 203; World War One, 473, 474, 475, *m 476,*

p 478, 482, 486–87, *m 486;* World War Two, 585, *m 602,* 603, 608
Franco, Francisco, 580
Franklin, Benjamin, 124, 129, 140, 159, 166, 177
Freedmen, 336–37; *see also* Black Americans
Freedmen's Bureau, 336
Freedom rides, 665
Free-Soilers, 300, 312
Frémont, John C., 294, 299, 315
French and Indian War, *p 138,* 140–42, *f 140, m 141,* 145, 147
French Revolution, 189–90
Frontier, 69, *p 95, p 98, m 100,* 117, *p 126,* 165, 263, *p 263;* Indian troubles on, 129, 174, 186, 203–4, *p 204,* 210, 213, 360, 362, *p 362;* settlement of, 127–29, 142, 353, 356, 359–61, *p 360;* Western, 203–4, 210, 231–33, 291–94, 353–56, *m 354,* 359–61
Fugitive Slave Act, 309, 310
Fur trade, 45, 73, 92, 140, 142, *m 173,* 219, 233

Gadsden Purchase, 305
Gage, John, 153–54
Garfield, James A., 408
Garrison, William Lloyd, 275, 276, 281
Garvey, Marcus, 502
George the Third, King, 153, 157, 158
Georgia, 225, 249, 318, 330; colonial, *m 74,* 75, 80–82, 165
Germany, 97, 158, 159, 457, *p 563;* Cold War, 633–35, 694–95, *p 694;* Hitler and Nazis (*see also* World War Two), 577–78, 579–80, 583–85, 610, *m 684;* reparations, 487, 488, 567; World War One, 473–76, *f 474, m 476,* 479–80, 481–82, *m 481,* 486–88, *m 486;* World War Two, 585, 589–92, *p 597,* 601–3, *m 602,* 604; zones of, 608, *m 608,* 610, 634–35
Gettysburg, Battle of, 330
Ghent, Treaty of, 209
G.I. Bill of Rights, 615, 651
Gilbert, Sir Humphrey, 55
Goldwater, Barry, 681
Gompers, Samuel, 415–16
Good Neighbor Policy, 573–74, *f 573*
Government: city, 392, 407, 426, 431–32; colonial, 56–57, 58, 62, 63–64, *f 64,* 68, 69, 73, 74, 129, 133–36; dishonesty in, 392, 407, 426, 494, 624; French colonial, 45; Great Depression and, 531, 536–38, 541–44, 547–50, 556; national, 172–73, 177–80, 180, 184–85, 196, 243–46, 249–51, 628; overseas ter-

ritories, 464–568; reform of, 431–32; Spanish colonial, 39
Grange, 420–21, p 420
Grant, Ulysses S., 327, 329–30, 338, 344, 407
Great Awakening, 123–24
Great Britain, 99, 139, 201–4, 291, 292, 305, 467, 468, 565, 583, 640, 647; and American Revolution, 154, 157–60, 163–66; boundary agreements with, 209, 215, 293; Civil War (American) and, 324, 329, 455–56; Cold War, 633–35, 647; cotton manufacturing, 225, 226; Florida, 142, 166; French and Indian War, p 138, 139–42, f 140, 145, 147; French Revolution, 189–90; French wars, p 138, 139–42, f 140, 189–90, 197, 201; fur trade, 140, 142; Northwest Territory, m 173, 190; Parliament, 67, p 146, 153; peace treaty of 1763, 142; South America and, 214, 215, 458; trade with, 195, 201–3, 203, 571; War of 1812, 204, 207–10; West Indies trade, 215; World War One, 473–76, m 476, 482, 486–87; World War Two, 585, 589, 591, 592, 602, m 602, 603, 607–10
Great Plains, p 352, 353–56, 359–62
Great Society, 681–84, 687
Greece, 591, m 634, 635
Guadalupe Hidalgo, Treaty of, 299
Guam, 464, 591, m 603, 604
Guantanamo naval base, 573, p 574

Hamilton, Alexander, 177, 184–85, 190, 191, 195–96
Hancock, John, 153–54
Harding, Warren G., p 492, 493–94, 495–96
Harlem Renaissance, 512–13
Harrison, Benjamin, 410
Harrison, William Henry, 204, 207, m 208, 210, p 256, 257, p 257
Harvard College, 122, f 123
Hawaii, 219, 305, m 456, 457–58
Hawkins, John, 49
Hay, John, 467, 468
Hayes, Rutherford B., 344, 407–8
Haymarket Riot, 415, p 415
Health, Education, and Welfare, Department of, 628
Henson, Josiah, 287
Hepburn Act, 438
Hiroshima, Japan, m 603, 604
Hitler, Adolf, 577–78, p 576; see also Germany
Home Owners Loan Corporation, 538
Homestead Act, 359
Homesteaders, p 352, 359
Hooker, Thomas, 68

Hoover, Herbert, 495–96, p 496, 529, 531, p 534, 535, 536, p 567, 572
House of Burgesses, 56–57
House of Representatives, 178, p 179, 245, 342, p 342, 408, 502, 536
Housing, 719; in cities, 222, 305, 390, 427, 502, 506, 658, 717; colonial, 93, p 98, p 108, 110, 117, 128; frontier, p 98, 117, 128, 360, p 360; modern 561, p 561; public, 622, 629, 670–78, 683; segregation in, 279, 280, 349
Housing and Urban Development, Department of, 683
Houston, Sam, 292
Howe, William, 164–65
Hughes, Charles Evans, 475
Humphrey, Hubert H., 682, 688–89
Hungary, m 602, 603, 647

Illinois, 233, 238, 249, 276, p 276, 315
Immigrants and immigration, 97–100, 305, 376, 384–85, p 384, 402–3, 427, p 498, 499–500, p 622; cities and, 390, 427; laws controlling, 451, 499–500, 622–23, 687–88; to Old Northwest, 233, 305; from South, 233, 291, 501, 596, 651; Westward, 231–33, p 289, p 290, 291, 293, 294, p 294, 359–61, 651; workers, 365, f 368, 383–85, 413, 499
Imperialism, 461
Inca Indians, m 32, 33, 38, p 39
Indentured servants, 81, 82, 98, 99, 103–4, 115
India, 26–27, m 640, 641
Indians, 31–34, m 32, p 33, 34, f 34, p 36, 37–39, p 39, 45, 62, 75, 79, 294; American Revolution and, 159, 165; French and Indian War, and, 140, 142, p 142; Spanish and, 37–38, p 39; troubles with, 69, 129, 142, 174, 186, 203–4, p 204, 212–13, 249, p 252, 362, p 362; Westward movement of, 249, f 251, p 252, 361–62, p 361
Indo-China, 589, m 603, 646
Indonesia, 640, m 640, 641
Industries, 210, 220–21, m 220, m 232, 233, 243, 347–48, 355–56, p 370, 371–74, 377, 523–26, 658–59, p 722, 723–24; Civil War, 324, 355–56, 371; colonial, 86, 91–92, 142, 145; in Depression, 530–31, 538, 549; government and, 368, p 376, 379, 432, 437, 439, 445, 446, 450, 495, 496, 525, 723; monopolies, see Trusts; muckrakers and, 426; protective tariffs (see also Tariffs), 238, 243, 409; workers, see Labor; World War One, 479,

480, p 480, 501, 517; World War Two, 592, p 594, 595–97, p 596
Initiative, 432
Injunction, 416, 450, 518, 616
Internal improvements, 243–45, 250–51
Internal Security Act, 624
Interstate Commerce Act, 368
Interstate Commerce Commission, 438, 445, 496
Iron industries, 92, p 221, m 232, 233, 348, 372, 377–78
Iroquois Indians, p 30, m 32, 33, 140
Isolation movement, 578, 580, f 580
Italy, 583, m 584; Ethiopian War, 578–79, p 579; World War One, m 476, m 486, 487; World War Two, 589, 590–91, 601–2, m 602

Jackson, Andrew, m 208, 209, f 209, 210, 213, 215, 245–46, p 246, p 248, 249–52, p 250, 255–56, 292
Jackson, Thomas "Stonewall," 324
Jacksonian Democracy, 255–56
Jamestown, p 54, 55–56, 103
Japan, 215, 291, 487, 565, 577, 583, p 638, 639; Chinese war, p 576, 577, 580, 589; World War Two, p 588, 589–92, 603–4, m 603, p 604, p 606, 608
Jay, John, 166, 190
Jefferson, Thomas, p 156, 159, 184, 185, 190–92, p 192, p 194, 196–97, 201–2, f 251
Johnson, Andrew, 335, 336, 537–38
Johnson, Lyndon B., 669, 671, 677, p 678, p 680, 681–84, p 683, p 686, 688–89, 699–700
Johnson, Tom, 431
Joliet, Louis, 44
Jones, John Paul, 165
Juarez, Benito, 455
Judicial review, 239
Judiciary Act, 184

Kansas, p 308, 311, m 311, 312, 356, p 421
Kansas-Nebraska Act, 311
Kearny, Stephen, 299
Kellogg, Frank, 565–66, p 566
Kellogg-Briand Pact, 566
Kennedy, John F., p 668, 669–72, p 671, p 672, 675–77, p 676, p 677, 693–96, 699
Kennedy, Robert F., 688–89
Kentucky, 186, 196, 227, 323
Khrushchev, Nikita, 647, p 692, 694, 695
King, Dr. Martin Luther, Jr., p 662, 665, 676, 684, 718, p 718, 719, f 719
Knights of Labor, 385, 414–15
Know-Nothing Party, 305

Knox, Henry, 184
Korean War, 622, *m 640,* 641–42, *f 641, p 642,* 645
Ku Klux Klan, 343–44, 500–1, *p 500*

Labor, 255, *p 412, p 414, p 594,* 595–97, *p 596,* 616, *p 616,* 638, *p 659;* and black Americans, 279, 385–86, 414, 501, 502, 596–97, 658, 717–18; colonial, 39, 75, 81, 82, 92–93, 98, 99, 103–6, 110, *p 111;* education and, 402–3, 513, 658; immigrant, 365, *f 368,* 383–85, 413, 499; New Deal and, 543–44; unemployment, 256–57, *p 318,* 501, 517, 529, **530**–31, *p 530, p 531,* 538, 670, 717–18, 724–25; working conditions and wages, 221–22, *f 227,* 255, 383–86, 413–14, 416, 428, 438–39, 451, 517–18, 544, 616, 622, 628, 660, 670, 723, 724; *see also* Indentured servants; Labor unions; Slavery
Labor unions, 221–22, 255, 365, 413–16, 451, 518, 595, 659–60, 717; law about, 616, 678; New Deal and, 543; strikes, 415, 416, *f 416,* 438–39, 450, 451, *p 451,* 517–18, *p 518,* 616, *p 617,* 660; *see also* Labor
La Follette, Robert, 432, 446, 495
Landon, Alfred M., 544
Laos, *m 640,* 646
La Salle, Robert, 44, *m 44*
Latin America, 456–57, 469–70, 567–68, *p 570,* 573–74, *f 573, p 624,* 675, 699–700
League of Nations, 485–86, 487, 488, 493, 577–79
Lee, Richard Henry, 159
Lee, Robert E., 324, 328, 330
Legislatures, 172, 255, *p 272,* 341–42, *p 421,* 432, 688; colonial, **56**, 129, *p 132,* 134–36, *p 136*
Lend-Lease Act, 585
Lewis, John L., 543–44, *p 544*
Lewis, Meriwether, 233
Lexington, Battle of, 154, *m 154,* 163
Liberia, 280–81, *p 280*
Liberty Bonds, 481
Liliuokalani, Queen, 457–58, *p 458*
Lincoln, Abraham, *p 314,* 317–18, 321, 323, *p 323, f 324,* 328–29, 330, 335–36, 455
Lindbergh, Charles, *f 507*
Lodge, Henry Cabot, 488
London Company, 55–56
Louisiana, 195, 196–97, 226, 227, 231, 318, 327, 344
Louisiana Purchase, 197, *m 197,* 240, *f 251, m 299*
Lovejoy, Elijah, 276, *p 276*
Loyalists, 159, *p 159*
Lundy, Benjamin, 275

"Lusitania," 475, *m 476*
Lyceum lectures, 269

MacArthur, Douglas, *p 606, p 638,* 639, *f 641,* 642
Macdonough, Thomas, 208, *m 208*
Macon's Bill Number 2, 203
Madison, James, 177, 191, 196, 203–4, *p 203*
Magazines, *p 264,* 269, 426, *p 426,* 554, 555
Magellan, Ferdinand, *p 24, m 27,* 28
Maine, *m 68,* 70, 215, 240, 274
Manifest Destiny, 291–94
Mann, Horace, 264
Mann-Elkins Act, 445
Manpower Development and Training Act, 670
Manufacturing, *see* Industries
Mao Tse-Tung, 641
Marbury against Madison, case of, 239
March on Washington, *p 674,* 676–77, *f 719*
Marquette, Father Jacques, 44
Marshall, John, 239
Marshall Plan, 636
Maryland, 225, 227, 323, 328; colonial, 57–59, *m 57,* 59, 80–82, 104, 133–36, *p 136*
Mass production, 523–24
Massachusetts, 174, 280; colonial (*see also* Massachusetts Bay, Plymouth Colony), 62–64, *m 63, m 68,* 70, 80–81, 88, 122, *p 122,* 152–54, 158, 163, *f 172*
Massachusetts Bay, 63–64, *m 63, f 64,* 67, 69–70
Matzeliger, Jan Ernst, *f 372*
Maya Indians, 31–32, *m 32*
Mayflower Compact, 62, *p 62*
McCarthy, Eugene, 688–89
McCarthy, Joseph, 623–24, 629, *p 629*
McClellan, George C., 328
McCulloch against Maryland, 239
McKinley, William, *p 406, p 408,* 422, *p 422,* 437, 462, 463
McNary-Haugen Bill, 519–20
Meat packing industry, 356, 371, 373, 378, 439, *p 439*
Medicare Act, 683
Meredith, James, *f 670*
Mexican Cession, 299–300, *m 299,* 303–4
Mexican War, *p 296,* 298–99, *m 298, p 300,* 303
Mexico, 37–39, *m 38,* 455, 470, *f 474;* Americans' rights in, 567, 573–74; Indians of, 31–32, *m 32, p 33, f 34,* 37; territories and, 291–92, 294, 297–99, 305

Mexico City, *p 296, m 298,* 299, *p 300*
Middle colonies, *p 78,* 80, 81, 86, 88, 92
Middle East, 591, 601, *m 602,* 647
Middle states, 160, 171, 219, 220–21
Middle West, 390, 596, 657
Midway Island, *m 456,* 457, *m 603,* 604; Battle of, **592**
Mining industries, 92, 353–56; *m 354,* 440
Minutemen, **154**
Missions, 39, *p 40,* 45, 294
Mississippi, 226, 318, 329, 341–42
Mississippi River and Valley, 44, 116, 186, 196, 231, 327, *m 328,* 329, 353
Missouri, 239–40, 323
Missouri Compromise, *m 238,* **240**, 300, *m 311,* 322
Money, 22, 88, 450; cheap and hard, **410**; Depression and, 530, 531, 536–38, 542–43, 549; paper money, 239, 246, 410, 450; *see also* Banking
Monopoly, *see* Trusts
Monroe Doctrine, *p 212,* 214–15, *p 454,* 455, 458
Monroe, James, 196, 197, 214–15, 237
Montcalm, General, *f 140,* 141
Montgomery, Alabama, 665, *f 719*
Moon landings, 705–7, *p 707; see also* Space
Morgan, J. P., 378, *p 379*
Motion pictures, *p 504,* 506–7, 525, 553, 556, 652
Mountain Men, *p 230, m 232,* **233**
Muckrakers, **426**
Munich Conference, *p 582,* 583
Music and musicians, 262–63, 398, *f 482,* 512, 513, *f 543, p 552,* 555–56, *f 556,* 652–53
Mussolini, Benito, 578, 580

Napoleon, 196–97, 203, 208
National Association for the Advancement of Colored People, 433, 501–2, *p 502,* 663–64
National Defense Education Act, 629, 651
National Housing Act, 622
National Labor Relations Act, 543, 548
National Labor Relations Board, 543
National Labor Union, 414
National Progressive Republican League, 445
National Recovery Administration, 538
National Road, *p 236,* 238, *m 244*

National Security Act, 617
Nationalist China, 608, 641, 645–46
Navigation Acts, 85–86, 142, 146
Nebraska, 311, *m 311*, 312, *p 360*, 365
Negroes, *see* Black Americans
Netherlands, the, 585, 640
Neutrality Act (1935), **579**; (1937), **580**; (1939), **585**
New Amsterdam, 45
New Deal, **535**–38, 541–44, 547–50, 628
New England, 171, 191, 203, 210, 219–20, 237, 267–68; colonies, *m 68, 70*, 80–81, 86–87, 92, 121–22, 123, *p 134*; Revolutionary War, 160, 163–64
New England Anti-Slavery Society, 275
New England Confederation, 70
New France, 44–45, *m 44*, 70
New Freedom, 449–51, 475
New Frontier, **670**–72, 675–78
New Hampshire (colonial), *m 68*, 69–70, 80–81
New Jersey (colonial), 73, *m 74*, 80, 81
New Mexico, 233, 297, *m 298*, 299, 303, 304, *m 304*, 355, 361
New Netherland, 45, 73, *p 102*
New Orleans, 142, 196, 227, 311, 327, 342, 366, 397
New Orleans, Battle of, *p 199*, *m 208*, 209, *f 209*
New South, 347–49; *see also* South
New World, 28, 31–45
New York (colonial), 45, 73, *m 74*, 80, 81, *p 84*, 88, 93
New York City, 148, 163, 164–65, *p 170*, *p 218*, 219, 222, *p 262*, 263, 280, 366, *p 391*, 397, *p 414*, 718
New York State, 163–64, 191, 220, 232, 267–68, 427
Newspapers, 122–23, 270, 275, 281, 554–55
Niagara Movement, 433
Nicolet, Jean, 44
Nineteenth Amendment, 432
Nixon, Richard M., 669, 689, 702, *p 710*, 711–14, *p 712*, 726
Norsemen, *p 17*, 18, 20
North Africa, 591, 601
North Atlantic Treaty Organization, *f 635*, 636, 647, 700
North Carolina, 225, 323, 348, *p 525*, 665; colonial, 55, 74, *m 74*, 80–82, 99, 129, 166
North Korea, *m 640*, 641–42, 645
North Viet Nam, *m 640*, 646, 695, 701–2, *p 702*, 711
Northeast, **219**–22, *m 220*, 233,

243–46, 250, 264, 305, 390, 596, 657
Northwest Ordinance, 173–74
Northwest Territory, 173–74, *m 173*, 186, *p 186*, 190
Northwestern Indians, *m 32*, 34
Nye, Gerald P., *f 580*
Nuclear weapons, 712; *see also* Atomic bomb

Office of Price Administration, 597–98
Office of Production Management, 592
Officeholding, 135–36, 172, 255–56, 274
Oglethorpe, James, 75
Ohio, 233, *p 287*
Ohio River and Valley, 140, 141, 142, 186, 231
Oil industry, 348, 373, 378, 426, 445, 567, 573–74
Oklahoma, 361, *p 519*
Old Northwest, **231**, *m 232*, 233, 264, 305
Old South, **226**
Old Southwest, **226**, 231, *m 232*
Open Door Policy, **467**
Oregon, 219, 233, 291, 293–94, *f 293*, 353
Oregon Country, 231, *m 232*, *m 299*
Oregon Trail, *p 290*, *m 292*, *p 293*
Oswald, Lee Harvey, 677

Paine, Thomas, 159
Panama, 468–69, *m 469*, 699
Panama Canal, 468–69, *p 468*, *m 469*, 567, *p 568*
Pan-American Conference, 456–57, *p 457*
Paris peace conference (1918), 487–88, *p 487*, *p 488*
Paris, Treaty of, 166
Parks, Rosa, 665
Paxton Boys, **129**
Peace Corps, *f 696*
Peace Treaty of 1763, **142**
Pearl Harbor, *p 588*, 590, *p 590*, *f 592*
Pendleton Civil Service Act, 408–9
Penn, William, 75
Pennsylvania, 191, *f 191*, 220, 372, *p 373*, *f 416*; colonial, 45, *m 74*, 75, 80, 81, 98, 99, 129
Perry, Matthew C., 215
Perry, Oliver Hazard, *p 206*, 207, *m 208*
Pershing, John J., 479, 482
Personal liberty laws, 309–10
Peru, *m 32*, 33, 38, *m 38*, *p 39*
Philadelphia, Pennsylvania, *p 77*, 88, 93, 153, 163, 165, *p 176*, 177, *p 199*, 219, 222, *p 240*, 366

Philippine Islands, 463, 464, *f 464*, 591, *m 603*, 604; independence, 568, 572–73, *p 572*, 640
Pierce, Franklin, 305
Pike, Zebulon, 233
Pilgrims, *p 60*, 61–62, *p 62*, *p 96*, *p 113*
Pioneer farmers, **127**
Pitt, William, 141
Pittsburgh, Pennsylvania, 348, 372, *p 381*, 507
Pizarro, Francisco, **38**, *m 38*, *p 39*
Plains Indians, *m 32*, 33, 361–62, *p 361*
Plantations, 57, 82, *p 82*, *p 228*; slavery, *p 108*, 109–11, *p 110*, *p 111*, *p 284*, 285
Playwrights, 511, 560, 653
Plessy against Ferguson, **349**
Plymouth Colony, 62, 63, *m 63*
Poets, 268–69, 511–13, 560
Poland, *m 486*, 487, 584–85, *m 584*, 610
Political machines and bosses, 392, 431, 432
Political parties, 190–91, 237, 246, 256, 300, 305, 312, 317, 318, 407, 409, 421–22, 445–46, *f 445*, 495
Polk, James K., 293, 297, 298, 300
Poll tax, 280, 348, 621, 672
Ponce de Leon, 37, *m 38*
Pontiac, Chief, 142, *p 142*
Poor People's Campaign, **718**–19
Population, 222, 231–32, 324, 361, 371–72, 389, 559, 657
Populist Party, 421–22, *p 421*, 426, 432–33
Portugal, 25, 26–27, *m 27*, *m 38*, 43
Post office, 445, *f 714*
Poverty, 660, 682–83, *p 682*, 713, 718–19, 725–26, *p 726*
Powderly, Terence V., 414
President, 179, 246, 338, 536, 617–18, 670, 688; assassinations of, 336, 408, *p 408*, 437
Proclamation of 1763, **142**
Progressive movement, 426–28, 443–46, 493
Progressive Party, **495**
Prohibition, 520, *p 520*, 554
Prophet, the, 203
Proprietary colonies, 55, **133**
Prosser, Gabriel, 285–86
Public works, **531**, *p 537*, 538, 541, 543, 544, 554
Public Works Administration, **538**
Pueblo Indians, *m 32*, 33
Puerto Rico, 213, *m 462*, 463, 464, *m 469*, 568
Pure Food and Drug Act, **439**
Puritans, 62–64, 67, 69, *p 70*, *p 113*

Quakers, 75, 135, 275

Quebec, 44, 45, *f 140,* 141, 158
Quota system, **499–500,** 625, 687–88

Radical Republicans, 336–38, 344
Radio, 507, *p 508,* 525, 553–54
Railroads, 305, 310–11, 324, *p 351,* *m 354,* 359, 364, 365–68, *m 366,* *p 367, f 368,* 373, 421, 438, 451, 480, 517, 526, 616, 665
Raleigh, Sir Walter, 55
Randolph, A. Philip, 596
Randolph, Edmund, 184
Raw materials, 22, 52, 75, 367, 371, 372, 461
Recall, 432
Reconstruction, 336–38, *p 340,* 341–44
Reconstruction Finance Corporation, 531
Referendum, 432
Reform and reformers, *p 272,* 273–76, *p 276; see also* Populist Party, Progressive movement
Regulators, **129**
Religion, 135, 171, 263, 275, 305, 495, 500, 651–52; and black Americans, 280, 281; colonial, 52, 58, 64, 67–68, 73, 75, *p 113,* 123–24, 129; in England, 51–52, *p 51,* 62, 75, 99; French and, 45, 100; Great Awakening, **123**–24; missions, **39,** *p 40,* 45, 294; revival meetings, 263, *p 263;* separation of church and state, 68
Reparations, 487, 488, 567
Republican Party (first), **191,** 192, 196, 203, 237, 238, 239; (second), **312,** 315, 316, 317–18, 336, 344, 407, 409, 445–46, 544
Revels, Hiram, 341–42
Revere, Paul, 154
Revival meetings, 263, *p 263*
Revolutionary War, **154,** *m 154, p 154,* 157–60, *p 159, p 160,* 163–66, *m 164, p 165,* 171, 184–85, 231, 264
Rhode Island (colonial), 67–68, 70, 80–81, 123, 133–37
Richmond, Virginia, 286, 327, 328, *m 328, p 334*
Riis, Jacob, 427
Roads, 232, *p 236,* 238, 239, 243–45, 249–50, 657–58
Roanoke Island, 55
Rockefeller, John D., 378
Rolfe, John, 56
Roosevelt Corollary, 469–70
Roosevelt, Franklin D., *p 533, p 534, p 546,* 550, 554, *p 570,* 580, 584, 585, 598, 603, *p 608,* 628; Good Neighbor Policy, **573**–74, *f 574;* New Deal, **535**–38, 541–44,

547–50; World War Two, 585, 589, 590, 607–8
Roosevelt, Theodore, *p 436,* 437–40, *p 438, p 440,* 443–46, *p 444, f 445, p 446, p 468,* 469
Royal colonies, 73, 74, 75, **133–36**
Russia, 481–82, 571; in World War One, 473, *m 476,* 481–82, 485, *m 486,* 487; *see also* Soviet Union

St. Louis, 233, 305, 311, 366
Samoa, *m 456,* 457
San Francisco, 294, *f 355,* 361, 608, *p 610, p 658*
San Martín, José de, 213, *p 214*
Saratoga, Battle of, 164, *m 164*
Scalawags, 341, 343
Schools, *see* Education
Scott, Dred, 315–16, *p 316*
Scott, Winfield, *p 296, m 298,* 299, 305
Second Continental Congress, 157, 159, 163, 172
Secret ballot, *p 430,* 432
Securities Exchange Act, 542
Sedition Act, 196
Segregation, 279–80, 348–49, 433, 621–22, *p 623,* 664–65, 668, *f 670,* 678, 717, 718
Selective Service Act, 479
Self-governing colonies, 133–36
Seminole Indians, 249
Senate, 178, 338, *p 338,* 342, *p 342,* 445, 488, *f 580,* 629
Separation of powers, 180
Serra, Father Junípero, 294
Settlement houses, 427, *p 428*
Seventeenth Amendment, 445
Seward, William, 456
Seymour, Horatio, 338
Share croppers, 348
Shays' Rebellion, 174, *p 174*
Sherman Anti-Trust Act, 379, 450
Sherman, William T., 330
Shipping, 190, *p 217,* 219, *m 220,* 526; World War One, 473–76, 479–80; World War Two, 585, 592, 601–2; *see also* Transportation, specific subjects
Sit-ins, 665, *p 665*
Sissle, Noble, *f 482*
Sixteenth Amendment, 445
Slave trade, 87, *p 102,* 105–6, *p 105,* 180, 227, 304, *p 310*
Slavery, 105, 163, 171–72, *f 172,* 226–28, 243, 275–76, *p 284,* 285–87, 309–10, *p 310,* 321; abolition of, 171, *f 172,* 316–17, 328–29, 330, 336; colonial, 39, 75, 82, 103–4, *p 104,* 105, *p 105, p 108,* 109–11, *p 110, p 111,* 115; Constitution and, 179–80, 227; Emancipation Proclamation, 328–

29; field hands and house servants, 109, 110, *p 110, p 111,* 227, *p 275;* revolts, **110**–11, 285–86, *p 286;* reform movements and, 274–76; rights and freedoms, 109, 110–11, 135; runaway slaves, 213, 249, 282, 287, 304, 309–10, *f 312;* in Spanish colonies, 38–39, 103–11; states divided as slave and free, *m 238,* 239–40, 292–94, 300, 303–4, *m 304, m 311,* 312; in territories, 173, *m 304,* 310–12, *m 311,* 315–16, 321, 322–23
Slidell, John, 297, 298
Slums, 222, **305,** 390, 622, 629, 658, 670
Smith, Alfred E., 495, *p 495*
Smith, John, 56
Smuggling, **86,** 146
Social Security Act, **544,** 548, 622, 628, 670
Sons of Liberty, 147–48, 152
South, 225–26, *m 226,* 231, 233, 243–46, 249–51, 269, 291, 501, 596, 657, 664–65; *see also* Southern states
South America, *m 27,* 28, *m 38,* 213–14, 458; Indians of 31, *m 32,* 33, 38, *p 39;* Spain and, 38–39, *m 38,* 213–14
South Carolina, 225, 251, 286, 318, 323, 344; colonial, 74–75, *m 74,* 80–82, 165
South Korea, *m 640,* 641–42, 645
South Viet Nam, *m 640,* 646, 695, 701–2, *p 702,* 711, *p 712*
Southeast Asia Treaty Organization, 646–47
Southern colonies, 80, 81–82, 86, 92, 103–4, *p 104, p 105, p 108,* 109–11, *p 110, p 111,* 123
Southern Democrats, 317
Southern states, 191, 225–26, *m 226;* agriculture, 171–72, 225–28, 285, 348; Civil War period, 318, 321–24, *m 322,* 327–30, 335; industries, *p 346,* 347, 348; New South, **347**–49; Reconstruction, 336–38, *p 340,* 341–44; Revolutionary War, 160, 165–66; slavery, *see* Slavery; Tariffs and, 243–44, 250–51; *see also* Confederate States of America
Southwest, 40, 226, 231
Southwestern Indians, *m 32,* 33
Soviet Union, 485, 487, 571–72, 584, *m 584,* 623, 696; atomic power, 636, 712; Cold War, **633**–35, 647, 700; Cuba, 693–94; Czechoslovakia, 700, *p 700;* Germany and, 633–35; space, 629, 705,

707; World War Two, 591, 592, 602, *m 602*, 603, 607–10; *see also* Russia

Space, 629, *p 649, p 691, p 704, 705–7, p 707*

Spain, 25, 27–28, *m 27*, 37–40, *m 38*, 43, *p 48*, 49, 75, 160, 186, 580, *m 584;* colonies of, 38–40, 213–14; Cuba and, 461–64; Florida, 38, *m 38*, 40, 42, 166, 195, 213; French and Indian War and, 141, 142; Indians and, 37–38, 294; Louisiana, 195, 196; Philippine Islands, 463, 464; slavery in colonies, 38–39, 103, 111

Spanish-American War, *p 460, m 461, 463–64*

Spoils system, 246, 401, 408

Sports, *f 392*, 395–97, *p 396, p 397*, 507, 534, 554; *see also* Amusements and recreation

Square Deal, 437

Stalin, Joseph, 607–8, 609, *p 609*

Stamp Act, 147, *p 147, p 148*

Stamp Act Congress, 148

Standard Oil Company, 378, 426, 445

Standard parts, 523–24

Stanton, Elizabeth Cady, 274, *f 274*

State banks, 252, 256, 257

States, 174, 184–85, 255–56, 432; constitutions of, 172, 255–56, 336, 337, 341, 342; legislatures of, 172, 255, *p 272*, 341–42, *p 421*, 432; rights of, 180, 239, 244, 249, 250–51; slavery, *see* Slavery

Steamboats, 233

Steel industries, 348, *p 370*, 372–73, 377–78, 517–18, *p 518*, 526, 616, *p 617*

Stephens, Alexander H., 321

Stevens, Thaddeus, 337, *p 338*, 344

Stevenson, Adlai, 627, 628

Stock market, *p 515*, 529–30, 542

Stowe, Harriet Beecher, 310

Strikes, *see* Labor unions

Submarines, 474–76, 479–80, 481, 592, 601

Suburbs, 506, *p 656*, 657

Suez Canal, 591, 601, *m 602*, 647

Sugar Act, 147

Sullivan, John L., *f 392*, 397

Sumner, Charles, 337, 344

Supreme Court, 179, 547–48, *p 548, f 689;* decisions of, 239, 249, 315–16, 321, 349, 368, 379, 451, 537, 538, 547, 548, 664, 665

Taft-Hartley Act, 616, 618, 622

Taft, William Howard, *p 442*, 443–46, *p 444, f 445*

Taney, Roger B., 316

Tarbell, Ida M., 426

Tariff Act (1816), 238, 239; (1828), 245, 251; (1832), 251

Tariffs, 238, 239, 243–45, 250–51, 257, 316, 372, 409, 410, 444, 449, 455, 493, 495, 496, 519, 531, 572–73, 671; reciprocal agreements, 571, 573

Taxation: colonial, 52, 124, 135, 146–48, *p 147, p 148*, 151–53, 173, 179, *f 191*, 196, 239, 372, 445, 449–50, 481, 493, 495, 496, 531, 597, 617, 677; *see also* Poll Tax; Tariffs

Taylor, Zachary, 298, *m 298*, 299, 300, 303, 304

Tea Act, 152–53

Tecumseh, 203, *p 204*

Telephone and telegraph, 374, 445

Television, 652, *f 652*

Temperance movement, *p 272*, 273–74

Tenant farmers, 348, 419, 519

Tennessee, 186, 227, 323, 327, 330, 336, *f 512*

Tennessee Valley Authority, *p 540*, 541, *m 542*

Territories, 173–74, *m 232, m 292, m 304, m 322;* slavery in *m 304*, 311–12, *m 311*, 315–16, 321, 322–23; overseas, 456, *m 456*, 457–58, 461, 463, 464, 468, 568

Texas, 226, 231, 233, 291, 291–93, 296–97, *m 299*, 299, 318, 348, 355–56

Theaters, 262–63, 397, 508, 511, 556, 560, 652

Thirteenth Amendment, 336

Tilden, Samuel J., 407

Tippecanoe, Battle of, 204

Tobacco, 56, 57–58, *m 57, p 58*, 82, *p 82*, 225, 226, *m 226*, 227, *m 232;* industries, 348, 445

Toleration Act, 58

Toussaint L'Ouverture, General, 197

Town meetings, 64, *p 134*

Towns, *see* Cities and towns

Townshend Acts, 151–52

Trade, 20, 22, 25, 32, 45, 219–20, 233, 367, 457; Chinese, 215, 219, 291, 467; colonial, 52, 85–88, *m 87*, 142, 146–48, *p 147, p 148*, 151–53; Embargo Act, 202; French and British interference with, 195, 201, 203; fur, 45, 73, 92, 140, 142, *m 173*, 219, 233; Japanese, 215, 291; laws controlling, 173, 179; reciprocal agreements, 571, 573; smuggling, 86, 146; South American, 214, 219; with Soviet Union, 571–72; tariffs, *see* Tariffs; triangular, 86–87; West Indian,

86–87, 215; World War One, 473–74

Trade Expansion Act, 670–71

Transportation, 34, *p 117*, 232–33, *p 242*, 243–45, *m 244*, 249–50, 305, 310–11, *p 351, p 364*, 365, 372, 468, 506, 525, 526; in cities, 391, *p 391*, 678; segregated, 280, 349, 665; *see also* Shipping

Transportation, Department of, 685

Travel, 506, 526; *see also* Transportation

Triangular trade, 86–87

Truman Doctrine, 635

Truman, Harry S., 598, 603, 604, 609, *p 613*, 616, 618, *p 618, p 620*, 621–24, *p 624*, 628, *f 641*, 642, 645, 646

Trusts, 378–79, 426, 437–38, 445, 450, 495, 496, 723

Truth, Sojourner, 281, *f 281*

Tubman, Harriet, 281, 287

Turkey, 473, *m 476, m 486, m 634*, 635

Turner, Nat, 286, *p 286*

Tuskegee Institute, *p 349, p 385*, 386, *p 386*

Twentieth Amendment, 536

Twenty-Fifth Amendment, 688

Twenty-Fourth Amendment, 672

Twenty-Second Amendment, 618

Tyler, John, 257, 293

Uncle Tom's Cabin (Stowe), 310

Underground Railroad, 287, *p 287*

Union, 322–24, *m 322, m 328*

Union Army, 323, *f 324*, 327–30, *p 329, p 330*

Union Pacific Railroad, 365, *m 366*

United Nations, 608–9, *p 610*, 636, 641–42, 647, 696

United States Steel Corporation, 378, 526

Universal Negro Improvement Association, 502

Urban League, 433, 501

Utah, 233, 303, 304, *m 304*, 353, 365

Van Buren, Martin, 256–57

Vaudeville, 397, 508

Venezuela, 458

Vera Cruz, Mexico, *m 298*, 299

Vermont, *m 68*, 186

Verrazano, Giovanni, 43

Versailles, Treaty of, 487–88, *p 488*, 567

Vesey, Denmark, 286

Veterans' Bureau, 493, 494

Veto, 134, 246

Vietcong, 646, 695, 700–2, *p 702*

Viet Nam, 640, *m 640*, 646, *p 646*, 695, 701–2, *p 702*

Virginia, 165, 166, 197, 225, 323, 327, 328, 330, *p 334;* colonial, 56–57, *p 56, m 57, p 58,* 80–82, 104, 110, 122, 129, *p 132;* slaves and slavery, 227, 286, *p 286*
Vista, 682, *p 682*
Vocational education, 402–3, 513, 658, 670
Voting, 245, *p 254, p 343,* 410, *p 430,* 432, *p 432;* in Colonial America, 135–36, *p 135, p 136;* right of, 172, 246, 255–56, 274, 279–80, 336, 337, 348, 362, 432, 505, 621, 672, 684
Voting Rights Act of 1965, 684

Wabash Railway Case, 368
Wages, *see* Labor
Wages and Hours Law, 544
Wake Island, *m 456,* 457, 591, *m 603*
Walker, David, 256
Walker, Q., *f 172*
Wallace, George C., 689
War Between the North and the South, 373; *see also* Civil War
War Hawks, 204
War Industries Board, 480
War of 1812, *p 200,* 204, *p 206,* 207–10, *m 208, p 210,* 213, 219
War on Poverty, 682
War Production Board, 595
Washington, Booker T., 386, *p 386,* 433
Washington, D.C., 185, 208–9, *m*
208, 304, 328, *p 408,* 674, 676–77, 718–19, *f 719*
Washington, George, 140, *p 170,* 177; as President, *p 182,* 183–84, 185, *p 185,* 186, 189–92; Revolutionary War, 157, 160, 163, *m 164,* 166, *p 166*
Washington Naval Conference, *p 564,* 565
Wayne, Anthony, 186, *p 186*
Weaver, Robert C., 683
Webster, Noah, 264, *f 269*
Webster-Ashburton Treaty, 215
West, 231–33, *m 232,* 244–46, 249–52, 291–94, 359–61, *m 554,* 657; land prices and sales, 232, 243–45, 250, 359; transportation, 232–33, *p 236,* 238, 250, *p 351, p 364,* 365
West Berlin, 694–95, *p 694*
West Indies, 27–28, *m 27,* 38, 86–87, 106, 215
Wheelwright, John, 69–70
Whigs, 256, 257, 312
Whisky Rebellion, *f 191*
White, Walter, 513
Whitman, Marcus, *f 293*
Whitney, Eli, 172, 225, 524
Williams, Roger, 67–68, *p 69*
Willkie, Wendell L., 585
Wilmot Proviso, 300
Wilson, Woodrow, 446, *p 448,* 449–50, 470, *p 472,* 473, *f 474,* 475–76, 485–88, *p 487*
Winthrop, John, 63, *f 64*
Wisconsin, 233, 315, 432
Wolfe, James, *f 140,* 141
Women, 403, 505; rights of, *p 136,* 274, *f 274,* 432, *p 432,* 505; workers, 221, *f 227,* 428, 505, *p 594,* 596
Women's Rights Convention, 274, *f 274*
Workers, *see* Labor
Works Progress Administration, 543, 549, 556, 560
World War One, *p 472,* 473–76, *p 475, m 476, p 478,* 479–82, *m 481, f 482, p 484, m 486,* 493, 501, *p 501, p 516,* 517, 520, 578; peace terms, 485–88, *m 486;* United States enters, 476; war debts, 566–67, 572, 578
World War Two, 595–98, 615, 616, 622, 651; in Europe, *m 584,* 585, 589–92, *p 600,* 601–3, *m 602,* 604; in Pacific, *f 588,* 589–92, 603–4, *m 603, p 604, p 606,* 639–40; peace plans, 607–10, 633–34; United States enters, 590–91
Wright brothers, 525
Writs of assistance, 146
Wyoming, 432, *p 432*

Yalta Meeting, 608
Yorktown, Battle of, *p 162, m 164,* 166, *p 166*
Young Plan, 567
Yugoslavia, *m 486,* 487, 591

Zimmerman Note, *f 474*

Amendment 26.   Lowering the Voting Age to 18 (1971)

Section 1.

The voting age was lowered to 18 in all federal, state, and local elections.

The right of citizens of the United States, who are 18 years of age or older, to vote shall not be denied or abridged by the United States or any state on account of age.

Section 2.

The Congress shall have the power to enforce this article by appropriate legislation.

PICTURE CREDITS

Cover Photograph: The Bay Bridge, San Francisco—Shostal
Maps: pp. 14–15 Harold K. Faye; all others Harbrace

KEY: *t*, top; *b*, bottom; *l*, left; *r*, right; *m*, middle; B. The Bettmann Archive Inc.; BB, Brown Brothers; C, Culver Pictures Inc.; HPS, Historical Pictures Service-Chicago; LOC, Library of Congress; NYHS, Courtesy the New-York Historical Society, N.Y.C.; NYPL, New York Public Library; UPI, United Press International Inc.; WW, Wide World Photos Inc.

P. 1, J. P. Charbonnier, from Photo Researchers; p. 2*t*, Dennis Brack, Black Star; *ml*, Adeline Haaga, Photo Researchers; *mr*, Fred J. Maroon, Photo Researchers; *b*, UPI; p.3*tl*, Declan Haun, Black Star; *tr*, Fred Ward, Black Star; *ml*, Fred Kaplan, Black Star; *mr & b*, UPI; p.4*t*, Farrell Grehan, Photo Researchers; *ml*, Jules Zalon, DPI; *mr*, Jean Paul Jallot, Photo Researchers; *b*, E. Dubrowsky, Black Star; p.5*t*, Rogers, Monkmeyer; *ml*; *mr*, Carl Schulfeld, Rapho-Guillumette Pictures; *b*, Harbrace; p. 6*t* (C. Evers), Flip Schulke, Black Star; (C. Stokes), UPI; (M. L. King), Steve Schapiro; (C. Chavez), Gerhard Gscheidle, Photophile; *ml*, Steve Schapiro, Black Star; *mr*, Gerhard Gscheidle, Photophile; *b*, Robert Houston, Black Star; p.7*tr*, Dennis Brack, Black Star; *ml*, Beth Bagby, Photophile; *mr*, J. Edward Bailey for TIME, © TIME Inc., 1970; *b*, Beth Bagby, Photophile; p.8*tr*, Bell Aerospace; *ml*, Grant Heilman; *mr & b*, Joe Munroe, Photo Researchers; p.9*tl*, Elliott Erwitt, Magnum Photos; *ml*, Office of Saline Water, USDI; *mr*, NASA photo; *bl*, Bethlehem Steel Corp.; *br*, Fred Lyon, Rapho-Guillumette Pictures; p.10*tr*, John H. Atkinson, Jr., DPI; *ml*, Katrina Thomas, Photo Researchers; *mr*, Harbrace; *bl & br*, Fred Kaplan, Black Star; p. 11*tr*, Moos-Hake/Greenberg; *ml*, Peter J. Kaplan; *mr*, George E. Joseph; *b* (concert), Peter J. Kaplan; (boating), Moos-Hake/Greenberg; p.12*tr & ml*, UPI; *mr*, Harbrace; *b*, UPI; p.13*t*, Merritt, Black Star; *m*, Naval Photographic Center; *b*, Harry Redl, Black Star; pp.17,18, LOC; p.20, B; p.22, Bodleian Library, Oxford; p.24, HPS; p.28, Rare Book Division NYPL, Astor, Lenox and Tilden Foundations; pp.30,33, Courtesy of the American Museum of Natural History; p.34, BB; p.36, C; p.39, LOC; p.40, Edith Reichman; p.42, Confederation Life Collection; p.48, Mariners Museum, Newport News, Va.; pp.50,51, B; p.52, Reproduced by Permission of the Fishmongers' Co., London; p.54,LOC; p.56, HPS; p.58, C; p.60, Courtesy of Kenneth M. Newman, The Old Print Shop, N.Y.C.; p.62, LOC; p.64, New England Mutual Life; pp.66,69, C; p.70, B; pp.72,77, LOC; p.78, NYPL, Astor, Lenox and Tilden Foundations; p.81, NYPL Picture Collection; p.82, C; p.84, NYHS; p.86, John Hancock Mutual Life Insurance Co.; p.88, C; p.93, Massachusetts Historical Society; p.95, C; p.96, From the original painting in the Woolaroc Museum, Bartlesville, Okla.; p.98, *Flax Scutching Bee* Linton Park, National Gallery of Art, Wash., D.C., Gift of Edgar William and Bernice Chrysler Garbisch; p.99, NYPL Picture Collection; p.100, NYHS; p.102, NYPL Picture Collection; p.104, Pictorial Parade; p.105, American Antiquarian Society; p.106*l & r*, Photo by Charles Uht, Courtesy of the Museum of Primitive Art; p.108, C; p.110, BB; p.111, Detail from *Washington as a Farmer at Mount Vernon*, Virginia Museum; p.113, NYHS; p.114, LOC; p.116, C; p.117, Records of the Public Buildings Service, photo no. 121-PS-2700 in the National Archives; p.118, *The End of the Hunt*, Artist Unknown, National Gallery of Art, Wash., D.C., Gift of Edgar William and Bernice Chrysler Garbisch; p.120, BB; p.122, U.S. Office of Education, Federal Security Agency;

p.123, NYPL; p.124, C; p.126, Fine Arts Collection, South Dakota State University; p.131, C; p.132, LOC; p.134, BB; p.135, National Life Insurance Co., p.138, State Historical Society of Wisconsin; p.140, B; p.142, BB; p.144, LOC; p.146, C; p.147*l*, Smithsonian Institution; *r*, LOC; p.148, LOC; p.150, B; p.152, C; p.153, LOC; p.156, BB; p.158, LOC; p.159, NYPL; p.160, LOC; p.162, Virginia State Library; p.165, Courtesy, U.S. Naval Academy Museum; p.166, C; p.169, State Historical Society of Wisconsin; p.170, LOC; p.172, C; p.174, The Granger Collection; p.176, Historical Society of Pennsylvania; p.178, Nebraska State Historical Society; p.180, B; p.182, C; p.185, HPS; p.190, Collection of I.B.M.; p.191, BB; p.194, From the Historical Paintings Collection of the Continental Insurance Co.; pp.199,200, Mariners Museum, Newport News, Va.; p.202, C; p.204, NYPL Picture Collection; p.206, Courtesy Lighthouse Gallery, Shelburne Museum, Shelburne, Vt.; p.209, B; p.212, C; p.214*l*, Charles Phelps Cushing, *r*, B; p.217, NYHS; p.218, Courtesy, Museum of the City of New York; p.221, BB; p.224, Detail from *The Cotton Exchange at New Orleans* by Degas, courtesy Musée de Pau. Photo by Giraudon; pp.227-230, LOC; p.235, Collection of the Boatmen's National Bank of St. Louis; p.236, B; p.240, Independence National Historical Park Collection, Philadelphia; p.242, NYPL I.N. Phelps Stokes Collection; p.245, The Granger Collection; p.246, NYHS; p.248, B; p.250, LOC; p.251, Woolaroc Museum, Bartlesville, Okla.; p.256, Courtesy, Kenneth M. Newman, The Old Print Shop, N.Y.C.; p.257, B; p.259, Detail from *Winter Scene in Brooklyn* in the Brooklyn Museum Collection; p.260, International Harvester; p.263, LOC; p.264, NYPL Godey's Magazine and Lady's Book, Feb., 1844; p.266, University of Michigan, Michigan Historical Collections; p.268*l*, BB; p.269, C; p.272, BB; p.274, Pictorial Parade; p.275, BB; p.276, C; p.278, HPS; p.280, The Granger Collection; pp.281,282, Sophia Smith Collection, Smith College; p.284, NYHS; p.286, C; p.287, Ohio Historical Society; p.289, Nelson Bagley-Atkins Museum (Nelson Fund) Kansas City, Mo.; p.290, The Church of Jesus Christ of Latter-Day Saints; p.293, C; p.294, Stanford University Museum, Stanford Collections; p.300, The Granger Collection; p.302, BB; p.307, National Park Service, photo by Lane Studio; p.308, C; p.310, BB; p.312, C; p.314, B; p.316, The Granger Collection; p.317, Western Reserve Historical Society; pp.318, 320, C; p.323,324, LOC; p.326, West Point Museum; p.329, LOC; p.330, Courtesy of the Cooper-Hewitt Museum of Design, Smithsonian Institution; p.333, National Archives; p.334, B; p.337, LOC, Harper's Weekly, June 24, 1866; p. 338, HPS; p.340, C; p.342, Illinois State Historical Library; p.343, LOC; pp.344,346, C; p.349, LOC; p.351, Smithsonian Institution; p.352, Fine Arts Collection, South Dakota State University; p.355, C; p.356, Courtesy Pitman Publishing Co.; p.358, Fine Arts Collection, South Dakota State University; p.360, S.D. Butcher Collection of the Nebraska State Historical Society; p.364, The Great Northern Railway Co.; p.367, The Metropolitan Museum of Art, Bequest of Moses Tanenbaum, 1937; p.370, Bethlehem Steel Corp.; p.372, From *A Pictorial History of the Negro in America*, by Langston Hughes and Milton Meltzer; p.373, C; p.374, LOC; p.376, B; p.378, UPI; p.379, C; p.381, NYPL; p.382, HPS; p.384, BB; p.385, Pictorial Parade; p.386, B; p.388, NYHS; p.391, LOC; p.392, C; pp.394,396, LOC; p.397, Detail from *Baseball Players Practicing* by Thomas Eakins, Museum of Art, Rhode Island School of Design; p.398, LOC; p.402, BB; p.403, NYPL Picture Collection; p.405, The Granger Collection; p.406, U.S. Army Photograph; p.408, LOC; p.409, B; p.410, LOC, Harper's Weekly, Nov. 17, 1888; p.412, BB;

p.414, HPS; p.415, B; pp.416,418, C; p.420, NYPL Picture Collection; p.421, B; pp.422,424, BB; p.426, NYPL; p.427, C; p.428, Ewing Galloway; pp.430,432, The Granger Collection; p.433, NAACP Photo; p.435, State Historical Society of Wisconsin; p.436, BB; p.438, Theodore Roosevelt Assoc.; p.439, BB; p.440, Theodore Roosevelt Assoc.; p.442, B; p.444, HPS; p.445, B; p.446, UPI; p.448, LOC; p.450, Photoworld; p.451, NYPL Picture Collection; p.453, LOC; p.454, NYPL, N.Y. Herald, Dec. 16, 1902; p.457, C; pp.458,460, LOC; p.464, U. S. Naval Academy; p.466, U. S. Signal Corps, photo no. 111-SC-88936 in the National Archives; p.468, Theodore Roosevelt Assoc.; p.470, BB; p.472, LOC; p.474, B; pp.478,480, C; p.482, UPI; p.484, BB; p.487, National Archives; p.488, Imperial War Museum, London; p.491, LOC; p.492, Gilloon Photo Agency; pp.494,495, WW; p.496, BB; p.498, UPI; p.500, BB; p.501, U.S. War Dept. General Staff, photo no. 165-WW-127-8 in the National Archives; pp.502, NAACP Photo; p.504, Penguin Photo; p.506, BB; p.507, C; p.508, Ewing Galloway; p.510, BB; p.512, C; pp.515-518, UPI; p.519, Franklin D. Roosevelt Library; p.520, B; p.522, Courtesy, U.S. Steel Corp. from *Steel Serves the Nation, 1901-1951*; p.524, Educational Affairs Dept.; Ford Motor Co.; p.525, Courtesy United Air Lines; pp.526,528, BB; p.530, WW; p.531, Franklin D. Roosevelt Library; p.533, WW; p.534, UPI; p.536, Franklin D. Roosevelt Library, ACME Photo; p.537, C; p.538, UPI; p.540, Tennessee Valley Authority; p.543, UPI; p.544, WW; p.546, credit not known; pp.548-550, LOC; p.552, Pictorial Parade; p.554, From *City Lights* © 1931 United Artists. NYPL Theatre Collection, Astor, Lenox, and Tilden Foundations; p.555, Photoworld; p.556, Pictorial Parade; p.558, Fine Arts Collection, South Dakota State University; p.560, Edward Steichen; p.561, Western Pennsylvania Conservancy, photo by Michael Fedison; p.563, Pictorial Parade; p.564, UPI; p.566, BB; p.567, UPI; p.568, Panama Canal Co.; pp.570,572, WW; p.573, BB; p.574, Pictorial Parade; p.576, WW; p. 578, Pictorial Parade; p.579, WW; p.580, UPI; p.582, WW; p.587, U.S. Army Photo; p.588, Navy Dept.; p.591, Franklin D. Roosevelt Library; p.592, BB; p.594, LOC; p.596, Ford Motor Co.; p.597, U.S. Army Photo; p.598, BB; p.600, U.S. Coast Guard, photo no. 26-WA-6J-3 in the National Archives; p.604, credit not known; p.606, UPI; p.609, U.S. Army Photo; p.610, UPI; pp.613,614, WW; p.616, LOC; pp.617-622, UPI; p.623, U.S. Army Photo; p.624, WW; p.626, Authenticated News International; pp.629-632, WW; pp.635,636, BB; pp.638,641,WW; p.642, UPI; p.644, U.S. Army Photo; p.646, Sully, Black Star; p.649, Ken Heyman; p.650, Harbrace; p.652, NYPL Picture Collection; p.653, Louis Goldman, Rapho-Guillumette Pictures; p.654*l*, Mottke Weissman, 654*r*, UPI; p.656, WW; p.659, Courtesy, Aluminum Co. of America; pp.660,662, WW; p.664, Burt Glinn, Magnum; p.665, WW; p.667, National Parks Service; p.668, UPI; p.670, WW; pp.671,672, UPI; p.674, Dan Budnik, Magnum; p.676, WW; p.677, Fred Ward, Black Star; p.678, WW; p.680, UPI; p.682, Lynn McLaren, Rapho-Guillumette Pictures; p.683, UPI; p.684, Hella Hammid, Rapho-Guillumette Pictures; pp.686-689, WW; pp.691-695, UPI; p.696, Paul Conklin, PIX; pp.698-702, UPI; p.704, NASA Photo; p.706, UPI; p.707, NASA Photo; p.709, WW; p.710, Pictorial Parade; p.712, UPI; p.713, Ernest Baxter, Black Star; pp.714-719, WW; p.720, UPI; p.722, Laurence Lowry, Rapho-Guillumette Pictures; p.724, De Wys Photos; p.725, Ken Heyman; p.726, UPI.

E
F
G
H 0